THE PROGRAMMER'S TECHNICAL REFERENCE:
MS-DOS, IBM PC & Compatibles

Dave Williams

SIGMA PRESS – Wilmslow, United Kingdom

Copyright ©, D. Williams, 1990

All Rights Reserved. No part of this publication may be reproduced, stored in a retrieval system, or transmitted in any form or by any means, electronic, mechanical, photocopying, recording or otherwise, without prior written permission.

First published in 1990 by

Sigma Press, 1 South Oak Lane, Wilmslow, Cheshire SK9 6AR, England.
Reprinted, 1992.

British Library Cataloguing in Publication Data

A CIP catalogue record for this book is available from the British Library.

ISBN: 1-85058-199-1

Typesetting and design by

Sigma Hi-Tech Services Ltd

Printed in Malta by

Interprint Ltd.

Distributed by

John Wiley & Sons Ltd., Baffins Lane, Chichester, West Sussex, England.

Acknowledgement of copyright names

Within this book, various proprietary trade names and names, as listed below, are protected by copyright and are mentioned for descriptive purposes:

UNIX, AT&T, Allied Telephone and Telegraph; *AST, RAMpage!* AST Corporation; *Atari, ST,* Atari Computer; *Borland, Turbo C, Turbo Pascal, Turbo Lightning,* Borland; *Amiga 2000,* Commodore Business Machines; *Compaq, Deskpro,* Compaq Computer Corporation; *Corona, Cordata, Cordata Computer;* 10-Net, Fox Research, Inc.; *Smartmodem,* Hayes; *IBM, PC, PCjr, PC/XT, PC/AT, XT/286, PS/2, TopView, DOS, PC-DOS, Micro Channel 3270 PC, RT PC, Token Ring,* IBM Corporation; *Intel, iAPX286, iAPX386, LIM EMS, Communicating Applications Standard,* Intel Corporation; *Logitech, Logimouse,* Logitech, Inc.; *Microsoft, MS, MS-DOS, OS/2, Xenix, Windows, Windows/286, Windows/386, Microsoft Networks, LIM EMS, XMA,* Microsoft Corp.; *Mouse Systems,* Mouse Systems Corp.; *Novell, NetWare,* Novell Corp.; *DesQview,* Quarterdeck Office Systems; *ARC,* SEAware, Inc.; *DoubleDOS,* Softlogic; *TaskView,* Sunny Hill Software; *Tandy,* Tandy Corp.; *Zenith, Z-100,* Zenith Radio Corporation; *ShowPartner, Paintbrush,* ZSoft Corporation; '*LIM 4.0*' and '*Expanded Memory Specification*' are copyright Lotus Development Corp, Intel Corp, and Microsoft Corp; '*EEMS*', '*AQA 3.1*' and '*Enhanced Expanded Memory Specification*' are copyright by Ashton-Tate, Quadram, and AST.Various other names are trademarks of their respective companiesFull acknowledgment is hereby made of all such protection.

Preface

This book is a technical reference. It is NOT a tutorial. It is intended to replace the various (expensive) references needed to program for the DOS environment, that stack of magazines threatening to take over your work area, and those odd tables and charts you can never find when you need them.

The various Microsoft and IBM publications and references don't always have the same information. This has caused some consternation about the 'undocumented' features to be found in DOS. In general, if a call doesn't appear in the IBM DOS Technical Reference it is considered 'undocumented' although it may be in common use.

Microsoft's offical policy toward DOS has been to put the burden of documenting and supporting their product to their vendors. Microsoft will not answer any questions concerning DOS directly since they don't officially support it. This leaves what information IBM and other OEMs (DEC, Zenith, et al) have chosen to publish, and the information obtained from programmers who've poked around inside it.

Now that Microsoft is selling MSDOS 3.3 and 4.0 over the counter they seem to be dragging their feet over whether they will have to support the generic version since it doesn't have an OEM name on it anymore. In view of their push to OS/2 (OS/2! Just Say No!) further support of DOS seems unlikely.

A project this size takes a LOT of time and effort. I've tried to verify as much of the information I've received as I could, but there's just too much for absolute certainty.

Contents

Chapter 1: DOS and the IBM PC 1

Chapter 2: CPU Port Assignments, System Memory Map, BIOS Data Area, Interrupts 00h to 09h 10

Chapter 3: The PC ROM BIOS 25

Chapter 4: DOS Interrupts and Function Calls 54

Chapter 5: Interrupts 22h Through 86h 98

Chapter 6: DOS Control Blocks and Work Areas 130

Chapter 7: DOS File Structure 140

Chapter 8: DOS Disk Information 151

Chapter 9: Installable Device Drivers 171

Chapter 10: Expanded and Enhanced Expanded Memory Specifications 185

Chapter 11: Conversion Between MSDOS and Foreign Operating Systems 208

Chapter 12: Microsoft Windows A.P.I. 210

Chapter 13: Network Interfacing 269

Chapter 14: Mouse Programming 300

Chapter 15: Register-Level Hardware Access 310

Chapter 16: Video Subsystems and Programming 315

Appendix 1: Keyboard Scan Codes 328

Appendix 2: Standard ASCII Character Codes 342

Appendix 3: ASCII Control Codes 345

Appendix 4: IBM PC Interrupt Usage 347

Appendix 5: List of IBM PC-XT-AT-PS/2 Diagnostic Error Codes 349

Appendix 6: Pinouts For Various Interfaces 358

Appendix 7: ANSI.SYS 370

Bibliography 374

Index 380

1

DOS and the IBM PC

Some History

Development of MS-DOS/PCDOS began in October 1980, when IBM began searching the market for an operating system for the yet-to-be-introduced IBM PC. Microsoft had no real operating system to sell, but after some research licensed Seattle Computer Products' 86-DOS operating system, which had been written by a man named Tim Paterson earlier in 1980 for use on that company's line of 8086, S100 bus micros. 86-DOS (also called QDOS, for Quick and Dirty Operating System) had been written as more or less a 16-bit version of CP/M, since Digital Research was showing no hurry in introducing CP/M-86.

This code was hurriedly polished up and presented to IBM for evaluation. IBM had originally intended to use Digital Research's CP/M operating system, which was the industry standard at the time. Folklore reports everything from obscure legal entanglements to outright snubbing of the IBM representatives by Digital. Irregardless, IBM found itself left with Microsoft's offering of "Microsoft Disk Operating System 1.0". An agreement was reached between the two, and IBM agreed to accept 86-DOS as the main operating system for their new PC. Microsoft purchased all rights to 86-DOS in July 1981, and "IBM PC-DOS 1.0" was ready for the introduction of the IBM PC in October 1981. IBM subjected the operating system to an extensive quality-assurance program, reportedly found well over 300 bugs, and decided to rewrite the programs. This is why PC-DOS is copyrighted by both IBM and Microsoft.

It is sometimes amusing to reflect on the fact that the IBM PC was not originally intended to run MS-DOS. The target operating system at the end of the development was for a (not yet in existence) 8086 version of CP/M. On the other hand, when DOS was originally written the IBM PC did not yet exist! Although PC-DOS was bundled with the computer, Digital Research's CP/M-86 would probably have been the main operating system for the PC except for two things - Digital Research wanted $495 for CP/M-86 (considering PC-DOS was essentially free) and many software developers found it easier to port existing CP/M software to DOS than to the new version of CP/M. Several computer magazines claimed that Digital Research aided IBM in writing DOS 4.0, which was subsequently licensed back to Microsoft, which has dropped further development of the operating system to tilt at the windmills of OS/2. OS/2? Not yet! After using DR-DOS 3.4 and noting its behaviour, I now tend to seriously doubt Digital had any dealings with PC-DOS 4.0.

MS-DOS and PC-DOS have been run on more than just the IBM-PC and clones. Some of the following have been done:

Hardware PC Emulation:

Commodore Amiga 2000	8088 or A2286D 80286 Bridge Board
IBM PC/AT	80286 AT adapter
Atari 400/800	Co-Power 88 board
Apple Macintosh	AST 80286 board
Atari ST	PC-Ditto II cartridge
Apple II	TransPC 8088 board, QuadRam QuadLink

Software PC Emulation:

Atari ST	PC-Ditto I
Apple Macintosh	SoftPC

DOS Emulation:

OS/2	DOS emulation in "Compatibility Box"
QNX	DOS window
SunOS	DOS window
Xenix	DOS emulation with DOSMerge

What is DOS?

DOS exists as a high-level interface between an application program and the computer. DOS stands for "Disk Operating System", which reflects the fact that its main original purpose was to provide an interface between the computer and its disk drives.

DOS now lets your programs do simple memory management, I/O from the system console, and assorted system tasks (time and date, etc) as well as managing disk operations. Versions 3.1 and up also incorporate basic networking functions.

With the introduction of installable device drivers and TSR (terminate but stay resident) programs in DOS 2.0, the basic DOS functions may be expanded to cover virtually any scale of operations required.

Other Operating Systems

There are a number of compatible replacements for Microsoft's MS-DOS. Some are:

Consortium Technologies MultiDOS	(multitasking, multiuser)
Digital Research Concurrent DOS	(multitasking)
Digital Research Concurrent DOS 386	(for 80386 computers)
Digital Research Concurrent DOS XM	(multitasking, multiuser)
Digital Research DR-DOS 3.31 and 4.0	(PC-DOS clones)
PC-MOS/386	(multitasking, multiuser)
Wendin-DOS	(multitasking, multiuser)
VM/386	(multitasking)

Various other operating systems are available for the IBM PC. These include:

Digital Research CP/M-86
Digital Research Concurrent CP/M-86 (multitasking)
Minix (multitasking UNIX workalike)
Pick (database-operating system)

QNX (multitasking, multiuser)
UNIX (various systems from IBM itself, Microsoft-SCO, Bell, and various UNIX clones, single and multi user) (AIX, Xenix, AT&T System V, etc.)

"Shell" programs exist which use DOS only for disk management while they more or less comprise a new operating system. These include:

DesQview
Windows
OmniView
GEM
TopView
TaskView

Specific Versions of MS/PC-DOS

DOS 1.x is essentially 86-DOS. DOS 2.x kept the multiple file layout (the two hidden files and COMMAND.COM) but for all practical purposes is an entirely different operating system with backwards compatibility with 1.x. I seriously doubt there has been much code from 1.x retained in 2.x. DOS 3.x is merely an enhancement of 2.x; there seems little justification for jumping a whole version number. DOS 4.0, originating as it did from outside Microsoft, can justify a version jump. Unfortunately, 4.x seems to have very little reason to justify its existence - virtually all of its core features can be found in one version or another of DOS 3.x.

DOS version nomenclature: major.minor.minor. The digit to the left of the decimal point indicates a major DOS version change. 1.0 was the first version. 2.0 added support for subdirectories, 3.0 added support for networking, 4.0 added some minimal support for Lotus-Intel-Microsoft EMS.

The first minor version indicates customization for a major application. For example, 2.1 for the PCjr, 3.3 for the PS/2s. The second minor version does not seem to have any particular meaning.

The main versions of DOS are:

PC-DOS 1.0	August 1981	original release
PC-DOS 1.1	May 1982	bugfix, double sided drive support
MS-DOS 1.25	June 1982	for early compatibles
PC-DOS 2.0	March 1983	for PC/XT, Unix-type subdirectory support
PC-DOS 2.1	October 1983	for PCjr, bugfixes for 2.0
MS-DOS 2.11	October 1983	compatible equivalent to PC-DOS 2.1
PC-DOS 3.0	August 1984	1.2 meg drive for PC/AT, some new system calls
PC-DOS 3.1	November 1984	bugfix for 3.0, implemented network support
MS-DOS 2.25	October 1985	compatible; extended foreign language support
PC-DOS 3.2	December 1985	720k 3.5 inch drive support for Convertible
PC-DOS 3.3	April 1987	for PS/2 series, 1.44 meg, multiple DOS partitions
MS-DOS 3.31	November 1987	over-32 meg DOS partitions, new function calls
PC-DOS 4.0	August 1988	minor EMS support, some new function calls
MS-DOS 4.01	January 1989	Microsoft version with some bugfixes

IBM's PC-DOS is considered to be the "standard" version of DOS; Microsoft has sold MS-DOS over the counter only since version 3.2 (previously, Microsoft sold its versions only to OEMs).

Most versions of DOS functionally duplicate the external DOS commands such as DISKCOPY, etc. Although Microsoft announced that they would sell MS-DOS 4.0 only to OEMs, they apparently changed the policy and are now selling it over the counter.

Some versions of MS-DOS varied from PC-DOS in the available external commands. Some OEMs only licensed the basic operating system code (the xDOS and xBIO programs, and COMMAND.COM) from Microsoft, and either wrote the rest themselves or contracted them from outside software houses like Phoenix. Most of the external programs for DOS 3.x and 4.x are written in "C" while the 1.x and 2.x utilities were written in assembly language. Other OEMs required customized versions of DOS for their specific hardware configurations, such as Sanyo 55x and early Tandy computers, which were unable to exchange their DOS with the IBM version.

At least two versions of DOS have been modified to be run entirely out of ROM. The Sharp PC5000 had MS-DOS 1.25 in ROM, and the Toshiba 1000 and some Tandy 1000 models have MS-DOS 2.11 in ROM. Digital Research has also announced its DR-DOS is available in a ROM version and Award Software is marketing DOS cards to OEMs as a plug-in.

PC-DOS 3.0 was extremely buggy on release. It does not handle the DOS environment correctly and there are numerous documented problems with the batch file parser. The network support code is also nonfunctional in this DOS version. It is recommended that users upgrade to at least version 3.1.

DEC MS-DOS versions 2.11 for the Rainbow had the ANSI.SYS device driver built into the main code. The Rainbow also used a unique quad density, single-sided floppy drive and its DOS had special support for it.

IBM had a version 1.85 of PC-DOS in April 1983, after the introduction of DOS 2.0. It was evidently for internal use only, supported multiple drive file searches (a primitive form of PATH), built in MODE commands for screen support, a /P parameter for TYPE for paused screens, an editable command stack like the public domain DOSEDIT.COM utility, and could be set up to remain completely resident in RAM instead of a resident/transient part like normal DOS. It is a pity some of the neat enhancements didn't make it into DOS 2.0. IBM also had an "internal use only" version 3.4, evidently used while developing DOS 4.0.

Some versions of DOS used in compatibles do not maintain the 1.x, 2.x, ... numbering system. Columbia Data Products computers labelled DOS 1.25 as DOS 2.0. Early Compaqs labelled DOS 2.0 as DOS 1.x. Other versions incorporated special features - Compaq DOS 3.31 and Wyse DOS 3.21 both support 32-bit file allocation tables in the same fashion as DOS 4.x.

According to PC Week Magazine, July 4, 1988, Arabic versions of MS-DOS are shipping with a hardware copy-protection system from Rainbow Technologies. This is similar to the short-lived system used by AutoCAD 2.52 and a very few other MS-DOS programs, where an adapter block is plugged into the parallel port and software makes use of coded bytes within the block. This type of copy protection has been common on Commodore products for several years, where it is called a "dongle".

The AutoCAD dongle was defeated by a small program written within weeks of version 2.52's debut. Version 2.62 was released 3 months later, without the dongle. The DOS dongle will, however, prevent the system from booting at all unless it is found.

This makes the Arabic version of MS-DOS the first copy-protected operating system, a dubious distinction at best. The modifications to the operating system to support the dongle are not known at this time. Frankly, it would seem that burning the operating system into ROMs would be cheaper and simpler.

Versions of DOS sold in Great Britain are either newer than those sold in the US or use a different numbering system. DOS 3.4, 4.0, 4.1, 4.2, and 4.3 had been released here between the US releases of 3.3 and 4.0.

Microsoft changed their OEM licensing agreements between DOS versions 2.x and 3.x. OEM versions of DOS 3.x must maintain certain data areas and undocumented functions in order to provide compatibility with the networking features of the operating system. For this reason, resident programs will be much more reliable when operating under DOS 3.x.

IBM's release of DOS 4.0 (and the immediate subsequent release of a bugfix) is a dubious step "forward". DOS 4.0 is the first version of DOS to come with a warranty; the catch is that IBM warrants it only for a very slim list of IBM-packaged software. 4.0 has some minor EMS support, support for large hard disks, and not much else. With its voracious RAM requirements and lack of compatibility with previous versions of DOS (many major software packages crash under DOS 4.0), plus the increase in price to a cool $150, there has been no great rush to go to the newest DOS

The Operating System Hierarchy

The Disk Operating System (DOS) and the ROM BIOS serve as an insulating layer between the application program and the machine, and as a source of services to the application program.

As the term 'system' might imply, DOS is not one program but a collection of programs designed to work together to allow the user access to programs and data. Thus, DOS consists of several layers of "control" programs and a set of "utility" programs.

The system hierarchy may be thought of as a tree, with the lowest level being the actual hardware. The 8088 or V20 processor sees the computer's address space as a ladder two bytes wide and one million bytes long. Parts of this ladder are in ROM, parts in RAM, and parts are not assigned. There are also various "ports" that the processor can use to control devices.

The hardware is normally addressed by the ROM BIOS, which will always know where everything is in its particular system. The chips may usually also be written to directly, by telling the processor to write to a specific address or port. This sometimes does not work as the chips may not always be at the same addresses or have the same functions from machine to machine.

DOS Structure

DOS consists of four components:

The boot record
The ROM BIOS interface (IBMBIO.COM or IO.SYS)
The DOS program file (IBMDOS.COM or MS-DOS.SYS)
The command processor (COMMAND.COM or aftermarket replacement)

The Boot Record

The boot record begins on track 0, sector 1, side 0 of every diskette formatted by the DOS FORMAT command. The boot record is placed on diskettes to produce an error message if you try to start up the system with a non-system diskette in drive A. For hard disks, the boot record resides on the first sector of the DOS partition. All media supported by DOS use one sector for the boot record.

Read Only Memory (ROM) BIOS Interface and Extensions

The file IBMBIO.COM or IO.SYS is the interface module to the ROM BIOS. This file provides a low-level interface to the ROM BIOS device routines and may contain extensions or changes to the system board ROMs. Some compatibles do not have a ROM BIOS to extend, and load the entire BIOS from disk (Sanyo 55x, Viasyn machines). Some versions of MS-DOS, such as those supplied to Tandy, are named IBMBIO.COM but are not IBM files.

These low-level interface routines include the instructions for performing operations such as displaying information on the screen, reading the keyboard, sending data out to the printer, operating the disk drives, and so on. It is the operating system's means of controlling the hardware. IBMBIO.COM contains any modifications or updates to the ROM BIOS that are needed to correct any bugs or add support for other types of hardware such as new disk drives. By using IBMBIO.COM to update the ROM BIOS on the fly when the user turns on their computer, IBM does not need to replace the ROM BIOS chip itself, but makes any corrections through the cheaper and easier method of modifying the IBMBIO.COM file instead.

IBMBIO.COM also keeps track of hardware operations on an internal stack or "scratch pad" area for the operating system to save information such as addresses it will need, etc. An example of the use for this stack can be seen when running a program such as a word processor. If you have told the word processor to save your letter, it will write the data to your disk. During this time, if you start typing some more information, the keyboard generates a hardware interrupt. Since you don't want the process of writing the information to the disk to be interrupted, DOS allocates a slot in the stack for the keyboard's hardware interrupt and when it gets a chance, (probably after the data has been written to the disk), it can process that interrupt and pick up the characters you may have been typing. The STACKS= command in DOS 3.2+'s CONFIG.SYS file controls the number of stack frames available for this purpose.

IBMBIO.COM also reads your CONFIG.SYS file and installs any device drivers (i.e. DEVICE=ANSI.SYS) or configuration commands it may find there.

The DOS Program

The actual DOS program is the file IBMDOS.COM or MS-DOS.SYS. It provides a high-level interface for user (application) programs. This program consists of file management routines, data blocking/deblocking for the disk routines, and a variety of built-in functions easily accessible by user programs.

When a user program calls these function routines, they accept high-level information by way of register and control block contents. When a user program calls DOS to perform an operation, these functions translate the requirement into one or more calls to IBMBIO.COM, MS-DOS.SYS or system hardware to complete the request.

The Command Interpreter

The command interpreter, COMMAND.COM, is the part you interact with on the command line. COMMAND.COM has three parts. IBM calls them the "resident portion", the "initialization portion" and the "transient portion".

IBM's original documentation spoke of installing alternate command interpreters (programs other than COMMAND.COM) with the SHELL= statement in CONFIG.SYS. Unfortunately, IBM chose not to document much of the interaction between IBMDOS.COM and IBM-BIO.COM. By the time much of the interaction was widely understood, many commercial software programs had been written to use peculiarities of COMMAND.COM itself.

Two programs exist that perform as actual "shells" by completely replacing COMMAND.COM and substituting their own command interpreter to use with the hidden DOS files. These are Command Plus, a commercial package, and the very interesting shareware 4DOS package. Both supply greatly enhanced batch language and editing capabilities.

Note: DOS 3.3+ checks for the presence of a hard disk, and will default to COMSPEC=C:\. Previous versions default to COMSPEC=A:\. Under some DOS versions, if COMMAND.COM is not immediately available for reloading (i.e., swapping to a floppy with COMMAND.COM on it) DOS may crash.

Resident Portion

The resident portion resides in memory immediately following IBMDOS.COM and its data area. This portion contains routines to process interrupts 22h (Terminate Address), 23h (Ctrl-Break Handler), and 24h (Critical Error Handler), as well as a routine to reload the transient portion if needed. For DOS 3.x, this portion also contains a routine to load and execute external commands, such as files with extensions of COM or EXE.

When a program terminates, a checksum is used to determine if the application program overlaid the transient portion of COMMAND.COM. If so, the resident portion will reload the transient portion from the area designated by COMSPEC= in the DOS environment. If COMMAND.COM cannot be found, the system will halt.

All standard DOS error handling is done within the resident portion of COMMAND.COM. This includes displaying error messages and interpreting the replies to the "Abort, Retry, Ignore, Fail?" message.

Since the transient portion of COMMAND.COM is so large (containing the internal commands and all those error messages), and it is not needed when the user is running an application it can be overlaid that program if that application needs the room. When the application is through, the resident portion of COMMAND.COM brings the transient portion back into memory to show the prompt. This is why you will sometimes see the message "Insert disk with COMMAND.COM". It needs to get the transient portion off the disk since it was overlaid with the application program.

The initialization portion of COMMAND.COM follows the resident portion and is given control during the boot-up procedure. This section actually processes the AUTOEXEC.BAT file. It also decides where to load the user's programs when they are executed. Since this code is only needed during start-up, it is overlaid by the first program which COMMAND.COM loads.

The transient portion is loaded at the high end of memory and it is the command processor itself. It interprets whatever the user types in at the keyboard, hence messages such as 'Bad command or file name' for when the user misspells a command. This portion contains all the internal commands (i.e. COPY, DIR, RENAME, ERASE), the batch file processor (to run .BAT files) and a routine to load and execute external commands which are either .COM or .EXE files.

The transient portion of COMMAND.COM produces the system prompt, (C), and reads what the user types in from the keyboard and tries to do something with it. For any .COM or .EXE files, it builds a command line and issues an EXEC function call to load the program and transfer control to it.

DOS Initialization

The system is initialized by a software reset (Ctrl-Alt-Del), a hardware reset (reset button), or by turning the computer on. The Intel 80x8x series processors always look for their first instruction at the end of their address space (0FFFF0h) when powered up or reset. This address contains a jump to the first instruction for the ROM BIOS.

Built-in ROM programs (Power-On Self-Test, or POST, in the IBM) check machine status and run inspection programs of various sorts. Some machines set up a reserved RAM area with bytes indicating installed equipment (AT and PCjr).

When the ROM BIOS finds a ROM on an adapter card, it lets that ROM take control of the system so that it may perform any set up necessary to use the hardware or software controlled by that ROM. The ROM BIOS searches absolute addresses 0C8000h through 0E0000h in 2K increments in search of a valid ROM. A valid ROM is determined by the first few bytes in the ROM. The ROM will have the bytes 55h, 0AAh, a length indicator and then the assembly language instruction to CALL FAR (to bring in a 'FAR' routine). A checksum is done on the ROM to verify its integrity, then the BIOS performs the CALL FAR to bring in the executable code. The adapter's ROM then performs its initialization tasks and hopefully returns control of the computer back to the ROM BIOS so it can continue with the booting process.

The ROM BIOS routines then look for a disk drive at A: or an option ROM (usually a hard disk) at absolute address C:800h. If no floppy drive or option ROM is found, the BIOS calls int 19h (ROM BASIC if it is an IBM) or displays an error message.

If a bootable disk is found, the ROM BIOS loads the first sector of data from the disk and then jumps into the RAM location holding that code. This code normally is a routine to load the rest of the code off the disk, or to 'boot' the system.

The following actions occur after a system initialization:

1. The boot record is read into memory and given control.

2. The boot record then checks the root directory to assure that the first two files are IBMBIO.COM and IBMDOS.COM. These two files must be the first two files, and they must be in that order (IBMBIO.COM first, with its sectors in contiguous order).
   Note: IBMDOS.COM need not be contiguous in version 3.x+.

3. The boot record loads IBMBIO.COM into memory.

4. The initialization code in IBMBIO.COM loads IBMDOS.COM, determines equipment status, resets the disk system, initializes the attached devices, sets the system parameters and loads any installable device drivers according to the CONFIG.SYS file in the root directory (if present), sets the low-numbered interrupt vectors, relocates IBMDOS.COM downward, and calls the firstbyte of DOS.
   Note: CONFIG.SYS may be a hidden file.

5. DOS initializes its internal working tables, initializes the interrupt vectors for interrupts 20h through 27h, and builds a Program Segment Prefix for COMMAND.COM at the lowest available segment. For DOS versions 3.10 up, DOS also initializes the vectors for interrupts

DOS and the IBM PC

0Fh through 3Fh. An initialization routine is included in the resident portion and assumes control during start-up. This routine contains the AUTOEXEC.BAT file handler and determines the segment address where user application programs may be loaded. The initialization routine is then no longer needed and is overlaid by the first program COMMAND.COM loads.

Note: AUTOEXEC.BAT may be a hidden file.

6. IBMBIO.COM uses the EXEC function call to load and start the top-level command processor. The default command processor is COMMAND.COM in the root directory of the boot drive. If COMMAND.COM is in a subdirectory or another command processor is to be used, it must be specified by a SHELL= statement in the CONFIG.SYS file. A transient portion is loaded at the high end of memory. This is the command processor itself, containing all of the internal command processors and the batch file processor. For DOS 2.x, this portion also contains a routine to load and execute external commands, such as files with extensions of COM or EXE. This portion of COMMAND.COM also produces the DOS prompt (such as 'A'), reads the command from the standard input device (usually the keyboard or a batch file), and executes the command. For external commands, it builds a command line and issues an EXEC function call to load and transfer control to the program.

Note 1. COMMAND.COM may be a hidden file.

2. For IBM DOS 2.x, the transient portion of the command processor contains the EXEC routine that loads and executes external commands. For MS-DOS 2.x+ and IBM DOS 3.x+, the resident portion of the command processor contains the EXEC routine.

3. IBMBIO only checks for a file named COMMAND.COM. It will load any file of that name if no SHELL= command is used.

That pretty much covers the boot-up process. After COMMAND.COM is loaded, it runs the AUTOEXEC.BAT file and then the user gets a prompt to begin working.

2

CPU Port Assignments, System Memory Map, BIOS Data Area, Interrupts 00h to 09h

Introduction

For consistency in this reference, all locations and offsets are in hexadecimal unless otherwise specified. All hex numbers are prefaced with a leading zero if they begin with an alphabetic character, and are terminated with a lowercase H (h). The formats vary according to common usage.

System Memory Map

The IBM PC handles its address space in 64k segments, divided into 16k fractions and then further then as necessary.

```
start   start   end
addr.   addr.   addr    usage
(dec)   (hex)

   *640k RAM Area*

0k                      start of RAM, first K is interrupt vector table
16k     00000-03FFF     PC-0 system board RAM ends
32k     04000-07FFF
48k     08000-0BFFF
64k     10000-13FFF     PC-1 system board RAM ends
80k     14000-17FFF
96k     18000-1BFFF
112k    1C000-1FFFF
128k    20000-23FFF
144k    24000-27FFF
160k    28000-2BFFF
176k    2C000-2FFFF

192k    30000-33FFF
208k    34000-37FFF
224k    38000-3BFFF
240k    3C000-3FFFF
```

CPU Ports Assignments, System Memory Data, BIOS Data Area 11

```
256k   40000-43FFF   PC-2 system board RAM ends
272k   44000-47FFF
288k   48000-4BFFF
304k   4C000-4FFFF

320k   50000-53FFF
336k   54000-57FFF
352k   58000-5BFFF
368k   5C000-5FFFF

384k   60000-63FFF
400k   64000-67FFF
416k   68000-6BFFF
432k   6C000-6FFFF

448k   70000-73FFF
464k   74000-77FFF
480k   78000-7BFFF
496k   7C000-7FFFF

512k   80000-83FFF
528k   84000-87FFF
544k   88000-8BFFF   the original IBM PC-1 BIOS limited memory to 544k
560k   8C000-8FFFF

576k   90000-93FFF
592k   94000-97FFF
609k   98000-9BFFF
624k   9C000-9FFFF   to 640k (top of RAM address space)

       A0000 ***** 64k ***** EGA address

640k   A0000-A95B0   MCGA 320x200 256 colour video buffer
             -AF8C0  MCGA 640x480 2 colour video buffer
             -A3FFF
656k   A4000-A7FFF
672k   A8000-ABFFF      this 64k segment may be used for contiguous DOS
688k   AC000-AFFFF      RAM with appropriate hardware and software

       B0000 ***** 64k ***** mono and CGA address

704k   B0000-B3FFF   4k  monochrome display    | PCjr and early Tandy 1000
720k   B4000-B7FFF                             | BIOS revector direct write to the
                                               | B8 area to the Video Gate Array
736k   B8000-BBFFF   16k CGA uses              | and reserved system RAM
756k   BC000-BFFFF                             |

       C0000 ***** 64k ************** expansion ROM

768k   C0000-C3FFF   16k EGA BIOS C000:001E EGA BIOS signature (letters IBM
784k   C4000-C5FFF
       C6000-C63FF   256 bytes Professional Graphics Display comm. area
       C6400-C7FFF
800k   C8000-CBFFF   16k hard disk controller BIOS, drive 0 default
       CA000             some 2nd floppy (high density) controller BIOS
816k   CC000-CDFFF   8k  IBM PC Network NETBIOS
       CE000-CFFFF

       D0000 ***** 64k ***** expansion ROM

832k   D0000-D7FFF   32k IBM Cluster Adapter   | PCjr first ROM cartridge
             DA000      voice communications   | address area.
848k   D4000-D7FFF                             | Common expanded memory
864k   D8000-DBFFF                             | board paging area.
880k   DC000-DFFFF                             |

       E0000 ***** 64k ***** expansion ROM

896k   E0000-E3FFF                             | PCjr second ROM cartidge
912k   E4000-E7FFF                             | address area
928k   E8000-EBFFF
```

12 *The Programmer's Technical Reference*

```
944k   EC000-EFFFF                              | spare ROM sockets on AT

 F0000 ***** 64k ***** system

960k   F0000-F3FFF   reserved by IBM             cartridge address
976k   F4000-                                    area (PCjr cartridge
       F6000         ROM BASIC Begins            BASIC)
992k   F8000-FB000
1008k  FC000-FFFFF   ROM BASIC and original
                     BIOS (Compatibility BIOS
                     in PS/2)
1024k          FFFFF end of memory (1024k) for 8088 machines

384k   100000-15FFFF 80286/AT extended memory area, 1Mb motherboard
15Mb   100000-FFFFFF 80286/AT extended memory address space
15Mb   160000-FDFFFF Micro Channel RAM expansion (15Mb extended memory)
128k   FE0000-FFFFFF system board ROM           (PS/2 Advanced BIOS)
```

Note that the ROM BIOS has a duplicated address space which causes it to 'appear' both at the end of the 1 megabyte real mode space and at the end of the 16 megabyte protected mode space. The addresses from 0E0000 to 0FFFFF are equal to 0FE0000 to 0FFFFFF. This is necessary due to differences in the memory addressing between Real and Protected Modes.

[handwritten: JUMP TO F000:FFF0 TO RE-BOOT COMPUTER (Processor Reset vector)]

PC Port Assignment

```
           hex address        Function                         Models
                                               PCjr |PC |XT |AT |CVT |M30 |PS2
0000-000F      8237 DMA controller                   PC
0010-001F      8237 DMA controller                              AT               PS2
0020-0027      8259A interrupt controller
0020-003F      8259A interrupt controller (AT)
0020-0021      Interrupt controller 1, 8259A        PC         AT               PS2
0040-0043      Programmable timer 8253              PC
0040-0047      Programmable timers                                               PS2
0040-005F      8253-5 programmable timers                      AT
               (note: 0041 was memory refresh in PCs. Not used in PS/2)
0060-0063      Keyboard controller 8255A            PC
0060-006F      8042 keyboard controller                        AT
0060           IOSGA keyboard input port                                         PS2
0061           speaker                        PCjr  PC   XT   AT   CVT
0061           IOSGA speaker control                                    M30      PS2
0061           On some clones, setting or clearing bit 2 controls Turbo mode
0062           IOSGA configuration control                             M30      PS2
0063           SSGA, undocumented                                                PS2
0064           keyboard auxiliary device                                         PS2
0065-006A      SSGA, undocumented                                                PS2
006B           SSGA, RAM enable/remap                                            PS2
006C-006F      SSGA, undocumented                                                PS2
0070           AT CMOS write internal register
0071           AT CMOS read internal register
0070-0071      CMOS real-time clock, NMI mask                                    PS2
0070-007F      CMOS real-time clock, NMI mask                  AT
0074-0076      reserved                                                          PS2
0800-008F      SSGA DMA page registers                                           PS2
0080-009F      DMA page registers, 74LS612                     AT
0090           central arbitration control port                (Micro Channel)
0091           card selected feedback                          (Micro Channel)
0092           system control port A                           (Micro Channel)
0093           reserved                                        (Micro Channel)
0094           system board setup                              (Micro Channel)
0096           POS 'CD SETUP' selector                         (Micro Channel)
00A0-00A1      Interrupt controller 2, 8259A                   AT               PS2
00A0-00AF      IOSGA NMI mask register                                           PS2
00B0-00BF      realtime clock/calendar, (undocumented)                           PS2
00C0-00DF      reserved                       PCjr  PC   XT   AT   CVT   M30
```

CPU Ports Assignments, System Memory Data, BIOS Data Area

Port	Function			
00C0-00DF	DMA controller 2, 8237A-5		AT	PS2
00E0-00EF	realtime clock/calendar, (undocumented)		M30	PS2
00F0-00FF	PS/2 math coprocessor I/O (Model 50+) (diskette IO on PCjr)			
0100-0101	PS/2 POS adapter ID response		(Micro Channel)	
0102-0107	PS/2 POS adapter configuration response		(Micro Channel)	
01F0-01F8	Fixed disk		AT	PS2
0200-0201	game-control adapter (joystick)			
0200-020F	Game controller	PC	AT	
0020-002F	IOSGA interrupt function			PS2
020C-020D	reserved by IBM			
0210-0217	expansion box (PC, XT)			
021F	reserved by IBM			
0278-027F	Parallel printer port 2		AT	
0278-027B	Parallel printer port 3			PS2
02B0-02DF	EGA (alternate)	PC	AT	
02E1	GPIB (adapter 0)		AT	
02E2-02E3	Data acquisition (adapter 0)		AT	
02F8-02FF	Serial communications (COM2)	PC	AT	PS2
0300-031F	Prototype card	PC	AT	
0320-032F	hard disk controller	PC		
0348-0357	DCA 3278			
0360-0367	PC Network (low address)			
0368-036F	PC Network (high address)		AT	
0378-037F	Parallel printer port 1	PC	AT	
0378-037B	Parallel printer port 2			PS2
0380-038F	SDLC, bi-synchronous 2	PC	AT	
0380-0389	BSC communications (alternate)	PC		
0390-0393	Cluster (adapter 0)	PC	AT	
03A0-03A9	BSC communications (primary)	PC	AT	
03B0-03BF	Monochrome/parallel printer adapter	PC	AT	
03B4-03B5	Video subsystem			PS2
03BA	Video subsystem			PS2
03BC-03BF	Parallel printer port 1			PS2
03C0-03CF	Enhanced Graphics Adapter			
03C0-03DA	Video subsystem and DAC			PS2
03D0-03DF	CGA, MCGA, VGA adapter control			
03F0-03F7	Floppy disk controller	PC	AT	PS2
03F8-03FF	Serial communications (COM1)	PC	AT	PS2
06E2-06E3	Data acquisition (adapter 1)		AT	
0790-0793	Cluster (adapter 1)	PC	AT	
0AE2-0AE3	Data acquisition (adapter 2)		AT	
0B90-0B93	Cluster (adapter 2)	PC	AT	
0EE2-0EE3	Data acquisition (adapter 3)		AT	
1390-1393	Cluster (adapter 3)	PC	AT	
22E1	GPIB (adapter 1)			
2390-2393	Cluster (adapter 4)	PC	AT	
42E1	GPIB (adapter 2)		AT	
62E1	GPIB (adapter 3)		AT	
82E1	GPIB (adapter 4)		AT	
A2E1	GPIB (adapter 5)		AT	
C2E1	GPIB (adapter 6)		AT	
E2E1	GPIB (adapter 7)		AT	

Notes:
1. These are functions common across the IBM range. The PCjr, PC-AT, PC Convertible and PS/2 (both buses) have enhancements. In some cases, the AT and PS/2 series ignore, duplicate, or reassign ports arbitrarily. If your code incorporates specific port addresses for video or system board control it would be wise to have your application determine the machine type and video adapter and address the ports as required.
2. I/O Addresses, hex 000 to 0FF, are reserved for the system board I/O. Hex 100 to 3FF are available on the I/O channel.
3. These are the addresses decoded by the current set of adapter cards. IBM may use any of the unlisted addresses for future use.
4. SDLC Communication and Secondary Binary Synchronous Communications cannot be used together because their port addresses overlap.
5. IOSGA = I/O Support Gate Array; SSGA = System Support Gate Array.

Reserved Memory Locations
Interrupt Vector Table

```
000-3FF   - 1k DOS interrupt vector table, 4 byte vectors for ints 00h-0FFh.
   30:00    used as a stack area during POST and bootstrap routines. This stack
to 3F:FF    area may be revectored by an application program.
```

The BIOS Data Area

addr.	size	description
40:00	word	COM1 port address These addresses are zeroed out in the OS/2
40:02	word	COM2 port address DOS Compatibility Box if any of the OS/2
40:04	word	COM3 port address COMxx.SYS drivers are loaded.
40:06	word	COM4 port address
40:08	word	LPT1 port address
40:0A	word	LPT2 port address
40:0C	word	LPT3 port address
40:0E	word	LPT4 port address (not valid in PS/2 machines)
40:0E	word	PS/2 pointer to 1k extended BIOS Data Area at top of RAM
40:10	word	equipment flag (see int 11h), bits:

```
           0     0       no floppy drive present
                 1       if floppy drive present (see bits 6&7)
           1     0       no math coprocessor installed
                 1       if 80x87 installed   (not valid in PCjr)
           2,3   system board RAM   (not used on AT or PS/2)
                 0,0   16k              0,1   32k
                 1,0   48k              1,1   64k
           4,5   initial video mode
                 0,0   no video adapter
                 0,1   40column colour  (PCjr default)
                 1,0   80column colour
                 1,1   MDA
           6,7   number of diskette drives
                 0,0   1 drive          0,1   2 drives
                 1,0   3 drives         1,1   4 drives
           8     0       DMA present
                 1       DMA not present (PCjr, Tandy 1400, Sanyo
                         55x)
           9,A,B number of RS232 serial ports
           C     game adapter  (joystick)
                 0       no game adapter
                 1       if game adapter
           D     serial printer (PCjr only)
                 0       no  printer
                 1       serial printer present
           E,F   number of parallel printers installed
Note    The IBM PC and AT store the settings of the system board switches or CMOS
        RAM setup information (as obtained by the BIOS in the Power-On Self Test
        (POST)) at addresses 40:10h and 40:13h. 00000001b indicates 'on',
        00000000b is 'off'.

40:12   byte   reserved (PC, AT) number of errors detected by infrared keyboard
               link (PCjr); POST status (Convertible)
40:13   word   available memory size in Kbytes (less display RAM in PCjr)
               this is the value returned by int 12h
40:15   word   reserved
40:17   byte   keyboard flag byte 0 (see int 9h)
               bit 7   insert mode on       3   alt pressed
                   6   capslock on          2   ctrl pressed
                   5   numlock on           1   left shift pressed
                   4   scrollock on         0   right shift pressed
40:18   byte   keyboard flag byte 1 (see int 9h)
               bit 7   insert pressed       3   ctrl-numlock (pause) toggled
                   6   capslock pressed     2   PCjr keyboard click active
                   5   numlock pressed      1   PCjr ctrl-alt-capslock held
                   4   scrollock pressed    0
```

CPU Ports Assignments, System Memory Data, BIOS Data Area

```
40:19   byte     storage for alternate keypad entry (not normally used)
40:1A   word     pointer to keyboard buffer head character
40:1C   word     pointer to keyboard buffer tail character
40:1E   32bytes  16 2-byte entries for keyboard circular buffer, read by int 16h
40:3E   byte     drive seek status - if bit=0, next seek will recalibrate by
                 repositioning to Track 0.
                 bit 3  drive D        bit 2  drive C
                     1  drive B            0  drive A
40:3F   byte     diskette motor status (bit set to indicate condition)
                 bit 7  write in progress   3  motor on (floppy 3)
                     6                      2  motor on  (floppy 2)
                     5                      1  B: motor on (floppy 1)
                     4                      0  A: motor on (floppy 0)
40:40   byte     motor off counter
                 starts at 37 and is decremented 1 by each system clock tick.
                 motor is shut off when count = 0.
40:41   byte     status of last diskette operation    where:
                 bit 7  timeout failure               3  DMA overrun
                     6  seek failure                  2  sector not found
                     5  controller failure            1  address not found
                     4  CRC failure                   0  bad command
40:42   7 bytes  NEC floppy controller chip status
40:49   byte     Video Control Data Area 1 from 0040:0049 through 0040:0066
                 current CRT mode (hex value)
                   00h 40x25 BW         (CGA)      01h 40x25 colour     (CGA)
                   02h 80x25 BW         (CGA)      03h 80x25 colour     (CGA)
                   04h 320x200 colour   (CGA)      05h 320x200 BW       (CGA)
                   06h 640x200 BW       (CGA)      07h monochrome       (MDA)
                 extended video modes   (EGA/MCGA/VGA or other)
                   08h lores,16 colour             09h med res,16 colour
                   0Ah hires,4 colour              0Bh n/a
                   0Ch med res,16 colour           0Dh hires,16 colour
                   0Eh hires,4 colour              0Fh hires,64 colour
40:4A   word     number of columns on screen, coded as hex number of columns
                 20 col = 14h   (video mode 8, low res 160x200 CGA graphics)
                 40 col = 28h
                 80 col = 46h
40:4C   word     screen buffer length in bytes
                 - (number of bytes used per screen page, varies with video mode)
40:4E   word     current screen buffer starting offset (active page)
40:50   8 words  cursor position pages 1-8
                 the first byte of each word gives the column (0-19, 39, or 79); the
                 second byte gives the row (0-24)
40:60   byte     end line for cursor    (normally 1)
40:61   byte     start line for cursor  (normally 0)
40:62   byte     current video page being displayed  (0-7)
40:63   word     base port address of 6845 CRT controller or equivalent
                 for active display         3B4h=mono, 3D4h=colour
40:65   byte     current setting of the CRT mode register
40:66   byte     current palette mask setting   (CGA)
40:67   5 bytes  temporary storage for SS:SP during shutdown (cassette interface)
40:6C   word     timer counter low word
40:6E   word     timer counter high word
40:69   byte     HD_INSTALL (Columbia PCs) (not valid on most clone computers)
                 bit 0     0  8 inch external floppy drives
                           1  5.25" external floppy drives
                     1,2      highest drive address which int 13 will accept (since
                              the floppy drives are assigned 0-3, subtract 3 to
                              obtain the number of hard disks installed)
                     4,5      # of hard disks connected to expansion controller
                     6,7      # of hard disks on motherboard controller (if bit 6 or
                              7 = 1, no A: floppy is present and the maximum number
                              of floppies from int 11 is 3)
40:70   byte     24 hour timer overflow 1 if timer went past midnight it is reset to
                 0 each time it is read by int 1Ah
40:71   byte     BIOS break flag (bit 7 = 1 means break key hit)
40:72   word     reset flag PCjr keeps 1234h here for softboot when a cartridge is
                 installed
                 bits 1234h = soft reset, memory check will be bypassed
                      4321h = preserve memory      (PS/2 other only)
                      5678h = system suspended     (Convertible)
```

```
                         9ABCh = manufacturing test mode (Convertible)
                         ABCDh = system POST loop mode    (Convertible)
40:74     byte    status of last hard disk operation; PCjr special disk control
40:75     byte    # of hard disks attached (0-2)      ; PCjr special disk control
40:76     byte    HD control byte; temp holding area for 6th param table entry
40:77     byte    port offset to current hd adapter ; PCjr special disk control
40:78  4 bytes    timeout value for LPT1,LPT2,LPT3,LPT4
40:7C  4 bytes    timeout value for COM1,COM2,COM3,COM4 (0-0FFh secs, default 1)
40:80     word    pointer to start of circular keyboard buffer, default 03:1E
40:82     word    pointer to end of circular keyboard buffer, default 03:3E
40:84             Video Control Data Area 2, 0040:0084 through 0040:008A
40:84     byte    rows on the screen minus 1 (EGA only)
40:84     byte    PCjr interrupt flag; timer channel 0   (used by POST)
40:85     word    bytes per character (EGA only)
40:85  2 bytes    (PCjr only) typamatic character to repeat
40:86  2 bytes    (PCjr only) typamatic initial delay
40:87     byte    mode options (EGA only)
                    bit 1   0   EGA is connected to a colour display
                            1   EGA is monochrome.
                    bit 3   0   EGA is the active display,
                            1   'other' display is active.
                  mode combinations:
                    bit 3   Bit 1    Meaning
                     0        0     EGA is active display and is colour
                     0        1     EGA is active display and is monochrome
                     1        0     EGA is not active, a mono card is active
                     1        1     EGA is not active, a CGA is active
40:87     byte    (PCjr only) current Fn key code
                            80h bit indicates make/break key code?
40:88     byte    feature bit switches (EGA only) 0=on, 1=off
                    bit 3      switch 4
                        2      switch 3
                        1      switch 2
                        0      switch 1
40:88     byte    (PCjr only) special keyboard status byte
                    bit 7  function flag   3 typamatic (0=enable,1=disable)
                        6  Fn-B break      2 typamatic speed (0=slow,1=fast)
                        5  Fn pressed      1 extra delay bef.typamatic (0=enable)
                        4  Fn lock         0 write char, typamatic delay elapsed
40:89     byte    PCjr, current value of 6845 reg 2 (horizontal synch)
                  used by ctrl-alt-cursor screen positioning routine in ROM
40:8A     byte    PCjr CRT/CPU Page Register Image, default 3Fh
40:8B     byte    last diskette data rate selected
                    bit 7,6 Starting data transfer rate to use
                         00       500 kb/sec
                         01       300 kb/sec
                         10       250 kb/sec
                         11       reserved
                      5,4 Last step rate selected
                       3  Ending data transfer rate to use
                       2  Reserved
                       1  Reserved
                       0  1  combination floppy/fixed disk controller detected
                          0  XT floppy only controller (for 360kb drive) detected
                       Data Transfer Rates
                       Kbits/sec    Media    Drive    Sectors/Track
                         250        360K     360K          9
                         300        360K     1.2M          9
                         500        1.2M     1.2M         15
                         250        720K     720K          9
                         250        720K     1.4M          9
                         500        1.4M     1.4M         18
40:8C     byte    hard disk status returned by controller
40:8D     byte    hard disk error returned by controller
40:8E     byte    hard disk interrupt (bit 7=working interrupt)
40:8F     byte    combo_card - status of drives 0 and 1
                    bit 7   reserved
                        6   drive type determined for drive 1
                        5   drive multiple data rate capability for drive 1
                             0     no multiple data rate
                             1     multiple data rate
```

CPU Ports Assignments, System Memory Data, BIOS Data Area   17

```
                    4     1 then drive 1 has 80 tracks
                          0 then drive 1 has 40 tracks
                    3     reserved
                    2     drive type determined for drive 0
                    1     drive multiple data rate capability for drive 0
                          0         no multiple data rate
                          1         multiple data rate
                    0  1            then drive 0 has 80 tracks
                       0            then drive 0 has 40 tracks
40:904    bytes media state drive 0, 1, 2, 3
                    floppy_media_state
                    bit 7,6 Data transfer rate
                          00 - 500 K/sec
                          01 - 300 K/sec
                          10 - 250 K/sec
                          11 - reserved
                    5     double stepping required
                    4     media/drive determined
                    3     reserved
                    2-0   present state
                          000   360k in 360k unestablished
                          001   360k in 1.2M unestablished
                          010   1.2M in 1.2M unestablished
                          011   360k in 360k established
                          100   360k in 1.2M established
                          101   1.2M in 1.2M established
                          110   reserved
                          111   none of the above
40:94  2 bytes  track currently seeked to drive 0, 1
40:96  byte     keyboard flag byte 3 (see int 9h)
40:97  byte     keyboard flag byte 2 (see int 9h)
40:98  dword    segment:offset pointer to users wait flag
40:9C  dword    users timeout value in microseconds
40:A0  byte     real time clock wait function in use
                bits 7     wait time elapsed and posted flag
                     6-1   reserved
                     0     int 15h, function 86h (WAIT) has occurred
40:A1  byte     LAN A DMA channel flags
40:A2  2 bytes  status LAN A 0,1
40:A4  dword    saved hard disk interrupt vector
40:A8  dword    EGA pointer to table of 7 parameters. Format of table:
                dword    pointer to 1472 byte table containing 64 video parms
                dword    reserved
                dword    reserved
                dword    reserved
                dword    reserved
                dword    reserved
                dword    reserved
40:B0  2 words  international support                              (Tandy 1000 TX)
40:B4  byte     keyboard NMI control flags                         (Convertible)
40:B4  byte     monochrome monitor hookup detect                   (Tandy 1000 TX)
                00h not present    0FFh   present
40:B5  dword    keyboard break pending flags                       (Convertible)
40:B5  byte     extended equipment detect    (5 bits)              (Tandy 1000 TX)
                bit 0 = 0    drive A is 5
                        1    drive A is 3
                    1 = 0    drive A is 5
                        1    drive A is 3
                    2 = 0    Tandy 1000 keyboard layout
                        1    IBM keyboard layout
                    3 = 0    CPU slow mode
                        1    CPU fast mode
                    4 = 0    internal colour video support enabled
                        1    internal colour video support disabled, external video
                             enabled (chg from mb'd to expansion card)
                    5 = 0    no external monochrome video installed
                        1    external monochrome video installed
40:B6  byte extended equipment detect    (1 bit)                   (Tandy 1000 TX)
             bit 0 = 0    drive C is 5
                     1    drive C is 3
40:B9  byte port 60 single byte queue                              (Convertible)
```

```
40:BA    byte     scan code of last key                          (Convertible)
40:BB    byte     pointer to NMI buffer head                     (Convertible)
40:BC    byte     pointer to NMI buffer tail                     (Convertible)
40:BD    16bytes  NMI scan code buffer                           (Convertible)
40:CE    word     day counter                          (Convertible and after)
to -04:8F         end of BIOS Data Area
```

DOS and BASIC Data Areas

```
40:90 -40:EF      reserved by IBM
04:F0  16bytes    Inter-Application Communications Area (for use by applications
04:FF             to transfer data or parameters to each other)
05:00    byte     DOS print screen status flag
                     00h    not active or successful completion
                     01h    print screen in progress
                     0FFh   error during print screen operation
05:01             Used by BASIC
05:02-03          PCjr POST and diagnostics work area
05:04    byte     Single drive mode status byte
                     00     logical drive A
                     01     logical drive B
05:05-0E          PCjr POST and diagnostics work area
05:0F             BASIC: SHELL flag (set to 02h if there is a current SHELL)
05:10    word     BASIC: segment address storage (set with DEF SEG)
05:12  4 bytes    BASIC: int 1Ch clock interrupt vector segment:offset storage
05:16  4 bytes    BASIC: int 23h ctrl-break interrupt segment:offset storage
05:1A  4 bytes    BASIC: int 24h disk error int vector segment:offset storage
05:1B-1F          Used by BASIC for dynamic storage
05:20-21          Used by DOS for dynamic storage
05:22-2C          Used by DOS for diskette parameter table. See int 1Eh for values
                  In DOS 1.0 this is located in the ROM BIOS, but in DOS 1.1 and
                  subsequently it is a part of DOS located at 05:22. The first byte
                  (out of eleven) of the Disk Parameter contains the hexadecimal
                  value CF in DOS 1.0 and DF in DOS 1.1 and later. DOS 1.0   24ms;
                  DOS 1.1    26ms
05:30-33          Used by MODE command
05:34-FF          Unknown - Reserved for DOS Model and BIOS ID
```

At absolute addresses:

```
0008:0047         IO.SYS or IBMBIO.COM IRET instruction. This is the dummy routine
                  that interrupts 01h, 03h, and 0Fh are initialized to during POST.
C000:001E         EGA BIOS signature (the letters IBM)
F000:FA6E         table of characters 00h-7Fh used by int 10h video BIOS.
                  The first 128 characters are stored here and each occupies 8
                  bytes. The high bit ones are somewhere on the video adapter card.
F000:FFF5         BIOS release date
F000:FFFE         PC model identification
```

ROM BIOS

```
copyright  model  sub-    revision   machine
date       byte   model
                  byte

09/02/86   FA     00       00        PS/2 Model 30
01/10/86   FB     00       01        XT
01/10/86   FB     00       00        XT-2 (early)    (640k motherboard)
05/09/86   FB     01       --        XT-2 (revised)  (640k motherboard)
01/10/84   FC     --       --        AT
06/10/85   FC     00       01        AT Model 239 6mHz (6.6 max governor)
11/15/85   FC     01       00        AT Model 319, 339 8mHz (8.6 max governor)
04/21/86   FC     02       00        XT/286
02/13/87   FC     04       00        PS/2 Model 50
02/13/87   FC     05       00        PS/2 Model 60
           FC     00                 7531/2 Industrial AT
```

```
                FC    06              7552 'Gearbox'
06/01/83        FD                    PCjr
11/08/82        FE                    XT, Portable PC, XT/370, 3270PC
04/24/81        FF                    PC-0                (16k motherboard)
10/19/81        FF                    PC-1                (64k motherboard)+
08/16/82        FF                    PC, XT, XT/370     (256k motherboard)
10/27/82        FF                    PC, XT, XT/370     (256k motherboard)
    1987        F8                    PS/2 Model 80
    1987        F8    01    00        PS/2 Model 80 20mHz
09/13/85        F9    00    00        Convertible
                2D                    Compaq PC          (4.77mHz original)
                9A                    Compaq Plus        (XT compatible)
```

The IBM PC System Interrupts (Overview)

The interrupt table is stored in the very lowest location in memory, starting at 0000:0000h. The locations are offset from segment 0, i.e. location 0000h has the address for int 0, etc. The table is 1024 bytes in length and contains 256 four byte vectors from 00h to 0FFh. Each address' location in memory can be found by multiplying the interrupt number by 4. For example, int 7 could be found by (7x4=28) or 1Bh (0000:001Bh).

These interrupt vectors normally point to ROM tables or are taken over by DOS when an application is run. Some applications revector these interrupts to their own code to change the way the system responds to the user. DOS provides int 21h function 25h to change interrupts from a high level; altering the interrupt vector table directly is not recommended, nor would it really get you anywhere.

Interrupt Address

```
Number  (Hex)     Type    Function
  0     00-03     CPU     Divide by Zero
  1     04-07     CPU     Single Step
  2     08-0B     CPU     Nonmaskable
  3     0C-0F     CPU     Breakpoint
  4     10-13     CPU     Overflow
  5     14-17     BIOS    Print Screen
  6     18-1B     hdw     Reserved
  7     1C-1F     hdw     Reserved
  8     20-23     hdw     Time of Day
  9     24-27     hdw     Keyboard
  A     28-2B     hdw     Reserved
  B     2C-2F     hdw     Communications (8259)
  C     30-33     hdw     Communications
  D     34-37     hdw     Disk
  E     38-3B     hdw     Diskette
  F     3C-3F     hdw     Printer
 10     40-43     BIOS    Video
 11     44-47     BIOS    Equipment Check
 12     48-4E     BIOS    Memory
 13     4C-4F     BIOS    Diskette/Disk
 14     50-53     BIOS    Serial Communications
 15     54-57     BIOS    Cassette, System Services
 16     58-5B     BIOS    Keyboard
 17     5C-5F     BIOS    Parallel Printer
 18     60-63     BIOS    ROM BASIC Loader
 19     64-67     BIOS    Bootstrap Loader
 1A     68-6B     BIOS    Time of Day
 1B     6C-6F     BIOS    Keyboard Break
 1C     70-73     BIOS    Timer Tick
 1D     74-77     BIOS    Video Initialization
 1E     78-7B     BIOS    Diskette Parameters
 1F     7C-7F     BIOS    Video Graphics Characters, second set
 20     80-83     DOS     General Program Termination
```

20   *The Programmer's Technical Reference*

```
    21      84-87       DOS     DOS Services Function Request
    22      88-8B       DOS     Called Program Termination Address
    23      8C-8F       DOS     Control Break Termination Address
    24      90-93       DOS     Critical Error Handler
    25      94-97       DOS     Absolute Disk Read
    26      98-9B       DOS     Absolute Disk Write
    27      9C-9F       DOS     Terminate and Stay Resident
  28-3F     A0-FF       DOS     Reserved for DOS
                               *29h   Fast Screen Write
                               *2Ah   Microsoft Networks - Session Layer Interrupt
                                2Fh   Multiplex Interrupt
                               *30h   Far jump instruction for CP/M-style calls
                                33h   Used by Microsoft Mouse Driver
  40-43    100-115      BIOS    Reserved for BIOS
                                40h   Hard Disk BIOS
                                41h   Hard Disk Parameters  (except PC1)
                                42h   Pointer to screen BIOS entry  (EGA, VGA, PS/2)
                                43h   Pointer to EGA initialization parameter table
    44     116-119      BIOS    First 128 Graphics Characters
  45-47    120-131      BIOS    Reserved for BIOS
                                45h   Reserved by IBM  (not initialized)
                                46h   Pointer to hard disk 2 params (AT, PS/2)
                                47h   Reserved by IBM  (not initialized)
    48     132-135      BIOS    PCjr Cordless Keyboard Translation
    49     136-139      BIOS    PCjr Non-Keyboard Scancode Translation Table
                                4Ah   Real-Time Clock Alarm (Convertible, PS/2)
  50-5F    140-17F      BIOS    Reserved for BIOS
                                5Ah   Cluster Adapter BIOS entry address
                               *5Bh   IBM  (cluster adapter?)
                                5Ch   NETBIOS interface entry port
  60-67    180-19F      User Program Interrupts (available for general use)
                                60h   10-Net Network
                                67h   Used by LIM & AQA EMS, EEMS
  68-7F    1A0-1FF      Reserved by IBM
                                6Ch   System Resume Vector (Convertible)
                                6Fh   some Novell and 10-Net API functions
                                70h   IRQ 8, Real Time Clock Interrupt (AT, PS/2)
                                71h   IRQ 9, LAN Adapter 1
                                72h   IRQ 10  (AT, XT/286, PS/2)   Reserved
                                73h   IRQ 11  (AT, XT/286, PS/2)   Reserved
                                74h   IRQ 12  Mouse Interrupt (PS/2)
                                75h   IRQ 13, Coprocessor Error
                                76h   IRQ 14, Hard Disk Controller (AT, PS/2)
                                77h   IRQ 15 (AT, XT/286, PS/2)   Reserved
                                7Ch   IBM REXX88PC command language
  80-85    200-217      ROM BASIC
  86-F0    218-3C3      Used by BASIC Interpreter When BASIC is running
  F1-FF    3C4-3FF      Reserved by IBM
                                0F1h-0FFh   Interprocess Communications Area
                               *0F8h   Set Shell Interrupt (OEM)
                               *0F9h   OEM SHELL service codes
                                0FAh   USART ready (RS-232C)
                                0FBh   USART RS ready (keyboard)
                               *0FEh   used on '283 & '386
                               *0FFh   used on '283 & '386
* = "undocumented"
```

The IBM-PC System Interrupts (in detail)

Interrupt 00h Divide by Zero
(0:0000h)
(processor error). Automatically called at end of DIV or IDIV operation that results in error. Normally set by DOS to display an error message and abort the program.

Interrupt 01h Single step
(0:0004h)

Taken after every instruction when CPU Trap Flag indicates single-step mode (bit 8 of FLAGS is 1). This is what makes the 'T' command of DEBUG work for single stepping. Is not generated after MOV to segment register or POP of segment register. (unless you have a very early 8088 with the microcode bug).

Interrupt 02h Non-maskable interrupt
(0:0008h)
Vector not disabled via CLI. Generated by NMI signal in hardware. This signal has various uses:

```
POST parity error:               all except PCjr and Convertible
80x87 coprocessor interrupt:     all except PCjr and Convertible
Keyboard interrupt:              PCjr, Convertible
I/O channel check:               Convertible, PS/2 50+
Disk controller power-on request: Convertible
System suspend:                  Convertible
Realtime clock:                  Convertible
System watchdog timer:           PS/2 50+
Timeout interrupt:               PS/2 50+
DMA timer time-out interrupt:    PS/2 50+
Infrared keyboard link:          PCjr
```

Interrupt 03h Breakpoint
(0:000Ch)
Taken when CPU executes the 1-byte int 3 (0CCh). Similar to 8080's

(internal)
RST instruction. Generally used to set breakpoints for DEBUG. Also used by Turbo Pascal versions 1,2,3 when {$U+} specified

Interrupt 04h Divide overflow
(0:0010h)
Generated by INTO instruction if OF flag is set. If flag isnot set,(internal) INTO is effectively a NOP. Used to trap any arithmetic errors when program is ready to handle them rather than immediately when they occur.

Interrupt 05h Print Screen
(0:0014h)
Service dumps the screen to the printer. Invoked by int 9 for shifted key 55 (PrtSc). Automatically called by keyboard scan when PrtSc key is pressed. Normally executes a routine to print the screen, but may call any routine that can safely be executed from inside the keyboard scanner. Status and result byte are at address 0050:0000.

(internal) BOUND Check Failed (80286+)
Generated by BOUND instruction when the value to be tested is less than the indicated lower bound or greater than the indicated upper bound.

```
entry   AH      05h
return  absolute address 50:0
        00h     print screen has not been called, or upon return from a call
                there were no errors
        01h     print screen is already in progress
        0FFh    error encountered during printing
note 1. Uses BIOS services to read the screen.
     2. Output is directed to LPT1.
     3. Revectored into GRAPHICS.COM if GRAPHICS.COM is loaded.
```

Interrupt 06h Reserved by IBM
(0:0018h)
(internal) Undefined Opcode (80286+)

Interrupt 07h Reserved by IBM
(0:00C0h)
(internal) No Math Unit Available (80286+)

Interrupt 08h Timer
(0:0020h)
55ms timer 'tick' taken 18.2 times per second. Updates BIOS clock and turns off diskette drive motors after 2 seconds of inactivity.
(IRQ0)
(internal) Double Fault (80286+ protected mode)
Called when multiple exceptions occur on one instruction, or an exception occurs in an exception handler. If an exception occurs in the double fault handler, the CPU goes into SHUTDOWN mode (which circuitry in the PC/AT converts to a reset).

```
entry    AH       08h
return   absolute addresses:
         40:6C    number of interrupts since power on (4 bytes)
         40:70    number of days since power on      (1 byte)
         40:67    day counter on all products after AT
         40:40    motor control count - gets decremented and shuts off diskette
                  motor if zero
note     Int 1Ch is invoked by int 08h as a user interrupt.
```

(internal) Double Fault (80286+ protected mode)
 Called when multiple exceptions occur on one instruction, or an exception occurs in an exception handler. If an exception occurs in the double fault handler, the CPU goes into SHUT DOWN mode (which circuitry in the PC/AT converts to a reset).

Interrupt 09h Keyboard
(0:0024h)
Taken whenever a key is pressed or released. This is normally a scan code, but may also be an ACK or NAK of a command on AT-type keyboards.
(IRQ1)
```
note     Stores characters/scan-codes in status at absolute addr. [0040:0017,18]
```

```
(internal) Math Unit Protection Fault (80286+ protected mode)
entry    AH       09h
return   at absolute memory addresses:
         40:17    bit
                  0        right shift key depressed
                  1        left shift key depressed
                  2        control key depressed
                  3        alt key depressed
                  4        ScrollLock state has been toggled
                  5        NumLock state has been toggled
                  6        CapsLock state has been toggled
                  7        insert state is active
         40:18    bit
                  0        left control key depressed
                  1        left alt key depressed
                  2        SysReq key depressed
                  3        Pause key has been toggled
                  4        ScrollLock key is depressed
                  5        NumLock key is depressed
                  6        CapsLock key is depressed
                  7        Insert key is depressed
         40:96    bit
                  0        last code was the E1h hidden code
                  1        last code was the E0h hidden code
                  2        right control key down
                  3        right alt key down
                  4        101 key Enhanced keyboard installed
                  5        force NumLock if rd ID & kbx
```

```
                6          last character was first ID character
                7          doing a read ID (must be bit 0)
        40:97   bit
                0          ScrollLock indicator
                1          NumLock indicator
                2          CapsLock indicator
                3          circus system indicator
                4          ACK received
                5          resend received flag
                6          mode indicator update
                7          keyboard transmit error flag
        40:1E   keyboard buffer (20h bytes)
        40:1C   buffer tail pointer
        40:72   1234h if ctrl-alt-del pressed on keyboard
   AL           scan code
note 1. Int 05h invoked if PrtSc key pressed.
     2. Int 1Bh invoked if Ctrl-Break key sequence pressed.
     3. Int 15h, AH=85h invoked on AT and after if SysReq key is pressed.
     4. Int 15h, AH=4Fh invoked on machines after AT.
     5. Int 16h, BIOS keyboard functions, uses this interrupt.
```

Interrupt 0Ah EGA Vertical Retrace
(0:0028h) used by EGA vertical retrace
(IRQ2)
Note: The TOPS and PCnet adapters use this IRQ line by default.

(internal) Invalid Task State Segment (80286+ protected mode)

Interrupt 0Bh Communications Controller (serial port) hdw. entry
(0:002Ch) Serial Port 2 (COM2)
(IRQ3)
Note 1. IRQ 3 may be used by SDLC (synchronous data-link control) or bisynchronous communications cards instead of a serial port.
  2. The TOPS and PCnet adapters use this interrupt request line as an alternate.
  3. On PS/2s, COM2 through COM8 share this interrupt.
  4. On many PCs, COM4 shares this interrupt.
  5. On the Commodore Amiga 2000 with the PC Bridge Board, this interrupt is used for communication between the Amiga system board and the Bridge Board. This was probably the lowest IRQ level they felt safe using, but limits the A2000's use of network cards, etc.

(internal) Not Present (80286+ protected mode)
Generated when loading a segment register if the segment descriptor indicates that the segment is not currently in memory. May be used to implement virtual memory.

Interrupt 0Ch Communications Controller (serial port) hdw. entry
(0:0030h) Serial Port 1 (COM1) or internal modem in PCjr or Convertible
(IRQ4)
Note 1. IRQ 4 may be used by SDLC (synchronous data-link control) or bisynchronous communications cards instead of a serial port.
  2. On some PCs, this interrupt is shared by COM3.
  3. Tandy computers use IRQ4 instead of IRQ5 for the hard disk interrupt.
  4. Best performance of mice sometimes happens when they are configured for IRQ4 instead of IRQ3, since some mouse drivers may lock system interrupts for long periods.

(internal) Stack Fault (80286+ protected mode)
Generated on stack overflow/underflow. Note that the 80286 will shut down in real mode if SP=1 before a push.

Interrupt 0Dh Alternate Printer, AT 80287
(0:0034h) used by hard disk on IBM and most compatibles, 60 Hz RAM
 (IRQ5)
refresh, LPT2 on AT, XT/286, and PS/2, dummy CRT vertical retrace on PCjr
Note: Various Tandy 1000 models may use this line for the 60Hhz RAM refresh or as 'optional bus interrupt'.

(internal) General Protection Violation (80286+)
Called in real mode when an instruction attempts to access a word operand located at offset 0FFFFh or a PUSH MEM or POP MEM instruction contains an invalid bit code in the second byte.

Interrupt 0Eh Diskette Interrupt
(0:0038h)
Generated by floppy controller on completion of an operation
 (IRQ6) (sets bit 8 of 40:3E)

(internal) Page Fault (80386+ native mode)

Interrupt 0Fh Reserved by IBM
(0:003Ch) IRQ7 used by PPI interrupt (LPT1, LPT2)
(IRQ7)
Note: Generated by the LPT1 printer adapter when printer becomes ready. Many printer adapters do not reliably generate this interrupt.

3

THE PC ROM BIOS

Calling the ROM BIOS

The BIOS services are invoked by placing the number of the desired function in register AH, subfunction in AL, setting the other registers to any specific requirements of the function, and invoking any of ints 10h through int 20h.

When the interrupt is called, all register and flag values are pushed into the stack. The interrupt address contains a pointer into an absolute address in the ROM BIOS chip address space. This location may be further vectored into the IBMBIO.COM (or equivalent) file or user file.

The address vector points to a particular BIOS command handler. The handler pops the register values, compares them to its list of functions, and executes the function if valid. When the function is complete, it may pass values back to the command handler. The handler will push the values into the stack and then return control to the calling program.

Most functions will return an error code; some return more information. Details are contained in the listings for the individual functions.

Register settings listed are the ones used by the BIOS. Some functions will return with garbage values in unused registers. Do not test for values in unspecified registers; your program may exhibit odd behaviour.

Interrupt 10h Video Service
(0:0040h) The BIOS Video Services may be found in Chapter 16.

(internal) Coprocessor Error (80286+)
Generated by the CPU when the -ERROR pin is asserted by the coprocessor (usually 80x87, but may be any multimaster CPU or alternate NDP such as Weitek, etc.). ATs and clones usually wire the coprocessor to use IRQ13, but not all get it right.

Interrupt 11h Equipment Check
(0:0044h) Reads the BIOS Data Area and returns two bytes of setup info. entry. No parameters are required

```
return  AX      Equipment listing word. Bits are:
                0    number of floppy drives
                     0    no drives
                     1    bootable (IPL) diskette drive installed
```

```
                 1     math chip
                       0         no math coprocessor (80x87) present
                       1         math coprocessor (80x87) present
        (PS/2)   2     0         mouse not installed
                       1         mouse installed
        (PC)     2,3   system board RAM
                       0,0       16k     (PC-0, PC-1)
                       0,1       32k
                       1,0       48k
                       1,1       64k     (PC-2, XT)
                       note 1. not commonly used. Set both bits to 1
                            2. both bits always 1 in AT
                 4,5   initial video mode
                       0,0 no video installed (use with dumb terminal)
                       0,1       40x25 colour   (CGA)
                       1,0       80x25 colour   (CGA, EGA, PGA, MCGA, VGA)
                       1,1       80x25 monochrome (MDA or Hercules, most superhires
                                 mono systems)
                 6,7   number of diskette drives (only if bit 0 is 1)
                       0,0       1 drives
                       0,1       2 drives
                       1,0       3 drives
                       1,1       4 drives
                 8     0         DMA present
                       1         no DMA (PCjr, some Tandy 1000s, 1400LT)
                 9,A,B number of RS232 serial ports (0-3)
                       0,0,0     none
                       0,0,1     1
                       0,1,0     2
                       0,1,1     3
                       1,0,0     4
                 C     0         no game I/O attached
                       1         game I/O attached (default for PCjr)
                 D     serial accessory installation
                       0         no serial accessories installed
                       1         Convertible - internal modem installed or PCjr -
                                 serial printer attached
                 E,F   number of parallel printers
                       0,0       none
                       0,1       one     (LPT1, PRN)
                       1,0       two     (LPT2)
                       1,1       three   (LPT3)
                       note      Models before PS/2 would allow a fourth parallel
                                 printer. Remapping of the BIOS in the PS/2s does
                                 not allow the use of LPT4.
```

Interrupt 12h Memory Size
(0:0048h) get system memory
```
entry   no parameters required
return  AX       number of contiguous 1K RAM blocks available for DOS
```
Note 1. This is the same value stored in absolute address 04:13h..
  2. For some early PC models, the amount of memory returned by this call is determined by the settings of the dip switches on the motherboard and may not reflect all the memory that is physically present.
  3. For the PC/AT, the value returned is the amount of functional memory found during the power-on self-test, regardless of the memory size configuration information stored in CMOS RAM.
  4. The value returned does not reflect any extended memory (above the 1 Mb boundary) that may be present on 80286 or 80386 machines.

Interrupt 13h Disk Functions
(0:0049h) The service calls for BIOS disk functions are located in Chapter 8.

Interrupt 14h Initialize and Access Serial Port For Int 14
(0:0050h) the following status is defined:

The PC ROM BIOS

```
            serial status byte:
            bits    0 delta clear to send
                    1 delta data set ready
                    2 trailing edge ring detector
                    3 delta receive line signal detect
                    4 clear to send
                    5 data set ready
                    6 ring indicator
                    7 receive line signal detect

            line status byte:
            bits    0 data ready
                    1 overrun error
                    2 parity error
                    3 framing error
                    4 break detect
                    5 transmit holding register empty
                    6 transmit shift register empty
                    7 time out   note: if bit 7 set then other bits are invalid
```

All routines have AH=function number and DX=RS232 card number (0 based). AL=character to send or received character on exit, unless otherwise noted.

```
entry   AH      00h     Initialize And Access Serial Communications Port
                        bit pattern: BBBPPSLL
                        BBB = baud rate:   110, 150, 300, 600, 1200,
                                           2400, 4800, 9600
                        PP  = parity:      01 = odd, 11 = even
                        S   = stop bits:   0 = 1, 1 = 2
                        LL  = word length: 10 = 7-bits, 11 = 8-bits
        AL      parms for initialization:
                bit pattern:
                0       word length
                1       word length
                2       stop bits
                3       parity
                4       parity
                5       baud rate
                6       baud rate
                7       baud rate
                word length     10      7 bits
                                11      8 bits
                stop bits       0       1 stop bit
                                1       2 stop bits
                parity          00      none
                                01      odd
                                11      even
                baud rate       000     110 baud
                                001     150 baud
                                010     300 baud
                                011     600 baud
                                100     1200 baud
                                101     2400 baud
                                110     4800 baud
                                111     9600 baud    (4800 on PCjr)
        DX      port number (0=COM1, 1=COM2, etc.)
return  AH      line status
        AL      modem status
note    To initialize the serial port to 9600 baud on PS/2 machines, seefns 04h
        and 05h.

Function 01h    Send Character in AL to Comm Port
entry   AH      01h
        AL      character
        DX      port number (0 - 3)
return  AH      RS232 status code
                bit     0       data ready
                        1       overrun error
                        2       parity error
                        3       framing error
```

```
                              4       break detected
                              5       transmission buffer register empty
                              6       transmission shift register empty
                              7       timeout
              AL        modem status
                        bit
                              0       delta clear-to-send
                              1       delta data-set-ready
                              2       trailing edge ring detected
                              3       change, receive line signal detected
                              4       clear-to-send
                              5       data-set-ready
                              6       ring received
                              7       receive line signal detected

Function 02h            Wait For A Character From Comm Port DX
entry   AH              02h
        DX              port number (0-3)
return  AL              character received
        AH              error code (see above)(00h for no error)

Function 03h            Fetch the Status of Comm Port DX (0 or 1)
entry   AH              03h
        DX              port (0-3)
return  AH              set bits (01h) indicate comm-line status
                        bit     7       timeout
                        bit     6       empty transmit shift register
                        bit     5       empty transmit holding register
                        bit     4       break detected ('long-space')
                        bit     3       framing error
                        bit     2       parity error
                        bit     1       overrun error
                        bit     0       data ready
        AL              set bits indicate modem status
                        bit     7       received line signal detect
                        bit     6       ring indicator
                        bit     5       data set ready
                        bit     4       clear to send
                        bit     3       delta receive line signal detect
                        bit     2       trailing edge ring detector
                        bit     1       delta data set ready
                        bit     0       delta clear to send

Function 04h              Extended Initialize               (Convertible, PS/2)
entry   AH              04h
        AL              break status
                        01h     if break
                        00h     if no break
        BH              parity
                        00h       no parity
                        01h       odd parity
                        02h       even parity
                        03h       stick parity odd
                        04h       stick parity even
        BL              number of stop bits
                        00h       one stop bit
                        01h       2 stop bits (1 if 5 bit word length)
        CH              word length
                        00h       5 bits
                        01h       6 bits
                        02h       7 bits
                        03h       8 bits
        CL              baud rate
                        00h       110
                        01h       150
                        02h       300
                        03h       600
                        04h       1200
                        05h       2400
                        06h       4800
                        07h       9600
```

```
                    08h       19200
            DX      comm port (0-3)
return      AH      line control status
            AL      modem status
note        Provides a superset of fn 00h capabilities for PS/2 machines.

Function 05h        Extended Communication Port Control      (Convertible, PS/2)
entry       AH      05h
            AL      00h       read modem control register
                    01h       write modem control register
            BL      modem control register
                bits 0        DTR data terminal ready
                     1        RTS request to send
                     2        out1
                     3        out2
                     4        loop
                     5,6,7    reserved
            DX      port number (0=COM1, 1=COM2, etc.)
return      AH      port status (see 00h above)
            AL      modem status (see 00h above)
            BL      modem control register (see 01h above)
```

FOSSIL Drivers

Interrupt 14h FOSSIL (Fido/Opus/Seadog Standard Interface Level) drivers
A FOSSIL is a device driver for handling the IBM PC serial communications ports in a standard fashion from an application (communications) program. A FOSSIL chains into the int 14h BIOS communications vector and replaces many functions with enhanced routines that may be easily accessed by an application.

For all functions, all registers not specifically containing a function return value must be preserved across the call.

```
entry       AH      00h       Set baud rate and parameters
            AL      byte
                    bits 7,6,5 baudrate
                    000       19200 baud
                    001       38400 baud
                    010       300 baud
                    011       600 baud
                    100       1200 baud
                    101       2400 baud
                    110       4800 baud
                    111       9600 baud
                    bits 4,3 parity
                    00        none
                    01        odd
                    10        none
                    11        even
                    bit 2 stop bits
                    0         1 stop bit
                    1         2 stop bits
                    bit 1 char length
                    0         5 bits plus value
                    other     optional
            DX      port number (NOP if DX=00FFh)
return      AX      status (see fn 03h)
note        Low-order 5 bits are undefined by FOSSIL 1.0 spec.

entry       AH      01h       Transmit character with wait
            AL      ASCII value of character to be sent
            DX      port number (NOP if DX=00FFh)
return      AX      status bits (see function 03h)
note        1 Character is queued for transmission. If there is room in the
            transmitter buffer when this call is made, the character will be stored
```

```
           and control returned to caller. If the buffer is full, the driver will
           wait for room. Use this function with caution when flow control is
           enabled.

entry   AH      02h     FOSSIL: Receive a character with wait
        DX      port number (0-3) (NOP if DX=00FFh)
return  AH      RS-232 status code (see AH=00h above)
        AL      ASCII value of character received from serial port
note    Will timeout if DSR is not asserted, even if function 03h returns data
        ready.

entry   AH      03h     FOSSIL: Request status
        DX      port number  (NOP if DX=00FFh)
return  AX      status bit mask
        AH      bit 0 set   RDA     input data is available in buffer
                    1 set   OVRN    input buffer overrun
                    2 N/A
                    3 N/A
                    4 N/A
                    5 set   THRE    room is available in output buffer
                    6 set   TSRE    output buffer is empty
                    7 N/A
        AL      bit 0 N/A
                    1 N/A
                    2 N/A
                    3 set           this bit is always set
                    4 N/A
                    5 N/A
                    6 N/A
                    7 set   DCD     carrier detect
note    Bit 3 of AL is always returned set to enable programs to use it as a
        carrier detect bit on hardwired (null modem) links.

entry   AH      04h     Initialize FOSSIL driver
        BX      4F50h                   (optional)
        DX      port number             (DX=00FFh special)
        ES:CX   pointer to ^C flag address (optional)
return  AX      1954h if successful
        BL      maximum function number supported (excluding 7Eh-0BFh)
        BH      revision of FOSSIL supported
note 1. DTR is raised when FOSSIL inits.
     2. Existing baudrate is preserved.
     3. If BX contains 4F50h, the address specified in ES:CX is that of a ^C flag
        byte in the application program, to be incremented when ^C is detected
        in the keyboard service routines. This is an optional service and only
        need be supported on machines where the keyboard service can't (or
        won't) perform an int 1Bh or int 23h when a control-C is entered.

entry   AH      05h     Deinitialize FOSSIL driver
        DX      port number  (DX=00FFh special)
return  none
note 1. DTR is not affected.
     2. Disengages driver from comm port. Should be done when operations on the
        port are complete.
     3. If DX=00FFh, the initialization that was performed when FOSSIL function
        04h with DX=00FFh should be undone.

entry   AH      06h     FOSSIL: Raise/lower DTR
        AL      DTR state to be set
                00h     lower DTR
                01h     raise DTR
        DX      comm port (NOP if DX=00FFh)
return  none
entry   AH      07h     FOSSIL: Return timer tick parameters
return  AH      ticks per second on interrupt number shown in AL
        AL      timer tick interrupt number (not vector!)
        DX      milliseconds per tick (approximate)

entry   AH      08h     FOSSIL: Flush output buffer
        DX      port number (NOP if DX=00FFh)
return  none
```

The PC ROM BIOS

```
note        Waits until all output is done.
entry   AH      09h     FOSSIL: Purge output buffer
        DX              port number (NOP if DX=00FFh)
return  none
note        Returns to caller immediately.

entry   AH      0Ah     FOSSIL: Purge input buffer
        DX              port number (NOP if DX=00FFh)
return  none
note 1. If any flow control restraint has been employed (dropping RTS or
        transmitting XOFF) the port will be 'released' by doing the reverse,
        raising RTS or sending XON.
     2. Returns to caller immediately.

entry   AH      0Bh     FOSSIL: Transmit no wait
        AL              ASCII character value to be sent
        DX              port number (NOP if DX=00FFh)
return  AX      0000h   character not accepted
                0001h   character accepted
note        This is exactly the same as the 'regular' transmit call except that if
            there is no space available in the output buffer a value of zero is
            returned in AX, if room is available a value 1 (one) is returned.

entry   AH      0Ch     FOSSIL: Nondestructive Read no Wait
        DX              port number (NOP if DX=00FFh)
return  AH              character
                0FFFFh  character not available
note 1. Reads async buffer.
     2. Does not remove keycode from buffer.

entry   AH      0Dh     FOSSIL: Keyboard read no wait
return  AX              IBM keyboard scan code or
                        0FFFFh if no keyboard character available
note 1. Use IBM-style function key mapping in the high order byte.
     2. Scan codes for non function keys are not specifically required but may be
        included.
     3. Does not remove keycode from buffer.

entry   AH      0Eh     FOSSIL: Keyboard input with wait
return  AX              IBM keyboard scan code
note        Returns the next character from the keyboard or waits if no
            character is available.

entry   AH      0Fh     Enable or Disable flow control
        AL              bit mask describing requested flow control
          bits 0        XON/XOFF on transmit (watch for XOFF while sending)
               1        CTS/RTS (CTS on transmit/RTS on receive)
               2        reserved
               3        XON/XOFF on receive (send XOFF when buffer near full)
               4-7      not used, FOSSIL spec calls for setting to 1
        DX              port number (NOP if DX=00FFh)
return  none
note 1. Bit 2 is reserved for DSR/DTR, but is not currently supported in any
        implementation.
     2. TRANSMIT flow control allows the other end to restrain the transmitter
        when you are overrunning it. RECEIVE flow control tells the FOSSIL to
        attempt to do just that if it is being overwhelmed.
     3. Enabling transmit Xon/Xoff will cause the FOSSIL to stop transmitting
        upon receiving an Xoff. The FOSSIL will resume transmitting when an Xon
        is received.
     4. Enabling CTS/RTS will cause the FOSSIL to cease transmitting when CTS is
        lowered. Transmission will resume when CTS is raised. The FOSSIL will
        drop RTS when the receive buffer reaches a predetermined percentage
        full. The FOSSIL will raise RTS when the receive buffer empties below
        the predetermined percentage full. The point(s) at which this occurs is
        left to the individual FOSSIL implementor.
     5. Enabling receive Xon/Xoff will cause the FOSSIL to send a Xoff when the
        receive buffer reaches a pre-determined percentage full. An Xon will be
        sent when the receive buffer empties below the predetermined percentage
        full. The point(s) at which this occurs is left to the individual FOSSIL
        implementor.
```

```
       6. Applications using this function should set all bits ON in the high
          nibble of AL as well.  There is a compatible (but not identical) FOSSIL
          driver implementation that uses the high nibble as a control mask.  If
          your application sets the high nibble to all ones, it will always work,
          regardless of the method used by any given driver.

entry    AH       10h      Extended Ctrl-C/Ctrl-K checking and transmit on/off
         AL       flags bit mask byte (bit set if activated)
           bits 0          enable/disable Ctrl-C/Ctrl-K checking
                1          disable/enable the transmitter
                2-7        not used
         DX       port number (NOP if DX=00FFh)
return   AX       status byte
                  0000h    control-C/K has not been received
                  0001h    control-C/K has been received
note     This is used primarily for programs that can't trust XON/XOFF at FOSSIL
         le vel (such as BBS software).

entry    AH       11h      FOSSIL: Set current cursor location.
         DH       row (line) 0-24
         DL       column     0-79
return   none
note 1.  This function looks exactly like the int 10h, fn 02h on the IBM PC. The
         cursor location is passed in DX: row in DH and column in DL. This
         function treats the screen as a coordinate system whose origin (0,0) is
         the upper left hand corner of the screen.
     2.  Row and column start at 0.

entry    AH       12h      FOSSIL: Read current cursor location.
return   DH       row (line)
         DL       column
note 1.  Looks exactly like int 10h/fn 03h in the IBM PC BIOS. The current cursor
         location (same coordinate system as function 16h) is passed back in DX.
     2.  Row and column start at 0.

entry    AH       13h      FOSSIL: Single character ANSI write to screen.
         AL       value of character to display
return   none
note     This call might not be reentrant since ANSI processing may be through DOS.

entry    AH       14h      FOSSIL: Enable or disable watchdog processing
         AL       00h      to disable watchdog
                  01h      to enable watchdog
         DX       port number (NOP if DX=00FFh)
return   none
note 1.  This call will cause the FOSSIL to reboot the system if Carrier Detect
         for the specified port drops while watchdog is turned on.
     2.  The port need not be active for this function to work.

entry    AH       15h      Write character to screen using BIOS support routines
         AL       ASCII code of character to display
return   none
note 1.  This function is reentrant.
     2.  ANSI processing may not be assumed.

entry    AH       16h      Insert or Delete a function from the timer tick chain
         AL       00h      to delete a function
                  01h      to add a function
         ES:DX    address of function
return   AX       0000h    successful
                  0FFFFh   unsuccessful

entry    AH       17h      FOSSIL: Reboot system
         AL       boot type
                  00h      cold boot
                  01h      warm boot
return   none

entry    AH       18h      FOSSIL: Read block
         CX       maximum number of characters to transfer
         DX       port number (NOP if DX=00FFh)
```

```
           ES:DI      pointer to user buffer
return     AX         number of characters transferred
note 1. This function does not wait for more characters to become available if
        the value in CX exceeds the number of characters currently stored.
     2. ES:DI are left unchanged by the call; the count of bytes actually
        transferred will be returned in AX.

entry      AH         19h     FOSSIL: Write block
           CX         maximum number of characters to transfer
           DX         port number  (NOP if DX=00FFh)
           ES:DI      pointer to user buffer
return     AX         number of characters transfered
note       ES and DI are not modified by this call.

entry      AH         1Ah     FOSSIL: Break signal begin or end
           AL         00h     stop sending 'break'
                      01h     start sending 'break'
           DX         port number  (NOP if DX=00FFh)
return     none
note 1. Resets all transmit flow control restraints such as an XOFF received from
        remote.
     2. Init (fn 04h) or UnInit (fn 05h) will stop an in-progress break.
     3. The application must determine the 'length' of the break.

entry      AH         1Bh     FOSSIL: Return information about the driver
           CX         size of user buffer in bytes
           DX         port number  (if DX=00FFh, port data will not be valid)
           ES:DI      pointer to user buffer
return     AX         number of characters transferred
           ES:DI      user buffer structure:
                      00h     word    size of structure in bytes
                      02h     byte    FOSSIL driver version
                      03h     byte    revision level of this specific driver
                      04h     dword   FAR pointer to ASCII ID string
                      08h     word    size of the input buffer in bytes
                      0Ah     word    number of bytes in input buffer
                      0Ch     word    size of the output buffer in bytes
                      0Eh     word    number of bytes in output buffer
                      10h     byte    width of screen in characters
                      11h     byte    screen height in characters
                      12h     byte    actual baud rate, computer to modem (see mask in
                                      function 00h)
note 1. The baud rate byte contains the bits that fn 00h would use to set the
        port to that speed.
     2. The fields related to a particular port (buffer size, space left in the
        buffer, baud rate) will be undefined if port=0FFh or an invalid port is
        contained in DX.
     3. Additional information will always be passed after these, so that the
        fields will never change with FOSSIL revision changes.

entry      AH         7Eh     FOSSIL: Install an external application function
           AL         code assigned to external application
           ES:DX      pointer to entry point
return     AX         1954h           FOSSIL driver present
                      not 1954h       FOSSIL driver not present
           BH         00h     failed
                      01h     successful
           BL         code assigned to application (same as input AL)
note 1. Application codes 80h-0BFh are supported. Codes 80h-83h are reserved.
     2. An error code of BH=00h with AX=1954h should mean that another external
        application has already been installed with the code specified in AL.
     3. Applications are entered via a FAR call and should make a FAR return.

entry      AH         7Fh     FOSSIL: Remove an external application function
           AL         code assigned to external application
           ES:DX      pointer to entry point
return     AX         1954h
           BH         00h     failed
                      01h     successful
           BL         code assigned to application (same as input AL)
```

Interrupt 15h Cassette I/O
(0:0054h) Renamed 'System Services' on PS/2 line. Issuing int 15h on an XT may cause a system crash. On AT and after, interrupts are disabled with CLI when the interrupt service routine is called, but most ROM versions do not restore interrupts with STI.

```
Function 00h     Turn Cassette Motor On                         (PC, PCjr only)
entry   AH       00h
return  CF       set on error
                 AH         error code
                            00h      no errors
                            01h      CRC error
                            02h      bad tape signals
                                     no data transitions (PCjr)
                            03h      no data found on tape
                                     not used (PCjr)
                            04h      no data
                                     no leader (PCjr)
                            80h      invalid command
                            86h      no cassette present
                                     not valid in PCjr
note    NOP for systems where cassette not supported.

Function 01h     Turn Cassette Motor Off                        (PC, PCjr only)
entry   AH       01h
return  CF       set on error
        AH       error code (86h)
note    NOP for systems where cassette not supported.

Function 02h     Read Blocks From Cassette                      (PC, PCjr only)
entry   AH       02h
        CX       count of bytes to read
        ES:BX    segment:offset + 1 of last byte read
return  CF       set on error
        AH       error code (01h, 02h, 04h, 80h, 86h)
        DX       count of bytes actually read
        ES:BX    pointer past last byte written
note 1. NOP for systems where cassette not supported.
     2. Cassette operations normally read 256 byte blocks.

Function 03h     Write Data Blocks to Cassette                  (PC, PCjr only)
entry   AH       03h
        CX       count of bytes to write
        ES:BX    pointer to data buffer

return  CF       set on error
        AH       error code (80h, 86h)
        CX       00h
        ES:BX    pointer to last byte written+1
note 1. NOP for systems where cassette not supported.
     2. The last block is padded to 256 bytes with zeroes if needed.
     3. No errors are returned by this service.

Function 0Fh     ESDI Format Unit Periodic Interrupt            (PS/2 50+)
entry   AH       0Fh
        AL       phase code
                 00h      reserved
                 01h      surface analysis
                 02h      formatting
return  CF       clear    if formatting should continue
                 set      if it should terminate
note 1. Called the BIOS on the ESDI Fixed Disk Drive Adapter/A during a format or
        surface analysis operation after each cylinder is completed.
     2. This function call can be captured by a program so that it will be
        notified as each cylinder is formatted or analyzed. The program can count
        interrupts for each phase to determine the current cylinder number.
     3. The BIOS default handler for this function returns with CF set.
```

```
Function 10h TopView API Function Calls                              (TopView)
entry   AH     00h      PAUSE    Give Up CPU Time
                        return 00h      after other processes run
               01h      GETMEM   allocate 'system' memory
                        BX       number of bytes to allocate
                        return ES:DI    pointer to a block of memory
               02h      PUTMEM   deallocate 'system' memory
                        ES:DI    pointer to previously allocated block
                        return   block freed
               03h      PRINTC   display character/attribute on screen
                        BH       attribute
                        BL       character
                        DX       segment of object handle for window
                        note     BX=0 does not display anything, it positions the
                                 hardware cursor.
               04h-09h unknown
               10h      unknown
                        AL       04h thru 12h
                        return   TopView - unimplemented in DV 2.0x pops up
                                 'Programming error' window in DV 2.0x
               11h      unknown
               12h      unknown
               13h      GETBIT   define a 2nd-level interrupt handler
                        ES:DI    pointer to FAR service routine
                        return BX       bit mask indicating which bit was
                                        allocated 0 if no more bits availble
               14h      FREEBIT  undefine a 2nd-level interrupt handler
                        BX       bit mask from int 15/fn1013h
               15h      SETBIT   schedule one or more 2nd-level interrupts
                        BX       bit mask for interrupts to post
                        return   indicated routines will be called at next ???
               16h      ISOBJ    verify object handle
                        ES:DI    possible object handle
                        return BX       -1 if ES:DI is a valid object handle
                                         0 if ES:DI is not
               17h      TopView - unimplemented in DV 2.00
                        return   pops up 'Programming Error' window in DV 2.00
               18h      LOCATE   Find Window at a Given Screen Location
                        BH       column
                        BL       row
                        ES       segment of object handle for ?
                                 (0 = use default)
                        return ES       segment of object handle for window which
                                        is visible at the indicated position
               19h      SOUND    Make Tone
                        BX       frequency in Hertz
                        CX       duration in clock ticks (18.2 ticks/sec)
                        return   immediately, tone continues to completion
                        note     If another tone is already playing, the new tone
                                 does not start until completion of the
                                 previous one. In DV 2.00, it is possible to
                                 enqueue about 32 tones before the process is
                                 blocked until a note completes. In DV 2.00, the
                                 lowest tone allowed is 20 Hz
               1Ah      OSTACK   Switch to Task's Internal Stack
                        return   stack switched
               1Bh      BEGINC   Begin Critical Region
                        return   task-switching temporarily disabled
                        note     Will not task-switch until End Critical
                                 Region (AH=101Ch) is called
               1Ch      ENDC     End Critical Region
                        return   task-switching enabled
               1Dh      STOP     STOP TASK
                        ES       segment of object handle for task to be stopped
                                 (= handle of main window for that task)
                        return   indicated task will no longer get CPU time
                        note     At least in DV 2.00, this function is ignored
                                 unless the indicated task is the current task.
               1Eh      START    Start Task
                        ES       segment of object handle for task to be started
                                 (= handle of main window for that task)
```

```
              return    Indicated task is started up again
       1Fh    DISPEROR  Pop-Up Error Window
              BX        bit fields:
                        0-12     number of characters to display
                        13,14    which mouse button may be pressed
                                 to remove window
                                 00         either
                                 01         left
                                 10         right
                                 11         either
                        15       beep if 1
              CH        width of error window (0 = default)
              CL        height of error window (0 = default)
              DS:DI     pointer to text of message
              DX        segment of object handle
              return BX status:
                        1          left button pressed
                        2          right button pressed
                        27         ESC key pressed
              note      Window remains on-screen until ESC or indicated
                        mouse button is pressed
       20h    TopView - unimplemented in DV 2.0x
              return    pops up 'Programming Error' window in DV 2.0x
       21h    PGMINT    Interrupt Another Task (TopView)
              BX        segment of object handle for task to interrupt
              DX:CX     address of FAR routine to jump to next time task
                        is run
              return    nothing?
              note      The current ES, DS, SI, DI, and BP are passed to
                        the FAR routine
       22h    GETVER    Get Version
              BX        00h
              return BX nonzero, TopView or compatible loaded
                     BH minor version
                     BL major version
              notes     TaskView v1.1C returns BX = 0001h
                        DESQview  v2.0 returns BX = 0A01h
       23h    POSWIN    Position Window
              BX        segment of object handle for parent window within
                        which to position the window (0 = full screen)
              CH        # columns to offset from position in DL
              CL        # rows to offset from position in DL
              DL        bit flags
                        0,1      horizontal position
                                 00         current
                                 01         center
                                 10         left
                                 11         right
                        2,3      vertical position
                                 00         current
                                 01         center
                                 10         top
                                 11         bottom
                        4        don't redraw screen if set
                        5-7      not used
              ES        segment of object handle for window to be
                        positioned
              return    nothing
       24h    GETBUF    Get Virtual Screen Information
              BX        segment of object handle for window (0=default)
              return CX size of virtual screen in bytes
                     DL 0 or 1, unknown
                     ES:DI address of virtual screen
       25h    USTACK    Switch Back to User's Stack
              return    stack switched back
              note      Call only after int 15h, fn101Ah
       26h-2Ah DesQview (TopView?) - unimplemented in DV 2.0x
              return    pops up 'Programming Error' window in DV 2.0x
       2Bh    POSTTASK  Awaken Task
              DesQview 2.0 (Top View?)
              BX        segment of object handle for task
```

```
                    2Ch       Start New Application in New Process
                              return  nothing
                              DesQview 2.0 (TopView?)
                              ES:DI   pointer to contents of .PIF/.DVP file
                              BX      size of .PIF/.DVP info
                              return  BX        segment of object handle for new task
                                                00h       if error
                    2Dh       Keyboard Mouse Control                              DesQview 2.0+
                              BL      subfunction
                                      00h       determine whether using keyboard mouse
                                      01h       turn keyboard mouse on
                                      02h       turn keyboard mouse off
                              return  (calling BL was 00h)
                                      BL        0         using real mouse
                                                1         using keyboard mouse

Function 11h      Topview commands
entry   AH        11h
        AL        various
note    In DesQview 2.0x, these function calls are identical to AH=0DEh, so those
        below.

Function 20h      PRINT.COM  (DOS internal)                       (AT, XT-286, PS/2 50+)
entry   AH        20h
        AL        subfunction
                  00h       unknown (PRINT)
                  01h       unknown (PRINT)
                  10h       sets up SysReq routine on AT, XT/286, PS/2
                  11h       completion of SysReq routine (software only)
note    AL=0 or 1 sets or resets some flags which affect what PRINT does when it
        tries to access the disk.

Function 21h      Read Power-On Self Test (POST) Error Log                (PS/2 50+)
entry   AH        21h
        AL        00h       read POST log
                  01h       write POST log
                            BH        device ID
                            BL        device error code
return  CF        set on error
        AH        status
                  00h       successful read
                            BX        number of POST error codes stored
                            ES:DI     pointer to error log
                  01h       list full
                  80h       invalid command
                  86h       function unsupported
note    The log is a series of words, the first byte of which identifies the error
        code and the second is the device ID.

Function 40h      Read/Modify Profiles                                    (Convertible)
entry   AH        40h
        AL        00h       read system profile in CX,BX
                  01h       write system profile from CX, BX
                  02h       read internal modem profile in BX
                  03h       write internal modem profile from BX
        BX        profile info
return  BX        internal modem profile (from 02h)
        CX,BX     system profile (from 00h)

Function 41h Wait On External Event                                       (Convertible)
entry   AH        41h
        AL        condition type
            bits 0-2         condition to wait for
                             0,0,0     any external event
                             0,0,1     compare and return if equal
                             0,1,0     compare and return if not equal
                             0,1,1     test and return if not zero
                             1,0,0     test and return if zero
                 3           reserved
                 4           0         user byte
                             1         port address
```

            5-7   reserved
      BH   condition compare or mask value
            condition codes:
            00h   any external event
            01h   compare and return if equal
            02h   compare and return if not equal
            03h   test and return if not zero
            04h   test and return if zero
      BL   timeout value times 55 milliseconds
            00h   if no time limit
      DX   I/O port address (if AL bit 4=1)
      ES:DI pointer to user byte (if AL bit 4=0)

Function 42h Request System Power Off   (Convertible)
entry   AH   42h
        AL   00h   to use system profile
                01h   to force suspend regardless of profile
return unknown

Function 43h Read System Status   (Convertible)
entry   AH   43h
return AL   status byte
        bit 0   LCD detached
            1   reserved
            2   RS232/parallel powered on
            3   internal modem powered on
            4   power activated by alarm
            5   standby power lost
            6   external power in use
            7   battery low

Function 44h (De)activate Internal Modem Power   (Convertible)
entry   AH   44h
        AL   00h   to power off
                01h   to power on
return unknown

Function 4Fh OS Hook - Keyboard Intercept   (except PC, PCjr, and XT)
entry   AH   4Fh
        AL   scan code, CF set
return AL   scan code
        CF   set   processing desired
                clear   scan code should not be used
note 1. Called by int 9 handler for each keystroke to translate scan codes.
     2. An OS or a TSR can capture this function to filter the raw keyboard data
        stream. The new handler can substitute a new scan code, return the same
        scan code, or return the carry flag clear causing the keystroke to be
        discarded. The BIOS default routine simply returns the scan code
        unchanged.
     3. A program can call Int 15h fn 0C0h to determine whether the host
        machine's BIOS supports keyboard intercept.

Function 70h   EEROM handler   (Tandy 1000HX)
entry   AH   00h   read from EEROM
               BL   00h
               01h   write to EEROM
               BL   word number to write (0-15)
               DX   word value to write
return DX   (AH=00h) word value
        CF   set on error (system is not a Tandy 1000 HX)

Function 80h OS Hook - Device Open   (AT, XT/286, PS/2)
entry   AH   80h
        BX   device ID
        CX   process ID
return CF   set on error
        AH   status
note 1. Acquires ownership of a logical device for a process.
     2. This call, along with fns 81h and 82h, defines a simple protocol that can
        be used to arbitrate usage of devices by multiple processes. A
        multitasking program manager would be expected to capture int 15h and

```
           provide the appropriate service.
        3. The default BIOS routine for this function simply returns with CF clear
           and AH=00h.

Function 81h      OS Hook - Device Close                    (AT, XT/286, PS/2)
entry    AH       81h
         BX       device ID
         CX       process ID
return   CF       set on error
         AH       status
note  1. Releases ownership of a logical device for a process.
      2. A multitasking program manager would be expected to capture int 15h and
         provide the appropriate service.
      3. The BIOS default routine for this function simply returns with the CF
         clear and AH=00h.

Function 82h      Program Termination                       (AT, XT/286, PS/2)
         AH       82h
         BX       device ID
return   CF       set on error
         AH       status
note  1. Closes all logical devices opened with function 80h.
      2. A multitasking program manager would be expected to capture int
         15h and provide the appropriate service.
      3. The BIOS default routine for this function simply returns with CF
         clear and AH=00h.

Function 83h      Event Wait                  (AT, XT/286, Convertible, PS/2 50+)
entry    AH       83h
         AL       00h       to set interval
                  01h       to cancel
         CX:DX    number of microseconds to wait (granularity is 976 micro seconds)
         ES:BX    pointer to semaphore flag (bit 7 is set when interval expires)
                  (pointer is to caller's memory)
return   CF       set (1) if function already busy
note  1. Requests setting of a semaphore after a specified interval or cancels a
         previous request.
      2. The calling program is responsible for clearing the semaphore before
         requesting this function.
      3. The actual duration of an event wait is always an integral multiple of
         976 microseconds. The CMOS date/clock chip interrupts are used to
         implement this function.
      4. Use of this function allows programmed, hardware-independent delays at a
         finer resolution than can be obtained through use of the MS-DOS Get Time
         function (int 21h/fn 2Ch) which returns time in hundredths of a second.

Function 84h      Read Joystick Input Settings              (AT, XT/286, PS/2)
entry    AH       84h
         DX       00h       to read the current switch settings (return in AL)
                  01h       to read the resistive inputs
return   CF       set on error
         (fn 00h)
         AL       switch settings (bits 7-4)
         (fn 01h)
         AX       stick A (X) value
         BX       stick A (Y) value
         CX       stick B (X) value
         DX       stick B (Y) value
note  1. An error is returned if DX does not contain a valid subfunction number.
      2. If no game adapter is installed, all returned values are 00h.
      3. Using a 250K Ohm joystick, the potentiometer values usually lie within
         the range 0-416 (0000h-01A0h).

Function 85h System Request (SysReq) Key Pressed        (except PC, PCjr, XT)
entry    AH       85h
         AL       00h       key pressed
                  01h       key released
return   CF       set on error
         AH       error code
note  1. Called by BIOS keyboard decode routine when the SysReq key is detected.
      2. The BIOS handler for this call is a dummy routine that always returns a
```

```
                          success status unless called with an invalid subfunction number in AL.
                    3. A multitasking program manager would be expected to capture int 15h so
                       that it can be notified when the user strikes the SysReq key.

Function 86h      Delay                                         (except PC, PCjr, XT)
          AH      86h
          CX,DX   number of microseconds to wait
return    CF      clear    after wait elapses
          CF      set      immediately due to error
note 1. Suspends the calling program for a specified interval in microseconds.
     2. The actual duration of the wait is always an integral multiple of 976
        microseconds.
     3. Use of this function allows programmed, hardware-independent delays at a
        finer resolution than can be obtained through use of the MS-DOS Get Time
        function (int 21h fn 2Ch) which returns time in hundredths of a second).

Function 87h      Memory Block Move                             (2-3-486 machines only)
          AH      87h
          CX      number of words to move
          ES:SI   pointer to Global Descriptor Table (GDT)
                  offset 00h-0Fh   reserved, set to zero
                         00h       null descriptor
                         08h       uninitialized, will be made into GDT descriptor
                         10h-11h   source segment length in bytes (2*CX-1 or greater)
                         12h-14h   24-bit linear source address
                         15h       access rights byte (always 93h)
                         16h-17h   reserved, set to zero
                         18h-19h   destination segment length in bytes (2*CX-1 or
                                   greater)
                         1Ah-1Ch   24-bit linear destination address
                         1Dh       access rights byte (always 93h)
                         1Eh-2Fh   reserved, set to zero
                         20h       uninitialized, used by BIOS
                         28h       uninitialized, will be made into SS descriptor
return    CF      set on error
          AH      status
                  00h      source copied into destination
                  01h      parity error
                  02h      exception interrupt error
                  03h      address line 20 gating failed
note 1. The GDT table is composed of six 8-byte descriptors to be used by the CPU
        in protected mode. The four descriptors in offsets 00h-0Fh and 20h-2Fh
        are filled in by the BIOS before the CPU mode switch.
     2. The addresses used in the descriptor table are linear (physical) 24-bit
        addresses in the range 000000h-0FFFFFFh - not segments and offsets -
        with the least significant byte at the lowest address and the most
        significant byte at the highest address.
     3. Interrupts are disabled during this call; use may interfere with the
        operation of comm programs, network drivers, or other software that
        relies on prompt servicing of hardware interrupts.
     4. This call is not valid in the OS/2 Compatibility Box.
     5. This call will move a memory block from any real or protected mode
        address to any other real or protected mode address.

Function 88h      Get Extended Memory Size                      (AT, XT/286, PS/2)
entry     AH      88h
return    AX      number of contiguous 1K blocks of extended memory starting at
                  address 1024k
note      This call will not work in the OS/2 Compatibility Box.

Function 89h      Switch Processor to Protected Mode            (AT, XT/286, PS/2)
entry     AH      89h
          BH      interrupt number for IRQ0, written to ICW2 of 8259 PIC #1
                  (must be evenly divisible by 8, determines IRQ0-IRQ7)
          BL      interrupt number for IRQ8, written to ICW2 of 8259 PIC #2
                  (must be evenly divisible by 8, determines IRQ8-IRQ15)
          ES:SI   pointer to 8-entry Global Descriptor Table for protected mode:
                  offset 00h       null descriptor, initialized to zero
                         08h       GDT descriptor
                         10h       IDT (Interrupt Descriptor Table) descriptor
                         18h       DS, user's data segment
```

```
                        20h     ES, user's extra segment
                        28h     SS, user's stack segment
                        30h     CS, user's code segment
                        38h     uninitialized, used to build descriptor for BIOS
                                code segment
return   CF     set on error
                AH      0FFh    error enabling address line 20
         CF     clear   function successful (CPU is in protected mode)
                AH      00h
                CS      user-defined selector
                DS      user-defined selector
                ES      user-defined selector
                SS      user-defined selector
note     The user must initialize the first seven descriptors; the eighth is
         filled in by the BIOS to provide addressability for its own execution.
         The calling program may modify and use the eighth descriptor for any
         purpose after return from this function call.

Function 90h    Device Busy Loop                        (except PC, PCjr, XT)
entry    AH     90h
         AL     predefined device type code:
                00h     disk                                     (may timeout)
                01h     diskette                                 (may timeout)
                02h     keyboard                                  (no timeout)
                03h     PS/2 pointing device                     (may timeout)
                80h     network
                                                                  (no timeout)
                0FCh    hard disk reset (PS/2)                   (may timeout)
                0FDh    diskette motor start                     (may timeout)
                0FEh    printer                                  (may timeout)
         ES:BX  pointer to request block for type codes 80h through 0FFh
                (for network adapters ES:BX is a pointer to network control block)
return   CF     1 (set) if wait time satisfied
                0 (clear) if driver must perform wait
note 1.  Used by NETBIOS.
     2.  Generic type codes are allocated as follows:
         00h-7Fh   non-reentrant devices; OS must arbitrate access serially
                   reusable devices
         80h-0BFh  reentrant devices; ES:BX points to a unique control block
         0C0h-0FFh wait-only calls, no complementary POST int 15/fn 91h call
     3.  Invoked by the BIOS disk, printer, network, and keyboard handlers prior
         to performing a programmed wait for I/O completion.
     4.  A multitasking program manager would be expected to capture int 15h/fn
         90h so that it can dispatch other tasks while I/O is in progress.
     5.  The default BIOS routine for this function simply returns with the CF
         clear and AH=00h.

Function 91h    Device POST                         (AT, XT/286, PS/2 50+)
entry    AH     91h
         AL     type code (see AH=90h above)
                00h-7Fh   serially reusable devices
                80h-0BFh  reentrant devices
         ES:BX  pointer to request block for type codes 80h through 0BFh
return   AH     00h
note 1.  Used by NETBIOS.
     2.  Invoked by the BIOS disk network, and keyboard handlers to signal that
         I/O is complete and/or the device is ready.
     3.  Predefined device types that may use Device POST are:
         00H  disk                  (may timeout)
         01H  floppy disk           (may timeout)
         02H  keyboard               (no timeout)
         03H  PS/2 pointing device  (may timeout)
         80H  network                (no timeout)
     4.  The BIOS printer routine does not invoke this function because printer
         output is not interrupt driven.
     5.  A multitasking program manager would be expected to capture int 15h/fn
         91h so that it can be notified when I/O is completed and awaken the
         requesting task.
     6.  The default BIOS routine for this function simply returns with the CF
         flag clear and AH=00h.
```

```
Function 0C0h Get System Configuration
                             (XT after 1/10/86, PC Convertible, XT/286, AT, PS/2)
entry   AH       0C0h
return  CF       set        if BIOS doesn't support call
        ES:BX    pointer to ROM system descriptor table
         bytes 00h-01h  number of bytes in the following table (norm. 16 bytes)
               02h      system ID byte; see Chapter 2 for interpretation
               03h      secondary ID distinguishes between AT and XT/286, etc.
               04h      BIOS revision level, 0 for 1st release, 1 for 2nd, etc.
               05h      feature information byte
                    bits 7      DMA channel 3 used by hard disk BIOS
                         6      second 8259 installed (cascaded IRQ2)
                         5      realtime clock installed
                         4      kbd intrcpt:int 15h, fn 04h called upon int 09h
                         3      wait for external event supported (int 15fn41)
                                used on Convertible; reserved on PS/2 systems
                         2      extended BIOS area allocated at 640k
                         1      bus is Micro Channel instead of PC
                         0      reserved
               06h      unknown (set to 0) (reserved by IBM)
               07h      unknown (set to 0) (reserved by IBM)
               08h      unknown (set to 0)
               09h      unknown (set to 0) (Award copyright here)
note 1. Int 15h is also used for the Multitask Hook on PS/2 machines. No register
        settings available yet.
     2. The 1/10/86 XT BIOS returns an incorrect value for the feature byte.

Function 0C1h   Return Extended BIOS Data Area Segment Address (PS/2)
entry   AH       0C1h
return  CF       set on error
        ES       segment of XBIOS data area
note 1. The XBIOS Data Area is allocated at the high end of conventional memory
        during the POST (Power-On-Self-Test) sequence.
     2. The word at 0040:0013h (memory size) is updated to reflect the reduced
        amount of memory available for DOS and application programs.
     3. The 1st byte in the XBIOS Data Area is initialized to its length in K.
     4. A program can determine whether the XBIOS Data Area exists by using int
        15h/fn 0C0h.

Function 0C2h   Pointing Device BIOS Interface (DesQview 2.x) (PS/2)
entry   AH       0C2h
        AL       00h      enable/disable pointing device
                          BH    00h      disable
                                01h      enable
                 01h      reset pointing device
                          Resets the system's mouse or other pointing device, sets
                          the sample rate, resolution, and other characteristics
                          to their default values.
                          return BH      device ID
                          note 1. After a reset operation, the state of the
                                  pointing device is as follows:
                                  disabled;
                                  sample rate at 100 reports per second;
                                  resolution at 4 counts per millimeter;
                                  scaling at 1 to 1.
                               2. The data package size is unchanged by this fn.
                               3. Apps can use the fn 0C2h subfunctions to
                                  initialize the pointing device to other parms,
                                  then enable the device with fn 00h.
                 02h      set sampling rate
                          BH    00h      10/second
                                01h      20/second
                                02h      40/second
                                03h      60/second
                                04h      80/second
                                05h      100/second (default)
                                06h      200/second
                 03h      set pointing device resolution
                          BH    00h      one count per mm
                                01h      two counts per mm
                                02h      four counts per mm  (default)
```

The PC ROM BIOS

```
                        03h       eight counts per mm
            04h     get pointing device type
                    return  BH      ID code for the mouse or other
                                    pointing device.
            05h     initialize pointing device interface
                    Sets the data package size for the system's mouse or
                    other pointing device, and initializes the resolution,
                    sampling rate, and scaling to their default values.
                    BH      data package size (1 - 8 bytes)
                    note    After this operation, the state of the
                            pointing device is as follows:
                            disabled;
                            sample rate at 100 reports per second;
                            resolution at 4 counts per millimeter;
                            and scaling at 1 to 1.
            06h     get status or set scaling factor
                    Returns the current status of the system's mouse or other
                    pointing device or sets the device's scaling factor.
                    BH      00h     return device status
                            return  BL      status byte
                            bits    0       set if right button pressed
                                    1       reserved
                                    2       set if left button pressed
                                    3       reserved
                                    4       0       1:1 scaling
                                            1       2:1 scaling
                                    5       0       device disabled
                                            1       device enabled
                                    6       0       stream mode
                                            1       remote mode
                                    7       reserved
                                    CL      resolution
                                            00h     1 count per millimeter
                                            01h     2 counts per millimeter
                                            02h     4 counts per millimeter
                                            03h     8 counts per millimeter
                                    DL      sample rate
                                            0Ah     10 reports per second
                                            14h     20 reports per second
                                            28h     40 reports per second
                                            3Ch     60 reports per second
                                            50h     80 reports per second
                                            64h     100 reports per second
                                            0C8h    200 reports per second
                            01h     set scaling at 1:1
                            02h     set scaling at 2:1
            07h     set pointing device handler address
                    Notifies BIOS pointing device driver of the address for a
                    routine to be called each time pointing device data is
                    available.
                    ES:BX   address user device handler
                    return  AL      00h
return  CF      set on error
        AH      status
                00h     successful
                01h     invalid function
                02h     invalid input
                03h     interface error
                04h     need to resend
                05h     no device handler installed
note 1. The values in BH for those functions that take it as input are stored in
        different locations for each subfunction.
     2. The user's handler for pointing device data is entered via a far call
        with four parameters on the stack:
        SS:SP+0Ah       status
        SS:SP+08h       x coordinate
        SS:SP+06h       y coordinate
        SS:SP+04h       z coordinate (always 0)
        The handler must exit via a far return without removing the parameters
        from the stack.
     3. The status parameter word passed to the user's handler is interpreted as
```

```
              follows:
              bits    0          left button pressed
                      1          right button pressed
                      2-3        reserved
                      4          sign of x data is negative
                      5          sign of y data is negative
                      6          x data has overflowed
                      7          y data has overflowed
                      8-0Fh      reserved

Function 0C3h Enable/Disable Watchdog Timeout   (PS/2 50+)
entry   AH      0C3h
        AL      00h       disable
                01h       enable
                          BX         timer counter
return  CF      set on error
note    The watchdog timer generates an NMI.

Function 0C4h Programmable Option Select                        (PS/2 50+)
entry   AH      04Ch
        AL      00h       return base POS register address
                01h       enable slot
                          BL         slot number
                02h       enable adapter
return  CF      set on error
        DX      base POS register address (if function 00h)
note 1. Returns the base Programmable Option Select register address, enables a
        slot for setup, or enables an adapter.
     2. Valid on machines with Micro Channel Architecture (MCA) bus only.
     3. After a slot is enabled with fn 01h, specific information can be obtained
        for the adapter in that slot by performing port input operations:
              Port      Function
              100h      MCA ID (low byte)
              101h      MCA ID (high byte)
              102h      Option Select Byte 1
                  bit 0      0        if disabled
                             1        if enabled
              103h      Option Select Byte 2
              104h      Option Select Byte 3
              105h      Option Select Byte 4
                        bits 6-7 are channel check indicators
              106h      Subaddress Extension (low byte)
              107h      Subaddress Extension (high byte)

Function 0DEh DesQview Services                                 (DesQview)
entry   AH      0DEh
        AL      00h       Get Program Name
                          return AX        offset into DESQVIEW.DVO of current
                                           program's record:
                                 byte      length of name
                                 n bytes   name
                                 2 bytes   keys to invoke program (second =
                                           00h if only one key used)
                                 word      ? (normally 0)
                                 byte      end flag: 00h for all but last
                                           entry, which is 0FFh
                01h       Update 'Open Window' Menu
                          return none
                          note    Reads DESQVIEW.DVO, disables Open menu if file
                                  not in current directory
                02h       unimplemented in DV 2.0x
                          return nothing (NOP in DV 2.0x)
                03h       unimplemented in DV 2.0x
                          return nothing (NOP in DV 2.0x)
                04h       Get Available Common Memory
                          return BX        bytes of common memory available
                                 CX        largest block available
                                 DX        total common memory in bytes
                05h       Get Available Conventional Memory
                          return BX        K of memory available
                                 CX        largest block available
```

The PC ROM BIOS

```
            DX       total conventional memory in K
    06h  Get Available Expanded Memory
         return  BX       K of expanded memory available
                 CX       largest block available
                 DX       total expanded memory in K
    07h  APPNUM  Get Current Program's Number
         return  AX       number of program as it appears
                          on the 'Switch Windows' menu
    08h  GET (unknown)
         return  AX       00h      unknown
                          01h      unknown
    09h  unimplemented in DV 2.00
         return  nothing (NOP in DV 2.00)
    0Ah  DBGPOKE Display Character on Status Line        (DV 2.0+)
         BL      character
         return  character displayed, next call will display
                     in next position (which wraps back to the start
                     of the line if off the right edge of screen)
         note 1. Displays character on bottom line of *physical*
                     screen, regardless of current size of window
                     (even entirely hidden)
              2. Does not know about graphics display modes, just
                     pokes the characters into display memory
    0Bh  APILEVEL Define Minimum API Level Required       (DV 2.0+)
         BL      API level. A value higher than 02h pops up 'You
                     need a newer version' error window in DV 2.00.
         BH      unknown
         return  AX       maximum API level?
    0Ch  GETMEM  Allocate 'System' Memory                 (DV 2.0+)
         BX      number of bytes
         return  ES:DI    pointer to allocated block
    0Dh  PUTMEM  Deallocate 'System' Memory               (DV 2.0+)
         ES:DI   pointer to previously allocated block
         return  nothing
    0Eh  Find Mailbox by Name                             (DV 2.0+)
         ES:DI   pointer to name to find
         CX      length of name
         return  BX       00h      not found
                          01h      found
                 DS:SI    object handle
    0Fh  Enable DesQview Extensions                       (DV 2.0+)
         return  AX and BX destroyed (seems to be bug, weren't
                     saved & restored)
         note 1. Sends a manager stream with opcodes 0AEh, 0BDh,
                     and 0BFh to task's window
              2. Enables an additional mouse mode
    10h  PUSHKEY  Put Key Into Keyboard Input Stream      (DV 2.0+)
         BH      scan code
         BL      character
         return  BX       unknown (sometimes, but not always, same
                              as BX passed in)
         note    A later read will get the keystroke as if it had
                     been typed by the user
    11h  Enable/Disable Auto Justification of Window      (DV 2.0+)
         BL      00h      viewport will not move automatically
                 nonzero  viewport will move to keep cursor visible
         return  none
    12h  unknown                                          (DV 2.0+)
         BX      00h      clear something?
                 nonzero  set something?
         return  none
```

Interrupt 16h Keyboard I/O

(0:0058h) Access the keyboard. Scancodes are found in Appendix 1. ASCII codes are found in Appendix 2.

```
Function  00h   Get Keyboard Input - read the next character in keyboard buffer,
                    if no key ready, wait for one.
entry   AH      00h
return  AH      scan code
```

```
          AL      ASCII character
note      Removes keystroke from buffer (destructive read)

Function 01h     Check Keystroke Buffer - Do Not Clear
entry     AH      01h
return    ZF      0 (clear) if character in buffer
                  1 (set)   if no character in buffer
          AH      scan code of character (if ZF=0)
          AL      ASCII character if applicable
note      Keystroke is not removed from buffer. The same character and scan code
          will be returned by the next call to Int 16h/fn 00h.

Function 02h     Shift Status - fetch bit flags indicating shift status
entry     AH      02h
return    AL      status byte (same as [0040:0017])
          bits 7  Insert on
               6  CapsLock on
               5  NumLock on
               4  ScrollLock on
               3  Alt key down
               2  Control key down
               1  Left shift (left caps-shift key) down
               0  Right shift (right caps-shift key) down
note      The keyboard flags byte is stored in the BIOS Data Area at 0000:0417h.

Function 03h     Keyboard - Set Repeat Rate            (PCjr, AT, XT/286, PS/2)
entry     AH      03h
          AL      00h     reset typematic defaults             (PCjr)
                  01h     increase initial delay               (PCjr)
                  02h     decrease repeat rate by 1            (PCjr)
                  03h     increase both delays by $^1/_2$      (PCjr)
                  04h     turn off typematic                   (PCjr)
                  05h     set typematic rate                   (AT, PS/2)
          BH      00h-03h for delays of 250ms, 500ms, 750ms, or 1 second
                          0,0     250ms
                          0,1     500ms
                          1,0     750ms
                          1,1     1 second
          BL      00h-1Fh for typematic rates of 30cps down to 2cps
                          00000 30      01011 10.9    10101 4.5
                          00001 26.7    01100 10      10110 4.3
                          00010 24      01101 9.2     10111 4
                          00011 21.8    01110 8.6     11000 3.7
                          00100 20      01111 8       11001 3.3
                          00101 18.5    10000 7.5     11010 3
                          00110 17.1    10001 6.7     11011 2.7
                          00111 16      10010 6       11100 2.5
                          01000 15      10011 5.5     11101 2.3
                          01001 13.3    10011 5.5     11110 2.1
                          01010 12      10100 5       11111 2
return    nothing
note      Subfunction 05h is available on ATs with ROM BIOS dated 11/15/85 and
          later, the XT/286, and the PS/2.

Function 04h     Keyboard Click Toggle                  (PCjr and Convertible)
entry     AH      04h
          AL      00h     for click off
                  01h     for click on
return    nothing

Function 05h     Keyboard Buffer Write          (AT or PS/2 with enhanced kbd)
                 (XT/286, PS/2, AT with 'Enhanced' keyboard)
entry     AH      05h
          CH      scan code
          CL      ASCII character
return    CF      set on error
          AL      01h     if buffer full
note      Places a character and scan code in the keyboard type-ahead buffer.
```

The PC ROM BIOS

```
Function 10h       Get Enhanced Keystroke And Read        (F11, F12 Enhanced Keyboard)
                   (XT/286, PS/2, AT with 'Enhanced' keyboard)
entry    AH        10h
return   AH        scan code
         AL        ASCII character if applicable
note 1. Reads a character and scan code from the keyboard type-ahead buffer.
     2. Use this function for the enhanced keyboard instead of Int 16h fn 00h. It
        allows applications to obtain the scan codes for the additional F11, F12,
        and cursor control keys.

Function 11h       Check Enhanced Keystroke               (F11-F12 on enhanced keyboard)
                   (XT/286, PS/2, AT with 'Enhanced' keyboard)
entry    AH        11h
return   ZF        0         (clear) if key pressed
                             AH      scan code
                             AL      ASCII character if applicable
                   1         if buffer is empty
note 1. Keystroke is not removed from buffer. The same char and scan code will be
        returned by the next call to Int 16h/fn 10h.
     2. Use this function for the enhanced keyboard instead of Int 16h/fn 00h. It
        allows applications to test for the additional F11, F12, and cursor
        control keys.

Function 12h       Extended Shift Status                  (F11, F12 Enhanced keyboard)
entry    AH        12h
return   AX        status word
                   AL bit    0         right Shift key depressed
                             1         left Shift key depressed
                             2         Control key depressed
                             3         Alt key depressed
                             4         ScrollLock state active
                             5         NumLock state active
                             6         CapsLock state active
                             7         insert state is active
                   AH bit    0         left Control key pressed
                             1         left Alt key depressed
                             2         right Control key pressed
                             3         right Alt key depressed
                             4         Scroll Lock key depressed
                             5         NumLock key depressed
                             6         CapsLock key depressed
                             7         SysReq key depressed
note     Use this function for the enhanced keyboard instead of int 16h/fn 02h.

Function  79h      pcAnywhere
entry    AH        79h       pcAnywhere function
         AL        00h       installation check
return   AX        0FFFFh    installed, otherwise not present

Function  79h      pcAnywhere
entry    AH        7Bh       Enable/Disable Operation
         AL        state
                   00h       disabled
                   01h       enabled
return   unknown

Function 0EDh      Borland Turbo Lightning API    (partial)
entry    AH        0EDh
         BH        0EDh
         BL        function
                   00h       installation check
                   02h       pointer to Lightning internal data structure lobyte
                   03h       pointer to Lightning internal data structure hibyte
                   04h       load auxiliary dictionary
                   06h       autoproof mode
                   0Fh       get number of substitutions (segment)
         DS:DI     pointer to string to be processed
return   AX        error code (unknown)

Function 0F0h      Set CPU speed        (Compaq 386)
entry    AH        0F0h      set speed
```

```
            AL      speed
                    00h       equivalent to 6 mHz 80286 (COMMON)
                    01h       equivalent to 8 mHz 80286 (FAST)
                    02h       full 16 mHz (HIGH)
                    03h       toggles between 8 mHz-equivalent and speed set by system
                              board switch (AUTO or HIGH)
                    04h-07h   unknown
                    08h       full 16 mHz except 8 mHz-equivalent during floppy disk
                              access
                    09h       specify speed directly
                    CX        speed value, 1 (slowest) to 50 (full), 3 ~=8088
return  none?
note    Used by Compaq DOS MODE command.

Function 0F1h   Read Current CPU Speed                                  (Compaq 386)
entry    AH     0F1h
return   AL     speed code (see function 0F0h above)
                if AL=09h, CX=speed code

Function 0F2h   Determine Attached Keyboard Type                        (Compaq 386)
entry    AH     0F2h
return   AL     type
                00h       if 11-bit AT keyboard is in use
                01h       if 9-bit PC keyboard is in use
```

Interrupt 17h Printer

(0:005Ch) access the parallel printer(s). AH is changed. All other registers left alone.

```
Function 00h    Print Character/send AL to printer DX (0, 1, or 2)
entry    AH     00h
         AL     ASCII character code
         DX     printer to be used
                00h       PRN or LPT1
                01h       LPT2
                02h       LPT3
return   AH     status byte
         bits 0          time out
              1          unused
              2          unused
              3          I/O error
              4          printer selected
              5          out of paper
              6          acknowledge
              7          not busy

Function 01h    Initialize Printer - set init line low, send 0Ch to printer DX
entry    AH     01h
         DX     printer port to be initialized (0,1,2)
return   status as below

Function 02h    Printer Status - read status of printer DX into AH
entry    AH     02h
         DX     printer port to be used (0,1,2)
return   AH     status byte
         bits 7      0         printer is busy
                     1         ready
              6      ACKnowledge line state
              5      out-of-paper line state
              4      printer selected line state
              3      I/O error
              2      unused
              1      unused
              0      time-out error
```

Interrupt 18h ROM BASIC

(0:0060h) Execute ROM BASIC at address 0F600h:0000h
```
entry    no parameters used
return   jumps into ROM BASIC on IBM systems
note 1. Often reboots a compatible.
```

2. Used by Turbo C 1.5. 2.0 and later do not use it.
3. On IBM systems, this interrupt is called if disk boot failure occurs.

Interrupt 19h Bootstrap Loader / Extended Memory VDISK ID
(0:0064h)

entry no parameters used
return nothing
note 1. Reads track 0, sector 1 into address 0000h:7C00h, then transfers control to that address. If no diskette drive available, transfers to ROM-BASIC via int 18h or displays loader error message.
2. Causes reboot of disk system if invoked while running. (no memory test performed).
3. If location 0000:0472h does not contain the value 1234h, a memory test will be performed before reading the boot sector.
4. VDISK from DOS 3.x+ traps this vector to determine when the CPU has shifted from protected mode to real mode. A detailed discussion can be found by Ray Duncan in PC Magazine, May 30, 1989.
5. Reportedly, some versions of DOS 2.x and all versions of DOS 3.x+ intercept int 19h in order to restore some interrupt vectors DOS takes over, in order to put the machine back to a cleaner state for the reboot, since the POST will not be run on the int 19h. These vectors are reported to be: 02h, 08h, 09h, 0Ah, 0Bh, 0Ch, 0Dh, 0Eh, 70h, 72h, 73h, 74h, 75h, 76h, and 77h. After restoring these, it restores the original int 19h vector and calls int 19h.

Interrupt 1Ah Time of Day
(0:0068h) Access the PC internal clock

```
Function 00h Read System Timer Tick Counter                      (except PC)
entry   AH      00h
return  AL      00h     if clock was read or written (via AH=0,1) within the
                        current 24-hour period.
                nonzero midnight was passed since last read
        CX:DX   tick count (high 16 bits in CX)
```
note 1. The returned value is the cumulative number of clock ticks since midnight. There are 18.2 clock ticks per second. When the counter reaches 1,573,040, it is cleared to zero, and the rollover flag is set.
2. The rollover flag is cleared by this function call, so the flag will only be returned nonzero once per day.
3. Int 1Ah/fn 01h can be used to set the counter to an arbitrary 32 bit value.

```
Function 01h Set Clock Tick Counter Value                        (except PC)
entry   AH      01h
        CX:DX   high word/low word count of timer ticks
return  none
```
note 1. The clock ticks are incremented by timer interrupt at 18.2065 times per second or 54.9254 milliseconds/count. Therefore:
```
                counts per second   18       (12h)
                counts per minute   1092     (444h)
                counts per hour     65543    (10011h)
                counts per day      1573040  (1800B0h)
```
2. The counter is zeroed when system is rebooted.
3. Stores a 32-bit value in the clock tick counter.
4. The rollover flag is cleared by this call.

```
Function 02h        Read Real Time Clock Time                    (AT and after)
entry   AH          02h
return  CH          hours in BCD
        CL          minutes in BCD
        DH          seconds in BCD
        DL          00h     standard time
                    01h     daylight savings time
        CF          0       if clock running
                    1       if clock not operating
note    Reads the current time from the CMOS time/date chip.
```

```
Function 03h      Set Real Time Clock Time                        (AT and after)
entry     AH      03h
          CH      hours in BCD
          CL      minutes in BCD
          DH      seconds in BCD
          DL      0 (clear) if standard time
                  1 (set)   if daylight savings time option
return    none
note      Sets the time in the CMOS time/date chip.

Function 04h      Read Real Time Clock Date                       (AT and after)
entry     AH      04h
return    CH      century in BCD (19 or 20)
          CL      year in BCD
          DH      month in BCD
          DL      day in BCD
          CF      0 (clear) if clock is running
                  1 (set)   if clock is not operating
note      Reads the current date from the CMOS time/date chip.

Function 05h      Set Real Time Clock Date                        (AT and after)
entry     AH      05h
          CH      century in BCD (19 or 20)
          CL      year in BCD
          DH      month in BCD
          DL      day in BCD
return    none
note      Sets the date in the CMOS time/date chip.

Function 06h      Set Real Time Clock Alarm                       (AT and after)
entry     AH      06h
          CH      hours in BCD
          CL      minutes in BCD
          DH      seconds in BCD
return    CF      set if alarm already set or clock inoperable
note 1.   Sets alarm in the CMOS date/time chip. Int 4Ah occurs at specified alarm
          time every 24hrs until reset with Int 1Ah/fn 07h.
     2.   A side effect of this function is that the clock chip's interrupt level
          (IRQ8) is enabled.
     3.   Only one alarm may be active at any given time.
     4.   The program using this function must place the address of its interrupt
          handler for the alarm in the vector for Int 4Ah.

Function 07h      Reset Real Time Clock Alarm    (AT and after)
entry     AH      07h
return    none
note 1.   Cancels any pending alarm request on the CMOS date/time chip.
     2.   This function does not disable the clock chip's interrupt level (IRQ8).

Function 08h Set Real Time Clock Activated Power On Mode          (Convertible)
entry     AH      08h
          CH      hours in BCD
          CL      minutes in BCD
          DH      seconds in BCD

Function 09h      Read Real Time Clock Alarm Time and Status
                                                 (Convertible and PS/2 Model 30)
entry     AH      09h
return    CH      hours in BCD
          CL      minutes in BCD
          DH      seconds in BCD
          DL      alarm status:
                  00h     if alarm not enabled
                  01h     if alarm enabled but will not power up system
                  02h     if alarm will power up system

Function 0Ah Read System-Timer Day Counter                                (PS/2)
entry     AH      0Ah
return    CF      set on error
          CX      count of days since Jan 1,1980
note      Returns the contents of the system's day counter.
```

The PC ROM BIOS

```
Function 0Bh  Set System-Timer Day Counter                    (PS/2)
entry    AH     0Bh
         CX     count of days since Jan 1,1980
return   CF     set on error
note     Stores an arbitrary value in the system's day counter.

Function 80h   Set Up Sound Multiplexor              (PCjr) (Tandy 1000?)
entry    AH     80h
         AL     sound source
                00h    source is 8253 timer chip, channel 2
                01h    source is cassette input
                02h    source is I/O channel 'audio in' line
                03h    source is TI sound generator chip
return   none
note     Sets up the source for tones that will appear on the PCjr's Audio Out bus
         line or RF modulator.

Function 1Ah   Read Time and Date                           (AT&T 6300)
entry    AH     0FEh
return   BX     days count (1=Jan 1, 1984)
         CH     hours
         CL     minutes
         DH     seconds
         DL     hundredths
note     Day count in BX is unique to AT&T/Olivetti computers.
```

Interrupt 1Bh Control-Break
(0:006Ch) This interrupt is called when the keyboard scanner of the IBM machines detects Ctrl and Break pressed at the same time.

Note 1. If the break occurred while processing an interrupt, one or more end of interrupt commands must be send to the 8259 Programmable Interrupt Controller.
2. All I/O devices should be reset in case an operation was underway at the time.
3. It is normally pointed to an IRET during system initialization so that it does nothing, but some programs change it to return a ctrl-C scan code and thus invoke int 23h.

Interrupt 1Ch Timer Tick
(0:0070h)
Note 1. Taken 18.2065 times per second
2. Normally vectors to dummy IRET unless PRINT.COM has been installed.
3. If an application moves the interrupt pointer, it is the responsibility of that application to save and restore all registers that may be modified.

Interrupt 1Dh Vector of Video Initialization Parameters
(0:0074h) This doubleword address points to 3 sets of 16-bytes containing data to initialize for video modes for video modes 0 & 1 (40 column), 2 & 3 (80 column), and 4, 5 & 6 (graphics) on the Motorola 6845 CRT controller chip.

```
6845 registers:
         R0     horizontal total (horizontal sync in characters)
         R1     horizontal displayed (characters per line)
         R2     horizontal sync position (move display left or right)
         R3     sync width (vertical and horizontal pulse: 4-bits each)
         R4     vertical total (total character lines)
         R5     vertical adjust (adjust for 50 or 60 Hz refresh)
         R6     vertical displayed (lines of chars displayed)
         R7     vertical sync position (lines shifted up or down)
         R8     interlace (bits 4 and 5) and skew (bits 6 and 7)
         R9     max scan line addr (scan lines per character row)
         R10    cursor start (starting scan line of cursor)
         R11    cursor stop (ending scan line of cursor)
         R12    video memory start address high byte (6-bits)
         R13    video memory start address low byte (8-bits)
         R14    cursor address high byte (6-bits)
```

```
            R15      cursor address low byte (8-bits)
6845 Video Init Tables:
        table for modes 0 and 1     \
        table for modes 2 and 3      \  each table is 16 bytes long and
        table for modes 4,5, and 6   /  contains values for 6845 registers
        table for mode 7            /
        4 words:    size of video RAM for modes 0/1, 2/3, 4/5, and 6/7
        8 bytes:    number of columns in each mode
        8 bytes:    video controller mode byte for each mode
note 1. There are 4 separate tables, and all 4 must be initialized if all video
        modes will be used.
     2. The power-on initialization code of the computer points this vector to
        the ROM BIOS video routines.
     3. IBM recommends that if this table needs to be modified, it should be
        copied into RAM and only the necessary changes made.
```

Interrupt 1Eh Vector of Diskette Controller Parameters

(0:0078h) Dword address points to data base table that is used by BIOS. Default location is at 0F000:0EFC7h. 11-byte table format:

```
            bytes:
            00h     4-bit step rate, 4-bit head unload time
            01h     7-bit head load time, 1-bit DMA flag
            02h     54.9254 ms counts - delay till motor off (36-38 typ)
            03h     sector size:
                    00h     128 bytes
                    01h     256 bytes
                    02h     512 bytes
                    03h     1024 bytes
            04h     last sector on track (8 or 9 typical)
            05h     inter-sector gap on read/write (42 typical)
            06h     data length for DMA transfers (0FFh typical)
            07h     gap length between sectors for format (80 typical)
            08h     sector fill byte for format (0F6h typical)
            09h     head settle time (in milliseconds) (15 to 25 typical)
                    DOS 1.0     0
                    DOS 1.10    0
                    DOS 2.10    15
                    DOS 3.1     1
            10h     motor start time (in 1/8 second intervals) (2 to 4 typ.)
                    DOS 2.10    2
note 1. This vector is pointed to the ROM BIOS diskette tables on system
        initialization
     2. IBM recommends that if this table needs to be modified, it should be
        copied into RAM and only the necessary changes made.
```

Interrupt 1Fh Ptr to Graphics Character Extensions (Graphics Set 2)

(0:007Ch) This is the pointer to data used by the ROM video routines to display characters above ASCII 127 while in CGA medium and high res graphics modes.

Note 1. Doubleword address points to 1K table composed of 28 8-byte character definition bit-patterns. First byte of each entry is top row, last byte is bottom row.
  2. The first 128 character patterns are located in system ROM.
  3. This vector is set to 000:0 at system initialization.
  4. Used by DOS' external GRAFTABL command.

4

DOS Interrupts and Function Calls

DOS Registers

DOS uses the following registers, pointers, and flags when it executes interrupts and function calls:

General Registers

register	definition	
AX	accumulator	(16 bit)
AH	accumulator high-order byte	(8 bit)
AL	accumulator low order byte	(8 bit)
BX	base	(16 bit)
BH	base high-order byte	(8 bit)
BL	base low-order byte	(8 bit)
CX	count (16 bit)	
CH	count high order byte	(8 bit)
CL	count low order byte	(8 bit)
DX	data	(16 bit)
DH	date high order byte	(8 bit)
DL	data low order byte	(8 bit)

Segment Registers

register	definition	
CS	code segment	(16 bit)
DS	data segment	(16 bit)
SS	stack segment	(16 bit)
ES	extra segment	(16 bit)

Index Registers

register	definition	
DI	destination index	(16 bit)
SI	source index	(16 bit)

Pointers

register	definition	
SP	stack pointer	(16 bit)
BP	base pointer	(16 bit)
IP	instruction pointer	(16 bit)

Flags
AF, CF, DF, IF, OF, PF, SF, TF, ZF

These registers, pointers, and flags are 'lowest common denominator' 8088-8086 CPU oriented. DOS makes no attempt to use any of the special or enhanced instructions available on the later CPUs which will execute 8088 code, such as the 80186, 80286, 80386, or NEV V20, V30, V40, or V50.

DOS Stacks

When DOS takes control after a function call, it switches to an internal stack. Registers which are not used to return information (other than AX) are preserved. The calling program's stack must be large enough to accommodate the interrupt system - at least 128 bytes in addition to other interrupts.

DOS actually maintains three stacks -

stack 1: 384 bytes (in DOS 3.1)
for functions 00h and for 0Dh and up, and for ints 25h and 26h.

stack 2: 384 bytes (in DOS 3.1)
for function calls 01h through 0Ch.

stack 3: 48 bytes (in DOS 3.1)
for functions 0Dh and above. This stack is the initial stack used by the int 21h handler before it decides which of the other two to use. It is also used by function 59h (get extended error), and 01h to 0Ch if they are called during an int 24h (critical error) handler. Functions 33h (get/set break flag), 50h (set process ID), 51h (get process ID) and 62h (get PSP address) donot use any DOS stack under DOS 3.x (under 2.x, 50h and 51h use stack number 2).

IBM and Microsoft made a change back in DOS 3.0 or 3.1 to reduce the size of DOS. They reduced the space allocated for scratch areas when interrupts are being processed. The default seems to vary with the DOS version and the machine, but 8 stack frames seems to be common. That means that if you get more than 8 interrupts at the same time, clock, disk, printer spooler, keyboard, com port, etc., the system will crash. It happens usually on a network. STACKS=16,256 means allow 16 interrupts to interrupt each other and allow 256 bytes for each for scratch area. Eight is marginal.

DOS 3.2 does some different stack switching than previous versions. The interrupts which are switched are 02h, 08h, 09h, 0Ah, 0Bh, 0Ch, 0Dh, 0Eh, 70h, 72h, 73h, 74h, 75h, 76h, and 77h. DOS 3.2 has a special check in the initialization code for a PCjr and don't enable stack switching on that machine. DOS 3.3 was changed so that no stack switching occurs on PC, PC-XT, or the PC-Portable, and defaults to 9 stacks of 128 bytes in an AT.

DOS Interrupts

Microsoft recommends that a program wishing to examine or set the contents of any interrupt vector use the DOS function calls 35h and 25h provided for those purposes and avoid referencing the interrupt vector locations directly.

DOS Services (quick list)

Interrupt 21h Function Call Request
(0:0084h)
DOS provides a wide variety of function calls for character device I/O, file management, memory management, date and time functions, execution of other programs, and more. They are grouped as follows:

call	description
00h	program terminate
01h-0Ch	character device I/O, CP/M compatibility format
0Dh-24h	file management, CP/M compatibility format
25h-26h	nondevice functions, CP/M compatibility format
27h-29h	file management, CP/M compatibility format
2Ah-2Eh	nondevice functions, CP/M compatibility format
2Fh-38h	extended functions
39h-3Bh	directory group
3Ch-46h	extended file management
47h	directory group
48h-4Bh	extended memory management
54h-57h	extended functions
5Eh-5Fh	networking
60h-62h	extended functions
63h-66h	enhanced foreign language support

List of DOS services:
* = undocumented

```
00h     terminate program
01h     get keyboard input
02h     display character to STDIO
03h     get character from STDAUX
04h     output character to STDAUX
05h     output character to STDPRN
06h     direct console I/O - keyboard to screen
07h     get char from std I/O without echo
08h     get char from std I/O without echo, checks for ^C
09h     display a string to STDOUT
0Ah     buffered keyboard input
0Bh     check STDIN status
0Ch     clear keyboard buffer and invoke keyboard function
0Dh     flush all disk buffers
0Eh     select disk
0Fh     open file with File Control Block
10h     close file opened with File Control Block
11h     search for first matching file entry
12h     search for next matching file entry
13h     delete file specified by File Control Block
14h     sequential read from file specified by File Control Block
15h     sequential write to file specified by File Control Block
16h     find or create firectory entry for file
17h     rename file specified by file control block
18h*    unknown
19h     return current disk drive
1Ah     set disk transfer area (DTA)
1Bh     get current disk drive FAT
1Ch     get disk FAT for any drive
1Dh*    unknown
1Eh*    unknown
1Fh*    read DOS disk block, default drive
20h*    unknown
```

21h	random read from file specified by FCB	
22h	random write to file specified by FCB	
23h	return number of records in file specified by FCB	
24h	set relative file record size field for file specified by FCB	
25h	set interrupt vector	
26h	create new Program Segment Prefix (PSP)	
27h	random file block read from file specified by FCB	
28h	random file block write to file specified by FCB	
29h	parse the command line for file name	
2Ah	get the system date	
2Bh	set the system date	
2Ch	get the system time	
2Dh	set the system time	
2Eh	set/clear disk write VERIFY	
2Fh	get the Disk Transfer Address (DTA)	
30h	get DOS version number	
31h	TSR, files opened remain open	
32h*	read DOS Disk Block	
33h	get or set Ctrl-Break	
34h*	INDOS Critical Section Flag	
35h	get segment and offset address for an interrupt	
36h	get free disk space	
37h*	get/set option marking character (SWITCHAR)	
38h	return country-dependent information	
39h	create subdirectory	
3Ah	remove subdirectory	
3Bh	change current directory	
3Ch	create and return file handle	
3Dh	open file and return file handle	
3Eh	close file referenced by file handle	
3Fh	read from file referenced by file handle	
40h	write to file referenced by file handle	
41h	delete file	
42h	move file pointer (move read-write pointer for file)	
43h	set/return file attributes	
44h	device IOCTL (I/O control) info	
45h	duplicate file handle	
46h	force a duplicate file handle	
47h	get current directory	
48h	allocate memory	
49h	release allocated memory	
4Ah	modify allocated memory	
4Bh	load or execute a program	
4Ch	terminate prog and return to DOS	
4Dh	get return code of subprocess created by 4Bh	
4Eh	find first matching file	
4Fh	find next matching file	
50h*	set new current Program Segment Prefix (PSP)	
51h*	puts current PSP into BX	
52h*	pointer to the DOS list of lists	
53h*	translates BPB (Bios Parameter Block, see below)	
54h	get disk verification status (VERIFY)	
55h*	create PSP: similar to function 26h	
56h	rename a file	
57h	get/set file date and time	
58h	get/set allocation strategy	(DOS 3.x)
59h	get extended error information	
5Ah	create a unique filename	
5Bh	create a DOS file	
5Ch	lock/unlock file contents	
5Dh*	network	
5Eh*	network printer	
5Fh*	network redirection	
60h*	parse pathname	
61h*	unknown	
62h	get program segment prefix (PSP)	
63h*	get lead byte table	(DOS 2.25)
64h*	unknown	
65h	get extended country information	(DOS 3.3)
66h	get/set global code page table	(DOS 3.3)
67h	set handle count	(DOS 3.3)

```
68h    commit file                       (DOS 3.3)
69h    disk serial number                (DOS 4.0)
6Ah    unknown
6Bh    unknown
6Ch    extended open/create              (DOS 4.0)
```

Calling the DOS Services

The DOS services are invoked by placing the number of the desired function in register AH, subfunction in AL, setting the other registers to any specific requirements of the function, and invoking int 21h.

When the interrupt is called, all register and flag values are pushed into the stack. Int 21h contains a pointer into an absolute address in the IBMDOS.COM file. This address is the main loop for the DOS command handler. The handler pops the register values, compares them to its list of functions, and executes the function if valid. When the function is complete, it may pass values back to the command handler. The handler will push the values into the stack and then return control to the calling program.

Most functions will return an error code; some return more information. Details are contained in the listings for the individual functions. Extended error return codes for most functions may be obtained by calling function 59h.

Register settings listed are the ones used by DOS. Some functions will return with garbage values in unused registers. Do not test for values in unspecified registers; your program may exhibit odd behaviour.

DS:DX pointers are the data segment register (DS) indexed to the DH and DL registers (DX). DX always contains the offset address, DS contains the segment address.

The File Control Block services (FCB services) were part of DOS 1.0. Since the release of DOS 2.0, Microsoft has recommended that these services not be used. A set of considerably more enhanced services (handle services) were introduced with DOS 2.0. The handle services provide support for wildcards and subdirectories, and enhanced error detection via function 59h.

The data for the following calls was compiled from various Intel, Microsoft, IBM, and other publications. There are many subtle differences between MSDOS and PCDOS and between the individual versions. Differences between the versions are noted as they occur.

There are various ways of calling the DOS functions. For all methods, the function number is loaded into register AH, subfunctions and/or parameters are loaded into AL or other registers, and call int 21 by one of the following methods:

A. call interrupt 21h directly (the recommended procedure).
B. perform a long call to offset 50h in the program's PSP.
  1. This method will not work under DOS 1.x.
  2. Though recommended by Microsoft for DOS 2.0, this method takes more time and is no longer recommended.
C. place the function number in CL and perform an intrasegment call to location 05h in the current code segment. This location contains a long call to the DOS function dispatcher.
  1. IBM recommends this method be used only when using existing programs written for different calling conventions (such as converting CP/M programs). This method should be avoided unless you have some specific use for it.
  2. AX is always destroyed by this method.

3. This method is valid only for functions 00h-24h.

There are also various ways of exiting from a program. (assuming it is not intended to be a TSR). All methods except call 4Ch must ensure that the segment register contains the segment address of the PSP.

A. Interrupt 21h, function 4Ch (Terminate with Result Code). This is the 'official' recommended method of returning to DOS.
B. Interrupt 21h, function 00h (Exit Program). This is the early style int 21 function call. It simply calls int 20h.
C. Interrupt 20h (Exit).
D. A JMP instruction to offset 00h (int 20h vector) in the Program Segment Prefix. This is just a roundabout method to call int 20h. This method was set up in DOS 1.0 for ease of conversion for CP/M programs. It is no longer recommended for use.
E. A JMP instruction to offset 05h (int 21 vector) in the Program Segment Prefix, with AH set to 00h or 4Ch. This is another CP/M type function.

Version Specific Information

Function Calls:

DOS 2.x   supports function calls 00h to 57h.

DOS 2.25   is the only version to support function 63h (foreign keyboard)

DOS 3.x   has more sophisticated error handling and detection function calls available than 2.x.

DOS 3.0   supports function calls 00h to 5Ch and 62h, including new and changed function calls for version 3.0:
- 3Dh   Open File
- 59h   Get Extended Error
- 5Ah   Create Temporary File
- 5Bh   Create New File
- 5Ch   Lock/Unlock File Access
- 62h   Get Program Segment Prefix Address

DOS 3.1   supports function calls 00h to 62h, including the new and changed function calls for DOS 3.1:
- 5E00h   Get Machine Name
- 5E02h   Set Printer Setup
- 5E03h   Get Printer Setup
- 5F02h   Get Redirection List Entry
- 5F03h   Redirect Device
- 5F04h   Cancel Redirection

DOS 3.2   supports the following new functions:
- 44h   extended IOCTL functions

DOS 3.3   supports the following new functions:
- 44h   extended IOCTL functions
- 65h   get extended country information   (DOS 3.3)
- 66h   get/set global code page table   (DOS 3.3)

         67h   set handle count   (DOS 3.3)
         68h   commit file   (DOS 3.3)
DOS 4.0 supports the following new functions:
         44h   extended IOCTL functions
         69h   disk serial number
         6Ch   extended open/create

DOS Services in Detail
Interrupt 20h Terminate Current Program
(0:0080h) Issue int 20h to exit from a program. This vector transfers to the logic in DOS to restore the terminate address, the Ctrl-Break address, and the critical error exit address to the values they had on entry to the program. All the file buffers are flushed and all handles are closed. You should close all files changed in length (see function calls 10h and 3Eh) before issuing this interrupt. If the changed file is not closed, its length, time, and date are not recorded correctly in the directory.

For a program to pass a completion code or an error code when terminating, it must use either function call 4Ch (Terminate a Process) or 31h (Terminate Process and Stay Resident). These two methods are preferred over using int 20h and the codes returned by them can be interrogated in batch processing.

Important: Before you issue an interrupt 20h, your program must ensure that the CS register contains the segment of its Program Segment Prefix.

Interrupt 20h DOS - Terminate Program
```
entry   no parameters
return  The following vectors are restored from the Program Segment Prefix:
        0Ah     Program Terminate
        0Eh     Control-C
        12h     Critical Error
note 1. IBM and Microsoft recommend using int 21 Fn 4Ch. Using int 20 is
        officially frowned upon since the introduction of DOS 2.0
     2. In DOS 3.2 at least, int 20h merely calls int 21h, fn 00h.
```

INT 21H   DOS services
           Function (hex)

* Indicates functions not documented in the IBM DOS Technical Reference.

Note: some functions have been documented in other Microsoft or licensed OEM documentation.

```
Function  00h   Terminate Program
     Ends program, updates, FAT, flushes buffers, restores registers
entry   AH      00h
        CS      segment address of PSP
return  none
note 1. Program must place the segment address of the PSP control block in CS
        before calling this function.
     2. The terminate, ctrl-break, and critical error exit addresses (0Ah, 0Eh,
        12h) are restored to the values they had on entry to the terminating
        program, from the values saved in the program segment prefix at
        locations PSP:000Ah, PSP:000Eh, and PSP:0012h.
     3. All file buffers are flushed and the handles opened by the process are
        closed.
     4. Any files that have changed in length and are not closed are not
```

recorded properly in the directory.
5. Control transfers to the terminate address.
6. This call performs exactly the same function as int 20h.
7. All memory used by the program is returned to DOS. DOS just goes up the chain of memory blocks and marks any that are owned by the PSP which is terminating as free.
8. Files opened with FCBs are not automatically closed.

```
Function  01h     Get Keyboard Input
     Waits for char at STDIN (if necessary), echoes to STDOUT
entry    AH      01h
return   AL      ASCII character from STDIN (8 bits)
note 1. Checks char for Ctrl-C, if char is Ctrl-C, executes int 23h.
     2. For function call 06h, extended ASCII codes require two function calls.
        The first call returns 00h as an indicator that the next call will be an
        extended ASCII code.
     3. Input and output are redirectable. If redirected, there is no way to
        detect EOF.

Function  02h     Display Output
     Outputs char in DL to STDOUT
entry    AH      02h
         DL      8 bit data (usually ASCII character)
return   none
note 1. If char is 08 (backspace) the cursor is moved 1 char to the left
        (nondestructive backspace).
     2. If Ctrl-C is detected after input, int 23h is executed.
     3. Input and output are redirectable. If redirected, there is no way to
        detect disk full.

Function  03h     Auxiliary Input
      Get (or wait until) character from STDAUX
entry    AH      03h
return   AL      ASCII char from auxiliary device
note 1. AUX, COM1, COM2 is unbuffered and not interrupt driven
     2. This function call does not return status or error codes. For greater
        control it is recommended that you use ROM BIOS routine (int 14h) or
        write an AUX device driver and use IOCTL.
     3. At startup, PC-DOS initializes the first auxiliary port (COM1) to 2400
        baud, no parity, one stop bit, and an 8-bit word. MSDOS may differ.
     4. If Ctrl-C is has been entered from STDIN, int 23h is executed.

Function  04h     Auxiliary Output
       Write character to STDAUX
entry    AH      04h
         DL      ASCII char to send to AUX
return   none
note 1. This function call does not return status or error codes. For greater
        control it is recommended that you use ROM BIOS routine (int 14h) or
        write an AUX device driver and use IOCTL.
     2. If Ctrl-C is has been entered from STDIN, int 23h is executed.
     3. Default is COM1 unless redirected by DOS.
     4. If the device is busy, this function will wait until it is ready.

Function  05h     Printer Output
      Write character to STDPRN
entry    AL      05h
         DL      ASCII code for character to send
return   none
note 1. If Ctrl-C is has been entered from STDIN, int 23h is executed.
     2. Default is PRN or LPT1 unless redirected with the MODE command.
     3. If the printer is busy, this function will wait until it is ready.

Function  06h     Direct Console I/O
       Get character from STDIN; echo character to STDOUT
entry    AH      06h
         DL      0FFh for console input, or 00h-0FEh for console output
return   ZF      set     no character available
                 clear   character received
         AL      ASCII code for character
note 1. Extended ASCII codes require two function calls. The first call
```

returns 00h to indicate the next call will return an extended code
2. If DL is not 0FFh, DL is assumed to have a valid character that is output to STDOUT.
3. This function does not check for Ctrl-C or Ctrl-PrtSc.
4. Does not echo input to screen.
5. If I/O is redirected, EOF or disk full cannot be detected.

Function 07h Direct Console Input Without Echo (does not check BREAK)
    Get or wait for char at STDIN, returns char in AL
entry   AH   07h
return   AL   ASCII character from standard input device
note 1. Extended ASCII codes require two function calls. The first call returns 00h to indicate the next call will return an extended code.
    2. No checking for Ctrl-C or Ctrl-PrtSc is done.
    3. Input is redirectable.

Function 08h   Console Input Without Echo   (checks BREAK)
    Get or Wait for char at STDIN, return char in AL
entry   AH   08h
return   AL   char from standard input device
note 1. Char is checked for Ctrl-C. If Ctrl-C is detected, executes int 23h.
    2. For function call 08h, extended ASCII characters require two function calls. The first call returns 00h to signify an extended ASCII code. The next call returns the actual code.
    3. Input is redirectable. If redirected, there is no way to check EOF.

Function 09h   Print String
    Outputs Characters in the Print String to the STDOUT
entry   AH   09h
         DS:DX   pointer to the Character String to be displayed
return none
note 1. The character string in memory must be terminated by a $ (24h). The $ is not displayed.
    2. Output to STDOUT is the same as function call 02h.
    3. The $ is not displayed but remains in AL forever unless popped.

Function 0Ah   Buffered Keyboard Input
    Reads characters from STDIN and places them in the buffer beginning at the third byte.
entry   AH   0Ah
         DS:DX   pointer to an input buffer
return none
note 1. Min buffer size = 1, max = 255.
    2. Char is checked for Ctrl-C. If Ctrl-C is detected, executes int 23h.
    3. Format of buffer DX:
       byte   contents
        1   Maximum number of chars the buffer will take, including CR. Reading STDIN and filling the buffer continues until a carriage return (or 0Dh) is read. If the buffer fills to one less than the maximum number the buffer can hold, each additional number read is ignored and ASCII 7 (BEL) is output to the display until a carriage return is read. (you must set this value)
        2   Actual number of characters received, excluding the carriage return, which is always the last character (the function sets is value)
       3-n   Characters received are placed into the buffer starting here. Buffer must be at least as long as the number in byte 1.
    4. Input is redirectable. If redirected, there is no way to check EOF.
    5. The string may be edited with the standard DOS editing commands as it is being entered.
    6. Extended ASCII characters are stored as 2 bytes, the first byte being zero.

Function 0Bh   Check Standard Input (STDIN) status
     Checks for character available at STDIN
entry   AH   0Bh
return   AL   0FFh   if a character is available from STDIN
                    00h   if no character is available from STDIN
note 1. Checks for Ctrl-C. If Ctrl-C is detected, int 23h is executed.
    2. Input can be redirected.
    3. Checks for character only, it is not read into the application

62   *The Programmer's Technical Reference*

    4. IBM reports that this call does not work properly under the DOSSHELL
       program in DOS 4.00 and 4.01. DOSSHELL will return all zeroes. This
       function works correctly from the command line or application.

```
Function  0Ch   Clear Keyboard Buffer & Invoke a Keyboard Function      (FCB)
     Dumps buffer, executes function in AL (01h, 06h, 07h, 08h, 0Ah only)
entry    AH      0Ch
         AL      function number (must be 01h, 06h, 07h, 08h, or 0Ah)
return   AL      00h     buffer was flushed, no other processing performed
                 other   any other value has no meaning
note 1. Forces system to wait until a character is typed.
     2. Flushes all type-ahead input, then executes function specified by AL
        (by moving it to AH and repeating the int 21 call).
     3. If AL contains a value not in the list above, the keyboard buffer is
        flushed and no other action is taken.

Function  0Dh   Disk Reset
     Flushes all currently open file buffers to disk
entry    AH      0Dh
return           none
note 1. Does not close files. Does not update directory entries; files changed
        in size but not closed are not properly recorded in the directory.
     2. Sets DTA address to DS:0080h
     3. Should be used before a disk change, Ctrl-C handlers, and to flush the
        buffers to disk.

Function  0Eh   Select Disk
     Sets the drive specified in DL (if valid) as the default drive
entry    AL      0Eh
         DL      new default drive number (0=A:,1=B:,2=C:,etc.)
return   AL      total number of logical drives (not necessarily physical)
note 1. For DOS 1.x and 2.x, the minimum value for AL is 2.
     2. For DOS 3.x and 4.x, the minimum value for AL is 5.
     3. The drive number returned is not necessarily a valid drive.
     4. For DOS 1.x: 16 logical drives are available, A-P.
        For DOS 2.x: 63 logical drives are available. (Letters are only used for
                     the first 26 drives. If more than 26 logical drives are
                     used, further drive letters will be other ASCII characters
                     ie {,], etc.
        For DOS 3.x: 26 logical drives are available, A-Z.
        For DOS 4.x: 26 logical drives are available, A-Z.

Function  0Fh   Open Disk File                                          (FCB)
     Searches current directory for specified filename and opens it
entry    AH      0Fh
         DS:DX   pointer to an unopened FCB
return   AL      00h     if file found
                 0FFh    if file not not found
note 1. If the drive code was 0 (default drive) it is changed to the actual
        drive used (1=A:,2=B:,3=C:, etc). This allows changing the default
        drive without interfering with subsequent operations on this file.
     2. The current block field (FCB bytes C-D, offset 0Ch) is set to zero.
     3. The size of the record to be worked with (FCB bytes E-F, offset 0Eh) is
        set to the system default of 80h. The size of the file (offset 10h) and
        the date (offset 14h) are set from information obtained in the root
        directory. You can change the default value for the record size (FCB
        bytes E-F) or set the random record size and/or current record field.
        Perform these actions after open but before any disk operations.
     4. With DOS 3.x the file is opened in compatibility mode (network).
     5. Microsoft recommends handle function call 3Dh be used instead.
     6. This call is also used by the APPEND command in DOS 3.2+
     7. Before performing a sequential disk operation on the file, you must set
        the Current Record field (offset 20h). Before performing a random disk
        operation on the file, you must set the Relative Record field (offset
        21h). If the default record size of 128 bytes is incorrect, set it to
        the correct value.

Function 10h Close File                                                 (FCB)
     Closes a File After a File Write
entry    AH      10h
         DS:DX   pointer to an opened FCB
```

```
return   AL      00h     if the file is found and closed
                 0FFh    if the file is not found in the current directory
```
note 1. This function call must be done on open files that are no longer needed, and after file writes to insure all directory information is updated.
  2. If the file is not found in its correct position in the current directory, it is assumed that the diskette was changed and AL returns 0FFh. This error return is reportedly not completely reliable with DOS version 2.x.
  3. If found, the directory is updated to reflect the status in the FCB, the buffers to that file are flushed, and AL returns 00h.
  4. There is a subtle but dangerous bug in this function. If a Close request is issued using a File Control Block that has not been previously activated by a successful Open command, the file's length will be truncated to zero and the clusters previously assigned to the file are left floating.

```
Function  11h   Search For First Matching Entry                        (FCB)
    Searches current disk & directory for first matching filename
entry    AH      11h
         DS:DX   pointer to address of FCB
return   AL      00h     successful match
                 0FFh    no matching filename found
```
note 1. The FCB may contain the wildcard character ? under Dos 2.x, and ? or * under 3.x and 4.x.
  2. The original FCB at DS:DX contains information to continue the search with function 12h, and should not be modified.
  3. If a matching filename is found, AL returns 00h and the locations at the Disk Transfer Address are set as follows:
     a. If the FCB provided for searching was an extended FCB, then the first byte at the disk transfer address is set to 0FFh followed by 5 bytes of zeros, then the attribute byte from the search FCB, then the drive number used (1=A, 2=B, etc) then the 32 bytes of the directory entry. Thus, the disk transfer address contains a valid unopened FCB with the same search attributes as the search FCB.
     b. If the FCB provided for searching was a standard FCB, then the first byte is set to the drive number used (1=A, 2=b, etc)), and the next 32 bytes contain the matching directory entry. Thus, the disk transfer address contains a valid unopened normal FCB.
  4. If an extended FCB is used, the following search pattern is used:
     a. If the FCB attribute byte is zero, only normal file entries are found. Entries for volume label, subdirectories, hidden or system files, are not returned.
     b. If the attribute byte is set for hidden or system files, or subdirectory entries, it is to be considered as an inclusive search. All normal file entries plus all entries matching the specified attributes are returned. To look at all directory entries except the volume label, the attribute byte may be set to hidden + system + directory (all 3 bits on).
     c. If the attribute field is set for the volume label, it is considered an exclusive search, and ONLY the volume label entry is returned.
  5. This call is also used by the APPEND command in DOS 3.2+

```
Function 12h   Search For Next Entry Using FCB                         (FCB)
    Search for next matching filename
entry    AH      12h
         DS:DX   pointer to the unopened FCB specified from the previous Search
                 First (11h) or Search Next (12h)
return   AL      00h     if matching filename found
                 0FFh    if matching filename was not found
```
note 1. After a matching filename has been found using function call 11h, function 12h may be called to find the next match to an ambiguous request. For DOS 2.x, ?'s are allowed in the filename. For DOS 3.x and 4.x, global (*) filename characters are allowed.
  2. The DTA contains info from the previous Search First or Search Next.
  3. All of the FCB except for the name/extension field is used to keep information necessary for continuing the search, so no disk operations may be performed with this FCB between a previous function 11h or 12h call and this one.
  4. If the file is found, an FCB is created at the DTA address and set up to open or delete it.

```
Function   13h   Delete File Via FCB                                              (FCB)
     Deletes file specified in FCB from current directory
entry    AH       13h
         DS:DX    pointer to address of FCB
return   AL       00h       file deleted
                  0FFh      if file not found or was read-only
note 1.  All matching current directory entries are deleted. The global filename
         character '?' is allowed in the filename.
     2.  Will not delete files with read-only attribute set.
     3.  Close open files before deleting them.
     4.  Requires Network Access Rights.

Function   14h   Sequential Disk File Read                                        (FCB)
     Reads record sequentially from disk via FCB
entry    AH       14h
         DS:DX    pointer to an opened FCB
return   AL       00h       successful read
                  01h       end of file (no data read)
                  02h       Data Transfer Area too small for record size specified or
                            segment overflow
                  03h       partial record read, EOF found
note 1.  The record size is set to the value at offset 0Eh in the FCB.
     2.  The record pointed to by the Current Block (offset 0Ch) and the Current
         Record (offset 20h) fields is loaded at the DTA, then the Current Block
         and Current Record fields are incremented.
     3.  The record is read into memory at the current DTA address as specified by
         the most recent call to function 1Ah. If the size of the record and
         location of the DTA are such that a segment overflow or wraparound would
         occur, the error return is set to AL=02h.
     4.  If a partial record is read at the end of the file, it is passed to the
         requested size with zeros and the error return is set to AL=03h.

Function   15h   Sequential Disk Write                                            (FCB)
     Writes record specified by FCB sequentially to disk
entry    AH       15h
         DS:DX    pointer to address of FCB
return   AL       00h       successful write
                  01h       diskette full, write cancelled
                  02h       disk transfer area (DTA. too small or segment wrap
note 1.  The data to write is obtained from the disk transfer area.
     2.  The record size is set to the value at offset 0Eh in the FCB.
     3.  This service cannot write to files set as read-only.
     4.  The record pointed to by the Current Block (offset 0Ch) and the Current
         Record (offset 20h) fields is loaded at the DTA, then the Current Block
         and Current Record fields are incremented.
     5.  If the record size is less than a sector, the data in the DTA is written
         to a buffer; the buffer is written to disk when it contains a full sector
         of data, the file is closed, or a Reset Disk (function 0Dh) is issued.
     6.  The record is written to disk at the current DTA address as specified by
         the most recent call to function 1Ah. If the size of the record and
         location of the DTA are such that a segment overflow or wraparound would
         occur, the error return is set to AL=02h.

Function   16h   Create A Disk File                                               (FCB)
     Search and open or create directory entry for file
entry    AH       16h
         DS:DX    pointer to an FCB
return   AL       00h       successful creation
                  0FFh      no room in directory
note 1.  If a matching directory entry is found, the file is truncated to zero
         bytes.
     2.  If there is no matching filename, a filename is created.
     3.  This function calls function 0Fh (Open File) after creating or truncating
         a file.
     4.  A hidden file can be created by using an extended FCB with the attribute
         byte (offset FCB-1) set to 2.

Function   17h   Rename File Specified by File Control Block                      (FCB)
     Renames file in current directory
entry    AH       17h
         DS:DX    pointer to an FCB (see note 4)
```

```
return   AL        00h       successfully renamed
                   0FFh      file not found or filename already exists
note 1. This service cannot rename read-only files
     2. The '?' wildcard may be used.
     3. If the '?' wildcard is used in the second filename, the corresponding
        letters in the filename of the directory entry are not changed.
     4. The FCB must have a drive number, filename, and extension in the usual
        position, and a second filename starting 6 bytes after the first, at
        offset 11h.
     5. The two filenames cannot have the same name.
     6. FCB contains new name starting at byte 17h.

Function  18h    Internal to DOS
  *   Unknown - reportedly not used
entry    AH        18h
return   AL        00h

Function  19h    Get Current Disk Drive
       Return designation of current default disk drive
entry    AH        19h
return   AL        current default drive (0=A, 1=B,etc.)
note     Some other DOS functions use 0 for default, 1=A, 2=B, etc.

Function  1Ah    Set Disk Transfer Area Address (DTA)
       Sets DTA address to the address specified in DS:DX
entry    AH        1Ah
         DS:DX     pointer to buffer
return   none
note 1. The default DTA is 128 bytes at offset 80h in the PSP. DOS uses the DTA
        for all file I/O.
     2. Registers are unchanged.
     3. No error codes are returned.
     2. Disk transfers cannot wrap around from the end of the segment to the
        beginning or overflow into another segment.

Function  1Bh    Get Current Drive File Allocation Table Information
       Returns information from the FAT on the current drive
entry    AH        1Bh
return   AL        number of sectors per allocation unit (cluster)
         CX        number of bytes per sector
         DS:BX     address of the current drive's media descriptor byte
         DX        number of allocation units (clusters) for default drive
note 1. Save DS before calling this function.
     2. This call returned a pointer to the FAT in DOS 1.x. Beginning with DOS
        2.00, it returns a pointer only to the table's ID byte.
     3. IBM recommends programmers avoid this call and use int 25h instead.

Function  1Ch    Get File Allocation Table Information for Specific Device
       Returns information on specified drive
entry    AH        1Ch
         DL        drive number (1=A, 2=B, 3=C, etc)
return   AL        number of sectors per allocation unit (cluster)
         DS:BX     address of media descriptor byte for drive in DL
         CX        sector size in bytes
         DX        number of allocation units (clusters)
note 1. DL = 0 for default.
     2. Save DS before calling this function.
     3. Format of media-descriptor byte:
        bits:   0       0   (clear)    not double sided
                        1   (set)      double sided
                1       0   (clear)    not 8 sector
                        1   (set)      8 sector
                2       0   (clear)    nonremovable device
                        1   (set)      removable device
                3-7         always set (1)
     4. This call returned a pointer to the FAT in DOS 1.x. Beginning with DOS
        2.00, it returns a pointer only to the table's ID byte.
     5. IBM recommends programmers avoid this call and use int 25h instead.

Function  1Dh    Not Documented by Microsoft
  *   Unknown - reportedly not used
```

```
entry    AH      1Dh
return   AL      00h

Function 1Eh    Not Documented by Microsoft
*     Unknown - reportedly not used
entry    AH      1Eh
return   AL      00h
note     Apparently does nothing.

Function 1Fh Get Default Drive Parameter Block
*        Same as function call 32h (below), except that the table is
         accessed from the default drive
entry    AH      1Fh
         other registers unknown
return   AL      00h     no error
                 0FFh    error
         DS:BX   pointer to DOS Disk Parameter Block for default drive.
note 1.  Unknown vector returned in ES:BX.
     2.  For DOS 2, 3, 4.x, this just invokes function 32h (undocumented, Read
         DOS Disk Block) with DL=0.

Function 20h    Unknown
*     Internal - does nothing?
entry    AH      20h
return   AL      00h

Function 21h Random Read from File Specified by File Control Block          (FCB)
     Reads one record as specified in the FCB into the current DTA.
entry    AH      21h
         DS:DX   address of the opened FCB
return   AL      00h     successful read operation
                 01h     end of file (EOF), no data read
                 02h     DTA too small for the record size specified
                 03h     end of file (EOF), partial data read
note 1.  The current block and current record fields are set to agree with the
         random record field. Then the record addressed by these fields is read
         into memory at the current Disk Transfer Address.
     2.  The current file pointers are NOT incremented this function.
     3.  If the DTA is larger than the file, the file is padded to the requested
         length with zeros.

Function 22h Random Write to File Specified by FCB                          (FCB)
     Writes one record as specified in the FCB to the current DTA
entry    AH      22h
         DS:DX   address of the opened FCB
return   AL      00h     successful write operation
                 01h     disk full; no data written (write was cancelled)
                 02h     DTA too small for the record size specified (write was
                         cancelled)
note 1.  This service cannot write to read-only files.
     2.  The record pointed to by the Current Block (offset 0Ch) and the Current
         Record (offset 20h) fields is loaded at the DTA, then the Current Block
         and Current Record fields are incremented.
     3.  If the record size is less than a sector, the data in the DTA is written
         to a buffer; the buffer is written to disk when it contains a full sector
         of data, the file is closed, or a Reset Disk (function 0Dh) is issued.
     4.  The current file pointers are NOT incremented this function.
     5.  The record is written to disk at the current DTA address as specified by
         the most recent call to function 1Ah. If the size of the record and
         location of the DTA are such that a segment overflow or wraparound
         would occur, the error return is set to AL=02h.

Function 23h    Get File Size                                               (FCB)
     Searches current subdirectory for matching file, returns size in FCB
entry    AH      23h
         DS:DX   address of an unopened FCB
return   AL      00h file found
                 0FFh file not found
note 1.  Record size field (offset 0Eh) must be set before invoking this function
     2.  The disk directory is searched for the matching entry. If a matching
         entry is found, the random record field is set to the number of records
```

in the file. If the value of the Record Size field is not an even
divisor of the file size, the value set in the relative record field is
rounded up. This gives a returned value larger than the actual file size
   3. This call is used by the APPEND command in DOS 3.2+

Function   24h   Set Relative Record Field   (FCB)
     Set random record field specified by an FCB
entry   AH   24h
          DS:DX   address of an opened FCB
return   Random Record Field of FCB is set to be same as Current Block
          and Current Record.
note 1. You must invoke this function before performing random file access.
      2. The relative record field of FCB (offset 21h) is set to be same as the
          Current Block (offset 0Ch) and Current Record (offset 20h).
      3. No error codes are returned.
      4. The FCB must already be opened.

Function   25h   Set Interrupt Vector
     Sets the address of the code DOS is to perform each time the specified
     interrupt is invoked.
entry   AH   25h
          AL   int number to reassign the handler to
          DS:DX   address of new interrupt vector
return   none
note 1. Registers are unchanged.
      2. No error codes are returned.
      3. The interrupt vector table for the interrupt number specified in AL is
          set to the address contained in DS:DX. Use function 35h (Get Vector) to
          get the contents of the interrupt vector and save it for later use.
      4. When you use function 25 to set an interrupt vector, DOS 3.2 doesn't
          point the actual interrupt vector to what you requested. Instead, it
          sets the interrupt vector to point to a routine inside DOS, which does
          this:
                  1. Save old stack pointer
                  2. Switch to new stack pointer allocated from DOS's stack pool
                  3. Call your routine
                  4. Restore old stack pointer
          The purpose for this was to avoid possible stack overflows when there are
          a large number of active interrupts. IBM was concerned (this was an IBM
          change, not Microsoft) that on a Token Ring network there would be a lot
          of interrupts going on, and applications that hadn't allocated very much
          stack space would get clobbered.

Function   26h   Create New Program Segment Prefix (PSP)
This service copies the current program-segment prefix to a new memory location
for the creation of a new program or overlay. Once the new PSP is in place, a DOS
program can read a DOS COM or over lay file into the memory location immediately
following the new PSP and pass control to it.
entry   AH   26h
          DX   segment number for the new PSP
return   Current PSP is copied to specified segment
note 1. Microsoft recommends you use the newer DOS service 4Bh (EXEC) instead.
      2. The entire 100h area at location 0 in the current PSP is copied into
          location 0 of the new PSP. The memory size information at location 6 in
          the new segment is updated and the current termination, ctrl-break, and
          critical error addresses from interrupt vector table entries for ints
          22h, 23h, and 24 are saved in the new program segment starting at 0Ah.
          They are restored from this area when the program terminates.

Function   27h   Random Block Read From File Specified by FCB
     Similar to 21h (Random Read) except allows multiple files to be read.
entry   AH   27h
          CX   number of records to be read
          DS:DX   address of an opened FCB
return   AL   00h   successful read
                  01h   end of file, no data read
                  02h   DTA too small for record size specified (read
                         cancelled)
                  03h   end of file
          CX   actual number of records read (includes partial if AL=03h)
note 1. The record size is specified in the FCB. The service updates the Current

           Block (offset 0Ch) and Current Record (offset 20h) fields to the next
           record not read.
       2. If CX contained 0 on entry, this is a NOP.
       3. If the DTA is larger than the file, the file is padded to the requested
           length with zeros.
       4. This function assumes that the FCB record size field (0Eh) is correctly
           set. If not set by the user, the default is 128 bytes.
       5. The record is written to disk at the current DTA address as specified by
           the most recent call to function 1Ah. If the size of the record and
           location of the DTA are such that a segment overflow or wraparound would
           occur, the error return is set to AL=02h.

Function 28h Random Block Write to File Specified in FCB
    Similar to 27h (Random Write) except allows multiple files to be read.
entry   AH   28h
         CX   number of records to write
         DS:DX   address of an opened FCB
return   AL   00h   successful write
                  01h   disk full, no data written
                  02h   DTA too small for record size specified (write cancelled)
         CX   number of records written
note 1. The record size is specified in the FCB.
     2. This service allocates disk clusters as required.
     3. This function assumes that the FCB Record Size field (offset 0Eh) is
         correctly set. If not set by the user, the default is 128 bytes.
     4. The record size is specified in the FCB. The service updates the Current
         Block (offset 0Ch) and Current Record (offset 20h) fields to the next
         record not read.
     5. The record is written to disk at the current DTA address as specified by
         the most recent call to function 1Ah. If the size of the record and
         location of the DTA are such that a segment overflow or wraparound would
         occur, the error return is set to AL=02h.
     6. If called with CX=0, no records are written, but the FCB's File Size
         entry (offset 1Ch) is set to the size specified by the FCB's Relative
         Record field (offset 21h).

Function 29h Parse the Command Line for Filename
    Parses a text string into the fields of a File Control Block
entry   AH   29h
         DS:SI   pointer to string to parse
         ES:DI   pointer to memory buffer to fill with unopened FCB
         AL   bit mask to control parsing
              bit 0   0   parsing stops if file separator found
                       1   causes service to scan past leading chars such as
                             blanks. Otherwise assumes the filename begins in the
                             first byte
                  1   0   drive number in FCB set to default (0) if string
                             contains no drive number
                       1   drive number in FCB not changed
                  2   0   filename in FCB set to 8 blanks if no filename no
                             string
                       1   filename in FCB not changed if string does not contain
                             a filename
                  3   0   extension in FCB set to 3 blanks if no extension in
                             string
                       1   extension left unchanged
                 4-7   must be zero
return   AL   00h   no wildcards in name or extension
                  01h   wildcards appeared in name or extension
                  0FFh   invalid drive specifier
         DS:SI   pointer to the first byte after the parsed string
         ES:DI   pointer to a buffer filled with the unopened FCB
note 1. If the * wildcard characters are found in the command line, this service
         will replace all subsequent chars in the FCB with question marks.
     2. This service uses the characters as filename separators
         DOS 1   : ; . , + / [ ] = " TAB SPACE
         DOS 2,3,4   : ; . , + = TAB SPACE
     3. This service uses the characters
         : ; . , + < > | / \ [ ] = " TAB SPACE
         or any control characters as valid filename separators.
     4. A filename cannot contain a filename terminator. If one is encountered,

all processing stops. The handle functions will allow use of some of these characters.
5. If no valid filename was found on the command line, ES:DI +1 points to a blank (ASCII 32).
6. This function cannot be used with filespecs which include a path
7. Parsing is in the form D:FILENAME.EXT. If one is found, a corresponding unopened FCB is built at ES:DI.

Function 2Ah Get Date
    Returns day of the week, year, month, and date
entry AH   2Ah
return CX   year   (1980-2099)
       DH   month   (1-12)
       DL   day   (1-31)
       AL   weekday 00h   Sunday
                      01h   Monday
                      02h   Tuesday
                      03h   Wednesday
                      04h   Thursday
                      05h   Friday
                      06h   Saturday
note 1. Date is adjusted automatically if clock rolls over to the next day, and takes leap years and number of days in each month into account.
     2. Although DOS cannot set an invalid date, it can read one, such as 1/32/80, etc.
     3. DesQview also accepts CX = 4445h and DX = 5351h, i.e. 'DESQ' as valid
     4. DOS will accept CH=0 (midnight) as a valid time, but if a file's time is set to exactly midnight the time will not be displayed by the DIR command.

Function 2Bh Set Date
    set current system date
entry AH   2Bh
       CX   year   (1980-2099)
       DH   month   (1-12)
       DL   day   (1-31)
return AL   00h   no error (valid date)
            0FFh   invalid date specified
note 1. On entry, CX:DX must have a valid date in the same format as returned by function call 2Ah.
     2. DOS 3.3+ also sets CMOS clock.
     3. Under the DesQview system shell, this is the DV_GET_VERSION check.
        entry AH   2Bh
               AL   01h   DesQ call
               CX   4445h 'DE'   (invalid date used
               DX   5351h 'SQ'   for DesQview ID)
        return AH   major version
               AL   minor version
               AX   0FFh   DesQ not installed (DOS error code)
     4. For DESQview 2.00+, installation check
        entry AH   2Bh
               AL   subfunction (DV v2.00+)
                      01h   Get Version
        return BX   version (BH = major, BL = minor)
        note   Early copies of v2.00 return 0002h.
                      02h   Get Shadow Buffer Info, and Start
        return BH   Shadowing rows in shadow buffer
               BL   columns in shadow buffer
               DX   segment of shadow buffer
                      04h   Get Shadow Buffer Info
        return BH   rows in shadow buffer
               BL   columns in shadow buffer
               DX   segment of shadow buffer
                      05h   Stop Shadowing
               CX   4445h ('DE')
               DX   5351h ('SQ')
        return AL   0FFh   if DESQview not installed
        note   In DESQview v1.x, there were no subfunctions; this call only identified whether or not DESQview was loaded.

```
Function  2Ch  Get Time
     Get current system time from CLOCK$ driver
entry   AH       2Ch
return  CH       hours   (0-23)
        CL       minutes (0-59)
        DH       seconds (0-59)
        DL       hundredths of a second (0-99)
note 1. Time is updated every 5/100 second.
     2. The date and time are in binary format.

Function  2Dh  Set Time
     Sets current system time
entry   AH       2Dh
        CH       hours   (0-23)
        CL       minutes (0-59)
        DH       seconds (0-59)
        DL       hundredths of seconds (0-99)
return  AL       00h       if no error
                 0FFh      if bad value sent to routine
note 1. DOS 3.3+ also sets CMOS clock.
     2. CX and DX must contain a valid time in binary.

Function  2Eh  Set/Reset Verify Switch
     Set verify flag
entry   AH       2Eh
        AL       00      to turn verify off (default)
                 01      to turn verify on
return  none
note 1. This is the call invoked by the DOS VERIFY command.
     2. Setting of the verify switch can be obtained by calling call 54h.
     3. This call is not supported on network drives.
     4. DOS checks this flag each time it accesses a disk.

Function  2Fh  Get Disk Transfer Address (DTA)
     Returns current disk transfer address used by all DOS read/write operations
entry   AH       2Fh
return  ES:BX    address of DTA
note 1. The DTA is set by function call 1Ah.
     2. Default DTA address is a 128 byte buffer at offset 80h in that program's
        Program Segment Prefix.

Function  30h  Get DOS Version Number
     Return DOS version and/or user number
entry   AH       30h
return  AH       minor version number  (i.e., DOS 2.10 returns AX = 0A02h)
        AL       major version number  (0 for DOS 1.x)
        BH       OEM ID number
                 00h     IBM
                 16h     DEC     (others not known)
        BL:CX    24-bit user serial number
note 1. If AL returns a major version number of zero, the DOS version is below
        1.28 for MSDOS and below 2.00 for PCDOS.
     2. IBM PC-DOS always returns 0000h in BX and CX.
     3. OS/2 v1.0 Compatibility Box returns a value of 10 for major version.
     4. Due to the OS/2 return and the fact that some European versions of DOS
        carry higher version numbers than IBM's DOS, utilities which check for a
        DOS version should not abort if a higher version than required is found
        unless some specific problems are known.

Function  31h  Terminate Process and Stay Resident
     KEEP, or TSR
entry   AH       31h
        AL       exit code
        DX       program memory requirement in 16 byte paragraphs
return  AX       return code (retrievable by function 4Dh)
note 1. Files opened by the application are not closed when this call is made.
     2. Memory can be used more efficiently if the block containing the copy of
        the DOS environment is deallocated before terminating. This can be done
        by loading ES with the segment contained in 2Ch of the PSP and issuing
        function call 49h (Free Allocated Memory).
     3. Unlike int 27h, more than 64k may be made resident with this call.
```

```
Function   32h   Read DOS Disk Block
   *   Retrieve the pointer to the drive parameter block for a drive
   entry      AH      32h
              DL      drive (0=default, 1=A:, etc.).
   return     AL      00h      if drive is valid
                      0FFh     if drive is not valid
              DS:BX   pointer to DOS Drive Parameter Table. Format of block:
   Bytes      Type    Value
   00h        byte    Drive: 0=A:, 1=B:, etc.
   01h        byte    Unit within device driver (0, 1, 2, etc.)
   02h-03h    word    Bytes per sector
   04h        byte    largest sector number in cluster (one less than sectors per
                      cluster)
   05h        byte    Cluster to sector shift (i.e., how far to shift-left the
                        bytes/sector to get bytes/cluster)
   06h-07h    word    Number of reserved (boot) sectors
   08h        byte    Number of copies of the FAT
   09h-0Ah    word    Number of root directory entries
   0Bh-0Ch    word    Sector # of 1st data. Should be same as # of sectors/track.
   0Dh-0Eh    word    largest possible cluster number (one more than the number of data
                      clusters)

   DOS 2.x only
   0Fh        byte    sectors for one copy of the FAT
   10h-11h    word    First sector of root directory
   12h-15h    dword   Address of device driver header for this drive
   16h        byte    Media Descriptor Byte for this drive
   17h        byte    0FFh indicates block must be rebuilt (DOS 3.x) 00h indicates
                      block device has been accessed
   18h-1Bh    dword   address of next DOS Disk Block (0FFFFh means last in chain)
   1Ch        word    starting cluster of current dir (0 = root)
   1Eh        64byts  ASCIIZ current directory path string
   22h        byte    Current Working Directory (2.0 only) (64 bytes)

   DOS 3.x
   0Fh        byte    number of sectors in one FAT copy
   10h        word    first sector of root directory
   12h        dword   address of device driver for this drive
   16h        byte    media descriptor byte for medium
   17h        byte    0FFh = block must be rebuilt, 00h indicates block accessed
   18h        dword   address of next device block, offset = 0FFFFh indicates last word
                      cluster at which to start search for free space when writing
   1Ch        word    00h, probably unused, values left from before
   1Eh        word    0FFFFh indicates block was built

   DOS 4.0
   0Fh        word    number of sectors in one FAT copy
   11h        word    first sector of root directory
   13h        dword   address of device driver for this drive
   17h        byte    media descriptor byte for medium
   18h        byte    0FFh = block must be rebuilt, 00h indicates block accessed
   19h        dword   address of next device block, offset = 0FFFFh indicates last
   1Dh        word    cluster at which to start search for free space when writing
   1Fh        word    unknown
   note 1. Use [BX+0D] to find no. of clusters (1000h, 16-bit FAT; if not, 12-bit
           (exact dividing line is probably a little below 1000h to allow for bad
           sectors, EOF markers, etc.)
        2. Short article by C.Petzold, PC Magazine  Vol.5,no.8, and the article
           'Finding Disk Parameters' in the May 1986 issue of PC Tech Journal.
        3. This call is mostly supported in OS/2 1.0's DOS Compatibility
           Box. The dword at 12h will not return the address of the next
           device driver when in the Compatibility Box.
        4. Used by CHKDSK.

Function   33h   Control-Break Check
      Get or set control-break checking at CON
   entry      AH      33h
              AL      00h      to test for break checking
                      01h      to set break checking
                      DL       00h      to disable break checking
                               01h      to enable break checking
```

```
                        02h     internal, called by PRINT.COM (DOS 3.1)
                        03h     unknown
                        04h     unknown
                        05h     boot drive (DOS 4.0+)
return     DL           break setting (AL=00h)
                        00h     if break=off
                        01h     if break=on
                        (if AL=05h) boot drive, A=1, B=2, etc)
           AL           0FFh    error

Function  34h  Return INDOS Flag
  *   Returns ES:BX pointing to Critical Section Flag, byte indicating whether it
      is safe to interrupt DOS.
entry    AH      34h
return   ES:BX   points to 1-byte DOS "critical section flag"

note 1. If byte is 0, it is safe to interrupt DOS. This was mentioned in some
        documentation by Microsoft on a TSR standard, and 'PC Magazine' reports
        it functions reliably under DOS versions 2.0 through 3.3. Chris Dunford
        (of CED fame) and a number of anonymous messages on the BBSs indicate it
        may not be totally reliable.
     2. The byte at ES:BX+1 is used by the Print program for this same purpose,
        so it's probably safer to check the WORD at ES:BX.
     3. Reportedly, examination of DOS 2.10 code in this area indicates that the
        byte immediately following this 'critical section flag' must be 00h to
        permit the PRINT.COM interrupt to be called. For DOS 3.0 and 3.1
        (except Compaq DOS 3.0), the byte before the 'critical section flag'
        must be zero; for Compaq DOS 3.0, the byte 01AAh before it must be zero.
     4. In DOS 3.10 this reportedly changed to word value, with preceding byte.
     5. This call is supported in OS/2 1.0's DOS Compatibility Box
     6. Gordon Letwin of Microsoft discussed this call on ARPAnet in 1984. He
        stated:
        a. this is not supported under any version of the DOS
        b. it usually works under DOS 2, but there may be circumstances when it
           doesn't (general disclaimer, don't know of a specific circumstance)
        c. it will usually not work under DOS 3 and DOS 3.1; the DOS is
           considerably restructured and this flag takes on additional
           meanings and uses
        d. it will fail catastrophically under DOS 4.0 and forward.
           Obviously this information is incorrect since the call works
           fine through DOS 3.3. Microsoft glasnost?

Function  35h  Get Vector
      Get interrupt vector
entry    AH      35h
         AL      interrupt number (hexadecimal)
return   ES:BX   address of interrupt vector
note     Use function call 25h to set the interrupt vectors.

Function  36h  Get Disk Free Space
      get information on specified drive
entry    AH      36h
         DL      drive number (0=default, 1=A:, 2=B:, etc)
return   AX      number of sectors per cluster
                 0FFFFh means drive specified in DL is invalid
         BX      number of available clusters
         CX      bytes per sector
         DX      clusters per drive
note 1. Mult AX * CX * BX for free space on disk.
     2. Mult AX * CX * DX for total disk space.
     3. Function 36h returns an incorrect value after an ASSIGN command. Prior to
        ASSIGN, the DX register contains 0943h on return, which is the free space
        in clusters on the HC diskette. After ASSIGN, even with no parameters,
        0901h is returned in the DX register; this is an incorrect value.
        Similar results occur with DD diskettes on a PC-XT or a PC-AT. This
        occurs only when the disk is not the default drive. Results are as
        expected when the drive is the default drive. Therefore, the
        circumvention is to make the desired drive the default drive prior to
        issuing this function call.
     4. Int 21h, function call 36h returns an incorrect value after an ASSIGN
        command. Prior to ASSIGN, the DX register contains 0943h on return, which
```

DOS Interrupts and Function Calls

is the free space in clusters on the HC diskette. After ASSIGN, even with no parameters, 0901h is returned in the DX register; this is an incorrect value. Similar results occur with DD diskettes on a PC-XT or a PC-AT. This occurs only when the disk is not the default drive. Results are as expected when the drive is the default drive. Therefore, the circumvention is to make the desired drive the default drive prior to issuing this function call.
  5. This function supercedes functions 1Bh and 1Ch.

```
Function    37h    SWITCHAR / AVAILDEV
   *     Get/set option marking character (is usually "/"), and device type
entry   AH         37h
        AL         00h        read switch character (returns current character in DL)
                   01h        set character in DL as new switch character
        (DOS 2.x.  02h        read device availability (as set by function AL=3)
                              into DL. A 0 means devices that devices must be accessed
                              in file I/O calls by /dev/device. A non-zero value means
                              that devices are accessible at every level of the
                              directory tree (e.g., PRN is the printer and not a file
                              PRN).
                              AL=2 to return flag in DL, AL=3 to set from DL (0
                              = set,1 = not set).
        (DOS 2.x)  03h        get device availability, where:
        DL         00h        means /dev/ must precede device names
                   01h        means /dev/ need not precede device names
return  DL                    switch character (if AL=0 or 1)
                              device availability flag (if AL=2 or 3)
        AL         0FFh       the value in AL was not in the range 0-3.
```
note 1. Functions 2 & 3 appear not to be implemented for DOS 3.x.
  2. It is documented on page 4.324 of the MS-DOS (version 2) Programmer's Utility Pack (Microsoft - published by Zenith).
  3. Works on all versions of IBM PC-DOS from 2.0 through 3.3.1.
  4. The SWITCHAR is the character used for "switches" in DOS command arguments (defaults to '/', as in "DIR/P"). '-' is popular to make a system look more like UNIX; if the SWITCHAR is anything other than '/', then '/' may be used instead of '\' for pathnames.
  5. Ignored by XCOPY, PKARC, LIST.
  6. SWITCHAR may not be set to any character used in a filename.
  7. In DOS 3.x you can still read the "AVAILDEV" byte with subfunction 02h but it always returns 0FFh even if you try to change it to 0 with subfunction 03h.
  8. AVAILDEV=0 means that devices must be referenced in an imaginary subdirectory "\dev" (similar to UNIX's /dev/*); a filename 'PRN.DAT' can be created on disk and manipulated like any other. If AVAILDEV != 0 then device names are recognized anywhere (this is the default): 'PRN.DAT' is synonymous with 'PRN:'.
  9. These functions reportedly are not supported in the same fashion in various implementations of DOS.
  10. Used by DOS 3.3 CHKDSK, BASIC, DEBUG.

```
Function    38h    Return Country-Dependent Information
                   (PCDOS 2.0, 2.1, MSDOS 2.00 only)
entry   AH         38h
        AL         function code   (must be 0 in DOS 2.x)
        DS:DX      pointer to 32 byte memory buffer for returned information
return  CF         set on error
        AX         error code (02h)
        BX         country code
        DS:DX      pointer to buffer filled with country information:
           bytes 00h,01h  date/time format
                          0000h    USA standard        H:M:S    M/D/Y
                          0001h    European standard   H:M:S    D/M/Y
                          0002h    Japanese standard   H:M:S    D:M:Y
                 02h      ASCIIZ string currency symbol
                 03h      byte of zeros
                 04h      ASCIIZ string thousands separator
                 05h      byte of zeros
                 06h      ASCIIZ string decimal separator
                 07h      byte of zeros
           24 bytes 08h-1Fh reserved
```

```
Function  38h     Get Country-Dependent Information
                  (PCDOS 3.x+, MSDOS 2.01+)
entry     AH      38h
          AL      function code
                  00h       to get current country information
                  01h-0FEh  country code to get information for, for countries with
                            codes less than 255
                  0FFh      to get country information for countries with a greater
                            than 255
                  BX        16 bit country code if AL=0FFh
          DS:DX   pointer to the memory buffer where the data will be returned
          DX      0FFFFh if setting country code rather than getting info
return    CF      0 (clear) function completed
                  1 (set) error
                     AX     error code
                            02h       invalid country code (no table for it)
          (if DX  0FFFFh)
          BX      country code (usually international telephone code)
          DS:DX   pointer to country data buffer
            bytes 0,1       date/time format
                            0         USA standard         H:M:S    M/D/Y
                            1         European standard    H:M:S    D/M/Y
                            2         Japanese standard    H:M:S    D:M:Y
            bytes 02h-06h   currency symbol null terminated
            byte  07h       thousands separator null terminated
            byte  08h       byte of zeros
            byte  09h       decimal separator null terminated
            byte  0Ah       byte of zeros
            byte  0Bh       date separator null terminated
            byte  0Ch       byte of zeros
            byte  0Dh       time separator null terminated
            byte  0Eh       byte of zeros
            byte  0Fh       currency format byte
                      bit 0      0    if currency symbol precedes the value
                                 1    if currency symbol is after the value
                          1      0    no spaces between value and currency symbol
                                 1    one space between value and currency symbol
                          2           set if currency symbol replaces decimal point
                          3-7         not defined by Microsoft
            byte  10h       number of significant decimal digits in currency
                            (number of places to right of decimal point)
            byte  11h       time format byte
                      bit 0      0    12 hour clock
                                 1    24 hour clock
                          1-7         unknown, probably not used
            bytes 12h-15h   address of case map routine (FAR CALL, AL = char)
                      entry   AL  ASCII code of character to be converted to
                                  uppercase
                      return  AL  ASCII code of the uppercase input character
            byte  16h       data-list separator character
            byte  17h       zeros
            bytes 18h-21h   5 words reserved
note 1. When an alternate keyboard handler is invoked, the keyboard routine is
        loaded into user memory starting at the lowest portion of available user
        memory. The BIOS interrupt vector that services the keyboard is
        redirected to the memory area where the new routine resides. Each new
        routine takes up about 1.6K of memory and has lookup tables that return
        values unique to each language. (KEYBxx in the DOS book) Once the
        keyboard interrupt vector is changed by the DOS keyboard routine, the new
        routine services all calls unless the system is returned to the US format
        by the ctrl-alt-F1 keystroke combination. This does not change the
        interrupt vector back to the BIOS location; it merely passes the table
        lookup to the ROM locations.
     2. Ctrl-Alt-F1 will only change systems with US ROMS to the US layout.
        Some systems are delivered with non-US keyboard handler routines in ROM
     3. Case mapping call: the segment/offset of a FAR procedure that performs
        country-specific lower-to-upper case mapping on ASCII characters 80h to 0
        0FFh. It is called with the character to be mapped in AL. If there is
        an uppercase code for the letter, it is returned in AL, if there is no
        code or the function was called with a value of less than 80h AL is
        returned unchanged.
```

            4. This call is fully implemented in MS-DOS version 2.01 and higher. It is
               in version 2.00 but not fully implemented (according to Microsoft).

Function 38h   Set Country Dependent Information
entry   AH   38h
         AL   code   country code to set information for, for countries with
                        codes less than 255
                0FFh   to set country information for countries with a code
                        greater than 255
         BX   16 bit country code if AL=0FFh
         DX   0FFFFh
return   CF   clear   successful
                set   if error
                        AX   error code (02h)

Function 39h   Create Subdirectory (MKDIR)
                Makes a subdirectory along the indicated path
entry   AH   39h
         DS:DX address of ASCIIZ pathname string
return   flag CF 0   successful
                1   error
                        AX   error code if any (03h, 05h)
note 1. The ASCIIZ string may contain drive and subdirectory.
      2. Drive may be any valid drive (not necessarily current drive).
      3. The pathname cannot exceed 64 characters.

Function 3Ah   Remove Subdirectory (RMDIR)
entry   AH   3Ah
         DS:DX address of ASCIIZ pathname string
return   CF   clear   successful
                set   AX   error code if any (3, 5, 16)
note 1. The ASCIIZ string may contain drive and subdirectory.
      2. Drive may be any valid drive (not necessarily current drive).
      3. The pathname cannot exceed 64 characters.

Function 3Bh   Change Current Directory (CHDIR)
entry   AH   3Bh
         DS:DX address of ASCIIZ string
return   flag CF 0   successful
                1   error
         AX   error code if any (03h)
note 1. The pathname cannot exceed 64 characters.
      2. The ASCIIZ string may contain drive and subdirectory.
      3. Drive may be any valid drive (not necessarily current drive).

Function 3Ch   Create A File (CREAT)
                Create a file with handle
entry   AH   3Ch
         CX   byte, attributes for file
                00h   normal
                01h   read only
                02h   hidden
                03h   system
         DS:DX address of ASCIIZ filename string
return   CF   0   successful creation
                1   error
         AX   16 bit file handle
                or error code (03h, 04h, 05h)
note 1. The ASCIIZ string may contain drive and subdirectory.
      2. Drive may be any valid drive (not necessarily current drive).
      3. If the volume label or subdirectory bits are set in CX, they are ignored
      4. The file is opened in read/write mode
      5. If the file does not exist, it is created. If one of the same name
         exists, it is truncated to a length of 0.
      6. Good practice is to attempt to open a file with fn 3Dh and jump to an
         error routine if successful, create file if 3Dh fails. That way an
         existing file will not be truncated and overwritten

Function 3Dh   Open A File
                Open disk file with handle
entry   AH   3Dh

```
            AL         access code byte
(DOS 2.x)   bits 0-2       file attribute
                              000     read only
                              001     write only
                              010     read/write
                 3-7       reserved, should be set to zero
(DOS 3.x)   bits 0-2       file attribute
                              000     read only
                              001     write only
                              010     read/write
                 3         reserved, should be set to zero
                 4-6       sharing mode (network)
                              000     compatibility mode (the way FCBs open files)
                              001     read/write access denied (exclusive)
                              010     write access denied
                              011     read access denied
                              100     full access permitted
                 7         inheritance flag
                              0       file inherited by child process
                              1       file private to child process
            DS:DX      address of ASCIIZ pathname string
return      CF set on error
            AX         error code (01h, 02h, 03h, 04h, 05h, 0Ch)
            AX         16 bit file handle
note 1. Opens any normal, system, or hidden file.
     2. Files that end in a colon are not opened.
     3. The real/write pointer is set at the first byte of the file and the
        record size of the file is 1 byte (the read/write pointer can be changed
        through function call 42h). The returned file handle must be used for
        all subsequent input and output to the file.
     4. If the file handle was inherited from a parent process or was duplicated
        by DUP or FORCEDUP, all sharing and access restrictions are also
        inherited.
     5. A file sharing error (error 01h) causes an int 24h to execute with an
        error code of 02h.

Function 3Eh       Close A File Handle
                   Close a file and release handle for reuse
entry    AH        3Eh
         BX        file handle
return   flag CF 0         successful close
                 1         error
         AX        error code if error (06h)
note 1. When executed, the file is closed, the directory is updated, and all
        buffers for that file are flushed. If the file was changed, the time and
        date stamps are changed to current.
     2. If called with the handle 00000h, it will close STDIN (normally the
        keyboard).

Function 3Fh       Read From A File Or Device
                   Read from file with handle
entry    AH        3Fh
         BX        file handle
         CX        number of bytes to read
         DS:DX     address of buffer
return   flag CF 0         successful read
                 1         error
         AX      0         pointer was already at end of file
                           or number of bytes read
                           or error code (05h, 06h)
note 1. This function attempts to transfer the number of bytes specified to a
        buffer location. It is not guaranteed that all bytes will be read. If
        AX < CX a partial record was read.
     2. If performed from STDIN (file handle 0000), the input can be redirected
     3. If used to read the keyboard, it will only read to the first CR.
     4. The file pointer is incremented to the last byte read.

Function 40h       Write To A File Or Device
                   Write to file with handle
entry    AH        40h
         BX        file handle
```

DOS Interrupts and Function Calls

```
           CX       number of bytes to write
           DS:DX    address of buffer
return     flag CF  0     successful write
                    1     error
           AX       number of bytes written
                    or error code  (05h, 06h)
```
note 1. This call attempts to transfer the number of bytes indicated in CX from a buffer to a file. If CX and AX do not match after the write, an error has taken place; however no error code will be returned for this problem. This is usually caused by a full disk.
  2. If the write is performed to STDOUT (handle 0001), it may be redirected
  3. To truncate the file at the current position of the file pointer, set the number of bytes in CX to zero before calling int 21h. The pointer can be moved to any desired position with function 42h.
  4. This function will not write to a file or device marked read-only.
  5. May also be used to display strings to CON instead of fn 09h. This function will write CX bytes and stop; fn 09h will continue to write until a $ character is found.
  6. This is the call that DOS actually uses to write to the screen in DOS 2.x and above.

```
Function  41h    Delete A File From A Specified Subdirectory        (UNLINK)
entry     AH     41h
          DS:DX  pointer to ASCIIZ filespec to delete
return    CF     0     successful
                 1     error
          AX     error code if any  (02h, 05h)
```
note 1. This function will not work on a file marked read-only.
  2. Wildcards are not accepted.

```
Function  42h    Move a File Read/Write Pointer  (LSEEK)
entry     AH     42h
          AL     method code byte
                 00h    offset from beginning of file
                 01h    offset from present location
                 02h    offset from end of file
          BX     file handle
          CX     most significant half of offset
          DX     least significant half of offset
return    AX     low offset of new file pointer
          DX     high offset of new file pointer
          CF     0     successful move
                 1     error
          AX     error code (01h, 06h)
```
note 1. If pointer is at end of file, reflects file size in bytes.
  2. The value in DX:AX is the absolute 32 bit byte offset from the beginning of the file.

```
Function  43h    Get/Set file attributes  (CHMOD)
entry     AH     43h
          AL     00h    get file attributes
                 01h    set file attributes
          CX     file attributes to set
                 bit 0    read only
                     1    hidden file
                     2    system file
                     3    volume label
                     4    subdirectory
                     5    written since backup (archive bit)
                     6,7  not used
                     8    shareable (Novell NetWare)
                     9,F  not used
          DS:DX  pointer to full ASCIIZ file name
return    CF     set if error
          AX     error code  (01h, 02h, 03h, 05h)
          CX     file attributes on get
                 attributes:
                 01h    read only
                 02h    hidden
                 04h    system
                 0FFh   archive
```

note: This call will not change the volume label or directory bits.

```
Function 44h   I/O Control for Devices (IOCTL)
               Get or Set Device Information
entry    AH    44h
         AL    00h    Get Device Information
                      BX       file or device handle
                      return DX       device info
                                      bit 7 set = character device
                                          bit 0      console input device
                                              1      console output device
                                              2      NUL device
                                              3      CLOCK$ device
                                              4      device is special
                                              5      binary (raw) mode
                                              6      not EOF
                                              12     network device (DOS 3.x)
                                              14     can process IOCTL control
                                                     strings (subfns 2-5)
                                      bit 7 clear = file
                                          bit 0-5    block device number
                                              6      file has not been written
                                              12     Network device (DOS 3.x)
                                              14     unknown       (DOS 3.x)
                                              15     file is remote (DOS 3.x)
               01h    Set Device Information
                      BX       device handle
                      DH       0   (DH must be zero for this call)
                      DL       device info to set (bits 0-7 from
                               function 0)
               note   DX bits:
                      0    1    console input device
                      1    1    console output device
                      2    1    null device
                      3    1    clock device
                      4    1    reserved
                      5    0    binary mode - don't check for control chars
                           1    cooked mode - check for control chars
                      6    0    EOF - End Of File on input
                      7         device is character device if set, if not, EOF is
                                0 if channel has been  written, bits 0-5 are
                                block device number
                      12        network device
                      14   1    can process control strings (AL 2-5, can only be
                                read, cannot be set)
                      15   n    reserved
               02h    Read Character Device Control String
                      BX       device handle
                      CX       number of bytes to read
                      DS:DX    pointer to control string buffer
                      return AX       number of bytes read
               03h    Write Device Control String
                      BX       device handle
                      CX       number of bytes to write
                      DS:DX    pointer to buffer
                      return AX       number of bytes written
               04h    Read From Block Device (drive number in BL)
                      BL       drive number (0=default)
                      CX       number of bytes to read
                      DS:DX    pointer to buffer
                      return AX       number of bytes read
               05h    Write Block Device Control String
                      BL       drive number (0=default)
                      CX       number of bytes to write
                      DS:DX    pointer to buffer
                      return AX       number of bytes transferred
               06h    Get Input Handle Status
                      BX       file or device handle
                      return AL       0FFh    device ready
                                      00h     device not ready
               07h    Get Output Handle Status
```

DOS Interrupts and Function Calls

```
              return  AL       00h       not ready
                               0FFh      ready
              note    For DOS 2.x, files are always ready for output.
     08h      Removable Media Bit                           (DOS 3.x+)
              BL       drive number (0=default)
              return  AX       00h       device is removable
                               01h       device is nonremovable
                               0Fh       invalid drive specification
     09h      Test whether Local or Network Device          (DOS 3.x+)
              BL       drive number (0=default)
              return  DX       attribute word, bit 12 set if
                               device is remote
     0Ah      Is Handle in BX Local or Remote?              (DOS 3.x+)
              BX       file handle
              return  DX (attribute word) bit 15 set if file is remote
              note    If file is remote, Novell Advanced NetWare
                      2.0 returns the number of the file server
                      on which the handle is located in CX.
     0Bh      Change Sharing Retry Count to DX              (DOS 3.x+)
              CX       delay (default=1)
              DX       retry count (default=3)
     0Ch      General IOCTL (DOS 3.3 [3.2?]) allows a device
              driver to prepare, select, refresh, and query Code Pages
              BX       device handle
              CH       category code
                       00h       unknown (DOS 3.3)
                       01h       COMn:   (DOS 3.3)
                       03h       CON     (DOS 3.3)
                       05h       LPTn:
              CL       function
                       45h       set iteration count
                       4Ah       select code page
                       4Ch       start code-page preparation
                       4Dh       end code-page preparation
                       65h       get iteration count
                       6Ah       query selected code page
                       6Bh       query prepare list
              DS:DX    pointer to parameter block. Format:
         (for CL=45h)  word     number of times output is
                                attempted driver assumes device is busy
 (for CL=4Ah,4Dh,6Ah)  word     length of data
                       word     code page ID
         (for CL=4Ch)  word     flags
                       word     length of remainder of parameter block
                       word     number of code pages following
                     n words    code page 1,...,N
         (for CL=6Bh)  word     length of following data
                       word     number of hardware code pages
                     n words    hardware code pages 1,...,N
                       word     number of prepared code pages
                     n words    prepared code pages 1,...,N
     0Dh      Block Device Request                          (DOS 3.3+)
              BL       drive number (0=default)
              CH       category code
                       08h       disk drive
              CL       subfunction
                       40h       set device parameters
                       41h       write logical device track
                       42h       format and verify logical device
                       60h       get device parameters
                       61h       read logical device track
                       62h       verify logical device track
              DS:DX    pointer to parameter block
   (for fns 40h, 60h)  byte     special functions
                                bit 0 set if fn to use current BPB, clear if
                                      Device BIOS Parameter Block field
                                      contains new default BPB
                                    1 set if function to use track fields
                                      only. Must be clear if CL=60h
                                    2 set if all sectors in track same size
                                      (should be set)
```

```
                              3-7 reserved
                      byte    device type
                              00h     320K/360K disk
                              01h     1.2M disk
                              02h     720K disk
                              03h     single-density 8-inch disk
                              04h     double-density 8-inch disk
                              05h     fixed disk
                              06h     tape drive
                              07h     other type of block device
                      word    device attributes
                         bit 0 set if nonremovable medium
                              1 set if door lock supported
                              2-15 reserved
                      word    number of cylinders
                      byte    media type
                              00h 1.2M disk (default)
                              01h 320K/360K disk
                   31 bytes   device BPB (see function 53h)
                      word    # of sectors per track (start of track
                              layout field)
                 N word pairs: number,size of each sector in track
(for functions 41h, 61h) byte  reserved, must be zero
                      word    number of disk head
                      word    number of disk cylinder
                      word    number of first sector to
                              read/write
                      word    number of sectors
                      dword   transfer address
(for functions 42h, 62h) byte  reserved, must be zero
                      word    number of disk head
                      word    number of disk cylinder
                      note    DOS 4.01 seems to ignore the high byte of the
                              number of directory entries in the BPB for
                              diskettes.
              0Eh     Get Logical Device Map (DOS 3.2+)
                      BL      drive number (0=default)
                      return  AL=0 block device has only one logical drive
                              assigned 1..n the last letter used to
                              reference the device (1=A:,etc) (1..26 DOS 3.0+)
              0Fh     Set Logical Device Map (DOS 3.2+)
                      BL      physical drive number (0=default)
                      note    Maps logical drives to physical drives, similar
                              to DOS's treatment of a single physical
                              floppy drive as both A: and B:
        BL      drive number:  0=default, 1=A:, 2=B:, etc.
        BX      file handle
        CX      number of bytes to read or write
        DS:DX   data or buffer
        DX      data
return  AX      number of bytes transferred
                or error code (call function 59h for extended error codes)
                or status 00h     not ready
                          0FFh    ready
        CF      set if error

Function  45h   Duplicate a File Handle (DUP)
entry   AH      45h
        BX      file handle to duplicate
return  CF      clear   AX      duplicate handle
                set     AX      error code  (04h, 06h)
note 1. If you move the pointed of one handle, the pointer of the other will also
        be moved.
     2. The handle in BX must be open.

Function  46h   Force Duplicate of a Handle (FORCEDUP or CDUP)
                Forces handle in CX to refer to the same file at the same
                position as BX
entry   AH      46h
        BX      existing file handle
        CX      new file handle
```

```
return   CF        clear     both handles now refer to existing file
                   set       error
                   AX        error code (04h, 06h)
note 1. If CX was an open file, it is closed first.
     2. If you move the read/write pointer of either file, both will move.
     3. The handle in BX must be open.

Function 47h       Get Current Directory
                   Places full pathname of current directory/drive into a buffer
entry    AH        47h
         DL        drive (0=default, 1=A:, etc.)
         DS:SI     pointer to 64-byte buffer area
return   CF        clear     DS:DI     pointer to ASCIIZ pathname of current directory
                   set       AX        error code (0Fh)
note:    String does not begin with a drive identifier or a backslash.

Function 48h       Allocate Memory
                   Allocates requested number of 16-byte paragraphs of memory
entry    AH        48h
         BX        number of 16-byte paragraphs desired
return   CF        clear     AX        segment address of allocated space
                             BX        maximum number paragraphs available
                   set       AX        error code (07h, 08h)
note:    BX indicates maximum memory availible only if allocation fails.

Function 49h       Free Allocated Memory
                   Frees specified memory blocks
entry    AH        49h
         ES        segment address of area to be freed
return   CF        clear     successful
                   set       AX        error code (07h, 09h)
note 1. This call is only valid when freeing memory obtained by function 48h.
     2. A program should not try to release memory not belonging to it.

Function 4Ah       Modify Allocated Memory Blocks (SETBLOCK)
                   Expand or shrink memory for a program
entry    AH        4AH
         BX        new size in 16 byte paragraphs
         ES        segment address of block to change
return   CF        clear     nothing
                   set       AX        error code (07h, 08h, 09h)
                   or        BX        max number paragraphs available
note 1. Max number paragraphs availible is returned only if the call fails.
     2. Memory can be expanded only if there is memory available.

Function 4Bh       Load or Execute a Program   (EXEC)
entry    AH        4Bh
         AL        00h       load and execute program. A PSP is built for the
                             program the ctrl-break and terminate addresses are set to
                             the new PSP.
                  *01h       load but don't execute (internal, DOS 3.x & DESQview)
                             (see note 1)
                  *02h       load but do not execute (internal, DOS 2.x only)
                   03h       load overlay (do not create PSP, do not begin execution)
         DS:DX     points to the ASCIIZ string with the drive, path, and filename to
                   be loaded
         ES:BX     points to a parameter block for the load
                   (AL=00h) word     segment address of environment string to passed
                                     (0=use current)
                            dword    pointer to the command line to be placed at
                                     PSP+80h
                            dword    pointer to default FCB to be passed at PSP+5Ch
                            dword    pointer to default FCB to be passed at PSP+6Ch
                   (*AL=01h) word    segment of environment (0 = use current)
                            dword    pointer to command line
                            dword    pointer to FCB 1
                            dword    pointer to FCB 2
                   (DOS 3.x+) dword  will hold SS:SP on return
                   (DOS 3.x+) dword  will hold program entry point (CS:IP) on return
                   (*AL=02h) word    segment of environment (0 = use current)
                            dword    pointer to command line
```

```
                        dword      pointer to FCB 1
                        dword      pointer to FCB 2
            (AL=03h)    word       segment address where file will be loaded
                        word       relocation factor to be applied to the image
return  CF    set       error
                        AX         error code (01h, 02h, 05h, 08h, 0Ah, 0Bh)
        CF    clear     if successful
              for fn 00h, process ID set to new program's PSP; get with function
                    62h
              for fn 01h and DOS 3.x+ or DESQview, process ID set to program's
                    PSP; get with function 62h
              for fn 01h and DOS 2.x, new program's initial stack and entry
                    point returned in registers
              for fn 02h, new program's initial stack and entry point are
                    returned in the registers
```
note 1. If you make this call with AL=1 the program will be loaded as if you made
        the call with AL=0 except that the program will not be executed.
        Additionally, with AL=1 the stack segment and pointer along with the
        program's CS:IP entry point are returned to the program which made the
        4B01h call. These values are put in the four words at ES:BX+0Eh. On
        entry to the call ES:BX points to the environment address, the command
        line and the two default FCBs. This form of EXEC is used by DEBUG.COM.
     2. Application programs may invoke a secondary copy of the command processor
        (normally COMMAND.COM) by using the EXEC function. Your program may pass
        a DOS command as a parameter that the secondary command processor will
        execute as though it had been entered from the standard input device. The
        procedure is:
        A. Assure that adequate free memory (17k for 2.x and 3.0, 23k for 3.1 up)
           exists to contain the second copy of the command processor and the
           command it is to execute. This is accomplished by executing function
           call 4Ah to shrink memory allocated to that of your current
           requirements. Next, execute function call 48h with BX=0FFFFh. This
           returns the amount of memory available.
        B. Build a parameter string for the secondary command processor in the
           form:
```
                        1 byte     length of parameter string
                        xx bytes   parameter string
                        1 byte     0Dh (carriage return)
```
           For example, the assembly language statement below would build the
           string to cause execution of the command FOO.EXE:
                        DB 19,"/C C:FOO",13
        C. Use the EXEC function call (4Bh), function value 0 to cause execution
           of the secondary copy of the command processor. (The drive,
           directory, and name of the command processor can be gotten from the
           COMSPEC variable in the DOS environment passed to you at PSP+2Ch.)
        D. Remember to set offset 2 of the EXEC control block to point to the
           string built above.
     3. All open files of a process are duplicated in the newly created process
        after an EXEC, except for files originally opened with the inheritance
        bit set to 1.
     4. The environment is a copy of the original command processor's
        environment. Changes to the EXECed environment are not passed back to the
        original. The environment is followed by a copy of the DS:DX filename
        passed to the child process. A zero value will cause the child process
        to inherit the environment of the calling process. The segment address
        of the environment is placed at offset 2Ch of the PSP of the program
        being invoked.
     5. This function uses the same resident part of COMMAND.COM, but makes a
        duplicate of the transient part.
     6. How EXEC knows where to return to: Basically the vector for int 22h
        holds the terminate address for the current process. When a process
        gets started, the previous contents of int 22h get tucked away in the
        PSP for that process, then int 22h gets modified. So if Process A EXECs
        process B, while Process B is running, the vector for int 22h holds the
        address to return to in Process A, while the save location in Process
        B's PSP holds the address that process A will return to when *it*
        terminates. When Process B terminates by one of the usual legal means,
        the contents of int 22h are (surmising) shoved onto the stack, the old
        terminate vector contents are copied back to int 22h vector from
        Process B's PSP, then a RETF or equivalent is executed to return
        control to process A.

DOS Interrupts and Functions Calls

7. To load an overlay file with 4B: first, don't de-allocate the memory that the overlay will load into. With the other 4Bh functions, the opposite is true--you have to free the memory first, with function 4Ah. Second, the 'segment address where the file will be loaded' (first item in the parameter block for sub-function 03) should be a paragraph boundary within your currently-allocated memory. Third, if the procedures within the overlay are FAR procs (while they execute, CS will be equal to the segment address of the overlay area), the relocation factor should be set to zero. On the other hand, if the CS register will be different from the overlay area's segment address, the relocation factor should be set to represent the difference. You determine where in memory the overlay file will load by using the segment address mentioned above. Overlay files are .EXEs (containing header, relocation table, and memory image).
8. When function 00h returns, all registers are changed, including the stack. You must resore SS, SP, and any other required registers.
9. PCDOS EXEC function 3 (overlay) lives in the transient piece of COMMAND.COM and gets loaded when needed, thus the requirement for enough free space to load the EXEC loader (about 1.5k). Under MSDOS the EXEC system call lives in system space.
10. If you try to overlay an .EXE file with the high/low switch set to load the in high memory nothing will happen. The high/Low switch is only for process creation, not for overlays.
11. DOS 2.x destroys all registers, including SS:SP.

```
Function    4Ch     Terminate a Process (EXIT)
                    Quit with ERRORLEVEL exit code
entry       AH      4Ch
            AL      exit code in AL when called, if any, is passed to next process
return      none
note  1. Control passes to DOS or calling program.
      2. Return code from AL can be retrieved by ERRORLEVEL or function 4Dh.
      3. All files opened by this process are closed, buffers are flushed, and the
         disk directory is updated.
      4. Restores: Terminate vector from PSP:000Ah
                   Ctrl-C vector from PSP:000Eh
                   Critical Error vector from PSP:0012h

Function    4Dh     Get Return Code of a Subprocess (WAIT)
                    Gets return code from functions 31h and 4Dh   (ERRORLEVEL)
entry       AH      4Dh
return      AL      exit code of subprogram (functions 31h or 4Ch)
            AH      circumstance which caused termination
                    00h       normal termination
                    01h       control-break or control-C
                    02h       critical device error
                    03h       terminate and stay resident (function 31h)
note    The exit code is only returned once (the first time).

Function    4Eh     Find First Matching File (FIND FIRST)
entry       AH      4Eh
            CX      search attributes
            DS:DX   pointer to ASCIIZ filename (with attributes)
return      CF      set     AX       error code (02h, 12h)
                    clear   data block written at current DTA
                            format of block is:   (info from BIX)
documented by Micro- |00h      1 byte     attribute byte of search
soft as 'reserved for|01h      1 byte     drive letter for search
DOS' use on subsqent |02h     11 bytes    the search name used
Find Next calls'     |0Ch      2 bytes    word value of last entry
function 4Fh         |0Fh      4 bytes    dword pointer to this DTA
                     |13h      2 bytes    word directory start
                       PC-DOS 3.10 (from INTERRUP.ARC)
                     |00h      1 byte     drive letter
                     |01h-0Bh  bytes      search template
                     |0Ch      1 byte     search attributes
                       DOS 2.x (and DOS 3.x except 3.1?)
                     |00h      1 byte     search attributes
                     |01h      1 byte     drive letter
                     |02h-0Ch  bytes      search template
                     |0Dh-0Eh  2 bytes    entry count within directory
```

```
                    |0Fh-12h  4 bytes    reserved
                    |13h-14h  2 bytes    cluster number of parent directory

                     15h      1 byte     file attribute
                     16h      2 bytes    file time
                     18h      2 bytes    file date
                     1Ah      2 bytes    low word of file size
                     1Ch      2 bytes    high word of file size
                     1Eh     13 bytes    name and extension of file found, plus
                                         1 byte of 0s. All blanks are moved from
                                         the name and extension, and if an
                                         extension is present it is preceded by a
                                         period.
note 1. This function does not support network operations.
     2. Wildcards are allowed in the filespec.
     3. If the attribute is zero, only ordinary files are found. If the volume
        label bit is set, only volume labels will be found. Any other attribute
        will return that attribute and all normal files together.
     4. To look for everything except the volume label, set the hidden, system,
        and subdirectory bits all to 1.

Function   4Fh      Find Next Matching File (FIND NEXT)
                    Find next ASCIIZ file
entry      AH       4Fh
return     CF       clear   data block written at current DTA
                    set     AX       error code (02h, 12h)
note 1. If file found, DTA is formatted as in call 4Eh
     2. Volume label searches using 4Eh/4Fh reportedly aren't 100% reliable under
        DOS 2.x. The calls sometimes report there's a volume label and point to a
        garbage DTA, and if the volume label is the only item they often won't
        find it. Most references recommend the use of the older FCB calls for
        dealing with the volume labels.
     3. This function does not support network operations.
     4. Use of this call assumes that the original filespec contained wildcards

Function   50h      'Used Internally by DOS' - Set PSP
   *                Set new Program Segment Prefix (current Process ID)
entry      AH       50h
           BX       segment address of new PSP
return     none - swaps PSPs regarded as current by DOS
note 1. By putting the PSP segment value into BX and issuing call 50h DOS stores
        that value into a variable and uses that value whenever a file call is
        made.
     2. Note that in the PSP (or PDB) is a table of 20 (decimal) open file
        handles. The table starts at offset 18h into the PSP. If there is an
        0FFh in a byte then that handle is not in use. A number in one of the
        bytes is an index into an internal FB table for that handle. For
        instance the byte at offset 18h is for handle 0, at offset 19h handle 1,
        etc. up to 13h. If the high bit is set then the file associated by the
        handle is not shared by child processes EXEC'd with call 4Bh.
     3. Function 50h is dangerous in background operations prior to DOS 3.x as it
        uses the wrong stack for saving registers (same as functions 0..0Ch in
        DOS 2.x)
     4. Under DOS 2.x, this function cannot be invoked inside an int 28h handler
        without setting the Critical Error flag.
     5. Open File information, etc. is stored in the PSP DOS views as current. If
        a program (eg. a resident program) creates a need for a second PSP, then
        the second PSP should be set as current to make sure DOS closes that as
        opposed to the first when the second application finishes.
     6. See PC Mag Vol.5, No 9, p.314 for discussion, also used in BCOPY.ASM
     7. Used by DOS 3.3 PRINT & DEBUG, DesQview 2.01, Windows 1.03, SYMDEB from
        MASM 4.0.

Function   51h      "Used Internally by DOS" - Get Program Segment Prefix
   *                Returns the PSP address of currently executing program
entry      AH       51h
return     BX       address of currently executing program
                    offset
                    00h     2 bytes    program exit point
                    02h     word       memory size in paragraphs
                    04h     byte       unused (0)
```

```
         05h   5 bytes    CP/M style entry point (far call to DOS)
         0Ah   word       terminate address (old int 22h)
         0Ch   word       terminate segment
         0Eh   word       break address (old int 23h)
         10h   word       break segment
         12h              error address (old int 24h)
         14h              error segment
         16h   word       parent PSP segment
         18h   20 bytes   DOS 2.0+ open files, 0FFh = unused
         2Ch   word       DOS 2.0+ environment segment
         2Eh   dword      far pointer to process's SS:SP
         32h   word       DOS 3.x+ max open files
         34h              DOS 3.x+ open file table address
         36h   dword      DOS 3.x+ open file table segment
         38h   24 bytes   unused by DOS versions before 3.3
         50h   3 bytes    DOS function dispatcher (FAR routine)
         53h   9 bytes    unused
         55h              FCB #1 extension
         5Ch   16 bytes   FCB #1, filled in from first cmdline argument
         6Ch   20 bytes   FCB #2, filled in from second cmdline argument
         80h   128 bytes  command tail / default DTA buffer
```
note 1. Used in DOS 2.x, 3.x uses 62h.
   2. Function 51h is dangerous in background operations prior to DOS 3.x as it uses the wrong stack for saving registers (same as functions 0..0Ch in DOS 2.x).
   3. 50h and 51h might be used if you have more than one process in a PC. For instance if you have a resident program that needs to open a file you could first call 51h to save the current ID and then call 50h to set the ID to your PSP.
   4. Under DOS 2.x, this function cannot be invoked inside an int 28h handler without setting the Critical Error flag.
   5. Used by DOS 3.3 PRINT, DEBUG.

```
Function  52h     'Used Internally by DOS' - IN-VARS
   *              Returns a FAR pointer to a linked list of DOS data variables
entry     AH      52h
return    ES:BX   pointer to the DOS list of lists, for disk information. Does not
                  access the disk, so information in tables might be incorrect if
                  disk has been changed. Returns a pointer to the following array
                  of longword pointers:
               Bytes   Value      Description
   (common)   -02h    word       segment of first memory control block available
                                    through MALLOC
               00h    dword      far pointer to first DOS Disk Parameter Block
               04h    dword      far pointer to linked list of DOS open file
                                    tables. (Open File Table List)
               08h    dword      far pointer to CLOCK$: device driver, whether
                                    installable or resident
               0Ch    dword      far pointer to actual CON: device driver, whether
                                    installable or resident
   (DOS 2.x only)
               10h    word       number of logical drives in system
               11h    word       largest logical sector size supported
               13h    dword      far pointer to first disk buffer used by
                                    the logical drives. The size of each
                                    sector buffer is equal to the logical
                                    sector size plus a 16 byte header.
                                    (Sector Buffer Header) The number of
                                    these buffers is set by CONFIG.SYS.
                                    (Sector Buffer Structure)
               17h    ----       beginning (not a pointer. The real
                                    beginning!) of NUL device driver. This
                                    is the first device on DOS's linked list
                                    of device drivers.
   (DOS 3.x+)
               10h    word       largest logical sector sector size
                                    supported (most versions of DOS are
                                    hardcoded to 200h)
               12h    dword      far pointer to sector buffer structure
                                    used by the logical drives. (Sector
                                    Buffer Structure)
```

```
           16h       dword     far pointer to drive path and seek
                               information table. (Drive Path Table)
           1Ah       dword     far pointer to a table of FCBs. This
                               table is only valid if FCBS=xx was used
                               in CONFIG.SYS
           1Eh       word      size of FCB table
           20h       byte      number of logical drives presently
                               supported
           21h       byte      value of LASTDRIVE= in CONFIG.SYS
                               (default 5)
           22h       ----      beginning (not a pointer-the real
                               beginning!) of the NUL device driver.
                               This is the first device on DOS's linked
                               list of device drivers.

note 1. This call is not supported in OS/2 1.0's DOS Compatibility Box.
     2. Used by DOS 4.0 MEM.EXE, DOS 3.3 ASSIGN.COM, PRINT.COM, SUBST.EXE.
     3. Disk Parameter Block
           offset    size      description
           00h       byte      disk unit number, 0=A, 1=B, etc. If this and the
                               next byte are 0FFh this entry is the end of the
                               list and is not valid
           01h       byte      disk unit number passed to the block device
                               driver responsible for this logical drive
           02h       word      the drive's logical sector size in bytes
           04h       byte      number of sectors per cluster -1. The number of
                               sectors per cluster must be a power of 2
           05h       byte      allocation shift. The shift value used to calcu
                               late the number of sectors from the number of
                               clusters without having to use division. Number
                               of sectors = number of clusters < allocation
                               shift.
           06h       word      number of reserved sectors at the beginning of
                               the logical drive. May contain partition information.
           08h       byte      number of FATs. Default 2
           09h       word      number of root directory entries
           0Bh       word      first sector containing data (disk files)
           0Dh       word      last cluster number. Number of clusters in data
                               area +1. If less than 0FF6h the FAT uses 12-bit
                               directory entries, otherwise 16 bit entries
           0Fh       byte      FAT size. Size of one FAT in logical sectors
           10h       word      sector number of first root directory entry
           12h       dword     far pointer to the block device driver
           16h       byte      media descriptor byte (see Chapter 8)
           17h       byte      media flag. If this is 0, the drive has been
                               accessed. If it is -1 or set to -1 DOS will
                               rebuild all data structures associated with this
                               drive on the next access
           18h       dword     far pointer to the next Disk Parameter Block

     4. Open File Table List
           offset    size      description
           00h       dword     far pointer to the next table in the list. If the
                               offset of this pointer is 0FFFFh, then the next
                               table is the final entry and invalid
           04h       word      number of table entries. Each table entry is 53
                               bytes long. There will be at least one entry in
                               each table except the terminal entry
           06h       ---       beginning of the Open File Table entries (note 5)

     5. Open File Table Entry (35h bytes long)
           offset    size      description
           00h       word      number of file handles referring to this file
           02h       byte      access mode (see function 3Dh)
           03h       word      unknown
           05h       word      Device Information Word (see function 44h/00h)
           06h       dword     far pointer to device info header if this is a
                               character device. If block device, this will be
                               a far pointer to the Disk Parameter Block
           07h       dword     pointer to device driver header if character device;
                               pointer to DOS Device Control Block if block device
```

DOS Interrupts and Functions Calls

```
        0Bh       word        starting cluster of file
        0Dh       word        file time in packed format
        0Fh       word        file date in packed format
        11h       dword       file size
        15h       dword       current offset in file
        19h       word        unknown
        1Bh       word        last cluster read
        1Dh       word        number of sector containing directory entry
        1Fh       byte        offset of directory entry within sector (byte offset/32)
        20h    11 bytes       filename in FCB format (no path, no period, blank padded)
        2Bh     6 bytes       PSP segment of file's owner
        2Dh     3 bytes       unknown - normally 0
        31h       word        PSP segment of file's owner
        33h-34h word          unknown - normally 0

  6. Sector Buffer Header:     (DOS 2.x+)
     offset    size        description
        00h       dword       pointer to next disk buffer, 0FFFFh if last
        04h     4 bytes       unknown
        08h       word        logical sector number
        10h     2 bytes       unknown
        12h       dword       pointer to DOS Device Control Block
  7. Sector Buffer Structure, followed by 512 byte buffer
     offset    size        description
        00h       dword       far pointer to the next sector buffer. Buffers are filled
                                in the order of their appearance on this linked list.
                                The last buffer is valid and has the value 0FFFFFFFFh
        04h       byte        drive number. This is the drive that the data currently
                                in the buffer refers to. 0FFh if never used.
        05h       byte        data type flags. Bit fields which show the area of the
                                drive the buffer refers to
                          bits 1      FAT data
                               2      subdirectory data
                               3      file data
                               5      contents of buffer may be overwritten if set
        06h       word        logical sector number of buffered data
        08h       word        access number
        0Ah       dword       far pointer to Disk Parameter Block
        0Eh       word        not used, normally 0

  8. Drive Path Table Entry    (array, one 51h-byte entry per drive):
     offset    size        description
        00h    64 bytes       current default ASCIIZ pathname with drive letter, colon,
                                and leading backslash
        44h       byte        flags byte. All valid entries contain a 40h, last entry
                                contains 00h
        45h       dword       far pointer to current Disk Parameter Block
        49h       word        current block or track/sector number for this directory.
                                0 if root dir, -1 if never accessed
        4Bh       dword       unknown. Usually -1
        4Fh       word        offset of '\' in current path field representing root of
                                directory of logical drive (2 if not SUBSTed or JOINed,
                                otherwise number of bytes in SUBST/JOIN path)

Function  53h       "Used Internally by DOS" - Translate BPB
    *               Translates BPB (BIOS Parameter Block, see below) into a DOS Disk
                    Block (see function call 32h).
entry     AH        53h
          DS:SI     pointer to BPB (BIOS Parameter Block)
          ES:BP     pointer to area for DOS Disk Block
                    Layout of Disk Block:
                    bytes           value
                    00h-01h bytes per sector, get from DDB bytes 02h-03h.
                    02h     sectors per cluster, get from (DDB byte 4) + 1
                    03h-04h reserved sectors, get from DDB bytes 06h-07h
                    05h     number of FATs, get from DDB byte 08h
                    06h-07h number of root dir entries, get from DDB bytes 09h-0Ah
                    08h-09h total number of sectors, get from:
                            ((DDB bytes 0Dh-0Eh) - 1) * (sectors per cluster (BPB
                            byte 2)) + (DDB bytes 0Bh-0Ch)
                    0Ah     media descriptor byte, get from DDB byte 16h
```

```
                      0Bh-0Ch number of sectors per FAT, get from DDB byte 0Fh
       return  unknown

       Function  54h    Get Verify Setting
                        Get verify flag status
       entry    AH      54h
       return   AL      00h if flag off
                        01h if flag on
       note     Flag can be set with function 2Eh.

       Function  55h    'Used Internally by DOS' - Create 'Child' PSP
          *               Create PSP: similar to function 26h (which creates a new
                        Program Segment Prefix at segment in DX) except creates a 'child'
                        PSP rather than copying the existing one.
       entry    AH      55h
                DX      segment number at which to create new PSP.
       return   unknown
       note  1. This call is similar to call 26h which creates a PSP except that unlike
                call 26h the segment address of the parent process is obtained from the
                current process ID rather than from the CS value on the stack (from the
                INT 21h call). DX has the new PSP value and SI contains the value to be
                placed into PSP:2 (top of memory).
             2. Function 55 is merely a substitute for function 26h. It will copy the
                current PSP to the segment address DX with the addition that SI is
                assumed to hold the new memory top segment. This means that function
                26h sets SI to the segment found in the current PSP and then calls
                function 55h.

       Function  56h    Rename a File
       entry    AH      56h
                DS:DX   pointer to ASCIIZ old pathname
                ES:DI   pointer to ASCIIZ new pathname
       return   CF      clear     successful rename
                        set   AX      error code (02h, 03h, 05h, 11h)
       note  1. Works with files in same logical drive only.
             2. Global characters not allowed in filename.
             3. The name of a file is its full pathname. The file's full pathname can be
                changed, while leaving the actual FILENAME.EXT unchanged. Changing the
                pathname allows the file to be 'moved' from subdirectory to subdirectory
                on a logical drive without actually copying the file.
             4. DOS 3.x allows renaming of directories.

       Function  57h    Get/Set a File's Date and Time
                        Read or modify time and date stamp on a file's directory entry
       entry    AH      57h
                AL      function code
                        00h       Get Date and Time
                        01h       Set Date and Time
                                  CX       time to be set
                                  DX       date to be set
                        02h       unknown (DOS 4.0+)
                        03h       unknown
                        04h       unknown (DOS 4.0+)
                BX      file handle
       return   CF      clear     CX       time of last write (if AL = 0)
                                  DX       date of last write (if AL = 0)
                        set   AX      error code (01h, 06h)
       note     Date/time formats are:
                CX bits 0Bh-0Fh hours (0-23)      DX bits 09h-0Fh year (relative to
                                                                     1980)
                        05h-0Ah minutes (0-59)            05h-08h month (0-12)
                        00h-04h #2 sec. incr. (0-29)      00h-04h day of the month
                                                                     (0-31)

       Function  58h    Get/Set Allocation Strategy    (DOS 3.x+)
       entry    AH      58h
                AL      00h       Get Current Strategy
                        01h       Set New Current Strategy
                BL      new strategy if AH=1
                        00h       First Fit - chooses the lowest block in memory which will
                                  fit (this is the default) (use first memory block large
```

```
                         enough)
               01h       Best Fit - chooses the smallest block which will fill the
                         request.
               02h       Last Fit - chooses the highest block which will fit.
return  CF     clear     (0)       successful
               set       (1)       error
                                   AX        error code (01h)
        AX     strategy code (CF=0)
note 1. Documented in Zenith DOS version 3.1, some in Advanced MSDOS.
     2. The set subfunction accepts any value in BL; 2 or greater means last fit.
        The get subfunction returns the last value set, so programs should check
        whether the value is greater than or equal to 2.
```

Function 59h   Get Extended Error Code (DOS 3.x+)

The Get Extended Error function call (59h) is intended to provide a commonset of error codes and to supply more extensive information about the error to the application. The information returned from function call 59h, in addition to the error code, is the error class, the locus, and the recommended action. The error class provides information about the error type (hardware, internal, system, etc.). The locus provides information about the area involved in the failure (serial device, block device, network, or memory). The recommended action provides a default action for programs that do not understand the specific error code.

Newly written programs should use the extended error support both from interrupt 24h hard error handlers and after any int 21h function calls. FCB function calls report an error by returning 0FFh in AL. Handle function calls report an error by setting the carry flag and returning the error code in AX. Int 21h handle function calls for DOS 2.x continue to return error codes 0-18. Int 24h handle function calls continue to return error codes 0-12. But the application can obtain any of the error codes used in the extended error codes table by issuing function call 59h. Handle function calls for DOS 3.x can return any of the error codes. However, it is recommended that the function call be followed by function call 59h to obtain the error class, the locus, and the recommended action.

The Get Extended Error function (59h) can always be called, regardless of whether the previous DOS call was old style (error code in AL) or new style (carry bit). It can also be used inside an int 24h handler. You can either check AL or the carry bit to see if there was no error, and call function 59h only if there was an error, or take the simple approach of always calling 59h and letting it tell you if there was an error or not. When you call function 59h it will return with AX=0 if the previous DOS call was successful.

```
entry   AH     59h
        BX     version code (0000 for DOS 3.0 and 3.1)
return  AX     extended error code:
               01h       Invalid function number
               02h       File not found
               03h       Path not found
               04h       Too many open files, no file handles left
               05h       Access denied
               06h       Invalid handle
               07h       Memory control blocks destroyed
               08h       Insufficient memory
               09h       Invalid memory block address
               0Ah       Invalid environment
               0Bh       Invalid format
               0Ch       Invalid access code
               0Dh       Invalid data
               0Eh       Reserved
               0Fh       Invalid drive was specified
               10h       Attempt to remove the current directory
               11h       Not same device
               12h       No more files
               13h       Attempt to write on write-protected diskette
               14h       Unknown unit
               15h       Drive not ready
               16h       Unknown command
               17h       Bad CRC check
               18h       Bad request structure length
               19h       Seek error
               1Ah       Unknown media type
```

	1Bh	Sector not found
	1Ch	Printer out of paper
	1Dh	Write fault
	1Eh	Read fault
	1Fh	General Failure
	20h	Sharing violation
	21h	Lock violation
	22h	Invalid disk change
	23h	FCB unavailable
	24h	Sharing buffer overflow
	25h	Reserved
	26h	"
	27h	"
	28h	"
	29h	"
	2Ah	"
	2Bh	"
	2Ch	"
	2Dh	"
	2Eh	"
	2Fh	"
	30h	"
	31h	Reserved
	32h	Network: request not supported (DOS 3.1 + MS Networks)
	33h	Remote computer not listening
	34h	Duplicate name on network
	35h	Network: name not found
	36h	Network: busy
	37h	Network: device no longer exists
	38h	NETBIOS command limit exceeded
	39h	Network: adapter hardware error
	3Ah	Incorrect response from network
	3Bh	Unexpected network error
	3Ch	Incompatible remote adapter
	3Dh	Print queue full
	3Eh	Not enough space for print file
	3Fh	Print file was deleted
	40h	Network: name was deleted
	41h	Network: Access denied
	42h	Network: device type incorrect
	43h	Network: name not found
	44h	Network: name limit exceeded
	45h	NETBIOS session limit exceeded
	46h	Temporarily paused
	47h	Network: request not accepted
	48h	Print or disk redirection paused (DOS 3.1 + MS Networks)
	49h	Reserved
	4Ah	"
	4Bh	"
	4Ch	"
	4Dh	"
	4Eh	"
	4Fh	Reserved
	50h	File exists
	51h	Reserved
	52h	Cannot make directory entry
	53h	Fail on interrupt 24h
	54h	Too many redirections
	55h	Duplicate redirection
	56h	Invalid password
	57h	Invalid parameter
	58h	Network: device fault
BH	class of error:	
	01h	Out of resource
	02h	Temporary situation
	03h	Authorization (denied access)
	04h	Internal
	05h	Hardware failure
	06h	System failure

```
                    07h     Application program error
                    08h     Not found
                    09h     Bad format
                    0Ah     Locked
                    0Bh     Media error (wrong volume ID, disk failure)
                    0Ch     Already exists
                    0Dh     Unknown
            BL      suggested action code:
                    01h     Retry
                    02h     Delayed retry
                    03h     Prompt user
                    04h     Abort after cleanup
                    05h     Immediate abort
                    06h     Ignore
                    07h     Retry after user intervention
            CH      locus (where error occurred):
                    01h     Unknown or not appropriate
                    02h     Block device
                    03h     Network related
                    04h     Serial device
                    05h     Memory related
note 1. Not all DOS functions use the carry flag to indicate an error. Carry
        should be tested only on those functions which are documented to use it.
     2. None of the DOS functions which existed before 2.0 use the carry
        indicator. Many of them use register AL as an error indication instead,
        usually by putting 0FFh in AL on an error. Most, but not all, the 'new'
        (2.x, 3.x) functions do use carry, and most, but not all, of the 'old'
        (1.x) functions use AL.
     3. On return, CL, DI, DS, DX, ES, BP, and SI are destroyed - save before
        calling this function if required.
     4. DOS 2.x Error Codes:  If you are using function calls 38h-57h with DOS
        2.x, to check if an error has occurred, check for the following error
        codes in the AX register:
call   error code        call    error code      call    error code
38h    2                 41h     2,3,5           4Ah     7,8,9
39h    3,5               42h     1,6             4Bh     1,2,3,5,8,10,11
3Ah    3,5,15            43h     1,2,3,5         4Eh     2,3,18
3Bh    3                 44h     1,3,5,6         4Fh     18
3Ch    3,4,5             45h     4,6             56h     2,3,5,17
3Dh    2,3,4,5,12        46h     4,6             57h     1,6
3Eh    6                 47h     15
3Fh    5,6               48h     7,8
40h    5,6               49h     7,9
     5. Note that extended error codes 13h through 1Fh correspond to error codes
        00h through 0Ch returned by int 24h.

Function   5Ah      Create Temporary File
                    Create unique filename (for temporary use) (DOS 3.x)
entry      AH       5Ah
           DS:DX    pointer to ASCIIZ directory pathname ending with a
                      backslash (\)
           CX       file attribute
return     CF       clear   DS:DX   new ASCIIZ pathname
                            AX      handle
                    set     AX      error code (03h, 05h)
note 1. The file created is not truly 'temporary'. It must be removed by the user.
     2. If the filename created already exists in the current directory, this
        function will call itself again with another unique filename until a
        unique filename is found.
     3. The temporary filename usually consists of mixed letters and numbers. No
        file extension appears to be generated.

Function   5Bh      Create a New File    (DOS 3.x+)
entry      AH       5Bh
           DS:DX    pointer to directory ASCIIZ pathname
           CX       file attribute
return     CF       clear   AX      file handle
                            DS:DX   new ASCIIZ pathname
                    set     AX      error code (03h, 04h, 05h, 50h)
note 1. Unlike function 3Ch, function 5Bh will fail if the file already exists.
     2. The new file is opened in read/write mode.
```

```
Function  5Ch       Lock/Unlock File Access    (DOS 3.x+)
entry     AH        5Ch
          AL        00h       To lock file
                    01h       To unlock file
          BX        file handle
          CX:DX     starting offset of region to lock
          SI:DI     size of region to lock
return    CF        clear     successful
                    set       AX        error code (01h, 06h, 21h)
note  1. Close all files before exiting or undefined results may occur.
      2. Programs spawned with EXEC inherit all the parent's file handles but not
         the file locks.

Function  5Dh       undocumented - Multifunction
*                   DOS Internal - partial (DOS 3.x+)
entry     AH        5Dh
          AL        subfunction
                    00h    Indirect Function Call
                           DS:DX   pointer to buffer containing register values AX,
                                   BX, CX, DX, SI, DI, DS, ES for a call to int 21h
                           return  as appropriate for function being called
                           note    Does not check AH. Out of range values will crash
                                   the system.
                    01h    SYNC?  (DOS 3.1+)
                           parameters unknown
                           note 1. Does something to each disk file in the System
                                   File Table which has been written to.
                                2. If remote file, calls int 2Fh/fn1107h.
                                3. Seems to update the time stamp of all open files
                                   which have been written to.
                    02h-05h Network functions? (DOS 3.1+)
                           parameters unknown
                           note    Error unless network is loaded.
                    06h    Get Address of Critical Error Flag
                           return  CX        unknown value
                                   DX        unknown value
                                   DS:SI     pointer to critical error flag
                    08h    (unknown - used by COMMAND.COM)
                    09h    (unknown - used by COMMAND.COM)
                    0Ah    Set Error Info (Error, Class, Action, and Locus)
                           DS:DX   address of 11-word error information table
                                   words 0 to 7: values of AX, BX, CX, DX, SI, DI,
                                                 DS, ES that function 59h will
                                                 return
                                   words 8 to 10: zero (reserved)
return    CX        unknown
          DX        unknown
          DS:SI     (for 06h) pointer to critical error flag
note  1. This call seems to have many different functions.
      2. Function 0Ah; DOS 3.1+.
      3. Function 06h; setting CritErr flag allows use of functions 50h/51h from
         int 28h under DOS 2.x by forcing the use of the correct stack.
      4. Functions 07h, 08h, 09h are identical in DOS 3.1 and call int 2Fh fn1125h.

Function  5Eh       Network Printer  (Partially documented by Microsoft)
                    DOS 3.1+ with Networks software
entry     AH        5Eh
          AL        00     Get Machine Name
                           DS:DX   pointer to 16-byte buffer for ASCIIZ name
                           return  CH        0         if name not defined
                                   CL        NETBIOS name number if CH  0
                                   DS:DX     pointer to identifier if CH  0
                           note    the ASCIIZ name is a 15 byte string padded to
                                   length with zeroes
                    01     Set Machine Name
                           DS:DX   pointer to ASCIIZ name
                           CH      unknown
                           CL      name number
                    02     Set Printer Control String
                           BX      redirection list index
                           CX      length of setup string (max 64 bytes)
```

DOS Interrupts and Function Calls

```
                              DS:SI    pointer to string buffer
                        03    Get Printer Control String
                              BX       redirection list index
                              ES:DI    pointer to string buffer
                              return  CX       length of setup string (max 64 bytes)
return    CF            clear  successful
                        set    error
                              AX       error code (01h for all listed subfunctions)
note 1. Used in IBM's & Microsoft's Network programs.
     2. Partial documentation in Fall 1985 Byte.
     3. These services require that the network software be installed.
     4. Partial documentation in Advanced MS-DOS.
     5. SHARE must be loaded or results can be unpredictable on 00h, or fail with
        02h or 03h.

Function  5Fh    Network Redirection
                 (DOS 3.1 + Microsoft Networks)
entry     AH     5Fh
          AL     *00h    Unknown
                 *01h    Unknown
                  02h    Get Redirection List Entry
                         BX       redirection list index
                         DS:SI    pointer to 16 byte buffer for local device name
                         ES:DI    pointer to 128 byte buffer for network name
                         return  BH       device status flag (bit 0=0 if valid)
                                                             (bit 0=1 if invalid)
                                 BL       device type
                                          03       printer device
                                          04       drive device
                                 CX       stored parameter value (user data)
                                 DS:SI    pointer to 16 byte local device
                                          name
                                 ES:DI    pointer to 128 byte network name
                         note    DX and BP are destroyed by this call!
                  03h    Redirect Device - Make Assign List Entry
                         Redirects a workstation drive or device to a server
                         directory or device.
                         BL       device type
                                  03       printer device
                                  04       file device
                         CX       stored parameter value
                         DS:SI    pointer to ASCIIZ source device name
                         ES:DI    pointer to destination ASCIIZ network path +
                                  ASCIIZ password
                  04h    Cancel Redirection Assignment
                         DS:SI    pointer to ASCIIZ device name or network path to
                                  be cancelled
return    CF     clear   successful
                 set     if error
                         AX       error code
                                  (fn 02h) 01h, 12h
                                  (fn 03h) 01h, 03h, 05h, 08h
                                  (fn 04h) 01h, 0Fh
note 1. Used in IBM's Network program.
     2. Partial documentation in Fall 1985 Byte.
     3. These services require that the network software be installed.
     4. Partial documentation in Advanced MS-DOS.
     5. SHARE must be loaded or the call will fail.
     6. The network device name requires a password.

Function  60h    undocumented - Parse pathname (DOS 3.x+)
    *            Perform name processing on a string (internal to DOS)
entry     AH     60h
          DS:SI  pointer to ASCIIZ source string (null terminated)
          ES:DI  pointer to destination 67 byte (?) ASCIIZ string buffer
return    ES:DI  buffer filled with qualified name in form (drive):(path)
          CF     0        no error
                 1        error
                          AX       error code (unknown)
note 1. Documented in Zenith 3.05 Tech Ref.
     2. All name processing is performed on the input string: string substitution
```

                is performed on the components, current drive/directories are prepended,
                . and .. are removed.
             3. Example: If current drive/directory is c:\test, myfile.x is translated
                to c:\test\myfile.x; ..\source\sample.asm is tranlated to c:\source\
                sample.asm.
             4. It is the caller's responsibility to make sure DS:SI does not point to a
                null string. If it does, SI is incremented, a null byte is stored at
                ES:DI, and the routine returns.
             5. Used by CHKDSK, at least in DOS 3.3, and DOS 3.x.
             6. If path string is on a JOINed drive, the returned name is the one that
                would be needed if the drive were not JOINed; similarly for a SUBSTed
                drive letter. Because of this, it is possible to get a qualified name
                that is not legal with the current combination of SUBSTs and JOINs.

Function 61h   undocumented - (DOS 3.x)
   *   Internal to DOS - parameters not known
entry   AH   61h
return   AL   0
note   Supposedly documented in Zenith DOS 3.05 Tech Ref.

Function 62h   Get Program Segment Prefix (PSP) (DOS 3.x+)
entry   AH   62h
return   BX   segment address of PSP

Function 63h   Get Lead Byte Table (MS-DOS 2.25 only)
                  Added in DOS 2.25 for additional foreign character set support.
entry   AH   63h
          AL   subfunction
                  00h   Get System Lead Byte Table Address
                  01h   Set/Clear Interim Console Flag
                           DL   0000h   to clear interim console flag
                                   0001h   to set interim console flag
                  02h   get interim console flag
return   DS:SI   pointer to lead byte table (AL = 00h)
          DL   interim console flag (AL = 02h)
note 1. Function 63h destroys all registers except SS:SP on return.
     2. Not supported in DOS 3.x or 4.x.
     3. Note fn 63h does not return errors in AL or CF.

Function 64h   Undocumented - Used internally by DOS
entry   AH   64h
          AL   00h   Get (something)
                  return   DL   unknown
                  01h   Set (something)
                           DL   unknown
                  02h   Get and set (something)
                           DL   new (something)
                  return   DL   old (something)
note   DOS 3.2+ internal function of some type? May be a network function.

Function 65h   Get Extended Country Information (DOS 3.3+)
                  Returns information about the selected country formats,
                  code pages, and conversion tables
entry   AH   65h
          AL   info ID code
                  01h   get general internationalization info
                  02h   get pointer to uppercase table
                  03h   unknown
                  04h   get pointer to filename uppercase table
                  05h   unknown
                  06h   get pointer to collating sequence table
                  07h   get pointer to double-byte character set table
          BX   code page (-1 = global code page)
          CX   size of buffer (=5)
          DX   country ID (-1 = current country)
          ES:DI   pointer to country information buffer
return   CF   set on error
                  AX   error code (unknown)
                           otherwise:
          CX   size of country information returned
          ES:DI   pointer to country information:

```
                    1 byte     info ID
         If info ID  1:
                    dword     pointer to information
         If info ID = 1:
                    word      size
                    word      country ID
                    word      code page
                   34 bytes   (see function 38h)
         If info ID = 2:
                    dword     pointer to uppercase table
                    word      table size
                  128 bytes uppercase equivalents (if any) of chars 80h-0FFh
         If info ID = 4:
                    dword     pointer to collating table
                    word      table size
                  256 bytes   values used to sort characters 00h-0FFh
         If info ID = 6:
                    dword     pointer to filename uppercase table
                    word      table size
                  128 bytes   uppercase equivalents (if any) of chars 80h-0FFh
         If info ID = 7: (DOS 4.0)
                    unknown

Function  66h      Get/Set Global Code Page Table (DOS 3.3+)
                   Query/reset code page defaults
entry     AH       66h
          AL       00h       Get Global Code Page
                   01h       Set Global Page
                             BX        active code page
                             DX        system code page (active page at boot time)
return    CF       clear     successful
                   set       AX        error code (unknown)
          if 00h             BX        active code page
                             DX        system code page (active page at boot time)
note      BX = active code page: 437 = US, 860 = Portugal, 863 = Canada (French)
                                 865 = Norway/Denmark, 850 = multilingual

Function  67h      Set Handle Count  (DOS 3.3+)
                   Supports more than 20 open files per process
entry     AH       67h
          BX       desired number of handles (max 255)
return    CF       clear if OK
          CF       set if error
                   AX        error code (unknown)
note      This function changes the 20-byte handle table pointer in the PSP
          to point to a new, larger handle table elsewhere in memory.

Function  68h      Commit File (DOS 3.3+)
                   Write all buffered data to disk
entry     AH       68h
          BX       file handle
return    CF       set       AX        error code (unknown)
                   clear     successful
note 1.   Faster and more secure method of closing a file in a network than current
          close commands.
     2.   This is effectively the same as DUPing the handle for a file and then
          closing the new one, except that this call won't fail if the system is
          out of handles.
     3.   If BX   20, no action is taken.

Function  69h      Disk Serial Number  DOS 4.0+ (US versions)
                   Handles 'Volume Serial Number' on disks formatted with 4.0+
entry     AH       69h       Get Volume Serial Number
          DS:DX    pointer to table
return    DS:DX    data table. Format:
                   word      unknown (zeroes on my system.
                   dword     disk serial number (binary)
                  11 bytes   volume label or 'NO NAME    ' if none
                   8 bytes   FAT type - string 'FAT12   ' or 'FAT16   '
note      The FAT type field refers to the number of bits per directory entry.
```

96 *The Programmer's Technical Reference*

```
Function  6Ah       Unknown   (DOS 4.0?)

Function  6Bh       Unknown   (DOS 4.0?)

Function  6Ch       Extended Open/Create  DOS 4.0+ (US)
                    Combines functions available with Open, Create, Create New, and
                    Commit File
entry     AH        6Ch
          AL        00h     reserved   [which means there might be other subfunctions?]
          BX        mode    format     0WF0 0000 ISSS 0AAA
                                       AAA is access code (read, write, read/
                                       write) SSS is sharing mode
                                       I      0       pass handle to child
                                              1       no inherit [interesting!]
                                       F      0       use int 24h for errors
                                              1       disable int 24h for all I/O on
                                                      this handle; use own error routine
                                       W      0       no commit
                                              1       auto commit on all writes
          CX        create attribute
          DL        action if file exists/does not exists
             bits 7-4      action if file does not exist
                           0000    fail
                           0001    create
                  3-0      action if file exists
                           0000    fail
                           0001    open
                           0010    replace/open
          DH        00h
          DS:SI     pointer to ASCIIZ file name
return    CF        set on error
          AX        error code (unknown)
                    clear
          AX        file handle
          CX        action taken
                    01h       file opened
                    02h       file created/opened
                    03h       file replaced/opened
Function  89h       undocumented - DOS_Sleep
   *                Not documented by Microsoft
entry     AH        89h
return    unknown
note  1. Function included in Microsoft C 4.0 startup code MSDOS.INC
      2. Debugging shows that the first instruction on entry to DOS compares AH
         with 64h (at least in DOS 3.2) and aborts the call if AH 64.
      3. Possibly used in European MSDOS 4.0?
```

Aftermarket Application Installed Function Calls

Novell Netware 2.11:
Novell no longer recommends the int 21h method for invoking the Netware functions. Int 21h will be supported indefinitely, but the net API calls for addressing the software through the Multiplex Interrupt (2Fh). You may address the API through int 2Fh in the same manner as int 21h; only the interrupt number is different.

Novell API calls are referenced in Chapter 13. Most functions from 0B6h through 0F9h are pre-empted by NetWare; if your software uses any of these calls for another purpose it will likely not run under NetWare.

Note: Novell (and most others') network software and SoftLogic's DoubleDOS conflict on the following int 21h functions 0EAh-0EEh. Netware must use int 2Fh functions instead of 21h functions if DoubleDOS will be used on the network.

```
Function  0EAh   DoubleDOS - Turn off task switching
entry     AX     0EAh
return    Task switching turned off.

Function  0EBh   DoubleDOS - Turn on task switching
entry     AH     0EBh
return    Task switching turned on.

Function  0ECh   DoubleDOS - Get virtual screen address
entry     AH     0ECh
return    ES     segment of virtual screen
note      Screen address can change if task switching is on!

Function  0EEh   DoubleDOS - Release Timeslice
                 Give away time to other tasks
entry     AH     0EEh
          AL     number of 55ms time slices to give away
return    Returns after giving away time slices.

Function  0FFh   CED    (CJ Dunford's DOS macro and command-line editor)
                 CED installable commands
entry     AH     0FFh
          AL     00h      Add Installable Command
                 01h      Remove Installable Command
                 02h      Reserved, may be used to test for CED installation
          BL     mode byte
              bit 0       callable from DOS prompt
                  1       callable from application
                  2-7     not used in public domain CED
          DS:SI  pointer to CR-terminated command name
          ES:DI  pointer to far routine entry point
return    CF     set on error
          AX     01h      invalid function
                 02h      command not found (subfunction 1 only)
                 08h      insufficient memory (subfunction 0 only)
                 0Eh      bad data (subfunction 0 only)
          AH     0FFh     if CED not installed
```

5

Interrupts 22h Through 86h

Interrupt 22h Terminate Address
(0:0088h)
This interrupt transfers control to the far (dword) address at this interrupt location when an application program terminates. The default address for this interrupt is 0:0088h through 0:008Bh. This address is copied into the program's Program Segment Prefix at bytes 0Ah through 0Dh at the time the segment is created and is restored from the PSP when the program terminates. The calling program is normally COMMAND.COM or an application. Do not issue this interrupt directly, as the EXEC function call does this for you. If an application spawns a child process, it must set the Terminate Address prior to issuing the EXEC function call, otherwise when the second program terminated it would return to the calling program's Terminate Address rather than its own. This address may be set with int 21, function 25h.

Interrupt 23h Ctrl-Break Exit Address
(0:008Ch)
If the user enters a Ctrl-Break during STDIN, STDOUT, STDPRN, or STDAUX, int 23h is executed. If BREAK is on, int 23h is checked on MOST function calls (notably 06h). If the user written Ctrl-Break routine saves all registers, it may end with a return-from-interrupt instruction (IRET) to continue program execution. If the user-written interrupt program returns with a long return, the carry flag is used to determine whether the program will be aborted. If the carry flag is set, the program is aborted, otherwise execution continues (as with a return by IRET). If the user-written Ctrl-Break interrupt uses function calls 09h or 0Ah, (Display String or Buffered Keyboard Input) then a three-byte string of 03h-0Dh-0Ah (ETX/CR/LF) is sent to STDOUT. If execution is continued with an IRET, I/O continues from the start of the line. When the interrupt occurs, all registers are set to the value they had when the original function call to DOS was made. There are no restrictions on what the Ctrl-Break handler is allowed to do, including DOS function calls, as long as the registers are unchanged if an IRET is used. If the program creates a new segment and loads a second program which itself changes the Ctrl-Break address, the termination of the second program and return to the first causes the Ctrl-Break address to be restored from the PSP to the value it had before execution of the second program.

Interrupt 24h Critical Error Handler
(0:0090h)
When an unrecoverable I/O error occurs, control is transferred to an error handler in the resident part of COMMAND.COM with an int 24h. This may be the standard DOS error handler (Abort, Retry, Ignore?) or a user-written routine.

DOS Interrupts 22h Through 86h

On entry to the error handler, AH will have its bit 7=0 (high order bit) if the error was a disk error (probably the most common error), bit 7=1 if not.

BP:SI contains the address of a Device Header Control Block from which additional information can be retrieved (see below). The register is set up for a retry operation and an error code is in the lower half of the DI register with the upper half undefined.

The user stack is in effect and contains the following from top to bottom:
```
     IP         DOS registers from the issuing int 24h
     CS         int 24h
     flags
     AX         user registers at time of original
     BX         int 21h request
     CX
     SI
     DI
     BP
     DS
     ES
     IP         from original int 21h
     CS         from the user to DOS
     flags
```

To reroute the critical error handler to a user-written critical error handler, the following should be done:

Before an int 24h occurs:
1. The user application initialization code should save the int 24h vector and replace the vector with one pointing to the user error routine.

When the int 24h occurs:
2. When the user error routine received control it should push the flag registers onto the stack and execute a far call to the original int 24h vector saved in step 1.
3. DOS gives the appropriate prompt, and waits for user input (Abort, Retry, Ignore, Fail). After the user input, DOS returns control to the user error routine instruction following the far call.
4. The user error routine can now do any tasks necessary. To return to the original application at the point the error occurred, the error routine needs to execute an IRET instruction. Otherwise, the user error routine should remove the IP, CS, and flag registers from the stack. Control can then be passed to the desired routine.

Int 24h provides the following values in registers on entry to the interrupt handler:
```
entry   AH        status byte (bits)
                  7       0         disk I/O hard error
                          1         other error - if block device, bad FAT
                                    - if char device, code in DI
                  6       unused
                  5       0         if IGNORE is not allowed
                          1         if IGNORE is allowed
                  4       0         if RETRY is not allowed
                          1         if RETRY is allowed
                  3       0         if FAIL  is not allowed
                          1         if FAIL  is allowed
                  2 \     disk area of error   00 = DOS area   01 = FAT
                  1 /                          10 = root dir   11 = data area
                  0       0         if read operation
                          1         if write operation
        AL        drive number if AH bit 7 = 1, otherwise undefined
                  If it is a hard error on disk (AH bit 7=0), register AL contains
                  the failing drive number (0=A:, 1=B:, etc.).
        BP:SI     address of a Device Header Control Block for which error
                  occurred. Block device if high bit of BP:SI+4 = 1
        DI        (low byte) error code (note: high byte is undefined) error code
```

```
                    description
      00h           attempt to write on write-protected diskette
      01h           unknown unit
      02h           drive not ready
      03h           unknown command
      04h           data error (bad CRC)
      05h           bad request structure length
      06h           seek error
      07h           unknown media type
      08h           sector not found
      09h           printer out of paper
      0Ah           write fault
      0Bh           read fault
      0Ch           general failure
      0Fh           invalid disk change                    (DOS 3.0+)
      10h           FCB unavailable                        (DOS 3.0+)
      11h           sharing buffer overflow                (DOS 3.0+)
```

The handler must return this information:

The registers are set such that if an IRET is executed, DOS responds according to (AL) as follows:

```
AL    00h    IGNORE the error
      01h    RETRY the operation
      02h    ABORT via int 22h (jump to terminate address)
      03h    FAIL the system call that is in progress (DOS 3.0+)
note 1. Be careful when choosing to ignore a response because this causes DOS to
        believe that an operation has completed successfully when it may not have.
     2. If the error was a character device, the contents of AL are invalid.
```

Other Errors

If AH bit 7=1, the error occurred on a character device, or was the result of a bad memory image of the FAT. The device header passed in BP:SI can be examined to determine which case exists. If the attribute byte high-order bit indicates a block device, then the error was a bad FAT. Otherwise, the error is on a character device.

If a character device is involved, the contents of AL are unpredictable, and the error code is in DI as above.

1. Before giving this routine control for disk errors, DOS performs several retries. The number of retries varies according to the DOS version.
2. For disk errors, this exit is taken only for errors occurring during an int 21h function call. It is not used for errors during an int 25h or 26h.
3. This routine is entered in a disabled state.
4. All registers must be preserved.
5. This interrupt handler should refrain from using DOS function calls. If necessary, it may use calls 01h through 12h. Use of any other call destroys the DOS stack and leaves DOS in an unpredictable state.
6. The interrupt handler must not change the contents of the device header.
7. If the interrupt handler handles errors itself rather than returning to DOS, it should restore the application program's registers from the stack, remove all but the last three words on the stack, then issue an IRET. This will return to the program immediately after the int 21h that experienced the error. Note that if this is done DOS will be in an unstable state until a function call higher than 12h is issued, therefore not recommended.
8. For DOS 3.x+, IGNORE requests (AL=0) are converted to FAIL for critical errors that occur on FAT or DIR sectors.
9. For DOS 3.10 up, IGNORE requests (AL=0) are converted to FAIL requests for network critical errors (50-79).

10. The device header pointed to by BP:SI is as follows:
```
dword   pointer to next device (0FFFFh if last device)
word    attributes:
        bit     15      1       if character device.
                                If bit 15 is 1:
                                  bit 0 = 1 if current standard input
                                  bit 1 = 1 if current standard output
                                  bit 2 = 1 if current NULL device
                                  bit 3 = 1 if current CLOCK device
                                0       if block device.
        bit     14              is the IOCTL bit
word            pointer to device driver strategy entry point
word            pointer to device driver interrupt entry point
8 bytes         character device named field for block devices. The first byte is
                the number of units.
```
11. To tell if the error occurred on a block or character device, look at bit 15 in the attribute field (WORD at BP:SI+4).
12. If the name of the character device is desired, look at the eight bytes starting at BP:SI+10.

Handling of Invalid Responses (DOS 3.0+)

A. If IGNORE (AL=0) is specified by the user and IGNORE is not allowed (bit 5=0), make the response FAIL (AL=3).
B. If RETRY (AL=1) is specified by the user and RETRY is not allowed (bit 4=0), make the response FAIL (AL=3).
C. If FAIL (AL=3) is specified by the user and FAIL is not allowed (bit 3=0), make the response ABORT. (AL=2)

Interrupt 25h Absolute Disk Read

Interrupt 26h Absolute Disk Write
(0:0094h, 0:0098h)
These transfer control directly to the device driver. On return, the original flags are still on the stack (put there by the INT instruction). This is necessary because return information is passed back in the current flags.

The number of sectors specified is transferred between the given drive and the transfer address. Logical sector numbers are obtained by numbering each sector sequentially starting from track 0, head 0, sector 1 (logical sector 0) and continuing along the same head, then to the next head until the last sector on the last head of the track is counted. Thus, logical sector 1 is track 0, head 0, sector 2; logical sector 2 is track 0, head 0, sector 3; and so on. Numbering then continues wih sector 1 on head 0 of the next track. Note that although the sectors are sequentially numbered (for example, sectors 2 and 3 on track 0 in the example above), they may not be physically adjacent on disk, due to interleaving. Note that the mapping is different from that used by DOS 1.10 for double-sided diskettes.

The request is as follows:

```
int 25 for Absolute Disk Read,    | except Compaq DOS 3.31 or DOS 4.0+
int 26 for Absolute Disk Write    | over-32Mb partitions
entry   AL      drive number (0=A:, 1=B:, etc)
        CX      number of sectors to read (int 25h) or write (int 26h)
        DS:BX   disk transfer address buffer (DTA)
        DX      first relative sector to read - beginning logical sector number
return  CF      set if error
        AL      error code issued to int 24h in low half of DI
        AH      01h     bad command
                02h     bad address mark
```

```
                    03h    write-protected disk
                    04h    requested sector not found
                    08h    DMA failure
                    10h    data error (bad CRC)
                    20h    controller failed
                    40h    seek operation failed
                    80h    attachment failed to respond
note 1. Original flags on stack! Be sure to pop the stack to prevent uncontrolled
        growth.
     2. Ints 25 and 26 will try rereading a disk if they get an error the first
        time.
     3. All registers except the segment registers are destroyed by these calls

int 25 for Absolute Disk Read,   | Compaq DOS 3.31 or DOS 4.0+
int 26 for Absolute Disk Write   | over-32Mb partitions
entry    AL       drive number (0=A:, 1=B:, etc)
         CX       0FFFFh
         DS:BX    packet address. Packet format:
                  dword    sector number
                  word     number of sectors to read
                  dword    transfer address
return   same as above?
note 1. Original flags on stack! Be sure to pop the stack to prevent uncontrolled
        growth.
     2. Partition is potentially 32M (and requires this form of the call) if bit
        1 of device attribute word in device driver is set.
```

Interrupt 27h Terminate And Stay Resident
(0:009Ch) (obsolete)

This vector is used by programs that are to remain resident when COMMAND.COM regains control.

After initializing itself, the program must set DX to its last address plus one relative to the program's initial DS or ES value (the offset at which other programs can be loaded), then execute interrupt 27h. DOS then considers the program as an extension of itself, so the program is not overlaid when other programs are executed. This is useful for loading programs such as utilities and interrupt handlers that must remain resident.

```
entry    CS       current program segment
         DX       last program byte + 1
return   none
note 1. This interrupt must not be used by .EXE programs that are loaded into the
        high end of memory.
     2. This interrupt restores the interrupt 22h, 23h, and 24h vectors in the
        same manner as interrupt 20h. Therefore, it cannot be used to install
        permanently resident Ctrl-Break or critical error handler routines.
     3. The maximum size of memory that can be made resident by this method is
        64K.
     4. Memory can be more efficiently used if the block containing a copy of the
        environment is deallocated before terminating. This can be done by
        loading ES  with the segment contained in 2Ch of the PSP, and issuing
        function call 49h (Free Allocated Memory).
     5. DOS function call 4Ch allows a program to pass a completion code to DOS,
        which can be interpreted with processing (see function call 31h).
     6. Terminate and stay resident programs do not close files.
     7. Int 21, function 31h is the preferred method to cause a program to remain
        resident because this allows return information to be passed and allows
        a program larger than 64K to remain resident.
     8. It is possible to make an EXE program resident with this call by putting
        a 27h in the second byte of the PSP and terminating with a RET FAR.
```

Interrupt 28h (not documented by Microsoft)
* DOS Idle Interrupt

Int 28h has been provided by DOS since release 2.0. The int 28h process is similar to the 'Timer Tick' process provided by BIOS via int 1Ch in that it is an 'outbound' (from DOS) call which an application can 'hook onto' to get service at a particular entry point. DOS normally only issues int 28h when it receives a function call (int 21h) from a foreground application with an argument in the range of 0 thru 12 (0Ch) in the AH register, or when it is idling waiting for keyboard input. In effect, when DOS issues int 28, it is saying to the background task 'I'm not doing anything hot right now, if you can use the time, go ahead'. This means that a foreground application which doesn't do many low-number DOS functions can preempt CPU time easily.

When int 28h is being issued it is usually safe to do DOS calls. You won't get int 28hs if a program is running that doesn't do its keyboard input through DOS. You should rely on the timer interrupt for these. It is used primarily by the PRINT.COM routines, but any number of other routines can be chained to it by saving the original vector and calling it with a FAR call (or just JMPing to it) at the end of the new routine.

Int 28h is not called at all when any non-trivial foreground task is running. As soon as a foreground program has a file open, int 28h no longer gets called. Could make a good driver for for a background program that works as long as there is nothing else going on in the machine.

DOS uses 3 separate internal stacks: one for calls 01h through 0Ch; another for calls 0Dh and above; and a third for calls 01h through 0Ch when a Critical Error is in progress. When int 28h is called, any calls above 0Ch can be executed without destroying the internal stack used by DOS at the time.

The byte which is pushed on the stack before an int 28h just indicates which stack area is being used by the current int 21h call. In DOS 3.1, the code sequence that calls int 28h looks like this:

```
PUSH    SS:[0304]
INT     28
POP     SS:[0304]
```

The low-order byte of the word pushed contains 1 if the int 21h call currently in progress is for services 1 through 0Ch, and 0 for service 0 and for 0Dh and up. Assuming that the last DOS call was not a reentrant one, this tells you which set of DOS services should be safe to call.

```
entry   no parameters available
return  none
note 1. The int 28h handler may invoke any int 21h function except functions 00h
           through 0Ch (and 50h/51h under DOS 2.x unless DOS CritErr flag is set).
     2. Apparently int 28h is also called during screen writes.
     3. Until some program installs its own routine, this interrupt vector simply
           points to an IRET opcode.
     4. Supported in OS/2 1.0's DOS Compatibility Box.
     5. It is possible, if you are careful, to enhance the background priority by
           providing more int 28h calls than DOS normally would issue.
     6. If the InDOS flag is zero on int 28h, then it was called by someone other
           than DOS, and the word on the stack should NOT be examined.
```

Interrupt 29h (not documented by Microsoft)
* Internal - Quick Screen Output

This method is extremely fast (much faster than DOS 21h subfunctions 2 and 9, for example), and it is portable, even to 'non-compatible' MS-DOS computers.

```
entry   AL      ASCII value for character to output to screen
return  unknown
note 1. Documented by Digital Research's DOS Reference as provided with the DEC
           Rainbow.
     2. If ANSI.SYS is installed, character output is filtered through it.
     3. Works on the IBM PC and compatibles, Wang PC, HP-150 and Vectra, DEC
           Rainbow, NEC APC, Texas Instruments PC and others.
     4. This interrupt is called from the DOS's output routines if output is
           going to a device rather than a file, and the device driver's attribute
           word has bit 3 (04h) set to '1'.
```

5. This call has been tested with MSDOS 2.11, PCDOS 2.1, PCDOS 3.1, PCDOS 3.2, PCDOS 3.3, PCDOS 4.01, and Compaq DOS 3.31.
6. Used in IBMBIO.COM as a vector to int 10, function 0Eh (write TTY) followed by an IRET.
7. Most of the fast ANSI device drivers use this interrupt - ZANSI.SYS, NANSI.SYS, and PCMag's ANSI.COM.

Interrupt 2Ah   Microsoft Networks - Session Layer Interrupt
* (not documented by Microsoft)

```
entry     AH       00h      Check Network BIOS Installed
                            return  AH       nonzero if installed
                   01h      Execute NETBIOS Request
                   02h      Set Net Printer Mode
                   03h      Get Shared-Device Status (Check Direct I/O)
                            AL       00h
                            DS:SI    pointer to ASCIIZ disk device name
                            return  CF       0        if allowed
                   04h      Execute NETBIOS
                            AL       00h      for error retry
                                     01h      for no retry
                            ES:BX    pointer to network control block
                            return  AX       0000h    for no error
                                    AH       01h      if error
                                    AL       error code (unknown)
                   05h      Get Network Resource Information
                            AL       00h
                            return  AX       reserved
                                    BX       number of network names
                                    CX       number of commands
                                    DX       number of sessions
                   06h      Network Print-Stream Control
                            note    NETBIOS 1.10
                   07h-19h  unknown
                   20h      unknown
                            note    AL=01h intercepted by DESQview 2.0.
                   80h      Begin DOS Critical Section
                            AL       1 to 6
                   81h      End DOS Critical Section
                            AL       1 to 6
                   82h      Server Hook
                            stack   AX from call to int 21h
                            return  stack unchanged
                            note    Called by the int 21h function dispatcher in DOS
                                    3.10+ for function 0 and functions greater than
                                    0Ch except 59h.
                   84h      Keyboard Busy Loop
                            note    Similar to DOS's int 28h.
```

Interrupt 2Bh   (not documented by Microsoft)
* Unknown - Internal Routine for DOS (IRET)

Interrupt 2Ch   (not documented by Microsoft)
* Unknown - Internal Routine for DOS (IRET)

Interrupt 2Dh   (not documented by Microsoft)
* Unknown - Internal Routine for DOS (IRET)

Interrupt 2Eh   (undocumented by Microsoft)   (DOS 2.0+)
* Internal Routine for DOS (Alternate EXEC)

This interrupt passes a command line addressed by DS:SI to COMMAND.COM. The command line must be formatted just like the unformatted parameter area of a Program Segment Prefix. That is, the first byte must be a count of characters, and the second and subsequent bytes must be a command line with parameters, terminated by a carriage return character.

When executed, int 2Eh will reload the transient part of the command interpreter if it is not currently in memory. If called from a program that was called from a batch file, it will abort the batch file. If executed from a program which has been spawned by the EXEC function, it will abort the whole chain and probably lock up the computer. Int 2Eh also destroys all registers including the stack pointer.

Int 2Eh is called from the transient portion of the program to reset the DOS PSP pointers using the above Functions #81 & #80, and then reenters the resident program.

When called with a valid command line, the command will be carried out by COMMAND.COM just as though you had typed it in at the DOS prompt. Note that the count does not include the carriage return. This is an elegant way to perform a SET from an application program against the master environment block for example.

```
entry   DS:SI   pointer to an ASCIIZ command line in the form:
                    count byte
                    ASCII string
                    carriage return
                    null byte
note 1. Destroys all registers including stack pointer.
     2. Seems to work OK in both DOS 2.x and 3.x.
     3. It is reportedly not used by DOS.
     4. As far as known, int 2Eh is not used by DOS 3.1, although it was called
        by COMMAND.COM of PCDOS 3.0, so it appears to be in 3.1 only for the
        sake of compatibility.
```

Interrupt 2Fh   Multiplex Interrupt

Interrupt 2Fh is the multiplex interrupt. A general interface is defined between two processes. It is up to the specific application using interrupt 2Fh to define specific functions and parameters.

This interrupt is becoming more commonly used as the availible interrupt 21 functions are getting to be in short supply. Int 2Fh doesn't require any support from DOS itself for it to be used in application programs. It's not handled by DOS, but by the programs themselves.

Every multiplex interrupt handler is assigned a specific multiplex number. The multiplex number is specified in the AH register; the AH value tells which program your request is directed toward. The specific function that the handler is to perform is placed in the AL register. Other parameters are places in the other registers as needed. The handlers are chained into the 2Fh interrupt vector and the multiplex number is checked to see if any other application is using the same multiplex number. There is no predefined method for assigning a multiplex number to a handler. You must just pick one. To avoid a conflict if two applications choose the same multiplex number, the multiplex numbers used by an application should be patchable. In order to check for a previous installation of the current application, you can search memory for a unique string included in your program. If the value you wanted in AH is taken but you don't find the string, then another application has grabbed that location.

Int 2Fh was not documented under DOS 2.x. There is no reason not to use int 2Fh as the multiplex interrupt in DOS 2.x. The only problem is that DOS 2.x does not initialize the int 2Fh vector, so when you try to chain to it like you are supposed to, it will crash. If your program checks the vector for being zero and initializes it itself or doesn't chain in that case, it will work for you n 2.x just the same as 3.x.

DOS 3.2 itself contains some int 2Fh handlers - it uses values of 08h, 13h, and 0F8h. There may be more. NLSFUNC from DOS 3.3 up uses part of int 2Fh and so does GRAFTABL.

For int 2Fh calls, register AH identifies which program is to handle the interrupt. AH values

106 *The Programmer's Technical Reference*

00h-7Fh are reserved for DOS, not that anyone cares much. Values 0C0h-0FFh are reserved for applications. Register AL contains the subfunction code if used.

```
Function  00h  unknown
               Reportedly somehow used by PRINT.COM in DOS 3.3+.

Function  01h  PRINT.COM
               PC-DOS 3.3's PRINT.COM hooks the following interrupt vectors:
               05h    PrintScreen Interrupt
               13h    BIOS Disk Interrupt
               14h    BIOS Serial Communications Interrupt
               15h    BIOS 'System Services' Interrupt
               17h    BIOS Printer Interrupt
               19h    Bootstrap Loader Interrupt
               1Ch    Timer Tick
               23h    Control-C Terminate Address
               24h    Critical Error Handler Address
               28h    DOS Idle Interrupt (undocumented)
               2Fh    Multiplex Interrupt

entry  AH      01h
               AL     01h
                      00h     PRINT   Get Installed State
                              This call must be defined by all int 2Fh handlers. It is
                              used by the caller of the handler to determine if the
                              handler is present. On entry,
         AL=0. On return, AL contains the installed state as follows:
               return AL      0FFh    installed
                              01h     not installed, not OK to install
                              00h     not installed, OK to install

                      01h     PRINT   Submit File
                      DS:DX   pointer to submit packet
                              format  byte    level
                                      dword   pointer to ASCIIZ filename
               return CF      set if error
                      AX      error code
               note   A submit packet contains the level (BYTE) and a pointer
                      to the ASCIIZ string (DWORD in offset:segment form). The
                      ASCIIZ string must contain the drive, path, and filename
                      of the file you want to print. The filename cannot
                      contain global filename characters.
               return CF      set if error
                      AX      error code

                      02h     PRINT Cancel File
                      On entry, AL=2 and DS:DX points to the ASCIIZ string for
                      the print file you want to cancel. Global filename
                      characters are allowed in the filename.
                      DS:DX   pointer to ASCIIZ file name to cancel (wildcards OK)
               return CF      set if error
                      AX      error code

                      03h     PRINT Remove All Files
               return CF      set if error
                      AX      error code

                      04h     PRINT Hold Queue/Get Status
                      This call holds the jobs in the print queue so that you
                      can scan the queue. Issuing any other code releases the
                      jobs. On entry, AL=4. On return, DX contains the error
                      count. DS:SI points to the print queue. The printqueue
                      consists of a series of filename entries. Each entry is
                      64 bytes long. The first entry in the queue is the file
                      currently being printed. The end of the queue is marked
                      by the entry having a null as the first character.
               return DX      error count
                      DS:SI   pointer to print queue (null-string
                              terminated list of 64-byte ASCIIZ filenames)
                      CF      set if error
                      AX      error code
```

```
                              01h      function invalid
                              02h      file not found
                              03h      path not found
                              04h      too many open files
                              05h      access denied
                              08h      queue full
                              09h      spooler busy
                              0Ch      name too long
                              0Fh      drive invalid
                  05h      PRINT restart queue
           return CF       set if error
                           AX      error code
                  06h      unknown - may be used in DOS 3.3+ PRINT

Function   05h  DOS 3.0+ Critical Error Handler
entry   AH      05h
        AL      00h      Installation Check
                return AL      00h      not installed, OK to
                                        install
                               01h      not installed, not OK to
                                        install
                               0FFh     installed
                note     This set of functions allows a user program to
                         partially or completely override the default
                         critical error handler in COMMAND.COM.
        AL      xxh      Handle Error - nonzero error code in AL (xxh
                         indicates nonzero extended error code)
                return CF       clear
                               ES:DI    pointer to ASCIIZ error message
                        AL      (?)
                        CF      set      use default error handler

Function   06h  ASSIGN
entry   AH      06h
        AL      00h      Installation Check
                01h      Get Memory Segment
return (AH=00h) AH       nonzero if ASSIGN is installed
       (AH=01h) ES       segment of ASSIGN work area

Function   08h  DRIVER.SYS
entry   AH      08h
        AL      00h      Installation Check
                return AL      00h      not installed, OK to install
                               01h      not installed, not OK to install
                               0FFh     installed
                01h      unknown

other parameters unknown

Function   10h  SHARE
entry   AH      10h
        AL      00h      Installation Check
return  AL      00h      not installed, OK to install
                01h      not installed, not OK to install
                0FFh     installed

Function   11h  Multiplex - Network Redirection
entry   AH      11h
        AL      00h      Installation Check
                return AL      00h      not installed, OK to install
                               01h      not installed, not OK to install
                               0FFh     installed
                01h-05h  unknown
                06h      Close Remote File
                07h-0Dh  unknown
                0Eh      Do Redirection
                         stack    word     function to execute
                         return   CF       set on error
                0Fh      Printer Setup
                10h-1Eh  unknown
```

```
            1Eh     Do Redirection
                        stack   word        function to execute
                        return  CF          set on error
            1Fh     Printer Setup
                        stack   word        function (?)
                        return  CF          set on error (?)
            20h-26h unknown

Function  12h   Multiplex, DOS 3.x Internal Services
entry  AH       12h
       AL       00h     Installation Check
                        return  AL      0FFh    for compatibility with other int
                                                2Fh functions
                01h     Close File (?)
                        stack   word value - unknown
                        return  BX          unknown
                                CX          unknown
                                ES:DI       pointer to unknown value
                        note    Can be called only from within DOS.
                02h     Get Interrupt Address
                        stack   word        vector number
                        return  ES:BX       pointer to interrupt vector
                                stack       unchanged
                03h     Get DOS Data Segment
                        return  DS          segment of IBMDOS.COM file
                04h     Normalize Path Separator
                        stack   word        character to normalize
                        return  AL          normalized character (forward slash
                                            turned to backslash)
                                stack       unchanged
                05h     Output Character
                        stack   word        character to output
                        return  stack       unchanged
                        note    Can be called only from within DOS.
                06h     Invoke Critical Error
                        return  AL          0-3 for Abort, Retry, Ignore, Fail
                        note    Can be called only from within DOS.
                07h     Move Disk Buffer (?)
                        DS:DI   pointer to disk buffer
                        return  buffer moved to end of buffer list
                        note    Can be called only from within DOS.
                08h     Decrement Word
                        ES:DI   pointer to word to decrement
                        return  AX          new value of word
                        note    Word pointed to by ES:DI decremented,
                                skipping zero.
                09h     unknown
                        DS:DI   pointer to disk buffer(?)
                        return  (?)
                        note    Can be called only from within DOS.
                0Ah     unknown
                        note    Can be called only from within DOS.
                0Bh     unknown
                        ES:DI   pointer to system file table entry (?)
                        return  AX      (?)
                        note    Can be called only from within DOS.
                0Ch     unknown
                        note    Can be called only from within DOS.
                0Dh     Get Date and Time
                        return  AX          current date in packed format
                                DX          current time in packed format
                        note    Can be called only from within DOS.
                0Eh     Do Something to All Disk Buffers (?)
                        return  DS:DI   pointer to first disk buffer
                        note    Can be called only from within DOS.
                0Fh     unknown
                        DS:DI   pointer to (?)
                        return  DS:DI pointer to (?)
                        note 1. Can be called only from within DOS.
                             2. Calls on function 1207h.
                10h     Find Dirty Buffer
```

Interrupts 22h Through 86h

```
         DS:DI    pointer to first disk buffer
         return   DS:DI    pointer to first disk buffer
                           which has clean flag clear
                  ZF       clear    if found
                           set      if not found
11h      Normalize ASCIIZ Filename
         DS:SI    pointer to ASCIIZ filename to normalize
         ES:DI    pointer to buffer for normalized filename
         return   destination buffer filled with uppercase
                           filename, with slashes turned to backslashes
12h      Get Length of ASCIIZ String
         ES:DI    pointer to ASCIIZ string
         return   CX       length of string
13h      Uppercase Character
         stack    word     character to convert to uppercase
         return   AL       uppercase character
                  stack    unchanged
14h      Compare FAR Pointers
         DS:SI    first pointer
         ES:DI    second pointer
         return   ZF       set if pointers are equal
                  ZF       clear if not equal
15h      unknown
         DS:DI    pointer to disk buffer
         stack    word     (?)
         return   stack unchanged
         note     Can be called only from within DOS.
16h      Get Address of System FCB
         BX       system file table entry number
         return   ES:DI pointer to system file table entry
17h      Set Default Drive (?)
         stack    word     drive (0=A:, 1=B:, etc)
         return   DS:SI    pointer to drive data block for
                           specified drive
                  stack    unchanged
         note     Can be called only from within DOS.
18h      Get Something (?)
         return   DS:SI pointer to (?)
19h      unknown
         stack    word     drive (0=default, 1=A:, etc)
         return   (?)
                  stack    unchanged
         note 1.  Can be called only from within DOS.
              2.  Calls function 1217h.
1Ah      Get File's Drive
         DS:SI    pointer to filename
         return   AL       drive
                           (0=default, 1=A:, etc, 0FFh=invalid)
1Bh      Set Something (?)
         CL       unknown
         return   AL       (?)
         note     Can be called only from within DOS.
1Ch      Checksum Memory
         DS:SI    pointer to start of memory to checksum
         CX       number of bytes
         DX       initial checksum
         return   DX       checksum
         note 1.  Can be called only from within DOS.
              2.  Used to determine when transient portion of
                  COMMAND.COM has been overlaid by application.
1Dh      unknown
1Eh      Compare Filenames
         DS:SI    pointer to first ASCIIZ filename
         ES:DI    pointer to second ASCIIZ filename
         return   ZF       set      if filenames equivalent
                           clear    if not
         note     Used by COPY command.
1Fh      Build Drive Info Block
         stack    word     drive letter
         return   ES:DI pointer to drive info block
                           (will be overwritten by next call)
```

```
                            stack unchanged
                    note    Can be called only from within DOS.
            20h     Get System File Table Number
                    BX      file handle
                    return  CF      set on error, error code in AL
                            AL          06h (invalid file handle)
                            CF      clear if successful
                                    byte ES:[DI]    system file table entry
                                                    number for file handle
            21h     unknown
                    DS:SI   pointer to (?)
                    return  (?)
                    note    Can be called only from within DOS.
            22h     unknown
                    SS:SI   pointer to (?)
                    return  nothing(?)
                    note    Can be called only from within DOS.
            23h     Check if Character Device (?)
                    return  DS:SI   pointer to device driver with same name
                                    as (?)
                    note    Can be called only from within DOS.
            24h     Delay
                    return  after delay of (?) ms
                    note    Can be called only from within DOS.
            25h     Get Length of ASCIIZ String
                    DS:SI   pointer to ASCIIZ string
                    return  CX      length of string

Function    14h     NLSFUNC.COM
entry   AH          14h
other parameters unknown

Function    15h     CD-ROM extensions
            Microsoft CD-ROM driver versions 1.0 through 2.0 will work only up
            to DOS 3.31. DOS 4.0 and up require 2.1 drivers.
entry   AH          15h     CD-ROM services
        AL          subfunctions
                    00h     Installation Check
                    BX      00h
                    return  BX      number of CD-ROM drive letters used
                            CX      starting drive letter (0=A:)
                    note    This installation check DOES NOT follow the format
                            used by other software.

                    01h     Get Drive Device List
                    ES:BX   pointer to buffer to hold drive letter list (5 bytes per
                            drive letter)
                    return  buffer filled, for each drive letter:
                            byte    subunit number in driver
                            dword   address of device driver header
                    02h     Get Copyright File Name
                    CX      drive number (0=A:)
                    ES:BX   pointer to 38-byte buffer for name of copyright file
                    return  CF      set if drive is not a CD-ROM drive
                            AX      error code (15h)

                    03h     Get Abstract File Name
                    ES:BX   pointer to 38-byte buffer for name of abstract file
                    CX      drive number (0=A:)
                    return  CF      set if drive is not a CD-ROM drive
                            AX      error code (15h)

                    04h     Get Bibliographic Doc File Name
                    CX      drive number (0=A:)
                    ES:BX   pointer to 38-byte buffer for name of bibliographic
                            documentation file
                    return  CF      set if drive is not a CD-ROM drive
                            AX      error code (15h)

                    05h     Read VTOC (Volume Table of Contents)
                    CX      drive number (0=A:)
```

Interrupts 22h Through 86h

```
DX         sector index (0=first volume descriptor,
           m1=second,...)
ES:BX      pointer to 2048-byte buffer
return     CF       set on error
                    AX        error code (15h, 21h)
           CF       clear if successful
                    AX        volume descriptor type
                              (1=standard, 0FFh=terminator, 00h=other)

06h        Turn Debugging On
BX         debugging function to enable
note       Reserved for development.

07h        Turn Debugging Off
BX         debugging function to disable
note       Reserved for development.

08h        Absolute Disk Read
CX         drive number (0=A:)
DX         number of sectors to read
ES:BX      pointer to buffer
SI:DI      starting sector number
return     CF       set on error
           AL       error code  (15h, 21h)

09h        Absolute Disk Write
CX         drive number (0=A:)
DX         number of sectors to write
ES:BX      pointer to buffer
SI:DI      starting sector number
note       Corresponds to int 26h and is currently reserved and
           nonfunctional.

0Ah        Reserved by Microsoft

0Bh        CD-ROM 2.00 - Drive Check
CX         drive number (0=A:)
return     BX       0ADADh if MSCDEX.EXE installed
           AX       0       if drive not supported
                    <> 0    if supported

0Ch        CD-ROM 2.00 - Get MSCDEX.EXE Version
return     BH       major version
           BL       minor version
note       MSCDEX.EXE versions prior to 1.02 return BX=0.

0Dh        CD-ROM 2.00 - Get CD-ROM Drive Letters
ES:BX      pointer to buffer for drive letter list
           (1 byte per drive)
return     Buffer filled with drive numbers (0=A:). Each byte
           corresponds to the drive in the same position for
           function 1501h.

0Eh        CDROM 2.00 - Get/Set Volume Descriptor Preference
BX         subfunction
           00h      Get Preference
           DX       00h
           return   DX        preference settings
           01h      Set Preference
           DH       volume descriptor preference
                    1        primary volume descriptor
                    2        supplementary volume descriptor
           DL       supplementary volume descriptor preference
                    1        shift-Kanji
           CX       drive number (0=A:)
           return   CF       set on error
                    AX       error code  (01h, 15h)

0Fh        CD-ROM 2.00 - Get Directory Entry
CX         drive number (0=A:)
ES:BX      pointer to ASCIIZ pathname
```

```
              SI:DI   pointer to 255-byte buffer for directory entry
       return CF      set on error
              AX      error code
              CF      clear if succesful
              AX      disk format (0=High Sierra, 1=ISO 9660)
       note   Directory entry format:
              byte    length of directory entry
              byte    length of XAR in LBN's
              dword   LBN of data, Intel (little-Endian) format
              dword   LBN of data, Motorola (big-Endian) format
              dword   length of file, Intel format
              dword   length of file, Motorola format
              ---High Sierra---
                  6 bytes date and time
                  byte    bit flags
                  byte    reserved
              ---ISO 9660---
                  7 bytes data and time
                  byte    bit flags
              ---both formats---
                  byte    interleave size
                  byte    interleave skip factor
                  word    volume set sequence number, Intel format
                  word    volume set sequence number, Motorola format
                  byte    length of file name
                  n bytes file name
                  byte    (optional) padding if filename is odd length
                  n bytes system data

       Error codes:
              01h     invalid function
              15h     invalid drive
              21h     not ready
```

Function 43h Microsoft Extended Memory Specification (XMS)
              The XMS version 2.00 for MS-DOS allows DOS programs to utilize
              additional memory found in 80286 and 80386 machines. With some
              restrictions, XMS adds about 64K to the 640K which DOS programs
              can access directly. XMS also provides DOS programs with a
              standard method of storing data in extended memory.

entry   AH   XMS (extended memory) services
              Perform a FAR call to the driver entry point with AH set
              to the function code
              00h   Get XMS Version Number
                      return AX   16 bit BCD version number (AX=0285h would
                                      be XMS version 2.85)
                              BX   driver internal revision number
                              DX   0000h   HMA does not exist
                                      0001h   HMA exists
                      note 1. No error codes are returned from this function.
                           2. DX indicates the presence of HMA, not its
                              availability.
              01h   Request High Memory Area (1M to 1M + 64K)
                      DX   HMA memory request in bytes (for TSR or
                              device drivers)
                              0FFFFh if application program
                      return AX   0000h   failure
                                      0001h   success
                              BL   error code (80h, 81h, 90h, 91h, 92h)
              02h   Release High Memory Area
                      return AX   0000h   failure
                                      0001h   success
                              BL   error code (80h, 81h, 90h, 93h)
              03h   Global Enable A20
                      return AX   0000h   failure
                                      0001h   success
                              BL   error code (80h, 81h, 82h)
                      note   Should only be used by programs which have
                              control of the HMA. The A20 line should be
                              turned off via Function 04h (Global Disable A20)
                              before a program releases control of the system.

Interrupts 22h Through 86h

- 04h Global Disable A20
  - return AX
    - 0000h failure
    - 0001h success
  - BL error code (80h, 82h, 94h)
  - note 1. This function attempts to disable the A20 line. It should only be used by programs which have control of the HMA.
    2. The A20 line should be disabled before a program releases control of the system.
- 05h Local Enable A20
  - return AX
    - 0000h failure
    - 0001h A20 is enabled
  - BL error code (80h, 81h, 82h)
  - note This function attempts to enable the A20 line. It should only be used by programs which need direct access to extended memory. Programs which use this function should call Function 06h (Local Disable A20) before releasing control of the system.
- 06h Local disable A20
  - return AX
    - 0000h failure
    - 0001h success
  - BL error code (80h, 81h, 82h, 94h)
  - note This function cancels a previous call to Fn 05h (Local Enable A20). It should only be used by programs which need direct access to extended memory. Previous calls to Fn 05h must be cancelled before releasing control of the system.
- 07h Query A20
  - return AX
    - 0000h failure
    - 0001h success (A20 line is physically enabled)
  - BL error code (00h, 80h, 81h)
- 08h Query Free Extended Memory
  - return AX size of largest free extended memory block in K
  - BL error code (80h, 81h, 0A0h)
  - DX total free extended memory in K
  - note The 64K HMA is not included in the returned value even if it is not in use.
- 09h Allocate Extended Memory Block
  - DX Amount of extended memory being requested in K-bytes
  - return AX
    - 0000h failure
    - BL error code (80h 81h A0h A1h)
    - 0001h success
    - DX 16 bit handle for memory block
- 0Ah Free Extended Memory Block
  - DX handle of block to free
  - return AX
    - 0000h failure
    - BL error code (80h, 81h, 0A2h, 0ABh)
    - 0001h success
- 0Bh Move Extended Memory Block
  - DS:SI pointer to EMM structure
    - 4 bytes number of bytes to move
    - 2 bytes source handle
    - 4 bytes offset into source block
    - 2 bytes destination handle
    - 4 bytes offset into destination block
  - return AX
    - 0000h failure
    - BL error code (80h, 81h, 82h, 0A3h, 0A4h, 0A5h, 0A6h, 0A7h, 0A8h, 0A9h)
    - 0001h success
- 0Ch Lock Extended Memory Block
  - DX XMS handle of block to lock
  - return AX
    - 0000h failure
    - BL error code (80h, 81h, 0A2h, 0ACh, 0ADh)
    - 0001h block is successfully locked

```
                            DX:BX    32-bit linear address of locked block
         0Dh    Unlock Extended Memory Block
                DX       XMS handle of block to unlock
                return AX       0000h    failure
                                BL       error code (80h, 81h, 0A2h, 0AAh)
                                0001h    success
         0Eh    Get EMB Handle Information
                DX       handle for which to get info
                return AX       0000h    failure
                                BL       error code (80h, 81h, 0A2h)
                                0001h    success
                                BH       block's lock count
                                BL       number of free handles left
                                DX       block size in K
                note     To get the block's base address, use Fn 0Ch (Lock
                         Extended Memory Block).
         0Fh    Reallocate Extended Memory Block
                BX       New size for the extended memory block in K
                DX       Unlocked extended memory block handle to
                         reallocate
                return AX       0000h    failure
                                BL       error code (80h, 81h,
                                         0A0h, 0A1h, 0A2h, 0ABh)
                                0001h    success
         10h    Request Upper Memory Block (nonEMS memory above 640K)
                DX       Size of requested memory block in paragraphs
                return AX       0000h    failure
                                BL       error code (80h, 0B0h, 0B1h)
                                DX       size of largest available block
                                         in paragraphs
                                0001h    success
                                BX       segment address of UMB
                                DX       actual block size in paragraphs
                note 1. UMBs are paragraph aligned.
                     2. To determine the size of the largest available
                        UMB, attempt to allocate one with a size of
                        0FFFFh.
         11h    Release Upper Memory Block
                DX       segment address of UMB to release
                return AX       0000h    failure
                                BL       error code (80h, 0B2h)
                                0001h    success

note 1. UMBs cannot occupy memory addresses that can be banked by EMS 4.0. EMS
        4.0 takes precedence over UMBs for physically addressable memory.
     2. Programs should make sure that at least 256 bytes of stack space is
        available before calling XMS API functions.
     3. On many machines, toggling the A20 line is a relatively slow operation.
     4. Error codes:
        80h     Function not implemented
        81h     VDISK was detected
        82h     An A20 error occurred
        8Eh     A general driver error
        8Fh     Unrecoverable driver error
        90h     HMA does not exist
        91h     HMA is already in use
        92h     DX is less than the /HMAMIN= parameter
        93h     HMA is not allocated
        0A0h    All extended memory is allocated
        0A1h    All available extended memory handles are allocated
        0A2h    Invalid handle
        0A3h    Source handle is invalid
        0A4h    Source offset is invalid
        0A5h    Destination handle is invalid
        0A6h    Destination offset is invalid
        0A7h    Length is invalid
        0A8h    Move has an invalid overlap
        0A9h    Parity error occurred
        0AAh    Block is not locked
        0ABh    Block is locked
        0ACh    Block lock count overflowed
```

Interrupts 22h Through 86h

```
              0ADh      Lock failed
              0B0h      Only a smaller UMB is available
              0B1h      No UMB's are available
              0B2h      UMB segment number is invalid
Function 5453h TesSeRact Standard for Ram-Resident Program Communication
entry    AX        5453h     TesSeRact function request
         CX        function select word:
              bits 0         function 00h (check install - required)
                   1         function 01h (return userparms - required)
                   2         function 02h (check hotkey)
                   3         function 03h (replace int 24h)
                   4         function 04h (return Data Pointer)
                   5         function 05h (set extra hotkeys)
                   6-7       undefined - reserved for future use
                   8         function 10h (enable TSR)
                   9         function 11h (disable TSR)
                   10        function 12h (release TSR from RAM)
                   11        function 13h (restart TSR)
                   12        function 14h (get current status)
                   13        function 15h (set TSR status)
                   14        function 16h (get popup type)
                   15        undefined - reserved for future use
                   16        function 20h (call user procedure)
                   17        function 21h (stuff keyboard)
                   18-31     undefined - reserved for future use
Functions:
         00h       Check Install
                   DS:SI     pointer to 8-character blank-padded name
                   return AX      0FFFFh   the TSR has already been loaded
                                           Any other value indicates that it is safe to
                                           install this TSR, using the ID number in CX
                             CX        TSR ID Number
         01h       Return User Parameters
                   CX        TSR ID number
                   return AX      00h       no matching TSR ID Number found
                             Otherwise,
                             ES:BX     pointer to TsrParms structure (note 3)
         02h       Check Hotkey
                             CL        scan code of hot key
                   return AX      0FFFFh   hotkey conflicts with TSR already loaded.
                                           Any other value means OK to use hotkey.
         03h       Replace Default Interrupt 24h Handler
                   CX        TSR ID number
                   DS:SI     pointer to new routine for int 24h
                   return AX      <>0      unable to install handler (invalid ID
                                           number)
                             00h       successful installation
         04h       Return TesSeRact Internal Data Area Pointer
                   CX        TSR ID number
                   return AX      00h       no matching TSR ID Number found.
                                           Otherwise, FAR pointer to TsrData structure
                             ES:BX     pointer to TSR's internal data area (note 4)
         05h       Set Multiple Hot Keys
                   CX        TSR ID number
                   DL        number of additional hot keys to allocate
                   DS:SI     pointer to table of hot keys
                        byte      hotkey scan code
                        byte      hotkey shift state
                        byte      flag value to pass to TSR (nonzero)
                   return AX      <>0      unable to install hotkeys (invalid ID
                                           number)
                             00h       successful set
         06h-0Fh not used
         10h       Enable TSR
                   CX        TSR ID number
                   return AX      <>0      unable to enable TSR (invalid ID number)
                             00h       TSR enabled
         11h       Disable TSR
                   CX        TSR ID number
                   return AX      <>0      unable to disable
```

```
    12h     Release TSR [unload from RAM]
            CX      TSR ID number
            return  AX      <>0     invalid TSR number
            note    If any interrupts used by TSR have been grabbed by
                    another TSR, the TesSeRact routines will wait until it
                    is safe to remove the indicated TSR from memory.
    13h     Restart TSR
            CX      TSR ID number of TSR which was unloaded but is still in
                    memory
            return  AX      <>0     unable to restart TSR
                                    (invalid ID #)
                            00h     success
    14h     Get TSR Status Word
            CX      TSR ID number
            return  AX      0FFFFh  invalid TSR ID Code
                            Any other value is current status flags
                    BX      bit flags
    15h     Set TSR Status Word
            CX      TSR ID number
            DX      new bit flags
            return  AX      <>0     unable to set status word
    16h     Get InDOS State at Popup
            CX      TSR ID number
            return  AX      0FFFFh  invalid TSR ID Code
                            Any other value is current status flags
                    BX      value of INDOS flag
    20h     Call User Procedure
            CX      TSR ID number
            ES:DI   pointer to user-defined data
            return  AX      <>0     unable to pass pointer (invalid ID #)
                            00h     success
    21h     Stuff Keyboard
            CX      TSR ID number
            DH      scan code flag
                    00h     buffer contains alternating ASCII & scan codes
                    <>0     buffer contains only ASCII codes
            DL      speed
                    00h     stuff keystrokes only when buffer is empty
                    01h     stuff up to four keystrokes per clock tick
                    02h     stuff up to 15 keystrokes per clock tick
            SI      number of keystrokes
            ES:DI   pointer to buffer to stuff
            return  AX      0F0F0h  user aborted paste with ^C or ^Break
                            <>0     unable to stuff buffer (invalid ID #)
                            00h     Success
    22h - 2Fh reserved
note 1. TesSeRact is based in part on work done by the Ringmaster Development
        Team, in efforts to develop a public domain TSR standard.
     2. Borland's THELP.COM popup help system for Turbo Pascal and Turbo C fully
        supports the TesSeRact API.
     3. TsrParms structure:
         8 bytes    blank-padded TSR name
         word       TSR ID number
         dword      bitmap of supported functions
         byte       scan code of primary hotkey
                    00h     pop up when shift states match
                    0FFh    no popup (if shift state also 0FFh)
         byte       shift state of primary hotkey
                    0FFh    no popup (if scan code also 0FFh)
         byte       number of secondary hotkeys
         dword      pointer to extra hotkeys set by fn 05h
         word       current TSR status flags
         word       PSP segment of TSR
         dword      DTA for TSR
         word       default DS for TSR
         dword      stack at popup
         dword      stack at background invocation
     4. TesSeRact TSR Internal Data Area
         byte       revision level of TesSeRact library
         byte       type of popup in effect
         byte       int 08h occurred since last invocation
```

```
        byte       int 13h occurred since last invocation
        byte       active interrupts
        byte       active soft interrupts
        byte       DOS major version
        byte       how long to wait before popping up
        dword      pointer to INDOS flag
        dword      pointer to DOS critical error flag
        word       PSP segment of interrupted program
        word       PSP segment of prog interrupted by INT 28
        dword      DTA of interrupted program
        dword      DTA of program interrupted by INT 28
        word       SS of interrupted program
        word       SP of interrupted program
        word       SS of program interrupted by INT 28
        word       SP of program interrupted by INT 28
        dword      INT 24 of interrupted program
        3 words    DOS 3+ extended error info
        byte       old BREAK setting
        byte       old VERIFY setting
        byte       were running MS WORD 4.0 before popup
        byte       MS WORD 4.0 special popup flag
        byte       enhanced keyboard call in use
        byte       delay for MS WORD 4.0
              11 times:
        dword      old interrupt vector
        byte       interrupt number
        dword      new interrupt vector

Function   64h   SCRNSAV2.COM
entry    AH      64h
         AL      00h      installation check
return   AL      00h      not installed
                 0FFh     installed
note   SCRNSAV2.COM is a screen saver for PS/2's with VGA by Alan Ballard.

Function  7Ah   Novell NetWare
entry    AH      7Ah
         AL      00h      installation check
return   AL      00h      not installed
                 0FFh     installed
         ES:DI   pointer to FAR entry point for routines otherwise accessed
                 through int 21h
note 1. Returns address of entry point for IPX and SPX.
     2. Parameters are listed under int 21.

Function  087h  APPEND
entry    AH      087h
         AL      00h      APPEND installation check
                 return   AH   0 if installed
                 01h      APPEND - unknown
                 02h      APPEND - version check
return   unknown

Function  088h  Microsoft Networks
entry    AH      088h
         AL      00h      network program installation check
                 return   AH   0 if installed
                          BX      installed component flags (test in this order!)
                             bits 2       messenger
                                  3       redirector
                                  6       server
                                  7       receiver
                                  other bits not used, do not test
                 01h      unknown
                 02h      unknown
                 03h      get current POST address
                          return   ES:BX    POST address
                 04h      set new POST address
                          ES:BX    new POST address
                 09h      network version check
```

```
Function  0AAh   VIDCLOCK.COM
entry     AH     0AAh
          AL     00h     installation check
return    AL     00h     not installed
                 0FFh    installed
note      VIDCLOCK.COM is a memory-resident clock by Thomas G. Hanlin III.

Function  0B0h   GRAFTABL.COM or DISPLAY.SYS
parameters unknown

Function  0BBh   Network Functions
entry     AH     0BBh
          AL     00h     net command installation check
                 01h, 02h unknown
                 03h     get server POST address
                 04h     get server POST address

Function  0D44Dh 4DOS Command Interpreter  (COMMAND.COM replacement)
entry     AX     0D44Dh  4DOS installation check
          BX     00h
return    If 4DOS is present in memory the following values will be returned:
          AX     44DDh
          BH     minor 4DOS version number
          BL     major 4DOS version number
                 (same format as DOS int 21h/fn 30)
          CX     4DOS PSP segment address
          DL     4DOS shell number (0 for the first shell, 1 for the second, etc.;
                 incremented each time a new copy of 4DOS is loaded over a root
                 copy, either in a different multitasker window or via nested
                 shells)
note 1.  If you issue this call with BX 0 you will invoke some other function of
         4DOS's low-memory server, and probably hang the system.
     2.  This function is available in swapping mode ONLY. Also note that this
         tells you if 4DOS is loaded in memory somewhere - but not whether it is
         the parent process of your program. For example if there is a root 4DOS
         shell and a secondary copy of COMMAND.COM this function will still work.
         However, you can determine if 4DOS is your parent process by comparing
         the value returned in the CX register with the PSP chain pointer at
         location 16 in your own PSP.

Function  0F7h   AUTOPARK.COM  (PD TSR hard disk parking utility)
entry     AH     0F7h
          AL     00h     installation check
                         return  AL      00h     not installed
                                         0FFh    installed
                 01h     set parking delay
                         BX:CX   32 bit count of 55ms timer ticks
note      AUTOPARK is a TSR HD parker by Alan D. Jones.

Function         Intel Communicating Applications Standard (CAS 1.01A)
entry     AH             (default; CAS multiplex number can be user-adjusted)
          AL     00h     Get Installed State
                         return  AL      00h     not installed
                                         01h     not installed, not OK to
                                                 install
                                         0FFh    installed
                         note    No errors are returned.
                 01h     Submit a Task
                         DS:DX   ptr to ASCIIZ path and name of Task Control File
                         return  AX      positive event handle or neg. error code
                         note    Files associated with a task must stay in
                                 existence until the task is complete or an error
                                 will result.
                 02h     Abort the Current Event
                         return  AX      event handle of aborted event or negative
                                         error code
                         note    Terminating an event is not instantaneous. It
                                 might take up to 30 seconds.
                 03h     reserved
                 04h     reserved
                 05h     Find First Entry in Queue
```

Interrupts 22h Through 86h

```
              CX       Status of the event you are seeking. This value
                       is compared with the field at offset 2 of the
                       Control File
                       0 - event has successfully completed
                       1 - event is waiting to be processed
                       2 - number has been dialed
                       3 - connection has been made (sending)
                       4 - connection has been made (receiving)
                       5 - event was aborted
                      -1 - chooses an event without regard to status
                       This value will probably be used most often
                       Other negative values match error codes in Control
                       File.
              DH       direction:
                       0 - Search forward chronologically (from the
                           first to the last occurring event)
                       1 - Search backward chronologically (from the
                           last to the first occurring event)
              DL       queue to search:
                       0 - Find first control file in Task Queue
                       1 - Find first control file in Receive Queue
                       2 - Find first control file in Log Queue
       return AX       0, if successful, or negative error code
              BX       event handle for this file
06h    Find Next Entry in Queue
              DL       queue to search:
                       0 - Find next control file in Task Queue
                       1 - Find next control file in Receive
                           Queue
                       2 - Find next control file in Log Queue
       return AX       0, if successful, or negative error code
              BX       event handle for this file
07h    Open a File
              BX       event handle
              CX       receive file number
                       0 - the Receive Control File
                       1 - first received file
                       2 - second received file
                       3 - third received file
                       n - nth received file
              DL       queue:
                       0 - open control file in Task Queue
                       1 - open control file in Receive Queue or the
                           received data
       file specified in the CX register.
                       2 - Open control file in Log Queue.
       return AX       0 if successful, or negative error code
              BX       DOS file handle for the requested file
08h    Delete a File
              BX       event handle
              CX       receive file number
                       0 - delete all files associated with a specific
                           Receive Control File (including the RCF)
                       1 - delete first received file associated with
                           the event handle
                       2 - delete the second received file associated
                           with the event handle.
                       n - delete the nth received file associated with
                           the event handle
              DL       queue:
                       0 - delete control file in Task Queue
                       1 - delete a file or files associated with an
                           event in the Receive Queue.
                       2 - delete control file in Log Queue. It is
                           strongly recommended that this function NOT
                           be used to delete individual Log Control
                           Files to maintain the integrity of the log.
       return AX       0 if successful, or negative error code
09h    Delete All Files (in a queue)
              DL       queue:
                       0 - delete all control files in the Task Queue
```

```
             1 - delete all control files in the Receive Queue
                 and all received files
             2 - delete all control files in the Log Queue
       return AX      0 if successful or negative error code
 0Ah   Get Event Date
       BX      event handle of event whose date you want to get
       DL      queue:
               0 - task queue
               1 - receive queue
               2 - log queue
       return AX      0 if successful or negative error code
              CX      year   (1980-2099)
              DH      month  (1-12)
              DL      day    (1-31)
 0Bh   Set Task Date
       BX      event handle
       CX      year   (1980-2099)
       DH      month  (1-12)
       DL      day    (1-31)
       return AX      0 if successful or negative error code
 0CH   Get Event Time
       BX      event handle
       DL      queue:
               0 - task queue
               1 - receive queue
               2 - log queue
       return AX      0 if successful or negative error code
              CH      hour    (0-23)
              CL      minutes (0-59)
              DH      seconds (0-59)
              DL      0
 0DH   Set Task Time
       BX      event handle
       CH      hour    (0-23)
       CL      minutes (0-59)
       DH      seconds (0-59)
       DL      unused
       return AX      0 if successful or negative error code
 0EH   Get External Data Block
       DS:DX points to a 256-byte EDB area
       return AX      0 if successful or negative error code
       note    EDB area is filled with the External Data Block
               block format: (values in decimal)
               Offset  Length   Description
                 0       1      CAS major version number
                 1       1      CAS minor version number
                 2      68      ASCIIZ path to directory containing
                                Resident Manager and CAS software.
                                The path must end with a backslash
                70      13      ASCIIZ name of current phonebook (the
                                CAS subdirectory is assumed)
                83      13      AZCIIZ name of current logo file (the
                                CAS subdirectory is assumed)
                96      32      ASCIIZ default sender name
               128      21      ASCIIZ CSID (CCITT fax device ID)
               149     107      Reserved
 0Fh   Get/Set Autoreceive State
       DL      function code:
               0 - get current autoreceive state
               1 - set current state to value in DH
       DH      # rings before answer or 0 to disable
       return AX      current state or negative error code
                      0 - Autoreceive disabled
                      positive # - # rings before hdw answers
 10h   Get Current Event Status
       DS:DX   pointer to a 444 byte status area
       return AX      0 if successful or negative error code
              BX      number of the current event (AX=0)
 11h   Get Queue Status
       DL      queue:
               0 - find status of Task Queue
```

Interrupts 22h Through 86h

```
                    1 - find status of Receive Queue
                    2 - find status of Log Queue
          return AX      # changes to queue since Resident Manager
                         started or negative error code If
                         changes exceeds 7FFFH, the count begins
                         again at 0.
                 BX      current # of Control Files in queue
                 CX      current # of received files
12h   Get Hardware Status
      DS:DX      pointer to a 128-byte status area
      return AX      0 if successful, negative if not
      DS:DX      pointer to filled 128-byte status area
13h   Run Diagnostics
      DL         Mode
                    0 - report progress of diagnostics
                    1 - start running diagnostics
      return     if DL=1, AX=0 or a negative error code.
                 if DL=0, AX=40h or positive number indicating
                         diagnostics passed. A negative value
                         indicates failure and containes the
                         error code
14h   Move Received File
      BX         event handle
      CX         receive file number
                 (must be nonzero to specify a received file)
                 1 - first received file
                 2 - second received file
                 3 - third received file
                 n - nth received file
      DS:DX      pointer to new ASCIIZ pathname and
                 filename. This file must not exist already
      return AX      0 if successful or negative error code
      note       The path to the new directory must exist. This
                 function cannot create directories.
15h   Submit a Single File to Send
      DS:DX      pointer to variable-length data area
      return AX      positive event handle or neg. error code
      note 1. variable-length data area format:
           Offset  Length    Description
                0    1       Transfer type:
                                0 - 200x200 dpi, facsimile mode
                                1 - 100x200 dpi, facsimile mode
                                2 - file transfer mode
                                3-127 - Reserved.
                1    1       Text size (if ASCII file, fax mode)
                                0 - 80-column
                                1 - 132-column
                                2-127 - reserved
                2    2       time to send, in DOS file time format
                4    2       date to send, in DOS file time format
                             note: Setting both the time and date
                                   fields to 0 schedules the file to be
                                   sent immediately
                6   32       ASCIIZ Destination Name  (To: field)
               38   80       ASCIIZ pathname of the file to send
              118   47       ASCIIZ phone number to call
              165   64       ASCIIZ application-specific tag field
              229    1       reserved; set to zero
              230    1       cover page flag:
                                0 - don't send cover page
                                1 - send cover page
                                2-127 - Reserved
              231   23       reserved; set to zero
              254  var       ASCIIZ cover text (if offset 230=1)
           2. The individual fields have the same meaning as in
              a Task Control File
           3. You must set all fields, except for the
              Application-Specific Tag field, before calling
              this function. However, you can set the
              Destination Name and Cover Text fields to an
              empty string 16h-80h Reserved by Intel for future
```

```
                        expansion
MSDOS 2Fh functions 01h (PRINT), 02h (ASSIGN), 10h (SHARE):
return   AX       Error
                  Codes      Description
                  01h        invalid function number
                  02h        file not found
                  03h        path not found
                  04h        too many open files
                  05h        access denied
                  06h        invalid handle
                  08h        queue full
                  09h        busy
                  0Ch        name too long
                  0Fh        invalid drive was specified
         CF       clear (0) if OK
                  set   (1) if error - error returned in AX
note 1. The multiplex numbers AH=0h through AH=7Fh are reserved for DOS.
        Applications should use multiplex numbers 80h through 0FFh.
     2. When in the chain for int 2Fh, if your code calls DOS or if you execute
        with interrupts enabled, your code must be reentrant/recursive.
     3. Important! In versions of DOS prior to 3.0, the int 2Fh vector was
        initialized to zero rather than being pointed into the DOS service area.
        You must initialize this vector manually under DOS 2.x.
```

Miscellaneous Interrupts - in numeric order

Interrupt 30h FAR jump instruction for CP/M-style calls
note The CALL 5 entry point does a FAR jump to here (not a vector!)

Interrupt 31h Unknown

Interrupt 32h Unknown

Interrupt 33h Used by Microsoft Mouse Driver Function Calls
See Chapter 14.

Interrupt 3Fh Overlay Manager Interrupt (Microsoft LINK.EXE)
Default overlay interrupt; may be changed with LINK command line switch.

Interrupt 40h Hard Disk BIOS
Pointer to disk BIOS entry when a hard disk controller is installed. The BIOS routines use int 30h to revector the diskette handler (original int 13h) here so int 40 may be used for hard disk control.

Interrupt 41h Hard Disk Parameters
Pointer to first Hard Disk Parameter Block, normally located in the controller card's ROM. This table may be copied to RAM and changed, and this pointer revectored to the new table.

```
note 1. XT, AT,XT/2, XT/286, PS/2 except ESDI disks
     2. format of parameter table is:
          word      cylinders
          byte      heads
          word      starting reduced write current cylinder (XT only, 0 for others)
          word      starting write pre-comp cylinder
          byte      maximum ECC burst length
          byte      control byte
             bits 0-2     drive option (XT only, 0 for others)
                  3       set if more than 8 heads
                  4       always 0
                  5       set if manufacturer's defect map on max cylinder+1
                  6       disable ECC retries
```

```
                7         disable access retries
        byte    standard timeout (XT only, 0 for others)
        byte    formatting timeout (XT only, 0 for others)
        byte    timeout for checking drive (XT only, 0 for others)
        word    landing zone    (AT, PS/2)
        byte    sectors/track   (AT, PS/2)
        byte    0   (zeroes)
    3. normally vectored to ROM table when system is initialized.
```

Interrupt 42h Pointer to screen BIOS entry
EGA, VGA, PS/2. Relocated (by EGA, etc.) video handler (original int 10h). Revectors int 10 calls to EGA BIOS. Also used by Zenith Z-100

Interrupt 43h Pointer to EGA graphics character table
The POST initializes this vector pointing to the default table located in the EGA ROM BIOS. (PC-2 and up). Not initialized if EGA not present. This vector was referred to (mistakenly) as the Video Parameters table in the original EGA BIOS listings.

Interrupt 44h Pointer to graphics character table
(0:0110h) This table contains the dot patterns for the first 128 characters in video modes 4,5, and 6, and all 256 characters in all additional graphics modes. Not initialized if EGA not present.

1. EGA/VGA/CONV/PS - EGA/PCjr fonts, characters 00h to 7Fh.
2. Novell NetWare - High-Level Language API.
3. This interrupt is not used by some EGA cards.
4. Also used by Zenith Z-100.

Interrupt 45h Reserved by IBM (not initialized)
also used by Zenith Z-100

Interrupt 46h Pointer to second hard disk parameter block
AT, XT/286, PS/2 (see int 41h) (except ESDI hard disks) (not initialized unless specific user software calls for it)

Interrupt 47h Reserved by IBM (not initialized)

Interrupt 48h Cordless Keyboard Translation
(0:0120h) This vector points to code to translate the cordless keyboard scancodes into normal 83-key values. The translated scancodes are then passed to int 9. (not initialized on PC or AT) (PCjr, XT [never delivered])

Interrupt 49h Non-keyboard Scan Code Translation Table Address (PCjr)
(0:0124h) This interrupt is used for operation of non-keyboard devices on the PCjr, such as the Keystronic Numeric Keypad. This interrupt has the address of a table used to translate non-keyboard scancodes (greater than 85 excepting 255). This interrupt can be revectored by a user application. IBM recommends that the default table be stored at the beginning of an application that required revectoring this interrupt, and that the default table be restored when the application terminates. (not initialized on PC or AT)

The PCjr BIOS can interpret scancodes other than those generated by the keyboard to allow for expansion. The keyboard generates scancodes from 01h to 055h, including 0FFh. Any scancodes above 55h (56h through 7Eh for make codes and 0D6h through 0FEh for break codes) are processed in the following manner:

1. if the incoming make code falls within the range of the translate table whose address is pointed to by int 49h, it is translated into the corresponding scancode. Any incoming break

124   *The Programmer's Technical Reference*

   codes above 0D5h are ignored.
2. if the new translated scancode is less than 56h, it is processed by the BIOS as a keyboard scancode and the same data is placed in the BIOS keyboard buffer.
3. if the translated scancode is higher than 55h or the incoming scancode is outside the range of the translate table, 40h is added creating a new extended scancode. The extended scancode is placed in the BIOS keyboard buffer with the character code of 00h (NUL). This utilitizes the range of 96h through 0BEh for scancodes 56h through 7Eh.

The default translate-table maps scancodes 56h through 6Ah to existing keyboard values. Codes 6Bh theough 0BEh are mapped (by adding 40h) to extended codes 0ABh through 0FEh since they are outside the range of the default translate table.

The format of the translate table is:
```
        0       length - the number of nonkeyboard scancodes that are
                mapped within the table (from 1 to n)
        1 to n  word  high byte 00h (NUL) byte scancode with low order
                byte representing the scancode mapped values relative to
                their input values within the range of 56h through 7Eh
```

With this layout, all keyboard scancodes can be intercepted through int 9h and and non-keyboard scancodes can be intercepted through int 48h.

Interrupt 4Ah Real-Time Clock Alarm (Convertible, PS/2)
(not initialized on PC or AT) Invoked by BIOS when real-time clock alarm occurs.

Interrupts 4Bh-4DhReserved by IBM (not initialized)

Interrupt 4Eh Reserved by IBM (not initialized)
Used instead of int 13h for disk I/O on TI Professional PC

Interrupt 4Fh Reserved by IBM (not initialized)

Interrupt 50-57 IRQ0-IRQ7 Relocation
IRQ0-IRQ7 relocated by DesQview (normally not initialized)
IRQ0-IRQ7 relocated by IBM 3278 Emulation Control Program

Interrupt 58h Reserved by IBM (not initialized)

Interrupt 59h Reserved by IBM (not initialized)
GSS Computer Graphics Interface (GSS*CGI)
```
entry   DS:DX   Pointer to block of 5 array pointers
return  CF      0
        AX      return code
        CF      1
        AX      error code
note 1. Int 59h is the means by which GSS*CGI language bindings communicate with
        GSS*CGI device drivers and the GSS*CGI device driver controller.
     2. Also used by the IBM Graphic Development Toolkit
```

Interrupt 5Ah Reserved by IBM (not initialized)
IBM Cluster Adapter BIOS entry address

Interrupt 5Bh Reserved by IBM (not initialized)

Interrupt 5Ah Cluster Adapter BIOS entry address
(normally not initialized)

Interrupt 5Bh Reserved by IBM (not initialized)
Used by cluster adapter?

Interrupt 5Ch NETBIOS interface entry port, TOPS
See Chapter 13

Interrupts 5Dh -5Fh Reserved by IBM (not initialized)

Interrupt 60h-67h User Program Interrupts
(available for general use) Various major programs make standardized use of this group of interrupts. Details of common use follows:

Interrupt 60h 10-Net Network
See Chapter 13.

Interrupt 60h FTP Driver - PC/TCP Packet Driver Specification
See Chapter 13.

Interrupt 67h Used by Lotus-Intel-Microsoft Expanded Memory Specification
and Ashton-Tate/Quadram/AST Enhanced Expanded Memory Specification. See Chapter 10.

Interrupt 68h Not Used (not initialized)
APPC/PC Network Interface. See Chapter 13.

Interrupts 69h -6Bh Not Used (not initialized)

Interrupt 6Ch System Resume Vector (Convertible)
(not initialized on PC) DOS 3.2 Realtime Clock update

Interrupt 6Dh Not Used (not initialized)
Paradise VGA - internal

Interrupt 6Eh Not Used (not initialized)

Interrupt 6Fh 10-Net API
See Chapter 13.

Interrupt 70h IRQ 8, Real Time Clock Interrupt (AT, XT/286, PS/2)

Interrupt 71h IRQ 9, Redirected to IRQ 8 (AT, XT/286, PS/2)
LAN Adapter 1 (rerouted to int 0Ah [IRQ2] by BIOS)

Interrupt 72h IRQ 10 (AT, XT/286, PS/2) Reserved

Interrupt 73h IRQ 11 (AT, XT/286, PS/2) Reserved

Interrupt 74h IRQ 12 Mouse Interrupt (PS/2)

Interrupt 75h IRQ 13, Coprocessor Error (AT)
BIOS Redirects NDP errors to int 2 (NMI).

Interrupt 76h IRQ 14, Hard Disk Controller (AT, XT/286, PS/2)

Interrupt 77h IRQ 15 (AT, XT/286, PS/2) Reserved

Interrupts 78h-79h Not Used

Interrupt 7Ah Reserved
Novell NetWare - Low-Level API
AutoCAD Device Interface

Interrupt 7Bh-7Eh Not Used by IBM

Interrupt 7Ch REXX-PC API
IBM REXX-PC macro language

```
entry    AX      0000h    Initialize
         DS:SI   pointer to null terminated name of program to be executed
         EB:BX   pointer to null terminated argument string to be passed to the
                 program
         DX:DI   pointer to an environment control block in the format:
                 dword   offset in segment to signature string
                         The segment is that contained in DX and the signature is
                         the uppercase ASCIIZ string 'REXX'.
                 dword   offset in DX to environment name ASCIIZ string
                         note: The environment name will be truncated if longer
                         than 32 characters.
                 dword   offset in DX to the file extension ASCIIZ string
                 dword   path search - word value of 0 or non-zero.
                         This controls the searching of the path for commands that
                         might be REXX programs. 0 means no search made, n-zero
                         means search first.
                 dword   x'AAAA'
                         This is a signature that allows REXXPC88 to call your own
                         defined routine when a command expression needs to be
                         processed.
                 DD      Segment:offset (standard INTEL format) of environment
                         work buffer, the first double word of the buffer MUST be
                         the entry point address of the environment service
                         routine to be called. The rest of the buffer may be used
                         in any way you choose and will NOT be examined or
                         modified by REXXPC88.
return   none
note  1. The only way to tell if the program exists and can be executed is by
         examining a value returned by the program in the next call described
         below. If the program returns an end of program indication and a string
         was expected instead, it means that the program was not found or could
         not be executed for some reason.
      2. All registers except SS and SP are destroyed. The caller must save any
         other registers of interest.
```

Function 01h Interpret REXX Command
This call tells REXXPC88 to interpret the REXXPC88 program until a value is produced.
```
entry    AX      0001h
return   DS:DX   points to a result string, terminated by a CR + LF + NULL. The
                 final result string (which marks the end of the program)
                 consists of nothing but EOF + NULL. REXXPC88 will continue to
                 return this 'end of program' string until reinitialized via an
                 AX=01h call as described above.
note     All registers except SS and SP are destroyed. The caller must save any
         other registers of interest.
```

Function 02h Termination
This call allows resident REXXPC88 extensions to terminate execution of a REXXPC88 program, typically after detecting an error.
```
entry    AX      0002h
         DS:SI   points to null terminated string to be displayed as an error
                 message before terminating the REXXPC88 program.
return   none
note     Terminates the REXXPC88 program and returns control to DOS.
```

Function 03h Load
This call tells REXXPC88 to look up a program variable and return its current value (if any).
```
entry    AX      0003h
         DS:SI   points to null terminated name of REXXPC88 program variable.
         DS:DX   points to the null terminated string value of the program
                 variable. DX is zero if the program variable is currently
                 undefined. This string is in REXXPC88's data area and must be
                 treated as read-only.
```

Interrupts 22h Through 86h

return none
note 1. All registers except SS and SP are destroyed. The caller must save any other registers of interest.

Function 04h Store
    This call tells REXXPC88 to store a null terminated string as the value of a program variable.
entry AX   0004h
       DS:SI   points to null terminated name of REXXPC88 program variable
       ES:BX   points to null terminated string to be assigned to the variable
return none
note 1. The string is copied into REXXPC88's data dictionary. If there is insufficient storage to store the string, REXXPC88 terminates execution of the program with an error message and returns to DOS.
    2. Registers: all registers except SS and SP are destroyed. The caller must save any other registers of interest.

Function 05h User-Written Extensions
entry AX   0005h
       SS:BP   points to a C stack frame containing a two-byte pointer to the null terminated function name, a two-byte integer specifying the number of arguments, and a two-byte pointer to an array of pointers (each two bytes) to the arguments (each argument is a null terminated string).
return DS:SI   must point to a null terminated result string. A pointer of NIL (DS = 0, SI = 0) is reserved by REXXPC88 and indicates that 'no REXXPC88 extensions answered the function'.
note 1. Registers: all registers except SS, SP, and BP are available for use.
    2. Stack: Since the amount of REXXPC88 stack space remaining for growth can't be ascertained by the user extension program, the user may wish to switch to a local stack if he requires more than about 128 bytes of stack growth.

Function 06h Queue
    This call tells REXXPC88 to place data on the data or external interrupt queue either FIFO or LIFO.
entry AX   06h
       BH   00h   Internal data queue accessible via PULL and PARSE PULL
               01h   External interrupt queue accessible via LINEIN(EXQUE)
       BL   00h   Queue data FIFO on selected queue
               01h   Queue data LIFO on selected queue
       DS:SI   points to null terminated string to be queued.
return AX   0000h Message queued successfully.
              0001h No REXXPC88 program running at current time. Message not queued.
              0002h Not enough storage available for message. Message not queued.
              0003h Either BH (queue number) or BL (FIFO/LIFO flag) out of range. Message not queued.
note 1. For the Internal data queue a string may not exceed 127 characters.
    2. For the External int. queue a string may not exceed available storage.
    3. Registers: all registers except SS and SP are destroyed. The caller must save any other registers of interest.

Function 07h Check for Loaded Extension
    This call provides a way for a REXXPC88 extension to find out if a copy is already loaded, and to exchange information with a resident version.
entry AX   0007h
       SS:BP   points to a C stack frame containing a two-byte pointer to the null terminated name of the REXXPC88 extension.
return If the extension is already loaded, then DS:SI points to an ASCIIZ string '1', and other registers are used as desired by the extension to communicate with its non-resident copy. (Generally, this involves pointing ES:BX to the resident portion's entry point). If the extension is not yet resident, then DS:SI points to an ASCIIZ '0'.
note   Registers: all registers except SS, SP and BP are available for use.

Function 08h Reserved
    This call is reserved for communication between REXXSYS.SYS and REXXIBMR.
entry AX   0008h
return none

```
entry    AX      0008h
return   none
Function 09h  Check for REXX Installed
         This call provides external applications a way to determine if REXXIBMR
         is installed.
entry    AX      09h
return   AX      0FFFFh  REXXIBMR is not installed
         AX      0AAAAh  REXXIBMR is installed
note     It is assumed that your application will inspect the value of the 7Ch
         interrupt vector prior to issuing this interrupt. If the vector is
         0000:0000 then REXXIBMR is not installed and this function will cause
         the system to crash.

Function 0Ah  Uninstall resident version of REXX
         This call is used to uninstall a resident version
entry    AX      000Ah
         BX      0AAAAh
return   AX      0000h   Resident version uninstalled
                 0001h   Resident version cannot uninstall, as one interrupt
                         vector has been modified by some other program in a non-
                         conforming manner.
                 0FFFFh  The installed resident version does NOT support
                         the uninstall request code (i.e., it is pre 0.55 level).
```

Interrupt 7Fh IBM 8514/A Graphics Adapter API
59 API functions available, parameters unknown.

1. Used by second copy of COMMAND set with SHELL=
2. Not used by COMMAND /C at DOS prompt

Interrupt 80h-85h Reserved by BASIC
Note   Interrupts 80h through 0ECh are apparently unused and not initialized in most clone systems.

Interrupt 86h Int 18 when relocated by NETBIOS

Interrupt 86h-0F0h Used by BASIC when BASIC interpreter is running

Interrupt 0E0h Digital Research CP/M-86 function calls

Interrupt 0E4h Logitech Modula-2 v2.0 Monitor Entry
```
entry    AX      05h     monitor entry
                 06h     monitor exit
         BX      priority
return   unknown
```

Interrupt 0EFh GEM interface (Digital Research)
```
entry    CX      0473h
         DS:DX   pointer to GEM parameter block
note     no other parameters are known
```

Interrupt 0F0h unknown
1. Used by secondary copy of COMMAND when SHELL= set
2. Not used by COMMAND /C at DOS prompt
3. Used by BASIC while in interpreter

Interrupts 0F1h-0FFh (absolute addresses 3C4h-3FFh)
Location of Interprocess Communications Area

Interrupt 0F8h Set Shell Interrupt (OEM)
Set OEM handler for int 21h calls from 0F9h through 0FFh
```
entry    AH      0F8h
         DS:DX   pointer to handler for Functions 0F9h thru 0FFh
note 1.  To reset these calls, pass DS and DX with 0FFFFh. DOS is set up to allow
         ONE handler for all 7 of these calls. Any call to these handlers will
```

```
         result in the carry bit being set and AX will contain 1 if they are not
         initialized. The handling routine is passed all registers just as the
         user set them. The OEM handler routine should be exited through an IRET.
    2.   10 ms interval timer (Tandy?)
```

Interrupt 0F9h Reserved

First of 8 SHELL service codes, reserved for OEM shell (WINDOW); use like HP Vectra user interface?

Interrupt 0FAh USART ready (RS-232C)

Interrupt 0FBh USART RS ready (keyboard)

Interrupt 0FCh Unknown

Interrupt 0FDh reserved for user interrupt

Interrupt 0FEh reserved by IBM

Interrupt 0FFh reserved by IBM

6

DOS Control Blocks and Work Areas

DOS Address Space

Contrary to popular belief, DOS is not limited to 640k of work space. This constraint is enforced by the mapping of ROM and video RAM into the default 1 megabyte CPU address space. Some MSDOS compatible machines, such as the Sanyo 55x series, can have as much as 768k of contiguous DOS workspace with the appropriate option boards. Since DOS has no real memory management, it cannot deal with a fragmented workspace. Fragmented RAM (such as RAM mapped into the option ROM address space) can be dealt with as a RAMdisk or other storage area by using a device driver or other software.

The 80386 CPU and appropriate control software can create a DOS workspace of more than one megabyte. Certain add-on boards can also add more than a megabyte of workspace, but only for specially written software. Since these are all proprietary schemes, little information is available at present.

Storage Blocks

A storage block is used by DOS to record the amount and location of allocated memory within the machine's address space.

A storage block, a Program Segment Prefix, and an environment area are built by DOS for each program currently resident in the address space. The storage block is used by DOS to record the address range of memory allocated to a program. It is used by DOS to find the next available area to load a program and to determine if there is enough memory to run that porogram. When a memory area is in use, it is said to be allocated. Then the program ends, or releases memory, it is said to be deallocated.

A storage block contains a pointer to the Program Segment Prefix associated with each program. This control block is constructed by IBMDOS for the purpose of providing standardized areas for DOS/program communication. Within the PSP are areas which are used to save interrupt vectors, pass parameters to the program, record disk directory information, and to buffer disk reads and writes. This control block is 100h bytes in length and is followed by the program module loaded by DOS.

The PSP contains a pointer to the environment area for that program. This area contains a copy of the current DOS SET, PROMPT, COMSPEC, and PATH values as well as any user-set variables. The program may examine and modify this information as desired.

Each storage block is 10h bytes long, although only 5 bytes are currently used by DOS. The first byte contains 4Dh (a capital M) to indicate that it contains a pointer to the next storage block. A 5Ah (a capital Z) in the first byte of a storage block indicatres there are no more storage blocks following this one (it is the end of the chain). The identifier byte is followed by a 2 byte segment number for the associated PSP for that program. The next 2 bytes contain the number of segments what are allocated to the program. If this is not the last storage block, then another storage block follows the allocated memory area.

When the storage block contains zero for the number of allocated segments, then no storage is allocated to this block and the next storage block immediately follows this one. This can happen when memory is allocated and then deallocated repeatedly.

IBMDOS constructs a storage block and PSP before loading the command interpreter (default is COMMAND.COM).

If the copy of COMMAND.COM is a secondary copy, it will lack an environment address at PSP+2Ch.

Disk Transfer Area (DTA)

DOS uses an area in memory to contain the data for all file reads and writes that are performed with FCB function calls. This are is known as the disk transfer area. This disk transfer area (DTA) is sometimes called a buffer. It can be located anywhere in the data area of your application program and should be set by your program.

Only one DTA can be in effect at a time, so your program must tell DOS what memory location to use before using any disk read or write functions. Use function call 1Ah (Set Disk Transfer Address) to set the disk transfer address. Use function call 2Fh (Get Disk Transfer Address) to get the disk transfer address. Once set, DOS continues to use that area for all disk operations until another function call 1Ah is issued to define a new DTA. When a program is given control by COMMAND.COM, a default DTA large enough to hold 128 bytes is established at 80h into the program's Program Segment Prefix.

For file reads and writes that are performed with the extended function calls, there is no need to set a DTA address. Instead, specify a buffer address when you issue the read or write call.

Program Segment Prefix

When DOS loads a program, it first sets aside a section of memory for the program called the program segment, or code segment. Then it constructs a control block called the program segment prefix, or PSP, in the first 256 (100h) bytes. Usually, the program is loaded directly after the PSP at 100h.

The PSP contains various information used by DOS to help run the program. The PSP is always located at offset 0 within the code segment. When a program recieves control certain registers are set to point to the PSP. For a COM file, all registers are set to point to the beginning of the PSP and the program begins at 100h. For the more complex EXE file structures, only DS and ES registers are set to point to the PSP. The linker determines the settings for the CS, IP, SS, and SP registers and may set the starting location in CS:IP to a location other than 100h.

IBMBIO provides an IRET instruction at absolute address 847h for use as a dummy routine for interrupts that are not used by DOS. This lets the interruptsdo nothing until their vectors are re-routed to their appropriate handlers.

The PSP (with offsets in hexadecimal) is formatted as follows:
(* = undocumented)

PROGRAM SEGMENT PREFIX

```
offset  size       C O N T E N T S
00h     2 bytes    int 20h
02h     2 bytes    segment address, end of allocation block
04h     1 byte     reserved, normally 0
05h     5 bytes    FAR call to MSDOS function dispatcher    (int 21h)
0Ah     4 bytes    previous termination handler interrupt vector (int 22h)
0Eh     4 bytes    previous contents of ctrl-C interrupt vector (int 23h)
12h     4 bytes    prev. critical error handler interrupt vector (int 24h)
16h     22 bytes   reserved for DOS
 *      2 bytes    (16) parent process' PSP
 *      20 bytes   (18) 'handle table ' used for redirection of files
2Ch     2 bytes    segment address of the program's environment block
2Eh     34 bytes   reserved, DOS work area
 *      4 bytes    (2Eh) stores the calling process's stack pointer when switching
                        to DOS's internal stack.
 *                 (32h) DOS 3.x max open files
 *      2 bytes    (3Ah) size of handle table  |these functions are in here
 *      4 bytes    3Ch) handle table address   |but reported addresses vary
50h     3 bytes    int 21h, RETF instruction
53h     2 bytes    reserved - unused?
55h     7 bytes    reserved, or FCB#1 extension
5Ch     16 bytes   default unopened File Control Block #1
6Ch     16 bytes   default unopened FCB #2 (overlaid if FCB #1 opened)
80h     1 byte     parameter length (number of chars entered after filename)
81h     ...        parameters
0FFh    128 bytes  command tail and default Disk Transfer Area (DTA)
```

1. The first segment of available memory is in segment (paragraph) form. For example, 1000h would respresent 64k.

2. Offset 2Ch contains the segment address of the environment.

3. Programs must not alter any part of the PSP below offset 5Ch.

PSP (comments)

offset 00h   contains hex bytes 'CD 20', the int 20h opcode. A program can end by making a jump to this location when the CS points to the PSP. For normal cases, int 21h/fn4Ch should be used.

offset 02h   contains the segment-paragraph address of the end of memory as reported by DOS. (which may not be the same as the real end of RAM). Multiply this number by 10h or 16 to get the amount of memory available. ex. 1000h would be 64k.

DOS Control Blocks and Work Areas

offset 04h 'reserved or used by DOS' according to Microsoft

offset 05h contains a long call to the DOS function dispatcher. Programs may jump to this address instead of calling int 21h if they wish. Used by BASIC and other CPM object-code translated programs. It is slower than standard int 21h.

offset 0Ah, 0Eh, 12h
vectors (IP, CS)

offset 16h PSP:16h is the segment address of the invoking program's PSP, which * will most often be COMMAND.COM but perhaps may be a secondary non-permanent COMMAND or a multitasking shell, etc. At any rate, the resident shell version of COMMAND.COM has PSP:16h = PSP, which indicates 'don't look any lower in memory' for the command interpreter. To find the beginning of the allocation chain, look backwards through the PSP link addresses until the link address is equal to the PSP segment address that it resides in. This should be COMMAND.COM. To find COMMAND.COM's environment, look at the word stored at offset 0BD3h (PC-DOS 3.1 only). This is a segment address, so look there at offset 0.

18h handle alias table (networking). Also you can make PRN go to CON, * CON go to PRN, ERR go to PRN, etc. 0FFh = available.

offset 2Ch is the segment:offset address of the environment for the program using this particular PSP. This pointer does not point to COMMAND.COM's environment unless it is a second copy of COMMAND.

offset 2Eh the DWORD at PSP+2Eh is used by DOS to store the calling process's * stack pointer when switching to DOS's own private stack - at the end of a DOS function call, SS:SP is restored from this address.

offset 32h, 34h
* table of number of file handles (up to 64k of handles!)

offset 40h 2 byte field points to the segment address of COMMAND.COM's PSP in * 'weird' EXE files produced by Digital Research RASMPC/LINKPC. EXE files created with these tools can cause all sorts of problems with standard MSDOS debugging tools.

offset 50h contains a long call to the DOS int 21 function dispatcher.

offset 5Ch, 65h, 6Ch
contain FCB information for use with FCB function calls. The first FCB may overlay the second if it is an extended call; your program should revector these areas to a safe place if you intend to use them.

offset 5Ch 16 bytes first command-line argument (formatted as uppercase 11 character filename)

offset 6Ch 16 bytes second command-line argument (formatted as uppercase 11 character filename)

offset 7Ch-7Fh
> 'reserved or used by DOS'

offset 80h   1 byte number of bytes in command line argument

offset 80h, 81h   *81h = first character after file name.*
> contain the length and value of parameters passed on the command line.

offset 81h   97 bytes unformatted command line and/or default DTA

offset 0FFh contains the DTA

The PSP is created by DOS for all programs and contains most of the information you need to know about a program running. You can change the environment for the current process, however, but for the parent process, DOS in this case, you need to literally backtrack to DOS or COMMAND.COM's PSP. In order to get there you must look at the current PSP. At offset 16h of the current PSP segment there is a 2 byte segment address to the parent or previous process PSP. From there you can manipulate the enviroment by looking at offset 2Ch.

Try this under debug and explore the addresses located at these offsets;

```
offset  length          description
 16h      2      segment address of parent process PSP
 2Ch      2      segment address of environment block.
```

Remember under debug you will have to backtrack two times.

```
Programs      Parent
command.com   none
debug.com     command.com
program       debug.com
```

Memory Control Blocks

DOS keeps track of allocated and available memory blocks, and provides four function calls for application programs to communicate their memory needs to DOS. These calls are:

```
48h --- allocate memory                  (MALLOC)
49h --- free allocated memory
4Ah --- modify allocated memory blocks   (SETBLOCK)
4Bh --- load or execute program          (EXEC)
```

DOS manages memory as follows:

DOS builds a control block for each block of memory, whether free or allocated. For example, if a program issues an 'allocate' (48h), DOS locates a block of free memory that satisfies the request, and then 'carves' the requested memory out of that block. The requesting program is passed the location of the first byte of the block that was allocated for it - a memory management control block, describing the allocated block, has been built for the allocated block and a second memory management control block describes the amount of space left in the original free block of memory. When you do a SETBLOCK to shrink an allocated block, DOS builds a memory management control block for the area being freed and adds it to the chain of control blocks. Thus, any program that changed memory that is not allocated to it stands a chance of destroying a DOS memory management control block. This causes unpredictable results that don't show up until an activity is performed where DOS uses its chain of control blocks. The normal result is a memory allocation error, which means a system reset will be required.

When a program (command or application program) is to be loaded, DOS uses the EXEC function call 4Bh to perform the loading. This is the same function call that is available to applications programs for loading other programs. This function call has two options:

Function 00h,   to load and execute a program (this is what the command processor uses to load and execute external commands)

Function 03h,   to load an overlay (program) without executing it.

Although both functions perform their loading in the same way (relocation is performed for EXE files) their handling of memory management is different.

FUNCTION 0
For function 0 to load and execute a program, EXEC first allocates the largest available block of memory (the new program's PSP will be at offset 0 in that block). Then EXEC loads the program. Thus, in most cases, the new program owns all the memory from its PSP to the end of memory, including memory occupied by the transient parent of COMMAND.COM. If the program were to issue its own EXEC function call to load and execute another program, the request would fail because no available memory exists to load the new program into.

Note For EXE programs, the amount of memory allocated is the size of the program's memory image plus the value in the MAX_ALLOC field of the file's header (offset 0Ch, if that much memory is available. If not, EXEC allocates the size of the program's memory image plus the value in the MIN_ALLOC field in the header (offset 0Ah). These fields are set by the Linker).

A well-behaved program uses the SETBLOCK function call when it receives control, to shrink its allocated memory block down to the size it really needs. A COM program should remember to set up its own stack before doing the SETBLOCK, since it is likely that the default stack supplied by DOS lies in the area of memory being used. This frees unneeded memory, which can be used for loading other programs.

If the program requires additional memory during processing, it can obtain the memory using the allocate function call and later free it using the free memory function call.

When a program is loaded using EXEC function call 00h exits, its initial allocation block (the block beginning with its PSP) is automatically freed before the calling program regains control. It is the responsibility of all programs to free any memory they allocate before exiting to the calling program.

FUNCTION 3
For function 3, to load an overlay, no PSP is built and EXEC assumes the calling program has already allocated memory to load the new program into - it will NOT allocate memory for it. Thus the calling program should either allow for the loading of overlays when it determines the amount of memory to keep when issuing the SETBLOCK call, or should initially free as much memory as possible. The calling program should then allocate a block (based on the size of the program to be loaded) to hold the program that will be loaded using the 'load overlay' call. Note that 'load overlay' does not check to see if the calling program actually owns the memory block it has been instructed to load into - it assumes the calling program has followed the rules. If the calling program does not own the memory into which the overlay is being loaded, there is a chance the program being loaded will overlay one of the control blocks that DOS uses to keep

track of memory blocks.

Programs loaded using function 3 should not issue any SETBLOCK calls since they don't own the memory they are operating in. (This memory is owned by the calling program.)

Because programs loaded using function 3 are given control directly by (and return contrrol directly to) the calling program, no memory is automatically freed when the called program exits. It is up to the calling program to determine the disposition of the memory that had been occupied by the exiting program. Note that if the exiting program had itself allocated any memory, it is responsible for freeing that memory before exiting.

Memory control blocks, sometimes called 'arena headers' after their UNIX counterpart, are 16 bytes long. Only the first 5 bytes are used. 16 bytes areused for the memory control block, which always starts at a paragraph boundary. When DOS call 48h is made to allocate 'x' many paragraphs of memory, the amount used up is actually one more than the figure in the BX register to provide space for the associated memory control block. The location of the memory control block is at the paragraph immediately before the segment value returned in AX by the DOS int 21h/fn 48h call i.e. ((AX-1):0).

MEMORY CONTROL BLOCK

```
Offset    Size       Function
  0       1 byte     ASCII M or Z
  1-2     2 bytes    PSP segment address of program owning this block of memory
  3-4     2 bytes    Size of next MCB in 16-byte paragraphs
  5-F     11 bytes   unused
```

byte 1   will always have the value of 4Dh or 5Ah. The value 5Ah (Z) indicates the block is the last in a chain, all memory above it is unused. 4Dh (M) means that the block is intermediate in a chain, the memory above it belongs to the next program or to DOS.

bytes 2,3   hold the PSP segment address of the program that owns the corresponding block of memory. A value of 0 means the block is free to be claimed, any other value represents a segment address.

bytes 3, 4   indicate the size in paragraphs of the memory block. If you know the address of the first block, you can find the next block by adding the length of the memory block plus 1 to the segment address of the control block. Finding the first block can be difficult, as this varies according to the DOS version and the configuration.

The remaining 11 bytes are not currently used by DOS, and may contain 'trash' characters left in memory from previous applications.

If DOS determines that the allocation chain of memory control blocks has been corrupted, it will halt the system and display the message 'Memory Allocation Error', and the system will halt, requiring a reboot.

Each memory block consists of a signature byte (4Dh or 5Ah) then a word which is the PSP value of the owner of the block (which allocated it), followed by a word which is the size in paragraphs of the block. The last block has a signature of 5Ah. All others have 4Dh. If the owner is 0000 then the block is free.

Once a memory control block has been created it should only be manipulated with the appropriate DOS function calls. Accidentally writing over any of the first 5 bytes of a memory control block can cause a memory allocation error and cause the system to lock up. If the first byte is overwritten with something other than an 'M' or a 'Z' then DOS will complain with an error return code of 7 signifying 'Memory Control Blocks destroyed'. However, should you change the ownership or block size bytes, you've had it.

When a .COM program is first loaded by DOS and given control, the memory control block immediately preceding the Program Segment Prefix contains the following data:

```
ID    = 'Z'
Owner = segment address of PSP (= CS register of .COM program)
Size  = number of available paragraphs in DOS memory pool
```

An .EXE file will have the following data in the memory control block for the program (just prior to the PSP):

```
ID    = 'M'
Owner = segment address of PSP (= DS register of program)
Size  = the number of paragraphs allocated to the program according to
        the information in the .EXE program header
```

In the case of an .EXE program file the amount of memory allocated depends on the contents of the program header which informs the DOS loader how much to allocate for each of the segments in the program. With an .EXE program file there will always be a 'Z' memory control block created in memory immediately after the end of the space allocated to the program itself.

One important fact to remember about DOS memory allocation is that blocks of RAM allocated by different calls to DOS function 48H will NOT be contiguous. At the very best, they will be separated by the 16 bytes of the memory control block, and at worst they could be anywhere in RAM that DOS manages to find a existing memory control block of sufficient size to accomodate the memory request.

DOS treats the memory control blocks as a kind of linked list (term used loosely). It uses the earlier MCBs to find the later ones by calculating the location of the next one from the size of the prior one. As such, erasing any of the MCB data in the chain of MCBs will upset DOS severely, as each call for a new memory allocation causes DOS to scan the whole chain of MCBs looking for a free one that is large enough to fulfill the request.

A separate MCB is created for the DOS environment strings at each program load, so there will be many copies of the environment strewn through memory when you have a lot of memory resident programs loaded. The memory control blocks for the DOS environment strings are not returned to the DOS memory pool if the program goes resident, as DOS will need to copy this enviroment for the next program loaded.

DOS Program Segment

When you enter an external command or call a program through the EXEC function call, DOS determines the lowest available address space to use as the start of available memory for the program being started. This area is called the Program Segment.

At offset 0 within the program segment, DOS builds the Program Segment Prefix control block. EXEC loads the program after the Program Segment Prefix (at offset 100h) and gives it control.

The program returns from EXEC by a jump to offset 0 in the Program Segment Prefix, by issuing an int 20h, or by issuing an int 21h with register AH=00h or 4Ch, or by calling location 50h in the PSP with AH=00h or 4Ch.

It is the responsibility of all programs to ensure that the CS register contains the segment address of the Program Segment Prefix when terminating by any of these methods except call 4Ch.

All of these methods result in returning to the program that issued the EXEC. During this returning process, interrupt vectors 22h, 23h, and 24h (Terminate, Ctrl-Break, and Critical Error Exit addresses) are restored from the values saved in the PSP of the terminating program. Control is then given to the terminate address.

When a program receives control, the following conditions are in effect:

For all programs:

1. The segment address of the passed environment is contained at offset 2Ch in the Program Segment Prefix.
2. The environment is a series of ASCII strings totalling less than 32k bytes in the form: 'NAME=value' The default environment is 160 bytes. Each string is a maximum of 127 bytes terminated by a byte of zeroes for a total of 128 bytes, and the entire set of strings is terminated by another byte of zeroes. Following the byte of zeroes that terminates the set of environment string is a set of initial arguments passed to a program that contains a word count followed by an ASCIIZ string. The ASCIIZ string contains the drive, path, and filename.ext of the executable program. Programs may use this area to determine where the program was loaded from. The environment built by the command processor (and passed to all programs it invokes) contains a COMSPEC=string at a minimum (the parameter on COMSPEC is the path used by DOS to locate COMMAND.COM on disk). The last PATH and PROMPT commands issued will also be in the environment, along with any environment strings entered through the SET command.

The environment that you are passed is actually a copy of the invoking process's environment. If your application terminates and stays resident through int 27h, you should be aware that the copy of the environment passed to you is static. That is, it will not change even if subsequent PATH, PROMPT, or SET commands are issued.

The size of the environment may be changed from its default of 160 bytes by using the SHELL= command in the CONFIG.SYS from in DOS version 3.1 up, or COMMAND.COM may be patched in earlier versions.

The environment can be used to transfer information between processes or to store strings for later use by application programs. The environment is always located on a paragraph boundary. This is its format:

```
    byte    ASCIIZ string 1
    byte    ASCIIZ string 2
      ....
    byte    ASCIIZ string n
    byte    of zeros (0)
```

Typically the environment strings have the form:

```
    NAME = VALUE
```

The length of NAME or VALUE can be anything desired as long as it still fits into the 123 byte space (4 bytes are used by 'SET'). Following the byte of zeros in the environment, a WORD indicates the number of other strings following.

If the environment is part of an EXECed command interpreter, it is followed by a copy of the DS:DX filename passed to the child process. A zero value causes the newly created process to inherit the parent's environment.

DOS Control Blocks and Work Areas

3. Offset 05h in the PSP contains code to invoke the DOS function dispatcher. Thus, by placing the desired function number in AH, a program can issue a long call to PSP+05h to invoke a DOS function rather than issuing an int 21h.

4. The disk transfer address (DTA) is set to 80h (default DTA in PSP).

5. File Control Blocks 5Ch and 6Ch are formatted from the first two parameters entered when the command was invoked. Note that if either parameter contained a path name, then the corresponding FCB will contain only a valid drive number. The filename field will not be valid.

6. An unformatted parameter area at 81h contains all the characters entered after the command name (including leading and imbedded delimiters), with 80h set to the number of characters. If the , , or | parameters were entered on the command line, they (and the filenames associated with them) will not appear in this area, because redirection of standard input and output is transparent to applications.

(For EXE files only)

7. DS and ES registers are set to point to the PSP.

8. CS, IP, SS, and SP registers are set to the values passed by the linker.

(For COM files only)

9. For COM files, offset 6 (one word) contains the number of bytes available in the segment.

10. Register AX reflects the validity of drive specifiers entered with the first two parameters as follows:

```
AH=0FFh if the second parameter contained an invalid drive specifier,
        otherwise AH=00h.
AL=0FFh is the first parameter contained an invalid drive specifier,
        otherwise AL=00h.
```

11. All four segment registers contain the segment address of the inital allocation block, that starts within the PSP control block. All of user memory is allocated to the program. If the program needs to invoke another program through the EXEC function call (4Bh), it must first free some memory through the SETBLOCK function call to provide space for the program being invoked.

12. The Instruction Pointer (IP) is set to 100h.

13. The SP register is set to the end of the program's segment. The segment size at offset 6 is rounded down to the paragraph size.

14. A word of zeroes is placed on top of the stack.

7

DOS File Structure

File Management Functions

Use DOS function calls to create, open, close, read, write, rename, find, and erase files. There are two sets of function calls that DOS provides for support of file management. They are:

```
* File Control Block function calls    (0Fh-24h)
* Handle function calls                 (39h-69h)
```

Handle function calls are easier to use and are more powerful than FCB calls. Microsoft recommends that the handle function calls be used when writing new programs. DOS 3.0 up have been curtailing use of FCB function calls; it is possible that future versions of DOS may not support FCB function calls.

The following table compares the use of FCB calls to Handle function calls:

FCB Calls	Handle Calls
Access files in current directory only.	Access files in ANY directory
Requires the application program to maintain a file control block to open, create, rename or delete a file. For I/O requests, the application program also needs an FCB	Does not require use of an FCB. Requires a string with the drive, path, and filename to open, create, rename, or delete a file. For file I/O requests, the application program must maintain a 16 bit file handle that is supplied by DOS.

The only reason an application should use FCB function calls is to maintain the ability to run under DOS 1.x. To to this, the program may use only function calls 00h-2Eh. Though the FCB function calls are frowned upon, many of the introductory assembly language programming texts use the FCB calls as examples.

FCB Function Calls

FCB function calls require the use of one File Control Block per open file, which is maintained by the application program and DOS. The application program supplies a pointer to the FCB and fills in the appropriate fields required by the specific function call. An FCB function call can perform file management on any valid drive, but only in the current logged directory. By using the current block, current record, and record length fields of the FCB, you can perform sequential I/O by using the sequential read or write function calls. Random I/O can be performed by filling in the random record and record length fields.

Several possible uses of FCB type calls are considered programming errors and should not be done under any circumstances to avoid problems with file sharing and compatibility with later versions of DOS.

Some errors are:

1. If program uses the same FCB structure to access more than one open file. By opening a file using an FCB, doing I/O, and then replacing the filename field in the file control block with a new filename, a program can open a second file using the same FCB. This is invalid because DOS writes control information about the file into the reserved fields of the FCB. If the program replaces the filename field with the original filename and then tries to perform I/O on this file, DOS may become confused because the control information has been changed. An FCB should never be used to open a second file without closing the one that is currently open. If more than one File Control Block is to be open concurrently, separate FCBs should be used.

2. A program should never try to use the reserved fields in the FCB, as the function of the fields may change with different versions of DOS.

3. A delete or a rename on a file that is currently open is considered an error and should not be attempted by an application program.

It is also good programming practice to close all files when I/O is done. This avoids potential file sharing problems that require a limit on the number of files concurrently open using FCB function calls.

Handle Function Calls

The recommended method of file management is by using the extended 'handle' set of function calls. These calls are not restricted to the current directory. Also, the handle calls allow the application program to define the type of access that other processes can have concurrently with the same file if the file is being shared.

To create or open a file, the application supplies a pointer to an ASCIIZ string giving the name and location of the file. The ASCIIZ string contains an optional drive letter, optional path, mandatory file specification, and a terminal byte of 00h. The following is an example of an ASCIIZ string:

```
    format:         [drive][path] FILENAME.EXT,0
    in MASM:        db 'A:\PATH\FILENAME.EXT',0
```

If the file is being created, the application program also supplies the attribute of the file. This is a set of values that defines the file read-only, hidden, system, directory, or volume label.

If the file is being opened, the program can define the sharing and access modes that the file is opened in. The access mode informs DOS what operations your program will perform on this file (read-only, write-only, or read/write) The sharing mode controls the type of operations other processes may perform concurrently on the file. A program can also control if a child process inherits the open files of the parent. The sharing mode has meaning only if file sharing is loaded when the file is opened.

To rename or delete a file, the appplication program simply needs to provide a pointer to the ASCIIZ string containing the name and location of the file and another string with the new name if the file is being renamed.

The open or create function calls return a 16-bit value referred to as the file handle. To do any I/O to a file, the program uses the handle to reference the file. Once a file is opened, a program no longer needs to maintain the ASCIIZ string pointing to the file, nor is there any need to stay in the same directory. DOS keeps track of the location of the file regardless of what directory is current.

Sequential I/O can be performed using the handle read (3Fh) or write (40h) function calls. The offset in the file that I/O is performed to is automatically moved to the end of what was just read or written. If random I/O is desired, the LSEEK (42h) function call can be used to set the offset into the file where I/O is to be performed.

Special File Handles

DOS reserves five special file handles for use by itself and applications programs. They are:

```
0000h    STDIN     standard input device        (input can be redirected)
0001h    STDOUT    standard output device       (output can be redirected)
0002h    STDERR    standard error output device (output cannot be redirected)
                   Note: DOS opens STDERR for both writing and reading. Since STDIN
                   can be redirected, using STDERR to read the keyboard is a re
                   liable way to ensure that your program is actually reading the
                   keyboard, if that's what you want to do.
0004h    STDAUX    standard auxiliary device
0005h    STDPRN    standard printer device (PRN, normally LPT1)
```

These handles are predefined by DOS and can be used by an application program. They do not need to be opened by a program, although a program can close these handles. STDIN should be treated as a read-only file, and STDOUT and STDERR should be treated as write-only files. STDIN and STDOUT can be redirected. All handles inherited by a process can be redirected, but not at the command line. These handles are very useful for doing I/O to and from the console device. For example, you could read input from the keyboard using the read (3Fh) function call and file handle 0000h (STDIN), and write output to the console screen with the write function call (40h) and file handle 0001h (STDOUT). If you wanted an output that could not be redirected, you could output it using file handle 0002h (STDERR). This is very useful for error messages that must be seen by a user.

File handles 0003h (STDAUX) and 0004h (STDPRN) can be both read from and written to. STDAUX is typically a serial device and STDPRN is usually a parallel device.

Raw and Cooked File I/O

Raw and cooked modes originated in the Unix world and were provided with DOS 2.x+. They apply only to character I/O (including the keyboard, screen, printer and serial ports - but not block devices like disk drives), and only to the 'new' 2.x file handle I/O functions (not the old FCB file I/O functions). Raw mode is called 'binary' mode in DOS 3.x+, and cooked mode is called 'ASCII'. The common raw-cooked convention is from DOS 2.x and other operating systems.

The five predefined DOS file handles are all devices, so the mode can be changed from raw to cooked via IOCTL. These handles are in cooked mode when initialized by DOS. Regular file handles that are not devices are always in raw mode and cannot be changed to cooked mode.

The predefined file handles STDIN (0000h) and STDOUT (0001h) and STDERR (0002h) are all duplicate handles. If the IOCTL function call is used to change the mode of any of these three handles, the mode of all three handles is changed. For example, if IOCTL was used to change STDOUT to raw, then STDIN and STDERR would also be changed to raw mode.

In the default cooked mode, DOS examines the character I/O data stream for certain special control characters, and takes specific actions if they are found. For example, Ctrl-C is treated as a Break interrupt, Ctrl-S pauses the screen display, and Ctrl-Z is treated as end-of-file. (If you try to send Ctrl-Z to a printer through a DOS file handle in cooked mode, DOS closes the printer file!) Also, input is buffered within DOS until a CR is detected - so you can't process each key as it is pressed.

In raw mode, DOS ignores special characters, passing them through without any special processing, and does not buffer input lines. So to use file handle I/O and send bit-mapped graphics to a printer through DOS, or process individual keystrokes immediately, or bypass Ctrl-C checking, you need to switch the file handle to raw mode. Raw mode is not automatically reset to cooked mode by DOS when a program terminates, so it is a good idea to reset the file into cooked mode before your program exits if the system was in cooked mode to begin with. I/O to files is done in raw mode.

To set a file handle into raw mode or back into cooked mode, use DOS IOCTL (int 21h Fn 44h, Chapter 4):

1. Get the current mode bits (Subfunction 0).
2. Check that the file is a character file. (If not, exit.)
3. Switch the cooked mode bit to raw or vice versa.
4. Set the mode bits (Subfunction 1).

Microsoft C v4 and later do NOT set raw mode for binary files. When running with the CON driver set to raw mode (to enhance display speed) programs compiled in MSC will crash the computer. A letter to Microsoft reporting this odd behaviour got the somewhat bizarre reply that 'Microsoft does not support the use of any TSRs' from their techs. Raw mode is clearly documented by both IBM and Microsoft, and their own tools should take it into account.

File I/O in Binary (Raw) Mode

The following is true when a file is read in binary mode:

1. The characters ^S (scroll lock), ^P (print screen), ^C (control break) are not checked for during the read. Therefore, no printer echo occurs if ^S or ^P are read.
2. There is no echo to STDOUT (0001h).

3. Read the number of specified bytes and returns immediately when the last byte is received or the end of file reached.

4. Allows no editing of the input using the function keys if the input is from STDIN (0000h).

The following is true when a file is written to in binary mode:

1. The characters ^S (scroll lock), ^P (print screen), ^C (control break) are not checked for during the write. Therefore, no printer echo occurs.

2. There is no echo to STDOUT (0001h).

3. The exact number of bytes specified are written.

4. Does not caret (^) control characters. For example, Ctrl-D is sent out as byte 04h instead of the two bytes ^ and D.

5. Does not expand tabs into spaces.

File I/O in ASCII (Cooked) Mode

The following is true when a file is read in ASCII mode:

1. Checks for the characters ^C, ^S, and ^P.

2. Returns as many characters as there are in the device input buffer, or the number of characters requested, whichever is less. If the number of characters requested was less than the number of characters in the device buffer, then the next read will address the remaining characters in the buffer.

3. If there are no more bytes remaining in the device input buffer, read a line (terminated by ^M) into the buffer. This line may be edited with the function keys. The characters returned terminated with a sequence of 0Dh, 0Ah (^M, ^J) if the number of characters requested is sufficient to include them. For example, if 5 characters were requested, and only 3 were entered before the carriage return (0Dh or ^M) was presented to DOS from the console device, then the 3 characters entered and 0Dh and 0Ah would be returned. However, if 5 characters were requested and 7 were entered before the carriage return, only the first 5 characters would be returned. No 0Dh, 0Ah sequence would be returned in this case. If less than the number of characters requested are entered when the carriage return is received, the characters received and 0Dh, 0Ah would be returned. The reason the 0Ah (linefeed or ^J) is added to the returned characters is to make the devices look like text files.

4. If a 1Ah (^Z) is found, the input is terminated at that point. No 0Dh, 0Ah (CR,LF) sequence is added to the string.

5. Echoing is performed.

6. Tabs are expanded.

The following is true when a file is written to in ASCII mode:

1. The characters ^S, ^P, and ^C are checked for during the write operation.

2. Expands tabs to 8-character boundaries and fills with spaces (20h).

3. Carets control chars, for example, ^ D is written as two bytes, ^ and D.
4. Bytes are output until the number specified is output or a ^ Z is encountered. The number actually output is returned to the user.

Number of Open Files Allowed

The number of files that can be open concurrently is restricted by DOS. This number is determined by how the file is opened or created (FCB or handle function call) and the number specified by the FCBS and FILES commands in the CONFIG.SYS file. The number of files allowed open by FCB function calls and the number of files that can be opened by handle type calls are independent of one another.

Restrictions on FCB Usage

If file sharing is not loaded using the SHARE command, there is no restriction on the number of files concurrently open using FCB function calls.

However, when file sharing is loaded, the maximum number of FCBs open is set by the the FCBS command in the CONFIG.SYS file.

The FCBS command has two values you can specify, 'm' and 'n'. The value for 'm' specifies the number of files that can be opened by FCBs, and the value 'n' specifies the number of FCBs that are protected from being closed.

When the maximum number of FCB opens is exceeded, DOS automatically closes the least recently used file. Any attempt to access this file results in an int 24h critical error message 'FCB not available'. If this occurs while an application program is running, the value specified for 'm' in the FCBS command should be increased.

When DOS determines the least recently used file to close, it does not include the first 'n' files opened, therefore the first 'n' files are protected from being closed.

Restrictions on Handle Usage

The number of files that can be open simultaneously by all processes is determined by the FILES command in the CONFIG.SYS file. The number of files a single process can open depends on the value specified for the FILES command. If FILES is greater than or equal to 20, a single process can open 20 files. If FILES is less than 20, the process can open less than 20 files. This value includes the three predefined handles STDIN, STDOUT, and STDERR. This means only 17 additional handles can be added. DOS 3.3+ includes a function to use more than 20 files per application.

Allocating Space to a File

Files are not necessarily written sequentially on a disk. Space is allocated as needed and the next location available on the disk is allocated as space for the next file being written. Therefore, if considerable file generation has taken place, newly created files will not be written in sequential sectors. However, due to the mapping (chaining) of file space via the File Allocation Table (FAT) and the function calls available, any file may be used in either asequential or random manner.

Space is allocated in increments called clusters. Cluster size varies according to the media type. An application program should not concern itself with the way that DOS allocates space to a file. The size of a cluster is only important in that it determines the smallest amount of space that can be allocated to a file. A disk is considered full when all clusters have been allocated to files.

MSDOS / PCDOS Differences

There is a problem of compatibility between MS-DOS and IBM PC-DOS having to do with FCB Open and Create. The IBM 1.0, 1.1, and 2.0 documentation of OPEN (call 0Fh) contains the following statement:

> 'The current block field (FCB bytes C-D) is set to zero [when an FCB is opened].'

This statement is NOT true of MS-DOS 1.25 or MS-DOS 2.00. The difference is intentional, and the reason is CP/M 1.4 compatibility. Zeroing that field is not CP/M compatible. Some CP/M programs will not run when machine translated if that field is zeroed. The reason it is zeroed in the IBM versions is that IBM specifically requested that it be zeroed. This is the reason for the complaints from some vendors about the fact that IBM MultiPlan will not run under MS-DOS. It is probably the reason that some other IBM programs don't run under MS-DOS.

Note: Do what all MS/PC-DOS systems programs do: Set every single FCB field you want to use regardless of what the documentation says is initialized.

.COM File Structure

The COM file structure was designed for DOS 1.0 and maximum compatibility with programs ported from the CP/M operating system. COM files normally comprise one segment only. A COM file is loaded as a memory image of the disk file and the Instruction Pointer is set to offset 100h within the program.

.EXE File Structure

The EXE file is the native mode for DOS. EXE files may make use of multiple segments for code, stack, and data. The design of the EXE file reflects the segmented design of the Intel 80x86 CPU architecture. EXE files may be as large as available memory and may make references to specific segment addresses.

The EXE files produced by the Linker program consist of two parts, control and relocation information and the load module itself.

The control and relocation information, which is described below, is at the beginning of the file in an area known as the header. The load module immediately follows the header. The load module begins in the memory image of the module contructed by the Linker.

DOS File Structure

When you are loading a file with the name *.EXE, DOS does NOT assume that it is an EXE format file. It looks at the first two bytes for a signature (the letters MZ) telling it that it is an EXE file. If it has the proper signature, then the load proceeds. Otherwise, it presumes the file to be a .COM format file.

If the file has the EXE signature, then the internal consistency is checked. Pre-2.0 versions of MSDOS did not check the signature byte for EXE files.

The .EXE format can support programs larger than 64K. It does this by allowing separate segments to be defined for code, data, and the stack, each of which can be up to 64K long. Programs in EXE format may contain explicit references to segment addresses. A header in the EXE file has information for DOS to resolve these references.

Offset	Size	CONTENTS
00h	BYTE	4Dh The Linker's signature to mark the file as a valid .EXE file (ASCII letters M and Z, for Mark Zbikowski,
01h	BYTE	5Ah one of the major DOS programmers at Microsoft)
02h-03h	WORD	Length of the image mod 512 (remainder after dividing the load module image size by 512)
04h-05h	WORD	Size of the file in 512 byte pages including the header.
06h-07h	WORD	Number of relocation table items following the header.
08h-09h	WORD	Size of the header in 16 byte (paragraphs). This is used to locate the beginning of the load module in the file
0Ah-0Bh	WORD	Minimum number of 16 byte paragraphs required above the end of the loaded program.
0Ch-0Dh	WORD	Max number of 16 byte paragraphs required above the end of the loaded program. If the minimum and maximum number of paragraphs are both zero, the program will be loaded as high in memory as possible.
0Eh-0Fh	WORD	Displacement in paragraphs of stack segment within load module. This size must be adjusted by relocation.
10h-11h	WORD	Offset to be in SP register when the module is given control (stack offset)
12h-13h	WORD	Word Checksum - negative sum of all the words in the file, ignoring overflow.
14h-15h	WORD	Offset for the IP register when the module is given control (initial instruction pointer)
16h-17h	WORD	Displacement in paragraphs of code segment within load. module. This size must be adjusted by relocation. (CS)
18h-19h	WORD	Displacement in bytes of first relocation item in the file.
1Ah-1Bh	WORD	Overlay number (0 for the resident part of the program)

The Relocation Table

The word at 18h locates the first entry in the relocation table. The relocation table is made up of a variable number of relocation items. The number of items is contained at offset 06h. The relocation item contains two fields - a 2 byte offset value, followed by a 2 byte segment value. These two fields represent the displacement into the load module before the module is given control. The process is called relocation and is accomplished as follows:

1. The formatted part of the header is read into memory. Its size is 1Bh.

2. A portion of memory is allocated depending on the size of the load module and the allocation numbers in offsets 0Ah and 0Ch. DOS always tries to allocate 0FFFFh paragraphs. Since this call will always fail, the function returns the amount of free memory. If this block is larger than the minimum specified at offset 0Ah and the loaded program size, DOS will allocate the size specified at offset 0Ch or the largest free memory space, whichever is less.

3. A Program Segment Prefix is built following the resident portion of the program that is performing the load operation.

4. The formatted part of the header is read into memory (its size is at offset 08h)

5. The load module size is determined by subtracting the header size from the file size. Offsets 04h and 08h can be used for this calculation. The actual size is downward adjusted based on the contents of offset 02h. Note that all files created by the Linker programs prior to version 1.10 always placed a value of 4 at this location, regardless of the actual program size. Therefore, Microsoft recommends that this field be ignored if it contains a value of 4. Based on the setting of the high/low loader switch, an appropriate segment is determined for loading the load module. This segment is called the start segment.

6. The load module is read into memory beginning at the start segment. The relocation table is an ordered list of relocation items. The first relocation item is the one that has the lowest offset in the file.

7. The relocation table items are read into a work area one or more at a time.

8. Each relocation table item segment value is added to the start segment value. The calculated segment, in conjunction with the relocation item offset value, points to a word in the load module to which is added the start segment value. The result is placed back into the word in the load module.

9. Once all the relocation items have been processed, the SS and SP registers are set from the values in the header and the start segment value is added to SS. The ES and DS registers are set to the segment address of the program segment prefix. The start segment value is added to the header CS register value. The result, along with the header IP value, is used to give the module control.

'NEW' .EXE Format (Microsoft Windows and OS/2)

The 'old' EXE format is documented here. The 'new' EXE format puts more information into the header section and is currently used in applications that run under Microsoft Windows. The linker that creates these files comes with the Microsoft Windows Software Development Kit and is called LINK4. If you try to run a Windows-linked program under DOS, you will get the error message 'This program requires Microsoft Windows'. The OS/2 1.x file format is essentially the same as the Windows format.

Standard File Control Block

The standard file control block is defined as follows, with offsets in hex:

```
                    FILE CONTROL BLOCK
offset   size           Function
0        1 byte    Drive number. For example:
                   Before open:   00h = default drive
                                  01h = drive A:
                                  02h = drive B: etc.
                   After open:    00h = drive C:
                                  01h = drive A:
                                  02h = drive B: etc.
```

DOS File Structure

Offset	Size	Description
1-8	8 bytes	An 0 is replaced by the actual drive number during open. Filename, left justified with blanks. If a reserved device name is placed here (such as PRN), do not include the optional colon.
9-B	3 bytes	Filename extension, left justified with trailing blanks.
C-D	2 bytes	Current block # relative to start of file, starting with 0 (set to 0 by the open function call). A block consists of 128 records, each of the size specified in the logical record size field. The current block number is used with the current record field (below) for sequential reads and writes.
E-F	2 bytes	Logical record size in bytes. Set to 80h by OPEN function. If this is not correct, you must set the value because DOS uses it to determine the proper locations in the file for all disk reads and writes.
10-13	4 bytes	File size in bytes. In this field, the first word is the low-order part of the size.

14-15	2 bytes	Date file was created or last updated.
		MM/DD/YY are mapped as follows:
		`15 14 13 12 11 10  9  8  7  6  5  4  3  2  1  0`
		`y  y  y  y  y  y  y  m  m  m  m  d  d  d  d  d`
		where: mm is 1-12
		dd is 1-31
		yy is 0-119 (1980-2099)

16-17	2 bytes	Time file was created or last updated.
		These bytes contain the time when the file was created or last updated.
		The time is mapped in the bits as follows:
		`      BYTE  16h                BYTE  17h`
		`F  E  D  C  B  A  9  8    7  6  5  4  3  2  1  0`
		`H  H  H  H  H  M  M  M    M  M  M  D  D  D  D  D`
		binary # hrs 0-23 binary # minutes 0-59 bin. # 2-sec incr
		note: The time is stored with the least significant byte first.

18-19	2 bytes	Reserved for DOS.
20	1 byte	Current relative record number (0-127) within the current block. This field and the Current Block field at offset 0Ch make up the record pointer. This field is not initialized by the OPEN function call. You must set this field before doing sequential read-write operations to the diskette.
21-25	4 bytes	Relative Record. Points to the currently selected record, counting from the beginning of the file starting with 0. This field is not initialized by the OPEN system call. You must set this field before doing a random read or write to the file. If the record size is less than 64 bytes, both words are used. Otherwise, only the first 3 bytes are used. Note that if you use the File Control Block at 5Ch in the program segment, the last byte of the FCB overlaps the first byte of the unformatted parameter area.

Note 1. An unopened FCB consists of the FCB prefix (if used), drive number, and filename.ext properly filled in. An open FCB is one in which the remaining fields have been filled in by the CREAT or OPEN function calls.

2. Bytes 0-5 and 32-36 must be set by the user program. Bytes 16-31 are set by DOS and must not be changed by user programs.

3. All word fields are stored with the least significant byte first. For example, a record length of 128 is stored as 80h at offset 14, and 00h at offset 15.

Extended File Control Block

The extended file control block is used to create or search for files in the disk directory that have special attributes.
It adds a 7 byte prefix to the FCB, formatted as follows:

EXTENDED FILE CONTROL BLOCK

```
Offset  Size      Function
00h     1 byte    Flag byte containing 0FFh to indicate an extended FCB
01h     4 bytes   Reserved by Microsoft
06h     2 bytes   Attribute byte
                  Refer to int 21h/fn11h (search first) for details on using the attribute
                  bits during directory searches. This function is present to allow
                  applications to define their own files as hidden (and thereby excluded
                  from normal directory searches) and to allow selective directory searches
```

Any reference in the DOS function calls to an FCB, whether opened or unopened, may use either a normal or extended FCB. If you are using an extended FCB, the appropriate register should be set to the first byte of the prefix, rather than the drive-number field.

Common practice is to refer to the extended FCB as a negative offset from the first byte of a standard File Control Block.

8

DOS Disk Information

The DOS Area

All disks and diskettes formatted by DOS are created with a sector size of 512 bytes. The DOS area (entire area for a diskette, DOS partition for hard disks) is formatted as follows:

DOS AREA

partition table	- variable size (hard disk only)
boot record	- 1 sector
first copy of the FAT	- variable size
second copy of the FAT	- same size as first copy
root directory	- variable size
data area	- variable depending on disk size

The following sections describe each of the allocated areas:

The Boot Record

The boot record resides on track 0, sector 1, side 0 of every diskette formatted by the DOS FORMAT program. For hard disks the boot record resides on the first sector of the DOS partition. It is put on all disks to provide an error message if you try to start up with a nonsystem disk in drive A:. If the disk is a system disk, the boot record contains a JMP instruction pointing to the first byte of the operating system.

If the device is IBM compatible, it must be true that the first sector of the first FAT is located at the same sector for all possible media. This is because the FAT sector is read before the media is actually determined. The information relating to the BPB for a particular media is kept in the boot sector for the media. In particular, the format of the boot sector is:

DOS BOOT RECORD

```
00h 3 bytes    JMP to executable code. For DOS 2.x, 3 byte near jump (0E9h).
               For DOS 3.x, 2 byte near jump (0EBh) followed by a NOP (90h)
03h 8 bytes    optional OEM name and version  (such as IBM 2.1)
0Dh byte       sectors per allocation unit (must be a power of 2)
0Eh 2 bytes    B   reserved sectors (starting at logical sector 0)
10h byte           number of FATs
```

```
11h  2 bytes       maximum number of root directory entries
13h  2 bytes   P   number of sectors in logical image (total number of sectors in
                   media, including boot sector directories, etc.). If logical
                   disk size is greater than 32Mb, this value is 0 and the actual
                   size is reported at offset 26h
15h  byte      B   media descriptor byte
16h  2 bytes       number of sectors occupied by a single FAT
18h  2 bytes       sectors per track
1Ah  2 bytes       number of heads
1Ch  2 bytes       number of hidden sectors
EXTENDED BOOT RECORD (DOS 4.0+)
1Eh  2 bytes       number of sectors per track
20h  2 bytes       number of heads
22h  2 bytes       number of hidden sectors
26h  4 bytes       total number of sectors in media (32MB or larger indicated here)
27h  byte          physical drive number
28h  byte          reserved
29h  byte          extended boot record signature
30h  4 bytes       volume serial number (assigned with a random function)
34h  11bytes       volume label
3Fh  8 bytes       reserved
```

The three words at the end return information about the media. The number of heads is useful for supporting different multihead drives that have the same storage capacity but a different number of surfaces. The number of hidden sectors is useful for drive partitioning schemes.

DOS 3.2 uses a table called the BIOS Parameter Block (BPB) to determine if a disk has a valid File Allocation Table. The BPB is located in the first sector of a floppy disk. Although the BPB is supposed to be on every formatted floppy disk, some earlier versions of DOS did not create a BPB and instead assumed that the FAT begins at the second sector of the disk and that the first FAT byte (Media Descriptor Byte) describes the disk format.

DOS 3.2 reads in the whole of the BPB and tries to use it - although strangely enough, it seems as if DOS is prepared to cope with a BPB that is more or less totally blank (it seems to ignore the descriptor byte and treat it as a DSDD 9-sector disk).

DOS 3.2 determines if a disk has a valid boot sector by examining the first byte of logical sector 0. If that byte it a jump instruction 0E9h, DOS 3.2 assumes the rest of the sector is a valid boot sector with a BPB. If the first byte is not 0E9h DOS 3.2 behaves like previous versions, assumes the boot sector is invalid and uses the first byte of the FAT to determine the media type. If the first byte on the disk happens to be 0E9h, but the disk does not have a BPB, DOS 3.2 will return a disk error message.

The real problems occur if some of the BPB data is valid and some isn't. Apparently some OEMs have assumed that DOS would continue to ignore the formatting data on the disk, and have failed to write much there during FORMAT except the media descriptor byte (or, worse, have allowed random junk to be written there). While this error is understandable, and perhaps even forgivable, it remains their problem, not IBMs, since the BPB area has always been documented as containing the format information that IBM DOS 3.2 now requires to be there.

The DOS File Allocation Table (FAT)

The File Allocation Table, or FAT, has three main purposes:

1. to mark bad sectors on the media

2. to determine which sectors are free for use

3. to determine the physical location(s) of a file on the media.

DOS uses one of two different schemes for defining the File Allocation Table:

1. a 12-bit FAT, for DOS 1.x, 2.x, all floppies, and small hard disks
2. a 16-bit FAT, for DOS 3.x+ hard disks from 16.8 to 32Mb

This section explains how DOS uses the FAT to convert the clusters of a file into logical sector numbers. It is recommended that system utilities use the DOS handle calls rather than interpreting the FAT, particularly since aftermarket disk partitioning or formatting software may have been used.

The FAT is used by DOS to allocate disk space for files, one cluster at a time. In DOS 4.0, clusters are referred to as 'allocation units'. It means the same things; the smallest logical portion of a drive.

The FAT consists of a 12 bit entry (1.5 bytes) for each cluster on the disk or a 16 bit (2 bytes) entry when a hard disk has more than 20740 sectors as is the case with fixed disks larger than 10Mb.

The first two FAT entries map a portion of the directory; these FAT entries contain indicators of the size and format of the disk. The FAT can be in a 12 or 16 bit format. DOS determines whether a disk has a 12 or 16 bit FAT by looking at the total number of allocation units on a disk. For all diskettes and hard disks with DOS partitions less than 20,740 sectors, the FAT uses a 12 bit value to map a cluster. For larger partitions, DOS uses a 16 bit value.

The second, third, and fourth bit applicable for 16 bit FAT bytes always contains 0FFFFh. The first byte is used as follows:

Media Descriptor Byte

MEDIA DESCRIPTOR BYTE

```
hex      meaning                              normally used
value
00       hard disk                            3.3+ extended DOS partition
ED       double sided   9 sector 80 track     Tandy 2000 720k 5 floppy
F0       double sided  18 sector diskette     PS/2 1.44 meg DSHD
F8       hard disk                            bootable hard disk at C:800
F9       double sided  15 sector diskette     AT 1.2 meg DSHD
         double sided   9 sector diskette     Convertible 720k DSQD
FA       IBM Displaywriter System disk        287k
FB       IBM Displaywriter System disk        1 meg
FC       single sided   9 sector diskette     DOS 2.0, 180k SSDD
FD       double sided   9 sector diskette     DOS 2.0, 360k DSDD
FE       single sided   8 sector diskette     DOS 1.0, 160k SSDD
FF       double sided   8 sector diskette     DOS 1.1, 320k SSDD

for 8 inch diskettes:
FD       double sided  26 sector diskette     IBM 3740 format DSSD
FE       single sided  26 sector diskette     IBM 3740 format SSSD
         double sided   8 sector diskette     IBM 3740 format DSDD
```

The third FAT entry begins mapping the data area (cluster 002).

Note: These values are provided as a reference. Therefore, programs should not make use of these values.

Each entry contains a hexadecimal character (or 4 for 16 bit FATs). () indicates the high order four bit value in the case of 16 bit FAT entries. They can be:

> (0)000h   if the cluster is unused and available

(0F)FF8h - (0F)FFFh   to indicate the last cluster of a file

> (X)XXXh   any other hexadecimal numbers that are the cluster number of the next cluster in the file. The cluster number is the first cluster in the file that is kept in the file's directory entry.

The values (0F)FF0h - (0F)FF7h are used to indicate reserved clusters. (0F)FF7h indicates a bad cluster if it is not part of the allocation chain. (0F)FF8h - (0F)FFFh are used as end of file markers.

The file allocation table always occupies the sector or sectors immediately following the boot record. If the FAT is larger than 1 sector, the sectors occupy consecutive sector numbers. Two copies of the FAT are written, one following the other, for integrity. The FAT is read into one of the DOS buffers whenever needed (open, allocate more space, etc).

12 Bit File Allocation Table

Obtain the starting cluster of the file from the directory entry.

Now, to locate each subsequent sector of the file:

1. Multiply the cluster number just used by 1.5 (each FAT entry is 1.5 bytes long).

2. The whole part of the product is offset into the FAT, pointing to the entry that maps the cluster just used. That entry contains the cluster number of the next cluster in the file.

3. Use a MOV instruction to move the word at the calculated FAT into a register.

4. If the last cluster used was an even number, keep the low order 12 bits of the register, otherwise, keep the high order 12 bits.

5. If the resultant 12 bits are (0FF8h-0FFFh) no more clusters are in the file. Otherwise, the next 12 bits contain the cluster number of the next cluster in the file.

To convert the cluster to a logical sector number (relative sector, such as that used by int 25h and 26h and DEBUG):

1. Subtract 2 from the cluster number

2. Multiply the result by the number of sectors per cluster.

3. Add the logical sector number of the beginning of the data area.

12-bit FAT if DOS partition is smaller than 32,680 sectors (16.340 MB).

16 Bit File Allocation Table

Obtain the starting cluster of the file from the directory entry. Now to locate each subsequent cluster of the file:

1. Multiply the cluster number used by 2 (each FAT entry is 2 bytes long).
2. Use the MOV word instruction to move the word at the calculated FAT offset into a register.
3. If the resultant 16 bits are (0FF8h-0FFFFh) no more clusters are in the file. Otherwise, the 16 bits contain the cluster number of the next cluster in the file.

Compaq DOS makes available a new disk type (6) with 32 bit partition values, allowing 512 megabytes per hard disk (Compaq DOS 3.3.1)

DOS Disk Directory

The FORMAT command initially builds the root directory for all disks. Its location (logical sector number) and the maximum number of entries are available through the device driver interfaces.

Since directories other than the root directory are actually files, there is no limit to the number of entries that they may contain.

All directory entries are 32 bytes long, and are in the following format:

```
offset    size              DISK DIRECTORY ENTRY
00h       8 bytes   Filename
                    The first byte of the filename indicates the file status.
                    The file status byte may contain the following values:
                    00h   Directory entry has never been used. This is used to
                          limit the length of directory searches, for performance
                          reasons.
                    05h   Indicates that the first character of the filename
                          actually has an 0EDh character.
                    0E5h  Filename has been used but the file has been erased.
                    2Eh   This entry is for a directory. If the second byte is
                          also 2Eh, the cluster field contains the cluster number
                          of this directory's parent directory. (0000h if the
                          parent directory is the root directory). Otherwise,
                          bytes 00h-0Ah are all spaces and the cluster field
                          contains the cluster number of the directory.
                    Any other character is the first character of a
                    filename. Filenames are left-aligned and if necessary
                    padded with blanks.
08h       3 bytes   Filename extension if any
                    Three characters, left-aligned and padded with blanks if
                    necessary. If there is no file extension, this field contains
                    all blanks
0Bh       1 byte    File attributes
                    The attribute byte is mapped as follows:
                    hex  bit                meaning
                    00h         (no bits set) normal; can be read or written without
                                restriction
                    01h   0     file is marked read-only. An attempt to open the
                                file for out put using int 21h/fn 3Dh will fail and
                                an error code will be returned. This value can be
                                used with other values below.
                    02h   1     indicates a hidden file. The file is excluded from
                                normal directory searches.
                    04h   2     indicates a system file. The file is excluded from
                                normal directory searches.
                    08h   3     indicates that the entry contains the volume label
                                in the first 11 bytes. The entry has no other usable
                                information and may exist only in the root directory.
```

```
              10h   4     indicates that the file is a subdirectory
              20h   5     indicates an archive bit. This bit is set to on
                          whenever the file is written to and closed. Used by
                          BACKUP and RESTORE.
                    6     reserved, set to 0
                    7     reserved, set to 0
              note 1. Bits 6 and 7 may be used in OS/2.
              note 2. Attributes 08h and 10h cannot be changed using
                      int21/43h.
              note 3. The system files IBMBIO.COM and IBMDOS.COM (or
                      customized equivalent) are marked as read-only,
                      hidden, and system files. Files can be marked hidden
                      when they are created.
              note 4. Read-only, hidden, system and archive attributes may
                      be changed with int21h/fn43h.
0Ch                 10 bytes   Reserved by DOS; value unknown
16h    2 bytes      File timestamp
              These bytes contain the time when the file was created or last
              updated. The time is mapped in the bits as follows:
                    B Y T E    16h              B Y T E    17h
                    F E D C B A 9 8    7 6 5 4 3 2 1 0
                    H H H H H M M M    M M M D D D D D
                    binary # hrs 0-23   binary # minutes 0-59 bin. # 2-sec incr
              note: The time is stored with the least significant byte first.
18h    2 bytes      File datestamp
              This area contains the date when the file was created or last
              updated. The mm/dd/yy are mapped in the bits as follows:
                    B Y T E    18h              B Y T E    19h
                    F E D C B A 9 8    7 6 5 4 3 2 1 0
                    Y Y Y Y Y Y Y M    M M M D D D D D
                    0-119 (1980-2099)        1-12     1-31
              note: The date is stored with the least significant byte first.
1Ah    2 bytes      First file cluster number
              * (reserved in DOS 2, documented in DOS 3+)
              This area contains the starting cluster number of the first
              cluster in the file. The first cluster for data space on all
              fixed disks and floppy disks is always cluster 002. The
              cluster number is stored with the least significant byte first.
1Ch    4 bytes      File size
              This area contains the file size in bytes. The first word
              contains the low order part of the size. Both words are stored
              with the least significant byte first.
```

The Data Area

Allocation of space for a file (in the data area) is done only when needed (it is not pre-allocated). The space is allocated one cluster (unit allocation) at a time. A cluster is always one or more consecutive sector numbers, and all of the clusters in a file are 'chained' together in the FAT.

The clusters are arranged on disk to minimize head movement for multisided media. All of the space on a track (or cylinder) is allocated before moving on to the next track. This is accomplished by using the sequential sector numbers on the lowest-numbered head, then all the sector numbers on the next head, and so on until all sectors of all heads of the track are used. Then the next sector used will be sector 1 of head 0 on the next track.

An interesting innovation that was introduced in MS-DOS 3.0: disk space that is freed by erasing a file is not re-used immediately, unlike earlier versions of DOS. Instead, free space is obtained from the area not yet used during the current session, until all of it is used up. Only then will space that is freed during the current session be re-used.

This feature minimizes fragmentation of files, since never-before-used space is always contiguous. However, once any space has been freed by deleting a file, that advantage vanishes at the next system boot. The feature also greatly simplifies un-erasing files, provided that the need to do an un-erase is found during the same session and also provided that the file occupies contiguous clusters.

However, when one is using programs which make extensive use of temporary files, each of which may be created and erased many times during a session, the feature becomes a nuisance; it forces the permanent files to move farther and farther into the inner tracks of the disk, thus increasing rather than decreasing the amount of fragmentation which occurs.

The feature is implemented in DOS by means of a single 16-bit 'last cluster used' (LCU) pointer for each physical disk drive; this pointer is a part of the physical drive table maintained by DOS. At boot time, the LCU pointer is zeroed. Each time another cluster is obtained from the free-space pool (the FAT), its number is written into the LCU pointer. Each time a fresh cluster is required, the FAT is searched to locate a free one; in older versions of DOS this search always began at Cluster 0000, but in 3.x it begins at the cluster pointed to by the LCU pointer.

For hard disks, the size of the file allocation table and directory are determined when FORMAT initializes it and are based on the size of the DOS partition.

Floppy Disk Types

The following tables give the specifications for floppy disk formats:

```
IBM PC-DOS disk formats:
                       # of       FAT size      DIR      total
                       sides      sectors   (entries)   sectors
                                sectors      DIR    sectors
                                /track    sectors   /cluster
160k  5¹/₄  DOS 1.0    1      8   (40)    1    4    64    1      320   Original PC-0, 16k mbd
320k  5¹/₄  DOS 1.1    2      8   (40)    1    7   112    2      360   PC-1, 64k mbd
180k  5¹/₄  DOS 2.0    1      9   (40)    2    4    64    1      640   PC-2, 256k mbd
360k  5¹/₄  DOS 2.0    2      9   (40)    2    7   112    2      720   PC/XT
1.2M  5¹/₄  DOS 3.0    2     15   (80)    7   14   224    1     2400   PC/AT, PC/RT, XT/286
720k  3¹/₂  DOS 3.2    2      9   (80)    3    7   112    2     1440   Convertible, PS/2 25+
1.44M 3¹/₂  DOS 3.3    2     18   (80)    9   14   224    1     2880   PS/2 50+

various MS-DOS disk formats:

200k  5¹/₄    *        1     10   (40)
400k  5¹/₄    * **     2     10   (40)
800k  5¹/₄    *        2     10   (80)
720k  5¹/₄  DOS2.11    2      9   (80)    3    7   112    2     1440   Tandy 2000 (discontinued)

*  Michtron DS-DOS 2.11 Plus and one version of MS-DOS 3.11 (vendor unknown)
** TallTree JFormat program

720k  5   DOS2.11  1   (80)                                DEC Rainbow  SS/HD (disc.)
720k  5   DOS2.11  2   variable number of sectors          Victor 9000 PC (discont'd)
                       per track, more sectors on
                       outer tracks than innertracks.
                       Special DSDD drive.
```

Files in the data area are not necessarily written sequentially. The data area space is allocated one cluster at a time, skipping over clusters already allocated. The first free cluster found is the next cluster allocated, regardless of its physical location on the disk. This permits the most efficient utilization of disk space because clusters freed by erasing files can be allocated for new files. Refer back to the description of the DOS FAT in this chapter for more information.

```
        SSDD     single sided, double density   (160-180k)    5¹/₄
```

```
DSDD     double sided, double density    (320-360k)    5¼
DSQD     double sided, quad density      (720k)        5¼, 3½
DSHD     double sided, high density      (1.2-1.44M)   5¼, 3½
```

Much of the trouble with AT 1.2 meg drives has been through the inadvertent use of quad density disks in the high density drives. The high density disks use a higher-coercivity media than the quads, and quads are not completely reliable as 1.2Mb. Make sure you have the correct disk for your application.

Hard Disk Layout

The DOS hard disk routines perform the following services:

1. Allow multiple operating systems to be installed on the hard disk at the same time.
2. Allow a user-selected operating system to be started from the hard disk.
   i. In order to share the hard disk among operating systems, the disk may be logically divided into 1 to 4 partitions. The space within a given partition is contiguous, and can be dedicated to a specific operating system. Each operating system may 'own' only one partition in DOS versions 2.0 through 3.2. DOS 3.3 introduced the 'Extended DOS Partition' which allows multiple DOS partitions on the same hard disk. FDISK (or a similar program from other DOS vendors) utility allows the user to select the number, type, and size of each partition. The partition information is kept in a partition table that is embedded in the master hard disk boot record on the first sector of the disk. The format of this table varies from version to version of DOS.
   ii. An operating system must consider its partition to be the entire disk, and must ensure that its functions and utilities do not access other partitions on the disk.
   iii. Each partition may contain a boot record on its first sector, and any other programs or data that you choose, including a different operating system. For example, the DOS FORMAT command may be used to format and place a copy of DOS in the DOS partition in the same manner that a diskette is formatted. You can use FDISK to designate a partition as 'active' (bootable). The master hard disk boot record causes that partition's boot record to receive control when the system is initialized. Additional disk partitions could be FORTH, UNIX, Pick, CP/M-86, OS/2, or the UCSD p-System.

SYSTEM INITIALIZATION

The boot sequence is as follows:

1. System initialization first attempts to load an operating system from diskette drive A. If the drive is not ready or a read error occurs, it then attempts to read a master hard disk boot record on the first sector of the first hard disk in the system. If unsuccessful, or if no hard disk is present, it invokes ROM BASIC in an IBM PC or displays a disk error message on most compatibles.
2. If initialization is successful, the master hard disk boot record is given control and it examines the partition table embedded within it. If one of the entries indicates an active (bootable) partition, its boot record is read from the partition's first sector and given control. If none of the partitions is bootable, ROM BASIC is invoked on an IBM PC or a disk error on most compatibles.
4. If any of the boot indicators are invalid, or if more than one indicator is marked as bootable, the message 'INVALID PARTITION TABLE' is displayed and the system stops.

5. If the partition's boot record cannot be successfully read within five retries due to read errors, the message 'ERROR LOADING OPERATING SYSTEM' appears and the system stops.

6. If the partition's boot record does not contain a valid 'signature', the message 'MISSING OPERATING SYSTEM' appears, and the system stops.

Note: When changing the size or location of any partition, you must ensure that all existing data on the disk has been backed up. The partitioning program will destroy the data on the disk.

System programmers designing a utility to initialize/manage a hard disk must provide the following functions at a minimum:

1. Write the master disk boot record/partition table to the disk's first sector to initialize it.

2. Perform partitioning of the disk - that is, create or update the partition table information (all fields for the partition) when the user wishes to create a partition. This may be limited to creating a partition for only one type of operating system, but must allow repartitioning the entire disk, or adding a partition without interfering with existing partitions (user's choice).

3. Provide a means for marking a user-specified partition as bootable and resetting the bootable indicator bytes for all other partitions at the same time.

4. Such utilities should not change or move any partition information that belongs to another operating system.

Boot Record/Partition Table

A boot record must be written on the first sector of all hard disks, and must contain the following:

1. Code to load and give control to the boot record for one of four possible operating systems.

2. A partition table at the end of the boot record. Each table entry is 16 bytes long, and contains the starting and ending cylinder, sector, and head for each of four possible partitions, as well as the number of sectors preceding the partition and the number of sectors occupied by the partition. The 'boot indicator' byte is used by the boot record to determine if one of the partitions contains a loadable operating system. FDISK initialization utilities mark a user-selected partition as 'bootable' by placing a value of 80h in the corresponding partition's boot indicator (setting all other partitions' indicators to 0 at the same time). The presence of the 80h tells the standard boot routine to load the sector whose location is contained in the following three bytes. That sector is the actual boot record for the selected operating system, and it is responsible for the remainder of the system's loading process (as it is from the diskette). All boot records are loaded at absolute address 0:7C00.

The partition table with its offsets into the boot record is: (except for Wyse DOS 3.2 with 32 bit allocation table, and DOS 3.3-up)

```
Offset  Partit'n  Purpose        Head      Sector  Cylinder
1BEh    part 1    begins      boot ind  H     S       cyl
```

```
1C2h                ends           syst ind   H          S          cyl
1C6h                relative sector           low word              high word
1CAh                # sectors                 low word              high word
1CEh     part 2     begins         boot ind   H          S          cyl
1D2h                ends           syst ind   H          S          cyl
1D6h                relative sector           low word              high word
1DAh                # sectors                 low word              high word
1DEh     part 3     begins         boot ind   H          S          cyl
1E2h                ends           syst ind   H          S          cyl
1E6h                relative sector           low word              high word
1EAh                # sectors                 low word              high word
1EEh     part 4     begins         boot ind   H          S          cyl
1F2h                ends           syst ind   H          S          cyl
1F6h                relative sector           low word              high word
1FAh                # sectors                 low word              high word
1FEh                signature      hex 55         hex AA
```

Boot indicator (boot ind): The boot indicator byte must contain 0 for a non-bootable partition or 80h for a bootable partition. Only one partition can be marked as bootable at a time.

System Indicator (sys ind): The sys ind field contains an indicator of the operating system that 'owns' the partition. IBM PC-DOS can only 'own' one partition, though some versions of MSDOS allow all four partitions to be used by DOS.

The system indicators are:

```
            System Indicator   (sys ind)
    00h     unknown or unspecified
    01h     DOS 12 bit FAT     (DOS 2.x all and 3.x under 10 Mb)
    04h     DOS 16 bit FAT     (DOS 3.0+. Not recognized by 2.x)
    0DBh    DRI Concurrent DOS
    0F2h    2nd DOS partition, some 3.2 and all 3.3+
```

There are bytes for XENIX, and other operating systems. Some manufacturers (such as Zenith, Wyse, and Tandon) diddle with these system bytes to implement more than one DOS partition per disk.

Cylinder (CYL) and Sector (S): The 1 byte fields labelled CYL contain the low order 8 bits of the cylinder number - the high order 2 bits are in the high order 2 bits of the sector (S) field. This corresponds with the ROM BIOS interrupt 13h (disk I/O) requirements, to allow for a 10 bit cylinder number.

The fields are ordered in such a manner that only two MOV instructions are required to properly set up the DX and CX registers for a ROM BIOS call to load the appropriate boot record (hard disk booting is only possible from the first hard disk in the system, where a BIOS drive number of 80h corresponds to the boot indicator byte).

All partitions are allocated in cylinder multiples and begin on sector 1, head 0, with the exception that the partition that is allocated at the beginning of the disk starts at sector 2, to account for the hard disk's master boot record.

Relative Sector (rel sect): The number of sectors preceding each partition on the disk is kept in the 4 byte field labelled 'rel sect'. This value is obtained by counting the sectors beginning with cylinder 0, sector 1, head 0 of the disk, and incrementing the sector, head, and then track values up to the beginning of the partition. This, if the disk has 17 sectors per track and 4 heads, and the second partition begins at cylinder 1, sector 1, head 0, and the partition's starting relative sector is 68 (decimal) - there were 17 sectors on each of 4 heads on 1 track allocated ahead of it. The field is stored with the least significant word first.

Number of sectors (#sects): The number of sectors allocated to the partition is kept in the '# of sects' field. This is a 4 byte field stored least significant word first.

Signature: The last 2 bytes of the boot record (55AAh) are used as a signature to identify a valid boot record. Both this record and the partition boot record are required to contain the signature at offset 1FEh.

Hard Disk Technical Information

Western Digital's hard disk installation manuals make the claim that MSDOS can support only 2 hard drives. This is entirely false, and their purpose for making the claim is unclear. DOS merely performs a function call pointed at the hard disk driver, which is normally in one of three locations; a ROM at absolute address C:800, the main BIOS ROM if the machine is an AT, or a device driver installed through the CONFIG.SYS file. Two hard disk controller cards can normally not reside in the same machine due to lack of interrupt arbitration. Perstor's ARLL controller and some cards marketed by Novell can coexist with other controllers. Perstor's technical department has had four controllers and eight hard disks in the same IBM XT functioning concurrently.

A valid hard disk has a boot record arranged in the following manner:

```
DB      drive   ; 0 or 80h  (80h marks a bootable, active partition)
DB      head1   ; starting heads
DW      trksec1 ; starting track/sector (CX value for INT 13)
DB      system  ; see below
DB      head2   ; ending head
DW      trksec2 ; ending track/sector
DD      sector1 ; absolute # of starting sector
DD      sector2 ; absolute # of last sector
```

The master disk boot record invokes ROM BASIC if no indicator byte reflects a bootable system.

When a partition's boot record is given control, it is passed its partition table entry address in the DS:SI registers.

Determining Hard Disk Allocation

DOS determines disk allocation using the following formula:

$$SPF = \frac{TS - RS - \dfrac{D * BPD}{BPS}}{CF + \dfrac{BPS * SPC}{BPC}}$$

where:

TS	total sectors on disk
RS	the number of sectors at the beginning of the disk that are reserved for the boot record. DOS reserves 1 sector.
D	The number of directory entries in the root directory.
BPD	the number of bytes per directory entry. This is always 32.
BPS	the number of bytes per logical sector. Typically 512, but you can specify a different number with VDISK.
CF	The number of FATS per disk. Usually 2. VDISK is 1.
SPF	the number of sectors per FAT. Maximum 64.

```
        SPC   The number of sectors per allocation unit.
        BPC   the number of bytes per FAT entry. BPC is 1.5 for 12 bit FATs. 2 for
              16 bit FATS.
```

To calculate the minimum partition size that will force a 16-bit FAT:

```
        CYL = (max clusters * 8)/(HEADS * SPT)
```

where:

```
    CYL             number of cylinders on the disk
    max clusters    4092 (maximum number of clusters for a 12 bit FAT)
    HEADS           number of heads on the hard disk
    SPT             sectors per track  (normally 17 on MFM)
```

DOS 2.0 uses a 'first fit' algorithm when allocating file space on the hard disk. Each time an application requests disk space, it will scan from the beginning of the FAT until it finds a contiguous piece of storage large enough for the file.

DOS 3.0 keeps a pointer into the disk space, and begins its search from the point it last left off. This pointer is lost when the system is rebooted. This is called the 'next fit' algorithm. It is faster than the first fit and helps minimize fragmentation.

In either case, if the FCB function calls are used instead of the handle function calls, the file will be broken into pieces starting with the first available space on the disk.

BIOS Disk Routines

Interrupt 13h Disk I/O - access the disk drives (floppy and hard disk)
(0:004Ch) These calls do not try rereading disk if an error is returned

```
Function 00h       Reset - reset the disk controller chip
entry     AH       00h
          DL       drive (if bit 7 is set both hard disks and floppy disks reset)
                   00h-7Fh   floppy disk
                   80h-0FFh  hard disk
return    AH       status (see 01h below)
note 1.  Forces controller chip to recalibrate read/write heads.
     2.  Some systems (Sanyo 55x) this resets all drives.
     3.  This function should be called after a failed floppy disk Read, Write,
         Verify, or Format request before retrying the operation.
     4.  If called with DL = 80h (i.e., selecting a hard drive), the floppy
         controller and then the hard disk controller are reset.
     5.  Function 0Dh allows the hard disk controller to be reset without
         affecting the floppy controller.

Function 01h       Get Status of Disk System
entry     AH       01h
          DL       drive (hard disk if bit 7 set)
                   00h-7Fh   floppy disk
                   80h-0FFh  hard disk
return    AH       00h
          AL       status of most recent disk operation
                   00h    successful completion, no errors
                   01h    bad command
                   02h    address mark not found
                   03h    tried to write on write-protected disk      (floppy only)
                   04h    sector not found
                   05h    reset failed                                 (hard disk)
                   06h    diskette removed or changed                  (floppy only)
                   07h    bad parameter table                          (hard disk)
                   08h    DMA overrun
                   09h    attempt to DMA across 64K boundary           (floppy only)
                   0Ah    bad sector detected                          (hard disk)
                   0Bh    bad track detected                           (hard disk)
                   0Ch    unsupported track or media type not found    (floppy disk)
```

DOS Disk Information

```
            0Dh      invalid number of sectors on format      (hard disk)
            0Eh      control data address mark detected       (hard disk)
            0Fh      DMA arbitration level out of range       (hard disk)
            10h      uncorrectable CRC/EEC on read
            11h      ECC corrected data error                 (hard disk)
            20h      controller failure
            40h      seek failed
            80h      timeout
            0AAh     drive not ready                          (hard disk)
            0BBh     undefined error                          (hard disk)
            0CCh     write fault                              (hard disk)
            0E0h     status error                             (hard disk)
            0FFh     sense operation failed                   (hard disk)
note   For hard disks, error code 11h (ECC data error) indicates that a
       recoverable error was detected during a preceding int 13h fn 02h
       (Read Sector) call.
```

```
Function 02h     Read Sectors - read one or more sectors from diskette
entry    AH      02h
         AL      number of sectors to read
         BX      address of buffer (ES=segment)
         CH      track (cylinder) number (0-39 or 0-79 for floppies)
                 (for hard disk, bits 8,9 in high bits of CL)
         CL      sector number (1 to 18, not value checked)
         DH      head number (0 or 1)
         DL      drive (0=A, 1=B, etc.) (bit 7=0)   (drive 0-7)
                 00h-7Fh    floppy disk
                 80h-FF0h   hard disk
         ES:BX   address to store/fetch data   (buffer to fill)
       [0000:0078]   dword pointer to diskette parameters
return   CF      0          successful
                 AL         number of sectors transferred
                 1          error
                 AH         status (00h, 02h, 03h, 04h, 08h, 09h, 10h,
                            0Ah, 20h, 40h, 80h)
```
note 1. Number of sectors begins with 1, not 0.
  2. Trying to read zero sectors is considered a programming error; results
     are not defined.
  3. For hard disks, the upper 2 bits of the 10-bit cylinder number are placed
     in the upper 2 bits of register CL.
  4. For hard disks, error code 11h indicates that a read error occurred that
     was corrected by the ECC algorithm; in this case, AL contains the burst
     length. The data read is good within the limits of the ECC code. If a
     multisector transfer was requested, the operation was terminated after
     the sector containing the read error.
  5. For floppy drives, an error may result from the drive motor being off at
     the time of the request. The BIOS does not automatically wait for the
     drive to come up to speed before attempting the read operation. The
     calling program should reset the floppy disk system with function 00h
     and retry the operation three times before assuming that the error
     results from some other cause.

```
Function 03h     Write Sectors - write from memory to disk
entry    AH      03h
         AL      number of sectors to write (1-8)
         CH      track number (for hard disk, bits 8,9 in high bits of CL)
         CL      beginning sector number
                 (if hard disk, high two bits are high bits of track #)
         DH      head number
         DL      drive number (0-7)
                 00h-7Fh    floppy disk
                 80h-FF0h   hard disk
         ES:BX   address of buffer for data
return   CF      0          success
                 AL         number of sectors written
                 1          error
                 AH         status (see 01h above)
```
note 1. Number of sectors begins with 1, not 0.
  2. Trying to write zero sectors is considered a programming error; results
     are not defined.
  3. For hard disks, the upper 2 bits of the 10-bit cylinder number are placed

in the upper 2 bits of register CL.
4. For floppy drives, an error may result from the drive motor being off at the time of the request. The BIOS does not automatically wait for the drive to come up to speed before attempting the read operation. The calling program should reset the floppy disk system with function 00h and retry the operation three times before assuming that the error results from some other cause.

```
Function 04h      Verify - verify that a write operation was successful
entry    AH       04h
         AL       number of sectors to verify (1-8)
         CH       track number   (for hard disk, bits 8,9 in high bits of CL)
         CL       beginning sector number
         DH       head number
         DL       drive number (0-7)
         DL       drive number (0-7)
                  00h-7Fh    floppy disk
                  80h-FF0h   hard disk
         ES:BX    address of buffer for data
return   CF       set on error
         AH       status (see 01h above)
         AL       number of sectors verified
```
note 1. With IBM PC, XT, and AT with ROM BIOS earlier than 11/15/85, ES:BX should point to a valid buffer.
2. For hard disks, the upper 2 bits of the 10-bit cylinder number are placed in the upper 2 bits of register CL.
3. This function can be used to test whether a readable media is in a floppy drive. An error may result from the drive motor being off at the time of the request since the BIOS does not automatically wait for the drive to come up to speed before attempting the verify operation. The requesting program should reset the floppy disk system with function 00h and retry the operation three times before assuming that a readable disk is not present.

```
Function 05h Format Track - write sector ID bytes for 1 track (floppy
             disk)
entry    AH       05h
         AL       number of sectors to create on this track
                     interleave (for XT hard disk only)
         CH       track (or cylinder) number (bits 8,9 in high bits of CL)
         CL       sector number
         DH       head number (0, 1)
         DL       drive number (0-3)
                  00h-7Fh    floppy disk
                  80h-0FFh   hard disk
         ES:BX    pointer to 4-byte address field (C-H-R-N) (except XT hard
                  disk)
                  byte 1 = (C) cylinder or track
                  byte 2 = (H) head
                  byte 3 = (R) sector
                  byte 4 = (N) bytes/sector (0 = 128, 1 = 256, 2 = 512, 3 =
                               1024)
return   CF       set if error occurred
         AH       status code (see 01h above)
```
note 1. Not valid for ESDI hard disks on PS/2.
2. For floppy disks, the number of sectors per track is taken from the BIOS floppy disk parameter table whose address is stored in the vector for int 1Eh.
3. When this function is used for floppies on ATs or the PS/2, it should be preceded by a call to int 13h/fn 17h to select the type of media to format.
4. For hard disks, the upper 2 bits of the 10-bit cylinder number are placed in the upper 2 bits of CL.
5. On the XT/286, AT, and PS/2 hard disks, ES:BX points to a 512-byte buffer containing byte pairs for each physical disk sector as follows:
```
Byte   Contents
 0     00h        good sector
       80h        bad sector
 1     sector number
```
For example, to format a track with 17 sectors and an interleave of two, ES:BX would point to the following 34-byte array at the beginning of a

DOS Disk Information

```
            512-byte buffer:
            db      00h, 01h, 00h, 0Ah, 00h, 02h, 00h, 0Bh, 00h, 03h, 00h, 0Ch
            db      00h, 04h, 00h, 0Dh, 00h, 05h, 00h, 0Eh, 00h, 06h, 00h, 0Fh
            db      00h, 07h, 00h, 10h, 00h, 08h, 00h, 11h, 00h, 09h
```

Function 06h   Hard Disk - format track and set bad sector flags
                                                     (PC2, PC-XT, and Portable)
entry   AH   06h
        AL   interleave value (XT only)
        CH   cylinder number (bits 8,9 in high bits of CL)
        CL   sector number
        DH   head
        DL   drive (80h-0FFh for hard disk)
        ES:BX   512 byte format buffer
                the first 2*(sectors/track) bytes contain f,n for each sector
                f   00h   good sector
                        80h   bad sector
                n   sector number
return CF   error
        AH   status code (see 01h above)

Function 07h   Hard Disk - format the drive starting at the desired track
                                                     (PC2, PC-XT and Portable)
entry   AH   07h
        AL   interleave value (XT only) (01h-10h)
        CH   cylinder number (bits 8,9 in high bits of CL) (00h-03FFh)
        CL   sector number
        DH   head number (0-7)
        DL   drive number (80h-0FFh, 80h=C, 81h=D,...)
        ES:BX   format buffer, size = 512 bytes
                the first 2*(sectors/track) bytes contain f,n for each sector
                f   00h   good sector
                        80h   bad sector
                n   sector number
return CF   set on error
        AH   status code (see 01h above)
note   Award AT BIOS routines are extended to handle more than 1024 cylinders.
        AL   number of sectors
        CH   cylinder number low 8 bits
        CL   sector number bits 0-5, bits 6-7 are high 2 cylinder bits
        DH   head number (bits 0-5) bits 6-7 are extended high cyls (1024)
        DL   drive number (0-1 for diskette, 80h-81h for hard disk)
        ES:BX   transfer address

Function 08h   Read Drive Parameters   (except PC, Jr)
entry   AH   08h
        DL   drive number
                00h-7Fh   floppy disk
                80h-0FFh   hard disk
return CF   set on error
        AH   status code (see above)
        BL   drive type (AT/PS2 floppies only)
                01h   if 360 Kb, 40 track, 5"
                02h   if 1.2 Mb, 80 track, 5"
                03h   if 720 Kb, 80 track, 3"
                04h   if 1.44 Mb, 80 track, 3"
        CH   low 8 bits of maximum useable value for cylinder number
        CL bits 6-7   high-order 2 bits of maximum cylinder number
                0-5   maximum sector number
        DH   maximum usable value for head number
        DL   number of consecutive acknowledging drives (0-2)
        ES:DI   pointer to drive parameter table
note   On the PC and PC/XT, this function is supported on hard disks only.

Function 09h   Initialize Two Fixed Disk Base Tables   (XT, AT, XT/286, PS/2)
                (install nonstandard drive)
entry   AH   09h
        DL   80h-0FFh hard disk number
return CF   set on error
        AH   status code (see 01h above)
                For PC, XT hard disks, the disk parameter block format is:

```
              00h-01h maximum number of cylinders
              02h     maximum number of heads
              03h-04h starting reduced write current cylinder
              05h-06h starting write precompensation cylinder
              07h     maximum ECC burst length
              08h     drive options
                   bits 7    1         disable disk access retries
                        6    1         disable ECC retries
                        3-5            set to 0
                        0-2            drive option
              09h     standard timeout value
              0Ah     timeout value for format drive
              0Bh     timeout value for check drive
              0Ch-0Fh reserved

              For AT and PS/2 hard disks:
              00h-01h maximum number of cylinders
              02h     maximum number of heads
              03h-04h reserved
              05h-06h starting write precompensation cylinder
              07h     maximum ECC burst length
              08h     drive options byte
                   bits 6-7  nonzero (10, 01, or 11) if retries disabled
                        5    1         if manufacturer's defect map present at
                                       maximum cylinder + 1
                        4              not used
                        3    1         if more than 8 heads
                        0-2            not used
              09h-0Bh reserved
              0Ch-0Dh landing zone cylinder
              0Eh     sectors per track
              0Fh     reserved
note 1. For the XT, int 41h must point to the Disk Parameter Block.
     2. For the AT and PS/2, Int 41h points to table for drive 0 and Int 46h
        points to table for drive 1.
     3. Initializes the hard disk controller for subsequent I/O operations using
        the values found in the BIOS disk parameter block(s).
     4. This function is supported on hard disks only.

Function 0Ah    Read Long    (Hard disk)                (XT, AT, XT/286, PS/2)
entry    AH     0Ah
         CH     cylinder number (bits 8,9 in high bits of CL)
         CL     sector number (upper 2 bits of cyl # in upper 2 bits of CL)
         DH     head number
         DL     drive ID (80h-0FFh hard disk)
         ES:BX  pointer to buffer to fill
return   CF     set on error
         AH     status code (see 01h above)
         AL     number of sectors actually transferred
note 1. A 'long' sector includes a 4 byte EEC (Extended Error Correction) code.
     2. Used for diagnostics only on PS/2 systems.
     3. This function is supported on fixed disks only.
     4. Unlike the normal Read Sector (02h) function, ECC errors are not
        automatically corrected. Multisector transfers are terminated after any
        sector with a read error.

Function 0Bh    Write Long                               (XT, AT, XT/286, PS/2)
entry    AH     0Bh
         AL     number of sectors
         CH     cylinder (bits 8,9 in high bits of CL)
         CL     sector number
         DH     head number
         DL     drive ID (80h-0FFh hard disk)
         ES:BX  pointer to buffer containing data
return   CF     set on error
         AH     status code (see 01h above)
         AL     number of sectors actually transferred
note 1. A 'long' sector includes a 4 byte EEC (Extended Error Correction) code.
     2. Used for diagnostics only on PS/2 systems.
     3. Valid for hard disks only.
```

```
Function 0Ch    Seek To Cylinder                          (except PC, PCjr)
entry   AH      0Ch
        CH      lower 8 bits of cylinder
        CL      upper 2 bits of cylinder in bits 6-7
        DH      head number
        DL      drive number (0 or 1)  (80h-0FFh for hard disk)
return  CF      set on error
        AH      status code (see 01h above)
note 1. Positions heads over a particular cylinder, but does not move anydata.
     2. This function is supported on hard disks only.
     3. The upper 2 bits of the 10-bit cylinder number are placed in the upper 2
        bits of CL.
     4. The Read Sector, Read Sector Long, Write Sector, and Write Sector Long
        functions include an implied seek operation and need not be preceded by
        an explicit call to this function.

Function 0Dh    Alternate Hard Disk Reset                 (except PC, PCjr)
entry   AH      0Dh
        DL      hard drive number (80h-0FFh hard disk)
return  CF      set on error
        AH      status code (see 01h above)
note 1. Not for PS/2 ESDI hard disks.
     2. Resets the hard disk controller, recalibrates attached drives (moves the
        read/write arm to cylinder 0), and prepares for subsequent disk I/O.
     3. This function is for hard disks only. It differs from fn 00h by not
        resetting the floppy disk controller.

Function 0Eh    Read Sector Buffer                        (XT, Portable, PS/2)
entry   AH      0Eh
        ES:BX   pointer to buffer
return  CF      set on error
        AH      status code (see 01h above)
        AL      number of sectors actually transferred
note 1. Transfers controller's sector buffer. No data is read from the drive.
     2. Used for diagnostics only on PS/2 systems.
     3. This fn is supported by the XT's hard disk adapter only. It is 'not
        defined' for hard disk adapters on the AT or PS/2.

Function 0Fh    Write sector buffer                       (XT, Portable)
entry   AH      0Fh
        ES:BX   pointer to buffer
return  CF      set if error
        AH      status code (see 01h above)
        AL      number of sectors actually transferred
note 1. Should be called before formatting to initialize the controller's sector
        buffer.
     2. Used for diagnostics only on PS/2 systems.
     3. Transfers data from system RAM to the hard disk adapter's internal sector
        buffer.
     4. No data is written to the physical disk drive.
     5. This fn is for the XT hard disk controller only. It is 'not defined' for
        AT or PS/2 controllers.

Function 10h    Test For Drive Ready                      (XT, AT, XT/286, PS/2)
entry   AH      10h
        DL      hard drive number 0 or 1 (80h-0FFh)
return  CF      set on error
        AH      status code (see 01h above)
note 1. Tests whether the specified hard disk drive is operational and
        returns the drive's status.
     2. This function is supported on hard disks only.
     3. Perstor and Novell controllers allow more than one hard drive.

Function 11h    Recalibrate Drive                         (XT, AT, XT/286, PS/2)
entry   AH      11h
        DL      hard drive number (80h-0FFh hard disk)
return  CF      set on error
        AH      status code (see 01h above)
note 1. Causes the HD controller to recalibrate itself for the specified drive,
        positioning the read/arm to cylinder 0, and returns the drive's status.
     2. This function is for hard disks only.
```

```
Function 12h      Controller RAM Diagnostics                    (XT, Portable, PS/2)
entry     AH      12h
return    CF      set on error
                  AH       status code (see fn 01h above)
note 1. Used for diagnostics only on PS/2 systems.
     2. Makes the hard disk controller carry out a built-in diagnostic test on
        its internal sector buffer.

Function 13h      Controller Drive Diagnostic                   (XT, Portable, PS/2)
entry     AH      13h
return    CF      set on error
                  AH       status code (see 01h above)
note 1. Used for diagnostics only on PS/2 systems.
     2. Causes HD controller to run internal diagnostic tests of the attached
        drive, indicating whether the test was passed by the returned status.
     3. This function is supported on XT HDs only.

Function 14h      Controller Internal Diagnostic                (AT, XT/286)
entry     AH      14h
return    CF      set on error
                  AH       status code (see 01h above)
note 1. OEM is Western Digital 1003-WA2 hard/floppy combination controller in AT
        and XT/286.
     2. Used for diagnostics only in PS/2 systems.
     3. Causes HD controller to do a built-in diagnostic self-test, indicating
        whether the test was passed by the returned status.
     4. This function is supported on hard disks only.

Function 15h      Get Disk Type                                 (except PC and XT)
entry     AH      15h
          DL      drive ID
                  00h-7Fh   floppy disk
                  80h-0FFh  fixed disk
return    CF      set on error
                  AH       error code (see 01h above)
          AH      disk type
                  00h       no drive is present
                  01h       diskette, no change detection present
                  02h       diskette, change detection present
                  03h       fixed disk
                  CX:DX     number of 512-byte sectors
note 1. Returns a code indicating the type of disk referenced by the specified
        drive code.
     2. This function is not supported on the PC or XT.

Function 16h      Get Disk Change Status (diskette)             (except PC, XT, & Jr)
entry     AH      16h
          DL      drive to check
return    CF      set on error
          AH      disk change status
                  00h       no disk change
                  01h       disk changed
          DL      drive that had disk change (00h-07Fh floppy disk)
note      Returns the status of the change line, indicating whether the disk in the
          drive may have been replaced since the last disk access. If this
          function returns with CF set, the disk has not necessarily been changed;
          the change line can be activated by simply unlocking and relocking the
          disk drive door without removing the floppy disk.

Function 17h      Set Disk Type for Format (diskette)           (except PC and XT)
entry     AH      17h
          AL      00h       not used
                  01h       160, 180, 320, or 360Kb diskette in 360kb drive
                  02h       360Kb diskette in 1.2Mb drive
                  03h       1.2Mb diskette in 1.2Mb drive
                  04h       720Kb diskette in 720Kb drive
          DL      drive number (0-7)
return    CF      set on error
          AH      status of operation (see 01h above)
note 1. This function is probably enhanced for the PS/2 series to detect 1.44 in
        1.44 and 720k in 1.44.
```

DOS Disk Information

```
        2. This function is not supported for floppy disks on the PC or XT.
        3. If the change line is active for the specified drive, it is reset.
        4. The BIOS sets the data rate for the specified drive and media type. The
           rate is 250k/sec for double-density media and 500k/sec for high density
           media. The proper hardware is required.

Function 18h   Set Media Type For Format (diskette)          (AT, XT2, XT/286, PS/2)
entry    AH      18h
         CH      lower 8 bits of number of tracks
         CL      high 2 bits of number of tracks (6,7) sectors per track (bits 0-5)
         DL      drive number (0-7)
return   CF      clear    no errors
         AH      00h      if requested combination supported
                 01h      if function not available
                 0Ch      if not supported or drive type unknown
                 80h      if there is no media in the drive
         ES:DI   pointer to 11-byte disk parameter table for media type
         CF      set      error code (see 01h above)
note 1. A floppy disk must be present in the drive.
     2. This function should be called prior to formatting a disk with Int 13h Fn
        05h so the BIOS can set the correct data rate for the media.
     3. If the change line is active for the specified drive, it is reset.

Function 19h   Park Hard Disk Heads                                          (PS/2)
entry    AH      19h
         DL      drive number (80h-0FFh)
return   CF      set on error
         AH      error code (see fn 01h)
note     This function is defined for PS/2 fixed disks only.

Function 1Ah   ESDI Hard Disk - Low Level Format                             (PS/2)
entry    AH      1Ah
         AL      Relative Block Address (RBA) defect table count
                 0       if no RBA table
                 0       if RBA table used
         CL      format modifiers byte
            bits 0       ignore primary defect map
                 1       ignore secondary defect map
                 2       update secondary defect map
                 3       perform extended surface analysis
                 4       generate periodic interrupt
                 5       reserved - must be 0
                 6       reserved - must be 0
                 7       reserved - must be 0
         DL      drive  (80h-0FFh)
         ES:BX   pointer to RBA defect table
return   CF      set on error
         AH      error code (see fn 01h above)
note 1. Initializes disk sector and track address fields on a drive attached to
        the IBM 'ESDI Fixed Disk Drive Adapter/A'.
     2. If periodic interrupt selected, int 15h/fn 0Fh is called after each
        cylinder is formatted
     3. If bit 4 of CL is set, Int 15h, AH=0Fh, AL=phase code after each cylinder
        is formatted or analyzed. The phase code is defined as:
                 0       reserved
                 1       surface analysis
                 2       formatting
     4. If bit 2 of CL is set, the drive's secondary defect map is updated to
        reflect errors found during surface analysis. If both bit 2 and bit 1
        are set, the secondary defect map is replaced.
     5. For an extended surface analysis, the disk should first be formatted by
        calling this function with bit 3 cleared and then analyzed by calling
        this function with bit 3 set.

Function 1Bh   ESDI Hard Disk - Get Manufacturing Header                     (PS/2)
entry    AH      1Bh
         AL      number of record
         DL      drive
         ES:BX   pointer to buffer for manufacturing header (defect list)
return   CF      set on error
         AH      status
```

note   Manufacturing header format (Defect Map Record format) can be found in
          the 'IBM 70Mb, 115Mb Fixed Disk Drives Technical Reference'.

Function 1Ch   ESDI Hard Disk - Get Configuration   (PS/2)
entry   AH   1Ch
         AL   0Ah   Get Device Configuration
                         DL   drive
                         ES:BX   pointer to buffer for device configuration
                                 (drive physical parameter)
                 0Bh   Get Adapter Configuration
                         ES:BX   pointer to buffer for adapter configuration
                 0Ch   Get POS Information
                         ES:BX   pointer to POS information
                 0Eh   Translate RBA to ABA
                         CH   low 8 bits of cylinder number
                         CL   sector number, high two bits of cylinder number
                                 in bits 6 and 7
                         DH   head number
                         DL   drive number
                         ES:BX   pointer to ABA number
return   CF   set on error
         AH   status (see 01h)
note 1. Device configuration format can be found in IBM ESDI Fixed Disk Drive
        Adapter/A Technical Reference.
     2. ABA (absolute block address) format can be found in IBM ESDI Adapter
        Technical Reference by using its Device Configuration Status Block.

9

Installable Device Drivers

Device Driver Format

A device driver is a handler for communication between the system software and hardware devices. The motherboard ROM and IBMBIO.COM or IO.SYS files contain the basic drivers for allowing DOS to talk to the console, disk drives, serial and parallel ports, clock, and other resources.

DOS has five builtin drivers, STDIN, STDOUT, STERR, STDPRN, or STDAUX. An 'installable' driver may be loaded in the CONFIG.SYS file, and either replace one of the built-in drivers or define a new resource, such as a mouse or expanded memory driver.

The device driver is a COM (memory image) file that contains all of the code needed to control an add-in device. An EXE file cannot be used since the EXE loader is part of COMMAND.COM, which is not present when the device driver is being loaded by IBMBIO.COM or IO.SYS. The COM file must not load at the usual ORG 100h. Since the driver does not use the Program Segment Prefix, it is simply loaded without offset, therefore the driver file must have an origin of 0 (ORG 0 or no ORG statement). Driver files should not have a declared stack segment.

DOS can install the device driver anywhere in memory, so care must be taken in any FAR memory references. You should not expect that your driver will be loaded in the same place every time.

Types of Devices

There are two types of devices: Character devices and Block devices. Their attributes are as follows:

Character devices are designed to do serial I/O in a byte-by-byte manner. These devices have names like CON, AUX, or PRN, and you can open channels (handles or FCBs) to do I/O much like a disk file. I/O may be in either cooked or raw mode. (see Chapter 7 for discussion of cooked and raw modes). Because character devices have only one name, they can only support one device.

Block devices are normally implemented as disk drives. They can do random I/O in pieces called blocks, which are usually the physical sector size of the disk. These devices are not named as character devices are, and cannot be opened directly. Instead they are accessed by using drive letters such as A, B, C, etc. Block devices can have units within them. In this way, a single block driver can be responsible for one or more disk drives. For example, the first block device driver can be responsible for drives A, B, C, and D. This means it has four units defined and therefore takes up four drive letters. The position of the driver in the chain of all drives determines the way in which the drive letters correspond, i.e, if a second block device driver defines three units, then those units are E, F, and G.

DOS 1.x allows 16 block devices. DOS 2.x allows 63, and DOS 3.x allows 26. It is recommended that drivers limit themselves to 26 devices for compatibility with DOS 3.x and 4.x. When DOS 2.x passes the Z: drivespec, the drivespecs get a little weird, such as ^, [, or #. DOS 3.x+ will return an error message.

Creating a Device Driver

To create a device driver that DOS can install, you must do the following:

1. Create a memory image (COM) file with a device header at the start of the file.

2. Originate the code (including the device header) at 0, instead of 100h.

3. Set the next device header field. Refer to 'Pointer to Next Device Header Attribute Field' for more information.

4. Set the attribute field of the device header. Refer to 'Attribute Field' for more information.

5. Set the entry points for the interrupt and strategy routines.

6. Fill in the name/unit field with the name of the character device or the unit number of the block device.

DOS always processes installable character device drivers before handling the default devices. So to install a new CON device, simply name the device CON. Be sure to set the standard input device and standard output device bits in the attribute field of a new CON device. The scan of the device list stops on the first match so the installable device driver takes precedence. For instance, installing ANSI.SYS replaces the built-in CON driver.

DOS doesn't care about the position of installed character devices versus block devices.

Structure of a Device Driver

A device driver consists of three major parts:
    a device header
    a strategy routine
    an interrupt routine

Device Header

The driver has a special header to identify it as a device and to define the strategy and interrupt entry points and its various attributes. This header is located at the beginning of the file. It contains a pointer to the next driver in the chain, the attributes of the device, offsets into the strategy and interrupt routines, and the device ID.

This is the format of the device header:

DEVICE HEADER

```
Offset Length  Description
00h    word    Pointer to next device header field, offset value
02h    word    Pointer to next device header field, segment value
04h    word    Attribute
06h    word    Pointer to device strategy routine (offset only)
08h    word    Pointer to device interrupt routine (offset only)
0Ah    8 bytes Name/Unit field
```

Pointer to Next Device Header Field

The device header field is a pointer to the device header of the next device driver. It is a doubleword field that is set by DOS at the time the device driver is loaded. The first word is the offset and the second word is the segment.

If you are loading only one device driver, set the device header field to -1 before loading the device. If you are loading more than one device driver, set the first word of the device driver header to the offset of the next device driver's header. Set the device driver header field of the last device driver to -1.

Attribute Field

The attribute field is a word field used to identify the type of device this driver is responsible for. This field distinguishes between block and character devices and determines which selected devices are given special treatment. That describes the attributes of the device driver to the system. The attributes are:

ATTRIBUTE FIELD

```
word   attr.  description
bits   set
 0      0    not current standard input device
        1    current standard input device
 1      0    not current standard output device
        1    current standard output device
 2      0    not current NUL device
        1    current NUL device
 3      0    not current CLOCK device
        1    current CLOCK device
 4      0    standard CON I/O routines should be used
        1    fast screen I/O (int 29h) should be used
 5 - 10      'reserved for DOS' - unknown - should be set to 0
11      0    doesn't support removable media  (default for DOS 2.x)
        1    supports removable media         (DOS 3.0+ only)
12           'reserved for DOS' - unknown - should be set to 0
13      0    IBM format      (block devices)
        1    non-IBM format  (block devices)
        1    output till busy (character devices)
14      0    doesn't support IOCTL
        1    supports IOCTL
```

```
         15      0    block device
                 1    character device
```

Note: if a bit in the attribute word is defined only for one type of device, a driver for the other type of device must set that bit to 0.

BIT 1   is the standard input and output bit. It is used for character devices only. Use this bit to tell DOS if your character device driver is the new standard input device or standard output device.

BIT 2   is the NUL attribute bit. It is used for character devices only. Use it to tell DOS if your character device driver is a NUL device. Although there is a NUL device attribute bit, you cannot reassign the NUL device or replace it with your own routine. This attribute exists for DOS so that DOS can tell if the NUL device is being used.

BIT 3   is the clock device bit. It is used for character devices only. Default is 0. You can use it to tell DOS if your character device driver is the new CLOCK device.

BIT 4   is the 'fast video output' bit. The default is 0, which uses the BIOS for writing to the screen. When set, this bit uses int 29h for much faster screen updates.

BITS 5-10 reserved for DOS, unknown. Should be set to 0.

BIT 11 is the open/close removable media bit. Use it to tell DOS if the device driver can handle removable media. This bit is valid for DOS 3.0+ only. This bit was reserved in DOS 2.x. Since DOS 2.x does not look at this bit, its use is backward compatible.

BIT 12 reserved for DOS, unknown. Should be set to 0.

BIT 13 is the non-IBM format bit. When used for block devices it affects the operation of the BUILD BPB (BIOS parameter block) device call. For character devices it indicates that the devices implements the OUTPUT UNTIL BUSY device call.

BIT 14 is the IOCTL bit. It is used for both character and block devices. Use it to tell DOS whether the device driver can handle control strings through the IOCTL function call 44h. If a device driver cannot process control strings, it should set bit 14 to 0. This way DOS can return an error if an attempt is made through the IOCTL function call to send or receive control strings to the device. If a device can process control strings, it should set bit 14 to 1. This way, DOS makes calls to the IOCTL input and output device function to send and receive IOCTL strings. The IOCTL functions allow data to be sent to and from the device without actually doing a normal read or write. In this way, the device driver can use the data for its own use, (for example, setting a baud rate or stop bits, changing form lengths, etc.) It is up to the device to interpret the information that is passed to it, but the information must not be treated as a normal I/O request.

BIT 15 is the device type bit. Use it to tell the system the that driver is a block or character device.

Pointer to Strategy Routine

This field contains a pointer to 'device strategy' function in the driver. This function is called whenever a request is made to the driver, and must store the location of the request header from DOS. This pointer is a word value, and so must be in the same segment as the device header.

Pointer to Interrupt Routine

This field contains a pointer to the function which activates driver routines to perform the command in the current request header. This is called by DOS after the call to the strategy function, and should reset to the request header address stored by 'strategy', to allow for the possibility of interrupts between the two calls. This pointer is a word value, and so must be in the same segment as the device header.

Name/Unit Field

This is an 8-byte field that contains the name of a character device or the number of units in a block device. For the character names, the name is left-justified and the space is filled to 8 bytes. For block devices, the number of units can be placed in the first byte. This is optional because DOS fills in this location with the value returned by the driver's INIT code. The other 7 bytes of the block device ID are reserved and should not be used.

Installing Device Drivers

DOS installs new device drivers dynamically at boot time by reading and processing the DEVICE command in the CONFIG.SYS file. For example, if you have written a device driver called RAMDISK, to install it put this command in the CONFIG.SYS file:

```
DEVICE=[drive][path] RAMDISK [parameters]
```

DOS makes a FAR call to the device driver at its strategy entry point first, using the request header to pass information describing what DOS wants the device driver to do.

This strategy routine does not perform the request but rather queues the request or saves a pointer to the request header. The second entry point is the interrupt routine and is called by DOS immediately after the strategy routine returns. The interrupt routine is called with no parameters. Its function is to perform the operation based on the queued request and set up any return information.

DOS passes the pointer to the request header in ES:BX. This structure consists of a fixed length header (Request Header) followed by data pertinent to the operation to be performed.

Note: It is the responsibility of the device driver to preserve the machine state. For example, save all registers on entry and restore them on exit.

The stack used by DOS has enough room on it to save all the registers. If more stack space is needed, it is the device driver's responsibility to allocate and maintain another stack.

All calls to execute device drivers are FAR calls. FAR returns should be executed to return to DOS.

Installing Character Devices

One of the functions defined for each device is INIT. This routine is called only once when the device is installed and never again. The INIT routine returns the following:

A. A location to the first free byte of memory after the device driver, like a TSR that is stored in the terminating address field. This way, the initialization code can be used once and then thrown away to save space.

B. After setting the address field, a character device driver can set the status word and return.

Installing Block Devices

Block devices are installed in the same way as character devices. The difference is that block devices return additional information. Block devices must also return:

A. The number of units in the block device. This number determines the logical names the devices will have. For example, if the current logical device letter is F at the time of the install call, and the block device driver INIT routine returns three logical units, the letters G, H, and I are assigned to the units. The mapping is determined by the position of the driver in the device list and the number of units in the device. The number of units returned by INIT overrides the value in the name/unit field of the device header.

B. A pointer to a BPB (BIOS Parameter Block) pointer array. This is a pointer to an array of 'N' word pointers there 'N' is the number of units defined. These word pointers point to BPBs. This way, if all of the units are the same, the entire array can point to the same BPB to save space. The BPB contains information pertinent to the devices such as the sector size, number of sectors per allocation unit, and so forth. The sector size of the BPB cannot be greater than the maximum allotted size set at DOS initialization time. This array must be protected below the free pointer set by the return.

C. The media descriptor byte. This byte is passed to devices so that they know what parameters DOS is currently using for a particular drive unit.

Block devices can take several approaches. They can be 'dumb' or 'smart'. A dumb device would define a unit (and therefore a BPB) for each possible media drive combination. Unit 0=drive 0;single side, unit 1=drive 0;double side, etc. For this approach, the media descriptor bytes would mean nothing. A smart device would allow multiple media per unit. In this case, the BPB table returned at INIT must define space large enough to accommodate the largest possible medias supported (sector size in BPB must be as large as maximum sector size DOS is currently using). Smart drivers will use the media descriptor byte to pass information about what media is currently in a unit.

Request Header

The request header passes the information describing what DOS wants the device driver to do.

When a valid device driver command code or function is called by your application program, DOS develops a data structure called the 'Request Header' in ES:BX and passes it to the strategy entry point. This structure consists of a 13-byte defined header which may be followed by other data bytes depending on the function requested. It is the device driver's responsibility to preserve the machine state, for example, saving all registers including flags on entry and restoring them on exit. There is enough room on the stack when strategy or interrupt is called to do about 20 pushes. If more stack is needed, the driver should set aside its own stack space. The fixed ('static') part of the request header is as follows:

REQUEST HEADER

```
Offset  Length       Field
00h     byte         Length in bytes of the request header
01h     byte         Unit code. Determines subunit to use in block devices
                     Has no meaning for character devices
```

```
02h      byte       Command code
03h      word       Status
05h      8 bytes    Reserved for DOS
0Ch      varies     Data appropriate for the operation
```

Request Header Length Field

The length in bytes of the total request header (0-255) plus any data at the end of the header.

Unit Code Field

The unit code field identifies which unit in a block device driver the request is for. For example, if a block device driver has three units defined, then the possible values of the unit code field would be 0, 1, and 2. This field is not valid for character devices.

Command Code Field

The command code invokes a specific device driver function. Functions 0 through 12 are supported in all device drivers. Functions 13-15 are available only in DOS 3.0 or higher. Some functions are relevant for either character or block devices but not both; nonetheless all functions must have an executable routine present even if it does nothing but set the done flag in the return status word in the request header.

The command code field in the request header can have the following values:

```
code name                       function
0    INIT                       initialize driver for later use (used once only)
1    MEDIA CHECK                block devices only, NOP for character devices
2    BUILD BPB                  block devices only, NOP for character devices
3    IOCTL input                called only if device has IOCTL bit set
4    INPUT                      read data
5    NON-DESTRUCTIVE INPUT NO
     WAIT                       character devices only
6    INPUT STATUS               character devices only
7    INPUT FLUSH                character devices only
8    OUTPUT                     write data
9    OUTPUT                     write data with verify
10   OUTPUT STATUS              character devices only
11   OUTPUT FLUSH               character devices only
12   IOCTL OUTPUT               called only if device has IOCTL bit is set
13   DEVICE OPEN                called only if OPEN/CLOSE/RM bit is set
14   DEVICE CLOSE               called only if OPEN/CLOSE/RM bit is set
15   REMOVABLE MEDIA            only if OPEN/CLOSE/RM bit set & device is block
16   OUTPUT UNTIL BUSY          only called if bit 13 is set & device is character
```

The individual command codes are described later in this chapter.

Status Field

The status word field is zero on entry and is set by the driver interrupt routine on return.

The status field in the request header contains:

DEVICE DRIVER STATUS FIELD

```
size   bit   definition
byte    0
        1
        2
```

```
         3    Error message return code
         4    (with bit 15=1)
         5
         6
         7
byte     8    DONE
         9    BUSY
         A    Reserved by DOS, unknown
         B
         C
         D
         E
         F    Error
```

The low 8 bits of the status word define an error message if bit 15 is set. These errors are:

00h	write protect violation	01h	unknown unit
02h	device not ready	03h	unknown command
04h	CRC error	05h	bad drive request structure length
06h	seek error	07h	unknown media
08h	sector not found	09h	printer out of paper
0Ah	write fault	0Bh	read fault
0Ch	general failure	0Dh	reserved
0Eh	reserved	0Fh	invalid disk change

BIT 8   is the done bit. If it is set, it means the operation is complete. The driver sets the bit to 1 when it exits.

BIT 9   is the busy bit. It is only set by status calls and the removable media call.

BITS 10-14 are reserved.

BIT 15   is the error bit. If this bit is set, the low 8 bits of the status word(7-0) indicate the error code.

Reserved For DOS

Official sources label this area as 'reserved for DOS'. Another source indicates that this consists of two double-word (4-byte) pointers to be used to maintain a linked list of request headers for this device and a list of all current device requests being processed by DOS. This was apparently to be used for the undelivered multitasking version of DOS.

Device Driver Functions

All strategy routines are called with ES:BX pointing to the request header. The interrupt routines get the pointers to the request header from the queue the strategy routines stores them in. The command code in the request header tells the driver which function to perform.

Note: All DWORD pointers are stored offset first, then segment.

INIT

```
Command code = 0        (all devices)
```

Installable Device Drivers

Performs all initialization required at DOS boot time to install the driver and set local driver variables. This function is called only once, when the driver is loaded.

```
      ES:BX    pointer to 26-byte request header and data structure
Format of structure:
  offset    length      field
   00h     13 bytes    request header
   0Dh      dword      number of units (not set by character devices)
   11h      dword      ending address of the driver's resident code
   15h      dword      pointer to BPB array (not set by character devices)/pointer
                         to remainder of arguments
   19h      byte       drive number (DOS 3.0+ only)
```

When INIT is called, the driver must do the following:

A. set the number of units (block devices only)

B. set up the pointer to the BPB array (block devices only)

C. perform any initialization code (to modems, printers, etc)

D. set the ending address of the resident program code

E. set the status word in the request header

To obtain information obtained from CONFIG.SYS to a device driver at INIT time, the BPB pointer field points to a buffer containing the information passed from CONFIG.SYS following the =. The buffer that DOS passes to the driver at INIT after the file specification contains an ASCII string for the file OPEN. The ASCII string (ending in 0h) is terminated by a carriage return (0Dh) and linefeed (0Ah). If there is no parameter information after the file specification, the file specification is immediately followed by a linefeed (0Ah). This information is read-only and only system calls 01h-0Ch and 30h can be issued by the INIT code of the driver.

The last byte parameter contains the drive letter for the first unit of a block driver. For example, 0=A, 1=B etc.

If an INIT routine determines that it cannot set up the device and wants to abort without using any memory, follow this procedure:

A. set the number of units to 0

B. set the ending offset address at 0

C. set the ending offset segment address to the code segment (CS)

Note: If there are multiple device drivers in a single memory image file, the ending address returned by the last INIT called is the one DOS uses. It is recommended that all device drivers in a single memory image file return the same ending address.

Media Check

```
command code = 1         (block devices only)
           Checks to see if disk had been changed since last access.

           ES:BX pointer to 19-byte request header and data structure
Format of structure:
offset    length    field
00h      13 bytes  request header
0Dh         byte   media descriptor from BPB
0Eh         byte   returned
```

```
0Fh        dword    returns a pointer to the previous volume ID (if bit
                    11=1 and disk change is returned) (DOS 3.0+)
```

When the command code field is 1, DOS calls MEDIA CHECK for a drive unit and passes its current media descriptor byte. See 'Media Descriptor Byte' later in this chapter for more information about the byte. MEDIA CHECK returns one of the following:

A. media not changed
B. media changed
C. not sure
D. error code

The driver must perform the following:

A. set the status word in the request header

B. set the return byte
```
    00h   don't know if media has been changed
    01h   media has not been changed
    -1    media has been changed
```

DOS 3.0+: If the driver has set the removable media bit 11 of the device header attribute word to 1 and the driver returns -1 (media changed), the driver must set the DWORD pointer to the previous volume identification field. If DOS determines that the media changed is an error, DOS generates an error 0Fh (invalid disk change) on behalf of the device. If the driver does not implement volume identification support, but has bit 11 set to 1, the driver should set a pointer to the string 'NO NAME',0.

Media Descriptor

Currently the media descriptor byte has been defined for a few media types. This byte should be identical to the media byte if the device has the non-IBM format bit off. These predetermined values are:

```
media descriptor byte =    1 1 1 1 1 0 0 0
 (numeric order)           7 6 5 4 3 2 1 0

        BIT             MEANING
         0         0    not double sided
                   1    double sided
         1         0    not 8 sector
                   1    8 sector
         2         0    nonremovable
                   1    REMOVABLE
        3-7        must be set to 1
```

Build BPB (BIOS Parameter Block)

```
command code = 2          (block devices only)

        ES:BX    pointer to 22-byte request header and data structure
Format of structure:
offset   length           field
00h      13 bytes    request header
0Dh         byte     media descriptor from DOS
0Eh         dword    transfer address (buffer address)
12h         dword    pointer to BPB table
```

DOS calls BUILD BPB under the following two conditions:

A. If 'media changed' is returned.

B. If 'not sure' is returned. If so, there are no used buffers. Used buffers are buffers with changed data that have not yet been written to the disk.

The driver must do the following:

A. set the pointer to the BPB.

B. set the status word in the request header.

The driver must determine the correct media type currently in the unit to return the pointer to the BPB table. The way the buffer is used (pointer passed by DOS) is determined by the non-IBM format bit in the attribute field of the device header. If bit 13=0 (device is IBM compatible), the buffer contains the first sector of the FAT (most importantly the FAT ID byte). The driver must not alter this buffer in this case. If bit 13=1 the buffer is a one sector scratch area which can be used for anything.

For drivers that support volume identification and disk change, the call should cause a new volume identification to be read off the disk. This call indicates that the disk has been legally changed.

If the device is IBM compatible, it must be true that the first sector of the first FAT is located at the same sector for all possible media. This is because the FAT sector is read before the media is actually determined.

The information relating to the BPB for a particular media is kept in the boot sector for the media. In particular, the format of the boot sector is:

For DOS 2.x, 3 byte near jump (0E9h). For DOS 3.x+, 2 byte near jump (0EBh) followed by a NOP (90h)

```
8 bytes      OEM name and version
   BYTE              sectors per allocation unit (must be a power of 2)
   WORD      B       reserved sectors (starting at logical sector 0)
   BYTE              number of FATs
   WORD      P       max number of root directory entries
   WORD              number of sectors in logical image (total number of sectors in
                     media, including boot sector directories, etc.)
             B
   BYTE              media descriptor
   WORD              number of sectors occupied by a single FAT
   WORD              sectors per track
   WORD              number of heads
   WORD              number of hidden sectors
```

The three words at the end return information about the media. The number of heads is useful for supporting different multihead drives that have the same storage capacity but a different number of surfaces. The number of hidden sectors is useful for drive partitioning schemes.

INPUT / OUTPUT (IOCTL)

```
command code = 3 IOCTL Read
               4 Read                  (block or character devices)
               8 Write                 (block or character devices)
               9 Write With Verify
              12 IOCTL Write
              16 Output Until Busy     (character devices only)

        ES:BX    pointer to 24-byte request header and data structure
```

```
Format of structure:
offset      length       field
00h         13 bytes     request header
0Dh         byte         media descriptor byte from BPB
0Eh         dword        transfer address (buffer address)
12h         word         byte/sector count
14h         word         starting sector number (block devices)
16h         dword        (DOS 3.0+) pointer to the volume ID if error code 0Fh is
                         returned
```

The driver must perform the following:

A. set the status word in the request header

B. perform the requested function

C. set the actual number of sectors or bytes transferred

No error checking is performed on an IOCTL I/O call. However, the driver must set the return sector or byte count to the actual number of bytes transferred.

Under certain circumstances a block device driver may be asked to do a write operation of 64k bytes that seems to be a 'wrap around' of the transfer address in the BIOS I/O packet. This arises due to an optimization added to write code in DOS. It will only happen in writes that are within a sector size of 64k on files that are being extended past the current end of file. It is allowable for the device driver to ignore the balance of the write that wraps around, if it so chooses. For example, a write of 10000h bytes worth of sectors with a transfer address of XXX:1 ignores the last two bytes. A user program can never request an I/O of more than 0FFFFh bytes and cannot wrap around (even to 0) in the transfer segment, so in that case the last two bytes can be ignored.

A program that uses DOS function calls can never request an input or output function of more than 0FFFFh bytes, therefore, a wrap around in the transfer (buffer) segment can never occur. It is for this reason you can ignore bytes that would have wrapped around in the transfer segment.

If the driver returns an error code of 0Fh (invalid disk change) it must put a DWORD pointer to an ASCIIZ string which is the correct volume ID to ask the user to reinsert the disk.

DOS 3.0+:

The reference count of open files on the field (maintained by the OPEN and CLOSE calls) allows the driver to determine when to return error 0Fh. If there are no open files (reference count=0) and the disk has been changed, the I/O is all right, and error 0Fh is not returned. If there are open files (reference count 0) and the disk has been changed, an error 0Fh condition may exist.

Nondestructive Input No Wait

```
command code = 5            (character devices only)
    Reads a character from input stream but does not remove it from the
    buffer

        ES:BX     pointer to 14-byte request header and data structure
Format of structure:
offset      length          field
00h         13 bytes        request header
0Dh         byte            read from device
```

The driver must do the following:

A. return a byte from the device

Installable Device Drivers

B. set the status word in the request header.

If the character device returns busy bit=0 (characters in the buffer), then the next character that would be read is returned. This character is not removed form the buffer (hence the term nondestructive input). This call allows DOS to look ahead one character.

Status

```
command codes =  6    Input Status     (character devices only)
                10    Output Status    (character devices only)
        Check for characters waiting in input buffer

        ES:BX   pointer to 13-byte request header
```

This driver must perform the following:

A. perform the requested function

B. set the busy bit

C. set the status word in the request header.

The busy bit is set as follows:

For input on unbuffered character devices: if the busy bit (bit 9) is 1 on return, a write request would wait for completion of a current request. If the busy bit is 0, there is no current request. Therefore, a write request would start immediately.

For input on buffered character devices: if the busy bit is 1 on return, a read request does to the physical device. If the busy bit is 0, there are characters in the device buffer and a read returns quickly. It also indicates that a user has typed something. DOS assumes all character devices have a type-ahead input buffer. Devices that do not have this buffer should always return busy=0 so that DOS does not hang waiting for information to be put in a buffer that does not exist.

Flush Input Buffers

```
command code = 7        (character devices only)
        Forces all data in buffers to specified device.

        ES:BX   pointer to 13-byte request header
```

This call tells the driver to flush (terminate) all pending requests that it has knowledge of. Its primary use is to flush the input queue on character devices.

The driver must set the status word in the request header upon return.

Flush Output Buffers

```
command code 11         (character devices only)
        Forces all data in buffers to specified device.

        ES:BX   pointer to 13-byte request header
```

This call tells the driver to flush all output buffers and discards any pending requests. Its primary use is to flush the output queue on character devices.

The driver must set the status word in the request header upon return.

Open or Close (DOS 3.0+)

```
command code = 13    Open     (block or character devices)
               14    Close    (block or character devices)

      ES:BX    pointer to 13-byte static request header
```

These calls are designed to give the device information about the current file activity on the device if bit 11 of the attribute word is set. On block devices, these calls can be used to manage local buffering. The device can keep a reference count. Every OPEN causes the device to increment the reference count. Every CLOSE causes the device to decrement the reference count. When the reference count is 0, if means there are no open files in the device. Therefore, the device should flush buffers inside the device it has written to because now the user can change the media on a REMOVABLE media drive. If the media had been changed, it is advisable to reset the reference count to 0 without flushing the buffers. This can be thought of as 'last close causes flush'. These calls are more useful on character devices. The OPEN call can be used to send a device initialization string. On a printer, this could cause a string to be sent to set the font, page size, etc. so that the printer would always be in a known state in the I/O stream. Similarly, a CLOSE call can be used to send a post string (like a form feed) at the end of an I/O stream. Using IOCTL to set these pre and post strings provides a flexible mechanism of serial I/O device stream control.

Since all processes have access to STDIN, STDOUT, STDERR, STDAUX, and STDPRN (handles 0, 1, 2, 3, and 4) the CON, AUX, and PRN devices are always open.

Removable Media (DOS 3.0+)

```
command code = 15       (block devices only)
        This call identifies the media type as removable or nonremovable.

        ES:BX   pointer to 13-byte static request header
```

To use this call, set bit 11 (removable media) of the attribute field to 1. Block devices can only use this call through a subfunction of the IOCTL function call (int 21h fn44h).

This call is useful because it allows a utility to know whether it is dealing with a nonremovable media drive or with a removable media drive. For example, the FORMAT utility needs to know whether a drive is removable or nonremovable because it prints different versions of some prompts.

Note: No error checking is performed. It is assumed that this call always succeeds.

10

Expanded and Enhanced Expanded Memory Specifications

History

The Lotus/Intel/Microsoft Expanded Memory Manager was originally a Lotus and Intel project and was announced as version 3.0 in the second quarter of 1985 primarily as a means of running larger Lotus worksheets by transparently paging unused sections to bank-switched memory. Shortly afterward Microsoft announced support of the standard and version 3.2 was subsequently released with support for Microsoft Windows. LIM 3.2 supported up to 8 megabytes of paged memory. The LIM 4.0 supports up to 32 megabytes of paged memory.

Uses of Expanded Memory

The most common use for expanded memory is as a RAMdisk outside of DOS memory. The Lotus 1-2-3 Release 2 spreadsheet and many of its imitators can use EMS for storing part of the spreadsheet. AutoCAD, DesignCAD, and some other CAD programs can make use of EMS, as well as disk caching, etc. The MultiEdit word processor can also use EMS, and it looks like new applications are slowly starting to join the ranks of EMS-aware software.

The most striking use of expanded memory is Quarterdeck's DesQview. DesQview and the AQA EEMS were designed for each other. When EEMS is available, DesQview can manage multiple DOS partitions as a true multitasking manager. A program running under DesQview sees EEMS as conventional memory.

DOS and Expanded Memory

DOS 4.0 supports expanded memory for the internal functions of BUFFERS as well as various external programs (FASTOPEN and VDISK, for example). 4.0 checks for the presence of the Expanded Memory Manager device driver and passes calls to it like any other application. DOS 4.0 had a number of bugs with its EMS functions (such as not recognizing various non-IBM EMS managers and performing operations with the EMS board prohibited by the LIM 4.0 specification it supposedly embraces). DOS 4.01 was quietly released immediately afterward but still has problems. I have a real IBM 2Mb Expanded Memory Adapter in my AT (at $1395, I may have the only one in captivity!). Under DOS 4.01, XMA2EMS.SYS will initialize only 1664k of my 2048k. The card passes its own ROM and disk diagnostics perfectly. VDISK will also not function, aborting with a 'not enough memory' error.

The bug in DOS 4.00 can cause DOS 4.00 to corrupt files or entire directories when running programs that use expanded memory. The problem arises when using the DOS 4.00 /X option with BUFFERS, FASTOPEN, and VDISK commands. DOS 4.0 makes assumptions that are fundamentally inconsistent with standard EMS 4.0 usage. EMS 4.0 contains functions for saving and restoring the entire memory mapping context. Programs that need to change the memory map use these functions to save the current map, map in whatever memory they need, and then restore the original map. These functions change the entire map, including the pages of memory being used by DOS 4.0 /X option. DOS 4.0, however, assumes that the map for its pages NEVER get changed. The result is that DOS 4.0 gets confused about which buffers are currently in memory and corrupts the file data and/or directory data that is buffered.

Since the only really practical use for EMS in DOS 4.0 is in BUFFERS=, and any cache program (including IBM's own IBMCACHE) will blow BUFFERS= away, there's not much reason to worry about DOS 4.0's supposed EMS functionality.

One very good and one very bad result should come about from DOS 4.0's EMS support. First, since IBM now officially recognizes EMS, sells EMS cards, and DOS supports EMS (somewhat), we may see more programs making better use of EMS hardware.

The bad result is that IBM, for some idiotic reason, chooses to refer to EMS as 'XMA'. There already *IS* an XMA standard, which is defined by Microsoft, which uses 80286/80386 extended over-1-megabyte memory in a fashion much like EMS. Unfortunately, the XMA standard is little-known and I've seen advertisements for 'XMA' expanded memory adapters (sigh). As if extended, expanded, enhanced expanded, EMS, EEMS, conventional, HMA, and XMA weren't confusing enough already.

What Was That Again?

Conventional Memory: Normal 0-640k address space, 8088 and 286/386 real mode
High Memory: the 384k between the end of 640 and the 1 meg limit of the 8088 microprocessor
High Memory Area: (HMA) the first 64k of the over-1-meg 286/386 address space
Extended Memory: the over-1-meg address space of the 286/386, including HMA Use of this memory is defined by the Microsoft Extended Memory Specification, or XMA
Expanded Memory: Paged memory swapped in and out of a predetermined area of the 0-1meg real mode address area. The current specifications are LIM 4.1 and AQA EEMS 3.2.
Display Memory: memory between 640k and 1 meg where memory-mapped RAM from video cards is accessed.

AST/QuadRAM/Ashton-Tate Enhanced Expanded Memory Specification

The AQA EEMS maintains upward compatibility with the LIM, but is a superset of functions.

Expanded and Enhanced Expanded Memory Specifications 187

The AQA EEMS permits its pages to be scattered throughout the unused portion of the machine's address space. On August 19, 1987, the new version of the Expanded Memory Specification (EMS) was announced by Lotus, Intel and Microsoft. This new version of the specification includes many features of the Enhanced Expanded Memory Specification (EEMS) originally developed by AST Research, Quadram and Ashton-Tate, although the three original sponsoring companies elected not to make the new specification upward compatible with EEMS. AST Research says that they will endorse EMS 4.0 without reservation.

The definitive document for the LIM-EMS is Intel part number 300275-004, August, 1987. The definitive document for the AQA EEMS standard is AST part number 00048-001 B, June, 1987.

Both of these documents are free for the asking (Intel will even send you a floppy with the latest drivers). Unfortunately, the Intel documentation makes determining which functions are not available under LIM 3.x a bit difficult. There are very few LIM 4.0 or EEMS cards in the hands of users; most hardware is LIM 3.1 or 3.2 spec.

EMS Address Space Map

Mapping of the EMS address space:

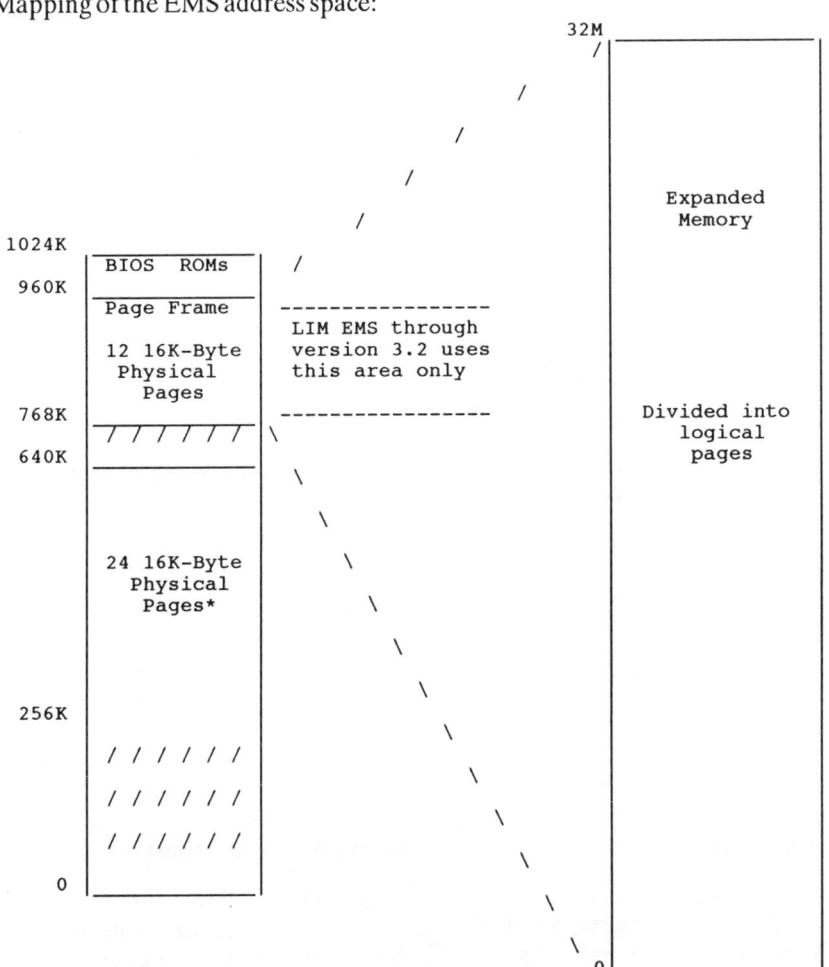

```
                                                32M  _____
                                                 /  |       |
                                                /   |       |
                                               /    |       |
                                              /     |       |
                                             /      |Expanded|
                                            /       |Memory |
1024K    _____        /                       |       |
        |BIOS  ROMs |       /                       |       |
 960K   |-----------|                               |       |
        |Page Frame |      -----------------        |       |
        |12 16K-Byte|      LIM EMS through          |       |
        | Physical  |      version 3.2 uses         |       |
        |  Pages    |      this area only           |       |
 768K   |-----------|      -----------------        |Divided into|
        |///////////|  \                            | logical    |
 640K   |_____|   \                           |  pages     |
        |           |    \                          |       |
        |           |     \                         |       |
        |           |      \                        |       |
        |24 16K-Byte|       \                       |       |
        | Physical  |        \                      |       |
        |  Pages*   |         \                     |       |
        |           |          \                    |       |
        |           |           \                   |       |
        |           |            \                  |       |
 256K   |           |             \                 |       |
        |           |              \                |       |
        |///////////|               \               |       |
        |///////////|                \              |       |
        |///////////|                 \             |       |
   0    |_____|                  \            |       |
                                        \           |       |
                                         \    0     |_____|
```

The page frame is located above the 640k system RAM area, anywhere from 0A000h to 0FFFFh. This area is used by the video adapters, network cards, and add-on ROMs (as in hard disk controllers). The page frames are mapped around areas that are in use.

Writing Programs That Use Expanded Memory

In order to use expanded memory, applications must perform these steps in the following order:

1. Determine if EMM is installed.
2. Determine if enough expanded memory pages exist for your application. (Function 3)
3. Allocate expanded memory pages (Functions 4 or 18).
4. Get the page frame base address (Function 2).
5. Map in expanded memory pages (Functions 5 or 17).
6. Read/write/execute data in expanded memory, just as if it were conventional memory.
7. Return expanded memory pages to expanded memory pool before exiting (Functions 6 or 18).

Programming Guidelines

The following section contains guidelines for programmers writing applications that use EMM.

1. Do not put a program's stack in expanded memory.
2. Do not replace interrupt 67h. This is the interrupt vector the EMM uses. Replacing interrupt 67h could result in disabling the Expanded Memory Manager.
3. Do not map into conventional memory address space your application doesn't own. Applications that use the EMM to swap into conventional memory space, must first allocate this space from the operating system. If the operating system is not aware that a region of memory it manages is in use, it will think it is available. This could have disastrous results. EMM should not be used to 'allocate' conventional memory. DOS is the proper manager of conventional memory space. EMM should only be used to swap data in conventional memory space previously allocated from DOS.
4. Applications that plan on using data aliasing in expanded memory must check for the presence of expanded memory hardware. Data aliasing occurs when mapping one logical page into two or more mappable segments. This makes one 16K-byte expanded memory page appear to be in more than one 16K-byte memory address space. Data aliasing is legal and sometimes useful for applications. Software-only expanded memory emulators cannot perform data aliasing. A simple way to distinguish software emulators from actual expanded memory hardware is to attempt data aliasing and check the results. For example, map one logical page into four physical pages. Write to physical page 0. Read physical pages 1-3 to see if the data is there as well. If the data appears in all four physical pages, then expanded memory hardware is installed in the system, and data aliasing is supported.
5. Applications should always return expanded memory pages to the expanded memory manager upon termination. These pages will be made available for other applications. If unneeded pages are not returned to the expanded memory manager, the system could run

out of expanded memory pages or expanded memory handles.
6. Terminate and stay resident programs (TSRs) should always save the state of the map registers before changing them. Since TSRs may interrupt other programs which may be using expanded memory, they must not change the state of the page mapping registers without first saving them. Before exiting, TSRs must restore the state of the map registers. The following sections describe the three ways to save and restore the state of the map registers.
   i. Save Page Map and Restore Page Map (Functions 8 and 9). This is the simplest of the three methods. The EMM saves the map register contents in its own data structures - the application does not need to provide extra storage locations for the mapping context. The last mapping context to be saved, under a particular handle, will be restored when a call to Restore Page Map is issued with the same handle. This method is limited to one mapping context for each handle and saves the context for only LIM standard 64K-byte page frames.
   ii. Get/Set Page Map (Function 15). This method requires the application to allocate space for the storage array. The EMM saves the mapping context in an array whose address is passed to the EMM. When restoring the mapping context with this method, an application passes the address of an array which contains a previously stored mapping context. This method is preferable if an application needs to do more than one save before a restore. It provides a mechanism for switching between more than one mapping context.
   iii. Get/Set Partial Page Map (Function 16). This method provides a way for saving a partial mapping context. It should be used when the application does not need to save the context of all mappable memory. This function also requires that the storage array be part of the application's data.
7. All functions using pointers to data structures must have those data structures in memory which will not be mapped out. Functions 22 and 23 (Alter Map & Call and Alter Map & Jump) are the only exceptions.

Page Frames

The bank switched memory chunks are referred to as 'page frames'. These frame consist of four 16K memory blocks mapped into some of the normally unused system ROM address area, 0C0000-0EFFFF. Each 16K page is independent of the other and they can map to discrete or overlapping areas of the 8 megabyte expanded memory address area. Most cards allow selection of addresses to prevent conflict with other cards, such as hard disk controllers and other expanded memory boards.

Calling the Manager

Applications programs communicate with the EMM device driver directly via user interrupt 67h. All communication between the application program and the driver by-passes DOS completely. To call the driver, register AH is loaded with the number of the EMM service requested; DX is loaded with the file handle; and interrupt 67h is called. ES:DI is used to pass the address of a buffer or array if needed.

On return AH contains 00h if the call was successful or an error code from 80h to 8Fh if unsuccessful.

Testing For the Presence of the Expanded Memory Manager

Before an application program can use the Expanded Memory Manager, it must determine whether the manager is present. The two recommended methods are the 'open handle' technique and the 'get interrupt vector' technique.

The majority of application programs can use either the 'open handle' or the 'get interrupt vector' method. However, if your program is a device driver or if it interrupts DOS during file system operations, you must use only the 'get interrupt vector' method.

Device drivers execute from within DOS and can't access the DOS file functions; programs that interrupt DOS during file operations have a similar restriction. During their interrupt processing procedures, they can't access the DOS file functions because another program may be using the system. Since the 'get interrupt vector' method doesn't require the DOS file functions, you must use it for programs of this type.

The 'Open Handle' Method

Most application programs can use the DOS 'Open Handle' method to test for the presence of the EMM. To use this method, follow these steps in order:

1. Issue an 'open handle' command (DOS function 3Dh) in 'read only' access mode (register AL = 0). This function requires your program to point to an ASCII string which contains the path name of the file or device in which you're interested (register set DS:DX contains the pointer). In this case the file is actually the reserved name of the expanded memory manager.

   You should format the ASCII string as follows:

   ```
   ASCII_device_name  DB  'EMMXXXX0', 0
   ```

   The ASCII codes for the capital letters EMMXXXX0 are terminated by a byte containing a value of zero.

2. If DOS returns no error code, skip Steps 3 and 4 and go to Step 5. If DOS returns a 'Too many open files' error code, go to Step 3. If DOS returns a 'File/Path not found' error code, skip Step 3 and go to Step 4.

3. If DOS returns a 'Too many open files' (not enough handles) status code, your program should invoke the 'open file' command before it opens any other files. This will guarantee that at least one file handle will be available to perform the function without causing this error. After the program performs the 'open file' command, it should perform the test described in Step 6 and close the 'file handle' (DOS function 3Eh). Don't keep the manager 'open' after this status test is performed since 'manager' functions are not available through DOS. Go to Step 6.

4. If DOS returns a 'File/Path not found", the memory manager is not installed. If your application requires the memory manager, the user will have to reboot the system with a disk containing the memory manager and the appropriate CONFIG.SYS file before proceeding.

Expanded and Enhanced Expanded Memory Specifications 191

5. If DOS doesn't return an error status code you can assume that either a device with the name EMMXXXX0 is resident in the system, or a file with this name is on disk in the current disk drive. Go to Step 6.

6. Issue an 'I/O Control for Devices' command (DOS function 44h) with a 'get device information' command (register AL = 0). DOS function 44h determines whether EMMXXXX0 is a device or a file. You must use the file handle (register BX) which you obtained in Step 1 to access the 'EMM' device. This function returns the 'device information' in a word (register DX). Go to Step 7.

7. If DOS returns any error code, you should assume that the memory manager device driver is not installed. If your application requires the memory manager, the user will have to reboot the system with a disk containing the memory manager and the appropriate CONFIG.SYS file before proceeding.

8. If DOS didn't return an error status, test the contents of bit 7 (counting from 0) of the 'device information' word (register DX) the function returned. Go to Step 9.

9. If bit 7 of the 'device information' word contains a zero, then EMMXXXX0 is a file, and the memory manager device driver is not present. If your application requires the memory manager, the user will have to reboot the system with a disk containing the memory manager and the appropriate CONFIG.SYS file before proceeding. If bit 7 contains a one, then EMMXXXX0 is a device. Go to Step 10.

10. Issue an 'I/O Control for Devices' command (DOS function 44h) with a 'get output status' command (register AL = 7). You must use the file handle you obtained in Step 1 to access the 'EMM' device (register BX). Go to Step 11.

11. If the expanded memory device driver is ready, the memory manager passes a status value of 0FFh in register AL. The status value is 00h if the device driver is not ready. If the memory manager device driver is 'not ready' and your application requires its presence, the user will have to reboot the system with a disk containing the memory manager and the appropriate CONFIG.SYS file before proceeding. If the memory manager device driver is 'ready', go to Step 12.

12. Issue a 'Close File Handle' command (DOS function 3Eh) to close the expanded memory device driver. You must use the file handle you obtained in Step 1 to close the 'EMM' device (register BX).

The 'Get Interrupt Vector' technique

Any type of program can use this method to test for the presence of the EMM.

Use this method (not the 'Open Handle' method) if your program is a device driver or if it interrupts DOS during file system operations.

Follow these steps in order:

1. Issue a 'get vector' command (DOS function 35h) to obtain the contents of interrupt vector array entry number 67h (addresses 0000:019Ch through 0000:019Fh). The memory manager uses this interrupt vector to perform all manager functions. The offset portion of this interrupt service routine address is stored in the word located at address 0000:019Ch; the segment portion is stored in the word located at address 0000:019Eh.

192 The Programmer's Technical Reference

2. Compare the 'device name field' with the contents of the ASCII string which starts at the address specified by the segment portion of the contents of interrupt vector address 67h and a fixed offset of 000Ah. If DOS loaded the memory manager at boot time this name field will have the name of the device in it. Since the memory manager is implemented as a character device driver, its program origin is 0000h. Device drivers are required to have a 'device header' located at the program origin. Within the 'device header' is an 8 byte 'device name field'. For a character mode device driver this name field is always located at offset 000Ah within the device header. The device name field contains the name of the device which DOS uses when it references the device. If the result of the 'string compare' in this technique is positive, the memory manager is present.

Terminate and Stay Resident (TSR) Program Cooperation

In order for TSR's to cooperate with each other and with other applications, a TSR must only remap the DOS partition it lives in. This rule applies at all times, even when no expanded memory is present.

Expanded Memory Services Quick List

```
         1 (40h) Get Manager Status
         2 (41h) Get Page Frame Segment
         3 (42h) Get Number of Pages
         4 (43h) Get Handle and Allocate Memory
         5 (44h) Map Memory
         6 (45h) Release Handle and Memory
         7 (46h) Get EMM Version
         8 (47h) Save Mapping Context
         9 (48h) Restore Mapping Context
        10 (49h) Reserved
        11 (4Ah) Reserved
        12 (4Bh) Get Number of EMM Handles
        12 (4Ch) Get Pages Owned By Handle
        14 (4Dh) Get Pages for All Handles
        15 (4Eh) Get Or Set Page Map

new LIM 4.0 specification:
        16 (4Fh) Get/Set Partial Page Map
        17 (50h) Map/Unmap Multiple Pages
        18 (51h) Reallocate Pages
        19 (52h) Handle Attribute Functions
        20 (53h) Get Handle Name
        21 (54h) Get Handle Directory
        22 (55h) Alter Page Map & Jump
        23 (56h) Alter Page Map & Call
        24 (57h) Move Memory Region
        25 (58h) Get Mappable Physical Address Array
        26 (59h) Get Expanded Memory Hardware
        27 (5Ah) Allocate Raw Pages
        28 (5Bh) Get Alternate Map Register Set
        29 (5Ch) Prepare Expanded Memory Hardware
        30 (5Dh) Enable OS/E Function Set
        31 (5Eh) Unknown
        32 (5Fh) Unknown
        33 (60h) (EEMS) Get Physical Window Array
        34 (61h) AST Generic Accelerator Card Support
```

Expanded Memory Services
Functions Defined in EMS 3.2 Specification

Interrupt 67h

```
Function 40h  Get Manager Status
LIM Function Call 1
              Returns a status code indicating whether the memory manager is
              present and the hardware is working correctly.
entry   AH    40h
return  AH    error status: 00h, 80h, 81h, 84h
note 1. Upward and downward compatible with both EMS and EEMS 3.2.
     2. This call can be used only after establishing that the EMS driver is in
        fact present
     3. Uses register AX
     4. This function doesn't require an EMM handle.

Function 41h  Get Page Frame Segment Address
LIM Function Call 2
              Obtain segment address of the page frame used by the EMM.
entry   AH    41h
return  AH    error status: 00h, 80h, 81h, 84h
        BX    page frame segment address (error code 0)
note 1. Upward and downward compatible with both EMS and EEMS 3.2.
     2. Uses registers AX & BX
     3. This function doesn't require an EMM handle.
     4. The value in BX has no meaning if AH   0.

Function 42h  Get Unallocated Page Count
LIM Function Call 3
              Obtain total number of logical expanded memory pages present in the
              system and the number of those pages not already allocated.
entry   AH    42h
return  AH    error status: 00h, 80h, 81h, 84h
        BX    00h    All EMS pages in have already been allocated. None are
                     currently available for expanded memory.
               value number of unallocated pages currently available
        DX    total number of EMS pages
note 1. Upward and downward compatible with both EMS and EEMS 3.2. Note that EMS
        and EEMS 3.2 had no mechanism to return the maximum number of handles
        that can be allocated by programs. This is handled by the EMS 4.0 new
        function 54h/02h.
     2. Uses registers AX, BX, DX
     3. This function doesn't require an EMM handle.

Function 43h  Get Handle and Allocate Memory
LIM Function Call 4
              Notifies the EMM that a program will be using extended memory,
              obtains a handle, and allocates a certain number of logical pages
              of extended memory to be controlled by that handle
entry   AH    43h
        BX    number of 16k logical pages requested (zero OK)
return  AH    error status: 00h, 80h, 81h, 84h, 85h, 87h, 88h, 89h
        DX    unique EMM handle (see note 2)
note 1. Upward compatible with both EMS and EEMS 3.2; EMS and EEMS 3.2 do not
        allow the allocation of zero pages (returns error status 89h). EMS 4.0
        does allow zero pages to be requested for a handle, allocating pages
        later using function 51h
     2. Your program must use this EMM handle as a parameter in any function that
        requires it. You can use up to 255 handles. The uppermost byte of the
        handle will be zero and cannot be used by the application.
     3. Regs AX & DX are used

Function 44h  Map Memory
LIM Function Call 5
              Maps one of the logical pages of expanded memory assigned to a
              handle onto one of the four physical pages within the EMM's page
              frame.
```

entry   AH   44h
        AL   physical page to be mapped (0-3)
        BX   the logical page to be mapped (zero through [number of pages
                allocated to the EMM handle - 1]). If the logical page number is
                0FFFFh, the physical page specified in AL will be unmapped (made
                inaccessible for reading or writing).
        DX   the EMM handle your program received from Function 4 (Allocate
                Pages).
return AH   error status: 00h, 80h, 81h, 83h, 84h, 8Ah, 8Bh
note 1. downward compatible with both EMS and EEMS 3.2; EMS and EEMS 3.2 do not
        support unmap (logical page 0FFFFh) capability. Also, EEMS 3.2 specified
        there were precisely four physical pages; EMS 4.0 uses the subfunctions
        of function 58h to return the permitted number of physical pages. This
        incorporates the functionality of function 69h ("function 42") of EEMS.
     2. uses register AX

Function 45h Release Handle and Memory
LIM Function Call 6
        Deallocates the logical pages of expanded memory currently assigned
        to a handle and then releases the handle itself.
entry   AH   45h
        DX   handle
return AH   error status: 00h, 80h, 81h, 83h, 84h, 86h
note 1. upward and downward compatible with both EMS and EEMS 3.2.
     2. uses register AX
     3. when a handle is deallocated, its name is set to all ASCII nulls (binary
        zeros).
     4. a program must perform this function before it exits to DOS or no other
        programs can use these pages or the EMM handle.

Function 46h Get EMM Version
LIM Function Call 7
        Returns the version number of the Expanded Memory Manager software.
entry   AH   46h
return AH   error status: 00h, 80h, 81h, 84h
        AL   version number byte (if AL=00h)
                binary coded decimal (BCD) format if version byte:
                high nibble: integer digit of the version number
                low nibble : fractional digit of version number
                i.e., version 4.0 is represented like this:
                        0100 0000
                         /   \
                         4 . 0
note 1. upward and downward compatible with both EMS and EEMS 3.2. It appears
        that the intended use for this function is to return the version of the
        vendor implementation of the expanded memory manager instead of the
        specification version.
     2. uses register AX

Function 47h Save Mapping Context
LIM Function Call 8
        Save the contents of the expanded memory page-mapping registers on
        the expanded memory boards, associating those contents with a
        specific EMM handle.
entry   AH   47h
        DX   caller's EMM handle (NOT current EMM handle)
return AH   error status: 00h, 80h, 81h, 83h, 84h, 8Ch, 8Dh
note 1. upward and downward compatible with both EMS and EEMS 3.2.
     2. This only saves the context saved in EMS 3.2 specification; if a driver,
        interrupt routine or TSR needs to do more, functions 4Eh (Page Map
        functions) or 4Fh (Partial Page Map functions) should be used.
     3. no mention is made about the number of save contexts to provide. AST
        recommends in their Rampage AT manual one save context for each handle
        plus one per possible interrupt (5 + handles).
     4. uses register AX
     5. this function saves the state of the map registers for only the 64K page
        frame defined in versions 3.x of the LIM. Since all applications written
        to LIM versions 3.x require saving the map register state of only this
        64K page frame, saving the entire mapping state for a large number of
        mappable pages would be inefficient use of memory. Applications that use
        a mappable memory region outside the LIM 3.x page frame should use

Expanded and Enhanced Expanded Memory Specifications   195

                functions 15 or 16 to save and restore the state of the map registers.

```
Function 48h Restore Page Map
LIM Function Call 9
             Restores the contents of all expanded memory hardware page-mapping
             registers to the values associated with the given handle by a
             previous function 08h (Save Mapping Context).
entry   AH   48h
        DX   caller's EMM handle (NOT current EMM handle)
return  AH   error status: 00h, 80h, 81h, 83h, 84h, 8Eh
note 1. upward and downward compatible with both EMS and EEMS 3.2.
     2. This only restores the context saved in EMS 3.2 specification; if a
        driver, interrupt routine or TSR needs to do more, functions 4Eh (Page
        Map functions) or 4Fh (Partial Page Map functions) should be used.
     3. uses register AX
     4. this function saves the state of the map registers for only the 64K page
        frame defined in versions 3.x of the LIM. Since all applications written
        to LIM versions 3.x require saving the map register state of only this
        64K page frame, saving the entire mapping state for a large number of
        mappable pages would be inefficient use of memory. Applications that use
        a mappable memory region outside the LIM 3.x page frame should use
        functions 15 or 16 to save and restore the state of the map registers.

Function 49h Reserved
LIM Function Call 10
             This function was used in EMS 3.0, but was no longer documented in
             EMS 3.2. It formerly returned the page mapping register I/O port
             array. Use of this function is discouraged, and in EMS 4.0 may
             conflict with the use of the new functions 16 through 30 (4Fh through
             5Dh) and functions 10 and 11. Functions 10 and 11 are specific to the
             hardware on Intel expanded memory boards and may not work correctly
             on all vendors' expanded memory boards.

Function 4Ah Reserved
LIM Function Call 11
             This function was used in EMS 3.0, but was no longer documented in
             EMS 3.2. It was formerly Get Page Translation Array. Use of this
             function is discouraged, and in EMS 4.0 may conflict with the use of
             the new functions (4Fh through 5Dh).

Function 4Bh Get Number of EMM Handles
LIM Function Call 12
             The Get Handle Count function returns the number of open EMM handles
             (including the operating system handle 0) in the system.
entry   AH   4Bh
return  AH   error status: 00h, 80h, 81h, 84h
        BX   handle count (AH=00h) (including the operating system handle
             [0]). max 255.
note 1. upward and downward compatible with EMS and EEMS 3.2.
     2. uses registers AX and BX

Function 4Ch Get Pages Owned by Handle
LIM Function Call 13
             Returns number of logical expanded memory pages allocated to a
             specific EMM handle.
entry   AH   4Ch
        DX   handle
return  AH   error status: 00h, 80h, 81h, 83h, 84h
        BX   pages allocated to handle, max 2048 because the EMM
             allows a maximum of 2048 pages (32M bytes) of expanded memory.
note 1. This function is upward compatible with EMS and EEMS 3.2.
     2. programmers should compare the number returned in BX with the maximum
        number of pages returned by function 42h register DX, total number of
        EMM pages. This should be an UNSIGNED comparison, just in case the spec
        writers decide to use 16 bit unsigned numbers (for a maximum space of
        one gigabyte) instead of signed numbers (for a maximum space of 512 mega
        bytes). Unsigned comparisons will work properly in either case
     3. uses registers AX and BX
Function 4Dh Get Pages for All Handles
LIM Function Call 14
             Returns an array containing all active handles and the number of
```

```
                        logical expanded memory pages associated with each handle.
   entry    AH          4Dh
            ES:DI       pointer to 1020 byte array to receive information on an array of
                        structures where a copy of all open EMM handles and the number of
                        pages allocated to each will be stored.
   return   AH          error status: 00h, 80h, 81h, 84h
            BX          number of active handles (1-255); array filled with 2-word en
                        tries, consisting of a handle and the number of pages allocated
                        to that handle. (including the operating system handle [0]). BX
                        cannot be zero because the operating system handle is always
                        active and cannot be deallocated.
   note 1.  NOT COMPATIBLE with EMS or EEMS 3.2, since the new special OS handle
            0000h is returned as part of the array. Unless benign use of this
            information is used (such as displaying the handle and count of pages
            associated with the handle) code should be changed to only work with
            handles between 01h and FFh and to specifically ignore handle 00h.
        2.  The array consists of an array of 255 elements. The first word of each
            element is the handle number, the second word contains the number of
            pages allocated.
        3.  There are two types of handles, 'standard' and 'raw'. The specification
            does not talk about how this function works when both raw and standard
            handles exist in a given system. There is no currently known way to
            differentiate between a standard handle and a raw handle in EMS 4.0.
        4.  uses registers AX and BX
```

Function 4Eh Get or Set Page Map
LIM Function Call 15
```
                        Gets or sets the contents of the EMS page-mapping registers on the
                        expanded memory boards. This group of four subfunctions is provided
                        for context switching required by operating environments and
                        systems. These functions are upward and downward compatible with
                        both EMS and EEMS 3.2; in addition, these functions now include the
                        functionality of EEMS function 6Ah ("function 43") involving all
                        pages. The size and contents of the map register array will vary
                        from system to system based on hardware vendor, software vendor,
                        number of boards and the capacity of each board in the system. Note
                        the array size can be determined by function 4Eh/03h. Use
                        these functions (except for 03h) instead of Functions 8 and 9 if you need
                        to save or restore the mapping context but don't want (or have) to
                        use a handle.

            00h         Get Page Map
                        This call saves the mapping context for all mappable memory regions
                        (conventional and expanded) by copying the contents of the mapping
                        registers from each expanded memory board to a destination array.
                        The application must pass a pointer to the destination array.
   entry    AH          4Eh
            AL          00h
            ES:DI       pointer to target array
   return   AH          error status: 00h, 80h, 81h, 84h, 8Fh
   note 1.  uses register AX
        2.  does not use an EMM handle

            01h         Set Page Map
                        This call the mapping context for all mappable memory regions
                        (conventional and expanded. by copying the contents of a source
                        array into the mapping registers on each expanded memory board in
                        the system. The application must pass a pointer to the source array
   entry    AH          4Eh
            AL          01h
            DS:SI       pointer to source array
   return   AH          error status: 00h, 80h, 81h, 84h, 8Fh, 0A3h
   note 1.  uses register AX
        2.  does not use an EMM handle

            02h         Get & Set Page Map
                        This call simultaneously saves the current mapping context and
                        restores a previous mapping context for all mappable memory regions
                        (both conventional and expanded). It first copies the contents of
```

Expanded and Enhanced expanded Memory Specifications 197

```
                the mapping registers from each expanded memory board in the system
                into a destination array. Then the subfunction copies the contents
                of a source array into the mapping registers on each of the expanded
                memory boards.
entry   AH      4Eh
        AL      02h
        DS:SI   pointer to source array
        ES:DI   pointer to target array
return  AH      error status: 00h, 80h, 81h, 84h, 8Fh, 0A3h
note    uses register AX

             03h  Get Size of Page Map Save Array
entry   AH      4Eh
        AL      03h
return  AH      error status: 00h, 80h, 81h, 84h, 8Fh
        AL      size in bytes of array
note 1. this subfunction does not require an EMM handle
     2. uses register AX
```

Functions New to EMS 4.0

```
Function 4Eh Get or Set Page Map
LIM Function Call 16
entry   AH      4Eh
        AL      00h     if getting mapping registers
                01h     if setting mapping registers
                02h     if getting and setting mapping registers at once
                03h     if getting size of page-mapping array
        DS:SI   pointer to array holding information (AL=01h, 02h)
        ES:DI   pointer to array to receive information (AL=00h, 02h)
return  AH      error status: 00h, 80h, 81h, 84h, 8Fh, 0A3h
        AL      bytes in page-mapping array (fn 03h only)
        ES:DI   array of received information (fn 00h, 02h)
note.   this function was designed to be used by multitasking operating systems
        and should not ordinarily be used by application software.

Function 4Fh Get/Set Partial Page Map
LIM Function Call 16
                These four subfunctions are provided for context switching required
                by interrupt routines, operating environments and systems. This set
                of functions provides extended functionality over the EEMS function
                6Ah (function 43) involving subsets of pages. In EEMS, a subset of
                pages could be specified by starting position and number of pages;
                in this function a list of pages is specified, which need not be
                contiguous. Interrupt routines can use this function in place of
                functions 47h and 48h, especially if the interrupt routine wants to
                use more than the standard four physical pages.

        AH      4Fh
        AL      subfunction
                00h     get partial page map
                        DS:SI   pointer to structure containing list of segments
                                whose mapping contexts are to be saved
                        ES:DI   pointer to array to receive page map
                01h     set partial page map
                        DS:SI   pointer to structure containing saved partial
                                page map
                02h     get size of partial page map
                        BX      number of mappable segments in the partial map to
                                be saved
return  AH      error status (00h): 00h, 80h, 81h, 84h, 8Bh, 8Fh, 0A3h
                error status (01h): 00h, 80h, 81h, 84h, 8Fh, 0A3h
                error status (02h): 00h, 80h, 81h, 84h, 8Bh, 8Fh
        AL      size of partial page map for subfunction 02h
        DS:SI   (call 00h) pointer to array containing the partial mapping con
                text and any additional information necessary to restore this
                context to its original state when the program invokes a Set
```

```
                    subfunction.
note       uses register AX

Function 50h Map/Unmap Multiple Pages
LIM Function Call 17
entry      AH      50h
           AL      00h      (by physical page)
                   01h      (by segment number)
           CX      contains the number of entries in the array. For example, if the
                   array contained four pages to map or unmap, then CX would
                   contain 4.
           DX      handle
           DS:SI   pointer to an array of structures that contains the information
                   necessary to map the desired pages.
return     AH      error status: 00h, 80h, 81h, 83h, 84h, 8Ah, 8Bh, 8Fh
note 1.  New function permits multiple logical-to-physical assignments to be made
         in a single call.(faster than mapping individual pages)
     2.  The source map array is an array of word pairs. The first word of a pair
         contains the logical page to map (0FFFFh if the physical page is to be
         totally unmapped) and the second word of a pair contains the physical
         page number (subfunction 00h) or the segment selector (subfunction 01h)
         of the physical page in which the logical page shall be mapped.
     3.  A map of available physical pages (by physical page number and segment
         selectors) can be obtained using function 58h/00h, Get Mappable Physical
         Address Array.
     4.  uses register AX
     5.  Both mapping and unmapping pages can be done simultaneously.
     6.  If a request to map or unmap zero pages is made, nothing is done and no
         error is returned.
     7.  Pages can be mapped or unmapped using one of two methods. Both methods
         produce identical results.
         A. A logical page and a physical page at which the logical page is to be
            mapped. This method is an extension of Function 5 (Map Handle Page).
         B. Specifies both a logical page and a corresponding segment address at
            which the logical page is to be mapped. While functionally the same
            as the first method, it may be easier to use the actual segment
            address of a physical page than to use a number which only
            represents its location. The memory manager verifies whether the
            specified segment address falls on the boundary of a mappable
            physical page. The manager then translates the segment address
            passed to it into the necessary internal representation to map the
            pages.

Function 51h Reallocate pages
LIM Function Call 18
                   This function allows an application to change the number of logical
                   pages allocated to an EMM handle.
entry      AH      51h
           BX      number of pages desired at return
           DX      handle
return     AH      error status: 00h, 80h, 81h, 83h, 84h, 87h, 88h
           BX      number of pages now associated with handle
note 1.  uses registers AX, BX
     2.  Logical pages which were originally allocated with Function 4 are called
         pages and are 16K bytes long. Logical pages which were allocated with
         Function 27 are called raw pages and might not be the same size as pages
         allocated with Function 4.
     3.  If the status returned in BX is not zero, the value in BX is equal to the
         number of pages allocated to the handle prior to calling this function.
         This information can be used to verify that the request generated the
         expected results.

Function 52h Get/Set Handle Attributes
LIM Function Call 19
entry      AH      52h
           AL      subfunction
                   00h      get handle attributes
                   01h      set handle attributes
                            BL      new attribute
                                    00h      make handle volatile
                                    01h      make handle non-volatile
```

Expanded and Enhanced expanded Memory Specifications

```
                        02h    get attribute capability
               DX              handle
return    AH                   error status: (function 00h) 00h, 80h, 81h, 83h, 84h, 8Fh, 91h
                               error status: (function 01h) 00h, 80h, 81h, 83h, 84h, 8Fh, 90h,
                                                            91h
                               error status: (function 02h) 00h, 80h, 81h, 84h, 8Fh
               AL              attribute (for subfunction 00h)
                        00h       handle is volatile
                        01h       handle is nonvolatile
               AL              attribute capability (for subfunction 02h)
                        00h       only volatile handles supported
                        01h       both volatile and non-volatile supported
```
note 1. uses register AX
   2. A volatile handle attribute instructs the memory manager to deallocate
      both the handle and the pages allocated to it after a warm boot. If all
      handles have the volatile attribute (default) at warm boot the handle
      directory will be empty and all expanded memory will be initialized to
      zero immediately after a warm boot.
   3. If the handle's attribute has been set to non-volatile, the handle, its
      name (if it is assigned one), and the contents of the pages allocated
      to the handle are all maintained after a warm boot.
   4. Most PCs disable RAM refresh signals for a considerable period during a
      warm boot. This can corrupt some of the data in memory boards.
      Non-volatile handles should not be used unless it is definitely known
      that the EMS board will retain proper function through a warm boot.
   5. subfunction 02h can be used to determine whether the memory manager can
      support the non-volatile attribute.
   6. Currently the only attribute supported is non-volatile handles and pages,
      indicated by the least significant bit.

Function 53h Handle Name Functions
LIM Function Call 20
            EMS handles may be named. Each name may be any eight characters. At
            installation, all handles have their name initialized to ASCII nulls
            (binary zeros). There is no restriction on the characters which may
            be used in the handle name (ASCII chars 00h through 0FFh). A name of
            eight nulls (zeroes) is special, and indicates a handle has no name.
            Nulls have no special significance, and they can appear in the
            middle of a name. The handle name is 64 bits of binary information
            to the EMM.
            Functions 53h and 54h provide a way of setting and reading the names
            associated with a particular handle. Function 53h manipulates names
            by number.
            When a handle is assigned a name, at least one character in the name
            must be a non-null character in order to distinguish it from a
            handle without a name.

            00h Get Handle Name
                 This subfunction gets the eight character name currently assigned to
                 a handle.
                 The handle name is initialized to ASCII nulls (binary zeros) three
                 times: when the memory manager is installed, when a handle is
                 allocated, and when a handle is deallocated.
```
entry     AH        53h
          AL        00h
          DX        handle
          ES:DI     pointer to 8-byte handle name array into which the name currently
                    assigned to the handle will be copied.
return    AH        error status: 00h, 80h, 81h, 83h, 84h, 8Fh
note      uses register AX

          01h  Set Handle Name
               This subfunction assigns an eight character name to a handle. A
               handle can be renamed at any time by setting the handle's name to a
               new value. When a handle is deallocated, its name is removed (set
               to ASCII nulls).
entry     AH        53h
          AL        01h
          DX        handle
          DS:SI     pointer to 8-byte handle name array that is to be assigned to the
                    handle. The handle name must be padded with nulls if the name is
```

199

```
                         less than eight characters long.
return    AH           error status: 00h, 80h, 81h, 83h, 84h, 8Fh, 0A1h
note      uses register AX

Function 54h Handle Directory Functions
LIM Function Call 21
              Function 54h manipulates handles by name.

          00h  Get Handle Directory
               Returns an array which contains all active handles and the names
               associated with each.
entry     AH           54h
          AL           00h
          ES:DI        pointer to 2550 byte target array
return    AH           error status: 00h, 80h, 81h, 84h, 8Fh
          AL           number of active handles
note   1. The name array consists of 10 byte entries; each entry has a word
          containing the handle number, followed by the eight byte (64 bit) name.
       2. uses register AX
       3. The number of bytes required by the target array is:
               10 bytes * total number of handles
       4. The maximum size of this array is:
               (10 bytes/entry) * 255 entries = 2550 bytes.

          01h  Search for Named Handle
               Searches the handle name directory for a handle with a particular
               name. If the named handle is found, this subfunction returns the
               handle number associated with the name.
entry     AH           54h
          AL           01h
          DS:SI        pointer to an 8-byte string that contains the name of the handle
                         being searched for
return    AH           error status: 00h, 80h, 81h, 84h, 8Fh, A0h, 0A1h
          DX           handle number
note      uses registers AX and DX

          02h  Get Total Handles
               Returns the total number of handles the EMM supports, including the
               operating system handle (handle value 0).
entry     AH           54h
          AL           02h
return    AH           error status: 00h, 80h, 81h, 84h, 8Fh
          BX           total number of handles available
note   1. This is NOT the current number of handles defined, but the maximum number
          of handles that can be supported in the current environment.
       2. uses registers AX and BX

Function 55h Alter Page Map and Jump (cross page branch)
LIM Function Call 22
              Alters the memory mapping context and transfers control to the
              specified address. Analogous to the FAR JUMP in the 8086 family
              architecture. The memory mapping context which existed before
              calling function is lost.
entry     AH           55h
          AL           00h       physical page numbers provided by caller
                       01h       segment addresses provided by caller
          DX           handle
          DS:SI        pointer to structure containing map and jump address
return    AH           error status: 00h, 80h, 81h, 83h, 84h, 8Ah, 8Bh, 8Fh
note   1. Flags and all registers except AX are preserved across the jump.
       2. uses register AX
       3. Values in registers which don't contain required parameters maintain the
          values across the jump. The values in registers (with the exception of
          AX) and the flag state at the beginning of the function are still in the
          registers and flags when the target address is reached.
       4. Mapping no pages and jumping is not considered an error. If a request to
          map zero pages and jump is made, control is transferred to the target
          address, and this function performs a far jump.

Function 56h Alter Page Map and Call (cross page call)
LIM Function Call 23
```

Expanded and Enhanced expanded Memory Specifications

        00h and 01h
            These subfunctions save the current memory mapping context, alter the specified memory mapping context, and transfer control to the specified address.

```
entry     AH      56h
          AL      00h  physical page numbers provided by caller
                  01h  segment addresses provided by caller
          DS:SI   pointer to structure containing page map and call address
          DX      handle
return    AH      error status: 00h, 80h, 81h, 83h, 84h, 8Ah, 8Bh, 8Fh
```
note 1. Flags and all registers except AX are preserved to the called routine. On return, flags and all registers except AX are preserved; AL is set to zero and AX is undefined.
     2. uses register AX
     3. Values in registers which don't contain required parameters maintain the values across the call. The values in registers (with the exception of AX) and the flag state at the beginning of the function are still in the registers and flags when the target address is reached.
     4. Developers using this subfunction must make allowances for the additional stack space this subfunction will use.

        02h Get Page Map Stack Space Size
            Since the Alter Page Map & Call function pushes additional information onto the stack, this subfunction returns the number of bytes of stack space the function requires.

```
entry     AH      56h
          AL      02h
return:   BX      number of bytes of stack used per call
          AH      error status: 00h, 80h, 81h, 84h, 8Fh
```
note 1. if successful, the target address is called. Use a RETF to return and restore mapping context
     2. uses registers AX, BX

Function 57h Move/Exchange Memory Region
LIM Function Call 24

        00h Move Memory Region
            Moves data between two memory areas. Includes moves between paged and non-paged areas, or between two different paged areas.

```
entry     AH      57h
          AL      00h
          DS:SI   pointer to request block
return    AH      error status: 00h, 80h, 81h, 83h, 84h, 8Ah, 8Fh, 92h,
                  93h, 94h, 95h, 96h, 98h, 0A2h
```
note 1. uses register AX

        01h Exchange Memory Region
            Exchanges data between two memory areas. Includes exchanges between paged and non-paged areas, or between two different paged areas.

```
entry     AH      57h
          AL      01h
          DS:SI   pointer to the data structure which contains the source and
                  destination information for the exchange.
return    AH      error status: 00h, 80h, 81h, 83h, 84h, 8Ah, 8Fh, 93h, 94h, 95h,
                  96h, 97h, 98h, 0A2h
```
note 1. The request block is a structure with the following format:
        dword   region length in bytes
        byte   0=source in conventional memory
                1=source in expanded memory
        word   source handle
        word   source offset in page or selector
        word   source logical page (expanded) or selector (conventional)
        byte   0=target in conventional memory
                1=target in expanded memory
        word   target handle
        word   target offset in page or selector
        word   target logical page (expanded) or selector (conventional)
     2. Expanded memory allocated to a handle is considered to be a linear array, starting from logical page 0 and progressing through logical page 1, 2, ... n, n+1, ... up to the last logical page in the handle.
     3. uses register AX

Function 58h Mappable Physical Address Array
LIM Function Call 25
   These functions let you obtain a complete map of the way physical
   memory is laid out in a vendor independent manner. This is a
   functional equivalent of EEMS function 68h ('function 41'). EEMS
   function 60h ('function 33') is a subset call of 68h.

         00h   Get Array
               Returns an array containing the segment address and physical page
               number for each mappable physical page in a system. This array
               provides a cross reference between physical page numbers and the
               actual segment addresses for each mappable page in the system.
entry   AH   58h
         AL   00h
         ES:DI pointer to target array
return   AH   error status: 00h, 80h, 81h, 84h, 8Fh
         CX   entries in target array
note 1. The information returned is in an array composed of word pairs. The first
         word is the physical page's segment selector, the second word the
         physical page number. Note that values are not necessarily returned in a
         particular order, either ascending/descending segment selector values or
         as ascending/descending physical page number.
     2. For compatibility with earlier EMS specifications, physical page zero
         contains the segment selector value returned by function 41h, and
         physical pages 1, 2 and 3 return segment selector values that correspond
         to the physical 16 KB blocks immediately following physical page zero.
     3. uses registers AX and CX
     4. The array is sorted in ascending segment order. This does not mean that
         the physical page numbers associated with the segment addresses are also
         in ascending order.

         01h   Get Physical Page Address Array Entries.
               Returns a word which represents the number of entries in the array
               returned by the previous subfunction. This number also indicates
               the number of mappable physical pages in a system.
entry   AH   58h
         AL   01h
return   AH   error status: 00h, 80h, 81h, 84h, 8Fh
         CX   number of entries returned by 58h/00h
note 1. multiply CX by 4 for the byte count.
     2. uses registers AX and CX

Function 59h Get Expanded Memory Hardware Information
LIM Function Call 26
   These functions return information specific to a given hardware
   implementation and to use of raw pages as opposed to standard pages.
   The intent is that only operating system code ever need use these
   functions.

         00h   Get EMS Hardware Info
               Returns an array containing expanded memory hardware configuration
               information for use by an operating system.
entry   AH   59h
         AL   00h
         ES:DI pointer to 10 byte target array
               The target array has the following format:
                 word: raw page size in paragraphs (multiples of 16 bytes)
                 word: number of alternate register sets
                 word: size of page maps (function 4Eh [15])
                 word: number of alternate registers sets for DMA
                 word: DMA operation -- see full specification
return   AH   error status: 00h, 80h, 81h, 84h, 8Fh, 0A4h
note 1. uses register AX
     2. This function is for use by operating systems only.
     3. This function can be disabled at any time by the operating system.

         01h   Get Unallocated Raw Page Count
               Returns the number of unallocated non-standard length mappable pages
               as well as the total number of non-standard length mappable pages
               of expanded memory
entry   AH   59h

```
return   AL        01h
         AH        error status: 00h, 80h, 81h, 84h, 8Fh
         BX        unallocated raw pages available for use
         DX        total raw 16k pages of expanded memory
note 1. uses registers AX, BX, CX
     2. An expanded memory page which is a sub-multiple of 16K is termed a raw
        page. An operating system may deal with mappable physical page sizes
        which are sub-multiples of 16K bytes.
     3. If the expanded memory board supplies pages in exact multiples of 16K
        bytes, the number of pages this function returns is identical to the
        number Function 3 (Get Unallocated Page Count) returns. In this case,
        there is no difference between a page and a raw page.

Function 5Ah Allocate Raw Pages
LIM Function Call 27
              Allocates the number of nonstandard size pages that the operating
              system requests and assigns a unique EMM handle to these pages.
entry    AH        5Ah
         AL        00h        allocate standard pages
                   01h        allocate raw pages
         BX        number of pages to allocate
return   AH        error status: 00h, 80h, 81h, 84h, 85h, 87h, 88h
         DX        unique raw EMM handle (1-255)
note 1. it is intended this call be used only by operating systems
     2. uses registers AX and DX
     3. for all functions using the raw handle returned in DX, the length of the
        physical and logical pages allocated to it are some non-standard length
        (that is, not 16K bytes).
     4. this call is primarily for use by operating systems or EMM drivers
        supporting hardware with a nonstandard EMS page size.

Function 5Bh Alternate Map Register Set - DMA Registers
LIM Function Call 28
entry    AH        00h       Get Alternate Map Register Set
                   01h       Set Alternate Map Register Set
                             BL    new alternate map register set number
                             ES:DI pointer to map register context save area if BL=0
                   02h       Get Alternate Map Save Array Size
                   03h       Allocate Alternate Map Register Set
                   04h       Deallocate Alternate Map Register Set
                             BL    number of alternate map register set
                   05h       Allocate DMA Register Set
                   06h       Enable DMA on Alternate Map Register Set
                             BL    DMA register set number
                             DL    DMA channel number
                   07h       Disable DMA on Alternate Map Register Set
                             BL    DMA register set number
                   08h       Deallocate DMA Register Set
                             BL    DMA register set number
return   AH        status: 00h, 02h  00h, 80h, 84h, 81h, 8Fh, 0A4h
                           01h      00h, 80h, 81h, 84h, 8Fh, 9Ah, 9Ch, 9Dh,
                                    0A3h, 0A4h
                           03h, 05h 00h 80h 81h 84h, 8Fh, 9Bh, 0A4h
                           04h      00h, 80h, 81h, 84h, 8Fh, 9Ch, 9Dh, 0A4h
                           06h, 07h 00h, 80h, 81h, 84h, 8Fh, 9Ah, 9Ch, 9Dh, 9Eh,
                                    9Fh, 0A4h
         BL        current active alternate map register set number if nonzero (AL=0)
         BL        number of alternate map register set; zero if not supported (AL=3)
         DX        array size in bytes (subfunction 02h)
         ES:DI     pointer to a map register context save area if BL=0 (AL=0)
note 1. this call is for use by operating systems only, and can be enabled or
        disabled at any time by the operating system
     2. This set of functions performs the same functions at EEMS function 6Ah
        subfunctions 04h and 05h ("function 43").
     3. 00h uses registers AX, BX, ES:DI
        01h uses register AX
        02h uses registers AX and DX
        03h uses registers AX and BX
        04h uses register AX
        05h uses registers AX, BX
        06h uses register AX
```

```
            07h uses register AX

Function 5Ch Prepare EMS Hardware for Warm Boot
LIM Function Call 29
             Prepares the EMM hardware for a warm boot.
entry    AH      5Ch
return   AH      error status: 00h, 80h, 81h, 84h
note 1. uses register AX
     2. this function assumes that the next operation that the operating system
        performs is a warm boot of the system.
     3. in general, this function will affect the current mapping context, the
        alternate register set in use, and any other expanded memory hardware
        dependencies which need to be initialized at boot time.
     4. if an application decides to map memory below 640K, the application must
        trap all possible conditions leading to a warm boot and invoke this
        function before performing the warm boot itself.

Function 5Dh Enable/Disable OS Function Set Functions
LIM Function Call 30
             Lets the OS allow other programs or device drivers to use the OS
             specific functions. This capability is provided only for an OS
             which manages regions of mappable conventional memory and cannot
             permit programs to use any of the functions which affect that
             memory, but must be able to use these functions itself.
entry    AH      5Dh
         AL      00h     enable OS function set
                 01h     disable OS function set
                 02h     return access key (resets memory manager, returns access
                         key at next invocation)
         BX,CX   access key returned by first invocation
return   BX,CX   access key, returned only on first invocation of function
         AH      status  00h, 80h, 81h, 84h, 8Fh, 0A4h
note 1. this function is for use by operating systems only. The operating system
        can disable this function at any time.
     2. 00h uses registers AX, BX, CX
        01h uses registers AX, BX, CX
        02h uses register AX
     3. 00h, 01h: The OS/E (Operating System/Environment) functions these
        subfunctions affect are:
        Function 26, Get Expanded Memory Hardware Information
        Function 28, Alternate Map Register Sets
        Function 30, Enable/Disable Operating System Functions

Function 5Eh Unknown
LIM Function call (not defined under LIM)

Function 5Fh Unknown
LIM Function call (not defined under LIM)

Function 60h EEMS - Get Physical Window Array
LIM Function call (not defined under LIM)
entry    AH      60h
         ES:DI   pointer to buffer
return   AH      status
         AL      number of entries
         buffer at ES:DI filled

Function 61h Generic Accelerator Card Support
LIM Function Call 34
entry    _  Contact AST Research for a copy of the Generic Accelerator Card
return   _  Driver (GACD) Specification
note        Can be used by accelerator card manufacturer to flush RAM cache,ensuring
            that the cache accurately reflects what the processor would see without
            the cache.

Function 68h EEMS - Get Addresses of All Page Frames in System
LIM Function Call (not defined under LIM)
entry    AH      68h
         ES:DI   pointer to buffer
return   AH      status
         AL      number of entries
```

Expanded and Enhanced expanded Memory Specifications

```
                buffer at ES:DI filled
note            Equivalent to LIM 4.0 function 58h

Function 69h EEMS - Map Page Into Frame
LIM Function Call (not defined under LIM)
entry   AH      69h
        AL      frame number
        BX      page number
        DX      handle
return  AH      status
note    Similar to EMS function 44h

Function 6Ah  EEMS - Page Mapping
LIM Function Call (not defined under LIM)
entry   AH      6Ah
        AL      00h     Save Partial Page Map
                        CH      first page frame
                        CL      number of frames
                        ES:DI   pointer to buffer which is to be filled
                01h     Restore Partial Page Map
                        CH      first page frame
                        CL      number of frames
                        DI:SI   pointer to previously saved page map
                02h     Save And Restore Partial Page Map
                        CH      first page frame
                        CL      number of frames
                        ES:DI   buffer for current page map
                        DI:SI   new page map
                03h     Get Size Of Save Array
                        CH      first page frame
                        CL      number of frames
                        return AL  size of array in bytes
                04h     Switch to Standard Map Register Setting
                05h     Switch to Alternate Map Register Setting
                06h     Deallocate Pages Mapped To Frames in Conventional Mem.
                        CH      first page frame
                        CL      number of frames
return  AH      status
note    Similar to LIM function 4Eh, except that a subrange of pages can be
        specified
```

Expanded Memory Manager Error Codes

EMM error codes are returned in AH after a call to the EMM (int 67h).

```
code    meaning
00h     function successful
80h     internal error in EMM software (possibly corrupted driver)
81h     hardware malfunction
82h     EMM busy (dropped in EEMS 3.2)
83h     invalid EMM handle
84h     function requested not defined - unknown function code in AH.
85h     no more EMM handles available
86h     error in save or restore of mapping context
87h     more pages requested than exist
88h     allocation request specified more logical pages than currently available
        in system (request does not exceed actual physical number of pages, but
        some are already allocated to other handles); no pages allocated
89h     zero pages; cannot be allocated (dropped in EMS 4.0)
8Ah     logical page requested to be mapped outside range of logical pages
        assigned to handle
8Bh     illegal page number in mapping request (valid numbers are 0 to 3)
8Ch     page-mapping hardware state save area full
8Dh     save of mapping context failed; save area already contains context
        associated with page handle
8Eh     restore of mapping context failed; save area does not contain context for
        requested handle
8Fh     subfunction parameter not defined (unknown function)
```

```
LIM 4.0 extended error codes:
90h     attribute type undefined
91h     warm boot data save not implemented
92h     move overlaps memory
93h     move/exchange larger than allocated region
94h     conventional/expanded regions overlap
95h     logical page offset outside of logical page
96h     region larger than 1 MB
97h     exchange source/destination overlap
98h     source/destination undefined or not supported
99h     (no status assigned)
9Ah     alternate map register sets supported, specified set is not
9Bh     all alternate map & DMA register sets allocated
9Ch     alternate map & DMA register sets not supported
9Dh     alternate map register or DMA set not defined, allocated or is currently
        defined set
9Eh     dedicated DMA channels not supported
9Fh     dedicated DMA channels supported; specified channel is not
0A0h    named handle could not be found
0A1h    handle name already exists
0A2h    move/exchange wraps around 1 MB boundary
0A3h    data structure contains corrupted data
0A4h    access denied
```

11

Conversion Between MSDOS and Foreign Operating Systems

Overview

Software portability is a popular topic in programming texts. In real life, very little software is ported from one system to another, and then normally only by necessity. When software must be portable, it is often written in a proprietary high-level language designed for system portability. InfoCom games and various CAD packages fall into this category.

From time to time the programmer may wish to target his software for a wider base of systems than the one he is currently working with. The usual reason is to broaden the market in which the software will be sold without having to write a specific version for each machine. In other cases it may be necessary to move existing software between machines when a particular machine becomes obsolete, but there is a heavy investment in software. Many companies have custom or proprietary software (engineering and inventory control are the most usual) which must be ported from such machines.

Programs from many different operating systems may be ported easily to MSDOS. Though single-tasking and single-user, MSDOS provides a rich applications program interface (API) for the programmer. Porting software *from* MSDOS to a foreign OS can frequently be a source of consternation to the programmer, as many functions taken for granted by DOS programmers (nondestructive keyboard read, for example) do not exist in most microcomputer and many mainframe operating systems.

When noncongruent function calls must be used between systems, it is probably best to build a macro library in whatever language is being used and simply pass parameters to it as a data structure. If data from a windowing OS such as AmigaDOS or MacOS is to be ported, use of a windowing shell is more efficient than trying to duplicate all the various functions yourself.

Porting of software depends on 'good' practice, i.e. placing hardware-dependent routines in their own modules or noting such use in the main code.

Special Considerations

When porting from machines using the Motorola 68000 or another processor with a large linear address space (non-segmented architecture) and you should take care that data structures moved from the ST to not exceed the 8088's 64k segment size limit. A program which requires structures larger than 64k could be ported to 80386 machines but the large structures would only be accessible in protected mode and would require switching in and out of protected mode to access the data. The difficulty involved would preclude such a solution unless absolutely necessary. A partial solution would be to port the software to a non-DOS OS having an MSDOS 'window' or emulation mode. Another solution would be to use one of the scientific number-crunching boards such as the MicroWay TransPuter module and pass structures back and forth to it.

If you are writing a program from scratch for multiple-platform operation, it would be wise to check into using a compiler vendor who supports the platforms in question. Some vendors have a wide range of products. For instance:

Borland:	Turbo Pascal	CP/M-80
		CP/M-86
		MSDOS
		MacIntosh
Lattice:	C	MSDOS
		Atari ST
		Amiga

Some vendors offer similar products to run under Unix, VMS, or OS/2 as well.

One thing MSDOS programmers may find to be eerily different is the way some other operating systems (Unix, for example) perform functions. In MSDOS, operating system functions are accessed by setting various CPU registers to specified values and calling the appropriate CPU interrupt. MSDOS' function dispatcher examines the values in the registers and takes the appropriate action.

'Portable' operating systems such as Unix and many networking systems cannot be certain of having any specific registers of CPU modes available, and thus build 'request packets' or 'call blocks', which are data structures the operating system can interpret, and then calling an interrupt. The OS kernel examines the structure and takes the appropriate action. Systems operating this way are (relatively) easily transported among CPU types and make both multitasking and multiprocessing much easier at the expense of some overhead.

Should it be necessary to do any extensive porting work, I highly recommend Arthur S. Tanenbaum's *'Operating System Design and Implementation'* by Prentice-Hall. Tanenbaum discusses operating systems from philosophy down to actual code and is an invaluable reference for anyone doing low-level OS programming.

Example Operating Systems
Atari ST

The Atari ST's operating system is called TOS, for Tramiel Operating System. TOS is single-user, single-tasking, and almost call-for-call compatible with MSDOS. Typically, the ST runs TOS as a low-level interface for Digital Research's GEM windowing environment.

Applications moved from MSDOS to TOS should require no unusual modifications, though applications moved from the Atari ST to MSDOS would be easiest to port by using GEM on the PC. TOS services are accessible through assembly language by manipulating the CPU registers, as in MSDOS. TOS duplicates the UNIX-style file handling calls of MSDOS but not the 'unsupported' CP/M style FCB calls.

CP/M

When Tim Paterson designed DOS he made it easy to port the CP/M functions to his new operating system. All CP/M-80 calls are duplicated in MSDOS. These are the so-called FCB or File Control Block calls which are now officially discouraged by IBM and Microsoft. Newer handle calls exist for most FCB calls. Porting software from MSDOS to CP/M may be difficult due to the sparseness of system calls and limited (64k address space) CPU resources. CP/M was written in a language called PL/M, but both CP/M and MSDOS were designed for easy use from an assembly-language level.

MacOS

Porting from MSDOS to the Apple MacIntosh OS should require no special handling. Porting from MacOS to MSDOS involves duplicating the massive windowing functions built into MacOS. Microsoft's Windows is a licensee of Apple and would probably be the best choice, though Aldus' PageMaker program uses DRI's GEM. The MacOS was written in Pascal and uses Pascal data structures and calling conventions.

AmigaDOS

AmigaDOS is a Unix variant with a windowing shell. Newer versions have the Bourne shell as an option for their CLI, or Command Line Interface. Most Amiga programs make little or no use of the piping or multitasking structures available under Unix and should not be too difficult to port. The Amiga's windowing and mouse routines are fairly simple and could be duplicated by a set of library routines or Quarterdeck's DesQview could be used, which would also duplicate the multitasking and interprocess data transfer available under AmigaDOS.

OS/2

Most new Microsoft language updates come with OS/2 and DOS variants. Microsoft Windows can duplicate most OS/2 windowing and piping functions if needed. Microsoft provides 'dual mode' libraries for programs to run under either DOS or OS/2. The official Microsoft interface to OS/2's 221 function calls is through the C language.

UNIX

Most versions of Unix appear very much like CP/M from the programmer's stand-point. Unix has memory management and hierarchic directory structures absent in CP/M. Most Unix systems use some sort of paged virtual memory and code generated by some Unix compilers tends to be very large. Should it be necessary to port a large Unix system to DOS, it would probably be best to use Quarterdeck's DesQview API and EEMS or LIM 4.0. Virtually all Unix software is written in C.

12

Microsoft Windows A.P.I.

Overview

First released in November 1985, Microsoft Windows was originally designed as a high-level interface for display, sort of like a super-ANSI.SYS driver. An application program running under Windows could write to its output device without knowing or caring if the display was a screen or a printer, or what the resolution of the output device was. Windows also includes graphics primitives for applications, arbitration for multiple programs accessing the screen or devices, and simple program-swapping and memory management capability.

Windows was a grand concept, and worthy of serious consideration. However, Microsoft pre-announced it by almost two years, and when the program finally did ship, it had a number of problems. Microsoft got snarled up in making Windows into a super-goombah pseudo-Macintosh 'operating environment' with enough code overhead to turn a standard AT into a reasonable facsimile of an asthmatic PCjr. It was SLOW. It was a RAM and disk hog, unsuitable for use on small floppy-based machines common at the time. It was expensive, priced four times higher than DOS, and programming in Windows required tools available only in the Windows Development kit, priced at a princely $350 (now $500). And as a final blow, it could not perform its task with normal DOS programs, requiring applications developed specially for Windows.

Later versions of Windows, tailored to the 80286 or 80386 processors, were able to increase the speed and functionality of the program somewhat. Despite the hard sell by some of the programmer types at PC-Magazine and others, Windows has been a dead player since its introduction. Interest in Windows picked up when Microsoft announced that programs running under Windows would be easy to port to the (then as yet unreleased) OS/2 operating system. Interest in Windows died again when OS/2's API turned out to be sufficiently different from Windows to make it about as difficult to port Windows applications as anything else.

Microsoft's original idea of a universal display interface would be very useful in today's world of multiple graphics standards, but few programmers want to haul Windows' overhead around. Microsoft could have made Windows an operating system in its own right, but has chosen not to do so. As part of their latest push, Microsoft has announced it will bundle Windows with MSDOS in the second half of 1989.

Programming Windows

The Windows Application Program Interface (API) is designed to be accessible through the linkable code libraries provided in the Windows Software Development Kit (SDK). The suggested calling conventions are set up for the 'C' programming language.

Windows has its own built-in mouse driver and will ignore any other drivers or mouse control utilities.

Versions

The following versions of Windows have been released:

```
        1.0      November 1985, original release
        1.03     (common to Zenith and aftermarket packaged products)
        2.0      third quarter 1987, overlapping windows, EMS support
        286      customized for maximum performance on the 80286 CPU
        386      customized for use of the 80386 special instructions
```

Various 'runtime kits' of Windows have been provided for some commercial software packages such as Ami or Ventura Publisher.

Windows 2.0 added increased output performance (claimed up to 400%) for Windows applications, enhanced data exchange support for non-Windows based applications, a new visual interface with overlapping windows (1.x windows could not overlap), support for running multiple applications in expanded memory, a new memory manager to allow efficient use of expanded memory hardware, allowing a single application to be larger than 640Kb, and for the user to switch rapidly between large applications which are running simultaneously.

All versions of Windows are reported to be backward-compatible.

Functions

The following function call listing is for Windows 1.03. Later versions of Windows have enhanced capabilities. All conventions are for the C language.

```
AccessResource
        Sets file pointer for read access to resource hResInfo.
entry   AccessResource()
        AccessResource(hInstance, hResInfo):nFile
        handle  hInstance;
        handle  hResInfo;
return  int (DOS file handle)

AddAtom
        Creates an atom for character string lpString.
entry   AddAtom()
        #undef  NoAtom
        AddAtom(lpString):wAtom
        lpStr   lpString;
return  atom

AddFontResource
        Adds font resource in lpFilename to system font table.
entry   AddFontResource()
        AddFontResource(lpFilename):nFonts
```

```
            lpStr     lpFilename;
return      short

AdjustWindowRect
            Converts client rectangle to a window rectangle.
entry       AdjustWindowRect()
            #undef    NoRect
            AdjustWindowRect(lpRect, lStyle, bMenu)
            lpRect    lpRect;
            long      lStyle;
            Boolean   bMenu;
return      void

AllocResource
            Allocates dwSize bytes of memory for resource hResInfo.
entry       AllocResource()
            AllocResource(hInstance, hResInfo, dwSize):hMem
            handle    hInstance;
            handle    hResInfo;
            dword     dwSize;
return      handle

AnsiLower
            Converts character string lpStr to lower-case.
entry       AnsiLower()
            AnsiLower(lpStr):cChar
            lpStr     lpStr;
return      byte

AnsiNext
            Returns long pointer to next character in string lpCurrentChar.
entry       AnsiNext()
            AnsiNext(lpCurrentChar):lpNextChar
            lpStr     lpCurrentChar;
return      lpStr

AnsiPrev
            Returns long pointer to previous character in string lpStart.
            lpCurrentChar points to current character.
entry       AnsiPrev()
            AnsiPrev(lpStart, lpCurrentChar):lpPrevChar
            lpStr     lpStart;
            lpStr     lpCurrentChar;
return      lpStr

AnsiToOem
            Converts ANSI string to OEM character string.
entry       AnsiToOem()
            AnsiToOem(lpAnsiStr, lpOemStr):bTranslated
            lpStr     lpAnsiStr;
            lpStr     lpOemStr;
return      Boolean

AnsiUpper
            Converts character string (or character if lpString high word is zero) to
            uppercase.
entry       AnsiUpper()
            AnsiUpper(lpStr):cChar
            lpStr     lpStr;
return      byte

AnyPopup
            Tells if a pop-up style window is visible on the screen.
entry       AnyPopup()
            AnyPopup():bVisible
return      Boolean

Arc
            Draws arc from X3, Y3 to X4, Y4, using current pen and moving
            counter-clockwise. The arc's centre is at centre of rectangle given by
            X1, Y1 and X2, Y2.
```

```
entry     Arc()
          #undef  NohDC
          Arc(hDC, X1, Y1, X2, Y2, X3, Y3, X4, Y4):BDrawn
          hDC     hDC;
          short   X1;
          short   Y1;
          short   X2;
          short   Y2;
          short   X3;
          short   Y3;
          short   X4;
          short   Y4;
return    Boolean

BeginPaint
          Prepares window for painting, filling structure at lpPaint with
          painting data.
entry     BeginPaint()
          #undef  NoRect
          #undef  NohDC
          BeginPaint(hWnd, lpPaint):hDC
          hWnd    hWnd;
 lpPaintStruct  lpPaint;
return    hDC

BitBlt
          Moves bitmap from source device to destination device. Source origin is
          at XSrc, YSrc. X,Y,,nWidth, nHeight give bitmap origin and dimensions on
          destination device. DwRop defines how source and destination bits are
          combined.
entry     BitBlt()
          #undef  NohDC
          BitBlt(hDestDC, X, Y, nWidth, nHeight, hSrcDC, XSrc, YSrc,
                 dwRop):bDrawn
          hDC     hDestDC;
          short   X;
          short   Y;
          short   nWidth;
          short   nHeight;
          hDC     hSrcDC;
          short   XSrc;
          short   YSrc;
          dword   dwRop;
return    Boolean

BringWindowToTop
          Brings pop-up or child window to top of stack of overlapping windows.
entry     BringWindowToTop()
          BringWindowToTop(hWnd)
          hWnd    hWnd;
return    void

BuildCommDCB
          Fills device control block lpDCB with control codes named by lpDef.
entry     BuildCommDCB()
          #undef  NoComm
          BuildCommDCB(lpDef, lpDCB):nResult
          lpStr   lpDef;
       DCB FAR * lpDCB;
return    short

CallMsgFilter
          Passes message and code to current message-filter function.
          Message-filter function is set using SetWindowsHook.
entry     CallMsgFilter()
          #undef  NoMsg
          CallMsgFilter(lpMsg, nCode):bResult
          lpMsg   lpMsg;
          int     nCode;
return    Boolean
```

CallWindowProc
        Passes message information to the function specified by lpPrevWndFunc.
entry   CallWindowProc()
        #undef NoWinMessages
        CallWindowProc(lpPrevWndFunc, hWnd, wMsg, wparam, lParam):lReply
        FarProc lpPrevWndFunc;
        hWnd   hWnd;
     unsigned wMsg;
        word   wparam;
        long   lParam;
return long

Catch
        Copies current execution environment to buffer lpCatchBuf.
entry   Catch()
        Catch(lpCatchBuf):Throwback
     lpCatchBuf lpCatchBuf;
return int

ChangeClipboardChain
        Removes hWnd from clipboard viewer chain, making hWndNext descendant of
        hWnd's ancestor in the chain.
entry   ChangeClipboardChain()
        #undef NoClipBoard
        ChangeClipboardChain(hWnd, hWndNext):bRemoved
        hWnd   hWnd;
        hWnd   hWndNext;
return Boolean

ChangeMenu
        Appends, inserts, deletes, or modifies a menu item in hMenu.
entry   ChangeMenu()
        #undef NoMenus
        ChangeMenu(hMenu, wIDChangeItem, lpNewItem, wIDNewItem,
                wChange):bChanged
        hMenu   hMenu;
        word   wIDChangeItem;
        lpStr   lpNewItem;
        word   wIDNewItem;
        word   wChange;
return Boolean

CheckDlgButton
        Places or removes check next to button, or changes state of 3-state
        button.
entry   CheckDlgButton()
        #undef NoCtlMgr
        CheckDlgButton(hDlg, nIDButton, wCheck)
        hWnd   hDlg;
        int   nIDButton;
        word   wCheck;
return void

CheckMenuItem
        Places or removes checkmarks next to pop-up menu items in hMenu.
entry   CheckMenuItem()
        #undef NoMenus
        CheckMenuItem(hMenu, wIDCheckItem, wCheck):bOldCheck
        hMenu   hMenu;
        word   wIDCheckItem;
        word   wCheck;
return Boolean

CheckRadioButton
        Checks nIDCheckButton and unchecks all other radio buttons in the group
        from nIDFirstButton to nIDLastButton.
entry   CheckRadioButton()
        #undef NoCtlMgr
        CheckRadioButton(hDlg, nIDFirstButton, nIDLastButton, nIDCheckButton)
        hWnd   hDlg;
        int   nIDFirstButton;

```
            int     nIDLastButton;
            int     nIDCheckButton;
return      void

ChildWindowFromPoint
            Determines which, if any, child window of hWndParent contains Point.
entry       ChildWindowFromPoint()
            #undef  NoPoint
            ChildWindowFromPoint(hWndParent, Point):hWndChild
            hWnd    hWndParent;
            point   Point;
return      hWnd

ClearCommBreak
            Clears communication break state from communication device nCid.
entry       ClearCommBreak()
            #undef  NoComm
            ClearCommBreak(nCid):nResult
            short   nCid;
return      short

ClientToScreen
            Converts client coordinates to equivalent screen coordinates in place
entry       ClientToScreen()
            #undef  NoPoint
            ClientToScreen(hWnd, lpPoint)
            hWnd    hWnd;
            lpPoint lpPoint;
return      void

ClipCursor
            Restricts the mouse cursor to a given rectangle on the screen.
entry       ClipCursor()
            #undef  NoRect
            ClipCursor(lpRect)
            lpRect  lpRect;
return      void

CloseClipboard
            Closes the clipboard
entry       CloseClipboard()
            #undef  NoClipBoard
            CloseClipboard():bClosed
return      Boolean

CloseComm
            Closes communication device nCid after transmitting current output buffer.
entry       CloseComm()
            #undef  NoComm
            CloseComm(nCid):nResult
            short   nCid;
return      short

CloseMetaFile
            Closes the metafile and creates a metafile handle.
entry       CloseMetaFile()
            CloseMetaFile(hDC):hMF
            handle  hDC;
return      handle

CloseSound
            Closes play device after flushing voice queues and freeing buffers.
entry       CloseSound()
            #undef  NoSound
            CloseSound()
return      int

CloseWindow
            Closes the specified window.
entry       CloseWindow()
            CloseWindow(hWnd):nClosed
```

```
               hWnd     hWnd;
       return  int

CombineRgn
               Combines, using nCombineMode, two existing regions into a new region.
       entry   CombineRgn()
                       #undef   NoRegion
                       CombineRgn(hDestRgn, hSrcRgn1, hSrcRgn2, nCombineMode):RgnType
                       hRgn     hDestRgn;
                       hRgn     hSrcRgn1;
                       hRgn     hSrcRgn2;
                       short    nCombineMode;
       return  short

CopyMetaFile
               Copies source metafile to lpFilename and returns the new metafile.
       entry   CopyMetaFile()
                       CopyMetaFile(hSrcMetaFile, lpFilename):hMF
                       handle   hSrcMetaFile;
                       lpStr    lpFilename;
       return  handle

CopyRect
               Makes a copy of an existing rectangle.
       entry   CopyRect()
                       #undef   NoRect
                       CopyRect(lpDestRect, lpSourceRect)
                       lpRect   lpDestRect;
                       lpRect   lpSourceRect;
       return  int

CountClipboardFormats
               Retrieves a count of the number of formats the clipboard can render.
       entry   CountClipboardFormats()
                       #undef   NoClipboard
                       CountClipboardFormats():nCount
       return  int

CountVoiceNotes
               Returns number of notes in voice queue nVoice.
       entry   CountVoiceNotes()
                       #undef   NoSound
                       CountVoiceNotes(nVoice):nNotes
                       int      nVoice;
       return  int

CreateBitmap
               Creates a bitmap having the specified width, height, and bit pattern.
       entry   CreateBitmap()
                       #undef   NoBitmap
                       CreateBitmap(nWidth, nHeight, cPlanes, cBitCount, lpBits):hBitmap
                       short    nWidth;
                       short    nHeight;
                       byte     cPlanes;
                       byte     cBitCount;
                       lpStr    lpBits;
       return  hBitmap

CreateBitmapIndirect
               Creates a bitmap with the width, height, and bit pattern given by
               lpBitmap.
       entry   CreateBitmapIndirect()
                       #undef   NoBitmap
                       CreateBitmapIndirect(lpBitmap):hBitmap
          Bitmap FAR * lpBitmap;
       return  hBitmap

CreateBrushIndirect
               Creates a logical brush with the style, colour, and pattern given by
               lpLogBrush.
       entry   CreateBrushIndirect()
```

```
               #undef   NoGDI
               #undef   NoBrush
               CreateBrushIndirect(lpLogBrush):hBrush
 LogBrush FAR * lpLogBrush;
return  hBrush

CreateCaret
        Creates caret or hWnd using hBitmap. If hBitmmap is NULL, creates solid
        flashing black block nWidth by nHeight pixels; if hBitmap is 1, caret is
        grey.
entry   CreateCaret()
        #undef   NoBitmap
        CreateCaret(hWnd, hBitmap, nWidth, nHeight)
        hWnd     hWnd;
        hBitmap  hBitmap;
        int      nWidth;
        int      nHeight;
return  void

CreateCompatibleBitmap
        Creates a bitmap that is compatible with the device specified by hDC.
entry   CreateCompatibleBitmap()
        #undef   NoHDC
        #undef   NoBitmap
        CreateCompatibleBitmap(hDC, nWidth, mnHeight):hBitmap
        hDC      hDC;
        short    nWidth;
        short    mnHeight;
return  hBitmap

CreateCompatibleDC
        Creates a memory display context compatible with the device specified by
        hDC.
entry   CreateCompatibleDC()
        #undef   NoHdc
        CreateCompatibleDC(hDC):hMemDC
        hDC      hDC;
return  hDC

CreateDC
        Creates a display context for the specified device.
entry   CreateDC()
        #undef   NohDC
        CreateDC(lpDriverName, lpDeviceName, lpOutput, lpInitData):hDC
        lpStr    lpDriverName;
        lpStr    lpDeviceName;
        lpStr    lpOutput;
        lpStr    lpInitData;
return  hDC

CreateDialog
        Creates a modeless dialogue box.
entry   CreateDialog()
        #undef   NoCtlmgr
        CreateDialog(hInstance, lpTemplateName, hWndParent,
        lpDialogFunc):hDlg
        handle   hInstance;
        lpStr    lpTemplateName;
        hWnd     hWndParent;
        farproc  lpDialogFunc;
return  hWND

CreateDiscardableBitmap
        Creates a discardable bitmap.
entry   CreateDiscardableBitmap()
        #undef   NohDC
        #undef   NoBitmap
        CreateDiscardableBitmap(hDC, X, Y):hBitmap
        hDC      hDC;
        short    X;
        short    Y;
```

```
return  hBitmap

CreateEllipticRgn
        Creates an elliptical region whose bounding rectangle is defined by X1,
        Y1, X2, and Y2.
entry   CreateEllipticRgn()
        #undef  NoRegion
        CreateEllipticRgn(X1, Y1, X2, Y2):hRgn
        short   X1;
        short   Y1;
        short   X2;
        short   Y2;
return  hRgn

CreateEllipticRgnIndirect
        Creates an elliptical region whose bounding rectangle is given by lpRect.
entry   CreateEllipticRgnIndirect()
        #undef  NoRect
        #undef  NoRegion
        CreateEllipticRgnIndirect(lpRect):hRgn
        lpRect  lpRect;
return  hRGN

CreateFont
        Creates a logical font having the specified characteristics.
entry   CreateFont()
        #undef  NoFont
        CreateFont(nheight, nWidth, nEscapement, nOrientation, nWeight,
        cItalic, cUnderline, cStrikeOut, nCharSet, cOutputPrecision,
        cClipPrecision, cQuality, cPitchAndFamily, lpFacename):hFont
        short   nheight;
        short   nWidth;
        short   nEscapement;
        short   nOrientation;
        short   nWeight;
        byte    cItalic;
        byte    cUnderline;
        byte    cStrikeOut;
        byte    nCharSet;
        byte    cOutputPrecision;
        byte    cClipPrecision;
        byte    cQuality;
        byte    cPitchAndFamily;
        lpStr   lpFacename;
return  hFont

CreateFontIndirect
        Creates a logical font with characteristics given by lpLogFont.
entry   CreateFontIndirect()
        #undef  NoGDI
        #undef  NoFont
        CreateFontIndirect(lpLogFont):hFont
  LogFont FAR * lpLogFont;
return  hFont

CreateHatchBrush
        Creates a logical brush having the specified hatched pattern and colour.
entry   CreateHatchBrush()
        #undef  NoBrush
        CreateHatchBrush(nIndex, rgbColor):Brush
        short   nIndex;
        dword   rgbColor;
return  hBrush

CreateIC
        Creates an information context for the specified device.
entry   CreateIC()
        #undef  NohDC
        CreateIC(lpDriverName, lpDeviceName, lpOutput, lpInitData):hIC
        lpStr   lpDriverName;
        lpStr   lpDeviceName;
```

```
            lpStr    lpOutput;
            lpStr    lpInitData;
return      hDC

CreateMenu
            Creates an empty menu.
entry       CreateMenu()
            #undef   NoMenus
            CreateMenu():hMenu
return      hMenu

CreateMetaFile
            Creates a metafile display context.
entry       CreateMetaFile()
            CreateMetaFile(lpFilename):hDC
            lpStr    lpFilename;
return      handle

CreatePatternBrush
            Creates a logical brush having the pattern specified by hBitmap.
entry       CreatePatternBrush()
            #undef   NoBitmap
            #undef   NoBrush
            CreatePatternBrush(hBitmap):hBrush
            hBitmap  hBitmap;
return      hBrush

CreatePen
            Creates a logical pen having the specified style, width, and colour.
entry       CreatePen()
            #undef   nOpen
            CreatePen(nPenStyle, nWidth, rgbColor):hPen
            short    nPenStyle;
            short    nWidth;
            dword    rgbColor;
return      hPen

CreatePenIndirect
            Creates a logical pen with the style, width, and colour given by lpLogPen.
entry       CreatePenIndirect()
            #undef   nOpen
            CreatePenIndirect(lpLogPen):hPen
     LogPen FAR * lpLogPen;
return      hPen

CreatePolygonRgn
            Creates a polygon region having nCount vertices as given by lpPoints.
entry       CreatePolygonRgn()
            #undef   NoPoint
            #undef   NoRegion
            CreatePolygonRgn(lpPoints, nCount, nPolyFillMode):hRgn
            lpPoint  lpPoints;
            short    nCount;
            short    nPolyFillMode;
return      hRgn

CreateRectRgn
            Creates a rectangular region.
entry       CreateRectRgn()
            #undef   NoRegion
            CreateRectRgn(X1, Y1, X2, Y2):hRgn
            short    X1;
            short    Y1;
            short    X2;
            short    Y2;
return      hRgn

CreateRectRgnIndirect
            Creates a rectangular region with the dimensions given by lpRect.
entry       CreateRectRgnIndirect()
            #undef   NoRect
```

```
                #undef  NoRegion
                CreatRectRgnIndirect(lpRect):hRgn
                lpRect  lpRect;
        return  hRgn

CreateSolidBrush
                Creates a logical brush having the specified solid colour.
        entry   CreateSolidBrush()
                #undef  NoBrush
                CreateSolidBrush(rgbColor):hBrush
                dword   rgbColor;
        return  hBrush

CreateWindow
                Creates tiled, pop-up, and child windows.
        entry   CreateWindow()
                CreateWindow(lpClassName, lpWindowName, dwStyle, X,Y,nWidth, nHeight,
                        hWndParent, hMenu, hInstance, lpParam):hWnd
                lpStr   lpClassName;
                lpStr   lpWindowName;
                dword   dwStyle;
                int     X;
                int     Y;
                int     nWidth;
                int     nHeight;
                hWnd    hWndParent;
                hMenu   hMenu;
                handle  hInstance;
                lpStr   lpParam;
        return  hWnd

DefWindowProc
                Provides default processing for messages an application chooses not to
                process.
        entry   DefWindowProc()
                #undef  NoWinMessages
                DefWindowProc(hWnd, wMsg, wParam, lParam):lReply
                hWnd    hWnd;
             unsigned   wMsg;
                word    wParam;
                long    lParam;
        return  long

DeleteAtom
                Deletes an atom nAtom if its reference count is zero.
        entry   DeleteAtom()
                #undef  NoAtom
                DeleteAtom(nAtom):nOldAtom
                atom    nAtom;
        return  atom

DeleteDC
                Deletes the specified display context.
        entry   DeleteDC()
                #undef  NohDC
                DeleteDC(hDC):bDeleted
                hDC     hDC;
        return  Boolean

DeleteMetaFile
                Deletes access to a metafile by freeing the associated system resources
        entry   DeleteMetaFile()
                DeleteMetaFile(hMF):bFreed
                handle  hMF;
        return  Boolean

DeleteObject
                Deletes the logical pen, brush, font, bitmap, or region by freeing all
                associated system storage.
        entry   DeleteObject()
                DeleteObject(hObject):bDeleted
```

```
                handle     hObject;
        return  Boolean

DestroyCaret
                Destroys the current caret and frees any memory it occupied.
        entry   DestroyCaret()
                DestroyCaret()
                hWnd       hWnd;
        return  int

CombineRgn
                Combines, using nCombineMode, two existing regions into a new region.
        entry   CombineRgn()
                #undef     NoRegion
                CombineRgn(hDestRgn, hSrcRgn1, hSrcRgn2, nCombineMode):RgnType
                hRgn       hDestRgn;
                hRgn       hSrcRgn1;
                hRgn       hSrcRgn2;
                short      nCombineMode;
        return  short

CopyMetaFile
                Copies source metafile to lpFilename and returns the new metafile.
        entry   CopyMetaFile()
                CopyMetaFile(hSrcMetaFile, lpFilename):hMF
                handle     hSrcMetaFile;
                lpStr      lpFilename;
        return  handle

CopyRect
                Makes a copy of an existing rectangle.
        entry   CopyRect()
                #undef     NoRect
                CopyRect(lpDestRect, lpSourceRect)
                lpRect     lpDestRect;
                lpRect     lpSourceRect;
        return  int

CountClipboardFormats
                Retrieves a count of the number of formats the clipboard can render.
        entry   CountClipboardFormats()
                #undef     NoClipboard
                CountClipboardFormats():nCount
        return  void

DestroyMenu
                Destroys the menu specified by hMenu and frees any memory it occupied.
        entry   DestroyMenu()
                #undef     NoMenus
                DetroyMenu(hMenu):bDestroyed
                hMenu      hMenu;
        return  Boolean

DestroyWindow
                Sends a WM_DESTROY message to hWnd and frees any memory it occupied.
        entry   DestroyWindow()
                DestroyWindow(hWnd):bDestroyed
                hWnd       hWnd;
        return  Boolean

DeviceModes
                Displays a dialogue box that prompts user to set printer modes.
        entry   DeviceModes()
                DeviceModes(hWnd, hItem, lpString, lpString):lpString
                hWnd       hWnd;
                handle     hItem;
                lpStr      lpString;
                lpStr      lpString;
        return  lpStr
```

```
DialogBox
        Creates a modal dialogue box.
entry   DialogBox()
        #undef  NoCtlMgr
        DialogBox(hInstance, lpTemplateName, hWndParent,
        lpDialogFuncc):nResult
        handle  hInstance;
        lpStr   lpTemplateName;
        hWnd    hWndParent;
        FarProc lpDialogFuncc;
return  int

DispatchMessage
        Passes message to window function of window specified in MSG structure.
entry   DispatchMessage()
        #undef  NoMsg
        DispatchMessage(lpMsg):lResult
        lpMsg   lpMsg;
return  long

DlgDirList
        Fills nIDListBox with names of files matching path specification.
entry   DlgDirList()
        #undef  NoCtlMgr
        #undef  NoCtlMgr
        DlgDirList(hDlg, lpPathSpec, nIDListBox, nIDStaticPath,
                wFiletype):nListed
        hWnd        hDlg;
        lpStr       lpPathSpec;
        int         nIDListBox;
        int         nIDStaticPath;
       unsigned wFiletype;
return  int

DlgDirSelect
        Copies current selection from nIDListBox to lpString.
entry   DlgDirSelect()
        #undef  NoCtlMgr
        #undef  NoCtlMgr
        DlgDirSelect(hDlg, lpString, nIDListBox):bDirectory
        hWnd    hDlg;
        lpStr   lpString;
        int     nIDListBox;
return  Boolean

DPtoLP
        Converts into logical points the nCount device points given by lpPoints
entry   DPtoLP()
        #undef  NoPoint
        #undef  NohDC
        DPtoLP(hDC, lpPoints, nCount):bConverted
        hDC     hDC;
        lpPoint lpPoints;
        short   nCount;
return  Boolean

DrawIcon
        Draws an icon with its upper left corner at X, Y.
entry   DrawIcon()
        #undef  NohDC
        #undef  NoDrawText
        DrawIcon(hDC, X, Y, hIcon):bDrawn
        hDC     hDC;
        int     X;
        int     Y;
        hIcon   hIcon;
return  Boolean

DrawMenuBar
        Redraws the menu bar.
entry   DrawMenuBar()
```

```
                #undef  NoMenus
                DrawMenuBar(hWnd)
                hWnd    hWnd;
return          void

DrawText
                Draws nCount characters of lpString in format specified by wFormat, using
                current text and background colours. Clips output to rectangle given by
                lpRect.
entry           DrawText()
                #undef  NoRect
                #undef  NohDC
                #undef  NoDrawText
                DrawText(hDC, lpString, nCount, lpRect, wFormat)
                hDC     hDC;
                lpStr   lpString;
                int     nCount;
                lpRect  lpRect;
                word    wFormat;
return          void

Ellipse
                Draws ellipse with centre at the centre of the given bounding rectangle.
                Draws border with current pen. Fills interior with current brush.
entry           Ellipse()
                #undef  NohDC
                Ellipse(hDC, X1, Y1, X2, Y2):bDrawn
                hDC     hDC;
                short   X1;
                short   Y1;
                short   X2;
                short   Y2;
return          Boolean

EmptyClipboard
                Empties clipboard, frees data handles, and assigns clipboard ownership to
                the window that currently has the clipboard open.
entry           EmptyClipboard()
                #undef  NoClipBoard
                EmptyClipboard():bEmptied
return          Boolean

EnableMenuItem
                Enables, disables, or greys a menu item, depending on wEnable.
entry           EnableMenuItem()
                #undef  NoMenus
                EnableMenuItem(hMenu, wIDEnableItem, wEnable):bEnabled
                hMenu   hMenu;
                word    wIDEnableItem;
                word    wEnable;
return          Boolean

EnableWindow
                Enables and disables mouse and keyboard input to the specified window.
entry           EnableWindow()
                EnableWindow(hWnd, bEnable):bDone
                hWnd    hWnd;
                Boolean bEnable;
return          Boolean

EndDialog
                Frees resources and destroys windows associated with a modal dialogue box.
entry           EndDialog()
                #undef  NoCtlMgr
                EndDialog(hDlg, nResult)
                hWnd    hDlg;
                int     nResult;
return          void

EndPaint
                Marks the end of window repainting; required after each BeginPaint call.
```

```
entry     EndPaint()
          #undef    NoRect
          #undef    NohDC
          EndPaint(hWnd, lpPaint)
          hWnd      hWnd;
  lpPaintStruct lpPaint;
return    void

EnumChildWindows
          Enumerates the child style windows belonging to hWndParent by passing
          each child window handle and lParam to the lpEnumFunc function.
entry     EnumChildWindows()
          EnumChildWindows(hWndParent, lpEnumFunc, lParam):bDone
          hWnd      hWndParent;
          FarProc   lpEnumFunc;
          long      lParam;
return    Boolean

EnumClipboardFormats
          Enumerates formats from list of available formats belonging to the
          clipboard.
entry     EnumClipboardFormats()
          #undef    NoClipBoard
          EnumClipboardFormats(wFormats):wNextFormat
          word      wFormats;
return    word

EnumFonts
          Enumerates fonts available on a given device, passing font information
           through lpData to lpFontFunc function.
entry     EnumFonts()
          #undef    NohDC
          EnumFonts(hDC, lpFacenname, lpFontfunc, lpData):nResult
          hDC       hDC;
          lpStr     lpFacenname;
          FarProc   lpFontfunc;
          lpStr     lpData;
return    short

EnumObjects
          Enumerates pens or brushes (depending on nObjectType) available on a
          device, passing object information through lpData to lpObjectFunc
          function.
entry     EnumObjects()
          #undef    NohDC
          EnumObjects(hDC, nObjectType, lpObjectFunc, lpData):nResult
          hDC       hDC;
          short     nObjectType;
          FarProc   lpObjectFunc;
          lpStr     lpData;
return    short

EnumProps
          Passes each property of hWnd, in turn, to the lpEnumFunc function
entry     EnumProps()
          EnumProps(hWnd, lpEnumFunc):nResult
          hWnd      hWnd;
          FarProc   lpEnumFunc;
return    int

EnumWindows
          Enumerates windows on the screen by passing handle of each tiled, iconic,
          pop-up, and hidden pop-up window (in that order) to the lpEnumFunc
          function.
entry     EnumWindows()
          EnumWindows(lpEnumFunc, lParam):bDone
          FarProc   lpEnumFunc;
          long      lParam;
return    Boolean
```

EqualRgn
Checks the two given regions to determine if they are identical.
```
entry   EqualRgn()
        #undef  NoRegion
        EqualRgn(hSrc1, hSrcRgn2):bEqual
        hRgn    hSrc1;
        hRgn    hSrcRgn2;
return  Boolean
```

Escape
Accesses device facilities not directly available through GDI.
```
entry   Escape()
        #undef  NohDC
        Escape(hDC, nEscape, nCount, lpInData, lpOutData):nResult
        hDC     hDC;
        short   nEscape;
        short   nCount;
        lpStr   lpInData;
        lpStr   lpOutData;
return  short
```

Escape - AbortDoc
Aborts the current job. lpInData, lpOutData, and nCount are not used.
```
entry   Escape()
        #undef  NohDC
        Escape(hDC, AbortDoc, nCount, lpInData, OutData):nResult
        hDC     hDC;
        short   AbortDoc;
        short   nCount;
        lpStr   lpInData;
        lpStr   OutData;
return  short
```

Escape - DraftMode
Turns draft mode off or on. lpInData points to 1 (on) or 0 (off). nCount is number of bytes at lpInData. lpOutData is not used.
```
entry   Escape()
        #undef  NohDC
        Escape(hDC, DraftMode, nCount, lpInData, lpOutData);nResult
        hDC     hDC;
        short   DraftMode;
        short   nCount;
        lpStr   lpInData;
        lpStr   lpOutData;
return  short
```

Escape - EndDoc
Ends print job started by StartDoc. nCount, lpInData, lpOutData are not used.
```
entry   Escape()
        #undef  NohDC
        Escape(hDC, EndDoc, nCount, lpInData, lpOutData):nResult
        hDC     hDC;
        short   ENDDOC;
        short   nCount;
        lpStr   lpInData;
        lpStr   lpOutData;
return  short
```

Escape - FlushOutput
Flushes output in device buffer; lpInData, lpOutData, and nCount are not used.
```
entry   Escape()
        #undef  NohDC
        Escape(hDC, FlushOutput, nCount, lpInData, lpOutData):nResult
        hDC     hDC;
        short   FlushOutput;
        short   nCount;
        lpStr   lpInData;
        lpStr   lpOutData;
return  short
```

Escape - GetColourTable
    Copies RGB colour table entry to lpOutData. lpInData is colour table
    index. nCount is not used.
entry   Escape()
        #undef NohDC
        Escape(hDC, GetColourTable, nCount, lpInData, lpOutData):nResult
        HDC   hDC;
        short   GetColourTable;
        short   nCount;
        lpStr   lpInData;
        lpStr   lpOutData;
return short

Escape - GetPhysPageSize
    Copies physical page size to POINT structure at lpOutData. lpInData and
    nCount are not used.
entry   Escape()
        #undef NohDC
        Escape(hDC, GetPhysPageSize, nCount, lpInData, lpOutData);nResult
        hDC   hDC;
        short   GetPhysPageSize;
        short   nCount;
        lpStr   lpInData;
        lpStr   lpOutData;
return short

Escape - GetPrintingOffset
    Copies printing offset to POINT structure at lpOutData. lpInData and
    nCount are not used.
entry   Escape()
        #undef NohDC
        Escape(hDC, GetPrintingOffset, nCount, lpInData,
        lpOutData):nResult
        HDC   hDC;
        short   GetPrintingOffset;
        short   nCount;
        lpStr   lpInData;
        lpStr   lpOutData;
return short

Escape - GetScalingFactor
    Copies scaling factors to POINT structure at lpOUtData. lpInData and
    nCount are not used.
entry   Escape()
        #undef NohDC
        Escape(hDC, GetScalingFactor, nCount, lpInData, lpOutData):nResult
        hDC   hDC;
        short   GetScalingFactor;
        short   nCount;
        lpStr   lpInData;
        lpStr   lpOutData;
return short

Escape - NewFrame
    Ends writing to a page. nCount, lpInData and lpOutData are not used.
entry   Escape()
        #undef NohDC
        Escape(hDC, NewFrame, nCount, lpInData, lpOutData):nResult
        hDC   hDC;
        short   NewFrame;
        short   nCount;
        lpStr   lpInData;
        lpStr   lpOutData;
return short

Escape - NextBand
    Ends writing to a band. lpOutData gives rectangle to hold device
    coordinates of next band. nCount and lpInData are not used.
entry   Escape()
        #undef NohDC
        Escape(hDC, NextBand, nCount, lpInData, lpOutData):nResult

Microsoft Windows A.P.I.

```
           hDC     hDC;
           short   NextBand;
           short   nCount;
           lpStr   lpInData;
           lpStr   lpOutData;
   return  short
```

Escape - QueryEcSupport
Tests whether an escape is supported by device driver. lpInData points to the escape. nCount is the number of bytes at lpInData. lpOutData is not used.
```
   entry   Escape()
           #undef  NohDC
           Escape(hDC, QueryEcSupport, nCount, lpInData, lpOutData):nResult
           hDC     hDC;
           short   QueryEcSupport;
           short   nCount;
           lpStr   lpInData;
           lpStr   lpOutData;
   return  short
```

Escape - SetAbortProc
Sets abort function for print job. lpInData, lpOutData, and nCount are not used.
```
   entry   Escape()
           #undef  NohDC
           Escape(hDC, SetAbortProc, nCount, lpInData, lpOutData):nResult
           hDC     hDC;
           short   SetAbortProc;
           short   nCount;
           lpStr   lpInData;
           lpStr   lpOutData;
   return  short
```

Escape - SetColourTable
Sets RGB colour table entry. lpInData points to table index and colour. lpOutData points to RGB colour value to be set by device driver. nCount is not used.
```
   entry   Escape()
           #undef  NohDC
           Escape(hDC, SetColourTable, nCount, lpInData, lpOutData):nResult
           hDC     hDC;
           short   SetColourTable;
           short   nCount;
           lpStr   lpInData;
           lpStr   lpOutData;
   return  short
```

Escape - StartDoc
Starts print job, spooling NewFrame calls under same job until it reaches ENDDOC. lpInData is name of document; nCount is its length. lpOutData not used.
```
   entry   Escape()
           #undef  NohDC
           Escape(hDC, StartDoc, nCount, lpInData, OutData):nResult
           hDC     hDC;
           short   StartDoc;
           short   nCount;
           lpStr   lpInData;
           lpStr   OutData;
   return  short
```

EscapeCommFunction
Executes escape function nFunc for communication device nCid.
```
   entry   EscapeCommFunction()
           #undef  NoComm
           EscapeCommFunction(nCid, nFunc):nResult
           short   nCid;
           int     nFunc;
   return  short
```

ExcludeClipRect
        Creates new clipping region from existing clipping region less the given
        rectangle.
entry   ExcludeClipRect()
        #undef NohDC
        ExcludeClipRect(hDC, X1, Y1, X2, Y2):nRgnType
        hDC   hDC;
        short   X1;
        short   Y1;
        short   X2;
        short   Y2;
return short

FatalExit
        Halts Windows and prompts through auxiliary port (AUX) for instructions
        on how to proceed.
entry   FatalExit()
        FatalExit(Code):Result
        int   Code;
return void

FillRect
        Fills given rectangle using the specified brush.
entry   FillRect()
        #undef NoBrush
        #undef NohDC
        #undef NoRect
        FillRect(hDC, lpRect, hBrush):nResult
        hDC   hDC;
        LPRECT lpRect;
        HBRUSH hBrush;
return int

FillRgn
        Fills given region with brush specified by hBrush.
entry   FillRgn()
        #undef NoBrush
        #undef NohDC
        #undef NoRegion
        FillRgn(hDC, hRgn, hBrush):bFilled
        hDC   hDC;
        hRgn   hRgn;
        hBrush hBrush;
return Boolean

FindAtom
        Retrieves atom (if any) associated with character string lpString.
entry   FindAtom()
        #undef NoAtom
        FindAtom(lpString):wAtom
        lpStr   lpString;
return atom

FindResource
        Locates resource lpname having lpType and returns handle for accessing
        and loading the resource.
entry   FindResource()
        FindResource(hInstance, lpname, lpType):hResInfo
        handle hInstance;
        lpStr   lpname;
        lpStr   lpType;
return handle

FindWindow
        Returns the handle of the window having the given class and caption.
entry   FindWindow()
        FindWindow(lpClassName, lpWindowname):hWnd
        lpStr   lpClassName;
        lpStr   lpWindowname;
return hWnd

Microsoft Windows A.P.I.

FlashWindow
        Flashes the given window once by inverting its active/inactive state.
entry   FlashWindow()
        FlashWindow(hWnd, bInvert):bInverted
        hWnd   hWnd;
        Boolean   bInvert;
return   Boolean

FloodFill
        Fills area of the display surface with current brush, starting at X, Y,
        and continuing in all directions to the boundaries with the given
        rgbColour.
entry   FloodFill()
        #undef   NohDC
        FloodFill(hDC, X, Y, rgbColour):bFilled
        hDC   hDC;
        short   X;
        short   Y;
        dword   rgbColour;
return   Boolean

FlushComm
        Flushes characters from nQueue of communication device nCid.
entry   FlushComm()
        #undef   NoComm
        FlushComm(nCid, nQueue):nResult
        short   nCid;
        int   nQueue;
return   short

FrameRect
        Draws border for the given rectangle using the specified brush.
entry   FrameRect()
        #undef   NoBrush
        #undef   NohDC
        #undef   NoRect
        FrameRect(hDC, lpRect, hBrush):nResult
        hDC   hDC;
        lpRect   lpRect;
        hBrush   hBrush;
return   int

FrameRgn
        Draws border for given region using hBrush. nWidth is width of vertical
        brush strokes. nHeight is height of horizontal strokes.
entry   FrameRgn()
        #undef   NoBrush
        #undef   NohDC
        #undef   NoRegion
        FrameRgn(hDC, hRgn, hBrush, nWidth, nHeight):bFramed
        hDC   hDC;
        hRgn   hRgn;
        hBrush   hBrush;
        short   nWidth;
        short   nHeight;
return   Boolean

FreeLibrary
        Removes library module hLibModule from memory if reference count is zero.
entry   FreeLibrary()
        FreeLibrary(hLibModule)
        handle   hLibModule;
return   handle

FreeProcInstance
        Removes the function instance entry at address lpProc.
entry   FreeProcInstance()
        FreeProcInstance(lpProc)
        FarProc lpProc;
return   void

FreeResource
Removes resource hResInfo from memory if reference count is zero.
```
entry   FreeResource()
        FreeResource(hResData):bFreed
        handle  hResData;
return  Boolean         Returns handle to the active window.
```

GetActiveWindow
```
entry   GetActiveWindow()
        GetActiveWindow():hWnd
return  hWnd
```

GetAtomHandle
Returns the handle (relative to the local heap) of the atom string.
```
entry   GetAtomHandle()
        #undef  NoAtom
        GetAtomHandle(wAtom):hMem
        atom    wAtom;
return  handle
```

GetAtomName
Copies character string (up to nSize characters) associated with wAtom to lpBuffer.
```
entry   GetAtomName()
        #undef  NoAtom
        GetAtomName(wAtom, lpBuffer, nSize):nLength
        atom    wAtom;
        lpStr   lpBuffer;
        int     nSize;
return  word
```

GetBitmapBits
Copies lCount bits of specified bitmap into buffer pointed to by lpBits.
```
entry   GetBitmapBits()
        #undef  NoBitmap
        GetBitmapBits(hBitmap, lCount, lpBits):lcopied
        hBitmap hBitmap;
        long    lCount;
        lpStr   lpBits;
return  long
```

GetBitmapDimension
Returns the width and height of the bitmap specified by hBitmap.
```
entry   GetBitmapDimension()
        #undef  NoBitmap
        GetBitmapDimension(hBitmap):ptDimensions
        hBitmap hBitmap;
return  dword
```

GetBkColour
Returns the current background colour of the specified device.
```
entry   GetBkColour()
        #undef  NohDC
        GetBkColour(hDC):rgbColour
        hDC     hDC;
return  dword
```

GetBkMode
Returns the background mode of the specified device.
```
entry   GetBkMode()
        #undef  NohDC
        GetBkMode(hDC):BkMode
        hDC     hDC;
return  short
```

GetBrushOrg
Retrieves the current brush origin for the given display context.
```
entry   GetBrushOrg()
        #undef  NoBrush
        GetBrushOrg(hDC):dwOrigin
        hDC     hDC;
```

```
       return  dword

GetBValue
        Retrieves the blue value of the given colour.
entry   GetBValue()
        GetBValue(rgbColour):cBlue

GetCaretBlinkTime
        Returns the current caret flash rate.
entry   GetCaretBlinkTime()
        GetCaretBlinkTime():wMSeconds
return  word

GetClassLong
        Retrieves information at nIndex in the WNDCLASS structure.
entry   GetClassLong()
        #undef  NoWinOffsets
        GetClassLong(hWnd, nIndex):long
        hWnd    hWnd;
        int     nIndex;
return  LONG

GetClassName
        Copies hWnd's class name (up to nMaxCount characters) into lpClassName.
entry   GetClassName()
        GetClassName(hWnd, nClassName, nMaxCount):nCopied
        hWnd    hWnd;
        lpStr   nClassName;
        int     nMaxCount;
return  int

GetClassWord
        Retrieves information at nIndex in the WNDCLASS structure.
entry   GetClassWord()
        #undef  NoWinOffsets
        GetClassWord(hWnd, nIndex):word
        hWnd    hWnd;
        int     nIndex;
return  word

GetClientRect
        Copies client coordinates of the window client area to lpRect.
entry   GetClientRect()
        #undef  NoRect
        GetClientRect(hWnd, lpRect)
        hWnd    hWnd;
        lpRect  lpRect;
return  void

GetClipboardData
        Retrieves data from the clipboard in the format given by wFormat.
entry   GetClipboardData()
        #undef  NoClipboard
        GetClipboardData(wFormat):hClipData
        word    wFormat;
return  handle

GetClipboardFormatName
        Copies wFormat's format name (up to nMaxCount characters) into
        lpFormatName.
entry   GetClipboardFormatName()
        #undef  NoClipboard
        GetClipboardFormatName(wFormat, lpFormatName, nMaxCount):nCopied
        word    wFormat;
        lpStr   lpFormatName;
        int     nMaxCount;
return  int

GetClipboardOwner
        Retrieves the window handle of the current owner of the clipboard.
entry   GetClipboardOwner()
```

```
            #undef  NoClipboard
            GetClipboardOwner():hWnd
return      hWnd

GetClipboardViewer
            Retrieves the window handle of the first window in the clipboard viewer
            chain.
entry       GetClipboardViewer()
            #undef  NoClipboard
            GetClipboardViewer():hWnd
return      hWnd

GetClipBox
            Copies dimensions of bounding rectangle of current clip boundary to
            lpRect.
entry       GetClipBox()
            #undef  NoRect
            #undef  NohDC
            GetClipBox(hDC, lpRect):nRgnType
            hDC     hDC;
            lpRect  lpRect;
return      short

GetCodeHandle
            Retrieves the handle of the code segment containing the given function.
entry       GetCodeHandle()
            GetCodeHandle(lpFunc):hInstance
            FarProc lpFunc;
return      handle

GetCommError
            Fills buffer lpStat with communication status of device nCid. Returns
            error code, if any.
entry       GetCommError()
            #undef  NoComm
            GetCommError(nCid, lpStat):nError
            short   nCid;
 ComStat FAR * lpStat;
return      short

GetCommEventMask
            Fills buffer lpStat with communication status of device nCid. Returns
            error code, if any.
entry       GetCommEventMask()
            #undef  NoComm
            GetCommEventMask(nCid, lpStat):nError
            short   nCid;
            int     lpStat;
return      word

GetCommState
            Fills buffer lpDCB with the device control block of communication
            device nCid.
entry       GetCommState()
            #undef  NoComm
            GetCommState(nCid, lpDCB):nResult
            short   nCid;
        DCB FAR * lpDCB;
return      short

GetCurrentPosition
            Retrieves the logical coordinates of the current position.
entry       GetCurrentPosition()
            #undef  NohDC
            GetCurrent Position(hDC):ptPos
            hDC     hDC;
return      dword

GetCurrentTask
            Returns task handle of the current task.
entry       GetCurrentTask()
```

Microsoft Windows A.P.I.

```
           GetCurrentTask():hTask
return     handle

GetCurrentTime
           Returns the time elapsed since the system was booted to the current time.
entry      GetCurrentTime()
           GetCurrentTime():lTime
return     long

GetCursorPos
           Stores mouse cursor position, in screen coordinates, in POINT structure.
entry      GetCursorPos()
           #undef  NoPoint
           GetCursorPos(lpPoint)
           lpPoinT lpPoint;
return     void

GetDC
           Retrieves the display context for the client area of the specified window.
entry      GetDC()
           #undef  NohDC
           GetDC(hWnd):hDC
           hWnd    hWnd;
return     hDC

GetDeviceCaps
           Retrieves the device-specific information specified by nIndex.
entry      GetDeviceCaps()
           #undef  NohDC
           GetDeviceCaps(hDC, nIndex):nValue
           hDC     hDC;
           short   nIndex;
return     short

GetDlgItem
           Retrieves the handle of a dialogue item (control) from the given dialogue
           box.
entry      GetDlgItem()
           #undef  NoCtlMgr
           GetDlgItem(hDlg, nIDDlgItem):hCtl
           hWnd    hDlg;
           int     nIDDlgItem;
return     hWnd

GetDlgItemInt
           Translates text of nIDDlgItem into integer value. Value at lpTranslated
           is zero if errors occur. bSigned is nonzero if minus sign might be
           present.
entry      GetDlgItemInt()
           #undef  NoCtlMgr
           GetDlgItemInt(hDlg, nIDDlgItem, lpTranslated, bSigned):wValue
           hWnd    hDlg;
           int     nIDDlgItem;
           Boolean FAR * lpTranslated;
           Boolean bSigned;
return     unsigned
GetDlgItemText
           Copies nIDDlgItem's control text (up to nMaxCount characters) into
           lpString.
entry      GetDlgItemText()
           #undef  NoCtlMgr
           GetDlgItemText(hDlg, nIDDlgItem, lpString, nMaxCount):nCopied
           hWnd    hDlg;
           int     nIDDlgItem;
           lpStr   lpString;
           int     nMaxCount;
return     int

GetDoubleClickTime
           Retrieves the current double-click time of the system mouse.
entry      GetDoubleClickTime()
```

```
                GetDoubleClickTime():wClickTime
return  word

GetEnvironment
        Copies to lpEnviron the environment associated with the device attached
        to a given port.
entry   GetEnvironment()
        GetEnvironment(lpPortName, lpEnviron, nmaxCount):nCopied
        lpStr   lpPortName;
        lpStr   lpEnviron;
        word    nmaxCount;
return  short

GetFocus
        Retrieves the handle of the window currently owning the input focus.
entry   GetFocus()
        GetFocus():hWnd
return  hWnd

GetGValue
        Retrieves the green value of the given colour.
entry   GetGValue()
        GetGValue(rgbColour):cGreen

GetInstanceData
        Copies nCount bytes of data from offset pData in instance hInstance to
        same offset in current instance.
entry   GetInstanceData()
        GetInstanceData(hInstance, pData, nCount):nBytes
        handle  hInstance;
        npStr   pData;
        int     nCount;
return  int

GetKeyState
        Retrieves the state of the virtual key specified by nVirtKey.
entry   GetKeyState()
        GetKeyState(nVirtKey):nState
        int     nVirtKey;
return  int


GetMapMode
        Retrieves the current mapping mode.
entry   GetMapMode()
        #undef  NohDC
        GetMapMode(hDC):nMapMode
        hDC     hDC;
return  short

GetMenu
        Retrieves a handle to the menu of the specified window.
entry   GetMenu()
        #undef  NoMenus
        GetMenu(hWnd):hMenu
        hWnd    hWnd;
return  HMENU

GetMenuString
        Copies wIDItem's menu label (up to nMaxCount characters) into lpString.
        wFlag is MF_BYPOSITION or MF_BYCOMMAND.
entry   GetMenuString()
        #undef  NoMenus
        GetMenuString(hMenu, wIDItem, lpString, nMaxCount, wFlag):nCopied
        hMenu   hMenu;
        word    wIDItem;
        lpStr   lpString;
        int     nMaxCount;
        word    wFlag;
return  int
```

```
GetMessage
        Retrieves message in range wMsgFilterMin to wMsgFilterMax; stores at
        lpMsg.
entry   GetMessage()
        #undef  NoMsg
        GetMessage(lpMsg, hWnd, wMsgFilterMin, wMsgFilterMax):bContinue
        lpMsg   lpMsg;
        hWnd    hWnd;
      unsigned  wMsgFilterMin;
      unsigned  wMsgFilterMax;
return  Boolean

GetMessagePos
        Returns mouse position, in screen coordinates, at the time of the last
        message retrieved by GetMessage.
entry   GetMessagePos()
        GetMessagePos():dwPos
return  dword

GetMessageTime
        Returns the message time for the last message retrieved by GetMessage.
entry   GetMessageTime()
        GetMessageTime():lTime
return  long

GetMetaFile
        Creates a handle for the metafile named by lpFilename.
entry   GetMetaFile()
        GetMetaFile(lpFilename):hMF
        lpStr   lpFilename;
return  handle

GetMetaFileBits
        Stores specified metafile as collection of bits in global memory block.
entry   GetMetaFileBits()
        GetMetaFileBits(hMF):hMem
        handle  hMF;
return  handle

GetModuleFileName
        Copies module filename (up to nSize characters) to lpFilename
entry   GetModuleFileName()
        GetModuleFileName(hModule, lpfilename, nSize):nLength
        handle  hModule;
        lpStr   lpfilename;
        int     nSize;
return  int

GetModuleHandle
        Returns module handle of module named by lpModuleName.
entry   GetModuleHandle()
        GetModuleHandle(lpModuleName):hModule
        lpStr   lpModuleName;
return  handle

GetModuleUsage
        Returns reference count of module hModule.
entry   GetModuleUsage()
        GetModuleUsage(hMModule):nCount
        handle  hMModule;
return  int

GetNearestColour
        Returns the device colour closest to rgbColour.
entry   GetNearestColour()
        #undef  NohDC
        GetNearestColour(hObject, nCount, lpObject):nCopied
        hDC     hObject;
        dword   nCount;
return  dword
```

GetObject
        Copies nCount bytes of logical data defining hObject to lpObject.
entry   GetObject()
        GetObject(hObject, NCount, lpObject):nCopied
        handle hObject;
        short   NCount;
        lpStr   lpObject;
return short

GetParent
        Retrieves the window handle of the specified window's parent (if any).
entry   GetParent()
        GetParent(hWnd):hWndParent
        hWnd   hWnd;
return hWnd

GetPixel
        Retrieves the RGB colour value of the pixel at the point specified by X and Y.
entry   GetPixel()
        #undef NohDC
        GetPixel(hDC, X, Y,):rgbcolour
        hDC   hDC;
        short   X;
        short   Y;
return dword

GetPolyFillMode
        Retrieves the current polygon-filling mode.
entry   GetPolyFillMode()
        #undef NohDC
        GetPolyFillMode(hDC):nPolyFillMode
        hDC   hDC;
return short

GetProcAddress
        Returns address of the function named by lpProcName in module hModule.
entry   GetProcAddress()
        GetProcAddress(hModule, lpProcName):lpAddress
        handle hModule;
        lpStr   lpProcName;
return FarProc

GetProfileInt
        Returns integer value named by lpKeyName in section lpSectionName from
        the WIN.INI file. If name or section not found, nDefault is returned.
entry   GetProfileInt()
        GetProfileInt(lpSectionName, lpKeyName, nDefault):nnKeyValue
        lpStr   lpSectionName;
        lpStr   lpKeyName;
        int   nDefault;
return int

GetProfileString
        Returns character string named by lpKeyName in section lpSectionName from
        the WIN.INI file. String is copied (up to nSize characters) to
        lpReturnedString. If name or section are not found, lpDefault is returned.
entry   GetProfileString()
        GetProfileString(lpSectionName, lpKeyName, lpDefault,
        lpReturnedString, nSize):nLength
        lpStr   lpSectionName;
        lpStr   lpKeyName;
        lpStr   lpDefault;
        lpStr   lpReturnedString;
        int   nSize;
return int

GetProp
        Retrieves data handle associated with lpString from window property list.
entry   GetProp()
        GetProp(hWnd, lpString):hData

```
            hWnd      hWnd;
            lpStr     lpString;
    return  handle

GetRelAbs
            Retrieves the relabs flag.
    entry   GetRelAbs()
            #undef    NohDC
            GetRelAbs(hDC):nRelAbsMode
            hDC       hDC;
    return  short

GetROP2
            Retrieves the current drawing mode.
    entry   GetROP2()
            #undef    NohDC
            GetROP2(hDC):nDrawMode
            hDC       hDC;
    return  short

GetRValue
            Retrieves the red value of the given colour.
    entry   GetRValue()
            GetRValue(rgbColour):cRed

GetScrollPos
            Retrieves current position of scroll bar elevator identified by hWnd and
            nBar.
    entry   GetScrollPos()
            #undef    NoScroll
            GetScrollPos(hWnd, nBar):nPos
            hWnd      hWnd;
            int       nBar;
    return  int

GetScrollRange
            Copies minimum and maximum scroll bar positions for given scroll bar to
            lpMinPos and lpMaxPos.
    entry   GetScrollRange()
            #undef    NoScroll
            GetScrollRange(hWnd, nBar, lpMinPos, lpMaxPos)
            hWnd      hWnd;
            int       nBar;
            lpInt     lpMinPos;
            lpInt     lpMaxPos;
    return  void

GetStockObject
            Retrieves a handle to a predefined stock pen, brush, or font.
    entry   GetStockObject()
            GetStockObject(nIndex):hObject
            short     nIndex;
    return  handle
GetStretchBltMode
            Retrieves the current stretching mode.
    entry   GetStretchBltMode()
            #undef    NohDC
            GetStretchBltMode(hDC):nStretchMode
            hDC       hDC;
    return  short

GetSubMenu
            Retrieves the menu handle of the pop-up menu at the given position in
            hmenu.
    entry   GetSubMenu()
            #undef    NoMenus
            GetSubMenu(hMenu, nPos):hPopupmenu
            hMenu     hMenu;
            int       nPos;
    return  hMenu
```

GetSysColour
    Retrieves the system colour identified by nIndex.
entry   GetSysColour()
        #undef NoColour
        GetSysColour(nIndex):rgbColour
        int   nIndex;
return dword

GetSysModalWindow
    Returns the handle of a system-modal window, if one is present.
entry   GetSysModalWindow()
        GetSysModalWindow():hWnd
return hWnd

GetSystemMenu
    Allows access to the System menu for copying and modification. bRevert is nonzero to restore the original System menu.
entry   GetSystemMenu()
        #undef NoMenus
        GetSystemMenu(hWnd, bRevert):hSysMenu
        hWnd   hWnd;
        Boolean bRevert;
return hMenu

GetSystemMetrics
    Retrieves information about the system metrics identified by nIndex.
entry   GetSystemMetrics()
        #undef NoSysMetrics
        GetSystemMetrics(nIndex):nValue
        int   nIndex;
return int

GetTempDrive
    Returns letter for the optimal drive for a temporary file. cDriveLOetter is a proposed drive.
entry   GetTempDrive()
        #undef NoOpenFile
        GetTempDrive(cDriveLetter):cOptDriveLetter
        byte   cDriveLetter;
return byte

GetTempFileName
    Creates a temporary filename.
entry   GetTempFileName()
        #undef NoOpenFile
        GetTempFileName(cDriveLetter, lpPrefixString, wUnique,
                        lpTempFileName):wUniqueNumber
        byte   cDriveLetter;
        lpStr   lpPrefixString;
        word   wUnique;
        lpStr   lpTempFileName;
return int

GetTextCharacterExtra
    Retrieves the current intercharacter spacing.
entry   GetTextCharacterExtra()
        #undef NohDC
        GetTextCharacterExtra(hDC):nCharExtra
        hDC   hDC;
return short

GetTextColour
    Retrieves the current text colour.
entry   GetTextColour()
        #undef NohDC
        GetTextColour(hDC):rgbColour
        hDC   hDC;
return dword

GetTextExtent
    Uses current font to compute width and height of text line given by

Microsoft Windows A.P.I. 239

```
              lpString.
     entry    GetTextExtent()
              #undef  NohDC
              GetTextExtent(hDC, lpString, nCount):dwTextExtents
              hDC      hDC;
              lpStr    lpString;
              short    nCount;
     return   dword

GetTextFace
              Copies the current font's facename (up to nCount characters) into
              lpFacename.
     entry    GetTextFace()
              #undef  NohDC
              GetTextFace(hDC, nCount, lpFacename):nCopied
              hDC      hDC;
              short    nCount;
              lpStr    lpFacename;
     return   short

GetTextMetrics
              Fills buffer given by lpMetrics with metrics for currently selected font.
     entry    GetTextMetrics()
              #undef  NoTextMetric
              #undef  NohDC
              GetTextMetrics(hDC, lpMetrics):bRetrieved
              hDC      hDC;
        lpTextMetric lpMetrics;
     return   Boolean

GetThresholdEvent
              Returns long pointer to a threshold flag. The flag is set if any voice
              queue is below threshold (i.e., below a given number of notes).
     entry    GetThresholdEvent()
              #undef  NoSound
              GetThresholdEvent():lpInt
     return   lpInt

GetThresholdStatus
              Returns a bit mask containing the threshold event status. If a bit is
              set, the given voice queue is below threshold.
     entry    GetThresholdStatus()
              #undef  NoSound
              GetThresholdStatus():fStatus
     return   int

GetUpdateRect
              Copies dimensions of bounding rectangle of window region that needs
              updating to lpRect. bErase is nonzero if background needs erasing.
              bUpdate is zero if window is up-to-date.
     entry    GetUpdateRect()
              #undef  NoRect
              #undef  NohDC
              GetUpdateRect(hWnd, lpRect, bErase):bUpdate
              hWnd     hWnd;
              lpRect   lpRect;
              Boolean bErase;
     return   Boolean

GetVersion
              Returns the current version of Windows.
     entry    GetVersion()
              GetVersion():wVersion
     return   word

GetViewportExt
              Retrieves the x and y-extents of the display context's viewport.
     entry    GetViewportExt()
              #undef  NohDC
              GetViewportExt(hDC):ptExtents
              hDC      hDC;
```

```
return  dword

GetViewportOrg
        Retrieves X and Y coordinates of the origin of the display context's
        viewport.
entry   GetViewportOrg()
        #undef  NohDC
        GetViewportOrg(hDC):ptOrigin
        hDC     hDC;
return  dword

GetWindowDC
        Retrieves display context for entire window, including caption bar,
 menus, scroll bars.
entry   GetWindowDC()
        #undef  NohDC
        GetWindowDC(hWnd):hDC
        hWnd    hWnd;
return  hDC

GetWindowExt
        Retrieves X and Y extents of the display context's window.
entry   GetWindowExt()
        #undef  NohDC
        GetWindowExt(hDC):ptExtents
        hDC     hDC;
return  dword

GetWindowLong
        Retrieves information identified by nIndex about the given window.
entry   GetWindowLong()
        #undef  NoWinOffsets
        GetWindowLong(hWnd, nIndex):long
        hWnd    hWnd;
        int     nIndex;
return  long

GetWindowOrg
        Retrieves X and Y coordinates of the origin of the display context's
        window.
entry   GetWindowOrg()
        #undef  NohDC
        GetWindowOrg(hDC):ptOrigin
        hDC     hDC;
return  dword

GetWindowRect
        Copies dimensions, in screen coordinates, of entire window (including
        caption bar, border, menus, and scroll bars..) to lpRect.
entry   GetWindowRect()
        #undef  NoRect
        GetWindowRect(hWnd, lpRect)
        hWnd    hWnd;
        lpRect  lpRect;
return  void

GetWindowText
        Copies hWnd's window caption (up to nMaxCount characters) into lpString.
entry   GetWindowText()
        GetWindowText(hWnd, lpString, nMaxCount):nCopied
        hWnd    hWnd;
        lpStr   lpString;
        int     nMaxCount;
return  int

GetWindowTextLength
        Returns the length of the given window's caption or text.
entry   GetWindowTextLength()
        GetWindowTextLength(hWnd):nLength
        hWnd    hWnd;
return  int
```

GetWindowWord
Retrieves information identified by nIndex about the given window.
```
entry   GetWindowWord()
        #undef  NoWinOffsets
        GetWindowWord(hWnd, nIndex):word
        hWnd    hWnd;
        int     nIndex;
return  word
```

GlobalAlloc
Allocates dwBytes of memory from the global heap. Memory type (e.g., fixed or moveable) is set by wFlags.
```
entry   GlobalAlloc()
        #undef  NoMemMgr
        GlobalAlloc(wFlags, dwBytes):hMem
        word    wFlags;
        dword   dwBytes;
return  handle
```

GlobalCompact
Compacts global memory to generate dwMinFree free bytes.
```
entry   GlobalCompact()
        #undef  NoMemMgr
        GlobalCompact(dwMinFree):dwLargest
        dword   dwMinFree;
return  dword
```

GlobalDiscard
Discards global memory block hMem if reference count is zero.
```
entry   GlobalDiscard()
        GlobalDiscard(hMem):hOldMem
```

GlobalFlags
Discards memory type of global memory block hMem.
```
entry   GlobalFlags()
        #undef  NoMemMgr
        GlobalFlags(hMem):wFlags
        handle  hMem;
return  word
```

GlobalFree
Removes global memory block hMem from memory if reference count is zero.
```
entry   GlobalFree()
        #undef  NoMemMgr
        GlobalFree(hmem):hOldMem
        handle  hmem;
return  handle
```

GlobalHandle
Retrieves the handle of the global memory if reference count is zero.
```
entry   GlobalHandle()
        #undef  NoMemMgr
        GlobalHandle(wMem):dwmem
        word    wMem;
return  dword
```

GlobalLock
Returns address of global memory block hMem, locks block in memory, and increases the reference count by one.
```
entry   GlobalLock()
        #undef  NoMemMgr
        GlobalLock(hMem):lpAddress
        handle  hMem;
return  lpStr
```

GlobalReAlloc
Reallocates the global memory block hMem to dwBytes and memory type wFlags.
```
entry   GlobalReAlloc()
        #undef  NoMemMgr
        GlobalReAlloc(hMem, dwBytes, wFlags):hNewMem
```

242   *The Programmer's Technical Reference*

```
            handle    hMem;
            dword     dwBytes;
            word      wFlags;
    return  handle

GlobalSize
            Returns the size, in bytes, of global memory block hMem.
    entry   GlobalSize()
            #undef    NoMemMgr
            GlobalSize(hMemmj):dwBytes
            handle    hMemmj;
    return  dword

GlobalUnlock
            Unlocks global memory block hMem and decreases the reference count by one.
    entry   GlobalUnlock()
            #undef    NoMemMgr
            GlobalUnlock(hMem):bResult
            handle    hMem;
    return  Boolean

GreyString
            Writes nCount characters of string at X, Y, using lpOutputFunc (or
            TextOut if NULL). Grays text using hBrush. lpData specifies output
            string (if lpOutputFunc is NULL) or data are passed to output function.
            nWidth and nHeight give dimensions of enclosing rectangle (if zero,
            dimensions are calculated).
    entry   GreyString()
            GreyString(hDC, hBrush, lpOutputFunc, lpData, nCount, X, Y, nWidth,
                    nHeight):bDrawn
            hDC       hDC;
            hBrush    hBrush;
            FarProc   lpOutputFunc;
            dword     lpData;
            int       nCount;
            int       X;
            int       Y;
            int       nWidth;
            int       nHeight;
    return  Boolean

HiByte
            Returns the high-order byte of nInteger.
    entry   HiByte()
            HiByte(nInteger):cHighByte

HideCaret
            Removes system caret from the given window.
    entry   HideCaret()
            HideCaret(hWnd)
            hWnd      hWnd;
    return  void

HiliteMenuItem
            Highlights or removes the highlighting from a top-level (menu-bar) menu
            item.
    entry   HiliteMenuItem()
            #undef    NoMenus
            HiliteMenuItem(hWnd, hMenu, wIDHiliteItem, wHilite):bHilited
            hWnd      hWnd;
            hMenu     hMenu;
            word      wIDHiliteItem;
            word      wHilite;
    return  Boolean

HIword
            Returns the high-order word of lInteger.
    entry   HIword()
            HIword(lInteger):wHighWord

InflateRect
```

Microsoft Windows A.P.I.

Expands or shrinks the rectangle specified by lpRect by X units on the left and right ends of the rectangle and Y units on the top and bottom.
entry   InflateRect()
           #undef NoRect
           InflateRect(lpRect, X, Y):nResult
           lpRect   lpRect;
           int   X;
           int   Y;
return int

InitAtomTable
Initializes atom hash table and sets it to nSize atoms.
entry   InitAtomTable()
           InitAtomTable(nSize):bResult
           int   nSize;
return Boolean

InSendMessage
Returns TRUE if window function is processing a message sent with SendMessage.
entry   InSendMessage()
           #undef NoWinMessages
           InSendMessage():bInSend
return Boolean

IntersectClipRect
Forms new clipping region from intersection of current clipping region and given rectangle.
entry   IntersectClipRect()
           #undef NohDC
           IntersectClipRect(hDC, X1, Y1, X2, Y2):nRgnType
           hDC   hDC;
           short   X1;
           short   Y1;
           short   X2;
           short   Y2;
return short

IntersectRect
Finds the intersection off two rectangles and copies it to lpDestRect.
entry   IntersectRect()
           #undef NoRect
           IntersectRect(lpDestRect, lpSrc1Rect, lpSrc2Rect):nIntersection
           lpRect   lpDestRect;
           lpRect   lpSrc1Rect;
           lpRect   lpSrc2Rect;
return int

InvalidateRect
Marks for repainting the rectangle specified by lpRect (in client coordinates). The rectangle is erased if bErase is nonzero.
entry   InvalidateRect()
           #undef NoRect
           InvalidateRect(hWnd, lpRect, bErase)
           hWnd   hWnd;
           lpRect   lpRect;
           Boolean bErase;
return void

InvalidateRgn
Marks hRgn for repainting. The region is erased if bErase is nonzero.
entry   InvalidateRgn()
           #undef NoRegion
       InvalidateRgn(hWnd, lpRect, bErase)
           hWnd   hWnd;
           hRgn   lpRect;
           Boolean bErase;
return void

InvertRect
Inverts the display bits of the specified rectangle.

```
        entry   InvertRect()
                #undef  NohDC
                #undef  NoRect
                InvertRect(hDC, lpRect):nResult
                hDC     hDC;
                LPRECT  lpRect;
        return  int

        InvertRgn
                Inverts the colours in the region specified by hRgn.
        entry   InvertRgn()
                #undef  NohDC
                #undef  NoRegion
                InvertRgn(hDC, hRgn):bInverted
                hDC     hDC;
                hRgn    hRgn;
        return  Boolean

        IsChild
                Returns TRUE if given window is a child of hParentWnd.
        entry   IsChild()
                IsChild(hParentWnd, hWnd):bChild
                hWnd    hParentWnd;
                hWnd    hWnd;
        return  Boolean

        IsClipboardFormatAvailable
                Returns TRUE if data in given format is available.
        entry   IsClipboardFormatAvailable()
                #undef  NoClipBoard
                IsClipboardFormatAvailable(wFormat):bAvailable
                word    wFormat;
        return  Boolean

        IsDialogMessage
                Determines whether lpMsg is intended for the given modeless dialogue box.
                If so, the message is processed and bUsed is nonzero
        entry   IsDialogMessage()
                #undef  NoMsg
                #undef  NoCtlMgr
                IsDialogMessage(hDlg, lpMsg):bUsed
                hWnd    hDlg;
                lpMsg   lpMsg;
        return  Boolean

        IsDlgButtonChecked
                Tests whether nIDButton is checked. For a 3-state button, returns 2 for
                greyed, 1 for checked, zero for neither.
        entry   IsDlgButtonChecked()
                #undef  NoCtlMgr
                IsDlgButtonChecked(hDlg, lpMsg):bUsed
                hWnd    hDlg;
                int     lpMsg;
        return  word

        IsIconic
                Specifies whether or not a window is open or closed (iconic).
        entry   IsIconic()
                IsIconic(hWnd):bIconic
                hWnd    hWnd;
        return  Boolean

        IsRectEmpty
                Determines whether or not the specified rectangle is empty.
        entry   IsRectEmpty()
                #undef  NoRect
                IsRectEmpty(lpRect):bEmpty
                lpRect  lpRect;
        return  Boolean

        IsWindow
```

Microsoft Windows A.P.I.

```
                Determines whether or not hWnd is a valid, existing window.
        entry   IsWindow()
                IsWindow(hWnd):bExists
                hWnd    hWnd;
        return  Boolean

IsWindowEnabled
                Specifies whether or not hWnd is enabled for mouse and keyboard input.
        entry   IsWindowEnabled()
                IsWindowEnabled(hWnd):bEnabled
                hWnd    hWnd;
        return  Boolean

IsWindowVisible
                Determines whether or not the given window is visible on the screen.
        entry   IsWindowVisible()
                IsWindowVisible(hWnd):bVisible
                hWnd    hWnd;
        return  Boolean

KillTimer
                Kills the timer event identified by hWnd and nIDEvent.
        entry   KillTimer()
                KillTimer(hWnd, nIDEvent):bKilled
                hWnd    hWnd;
                short   nIDEvent;
        return  Boolean

LineDDA
                Computes successive points in line starting at X1, Y1 and ending at X2,
                Y2, passing each point and lpData parameter to lpLineFunc function.
        entry   LineDDA()
                LineDDA(X1, Y1, X2, Y2, lpLineFunclpData)
                short   X1;
                short   Y1;
                short   X2;
                short   Y2;
                FarProc lpLineFunclpData;
        return  void

LineTo
                Draws line with current pen from the current position up to, but not
                including, the point X, Y.
        entry   LineTo()
                #undef  NohDC
                LineTo(hDC, X, Y):bDrawn
                hDC     hDC;
                short   X;
                short   Y;
        return  Boolean

LoadAccelerators
                Loads accelerator table named by lpTableName.
        entry   LoadAccelerators()
                LoadAccelerators(hInstance, lpTableName):hRes
                handle  hInstance;
                lpStr   lpTableName;
        return  handle

LoadBitmap
                Loads bitmap resource named by lpBitmapName.
        entry   LoadBitmap()
                #undef  NoBitmap
                LoadBitmap(hInstance, lpBitmapName):hBitmap
                handle  hInstance;
                lpStr   lpBitmapName;
        return  hBitmap

LoadCursor
                Loads cursor resource named by lpCursorName.
        entry   LoadCursor()
```

LoadCursor

```
        LoadCursor(hInstance, lpCursorName):hCursor
        handle  hInstance;
        lpStr   lpCursorName;
return  hCursor
```

LoadIcon

Loads icon resource named by lpIconName.
```
entry   LoadIcon()
        LoadIcon(hInstance, lpIconName):hIcon
        handle  hInstance;
        lpStr   lpIconName;
return  hIcon
```

LoadLibrary

Loads the library module named by lpLibFilename.
```
entry   LoadLibrary()
        LoadLibrary(lpLibFileName):hLibModule
        lpStr   lpLibFileName;
return  handle
```

LoadMenu

Loads menu resource named by lpMenuName.
```
entry   LoadMenu()
        #undef  NoMenus
        LoadMenu(hInstance, lpMenuName):hMenu
        handle  hInstance;
        lpStr   lpMenuName;
return  hMenu
```

LoadResource

Loads the resource hResInfo and returns a handle to the resource.
```
entry   LoadResource()
        LoadResource(hInstance, hResInfo):hResData
        handle  hInstance;
        handle  hResInfo;
return  handle
```

LoadString

Loads string resource wID into the buffer lpBuffer. Up to nBufferMax characters are copied.
```
entry   LoadString()
        LoadString(hInstance, wID, lpBuffer, nBufferMax):nSize
        handle  hInstance;
        unsigned wID;
        lpStr   lpBuffer;
        int     nBufferMax;
return  int
```

LoByte

Returns the low-order byte of nInteger.
```
entry   LoByte()
        LoByte(nInteger):cLowByte
```

LocalAlloc

Allocates wBytes of memory from the local heap. Memory type (e.g., fixed or moveable) is set by wFlags.
```
entry   LocalAlloc()
        #undef  NoMemMgr
        LocalAlloc(wFlags, wBytes):hMem
        word    wFlags;
        word    wBytes;
return  handle
```

LocalCompact

Compacts local memory to generate wMinFree free bytes.
```
entry   LocalCompact()
        #undef  NoMemMgr
        LocalCompact(wMinFree):wLargest
        word    wMinFree;
return  word
```

LocalDiscard
Discards local memory block hMem if reference count is zero.
entry   LocalDiscard()
```
LocalDiscard(hmem):hOldMem
```

LocalFlags
Returns memory type of local memory block hMem.
entry   LocalFlags()
```
#undef   NoMemMgr
LocalFlags(hmem):wFlags
handle  hmem;
```
return   word

LocalFree
Frees local memory block hMem from memory if reference count is zero.
entry   LocalFree()
```
#undef   NoMemMgr
LocalFree(hMem):hOldMem
handle  hMem;
```
return   handle

LocalFreeze
Prevents compaction of the local heap.
entry   LocalFreeze()
```
LocalFreeze(Dummy)
```

LocalHandle
Retrieves the handle of the local memory object whose address is wMem.
entry   LocalHandle()
```
#undef   NoMemMgr
LocalHandle(wMem):hmem
word    wMem;
```
return   handle

LocalHandleDelta
Sets the entry count for each new handle table created in the local heap.
entry   LocalHandleDelta()
```
LocalHandleDelta(nNewDelta):nCurrentDelta
```

LocalInit
Initializes the local heap.
entry   LocalInit()
```
#undef   NoMemMgr
LocalInit(wValue, pString, pString):bResult
     word    wValue;
char NEAR * pString;
char NEAR * pString;
```
return   Boolean

LocalLock
Returns the address of the local memory block hMem, locks the block in memory, and increases the reference count by one.
entry   LocalLock()
```
#undef   NoMemMgr
LocalLock(hMem):pAddress
handle  hMem;
```
return   char NEAR *

LocalMelt
Permits compaction of the local heap.
entry   LocalMelt()
```
LocalMelt(Dummy)
```

LocalNotify
Sets the callback function for handling notification messages from local memory.
entry   LocalNotify()
```
#undef   NoMemMgr
LocalNotify(lpFunc):lpPrevFunc
FarProc lpFunc;
```
return   FarProc

LocalReAlloc
Reallocates the local memory block hMem to wBytes and memory type wFlags.
entry   LocalReAlloc()
        #undef   NoMemMgr
        LocalReAlloc(hMem, wBytes, wFlags):hNewMem
        handle   hMem;
        word   wBytes;
        word   wFlags;
return handle

LocalSize
Returns the size, in bytes, of local memory block hMem.
entry   LocalSize()
        #undef   NoMemMgr
        LocalSize(hmem):wBytes
        handle   hmem;
return word

LocalUnlock
Unlocks local memory block hMem and decreases the reference count by one.
entry   LocalUnlock()
        #undef   NoMemMgr
        LocalUnlock(hMem):bResult
        handle   hMem;
return Boolean

LockData
Locks the data segment in memory.
entry   LockData()
        LockData(Dummy):hMem

LockResource
Returns the memory address of the resource hResInfo, locks the resource in memory, and increases the reference count by one.
entry   LockResource()
        LockResource(hResInfo):lpResInfo
        handle   hResInfo;
return lpStr

LockSegment Function
Locks the segment whose segment address is wSegment.
entry   LockSegment()
        #undef   NoMemMgr
        LockSegment(wSegment):hSegment
        word   wSegment;
return handle

LOword
Returns the low-order word of lInteger.
entry   LOword()
        LOword(lIntger):wLowWord

LPtoDP
Converts logical points into device points.
entry   LPtoDP()
        #undef   NoPoint
        #undef   NohDC
        LPtoDP(hDC, lpPoints, nCount):bConverted
        hDC   hDC;
        LPPoint lpPoints;
        short   nCount;
return Boolean

MakeIntAtom
Casts an integer for use as an argument in AddAtom.
entry   MakeIntAtom()
        MakeIntAtom(wInteger):nAtom

MakeIntResource
Casts an integer for use as an argument in AddAtom.
entry   MakeIntResource()

Microsoft Windows A.P.I. 249

```
            MakeIntResource(nInteger):lpIntegerID
MakeLong
            Creates an unsigned long integer.
    entry   MakeLong()
            MakeLong(nLowWord, nHighWord):dwInteger

MakePoint
            Converts a long value into a Point structure.
    entry   MakePoint()
            MakePoint(lValue):ptPoint

MakeProcInstance
            Returns function instance address for function lpProc. Calls to the
            instance address ensure that the function uses the data segment of
            instance hInstance.
    entry   MakeProcInstance()
            MakeProcInstance(lpProc, hInstance):lpAddress
            FarProc  lpProc;
            handle   hInstance;
    return  FarProc

MapDialogRect
            Converts the dialogue box coordinates given in lpRect to client
            coordinates.
    entry   MapDialogRect()
            #undef  NoRect
            #undef  NoCtlMgr
            MapDialogRect(hDlg, lpRect)
            hWnd    hDlg;
            lpRect  lpRect;
    return  void

Max
            Returns the maximum value of A and B.
    entry   max()
            max(A, B):nMaximum

MessageBeep
            Generates a beep at the system speaker when a message box is displayed.
    entry   MessageBeep()
            #undef  NoMb
            MessageBeep(wType):bBeep
            word    wType;
    return  Boolean

MessageBox
            Creates a window with given lpText and lpCaption containing the
            predefined icons and push buttons defined by wType.
    entry   MessageBox()
            #undef  NoMb
            MessageBox(hWndParent, lpText, lpCaption, wType):nMenuItem
            hWnd    hWndParent;
            lpStr   lpText;
            lpStr   lpCaption;
            word    wType;
    return  int

Min
            Returns the minimum value of A and B.
    entry   min()
            min(A, B):nMinimum

MoveTo
            Moves the current position to the point specified by X and Y.
    entry   MoveTo()
            #undef  NohDC
            MoveTo(hDC, X, Y):ptPrevPos
            hDC     hDC;
            short   X;
            short   Y;
```

```
        return  dword

MoveWindow
        Causes WM_SIZE message to be sent to hWnd. X, Y, nWidth, and nHeight give
        the new size of the window.
entry   MoveWindow()
        MoveWindow(hWnd, X, Y, nWidth, nHeight, bRepaint)
        hWnd    hWnd;
        int     X;
        int     Y;
        int     nWidth;
        int     nHeight;
        Boolean bRepaint;
return  void

OemToAnsi
        Converts the OEM character string to an ANSI string.
entry   OemToAnsi()
        OemToAnsi(lpOemStr, lpAnsiStr):bTranslated
        lpStr   lpOemStr;
        lpStr   lpAnsiStr;
return  Boolean

OffsetClipRgn
        Moves clipping region X units along the X-axis and Y units along the
        Y-axis.
entry   OffsetClipRgn()
        #undef  NohDC
        OffsetClipRgn(hDC, X, Y):nRgnType
        hDC     hDC;
        short   X;
        short   Y;
return  short

OffsetRect
        Moves given rectangle X units along the X-axis and Y units along the
        Y-axis.
entry   OffsetRect()
        #undef  NoRect
        OffsetRect(lpRect, X, Y):nResult
        lpRect  lpRect;
        int     X;
        int     Y;
return  int

OffsetRgn
        Moves the given region X units along the X-axis and Y units along
        the Y-axis.
entry   OffsetRgn()
        #undef  NoRegion
        OffsetRgn(hRgn, X, Y):nRgntype
        hRgn    hRgn;
        short   X;
        short   Y;
return  short

OpenClipboard
        Opens clipboard; prevents other applications from modifying its contents.
entry   OpenClipboard()
        #undef  NoClipBoard
        OpenClipboard(hWnd):bOpened
        hWnd    hWnd;
return  Boolean

OpenComm
        Opens communication device named by lpCommName. Transmit-queue and
        receive-queue sizes are set by wInQueue and wOutQueue.
entry   OpenComm()
        #undef  NoComm
        OpenComm(lpComName, wInWueue, wOutQueue):nCid
        lpStr   lpComName;
```

```
               word    wInWueue;
               word    wOutQueue;
       return  short

OpenFile
               Creates, opens, reopens, or deletes file named by lpFileName.
       entry   OpenFile()
                       #undef   NoOpenFile
                       OpenFile(lpFileName, lpReOpenBuff, wStyle):nFile
               lpStr   lpFileName;
           lpOfStruct  lpReOpenBuff;
               word    wStyle;
       return  int

OpenIcon
               Opens the specified window.
       entry   OpenIcon()
                       OpenIcon(hWnd):bOpened
               hWnd    hWnd;
       return  Boolean


OpenSound
               Opens the play device for exclusive use.
       entry   OpenSound()
                       #undef   NoSound
                       OpenSound():nVoices
       return  int

PaintRgn
               Fills the region specified by hRgn with the currently selected brush.
       entry   PaintRgn()
                       #undef   NohDC
                       #undef   NoRegion
                       PaintRgn(hDC, hRgn):bFilled
               hDC     hDC;
               hRgn    hRgn;
       return  Boolean

PatBlt
               Creates a bit pattern on the specified device, using dwRop to combine the
               current brush with the pattern already on the device.
       entry   PatBlt()
                       #undef   NohDC
                       PatBlt(hDC, X, Y, nWidth, nHeight5, dwRop):bDrawn
               hDC     hDC;
               short   X;
               short   Y;
               short   nWidth;
               short   nHeight5;
               dword   dwRop;
       return  Boolean

PeekMessage
               Checks application queue and places message (if any) at lpMsg.
       entry   PeekMessage()
                       #undef   NoMsg
                       PeekMessage(lpMsg, hWnd, wMsgFilterMin, wMsgFilterMax,
                                   bRemoveMsg):bPresent
               lpMsg   lpMsg;
               hWnd    hWnd;
           unsigned    wMsgFilterMin;
               word    wMsgFilterMax;
               Boolean bRemoveMsg;
       return  Boolean

Pie
               Draws arc starting at X3, Y3 and ending at X4, Y4 and connects centre and
               two endpoints, using current pen. Moves counter-clockwise. Fills with
               current brush. Arc's centre is centre of bounding rectangle given by X1,
               Y1, X2, Y2.
```

```
        entry   Pie()
                #undef  NohDC
                Pie(hDC, X1, Y1, X2, Y2, X3, Y3, X4, Y4):bDrawn
                hDC     hDC;
                short   X1;
                short   Y1;
                short   X2;
                short   Y2;
                short   X3;
                short   Y3;
                short   X4;
                short   Y4;
        return  Boolean

        PlayMetaFile
                Plays the contents of the specified metafile on the given device context.
        entry   PlayMetaFile()
                #undef  NohDC
                PlayMetaFile(hDC, hMF):bPlayed
                hDC     hDC;
                handle  hMF;
        return  Boolean

        Polygon
                Draws a polygon by connecting the nCount vertices given by lpPoints.
        entry   Polygon()
                #undef  NoPoint
                #undef  NohDC
                Polygon(hDC, lpPoints, nCount):bDrawn
                hDC     hDC;
                LPPoint lpPoints;
                short   nCount;
        return  Boolean

        Polyline
                Draws a set of line segments, connecting the nCount points given by
                lpPoints.
        entry   Polyline()
                #undef  NoPoint
                #undef  NohDC
                Polyline(hDC, lpPoints, nCount):bDrawn
                hDC     hDC;
                LPPoint lpPoints;
                short   nCount;
        return  Boolean

        PostAppMessage
                Posts message to application; returns without waiting for processing.
        entry   PostAppMessage()
                #undef  NoWinMessages
                PostAppMessage(hTask, wMsg, wParam, lParam):bPosted
                handle    hTask;
                unsigned  wMsg;
                word      wParam;
                long      lParam;
        return  Boolean

        PostMessage
                Places message in application queue; returns without waiting for
                processing.
        entry   PostMessage()
                #undef  NoWinMessages
                PostMessage(hWnd, wMsg, wParam, lParam):bPosted
                hWnd      hWnd;
                unsigned  wMsg;
                word      wParam;
                long      lParam;
        return  Boolean

        PostQuitMessage
                Posts a WM_QUIT message to the application and returns immediately.
```

```
entry     PostQuitMessage()
          #undef   NoWinMessages
          PostQuitMessage(nExitCode)
          int      nExitCode;
return    void

PtInRect
          Indicates whether or not a specified point lies within a given rectangle.
entry     PtInRect()
          #undef   NoPoint
          #undef   NoRect
          PtInRect(lpRect, Point):bInRect
          lpRect   lpRect;
          Point    Point;
return    Boolean

PtInRegion
          Tests if X, Y is within the given region.
entry     PtInRegion()
          #undef   NohDC
          #undef   NoRegion
          PtInRegion(hRgn, S, Y):bSuccess
          hRgn     hRgn;
          short    S;
          short    Y;
return    Boolean

PtVisible
          Tests if  X, Y is within the clipping region of the given display context.
entry     PtVisible()
          #undef   NohDC
          PtVisible(hDC, X, Y):bVisible
          hDC      hDC;
          short    X;
          short    Y;
return    Boolean

ReadComm
          Reads up to nSize bytes from the communication device nCid into buffer
          lpBuf.
entry     ReadComm()
          #undef   NoComm
          ReadComm(nCid, lpBuf, nSize):nBytes
          short    nCid;
          lpStr    lpBuf;
          int      nSize;
return    short
Rectangle
          Draws rectangle, using current pen for border and current brush for
          filling.
entry     Rectangle()
          #undef   NohDC
          Rectangle(hDC, X1, Y1, X2, Y2):bDrawn
          hDC      hDC;
          short    X1;
          short    Y1;
          short    X2;
          short    Y2;
return    Boolean

RectVisible
          Determines if any part of given rectangle lies within clipping region.
entry     RectVisible()
          #undef   NohDC
          #undef   NoRect
          RectVisible(hDC,lpRect):bVisible
          hDC      hDC;
          lpRect   lpRect;
return    Boolean

RegisterClass
```

RegisterClass
Registers a window class.
```
entry   RegisterClass()
        #undef  NoBrush
        #undef  NoWndClass
        RegisterClass(lpWndClass):bRegistered
    lpWndClass  lpWndClass;
return  Boolean
```

RegisterClipboardFormat
Registers a new clipboard format whose name is pointed to by lpFormatName.
```
entry   RegisterClipboardFormat()
        #undef  NoClipBoard
        RegisterClipboardFormat(lpFormatName):wFormat
        lpStr   lpFormatName;
return  word
```

RegisterWindowMessage
Defines a new window message that is guaranteed to be unique.
```
entry   RegisterWindowMessage()
        #undef  NoWinMessages
        RegisterWindowMessage(lpString):wMsg
        lpStr   lpString;
return  unsigned
```

ReleaseCapture
Releases mouse input and restores normal input processing.
```
entry   ReleaseCapture()
        ReleaseCapture()
return  void
```

ReleaseDC
Releases a display context when an application is finished drawing in it.
```
entry   ReleaseDC()
        #undef  NohDC
        ReleaseDC(hWnd, hDC):nReleased
        hWnd    hWnd;
        hDC     hDC;
return  int
```

RemoveFontResource
Removes from the font table the font resource named by lpFilename.
```
entry   RemoveFontResource()
        RemoveFontResource(lpFilename):bSuccess
        lpStr   lpFilename;
return  Boolean
```

RemoveProp
Removes lpString from property list; retrieves corresponding data handle.
```
entry   RemoveProp()
        RemoveProp(hWnd, lpString):hData
        hWnd    hWnd;
        lpStr   lpString;
return  handle
```

ReplyMessage
Replies to message without returning control to the SendMessage caller.
```
nentry  ReplyMessage()
        #undef  NoWinMessages
        ReplyMessage(lReply)
        long    lReply;
return  void
```

RestoreDC
Restores display context given by hDC to previous state given by nSavedDC.
```
entry   RestoreDC()
        #undef  NohDC
        RestoreDC(hDC, nSavedDC):bRestored
        hDC     hDC;
        short   nSavedDC;
return  Boolean
```

RGB
: Creates an RGB colour value from individual red, green, and blue values.
entry
: RGB()
  RGB(r,g,b):dword
return
: none

RoundRect
: Draws rounded rectangle, using current pen for border, current brush for filling.
entry
: RoundRect()
  #undef NohDC
  RoundRect(hDC, X1, Y1, X2, Y2.X3, Y3):bDrawn
  hDC   hDC;
  short   X1;
  short   Y1;
  short   X2;
  short   Y2 . X3;
  short   Y3;
return
: Boolean

SaveDC
: Saves the current state of the display context hDC.
entry
: SaveDC()
  #undef NohDC
  SaveDC(hDC):nSavedDC
  hDC   hDC;
return
: short

ScreenToClient
: Converts the screen coordinates at lpPoint to client coordinates.
entry
: ScreenToClient()
  #undef NoPoint
  ScreenToClient(hWnd,lpPoint)
  hWnd   hWnd;
  lpPoint lpPoint;
return
: void

ScrollWindow
: Moves contents of client area XAmount along screen's x-axis and YAmount units along y-axis (right for positive XAmount; down for positive YAmount).
entry
: ScrollWindow()
  #undef NoRect
  ScrollWindow(hWnd, XAmount, YAmount, lpRect, lpClipRect)
  hWnd   hWnd;
  int   XAmount;
  int   YAmount;
  lpRect lpRect;
  lpRect lpClipRect;
return
: void

SelectClipRgn
: Selects given region as current clipping region for the specified display context.
entry
: SelectClipRgn()
  #undef NohDC
  #undef NoRegion
  SelectClipRgn(hDC, hRgn):nRgnType
  hDC   hDC;
  hRgn   hRgn;
return
: short

SelectObject
: Selects hObject as current object, replacing previous object of same type.
entry
: SelectObject()
  #undef NohDC
  SelectObject(hDC, hObject):hOldObject
  hDC   hDC;
  handle hObject;
return
: handle

SendDlgItemMessage
       Sends a message to nIDDlgItem within the dialogue box specified by hDlg.
entry SendDlgItemMessage()
       #undef NoCtlMgr
       SendDlgItemMessage(hDlg, nIDDlgItem, wMsg, wParam, lParam):lResult
       hWnd   hDlg;
       int   nIDDlgItem;
       unsigned wMsg;
       word   wParam;
       long   lParam;
return long

SendMessage
       Sends a message to a window or windows.
entry SendMessage()
       #undef NoWinMessages
       SendMessage(hWnd, wMsg, wParam, lParam):lReply
       hWnd   hWnd;
       unsigned wMsg;
       word   wParam;
       long   lParam;
return long

SetActiveWindow
       Makes a tiled or pop-up style window the active window.
entry SetActiveWindow()
       SetActiveWindow(hWnd):hWndPrev
       hWnd   hWnd;
return hWnd

SetBitmapBits
       Sets bitmap bits to values given at lpBits. dwCount is byte count at
       lpBits.
entry SetBitmapBits()
       #undef NoBitmap
       SetBitmapBits(hBitmap, dwCount, lpBits):bCopied
       hBitmap hBitmap;
       dword   dwCount;
       lpStr   lpBits;
return Boolean

SetBitmapDimension
       Associates a width and height, in 0.1 millimeter units, with a bitmap.
entry SetBitmapDimension()
       #undef NoBitmap
       SetBitmapDimension(hBitmap, X, Y):ptOldDimensions
       hBitmap hBitmap;
       short   X;
       short   Y;
return Dword

SetBkColour
       Sets the background colour to the device colour closest to rgbColour.
entry SetBkColour()
       #undef NohDC
       SetBkColour(hDC, rgbColour):nOldColour
       hDC   hDC;
       dword   rgbColour;
return dword

SetBkMode
       Sets the background mode used with text, hatched brushes, and line styles.
entry SetBkMode()
       #undef NohDC
       SetBkMode(hDC, nBkMode):nOldMode
       hDC   hDC;
       short   nBkMode;
return short

SetBrushOrg
       Sets the origin of all brushes selected into the given display context.

SetBrushOrg

```
entry     SetBrushOrg()
          #undef  NoBrush
          SetBrushOrg(hDC, X, Y):dwOldOrigin
          hDC     hDC;
          int     X;
          int     Y;
return    dword
```

SetCapture

Causes mouse input to be sent to hWnd, regardless of mouse cursor position.
```
enter     SetCapture()
          SetCapture(hWnd):hWndPrev
          hWnd    hWnd;
return    hWnd
```

SetCaretBlinkTime

Establishes the caret flash rate.
```
entry     SetCaretBlinkTime()
          SetCaretBlinkTime(wMSeconds)
          word    wMSeconds;
return    void
```

SetCaretPos

Moves caret to the position specified by X and Y.
```
entry     SetCaretPos()
          SetCaretPos(X, Y)
          int     X;
          int     Y;
return    void
```

SetClassLong

Replaces long value at nIndex in the WNDCLASS structure.
```
entry     SetClassLong()
          #undef  NoWinOffsets
          SetClassLong(hWnd, nIndex, lNewLong):lOldLong
          hWnd    hWnd;
          int     nIndex;
          long    lNewLong;
return    long
```

SetClassWord

Replaces word at the given nIndex in the WNDCLASS structure.
```
entry     SetClassWord()
          #undef  NoWinOffsets
          SetClassWord(hWnd, nIndex, wNewWord):wOldword
          hWnd    hWnd;
          int     nIndex;
          word    wNewWord;
return    word
```

SetClipboardData

Copies hMem, a handle for data having wFormat format, into the clipboard.
```
entry     SetClipboardData()
          #undef  NoClipboard
          SetClipboardData(wformat, hMem):hClipData
          word    wformat;
          handle  hMem;
return    handle
```

SetClipboardViewer

Adds hWnd to clipboard viewer chain. hWndNext is next window in chain.
```
entry     SetClipboardViewer()
          #undef  NoClipboard
          SetClipboardViewer(hWnd):hWndNext
          hWnd    hWnd;
return    hWnd
```

SetCommBreak

Sets a break state on communication device nCid and suspends character transmission.

```
entry   SetCommBreak()
        #undef   NoComm
        SetCommBreak(nCid):nResult
        short    nCid;
return  short

SetCommEventMask
        Sets the event mask of the communication device nCid.
entry   SetCommEventMask()
        #undef   NoComm
        SetCommEventMask(nCid, nEvtMask):lpEvent
        short    nCid;
        word     nEvtMask;
return  word FAR *

SetCommState
        Sets a communication device to the state specified by the device control
        block lpDCB. The device to be set is identified by the ID field of the
        control block.
entry   SetCommState()
        #undef   NoComm
        SetCommState(lpDCB):nResult
        DCB FAR * lpDCB;
return  short


SetCursor
        Sets cursor shape in hCursor, removes cursor from screen if hCursor is
        NULL.
entry   SetCursor()
        SetCursor(hCursor):hOldCursor
        hCursor  hCursor;
return  hCursor

SetCursorPos
        Sets position of mouse cursor to screen coordinates given by X and Y.
entry   SetCursorPos()
        SetCursorPos(X, Y)
        int      X;
        int      Y;
return  void

SetDlgItemInt
        Sets text of nIDDlgItem to string representing an integer.
entry   SetDlgItemInt()
        #undef   NoCtlMgr
        SetDlgItemInt(hDlg, nIDDlgItem, wValue, bSigned)
        hWnd     hDlg;
        int      nIDDlgItem;
        unsigned wValue;
        Boolean  bSigned;
return  void

SetDlgItemText
        Sets caption or text of nIDDlgItem to lpString.
entry   SetDlgItemText()
        #undef   NoCtlMgr
        SetDlgItemText(hDlg, nIDDlgItem, lpString)
        hWnd     hDlg;
        int      nIDDlgItem;
        lpStr    lpString;
return  void

SetEnvironment
        Copies data at lpEnviron to environment associated with device attached
        to given port.
entry   SetEnvironment()
        SetEnvironment(lpPortName, lpEnviron, nCount):nCopied
        lpStr    lpPortName;
        lpStr    lpEnviron;
        word     nCount;
```

```
       return   short

SetFocus
              Assigns the input focus to the window specified by hWnd.
       entry   SetFocus()
               SetFocus(hWnd):hWndPrev
               hWnd     hWnd;
       return  hWnd

SetMapMode
              Sets the mapping mode of the specified display context.
       entry   SetMapMode()
               #undef   NohDC
               SetMapMode(hDC, nMapMode):nOldMapMode
               hDC      hDC;
               short    nMapMode;
       return  short

SetMenu
              Sets window menu to hmenu. Removes menu if hMenu is NULL.
       entry   SetMenu()
               #undef   NoMenus
               SetMenu(hWnd, hMenu):bSet
               hWnd     hWnd;
               hMenu    hMenu;
       return  Boolean

SetMetaFileBits
              Creates memory metafile from data in the given global memory block.
       entry   SetMetaFileBits()
               SetMetaFileBits(hMem):hMF
               handle   hMem;
       return  handle

SetPixel
              Sets pixel at X, Y to the device colour closest to rgbColour.
       entry   SetPixel()
               #undef NohDC
               SetPixel(hDC, X, Y, rgbColour):rgbActualColour
               hDC      hDC;
               short    X;
               short    Y;
               dword    rgbColour;
       return  dword

SetPolyFillMode
              Sets the polygon-filling mode for the specified display context.
       entry   SetPolyFillMode()
               #undef   NohDC
               SetPolyFillMode(hDC, nPolyFillMode):nOldPolyFillMode
               hDC      hDC;
               short    nPolyFillMode;
       return  short

SetPriority
              Sets the task priority of the task hTask, and returns new priority.
       SetPriority()
               SetPriority(hTask, nChangeAmount):nNew
               handle   hTask;
               int      nChangeAmount;
       return  int

SetProp
              Copies string and data handle to property list of hWnd.
       entry   SetProp()
               SetProp(hWnd, lpString, hData):bSet
               hWnd     hWnd;
               lpStr    lpString;
               handle   hData;
       return  Boolean
```

SetRect

Fills RECT structure at lpRect with given coordinates.

```
entry   SetRect()
        #undef  NoRect
        SetRect(lpRect, X1, Y1, X2, Y2):nResult
        lpRect  lpRect;
        int     X1;
        int     Y1;
        int     X2;
        int     Y2;
return  int
```

SetRectEmpty

Sets the rectangle to an empty rectangle (all coordinates are zero).

```
entry   SetRectEmpty()
        #undef  NoRect
        SetRectEmpty(lpRect):nResult
        lpRect  lpRect;
return  int
```

SetRelAbs

Sets the relabs flag.

```
entry   SetRelAbs()
        #undef  NohDC
        SetRelAbs(hDC, nRelAbsMode):nOldRelAbsMode
        hDC     hDC;
        short   nRelAbsMode;
return  short
```

SetResourceHandler

Sets the function address of the resource handler for resources with type lpType. A resource handler provides for loading of custom resources.

```
entry   SetResourceHandler()
        SetResourceHandler(hInstance, lpType, lpLoadFunc):lpLoadFunc
        handle  hInstance;
        lpStr   lpType;
        FarProc lpLoadFunc;
return  FARPROC
```

SetROP2

Sets the current drawing mode.

```
entry   SetROP2()
        #undef  NohDC
        SetROP2(hDC, nDrawMode):nOldDrawMode
        hDC     hDC;
        short   nDrawMode;
return  short
```

SetScrollPos

Sets scroll bar elevator to nPos; redraws scroll bar if bRedraw is nonzero.

```
entry   SetScrollPos()
        #undef  NoScroll
        SetScrollPos(hWnd, nBar, nPos, bRedraw):nOldPos
        hWnd    hWnd;
        int     nBar;
        int     nPos;
        Boolean bRedraw;
return  int
```

SetScrollRange

Set minimum and maximum scroll bar positions for a given scroll bar.

```
entry   SetScrollRange()
        #undef  NoScroll
        SetScrollRang(hWnd, nBar, nMinPos, nMaxPos, bRedraw)
        hWnd    hWnd;
        int     nBar;
        int     nMinPos;
        int     nMaxPos;
        Boolean bRedraw;
return  void
```

```
SetSoundNoise
        Sets the source and duration of a noise from the play device
entry   SetSoundNoise()
        #undef  NoSound
        SetSoundNoise(nSource, nDuration):nResult
        int     nSource;
        int     nDuration;
return  int

SetStretchBltMode
        Sets the stretching mode for the StretchBlt function.
entry   SetStretchBltMode()
        #undef  NohDC
        SetStretchMode(hDC, nStretchMode):nOldStretchMode
        hDC     hDC;
        short   nStretchMode;
return  short

SetSysColours
        Changes one or more system colours.
entry   SetSysColours()
        #undef  NoColour
        SetSysColours(nChange, lpSysColour, lpColourValues)
        int     nChange;
        lpInt   lpSysColour;
    long FAR *  lpColourValues;
return  void

SetSysModalWindow
        Makes the specified window a system-modal window.
entry   SetSysModalWindow()
        SetSysModalWindow(hWnd):hPrevWnd
        hWnd    hWnd;
return  hWnd

SetTextCharacterExtra
        Sets the amount of intercharacter spacing.
entry   SetTextCharacterExtra()
        #undef  NohDC
        SetTextCharacterExtra(hDC, nCharExtra):nOldCharExtra
        hDC     hDC;
        short   nCharExtra;
return  short

SetTextColour
        Sets text colour to the device colour closest to rgbColour.
entry   SetTextColour()
        #undef  NohDC
        SetTextcolour(hDC, rgbColour):rgbOldColour
        hDC     hDC;
        dword   rgbColour;
return  dword

SetTextJustification
        Prepares GDI to justify a text line using nBreakExtra and nBreakCount.
entry   SetTextJustification()
        #undef  NohDC
        SetTextJustification(hDC, nBreakExtra, nBreakCount):nSet
        hDC     hDC;
        short   nBreakExtra;
        short   nBreakCount;
return  short

SetTimer
        Creates system timer event identified by nIDEvent. wElapse is elapsed
        milliseconds. lpTimerFunc receives timer messages; if NULL, messages go
        to application queue.
entry   SetTimer()
        SetTimer(hWnd, nIDEvent, wElapse, lpTimerFunc):nIDNewEvent
        hWnd    hWnd;
        short   nIDEvent;
```

```
                unsigned   wElapse;
                FarProc    lpTimerFunc;
        return  short

SetViewportExt
                Sets the X and Y extents of the viewport of the specified display context.
        entry   SetViewportExt()
                #undef    NohDC
                SetViewportExt(hDC, X, Y):ptOldExtents
                hDC       hDC;
                short     X;
                short     Y;
        return  Dword

SetViewportOrg
                Sets the viewport origin of the specified display context.
        entry   SetViewportOrg()
                #undef    NohDC
                SetViewportOrg(hDC, X, Y):ptOldOrigin
                hDC       hDC;
                short     X;
                short     Y;
        return  Dword
SetVoiceAccent
                Places an accent (tempo, volume, mode, and pitch) in the voice queue
                nVoice.
        entry   SetVoiceAccent()
                #undef    NoSound
                SetVoiceAccent(nVoice, nTempo, nVolume, nMmode, nPitch):nResult
                int       nVoice;
                int       nTempo;
                int       nVolume;
                int       nMmode;
                int       nPitch;
        return  int

SetVoiceEnvelope
                Places the envelope (wave shape and repeat count) in the voice queue
                nVoice.
        entry   SetVoiceEnvelope()
                #undef    NoSound
                SetVoiceEnvelope(nVoice, nShape, nRepeat):nResult
                int       nVoice;
                int       nShape;
                int       nRepeat;
        return  int

SetVoiceNote
                Places a note in the voice queue nVoice.
        entry   SetVoiceNote()
                #undef    NoSound
                SetVoiceNote(nVoice, nValue, nLength, nCdots):nResults
                int       nVoice;
                int       nValue;
                int       nLength;
                int       nCdots;
        return  int

SetVoiceQueueSize
                Allocates nBytes of memory for the voice queue nVoice.
        entry   SetVoiceQueueSize()
                #undef    NoSound
                SetVoiceQueueSize(nVoice, nBytes):nResult
                int       nVoice;
                int       nBytes;
        return  int
        note    Default is 192 bytes.

SetVoiceSound
                Places a sound (frequency and duration) in the voice queue nVoice.
        entry   SetVoiceSound()
```

```
            #undef  NoSound
            SetVoiceSound(nVoice, nFrequency, nDuration):nResult
            int     nVoice;
            int     nFrequency;
            int     nDuration;
return      int

SetVoiceThreshold
            Sets the threshold level to nNotes for the voice queue nVoice.
entry       SetVoiceThreshold()
            #undef  NoSound
            SetVoiceThreshold(nVoice, nNotes):nResult
            int     nVoice;
            int     nNotes;
return      int

SetWindowExt
            Sets the X and Y extents of the window of the specified display context.
entry       SetWindowExt()
            #undef  NohDC
            SetWindowExt(hDC, X, Y):ptOldExtents
            hDC     hDC;
            short   X;
            short   Y;
return      dword

SetWindowLong
            Changes the window attribute identified by nIndex.
entry       SetWindowLong()
            #undef  NoWinOffsets
            SetWindowLong(hWnd, nIndex, lNewLong):lOldLong
            hWnd    hWnd;
            int     nIndex;
            long    lNewLong;
return      long

SetWindowOrg
            Sets the window origin of the specified display context.
entry       SetWindowOrg()
            #undef  NohDC
            SetWindowOrg(hDC, X, Y):ptOldOrigin
            hDC     hDC;
            short   X;
            short   Y;
return      dword

SetWindowsHook
            Installs a system and/or application hook function.
entry       SetWindowsHook()
            #undef  NoWH
            SetWindowsHook(nFilterType, lpFilterFunc):lpPrevFilterFunc
            int     nFilterType;
            FarProc lpFilterFunc;
return      FarProc

SetWindowText
            Sets window caption (if any) or text (if a control) to lpString.
entry       SetWindowText()
            SetWindowText(hWnd, lpString)
            hWnd    hWnd;
            lpStr   lpString;
return      void

SetWindowWord
            Changes the window attribute specified by nIndex.
entry       SetWindowWord()
            #undef  NoWinOffsets
            SetWindowWord(hWnd, nIndex, nNewWord):wOldWord
            hWnd    hWnd;
            int     nIndex;
            word    nNewWord;
```

```
         return  word

ShowCaret
         Displays newly-created caret or redisplays hidden caret.
entry    ShowCaret()
         ShowCaret(hWnd)
         hWnd    hWnd;
return   void

ShowCursor
         Adds 1 to cursor display count if bShow is nonzero.  Subtracts 1 if bShow
         is zero.
entry    ShowCursor()
         ShowCursor(bShow):nCount
         Boolean bShow;
return   int

ShowWindow
         Displays or removes the given window as specified by nCmdShow.
entry    ShowWindow()
         ShowWindow(hWnd, nCmdShow):bShown
         hWnd    hWnd;
         int     nCmdShow;
return   Boolean

SizeofResource
         Returns the size, in bytes, of resource hResInfo.
entry    SizeofResource()
         SizeofResource(hInstance, hResInfo):wBytes
         handle  hInstance;
         handle  hResInfo;
return   word

StartSound
         Starts play in each voice queue.
entry    StartSound()
         #undef  NoSound
         StartSound():nResult
return   int

StopSound
         Stops playing all voice queues and flushes the contents of the queues.
entry    StopSound()
         #undef  NoSOund
         StopSound():nResult
return   int

StretchBlt
         Moves bitmap from source rectangle into destination rectangle, stretching
         or compressing as necessary.  Source origin is at XSrc, YSrc.  X, Y,
         nWidth, and nHeight give origin and dimensions of rectangle on
         destination device.  dwROP defines how source and destination bits are
         combined.
entry    StretchBlt()
         #undef  NohDC
         StretchBlt(hDestDC, X, Y, nWidth, nHeight, hSrcDC, XSrc, YSrc,
                 nSrcWidth, nSrcHeight, dwROP):bDrawn
         hDC     hDestDC;
         short   X;
         short   Y;
         short   nWidth;
         short   nHeight;
         hDC     hSrcDC;
         short   XSrc;
         short   YSrc;
         short   nSrcWidth;
         short   nSrcHeight;
         dword   dwROP;
return   Boolean
```

SwapMouseButton
Swaps the meaning of the left and right mouse buttons if bSwap is TRUE.
```
entry     SwapMouseButton()
          SwapMouseButton(bSwap):bSwapped
          Boolean bSwap;
return    Boolean
```

SyncAllVoices
Places a sync mark in each voice queue. Voices wait at the sync mark until all queues have encountered it.
```
entry     SyncAllVoices()
          #undef  NoSound
          SyncAllVoices():nResult
return    int
```

TextOut
Writes character string using current font and starting at X, Y.
```
entry     TextOut()
          #undef  NohDC
          TextOut(hDC, X, Y, lpString, nCount):bDrawn
          hDC     hDC;
          short   X;
          short   Y;
          lpStr   lpString;
          short   nCount;
return    Boolean
```

Throw
Restores the execution environment to the values in buffer lpCatchBuf. Execution continues at the location specified by the environment with the return value nThrowBack available for processing.
```
entry      Throw()
           Throw(lpCatchBuf, nThrowBacki)
     lpCatchBuf lpCatchBuf;
           int     nThrowBacki;
return     void
```

TranslateAccelerator
Processes keyboard accelerators for menu commands.
```
entry     TranslateAccelerator()
          #undef  NoMsg
          TranslateAccelerator(hWnd, hAccTable, lpMsg):nTranslated
          hWnd    hWnd;
          handle  hAccTable;
          lpMsg   lpMsg;
return    int
```

TranslateMessage
Translates virtual keystroke messages into character messages.
```
entry     TranslateMessage()
          #undef  NoMsg
          TranslateMessage(lpMsg):bTranslated
          lpMsg   lpMsg;
return    Boolean
```

TransmitCommChar
Places the character cChar at the head of the transmit queue for immediate transmission.
```
entry     TransmitCommChar()
          #undef  NoComm
          TransmitCommChar(nCid, cChar):nResult
          short   nCid;
          char    cChar;
return    short
```

UngetCommChar
Makes the character cChar the next character to be read from the receive queue.
```
entry     UngetCommChar()
          #undef  NoComm
          UngetCommChar(nCid, cChar):nResult
```

```
            short   nCid;
            char    cChar;
return      short
```

UnionRect
Stores the union of two rectangles at lpDestRect.
```
entry       UnionRect()
            #undef  NoRect
            UnionRect(lpDestRect, lpSrc1Rect, lpSrc2Rect):nUnion
            lpRect  lpDestRect;
            lpRect  lpSrc1Rect;
            lpRect  lpSrc2Rect;
return      int
```

UnlockData
Unlocks the data segment.
```
entry       UnlockData()
            UnlockData(Dummy)
```

UnlockSegment
Unlocks the segment whose segment address is wSegment.
```
entry       UnlockSegment()
            #undef  NoMemMgr
            UnlockSegment(wSegment):hMem
            word    wSegment;
return      handle
```

UnrealizeObject
Directs GDI to reset the origin of the given brush the next time it is selected.
```
entry       UnrealizeObject()
            #undef  NoBrush
            UnrealizeObject(hBrush):bUnrealized
            hBrush  hBrush;
return      Boolean
```

UpdateWindow
Notifies application when parts of a window need redrawing after changes.
```
entry       UpdateWindow()
            UpdateWindow(hWnd)
            hWnd    hWnd;
return      void
```

ValidateRect
Releases from repainting rectangle specified by lpRect (in client coordinates). If lpRect is NULL, entire window is validated.
```
entry       ValidateRect()
            #undef  NoRect
            ValidateRect(hWnd, lpRect)
            hWnd    hWnd;
            lpRect  lpRect;
return      void
```

ValidateRgn
Releases hRgn from repainting. If hRgn is NULL, entire region is validated.
```
entry       ValidateRgn()
            #undef  NoRegion
            ValidateRgn(hWnd, hRgn)
            hWnd    hWnd;
            hRgn    hRgn;
return      void
```

WaitMessage
Yields control to other applications when application has no tasks to perform.
```
entry       WaitMessage()
            #undef  NoWinMessages
            WaitMessage()
return      void
```

WaitSoundState
```
        Waits until the play driver enters the state nState.
entry   WaitSoundState()
        #undef  NoSound
        WaitSoundState(nState):nResult
        int     nState;
return  int
```

WindowFromPoint
```
        Identifies the window containing Point (in screen coordinates).
entry   WindowFromPoint()
        #undef  NoPoint
        WindowFromPoint(Point):hWnd
        Point   Point;
return  hWnd
```

WinMain
```
        Serves as entry point for execution of a Windows application.
entry   WinMain()
        WinMain(hInstance, hPrevInstance, lpCmdLine, nCmdShow):nExitCode
```

WndProc
```
        Processes  messages sent to it by Windows or the application's main
        function.
entry   WndProc()
        WndProc(hWnd, wMsg, wParam, lParam):lReply
```

WriteComm
```
        Writes up to nSize bytes from buffer lpBuf to communication
        device nCid.
entry   WriteComm()
        #undef  NoComm
        WriteComm(nCid, lpBuf, nSize):nbytes
        short   nCid;
        lpStr   lpBuf;
        int     nSize;
return  short
```

WriteProfileString
```
        Copies character string lpString to the WIN.INI file. The string replaces
        the current string named by lpKeyName in section lpSectionname. If the
        key or section does not exist, a new key and section are created.
entry   WriteProfileString()
        WriteProfileString(lpApplicationName, lpKeyName, lpString):bResult
        lpStr   lpApplicationName;
        lpStr   lpKeyName;
        lpStr   lpString;
return  Boolean
```

Yield
```
        Halts the current task and starts any waiting task.
entry   Yield()
        Yield():bResult
return  Boolean
```

Errors

The following error codes are returned by Windows 1.03:

```
        Error               Description
        001h    Insufficient memory for allocation
        002h    Error reallocating memory
        003h    Memory cannot be freed
        004h    Memory cannot be locked
        005h    Memory cannot be unlocked
        007h    Window handle not valid
        008h    Cached display contexts are busy
```

010h	Clipboard already open
013h	Mouse module not valid
014h	Display module not valid
015h	Unlocked data segment should be locked
016h	Invalid lock on system queue
100h	Lock memory errors
140h	Local heap is busy
180h	Invalid local handle
1C0h	LocalLock count overflow
1F0h	LocalUnlock count underflow
200h	Global memory errors
240h	Critical section problems
280h	Invalid global handle
2C0h	GlobalLock count overflow
2F0h	GlobalUnlock count underflow
300h	Task schedule errors
301h	Invalid task ID
302h	Invalid exit system call
303h	Invalid BP register chain
400h	Dynamic loader/linker errors
401h	Error during boot process
402h	Error loading a module
403h	Invalid ordinal reference
404h	Invalid entry name reference
405h	Invalid start procedure
406h	Invalid module handle
407h	Invalid relocation record
408h	Error saving forward reference
409h	Error reading segment contents
410h	Error reading segment contents
411h	Insert disk for specified file
412h	Error reading non-resident table
4FFh	int 3Fh handler unable to load segment
500h	Resource manager/user profile errors
501h	Missing resource table
502h	Bad resource type
503h	Bad resource type
504h	Bad resource type
505h	Error reading resource
600h	Atom manager errors
700h	Input/output package errors

13

Network Interfacing

Interrupt 60h FTP Driver - PC/TCP Packet Driver Specification
The handler for the interrupt will start with a 3-byte jump instruction, followed by the ASCIIZ string 'PKT DRVR'. To find the interrupt being used by the driver, an application should scan through interrupt vectors 60h to 80h until it finds one with the 'PKT DRVR' string.

Network Interface classes/types:

```
Class    01h      Ethernet/IEEE 802.3
                  01h     3COM 3C500/3C501
                  02h     3COM 3C505
                  03h     MICOM-Interlan NI5010
                  04h     BICC Data Networks 4110
                  05h     BICC Data Networks 4117
                  06h     MICOM-Interlan NP600
                  08h     Ungermann-Bass PC-NIC
                  09h     Univation NC-516
                  0Ah     TRW PC-2000
                  0Bh     MICOM-Interlan NI5210
                  0Ch     3COM 3C503
                  0Dh     3COM 3C523
                  0Eh     Western Digital WD8003
                  0Fh     Spider Systems S4
Class    02h      ProNET-10
         01h      Proteon p1300
Class    03h      IEEE 802.5/ProNet-4
         01h      IBM Token-Ring Adapter
         02h      Proteon p1340
         03h      Proteon p1344
Class    04h      Omninet
Class    05h      Appletalk
Class    06h      Serial Line
Class    07h      StarLAN
Class    08h      ARCnet
                  01h     Datapoint RIM

entry    AX       01FFh   Get Class
         BX       handler returned by function 02h
return   CF       set on error
         DH       error code
                  01h     invalid handle number
                  02h     no interfaces of the specified class found
                  03h     no interfaces of the specified type found
                  04h     no interfaces of the specified number found
                  05h     bad packet type
                  06h     interface does not support multicast messages
                  07h     this packet driver cannot terminate
                  08h     invalid receiver mode
```

```
                        09h       insufficient space
                        0Ah       type accessed but never released
                        0Bh       bad command
                        0Ch       packet could not be sent
            CF          clear if successful
            BX          version
            CH          class
            DX          type
            CL          number
            DS:SI       pointer to name
            AL          driver type
                        01h       basic
                        02h       extended
                        0FFh      not installed
entry       AH          02h - FTP Driver - Access Type
            AL          interface class
            BX          interface type
            CX          length of type
            DL          interface number
            DS:SI       pointer to type
            ES:DI       pointer to receiver
return      CF          set on error
                        DH        error code (see above)
            CF          clear if successful
            AX          handle
note        Receiver called with:
            AX          subfunction
                        00h       application to return pointer to buffer in ES:DI
                                  ES:DI     0:0 means throw away packet
                        01h       copy to DS:SI buffer completed
            BX          handle
            CX          buffer length when a packet is received

entry       AH          03h - FTP Driver - Release Type
            BX          handle
return      CF          set on error
                        DH        error code (see above)
            CF          clear if successful

entry       AH          04h - FTP Driver - Send Packet
            CX          length
            DS:SI       pointer to buffer
return      CF          set on error
                        DH        error code (see above)

entry       AH          05h - FTP Driver - Terminate Driver For Handle
            BX          handle
return      CF          set on error
                        DH        error code (see above)

entry       AH          06h - FTP Driver - Get Address
            BX          handle
            CX          length
            ES:DI       pointer to buffer
return      CF          set on error
                        DH        error code (see above)
            CF          clear if successful
            CX          length
note        Copies the local net address associated with the handle into the buffer

entry       AH          07h - FTP Driver - Reset Interface
            BX          handle
return      CF          set on error
                        DH        error code (see above)

Interrupt 60h           10-Net Network
entry       AH          11h       Lock and Wait
            AL          drive number or 0
            DX          number of seconds to wait
            ES:SI       Ethernet address or 0
```

Network Interfacing

```
              DS:BX    pointer to 31-byte ASCIIZ semaphore name
return   AL            status
                       00h     successful
                       01h     timeout
                       02h     server not responding
                       03h     invalid semaphore name
                       04h     semaphore list is full
                       05h     invalid drive ID
                       06h     invalid Ethernet address
                       07h     not logged in
                       08h     write to network failed
                       09h     semaphore already logged for this CPU

entry    AH            12h     Lock
         AL            drive number or 0 for default
         ES:SI         Ethernet address or 0
         DS:BX         pointer to 31-byte ASCIIZ semaphore name
return   AL            status (see function 11h)
                       01h     semaphore currently logged
note     Unlike function 11h, this function returns immediately.

entry    AH            13h     Unlock
         AL            drive number or 0
         ES:SI         Ethernet address or 0
         DS:BX         pointer to 31-byte ASCIIZ semaphore name
return   AL            status (see function 11h)
                       01h     semaphore not logged

entry    AH            20h - FTP Driver - Set Receive Mode
         BX            handle
         CX            mode
                       01h     turn off receiver
                       02h     receive only packets sent to this interface
                       03h     mode 2 plus broadcast packets
                       04h     mode 3 plus limited multicast packets
                       05h     mode 3 plus all multicast packets
                       06h     all packets
return   CF            set on error
         DH            error code

entry    AH            21h - FTP Driver - Get Receive Mode
         BX            handle
return   CF            set on error
         DH            error code (see function 01h above)
         CF            clear if successful
         AX            mode

entry    AH            24h - FTP Driver - Get Statistics
         BX            handle
return   CF            set on error
         DH            error code
         CF            clear if successful
         DS:SI         pointer to statistics buffer
                       dword    packets in
                       dword    packets out
                       dword    bytes in
                       dword    bytes out
                       dword    errors in
                       dword    errors out
                       dword    packets dropped

Interrupt 5Ch    NETBIOS interface entry port, TOPS
entry    AH            5Ch
         ES:BX         pointer to network control block
                       Subfunction in first NCB field (or with 80h for non-waiting call)
                       10h     start session with NCB_NAME name (call)
                       11h     listen for call
                       12h     end session with NCB_NAME name (hangup)
                       14h     send data via NCB_LSN
                       15h     receive data from a session
                       16h     receive data from any session
```

```
                   17h      send multiple data buffers
                   20h      send unACKed message (datagram)
                   21h      receive datagram
                   22h      send broadcast datagram
                   23h      receive broadcast datagram
                   30h      add name to name table
                   31h      delete name from name table
                   32h      reset adapter card and tables
                   33h      get adapter status
                   34h      status of all sessions for name
                   35h      cancel
                   36h      add group name to name table
                   70h      unlink from IBM remote program (no F0h function)
                   71h      send data without ACK
                   72h      send multiple buffers without ACK
                   78h      find name
                   79h      token-ring protocol trace
return    AL       status
                   00h      successful
                   01h      bad buffer size
                   03h      invalid NETBIOS command
                   05h      timeout
                   06h      receive buffer too small
                   08h      bad session number
                   09h      LAN card out of memory
                   0Ah      session closed
                   0Bh      command has been cancelled
                   0Dh      name already exists
                   0Eh      local name table full
                   0Fh      name still in use, can't delete
                   11h      local session table full
                   12h      remote PC not listening
                   13h      bad NCB_NUM field
                   14h      no answer to CALL or no such remote
                   15h      name not in local name table
                   16h      duplicate name
                   17h      bad delete
                   18h      abnormal end
                   19h      name error, multiple identical names in use
                   1Ah      bad packet
                   21h      network card busy
                   22h      too many commands queued
                   23h      bad LAN card number
                   24h      command finished while cancelling
                   26h      command can't be cancelled
                   0FFh     NETBIOS busy
return    AL       error code (0 if none)
note 1.  When the NETBIOS is installed ints 13h and 17h are interrupted by the
         NETBIOS. Int 18h is moved to int 86h and one of int 02h or 03h is used
         by NETBIOS. Also, NETBIOS extends the int 15h/fns 90h and 91h functions
         (scheduler functions).
     2.  Normally not initialized.
     3.  TOPS network card uses DMA 1, 3 or none.
     4.  Sytek PCnet card uses DMA 3.
     5.  Structure of Network Control Block:
             byte        ncb_command
             byte        ncb_retcode
             byte        ncb_lsn
             byte        ncb_num
             dword       pointer to ncb_buffer
             word        ncb_length
             16 bytes    ncb_callname
             16 bytes    ncb_name
             byte        ncb_rto
             byte        ncb_sto
             dword       pointer to ncb_post
             byte        ncb_lana_num
             byte        ncb_cmd_cplt
             14 bytes    ncb_reserve
     6.  Structure name:
             16 bytes    nm_name
```

```
            byte      nm_num
            byte      nm_status
         7. Structure A-status:
            6 bytes   as_ID
            byte      as_jumpers
            byte      as_post
            byte      as_major
            byte      as_minor
            word      as_interval
            word      as_crcerr
            word      as_algerr
            word      as_colerr
            word      as_abterr
            dword     as_tcount
            dword     as_rcount
            word      as_retran
            word      as_xresrc
            8 bytes   as_res0
            word      as_ncbfree
            word      as_ncbmax
            word      as_ncbx
            4 bytes   as_res1
            word      as_sespend
            word      as_msp
            word      as_sesmax
            word      as_bufsize
            word      as_names
           16 name    structures  as_name

Interrupt  6Fh  10-Net
entry   AH       00h       Login
        DS:DX    pointer to login record
                 8 bytes   user name
                 8 bytes   password
                12 bytes   name of SuperStation
return  CL       security level
        AX       status
                 0000h     successful
                 01FFh     time out on response
                 02FFh     network (hardware) error
                 03FFh     invalid password
                 04FFh     local resource not available
                 05FFh     server resource not available
                 06FFh     already logged in under different name
                 07FFh     login security failure (node)
                 08FFh     not logged in
                 09FFh     position calc error
                 0AFFh     receive subfunction does not equal send subfunction
                           (i.e. read, write)
                 0BFFh     request function not in range
                 0CFFh     no more server file handle entries left
                 0DFFh     no more shared file table entries left
                 0EFFh     no more user file handle entries left
                 0FFFh     chat permit not on
                 10FFh     not a server on request
                 11FFh     no transporter board error
                 12FFh     time out on send
                 13FFh     item not found (spool item not in queue)
                 14FFh     DOS access incompatible
                 15FFh     record already locked
                 16FFh     invalid parameter
                 17FFh     record lock time out error
                 18FFh     currently spooling to named device
                 19FFh     dropped receive message (throttle)
                 1AFFh     open sharing violation
                 1BFFh     no more tuf entries left
                 1CFFh     not file owner on open
                 1DFFh     read security not passed
                 1EFFh     write security not passed
                 1FFFh     group security not passed
                 20FFh     security file failure
```

```
                    21FFh    activity file failure
                    22FFh    spool control file failure
                    23FFh    device not mounted (spooling)
                    24FFh    spool file has not been terminated
                    25FFh    device not mounted or is not being shared
                    26FFh    duplicate node ID
                    27FFh    file not found error
                    28FFh    no more files
                    29FFh    unknown internal system error
                    2AFFh    print queue is full or corrupted
                    2BFFh    invalid function
                    2CFFh    invalid handle
                    2DFFh    too many files opened
                    2EFFh    path not found
                    2FFFh    named file is active
                    0FF01h   timeout
                    0FF02h   network error
                    0FF03h   invalid password
                    0FF04h   no local buffer
                    0FF05h   superstation not available
                    0FF06h   node already logged in
                    0FF07h   login not valid from this node
                    0FF08h   node ID already in use
                    0FF16h   invalid parameter (bad length, invalid node ID, etc)
                    0FF17h   record locked by another user
                    0FF18h   sent message has been dropped

         AH         01h      Logoff
         DS:DX      pointer to superstation ID or nulls (12 bytes)
return   CX         number of files closed
         AX         status (see function 00h)
                    0FF08h   superstation ID not already logged in

entry    AH         02h      Status of Node
         DS:DX      pointer to 512-byte record
              8 bytes    user name (0 if none)
              byte       station type
                         00h      workstation
                         01h      superstation
                         02h      gateway station
                         03h      gateway active
                         04h      logged into multiple superstations
                         05h      reserved
             24 bytes    list of superstations logged into more than one
                         superstation
             12 bytes node ID
              word       message count for this station (send for user node,
                         receive for superstations)
              for superstations only:
                  word       drives allocated (bit 0=A:, bit 1=B:,...)
                  byte       user service flag
                       bit 7      gate
                           6      print permit on
                           5      ?
                           4      SUBMIT is on
                           3      mail waiting for node
                           2      calendar waiting for you
                           1      news waiting for you
                           0      mail waiting for you
                  byte       printers allocated (bit 0=LPT1,...)
                  byte       number of unprinted spool files
                  byte       number of opened files
                  byte       number of logged on nodes
                  byte       primary drive (1=A:)
                  byte       reserved
              n bytes    list of logged on node IDs (each 12 bytes, max 37 IDs)
                         (continues at offset 1F4h)
              3 bytes    time: sec/min/hrs
              3 bytes    date: day/mon/year (since 1980)
return   CF         set on error
         AX         error code (see function 00h)
```

```
entry     AH       03h       Get Address of Configuration Table
          DS:DI    pointer   to node ID (optional)
return    ES:BX    pointer   to record (actually starts at [BX-41])
                   word      local device table address
                   word      extended network error mapping table address
                   word      shared device table address
                   word      mounted device table address
                   byte      receive buffer counter
                   byte      collect buffer counter
                   word      TUF address
                   byte      enable flag
                   byte      FCB keep flag
                   word      reserved
---up to here, 10-Net v3.3---
                   word      count of dropped Send6F
                   word      buffer start address
                   word      comm driver base address
                   word      send/receive retry count
                   byte      number of 550ms loops before timeout
                   word      UFH address
                   word      CDIR address
                   word      LTAB address
                   word      SFH address
                   word      FTAB address
                   word      RLTAB address
                   word      SMI address
                   word      NTAB address
          ES:BX    pointer   to word address of first CT_DRV
                   byte      number of DRV entries
                 8 bytes     login name
                12 bytes     node ID (blank-padded)
                 6 bytes     node address
                   byte      flag
                   byte      CT_CFLG (chat permit)
                      bit 0          CHAT permit
                          1          sound bell
                          2-7        ?
                   byte      CT_PSFLG
                      bit 0          SUBMIT permit
                          1          SUBMIT received
                          2          SUBMIT active
                          3          CHAT called FOXPTRM
                          4          KB initiated
                          5          PRINT permit
                          6-7        ?
                   byte      in 10-Net flag
                   word      receive message count
                   word      send message count
                   word      retry count
                   word      failed count
                   word      driver errors
                   word      dropped responses/CHATs
                 9 bytes     LIST ID/NTAB address (3 entries, LPT1-3)
                 6 bytes     AUX ID/NTAB address (2 entries, COM1-2)
                   byte      active CB channel
                   byte      received 6F messages on queue
                 9 bytes     activity counters for channels 1-9
---beyond here, 10-Net v3.3---
                   byte      bit 0          RS232 gate
                                 1          Send6F gate (user set)
                                 2-7        ?
                   dword     pointer into gate (user set)
                   dword     pointer into 10-Net send
                 N words     addresses of timer blocks

entry     AH       04h       Send
          DS:BX    pointer   to record
                12 bytes     receiving node's ID
                             if first byte has high-order bit set, message is directed
                                to the CT_RGATE vector at the receiver
```

276   *The Programmer's Technical Reference*

```
                           if second byte is 00h, first byte is taken as a CB
                                 channel number and delivered to all nodes on same
                                 channel
                    word   length of data at DX
          DS:DX     pointer to data (max 1024 bytes)
return    CF        set on error
          AX        error code (see function 00h)

entry     AH        05h    Receive
          CX        number of seconds before timeout
          DS:DX     pointer to receive buffer
              12 bytes     sending node's ID
                    word   length of message
               N bytes     message (maximum 1024 bytes)
return    CF        set on error
          AX        error code (see function 00h)
          CF        clear if successful
          AH        0FEh if dequeued message is a CB message

entry     AH        07h    Lock Handle
          BX        file handle
          CX:DX     starting offset in file
          SI        record length
return    CF        set on error
          AX        error code (see also function 00h)
                    02h    file not found

entry     AH        08h    Unlock Handle
          BX        file handle
          AL        mode
                    00h    unlock all
                    01h    unlock record at CX:DX
return    CF        set on error
          AX        error code (see also function 00h)
                    02h    file not found

entry     AH        09h    Submit
          DS:BX     pointer to record
              12 bytes     destination node ID (must be logged in)
                    word   length+2 of following 'command line' text
               n bytes     command line text (<=100 bytes), system adds CR
return    none?

entry     AH        0Ah    Chat
          DS:BX     pointer to control parameters
               8 bytes     sender ID, if nulls defaults to node's userID
               8 bytes     destination user ID, 'EVERYONE' may be used
              12 bytes     destination node ID
          DS:DX     pointer to chat message
                    word   length+2 of following text
               n bytes     text, max 101 bytes

entry     AH        0Bh    Lock Semaphore, Return Immediately
          AL        drive number or 00h
          ES:SI     Ethernet address or 00h
          DS:BX     pointer to 31-byte ASCIIZ semaphore name
return    AL        status
                    00h    successful
                    01h    semaphore currently locked
                    02h    server not responding
                    03h    invalid semaphore name
                    04h    semaphore list is full
                    05h    invalid drive ID
                    06h    invalid Ethernet address
                    07h    not logged in
                    08h    write to network failed
                    09h    semaphore already logged in this CPU
note      Same as int 60h/fn 12h.

entry     AH        0Ch    Unlock Semaphore
          AL        drive number or 0
```

Network Interfacing

```
           ES:SI      Ethernet address or 0
           DS:BX      pointer to 31-byte ASCIIZ semaphore name
return     AL         status (see AH=0Bh)
                      01h     semaphore not locked
note       Same as int 60h/fn13h.

entry      AH         0Dh     Who
           AL         type code
                      01h     return superstations only
                      02h     return non-superstations only
                      otherwise return all
           CX         length of data
           DS:DX      pointer to array of records to be filled
                12 bytes   node ID
                   byte    flags
                      bit 1          workstation
                          2          superstation
                          3          xgate
                          4          active gate
                          5-7        ?
                   (if AL=01h, record continues)
                   byte    version number
                   word    level number of 10Net software in responding node
                   (if AL=02h, record continues)
                 8 bytes   user ID
                   byte    version number
                   word    level number
return     CL         number of records returned (responding stations)

entry      AH         0Eh     Spool/Print
           DS:DX      pointer to record
                   word    operation code
                           00h     initiate spool
                           01h     abort print
                           02h     close spool
                           03h     delete spool
                           04h     print
                           05h     get report info
                           06h     set chat template
                           07h     queue
                           08h     return queue
                           09h     queue non-spooled file for printing
                11 bytes   file name in FCB format
                (if operation code = 00h or 06h, record continues)
                   byte    notification
                      bit 0          notify at print start
                          1          notify server operator/reply
                          2          notify at print completion
                          3          explicit queuing only
                          4          reserved
                          5          no form feed
                          6          do ID page
                          7          queue to top
                   byte    days to keep (0FFh=forever)
                   byte    bits 0,1: device (1=LPT1)
                           bits 4-7: remote drive to store spool file
                                   (1=A,...)
                   word    length of following data area
                 n bytes   up to 64 bytes of description
                (if operation code = 03h, record continues)
                 8 bytes   user ID to associate with filename
                (if operation code = 04h, record continues)
                   word    block number
                 8 bytes user ID to associate with filename
                (if operation code = 05h, record continues)
                   byte    RRN to start retrieve
                   byte    bits 0,1  local print device (LPTx)
                           bit 3     if set, return entries for all users
                           bits 4-7  not used?
                   word    length of following area
                 n bytes   up to 1500 bytes to receive $SCNTL records returned
```

```
            (if operation code = 07h, record continues)
                    byte     queue number
                    byte     bits 0,1  local print device (LPTx)
                             bits 2-7  not used?
                    word     number of bytes of test print to be done
                    byte     test code
                             01h    print device
                             02h    test print count
                             03h    PRN
            (if operation code = 08h, record continues)
                    byte     queue location or $SCNTL location to start access
                             returns next item for access:
                             00h-7Fh queued items
                             80h-FEh non-queued, non-printed items
                             0FFh    no more items
                    word     unused
                    word     length of following area
                 n bytes     up to 64 bytes to receive $SCNTL records (see note)
            (if operation code = 09h, record continues)
                 3 bytes     unused
                 n bytes     path to non-spooled file to be queued for printing
return  CF              set on error
                  AX         error code (see also function 00h)
                             0FF17h  device not mounted
                             0FF18h  already spooling to named device
note    $SCNTL record:
     8 bytes    user ID
    11 bytes    filename in FCB format
     6 bytes    node ID
     3 bytes    creation date
       byte     flags
            bit 0         notify at start
                1         notify server operator/reply
                2         notify at completion
                3         explicit queueing only
                4         reserved
                5         no form feed at end
                6         do ID page
                7         queue to top
       byte     retention time in days
       byte     printing device (LPTx)
     3 bytes    date last printed (0=never)
       byte     device containing spool file
       word     bytes to print for test print
       word     block number to start print
       byte     reserved

entry   AH      10h     Attach/Detach Printer
        AL      subfunction
                00h     initiate spooling if LPT1 is mounted
                01h     terminate spooling if LPT1 is mounted

entry   AH      11h     Lock FCB
        AL      mode
                01h     sequential
                02h     random
                03h     random block
        CX      number of records
        DS:DX   pointer to FCB
return  CF      set on error
        AX      error code (see also function 00h)
                02h     file not found

entry   AH      12h     Unlock FCB
        AL      mode
                00h     sequential
                01h     random
                02h     random block
        CX      number of records
        DS:DX   pointer to FCB
return  CF      set on error
```

Network Interfacing

```
                    AX       error code (see also function 00h)
                             02h     file not found
entry     AH        13h      10-Net v3.3 - Get Remote Configuration Table
                             Address
          DS:DX     pointer to node ID, 12 bytes blank-padded
return    CF        set on error
                    AX       error code (see function 00h)
          CF        clear if successful
                    ES:BX    configuration table address on given machine

entry     AH        14h      10-Net v3.3 - Get Remote Memory
          BX:SI     address of remote memory
          CX        length (<=1024 bytes)
          DS:DX     pointer to node ID, 12 bytes blank-padded
          DS:DI     pointer to area to receive remote memory image
return    CF        set on error
                    AX       error code (see function 00h)
          CF        clear if successful
                    CX       amount of memory copied to DS:SI

entry     AH        15h      Shared Device Information
          AL        01h      10-Net v3.3 - Get Shared Device Entry
                    BX       zero-based index
                    DS:SI    pointer to node ID, 12 bytes blank-padded
                    ES:DI    pointer to 85-byte buffer
          return    CF       set on error
                             AX       error code (see function 00h)
                    CF       clear if successful
                             ES:DI buffer contains shared device table entry of
                             BXth device:
                                  8 bytes    device
                                  8 bytes    alias
                                 64 bytes    path
                                  8 bytes    password
                                    byte     access
                                  4 bytes    mask

                    02h      10-Net v3.3 - Set Shared Device Entry
                    DS:SI    pointer to node ID, 12 bytes blank-padded
                    ES:DI    pointer to valid shared device table entry
          return    CF       set on error
                             AX       error code (see function 00h)

                    03h      10-Net v3.3 - Delete Shared Device Entry
                    BX       zero-based index
                    DS:SI    pointer to node ID, 12 bytes blank-padded
          return    CF       set on error
                             AX       error code (see function 00h)

entry     AH        17h      10-Net v3.3 - Mount
          AL        local drive number (0=A:)
          BL        remote drive letter or '1'..'3' for LPTx or '4' or '5' for COMx
          DS:DX     pointer to node ID, 12 bytes blank-padded
return    CF        set on error
                    AX       error code (see function 00h)

entry     AH        18h      10-NET v3.3 - Unmount
          AL        local drive number (0=A:)
          BL        type
                    00h         disk
                    01h-03h     LPTx
                    04h,05h     COMx
return    CF        set on error
                    AX       error code (see function 00h)
```

Interrupt 68h APPC/PC

```
Function 01h       APPC/PC
entry    AH        01h
         DS:DX     pointer to control block
```

```
        12 bytes    reserved
        word        verb (action)
         6 bytes    0
        dword       (high byte first) return code
                    0000h       successful
                    0001h       BAD_TP_ID
                    0002h       BAD_CONV_ID
                    0003h       bad logical unit ID
                    0008h       no physical unit attached
                    0110h       bad state
                    01B1h       BAD_PART_LUNAME
                    01B2h       bad mode name
                    0201h       physical unit already active
                    0211h       logical unit already active
                    0212h       BAD_PART_SESS
                    0213h       BAD_RU_SIZES
                    0214h       BAD_MODE_SESS
                    0216h       BAD_PACING_CNT
                    0219h       EXTREME_RUS
                    021Ah       SNASVCMG_1
                    0223h       SSCP_CONNECTED_LU
                    0230h       invalid change
                    0243h       too many TPs
                    0272h       adapter close failure
                    0281h       GET_ALLOC_BAD_TYPE
                    0282h       unsuccessful
                    0283h       DLC failure
                    0284h       unrecognized DLC
                    0286h       duplicate DLC
                    0301h       SSCP_PU_SESSION_NOT_ACTIVE
                    0302h       data exceeds RU size
                    0401h       invalid direction
                    0402h       invalid type
                    0403h       segment overlap
                    0404h       invalid first character
                    0405h       table error
                    0406h       conversion error
                    0F0010000h  APPC disabled
                    0F0020000h  APPC busy
                    0F0030000h  APPC abended
                    0F0040000h  incomplete
if verb = 1B00h (DISPLAY), control block continues
        word        0
         8 bytes    (high byte first) logical unit ID
         8 bytes    (high byte first) partner logical unit name
         8 bytes    (high byte first) mode name
        byte        logical unit session limit
        byte        partner logical unit session limit
        byte        mode maximum negotiable session limit
        byte        current session limit
        byte        minimum negotiated winner limit
        byte        maximum negotiated loser limit
        byte        active session count
        byte        active CONWINNER session count
        byte        active CONLOSER session count
        byte        session termination count
        byte        bit 7: SESSION_TERMINATION_TARGET_DRAIN
                    bit 6: SESSION_TERMINATION_SOURCE_DRAIN
if verb=2000h (Attach Physical Unit), control block continues
        word        0
        byte        version
        byte        release
         8 bytes    (high byte first) net name
         8 bytes    (high byte first) physical unit name
         8 bytes    0
        dword       pointer to SYSTEM_LOG_EXIT routine, 0FFFFFFFFh means
                    don't log errors
        dword       0
        byte        0           RETURN_CONTROL: COMPLETE
                    1           RETURN_CONTROL: INCOMPLETE
if verb=2100h (Attach Logical Unit), control block continues
```

Network Interfacing

```
        word     70   offset to partner logical unit record
 8 bytes         (high byte first) logical unit name
 8 bytes         (high byte first) logical unit ID
        byte     logical unit local address
        byte     logical unit session limit
        dword    pointer to CREATE_TP_EXIT routine,
                 0FFFFFFFFh     reject incoming ALLOCATEs
                 00000000h      queue ALLOCATEs
        dword    0
        dword    pointer to SYSTEM_LOG_EXIT routine, 0FFFFFFFFh means
                 don't log errors
        dword    0
        byte     maximum TPs
        byte     queue depth
        dword    pointer to LU_LU_PASSword_EXIT routine, 0FFFFFFFFh means
                 no password exit
        dword    0
        word     total length of partner records
                 for each partner logical unit:
                     word     length of this partner logical unit record
                     word     42   offset to mode records
                 8 bytes      (high byte first) partner logical unit name
                     byte     partner logical unit security capabilities
                         bit 7         already verified
                             6         conversation level security
                             5         session level security
                             4-0       not used?
                     byte     partner logical unit session limit
                     word     partner logical unit maximum MC_SEND_LL
                 8 bytes      (high byte first) partner logical unit DLC name
                     byte     partner logical unit adapter number
                17 bytes      (counted string) partner logical unit adapter
                              address
                     word     total length of mode records
                              for each mode:
                                  word     16   length of this mode record
                              8 bytes      (high byte first) mode name
                                  word     RU_SIZE high bound
                                  word     RU_SIZE low bound
                                  byte     mode maximum negotiable session limit
                                  byte     pacing size for receive
       if verb=2200h (Detach Logical Unit), control block continues:
            8 bytes     (high byte first) logical unit ID
                byte    0
       if verb=2700h (Detach Physical Unit), control block continues:
                byte    Physical Unit type
                        00h    hard
                        01h    soft
       if verb=2B00h (Activate DLC), control block continues:
            8 bytes     (high byte first) DLC name
                byte    adapter number
                Routines defined by LU_LU_PASSword_EXIT, CREATE_TP_EXIT, and
                SYSTEM_LOG_EXIT pointers are called by pushing the dword pointer
                to the verb on the stack and then performing a FAR call.
ACCESS_LU_LU_PW verb:
    12 bytes     reserved
       word      1900h
     8 bytes     (high byte first) logical unit ID
     8 bytes     (high byte first) logical unit name
     8 bytes     (high byte first) partner logical unit name
    17 bytes     (counted string) partner fully qualified logical unit name
       byte      password available (0=no, 1=yes)
     8 bytes     password
CREATE_TP verb:
    12 bytes     reserved
       word      2300h
     6 bytes     0
       dword     (high byte first) sense code
                 00000000h      Ok
                 080F6051h      SECURITY_NOT_VALID
                 084B6031h      TP_NOT_AVAIL_RETRY
```

```
                  084C0000h     TP_NOT_AVAIL_NO_RETRY
                  10086021h     TP_NAME_NOT_RECOGNIZED
                  10086034h     CONVERSATION_TYPE_MISMATCH
                  10086041h     SYNC_LEVEL_NOT_SUPPORTED
    8 bytes       (high byte first) TP ID
    8 bytes       (high byte first) logical unit ID
    dword         (high byte first) conversation ID
    byte          0 basic conversation, 1 mapped conversation
    byte          0 no sync level, 1 confirm
    byte          reserved
   65 bytes       (counted string) transaction program name
    6 bytes       0
    word          length of ERROR_LOG_DATA to return
    dword         pointer to ERROR_LOG_DATA buffer
    8 bytes       (high byte first) partner logical unit name
   18 bytes       (counted string) partner fully qualified logical unit name
    8 bytes       (high byte first) mode name
   12 bytes       0
   11 bytes       (counted string) password
   11 bytes       (counted string) user ID
    byte          0 verification should be performed
                  1 already verified
SYSLOG verb:
   12 bytes       reserved
    word          2600h
   10 bytes       0
    word          (high byte first) type
    dword         (high byte first) subtype
    dword         pointer to ADDITIONAL_INFO
    dword         (high byte first) conversation ID
    8 bytes       (high byte first) TP ID
    8 bytes       (high byte first) physical unit or logical unit name
    word          length of data
    dword         pointer to data
    byte          0

Function 02h     APPC/PC
entry    AH      02h
         DS:DX   pointer to control block
              12 bytes   reserved
                 word    verb (action)
                 byte    00h     if basic verb
                         01h     if MC_ (mapped conversation) form of verb
               5 bytes   0
                 word    (high byte first) primary return code
                         0000h   successful
                         0001h   parameter check
                         0002h   state check
                         0003h   allocation error
                         0005h   deallocate abended
                         0006h   deallocate abended program
                         0007h   deallocate abended SVC
                         0008h   deallocate abended timer
                         0009h   deallocate normal return
                         000Ah   data posting blocked
                         000Bh   posting not active
                         000Ch   PROG_ERROR_NO_TRUNC
                         000Dh   PROG_ERROR_TRUNC
                         000Eh   PROG_ERROR_PURGING
                         000Fh   CONV_FAILURE_RETRY
                         0010h   CONV_FAILURE_NO_RETRY
                         0011h   SVC_ERROR_NO_TRUNC
                         0012h   SVC_ERROR_TRUNC
                         0013h   SVC_ERROR_PURGING
                         0014h   unsuccessful
                         0018h   CNOS partner logical unit reject
                         0019h   conversation type mixed
                         F001h   APPC disabled
                         F002h   APPC busy
                         F003h   APPC abended
                         F004h   incomplete
```

Network Interfacing

```
            dword    (high byte first) error code
                     0001h    bad TP ID
                     0002h    bad conversation ID
                     0004h    allocation error, no retry
                     0005h    allocation error, retry
                     0006h    data area crosses segment boundary
                     0010h    bad TPN length
                     0011h    bad CONV length
                     0012h    bad SYNC level
                     0013h    bad security selection
                     0014h    bad return control
                     0015h    SEC_TOKENS too big
                     0016h    PIP_LEN incorrect
                     0017h    no use of SNASVCMG
                     0018h    unknown partner mode
                     0031h    confirm: SYNC_NONE
                     0032h    confirm: bad state
                     0033h    confirm: NOT_LL_BDY
                     0041h    confirmed: bad state
                     0051h    deallocate: bad type
                     0052h    deallocate: flush bad state
                     0053h    deallocate: confirm bad state
                     0055h    deallocate: NOT_LL_BDY
                     0057h    deallocate: log_LL_WRONG
                     0061h    flush: not send state
                     0091h    post on receipt: invalid length
                     0092h    post on receipt: not in receive state
                     0093h    post on receipt: bad fill
                     00A1h    prepare to receive: invalid type
                     00A2h    prepare to receive: unfinished LL
                     00A3h    prepare to receive: not in send state
                     00B1h    receive and wait: bad state
                     00B2h    receive and wait: NOT_LL_BDY
                     00B5h    receive and wait: bad fill
                     00C1h    receive immediate: not in receive state
                     00C4h    receive immediate: bad fill
                     00E1h    request to send: not in receive state
                     00F1h    send data: bad LL
                     00F2h    send data: not in send state
                     0102h    send error: log LL wrong
                     0103h    send error: bad type
                     0121h    test: invalid type
                     0122h    test: not in receive state
         8 bytes     (high byte first) TP_ID
           dword     (high byte first) conversation ID
if verb=0100h (Allocate or MC_Allocate), control block continues:
           byte      (MC_Allocate only) 0 basic conversation
                                        1 mapped conversation
           byte      SYNC_LEVEL
                     00h      none
                     01h      confirm
           word      0
           byte      RETURN_CONTROL
                     00h      when session allocated
                     01h      immediate
                     02h      when session free
         8 bytes     0
         8 bytes     (high byte first) partner logical unit name
         8 bytes     (high byte first) mode name
        65 bytes     (counted string) TP name
           byte      Security
                     00h      none
                     01h      same
                     02h      pgm
        11 bytes     0
        11 bytes     (counted string) password
        11 bytes     (counted string) user ID
           word      PIP_DATA length
           dword     pointer to PIP_DATA
if verb=0300h (Confirm or MC_Confirm), then control block
continues:
```

```
                byte      request to send received (0=no, 1=yes)
if verb=0400h (Confirmed or MC_Confirmed), no additional fields
if verb=0500h (Deallocate or MC_Deallocate), control block continues:
                byte      0
                byte      Type
                          00h       SYNC_LEVEL
                          01h       FLUSH
                          02h       ABEND_PROC
                          03h       ABEND_SVC
                          04h       ABEND_TIMER
                          05h       ABEND
                word      (MC_Deallocate only) length of error log data
                dword     (MC_Deallocate only) pointer to error log data
if verb=0600h (Flush or MC_Flush), no additional fields
if verb=0700h (Get_Attributes or MC_Get_Attributes), control block
continues:
                8 bytes   (high byte first) logical unit ID
                byte      0
                byte      SYNC_LEVEL (0=none, 1=confirm)
                8 bytes   (high byte first) mode name
                8 bytes   (high byte first) own net name
                8 bytes   (high byte first) own logical unit name
                8 bytes   (high byte first) partner logical unit name
                18 bytes  (counted string) partner's fully qualified logical unit
                          name
                byte      0
                11 bytes  (counted string) user ID
if verb=0800h (Get_Type), then control block continues:
                byte      type (0=basic conversation, 1=mapped conversation)
if verb=0900h (Post_on_Receipt), then control block continues:
                word      maximum length
                byte      fill (0=buffer, 1=LL)
if verb=0A00h (Prepare_to_Receive or MC_Prepare_to_Receive):
                byte      type (0=SYNC_LEVEL, 1=FLUSH)
                byte      locks (0=short, 1=long)
if verb=0B00h (Receive_and_Wait or MC_Receive_and_Wait),
                control block continues:
                byte      What Received
                          00h       data
                          01h       data complete
                          02h       data incomplete
                          03h       confirm
                          04h       confirm send
                          05h       confirm deallocate
                          06h       send
                byte      (MC_Receive_and_Wait only) fill (0=buffer, 1=LL)
                byte      Request_to_Send_Received (0=no, 1=yes)
                word      maximum length
                word      data length
                dword     pointer to data
if verb=0C00h (Receive_Immediate or MC_Receive_Immediate),
                control block continues:
                byte      What Received
                          00h       data
                          01h       data complete
                          02h       data incomplete
                          03h       confirm
                          04h       confirm send
                          05h       confirm deallocate
                          06h       send
                byte      (MC_Receive_Immediate only) fill (0=buffer, 1=LL)
                byte      Request_to_Send_Received (0=no, 1=yes)
                word      maximum length
                word      data length
                dword     pointer to data
if verb=0E00h (Request_to_Send or MC_Request_to_Send), no additional
                fields
if verb=0F00h (Send_Data or MC_Send_Data), control block continues:
                byte      request to send received (0=no, 1=yes)
                byte      0
                word      data length
```

Network Interfacing

```
                dword     pointer to data
      if verb=1000h       (Send_Error or MC_Send_Error)
                byte      request to send received (0=no, 1=yes)
                byte      type (0=program, 1=SVC)
                dword     0
                word      (MC_Send_Error only) LOG_DATA length
                dword     (MC_Send_Error only) pointer to LOG_DATA
      if verb=1200h       (Test or MC_Test), then control block continues:
                byte      (MC_Test only) test
                          (0=posted, 1=request_to_send received)
                          note   error code has different interpretations for:
                          0      posted data
                          1      posted not data (primary return code = 0)
                          1      bad TP_ID (primary return code = 1)
      if verb=1300h       (Wait), then control block continues:
                byte      number of conversations to wait on
                          note   error codes have interpretations as for 1200h
                                 (Test) above

Function  03h   APPC/PC
entry     AH    03h
          DS:DX pointer to control block
                12 bytes reserved
                word      verb (action)
                6 bytes   0
                dword     (high byte first) return code (see AH=01h)
                word      0
                8 bytes   (high byte first) logical unit ID
      if verb=2400h       (TP Started), control block continues:
                8 bytes   (high byte first) TP ID
      if verb=2800h       (Get ALLOCATE), control block continues:
                byte      Type
                          00h    dequeue
                          01h    test
                dword     pointer to CREATE_TP record
      if verb=2A00h       (Change Logical Unit). control block continues:
                dword     pointer to CREATE_TP_EXIT routine
                          0FFFFFFFFh reject incoming ALLOCATEs
                          00000000h  queue ALLOCATEs
                dword     0
                dword     pointer to SYSTEM_LOG_EXIT routine, 0FFFFFFFFh means
                          don't log errors
                dword     0
                byte      maximum TPs
                byte      QUEUE_ALLOCATEs
                          00h    stop
                          01h    resume
                dword     pointer to LU_LU_PASSword_EXIT routine, 0FFFFFFFFh means
                          no exit
                dword     0

Function  04h   APPC/PC
entry     AH    04h
          DS:DX pointer to control block
                12 bytes reserved
                word      verb (action)
                          2500h  TP_ENDED
                          2900h  TP_VALID
                6 bytes   0
                dword     (high byte first) return code (see AH=01h)
                word      0
                8 bytes   (high byte first) TP_ID
                dword     pointer to CREATE_TP record (only if verb = 2900h)

Function  05h   Transfer Message Data
entry     AH    05h
          DS:DX pointer to control block
                12 bytes reserved
                word      1C00h
                byte      00h    user defined
                          01h    NMVT
```

```
                        02h      alert subvectors
                        03h      PDSTATS subvectors
            5 bytes     0
            dword       (high byte first) return code (see AH=01h)
            12 bytes    0
            byte        if bit 0 clear, add correlation subvector
                        if bit 1 clear, add product set ID subvector
                        if bit 2 clear, do SYSLOG
                        if bit 3 clear, send SSCP_PU_SESSION
                        bits 4-7 unknown
            byte        0
            word        length of data
            N bytes     data
Function  06h     Change Number of Sessions
entry     AH      06h
          DS:DX   pointer to control block
            12 bytes    reserved
            word        1500h
            6 bytes     0
            word        (high byte first) primary return code (see AH=02h)
            dword       (high byte first) secondary return code (see AH=01h)
                        0000h    accepted
                        0001h    negotiated
                        0003h    bad logical unit ID
                        0004h    allocation failure, no retry
                        0005h    allocation failure, retry
                        0151h    can't raise limits
                        0153h    all modes must reset
                        0154h    bad SNASVCMG limits
                        0155h    minimum greater than total
                        0156h    mode closed (prim return code = 1)
                                 CNOS mode closed (prim return code = 18h)
                        0157h    bad mode name (prim return code = 1)
                                 CNOS bad mode name (prim return code = 18h)
                        0159h    reset SNA drains
                        015Ah    single not SRC response
                        015Bh    bad partner logical unit
                        015Ch    exceeds maximum allowed
                        015Dh    change SRC drains
                        015Eh    logical unit detached
                        015Fh    CNOS command race reject
            8 bytes     (high byte first) logical unit ID
            8 bytes     blanks
            8 bytes     (high byte first) partner logical unit name
            8 bytes     (high byte first) mode name
            byte
               bit 7             use MODE_NAME_SELECT_ALL rather than MODE_NAME
                   6             set negotiable values
                   5-0           ?
            byte        partner logical unit mode session limit
            byte        minimum CONWINNERS_SOURCE
            byte        maximum CONWINNERS_TARGET
            byte        automatic activation
            byte        0
            byte        Drain
               bit 7             drain target
                   6             drain source
                   5             target responsible, not source
                   4-0           ?

Function  07h     Passthrough
entry     AH      07h
          DS:DX   pointer to control block
                  (format depends on application subsystem)
return    unknown


Function  0FAh    Enable/Disable APPC
entry     AH      0FAh
          AL bit 0      0        enable
```

Network Interfacing

```
                         1        disable
return   unknown

Function  0FBh   Convert
entry    AH       0FBh
         DS:DX   pointer to control block
              12 bytes   reserved
                 word    1A00h
               6 bytes   0
                 dword   (high byte first) return code
                 byte    conversion
                             00h    ASCII to EBCDIC
                             01h    EBCDIC to ASCII
                 byte    character set
                             00h    AE
                             01h    A
                             02h    G
                 word    length of string to convert
                 dword   pointer to source
                 dword   pointer to target
return   unknown

Function  0FCh   Enable/Disable Message Tracing
entry    AH       0FCh
         AL       00h     disable tracing
                  01h     enable tracing
         DX       number of bytes to keep (0=all)
return   unknown

Function  0FDh   Enable/Disable API Verb Tracing
entry    AH       0FDh
         AL       00h     disable tracing
                  01h     enable tracing
return   none

Function  0FEh   Trace Destination
entry    AH       0FEh
         AL       trace destinations
                  bits
                    0       storage (DS:DX pointer to trace stats record)
                    1       display
                    2       file (trace written to file OUTPUT.PC)
                    3       printer
return   unknown
note 1.  Do not move record while trace is active.
     2.  Trace Statistics Record
         dword   pointer to storage trace buffer
         word    max number of 80-byte records in trace
         word    (high-order byte first) current record number (must init to 0)
         dword   (high-order byte first) number of records written (init to 0)
         dword   reserved

Function  0FFh   Set Passthrough
entry    AH       0FFh
         DS:DX   pointer to passthrough exit routine
return   unknown

Interrupt 6Fh    Novell NetWare - PCOX API (3270 PC terminal interface)
Interrupt 6Fh    10-Net Network API
entry    AH       00h     Login
         DS:DX   login record
               8 bytes   user name
               8 bytes   password
              12 bytes   name of super-station
                 return  CL     security level
                         AX     status
                                0000h    good login
                                0FF01h   no response from superstation
                                0FF02h   network error
                                0FF03h   invalid password
                                0FF04h   no local buffer
```

```
                         0FF05h    superstation not available
                         0FF06h    node already logged in
                         0FF07h    login not valid from this node
                         0FF08h    node ID already in use
01h       Logoff
return    CX             number of files closed
          AX             status
                         0000h     successful
                         0FF08h    superstation ID not already logged in
02h       Status of node
DS:DX     pointer to 512-byte record
        8 bytes          user name (0 if none)
          byte           station type
                         00h       workstation
                         01h       superstation
                         04h       logged into multiple superstations
       24 bytes list of superstations logged into more than one
          superstation
       12 bytes node ID
          word           message count for this station (send for user
                         node, receive for superstations)
                         for superstations only:
          word           drives allocated (bit 0=A:, bit 1=B:,...)
          byte           user service flag
                bit 0         mail waiting for you
                    1         news waiting for you
                    2         calendar waiting for you
                    3         mail waiting for node
                    4         SUBMIT is on
                    5-7       ?
          byte           printers allocated (bit 0=LPT1,...)
          byte           number of unprinted spool files
          byte           number of opened files
          byte           number of logged on files
          byte           primary drive (1=A:)
          byte           reserved
        n bytes          list of logged on node IDs (each 12 bytes, max 38
                         IDs)
return    CF             set on error
          AX             error code
                         0FF01h    no response from node
                         0FF02h    network error
                         0FF04h    no local buffer
                         0FF16h    invalid node ID
03h       Get Address of Configuration Table
return    ES:BX          pointer to record (actually starts at [BX-25])
                word     count of dropped Send6F
                word     buffer start address
                word     comm driver base address
                word     send/receive retry count
                byte     number of 550ms loops
                word     UFH address
                word     CDIR address
                word     LTAB address
                word     SFH address
                word     FTAB address
                word     RLTAB address
                word     SMI address
                word     NTAB address
          ES:BX          pointer to word address of first CT_DRV
                byte     number of DRV entries
              8 bytes    login name
             12 bytes    node ID
              6 bytes    node address
                byte     flag
                byte     CT_CFLG
                    bit 0         CHAT permit
                        1         sound bell
                byte     CT_PSFLG
                         0         SUBMIT permit
                         1         SUBMIT received
```

Network Interfacing

```
                              2       SUBMIT active
                              3       CHAT called FOXPTRM
                              4       KB initiated
                              5       PRINT permit
                              6,7     ?
                  byte        reserved
                  word        receive message count
                  word        send message count
                  word        retry count
                  word        failed count
                  word        driver errors
                  word        dropped responses/CHATs
                  9 bytes     list ID/NTAB address (3 entries-LPT1-3?)
                  6 bytes     AUX ID/NTAB address (2 entries-COM1-2?)
                  byte        active CB channel
                  byte        received int 6Fh messages on queue
                  9 bytes     activity counters for channels 1-9
04h     Send
        DS:BX     pointer to record
                  12 bytes    receiving node's ID
                  word        length of data at DX
        DS:DX     pointer to data (max 1024 bytes)
return  CF        set on error
        AX        error code
                  0FF01h      timeout
                  0FF02h      network error
                  0FF04h      no local buffer
                  0FF16h      invalid parameter (bad length)
05h     Receive
        CX        number of seconds before timeout
        DS:DX     pointer to receive buffer
                  12 bytes    sending node's ID
                  word        length of message
                  n bytes     message (maximum 1024 bytes)
return  CF        set on error
        AX        error code
                  0FF01h      timeout
                  0FF18h      sent message has been dropped
06h     Unknown
07h     Lock Handle
        BX        file handle
        CX:DX     starting offset in file
        SI        record length
return  CF        set on error
        AX        error code
                  0FF01h      timeout
                  02h         file not found
                  0FF17h      record locked by another user
08h     Unlock Handle
        BX        file handle
        AL        mode
                  00h         unlock all
                  01h         unlock record at CX:DX
return  CF        set on error
        AX        error code
                  02h         file not found
0Bh     Lock Semaphore, Return Immediately
        AL        drive number or 0
        ES:SI     Ethernet address or 0
        DS:BX     pointer to 31-byte ASCIIZ semaphore name
return  AL        status
                  00h         successful
                  01h         semaphore currently locked
                  02h         server not responding
                  03h         invalid semaphore name
                  04h         semaphore list is full
                  05h         invalid drive ID
                  06h         invalid Ethernet address
                  07h         not logged in
                  08h         write to network failed
                  09h         semaphore already logged in this CPU
```

```
        0Ch     unlock semaphore
                AL      drive number or 0
                ES:SI   Ethernet address or 0
                DS:BX   pointer to 31-byte ASCIIZ semaphore name
        return  AL      status (see AH=0Bh)
                        1 semaphore not locked
        0Dh     Who
                CX      length of data
                DS:DX   pointer to array of records to be filled
                    12 bytes  node ID
                       byte   flag (1=workstation,
                              2=superstation)
        return  CL      number of records returned (responding stations)
        0Eh     spool/print
                DS:DX   pointer to record
                    word    00h     initiate spool
                            01h     abort print
                            02h     close spool
                            03h     delete spool
                            04h     print
                            05h     get report info
                 11 bytes file name
                    byte    notification
                        bit 0       no notification
                            1       notify at print start
                            2       notify at print start and reply?
                            3       notify at print completion
                            4       ?
                            5       no form feed
                            6       do ID page
                            7       ?
                    byte    days to keep (0FFh=forever)
                    byte    device (1=LPT1)
                    word    length of following data area
                  n bytes   $SCNT records returned if code in first word is
                            05h
        return  CF      set on error
                AX      error code
                        0FF16h  invalid parameter
                        0FF17h  device not mounted
                        0FF18h  already spooling to named device
        11h     Lock FCB
                AL      mode
                        00h     sequential
                        01h     random
                        02h     random block
                DS:DX   pointer to FCB
        return  CF      set on error
                AX      02h     file not found
                        0FF01h  timeout
                        0FF17h  record locked by another user
        12h     Unlock FCB
                AL      mode
                        00h     sequential
                        01h     random
                        02h     random block
                DS:DX   pointer to FCB
        return  CF      set on error
                AX      02h     file not found
```

Aftermarket Application Installed Function Calls

Novell Netware 2.11

Novell no longer recommends the int 21h method for invoking the Netware functions. Int 21h will be supported indefinitely, but the net API calls for addressing the software through the Multiplex Interrupt (2Fh). You may address the API through int 2Fh in the same manner as int 21h; only the interrupt number is different.

```
Function  0B6h  Novell NetWare SFT Level II - Extended File Attributes
entry     AH       0B6h
          AL       00h       Get Extended File Attributes)
                   01h       Set Extended File Attributes)
          CL       attributes
              bit 0-3        ?
                  4          transaction tracking file
                  5          indexing file    (to be implemented)
                  6          read audit       (to be implemented)
                  7          write audit      (to be implemented)
          DS:DX    pointer to ASCIIZ pathname
return    CF       set on error
          AL       error code
                   0FFh      file not found
                   8Ch       caller lacks privileges
          CL       current extended file attributes

Function  0B7h  unknown or not used. Novell?

Function  0B8h  Novell Advanced NetWare 2.0+ - Printer Functions
entry     AH       0B8h
          AL       00h       Get Default Print Job Flags)
                   01h       Set Default Capture Flags)
                   02h       Get Specific Capture Flags)
                   03h       Set Specific Print Job Flags)
                   04h       Get Default Local Printer)
                   05h       Set Default Local Printer)
                   06h       Set Capture Print Queue)
                   07h       Set Capture Print Job)
                   08h       Get Banner User Name)
                   09h       Set Banner User Name)
          CX       buffer size
          ES:BX    pointer to buffer
return    none

Function  0BBh Novell NetWare 4.0 - Set End Of Job Statush
entry     AH 0BBh
          AL       new EOJ flag
                   00h       disable EOJs
                   otherwise enable EOJs
return    AL       old EOJ flag

Function  0BCh  Novell NetWare 4.6 - Log Physical Recordh
entry     AH       0BCh
          AL       flags
              bit 0          lock as well as log record
                  1          non-exclusive lock
                  2-7        ?
          BX       file handle
          CX:DX    offset
          BP       timeout in timer ticks (1/18 sec)
          SI:DI    length
return    AL       error code

Function  0BDh  Novell NetWare 4.6 - Release Physical Recordh
entry     AH 0BDh
          BX       file handle
          CX:DX    offset
return    AL       error code

Function  0BEh  Novell NetWare 4.6 - Clear Physical Recordh
entry     AH 0BEh
          BX       file handle
          CX:DX    offset
return    AL       error code

Function  0BFh  Novell NetWare 4.6 - Log Record (FCB)
entry     AH       0BFh
          AL       flags
              bit 0          lock as well as log record
                  1          non-exclusive lock
```

```
                    2-7        ?
          DS:DX     pointer to FCB
          BX:CX     offset
          BP        timeout in timer ticks (1/18 sec)
          SI:DI     length
return    AL        error code

Function  0C0h   Novell NetWare 4.6 - Release Record (FCB)
entry     AH        0C0h
          DS:DX     pointer to FCB
          BX:CX     offset
return    AL        error code

Function  0C1h   Novell NetWare 4.6 - Clear Record (FCB)
entry     AH        0C1h
          DS:DX     pointer to FCB
          BX:CX     offset
return    AL        error code

Function 0C2h Novell NetWare 4.6 - Lock Physical Record Seth
entry     AH   0C2h
          AL        flags
              bit 0        ?
                  1        non-exclusive lock
                  2-7      ?
          BP        timeout in timer ticks (1/18 sec)
return    AL        error code

Function 0C3h Novell NetWare 4.6 - Release Physical Record Seth
entry          0C3h
return    AL        error code

Function 0C4h Novell NetWare 4.6 - Clear Physical Record Seth
entry     AH   C4h
return    AL        error code

Function  0C5h   Novell NetWare 4.6 - Semaphores
entry     AH        0C5h
          AL        00h       Open Semaphore)
                    DS:DX     pointer semaphore name
                    CL        initial value
                    return    CX:DX     semaphore handle
                              BL        open count
                    01h       Examine Semaphore)
                    return    CX        semaphore value (sign extended)
                              DL        open count
                    02h       Wait On Semaphore)
                              BP        timeout in timer ticks (1/18 sec)
                    03h       Signal Semaphore)
                    04h       Close Semaphore)
          CX:DX     semaphore handle (except function 00h)
return    AL        error code

Function  0C6h   Novell NetWare 4.6 - Get or Set Lock Mode
entry     AH        0C6h
          AL        00h       set old 'compatibility' mode
                    01h       set new extended locks mode
                    02h       get lock mode
return    AL        current lock mode

Function  0C7h   Novell NetWare 4.0 - TTS
entry     AH        0C7h
          AL        00h       TTS Begin Transaction (NetWare SFT level II)
                    01h       TTS End Transaction   (NetWare SFT level II)
                    02h       TTS Is Available      (NetWare SFT level II)
                    03h       TTS Abort Transaction (NetWare SFT level II)
                    04h       TTS Transaction Status)
                    05h       TTS Get Application Thresholds)
                    06h       TTS Set Application Thresholds)
                    07h       TTS Get Workstation Thresholds)
                    08h       TTS Set Workstation Thresholds)
```

Network Interfacing

```
return  AL      varies according to function called
                (00h)   error code
                        CX:DX   transaction reference number
                (01h)   error code
                (02h)   completion code
                        00h     TTS not available
                        01h     TTS available
                        0FDh    TTS available but disabled
                (03h)   error code
                (04h-08h) unknown

Function 0C8h   Novell NetWare 4.0 - Begin Logical File Locking
entry   AH      0C8h
                if function 0C6h lock mode 00h:
                DL      mode
                        00h     no wait
                        01h     wait
                if function 0C6h lock mode 01h:
                BP      timeout in timer ticks (1/18 sec)
return  AL      error code

Function 0C9h   Novell NetWare 4.0 - End Logical File Locking
entry   AH      0C9h
return  AL      error code

Function 0CAh   Novell NetWare 4.0  Log Personal File (FCB)
entry   AH      0CAh
        DS:DX   pointer to FCB
                if function 0C6h lock mode 01h:
                AL      log and lock flag
                        00h     log file only
                        01h     lock as well as log file
                BP      timeout in timer ticks (1/18 sec)
return  AL      error code

Function 0CBh   Novell NetWare 4.0 - Lock File Set
entry   AH      0CBh
                if function 0C6h lock mode 00h:
                DL      mode
                        00h     no wait
                        01h     wait
                if function 0C6h lock mode 01h:
                BP      timeout in timer ticks (1/18 sec)
return  AL      error code

Function 0CCh   Novell NetWare 4.0 - Release File (FCB)
entry   AH      0CCh
        DS:DX   pointer to FCB
return  none

Function 0CDh   Novell NetWare 4.0 - Release File Set
entry   AH      0CDhhreturn   none

Function 0CEh   Novell NetWare 4.0 - Clear File (FCB)
entry   AH      0CEh
        DS:DX   pointer to FCB
return  AL      error code

Function 0CFh   Novell NetWare 4.0 - Clear File Set
entry   AH      0CFhhreturn   AL      00h

Function 0D0h   Novell NetWare 4.6 - Log Logical Record
entry   AH      0D0h
        DS:DX   pointer record string
                if function 0C6h lock mode 01h:
                AL      flags
                        bit 0   lock as well as log the record
                            1   non-exclusive lock
                            2-7 ?
                BP      timeout in timer ticks (1/18 sec)
return  AL      error code
```

```
Function  0D1h  Novell NetWare 4.6 - Lock Logical Record Seth
entry     AH  0D1h
                   if function 0C6h lock mode 00h:
          DL       mode
                   00h     no wait
                   01h     wait
                   if function 0C6h lock mode 01h:
          BP       timeout in timer ticks (1/18 sec)
return    AL       error code

Function  0D2h  Novell NetWare 4.0 - Release Logical Record Seth
entry     AH  0D2h
          DS:DX    pointer to record string
return    AL       error code

Function  0D3h  Novell NetWare 4.0 - Release Logical Record Seth
entry     AH  0D3h
return    AL       error code

Function  0D4h  Novell NetWare 4.0 - Clear Logical Record Seth
entry     AH    0D4h
          DS:DX    pointer to record string
return    AL       error code

Function 0D5h Novell NetWare 4.0 - Clear Logical Record Seth
entry     AH  0D5h
return    AL       error code

Function  0D6h  Novell NetWare 4.0 - End Of Jobh
entry     AH    0D6h
return    AL       error code

Function  0D7h  Novell NetWare 4.0 - System Logouth
entry     AH    0D7h
return    AL       error code

Functions 0D8h, 0D9h unknown - Novell NetWare?

Function  0DAh  Novell NetWare 4.0 - Get Volume Statistics
entry     AH       0DAh
          DL       volume number
          ES:DI    pointer to reply buffer
return    AL       00h
                   reply buffer
                   word     sectors/block
                   word     total blocks
                   word     unused blocks
                   word     total directory entries
                   word     unused directory entries
                16 bytes    volume name, null padded
                   word     removable flag, 0 = not removable

Function 0DBh Novell NetWare 4.0 - Get Number Of Local Drivesh
entry     AH  0DBh
return    AL       number of local disks

Function  0DCh  Novell NetWare 4.0 - Get Station Number (Logical ID)
entry     AH       0DCh
return    AL       station number
                   00h     if NetWare not loaded or this machine is a
                           non-dedicated server
          CX       station number in ASCII

Function  0DDh  Novell NetWare 4.0 - Set Error Modeh
entry     AH       0DDh
          DL       error mode
                   00h     display critical I/O errors
                   01h     extended errors for all I/O in AL
                   02h     extended errors for critical I/O in AL
return    AL       previous error mode
```

```
Function  0DEh   Novell NetWare 4.0 - Get/Set Broadcast Mode
entry     AH       0DEh
          AL       broadcast mode
                   00h     receive console and workstation broadcasts
                   01h     receive console broadcasts only
                   02h     receive no broadcasts
                   03h     store all broadcasts for retrieval
                   04h     get broadcast mode
                   05h     disable shell timer interrupt checks
                   06h     enable shell timer interrupt checks
return    AL       old broadcast mode

Function  0DFh   Novell NetWare 4.0 - Capture
entry     AH       0DFh
          AL       00h     Start LPT Capture)
                   01h     End LPT Capture)
                   02h     Cancel LPT Capture)
                   03h     Flush LPT Capture)
                   04h     Start Specific Capture)
                   05h     End Specific Capture)
                   06h     Cancel Specific Capture)
                   07h     Flush Specific Capture)
return    AL       error code

Function  0E0h   Novell NetWare - Print Spooling
entry     AH       0E0h
          DS:SI    pointer to request buffer
                   subfunction in third byte of request buffer:
                   00h     spool data to a capture file
                   01h     close and queue capture file
                   02h     set spool flags
                   03h     spool existing file
                   04h     get spool queue entry
                   05h     remove entry from spool queue
                   06h     get printer status
                   09h     create a disk capture file
          ES:DI    pointer to reply buffer
return    AL       error code

Function  0E1h   Novell NetWare 4.0 - Broadcast Messages
entry     AH       0E1h
          DS:SI    pointer to request buffer
                   subfunction in third byte of request buffer:
                   00h     send broadcast message
                   01h     get broadcast message
                   02h     disable station broadcasts
                   03h     enable station broadcasts
                   04h     send personal message
                   05h     get personal message
                   06h     open message pipe
                   07h     close message pipe
                   08h     check pipe status
                   09h     broadcast to console
          ES:DI    pointer to reply buffer
return    AL       error code

Function  0E2h   Novell NetWare 4.0 - Directory Functions
entry     AH       0E2h
          DS:SI    pointer to request buffer
          ES:DI    pointer to reply buffer
                   subfunction in third byte of request buffer:
                   00h     Set Directory Handle)
                   01h     Get Directory Path)
                   02h     Scan Directory Information)
                   03h     Get Effective Directory Rights)
                   04h     Modify Maximum Rights Mask)
                   05h     unknown
                   06h     Get Volume Name)
                   07h     Get Volume Number)
                   08h     unknown
```

```
                    09h     unknown
                    0Ah     Create Directory)
                    0Bh     Delete Directory)
                    0Ch     Scan Directory For Trustees)
                    0Dh     Add Trustee To Directory)
                    0Eh     Delete Trustee From Directory)
                    0Fh     Rename Directory)
                    10h     Purge Erased Files)
                    11h     Restore Erased File)
                    12h     Allocate Permanent Directory Handle)
                    13h     Allocate Temporary Directory Handle)
                    14h     Deallocate Directory Handle)
                    15h     Get Volume Info With Handle)
                    16h     Allocate Special Temporary Directory Handle)
                    17h     retrieve a short base handle (Advanced NetWare 2.0)
                    18h     restore a short base handle (Advanced NetWare 2.0)
                    19h     Set Directory Information)
return   AL         error code

Function 0E3h       Novell NetWare 4.0 - Connection Control
entry    AH         E3h
         DS:SI      pointer to request buffer
         ES:DI      pointer to reply buffer
                    subfunction in third byte of request buffer
                    00h     login
                    01h     change password
                    02h     map user to station set
                    03h     map object to number
                    04h     map number to object
                    05h     get station's logged information
                    06h     get station's root mask (obsolete)
                    07h     map group name to number
                    08h     map number to group name
                    09h     get memberset M of group G
                    0Ah     Enter Login Area)
                    0Bh     unknown
                    0Ch     unknown
                    0Dh     Log Network Message)
                    0Eh     get disk utilization (Advanced NetWare 1.0)
                    0Fh     scan file information (Advanced NetWare 1.0)
                    10h     set file information (Advanced NetWare 1.0)
                    11h     get file server information (Advanced NetWare 1.0)
                    12h     unknown
                    13h     get internet address (Advanced NetWare 1.02)
                    14h     login to file server (Advanced NetWare 2.0)
                    15h     get object connection numbers (Advanced NetWare 2.0)
                    16h     get connection information (Advanced NetWare 1.0)
                    17h-31h unknown
                    32h     create object (Advanced NetWare 1.0)
                    33h     delete object (Advanced NetWare 1.0)
                    34h     rename object (Advanced NetWare 1.0)
                    35h     get object ID (Advanced NetWare 1.0)
                    36h     get object name (Advanced NetWare 1.0)
                    37h     scan object (Advanced NetWare 1.0)
                    38h     change object security (Advanced NetWare 1.0)
                    39h     create property (Advanced NetWare 1.0)
                    3Ah     delete property (Advanced NetWare 1.0)
                    3Bh     change property security (Advanced NetWare 1.0)
                    3Ch     scan property (Advanced NetWare 1.0)
                    3Dh     read property value (Advanced NetWare 1.0)
                    3Eh     write property value (Advanced NetWare 1.0)
                    3Fh     verify object password (Advanced NetWare 1.0)
                    40h     change object password (Advanced NetWare 1.0)
                    41h     add object to set (Advanced NctWare 1.0)
                    42h     delete object from set (Advanced NetWare 1.0)
                    43h     is object in set? (Advanced NetWare 1.0)
                    44h     close bindery (Advanced NetWare 1.0)
                    45h     open bindery (Advanced NetWare 1.0)
                    46h     get bindery access level (Advanced NetWare 1.0)
                    47h     scan object trustee paths (Advanced NetWare 1.0)
                    48h-0C7h unknown
```

Network Interfacing

```
                    0C8h    Check Console Privileges)
                    0C9h    Get File Server Description Strings)
                    0CAh    Set File Server Date And Time)
                    0CBh    Disable File Server Login)
                    0CCh    Enable File Server Login)
                    0CDh    Get File Server Login Status)
                    0CEh    Purge All Erased Files)
                    0CFh    Disable Transaction Tracking)
                    0D0h    Enable Transaction Tracking)
                    0D1h    Send Console Broadcast)
                    0D2h    Clear Connection Number)
                    0D3h    Down File Server)
                    0D4h    Get File System Statistics)
                    0D5h    Get Transaction Tracking Statistics)
                    0D6h    Read Disk Cache Statistics)
                    0D7h    Get Drive Mapping Table)
                    0D8h    Read Physical Disk Statistics)
                    0D9h    Get Disk Channel Statistics)
                    0DAh    Get Connection's Task Information)
                    0DBh    Get List Of Connection's Open Files)
                    0DCh    Get List Of Connections Using A File)
                    0DDh    Get Physical Record Locks By Connection and File)
                    0DEh    Get Physical Record Locks By File)
                    0DFh    Get Logical Records By Connection)
                    0E0h    Get Logical Record Information)
                    0E1h    Get Connection's Semaphores)
                    0E2h    Get Semaphore Information)
                    0E3h    Get LAN Driver's Configuration Information)
                    0E4h    unknown
                    0E5h    Get Connection's Usage Statistics)
                    0E6h    Get Object's Remaining Disk Space)
                    0E7h    Get Server LAN I/O Statistics)
                    0E8h    Get Server Miscellaneous Information)
                    0E9h    Get Volume Information)
return   AL         error code

Function 0E4h       DoubleDOS
entry    AH         0E4h
         AL         00h     Check status
return   AL         0 if DoubleDOS is active

Function 0E4h       Novell NetWare 4.0 - Set File Attributes (FCB)
entry    AH         0E4h
         CL         file attributes byte
              bit   0         read only
                    1         hidden
                    2         system
                    3-6       undocumented
                    7         shareable
         DX:DX      pointer to FCB
return   AL         error code

Function 0E5h       Novell NetWare 4.0 - Update File Size (FCB)
entry    AH         0E5h
         DS:DX      pointer to FCB
return   AL         error code

Function 0E6h       Novell NetWare 4.0 - Copy File To File (FCB)
entry    AH         0E6h
         CX:DX      number of bytes to copy
         DS:SI      pointer to source FCB
         ES:DI      pointer to destination FCB
return   AL         error code

Function 0E7h       Novell NetWare 4.0 - Get File Server Date and Timeh
entry    AH         0E7h
         DS:DX      pointer to 7-byte reply buffer
                    byte    year - 1900
                    byte    month
                    byte    day
                    byte    hours
```

```
                    byte     minutes
                    byte     seconds
                    byte     day of week (0 = Sunday)
return   unknown

Function   0E7h   Novell NetWare 4.6 - Set FCB Re-open Mode
entry    AH       0E8h
         DL       mode
                  00h      no automatic re-open
                  01h      auto re-open
return   AL       error code

Function   0E9h   Novell NetWare 4.6 - Shell's 'Get Base Status'
entry    AH       0E9h
         AL       00h      Get Directory Handle
         DX       drive number to check (0 = A:)
return   AL       network pathbase
         AH       base flags:
                  00h      drive not currently mapped to a base
                  01h      drive is mapped to a permanent base
                  02h      drive is mapped to a temporary base
                  03h      drive exists locally

Function   0EAh   Novell NetWare 4.6 - Return Shell Version
entry    AH       0EAh
         AL       00h      get specialized hardware information
                           return   AL       hardware type
                                             00h      IBM PC
                                             01h      Victor 9000
                  01h      Get Workstation Environment Information)
         ES:DI    pointer to 40-byte buffer
                  return   buffer filled with three null-terminated entries:
                           major operating system
                           version
                           hardware type
return   AH       00h if MSDOS system

Function   0EBh   Novell NetWare 4.6 - Log File
entry    0EBh     Log File
         DS:DX    pointer to ASCIIZ filename
                  if function 0C6h lock mode 01h:
                  AL       flags
                           00h      log file only
                           01h      lock as well as log file
                  BP       timeout in timer ticks (1/18 second)
return   AL       error code

Function   0ECh   Novell NetWare 4.6 - Release Fileh
entry    AH       0ECh
         DS:DX    pointer to ASCIIZ filename
return   none

Function   0EDh   Novell NetWare - Clear Fileh
entry    AH       0EDh
         DS:DX    pointer to ASCIIZ filename
return   AL       error code

Function   0EEh   Novell NetWare - Get Node Address (Physical ID)
entry    AH       0EEh
return   CX:BX:AX = six-byte address

Function   0EFh   Novell Advanced NetWare 1.0+ - Get Drive Info
entry    AH       0EFh
         buffer   00h      Get Drive Handle Table)
                  01h      Get Drive Flag Table)
                  02h      Get Drive Connection ID Table)
                  03h      Get Connection ID Table)
                  04h      Get File Server Name Table)
return   ES:DI    pointer to shell status table
```

Network Interfacing

```
Function  0F0h  Novell Advanced NetWare 1.0+ - Connection ID
entry     AH    0F0h
          AL    00h     Set Preferred Connection ID)
                01h     Get Preferred Connection ID)
                02h     Get Default Connection ID)
                03h     LPT Capture Active)
                04h     Set Primary Connection ID)
                05h     Get Primary Connection ID)
                06h     Get Printer Status)
          DL    preferred file server
return    AL    selected file server

Function  0F1h  Novell Advanced NetWare 1.0+ - File Server Connection
entry     AH    0F1h
          AL    00h     Attach To File Server)
                  DL        preferred file server
                01h     Detach From File Server)
                02h     Logout From File Server)
return    AL    completion code

Function  0F1h  Novell NetWare - unknown
entry     AH    0F2h
return    unknown

Function  0F3h  Novell Advanced NetWare 2.0+ - File Server File Copy
entry     AH    0F3h
          ES:DI pointer to request string
                word    source file handle
                word    destination file handle
                dword   starting offset in source
                dword   starting offset in destination
                dword   number of bytes to copy
return    AL    status/error code
          CX:DX number of bytes copied

Function  0F3h  Novell NetWare
                File Server File Copyh
entry     AH    0F3h
return    unknown
```

14

Mouse Programming

General Information

The current generation of PC mice are all based on the Microsoft design originally introduced in June 1983. The Microsoft design (now de facto industry standard) uses a CPU software interrupt and a set of interrupt function calls to interpret data obtained from the pointing device. The original Microsoft mice used a card plugged into the system bus and a proprietary connection to the mouse. Later designs and most clones use a serial connection, a major exception being the IBM PS/2 series' 'pointing device port'.

There are various types of mice on the market. Various arrangements of wheels, balls, or a light-reflecting grid are used to detect mouse motion. Other systems often emulate the mouse in software while providing a different hardware implementation. These include trackballs, some joysticks, and some touch pads (such as the Koala pad). There is at least one program which will let a standard joy-stick emulate a mouse. Trackballs and joy-sticks are useful when desk space is at a premium. Most of these devices communicate with the system through some form of the Microsoft mouse API.

Mouse movement is defined in terms of mickeys (according to Bill Gates, this unit of measurement was named for the cartoon character Mickey Mouse). There are approximately 200 mickeys per inch of mouse movement. The mouse polls the current mickey count and sends the information to the mouse driver at regular intervals.

The mouse driver transforms the mickey count into screen pixels. The number of mickeys required to move the cursor one pixel is adjustable through a function call. The default mickey-to-pixel ratio is 1:1 on the X axis (horizontal) and 2:1 on the Y axis (vertical).

In graphics modes the mouse cursor can be moved one pixel at a time. In text modes the mouse cursor usually moves one character cell at a time. For example, on a Hercules screen in text mode, the smallest increment the mouse cursor can move is 9 pixels horizontally or 14 vertically.

When the mouse is moved, the cursor moves a set amount. In order to allow fine positioning of the cursor, the ratio between mouse movement and cursor movement must be small. This would make it difficult to make large adjustments of cursor position without excessive mouse movement. To solve this problem, some simple mouse drivers implement a 'double-speed threshold'. The mouse and cursor move in a 1:1 ratio up to a certain speed (mickeys per second) and then

Mouse Programming

the driver multiplies the mickey count by two before processing it, effectively doubling the cursor speed. Double-speed mouse drivers are common.

A better solution is the 'ballistic' driver. The mouse driver monitors the mickey count and modifies the count according to an arithmetic function or table. The mickey/pixel rate is varied in a smooth ratio from slowest to fastest.

The Microsoft mouse driver is not re-entrant. That is, a driver function may not call another driver function and return to its previous state.

Register Usage

The mouse driver is accessed much the same as DOS. Appropriate values are placed in the CPU registers and interrupt 33h is called. On return, the requested action is performed and whatever return codes are given are in he registers.

With the Microsoft Mouse device driver the registers are used as follows:

```
AX           mouse event flags:
             bit         significance
             0           mouse movement
             1           left button pressed
             2           left button released
             3           right button pressed
             4           right button released
             5-15        reserved
BX           button state
             bit         significance
             0           left button is down
             1           right button is down
             2-15        reserved
CX           X coordinate
DX           Y coordinate
DS           mouse driver data segment
DI           raw horizontal mickey count
SI           raw vertical mickey count
```

Interrupt 33h Function Requests
Interrupt 33h Microsoft Mouse Driver Extensions

The Microsoft mouse driver hooks into the int 10h video BIOS vector and watches for a change in screen mode. The mouse driver will automatically adapt to any supported BIOS video mode. The Microsoft driver makes 35 functions available to applications. Other brands of mouse drivers may add more. The mouse driver does not check input values, so all registers used by a call must be set by the application program.

Function Requests

```
Function  00h    Reset Driver and Read Status
  entry   AX     0000h
  return  AX     status
                 0000h    hardware or driver not installed
                 0FFFFh   reset successful
          BX     number of buttons
                 0000h    other than two
                 0002h    two buttons
```

```
                    0003h    Mouse Systems mouse
note 1. Checks current screen mode and resets mouse mode if required.
     2. Hides cursor and positions it to centre of screen, sets all defaults.
Function  01h     Show Mouse Cursor
entry     AX      0001h
return    none

Function  02h     Hide Mouse Cursor
entry     AX      0002h
return    none
note      Multiple calls to hide the cursor will require multiple calls to function
          01h to unhide it.

Function  03h     Get Button Status
entry     AX      0003h
return    BX      button status byte
               bits 0     left button
                    1     right button
                    2     middle button (Mouse Systems mouse)
                    3-7   not used
          CX      column
          DX      row
note      If bit is 0, button is normal. If bit is 1, button is pressed.

Function  04h     Set Mouse Cursor Position
entry     AX      0004h
          CX      column
          DX      row
return    none
note      PCM v8n8 reports Microsoft as saying, 'If the screen is not in a mode
          with a cell size of 1x1, the parameter values are rounded to the nearest
          horizontal or vertical coordinate values permitted for the current
          screen mode.' Mefford reports that the Microsoft driver actually
          truncates instead of rounding. This may explain the reported tendencies
          of some Microsoft products toward not recognizing non-MS mice.

Function  05h     Return Button Press Data
entry     AX      0005h
          BX      button ID byte (BL)
               bits 0     left
                    1     right
                    2     middle (Mouse Systems mouse)
return    AX      button states (AL)
               bits 0     left button
                    1     right button
                    2     middle button (Mouse Systems mouse)
          BX      # times specified button pressed since last call
          CX      column at time specified button was last pressed
          DX      row at time specified button was last pressed
note      If bit is 0, button is normal. If bit is 1, button is pressed.

Function  06h     Return Button Release Data
entry     AX      0006h
          BX      button ID byte (BL)
               bits 0     left
                    1     right
                    2     middle (Mouse Systems mouse)
return    AX      button states (AL)
               bits 0     left button
                    1     right button
                    2     middle button (Mouse Systems mouse)
          BX      no. of times specified button released since last call
          CX      column at time specified button was last released
          DX      row at time specified button was last released
note      If bit is 0, button is normal. If bit is 1, button is pressed.

Function  07h     Define Horizontal Cursor Range
entry     AX      0007h
          CX      minimum column
          DX      maximum column
return    none
```

Mouse Programming

```
Function  08h     Define Vertical Cursor Range
entry     AX      0008h
          CX      minimum row
          DX      maximum row
return    none
note      If the minimum value is greater than the maximum value, the values are
          swapped.

Function  09h     Define Graphics Cursor
entry     AX      0009h
          BX      column of cursor hot spot in bitmap (-16 to 16)
          CX      row of cursor hot spot    (-16 to 16)
          ES:DX   pointer to bitmap
              16 words    screen mask
              16 words    cursor mask
return    none
note      Each word defines the sixteen pixels of a row, low bit rightmost.

Function  0Ah     Define Text Cursor
entry     AX      000Ah
          BX      select hardware/software text cursor
                  00h      software
          CX      screen mask value or scan line start
          DX      cursor mask value or scan line stop
                  01h      hardware
return    none
note      When the software cursor is selected, the char/attribute data at the
          current screen position is ANDed with the screen mask and then XORed
          with the cursor mask.

Function  0Bh     Read Motion Counters
entry     AX      000Bh
return    CX      number of mickeys mouse moved horiz. since last call
          DX      number of mickeys mouse moved vertically
note 1.   A mickey is the smallest increment the mouse can sense.
     2.   Positive values indicate up/right.
     3.   This call ignores overflow and sets mickey count to 0 on completion.

Function  0Ch     Define Interrupt Subroutine Parameters
entry     AX      000Ch
          CX      bit mask
              bit 0        call if mouse moves (note 3)
                  1        call if left button pressed
                  2        call if left button released
                  3        call if right button pressed
                  4        call if right button released
                  5        call if middle button pressed  (Mouse Systems)
                  6        call if middle button released (Mouse Systems)
                  7-15     not used
          DX      address of FAR routine (note 4)
return    unknown
note 1.   When the subroutine is called, it is passed these values:
          AH      condition mask (same bit assignments as call mask)
          BX      button state
          CX      cursor column
          DX      cursor row
          DI      vertical mickey count
          SI      horizontal mickey count
     2.   According to PCM v8n8, the DI and SI registers shown above are correct
          for the Microsoft Mouse and were shown reversed in some versions of the
          Microsoft Mouse Programmer's Reference Guide.
     3.   The Microsoft documentation reads 'cursor' instead of 'mouse'. The
          Microsoft driver looks at mouse position, though. (PCM v8n8). Logitech
          and Mouse Systems watch for cursor position.
     4.   The complete call is DS:DX. The segment value (DS) is taken care of by
          the mouse driver. You need only pass DX.

Function  0Dh     Light Pen Emulation On
entry     AX      000Dh
return    none
note 1.   Light pen emulation is on by default when using the Microsoft driver.
```

```
           2. If a real light pen is present in the system, fn 0Eh must be used to
              disable emulation.
Function  0Eh     Light Pen Emulation Off
entry     AX      000Eh
return    none

Function  0Fh     Define Mickey/Pixel Ratio
entry     AX      000Fh
          CX      mickeys per 8 pixels horizontally   (default 8)
          DX      mickeys per 8 pixels vertically     (default 16)
return    none

Function  10h     Define Screen Region for Updating (Conditional Off)
entry     AX      0010h
          DX      pointer to region you want to update (note 2)
return    none
note  1. Mouse cursor is hidden during updating, and needs to be explicitly turned
         on again.
      2. The complete call is DS:DX. The segment value (DS) is taken care of by
         the mouse driver. You need only pass DX.
      3. Array format:
         offset  value
         01h     left x-screen coordinate
         02h     top y-screen coordinate
         03h     right x-screen coordinate
         04h     bottom y-screen coordinate

Function  11h     not documented by Microsoft

Function  12h     Set Large Graphics Cursor Block
entry     AX      0012h
          BH      cursor width in words
          CH      rows in cursor
          BL      horizontal hot spot (-16 to 16)
          CL      vertical hot spot (-16 to 16)
          DX      pointer to bit map of screen and cursor maps (note 2)
return    AH      0FFFFh  successful
note  1. PC Mouse. Not documented by Microsoft
      2. The complete call is DS:DX. The segment value (DS) is taken care of by
         the mouse driver. You need only pass DX.

Function  13h     Define Double-Speed Threshold
entry     AX      0013h
          DX      threshold speed in mickeys/second,
                  0000h   default of 64/second
return    none
note             If speed exceeds threshold, the cursor's on-screen motion is doubled.

Function  14h     Exchange Interrupt Subroutines
entry     AX      0014h
          BX:DX   pointer to FAR routine
          CX      call mask (see function 000Ch)
return    BX:DX   FAR address of previous interrupt routine
          CX      call mask of previous interrupt routine

Function  15h     Return Driver State Storage Requirements
entry     AX      0015h
return    BX      size of buffer needed to store driver state

Function  16h     Save Driver State
entry     AX      0016h
          DX      offset into buffer
return    none

Function  17h     Restore Driver State
entry     AX      0017h
          DX      offset into buffer containing saved state
return    none

Function  18h-1Ch not documented by Microsoft
```

Mouse Programming

```
Function  18h       Set Alternate Mouse User Handler
entry     AX        0018h
          CX        call mask
              bit 0         call if mouse moves
                  1         call if left button pressed
                  2         call if left button released
                  3         call if right button pressed
                  4         call if right button released
                  5         call if shift button pressed during event
                  6         call if ctrl key pressed during event
                  7         call if alt key pressed during event
                  8-15      not used
          DX        offset to user subroutine
return    AX        0FFFFh  error
note 1. When the subroutine is called, it is passed the following values:
          AX        condition mask (same bit assignments as call mask)
          BX        button state
          CX        cursor column
          DX        cursor row
          DI        horizontal mickey count
          SI        vertical mickey count
     2. Up to three handlers can be defined by separate calls to this function.

Function  19h       Return User Alternate Interrupt Vector
entry     AX        0019h
          CX        call mask (same as 0018h above)
return    AX        status   0FFFFh no vector or mask found
          BX:DX     pointer to user interrupt vector (0 if AX=0FFFFh)
          CX        call mask (0 if AX=0FFFFh)
note      Attempts to find a user event handler (defined by function 18h) whose
          call mask matches CX.

Function  1Ah       Set Mouse Sensitivity
entry     AX        001Ah
          BX        horizontal speed
          CX        vertical speed
          DX        double speed threshold in mickeys/second,
                    0000h    sets default of 64/second
return    none

Function  1Bh       Return Mouse Sensitivity
entry     AX        001Bh
return    BX        horizontal speed
          CX        vertical speed
          DX        double speed threshold

Function  1Ch       Set Mouse Interrupt Rate
entry     AX        001Ch
          BX        interrupt rate desired (BL)
                    00h      no interrupts allowed
                    01h      30 interrupts per second
                    02h      50 interrupts per second
                    03h      100 interrupts per second
                    04h      200 interrupts per second
                    04h-FFh not defined
return    none
note      If a value larger than 04h is used, the Microsoft InPort driver may be
          have unpredictably.

Function  1Dh       Define Display Page Number
entry     AX        001Dh
          BX        display page number
note      The cursor will be displayed on the specified page.

Function  1Eh       Return Display Page Number
entry     AX        001Eh
return    BX        display page number

Function  1Fh       Disable Mouse Driver
entry     AX        001Fh
return    AX        001Fh    successful
```

```
                   0FFFFh   unsuccessful
         ES:BX     old int 33h vector
note 1.  Restores vectors for int 10h and int 71h (8086) or int 74h (286/386).
     2.  If you restore int 33h to ES:BX, driver will be completely disabled.

Function  20h      Enable Mouse Driver
entry     AX       0020h
return    none
note      Restores vectors for int 10h and int 71h (8086) or int 74h (286/386)
          which were removed by function 1Fh.

Function  21h      Software Reset
entry     AX       0021h
return    AX       0021h    mouse driver not installed
                   0FFFFh   mouse driver installed
          BX       0002h    mouse driver is installed
note      Identical to function 0000h, but does not reset the mouse.

Function  22h      Set Message Language
entry     AX       0022h
          BX       language number (BL)
                   00h      English
                   01h      French
                   02h      Dutch
                   03h      German
                   04h      Swedish
                   05h      Finnish
                   06h      Spanish
                   07h      Portuguese
                   08h      Italian
                   other values not used
return    none
note      Values other than 00h are valid only for Microsoft international mouse
          driver software.

Function  23h      Get Message Language
entry     AX       0023h
return    BX       current language number (BL)
note      See function 0022h.

Function  24h      Get Software Version, Mouse Type, and IRQ Number
entry     AX       0024h
return    AX       0FFFFh  on error, else
          BH       major version
          BL       minor version
          CH       mouse interface type
                   01h      bus mouse
                   02h      serial mouse
                   03h      Microsoft InPort
                   04h      IBM PS/2 Pointing Device port
                   05h      Hewlett-Packard mouse
          CL       IRQ interrupt request number
                   00h      PS/2 pointing device
                   01h      not defined
                   02h      IRQ2
                   03h      IRQ3
                   ...      ...
                   07h      IRQ7)

Function  42h      PCMouse - Get MSmouse Storage Requirements
entry     AX       0042h
return    AX       0FFFFh  successful
          BX       buffer size in bytes for functions 50h and 52h
                   00h      MSmouse not installed
                   42h      functions 42h, 50h, and 52h not supported

Function  43-49h   unknown

Function  50h      PCmouse - Save MSmouse State
entry     AH       50h
          BX       buffer size
```

Mouse Programming

```
              ES:DX    pointer to buffer
return        AX       0FFFFh  successful

Function 51h           unknown

Function 52h           PCMouse - Save MSmouse State
entry         AH       50h
              BX       buffer size
              ES:DX    pointer to buffer
return        AX       0FFFFh  successful
```

Interrupt 10h (Video BIOS) Microsoft Mouse Driver EGA Support
The following functions are appended to BIOS int 10h and implemented as the EGA Register Interface Library:

```
              0F0h     read one register
              0F1h     write one register
              0F2h     read consecutive register range
              0F3h     write consecutive register range
              0F4h     read non-consecutive register set
              0F5h     write non-consecutive register set
              0F6h     revert to default register values
              0F7h     define default register values
              0FAh     get driver status

Function 0F0h          Microsoft Mouse driver EGA support - Read One Register
entry         AH       0F0h
              BH       pointer for register/data chips
              BL       pointer
              DX       port number
                       (pointer/data chips)
                       00h    CRT Controller (25 registers)     (3B4h mono, 3D4h colour)
                       08h    sequencer (5 registers)                        (3C4h)
                       10h    graphics controller (9 registers)              (3CEh)
                       18h    attribute controller (20 registers)            (3C0h)
                       (single registers)
                       20h    miscellaneous output register                  (3C2h)
                       28h    Feature Control register        (3BAh mono, 3DAh colour)
                       30h    graphics 1 position register                   (3CCh)
                       38h    graphics 2 position register                   (3CAh)
return        BL       data
note          All other registers are restored.

Function 0F1h          Microsoft Mouse driver EGA support - Write One Register
entry         AH       0F1h
              BH       pointer for pointer/data chips (ignored for single registers)
              BL       pointer for pointer/data chips or data for single registers
              DX       port number (see function 0F0h)
return        BH and DX are not restored, all other registers are restored

Function 0F2h          Microsoft Mouse driver EGA support - Read Register Range
entry         AH       0F2h
              CH       starting pointer value
              CL       number of registers (must be 1)
              DX       port number
                       00h    CRT controller          (3B4h mono modes, 3D4h colour modes)
                       08h    sequencer                                      (3C4h)
                       10h    graphics controller                            (3CEh)
                       18h    attribute controller                           (3C0h)
              ES:BX    pointer to buffer, CL bytes
return        CX is not restored, all other registers are restored

Function 0F3h          Microsoft Mouse driver EGA support - Write Register Range
entry         AH       0F3h
              CH       starting register
              CL       number of registers (must be 1)
              DX       port number
                       00h    CRT controller          (3B4h mono modes, 3D4h colour modes)
                       08h    sequencer                                      (3C4h)
                       10h    graphics controller                            (3CEh)
```

```
                        18h     attribute controller            (3C0h)
            ES:BX   pointer to buffer, CL bytes
return      BX, CX, DX are not restored, all other registers are restored
Function 0F4h   Microsoft Mouse driver EGA support - Read Register Set
entry       AH      0F4h
            CX      number of registers (must be 1)
            ES:BX   pointer to 4-byte table of records in this format:
                byte 0-2     port number
                             (pointer/data chips)
                                00h     CRTC          (3B4h mono modes, 3D4h colour modes)
                                08h     sequencer                (3C4h)
                                10h     graphics controller      (3CEh)
                                18h     attribute controller     (3C0h)
                             (single registers)
                                20h     miscellaneous output register  (3C2h)
                                28h     Feature Control register (3BAh mono modes,
                                        3DAh colour)
                                30h     graphics 1 position register   (3CCh)
                                38h     graphics 2 position register   (3CAh)
                byte 1       must be zero
                byte 2       pointer value (0 for single registers)
                byte 3       EGA Register Interface fills in data read from register
                             specified in bytes 0-2.
return      CX is not restored, all other registers are restored

Function 0F5h   Microsoft Mouse driver EGA support - Read Register Set
entry       AH      0F5h
            CX      number of registers (must be greater than 1)
            ES:BX   pointer to 4-byte table of records in this format:
                byte 0-2     port number
                             (pointer/data chips)
                                00h     CRT controller (3B4h mono modes,3D4h colour modes)
                                08h     sequencer                (3C4h)
                                10h     graphics controller      (3CEh)
                                18h     attribute controller     (3C0h)
                             (single registers)
                                20h     miscellaneous output register  (3C2h)
                                28h     Feature Control register (3BAh mono modes,
                                        3DAh colour)
                                30h     graphics 1 position register   (3CCh)
                                38h     graphics 2 position register   (3CAh)
                byte 1       must be zero
                byte 2       pointer value (0 for single registers)
                byte 3       data to be written to register specified in bytes 0-2.
return      CX is not restored, all other registers are restored

Function 0F6h   MS Mouse driver EGA support - Revert to Default Registers
entry       AH      0F6h
return      all registers restored

Function 0F7h   MS Mouse driver EGA support - Define Default Register Table
entry       AH      0F7h
            CX      VGA colour select flag
                    5448h   allows EGA Register Interface to recognise byte
                            offset 14h of the table pointed to by ES:BX as the value
                            for the VGA colour select register
            DX      port number
                    (pointer/data chips)
                       00h      CRT controller        (3B4h mono modes, 3D4h colour modes)
                       08h      sequencer                      (3C4h)
                       10h      graphics controller            (3CEh)
                       18h      attribute controller           (3C0h)
                    (single registers)
                       20h      miscellaneous output register  (3C2h)
                       28h      Feature Control register   (3BAh mono, 3DAh colour)
                       30h      graphics 1 position register   (3CCh)
                       38h      graphics 2 position register   (3CAh)
            ES:BX   pointer to table of one byte entries, one byte to be
                    written to each register (all registers must be written)
return      BX and DX are not restored, all other registers are restored
```

```
Functions 0F8h, 0F9h unknown

Function 0FAh    Microsoft Mouse driver EGA support - Interrogate Driver
entry    AH      0FAh
         BX      00h
return   AX      restored
         BX      0000h   if mouse driver not present
         ES:BX   pointer to EGA Register Interface version number, if present:
                 byte 0  major release number
                 byte 1  minor release number (in 100ths)
```

15

Register-Level Hardware Access

8255 Peripheral Interface Chip (PIC)

The Intel 8255 has 3 1-byte registers, referred to as ports A, B, or C. They are located at port addresses 60h-62h. Ports A and C are read-only, B is read/write. In the IBM PC, setting bit 7 of port B changes information in port A, and setting bit 2 determines the contents of the lower 4 bits of port C. (bit 3 in the XT)

```
60h     port A   read-only
        byte     (normal)     8-bit scancodes from keyboard   (all machines)
                 (PC: port B bit 7-1)   equipment byte as returned by int 11h
                 bit 0        0 = no diskette drives installed
                     1        not used
                     2,3      banks of RAM on motherboard
                     4,5      display
                              1,1     monochrome
                              1,0     80x25 colour
                              0,1     40x25 colour
                     6,7      number of diskette drives

61h     port B   read/write
        byte
                 bit 0        PC,XT,jr    controls gate of 8253 timer chip channel 2
                     1        PC,XT,jr    output to speaker
                     2        PC          select contents of port C
                     3        PC,jr       0    text mode (default)
                                          1    graphics mode
                              XT          select contents of port C
                     4        PC,XT       0    enable RAM  (default)
                                          1    disable RAM (not very useful)
                     5        PC,XT       0    enable expansion slot error signals
                                          1    disable expansion slot error signals
                     5,6      jr          select sound source
                                          0,0  8253 chip
                                          0,1  cassette port
                                          1,0  sound line on expansion bus
                                          1,1  TI 76496 sound chip
                     7        PC          select contents of port A, acknowledge keyboard
                              XT          keyboard acknowledge only

62h     port C   read only
        (when port B bit 2=1 on PC or port B bit 3=1 on XT)
        byte
                 bit 0-3      PC          bottom half of configuration switch 2
                                          (RAM in expansion slots)
                     0        PCjr        1    incoming keystroke lost
                     1        XT          0    no math coprocessor installed (default)
                                          1    math coprocessor installed
```

Register-Level Hardware Access

```
           2         PCjr         0    modem card installed
           2,3       XT                banks of RAM on system board
           3         PCjr         0    128k RAM upgrade installed
                                  1    64k RAM (default)
           4         PC,jr             cassette input
                     XT                not used
           5         PC,XT,jr          output of 8253 channel 2
           6         PC,XT        1    expansion slot error check
                     jr           1    keyboard data
           7         PC,XT        1    parity error check
                     jr           0    keyboard cable connected
                                  1    keyboard cable not connected (default)
(when port B bit 2=0 on PC or port B bit 3=0 on XT)
      bit 0-3        PC                top half of configuration switch 2 (unused)
           0,1       XT                display type
                                  1,1  monochrome
                                  1,0  80x25 colour
                                  0,1  40x25 colour
           2,3       XT                number of diskette drives
           4,7       PC,XT             same as if port B bit 2=1
```

The AT keeps its configuration settings in a Motorola MC146818 chip along with the real-time clock. It has no 8255 chip as such, although the same port addresses are used to control the timer chip and receive data from the keyboard. The chip has 64 registers numbered 00h-3Fh. To read a register, first send its number to port address 70h and then read it from 71h.

CMOS RAM map, PC/AT:

```
         offset          contents
         00h             Seconds
         01h             Second Alarm
         02h             Minutes
         03h             Minute Alarm
         04h             Hours
         05h             Hour Alarm
         06h             Day of the Week
         07h             Day of the Month
         08h             Month
         09h             Year
         0Ah             Status Register A
         0Bh             Status Register B
         0Ch             Status Register C
         0Dh             Status Register D
         0Eh             Diagnostic Status Byte
         0Fh             Shutdown Status Byte
         10h             Disk Drive Type for Drives A: and B:
                         The drive-type bytes use bits 0:3 for the first drive
                         and 4:7 for the other Disk drive types:
                         00h       no drive present
                         01h       double sided 360k
                         02h       high capacity (1.2 meg)
                         03h-0Fh   reserved
         11h             (AT):Reserved    (PS/2):drive type for hard disk C:
         12h             (PS/2):drive type for hard disk D:
                         (AT, XT/286):hard disk type for drives C: and
                          D: Format of drive-type entry for AT, XT/286:
                             0     number of cyls in drive (0-1023 allowed)
                             2     number of heads per drive (0-15 allowed)
                             3     starting reduced write compensation (not used
                                   on AT)
                             5     starting cylinder for write compensation
                             7     max. ECC data burst length, XT only
                             8     control byte
                                   Bit
                                   7     disable disk-access retries
                                   6     disable ECC retries
                                   5-4   reserved, set to zero
                                   3     more than 8 heads
                                   2-0   drive option on XT (not used by AT)
```

```
                9         timeout value for XT (not used by AT)
                12        landing zone cylinder number
                14        number of sectors per track (default
                          17, 0-17 allowed)
    13h         Reserved
    14h         Equipment Byte (corresponds to sw. 1 on PC and XT)
    15h-16h     Base Memory Size      (low,high)
    17h-18h     Expansion Memory Size (low,high)
    19h-20h     Reserved
                (PS/2) POS information Model 50 (60 and 80 use a 2k
                CMOS RAM that is not accessible through software)
    21h-2Dh     Reserved (not checksummed)
    2Eh-2Fh     Checksum of bytes 10 through 20   (low,high)
    30h-31h     Exp. Memory Size as Determined by POST (low,high)
    32h         Date Century Byte
    33h         Information Flags (set during power-on)
    34h-3Fh     Reserved
 3. The alarm function is used to drive the BIOS WAIT function (int
    15h function 90h).
 4. To access the configuration RAM write the byte address (00-3Fh)
    you need to access to I/O port 70h, then access the data via I/O
    port 71h.
 5. CMOS RAM chip is a Motorola 146818.
 6. The equipment byte is used to determine the configuration for the
    POST power-on diagnostics.
 7. Bytes 00-0Dh are defined by the chip for timing functions, bytes
    0Eh-3Fh are defined by IBM.
 8. Compaq 386 uses came CMOS chip as IBM AT. Extra functions:
    byte 45 (2Dh) stores additional info not maintained by AT.
       bit 0    indicates is Compaq dual-mode monitor installed
           1    indicates whether keyclick is enabled
           2    not used
           3    if non-Compaq graphics adapter installed
```

8259 Interrupt Controller

The 8259 Interrupt Controller chip provides vital support services for the CPU. In a typical PC, interrupt signals can originate from several different places (i.e. keyboard, disk drive, etc.). The 8088, however, has only one input line on which to receive an interrupt signal. The 8259 chip is therefore employed to manage the various interrupt sources and present a single, controllable interrupt signal to the central processor.

As configured for use in the PC, the 8259 chip can accept up to eight independent signals numbered 0 through 7. For each interrupt it receives, the 8259 can present an interrupt signal to the CPU. Furthermore it presents to the CPU a unique interrupt type code for each of the eight interrupt sources. This allows us to assign a unique interrupt service routine to each different interrupt source. The eight signal inputs to the 8259 are wired onto the control bus so that any device tied into the bus system can access this interrupt mechanism. On the control bus, the signals are named IRQ0 through IRQ7.

Because each signal is independent, provision must be made for the possibility of two or more signals occurring at the same time. The 8259 manages such an event by holding on to the secondary interrupt(s) while the processor services the first. When that interrupt has been serviced, the next one is signalled to the processor. For events that occur at exactly the same moment, the 8259 passes them to the processor in a priority order, where interrupt source 0 has the highest priority and interrupt source 7 has the lowest. One very important consequence of this scheme is that the CPU must indicate to the 8259 when it has completed the servicing of each interrupt. This must be kept in mind whenever an interrupt service routine is written.

Because it has been designed for use in many different applications, the 8259 is an extremely complex chip. Fortunately most of this complexity is handled by the BIOS, which programs the proper configuration information into the 8259 on power-up. The 8259 is thus configured to signal interrupt type codes 08h-0Fh to correspond with interrupt sources 0-7. Note that the two highest-priority interrupts, IRQ0 and IRQ1, are wired directly on the system board. The rest of the interrupt sources are obtained from adapter cards plugged into the expansion slots.

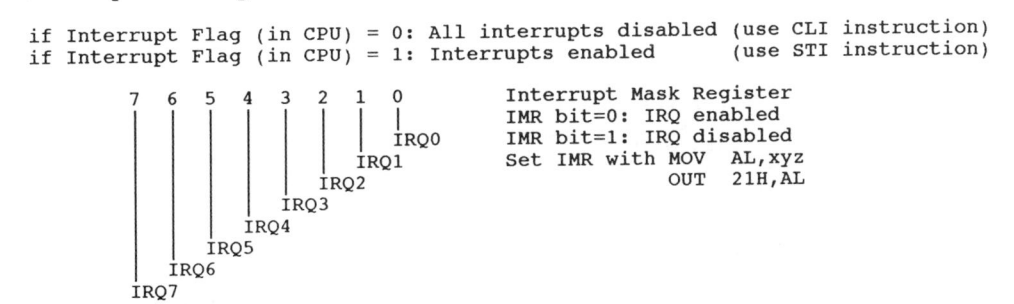

Programming the 8259 consists of two basic actions. First, you can enable or disable each interrupt source independently by writing a value into the interrupt mask register, or IMR. The IMR is a one-byte register within the 8259 that we can access via I/O port 21h. Each bit in the IMR corresponds to the interrupt source with its bit number (i.e. bit 0-IRQ0, bit 1-IRQ1, etc). If a bit in the IMR is 0, then its corresponding interrupt source in enabled. A signal appearing on that input to the 8259 will cause an interrupt to be sent to the CPU. If the IMR bit is 1, then the interrupt source is disabled (or masked) and cannot generate an interrupt. Keep in mind that the state of the interrupt flag within the CPU will ultimately determine whether or not any interrupt signal is received.

The second 8259 programming action that we must be concerned with is the signalling of the end of an interrupt service routine. This is accomplished by sending the 'end of interrupt' (EOI) command, represented by 20h, to the interrupt command register within the 8259. Coincidentally, this one-byte register is accessed via I/O port 20h.

Interrupt Sources

```
8259 Input         Type Code            Device
   IRQ0               08h               system timer (channel 0)
   IRQ1               09h               keyboard
   IRQ2               0Ah               EGA and CGA
   IRQ3               0Bh               COM2
   IRQ4               0Ch               COM1
   IRQ5               0Dh               hard disk
   IRQ6               0Eh               floppy drive
   IRQ7               0Fh               parallel printer
```

Interrupt Mask Register:

```
if Interrupt Flag (in CPU) = 0: All interrupts disabled (use CLI instruction)
if Interrupt Flag (in CPU) = 1: Interrupts enabled      (use STI instruction)

        7 6 5 4 3 2 1 0         Interrupt Mask Register
        | | | | | | | |         IMR bit=0: IRQ enabled
        | | | | | | | IRQ0      IMR bit=1: IRQ disabled
        | | | | | | IRQ1        Set IMR with MOV   AL,xyz
        | | | | | IRQ2                         OUT 21H,AL
        | | | | IRQ3
        | | | IRQ4
        | | IRQ5
        | IRQ6
        IRQ7
```

16

Video Subsystems and Programming

Quick List of Interrupt 10h Functions

00h	Determine or Set Video State	
01h	Set Cursor Type	
02h	Set Cursor Position	
03h	Read Cursor Position	
04h	Read Light Pen	
05h	Select Active Page	
06h	Scroll Page Up	
07h	Scroll Page Down	
08h	Read Character Attribute	
09h	Write Character and Attribute	
0Ah	Write Character	
0Bh	Set Colour Palette	
0Ch	Write Dot	
0Dh	Read Dot	
0Eh	Write TTY	
0Fh	Return Current Video State	
10h	Set Palette Registers	
11h	Character Generator Routine	
12h	Alternate Select	
13h	Enhanced String Write	
14h	Load LCD Character Font	
15h	Return Physical Display Parameters	
1Ah	Display Combination Code	
1Bh	Functionality/State Information	
1Ch	Save/Restore Video State	
40h	Set Graphics Mode	(Hercules Graphics Card)
41h	Set Text Mode	(Hercules Graphics Card)
42h	Clear Current Page	(Hercules Graphics Card)
43h	Select Drawing Page	(Hercules Graphics Card)
44h	Select Drawing Function	(Hercules Graphics Card)
45h	Select Page to Display	(Hercules Graphics Card)
46h	Draw One Pixel	(Hercules Graphics Card)
47h	Find Pixel Value	(Hercules Graphics Card)
48h	Move to Point	(Hercules Graphics Card)
49h	Draw to Point	(Hercules Graphics Card)
4Ah	Block Fill	(Hercules Graphics Card)
4Bh	Display Character	(Hercules Graphics Card)
4Ch	Draw Arc	(Hercules Graphics Card)
4Dh	Draw Circle	(Hercules Graphics Card)
4Eh	Fill Area	(Hercules Graphics Card)
6Ah	Direct Graphics Interface Standard	(DGIS)
6Fh	Set Video Mode	(VEGA Extended EGA/VGA)

Video Subsystems and Programming

```
        70h     Get Video RAM Address                       (Tandy 1000)
        71h     Get INCRAM Addresses                        (Tandy 1000)
        72h     Scroll Screen Right                         (Tandy 1000)
        73h     Scroll Screen Left                          (Tandy 1000)
        81h     unknown                                        (DesQview)
        82h     Get Current Window Info                        (DesQview)
        0BFh    Compaq Portable Extensions
        0F0h    Microsoft Mouse driver EGA support - Read One Register
        0F1h    Microsoft Mouse driver EGA support - Write One Register
        0F2h    Microsoft Mouse driver EGA support - Read Register Range
        0F3h    Microsoft Mouse driver EGA support - Write Register Range
        0F4h    Microsoft Mouse driver EGA support - Read Register Set
        0F5h    Microsoft Mouse driver EGA support - Read Register Set
        0F6h    Microsoft Mouse driver EGA support - Revert to Default
                                                            Registers
        0F7h    Microsoft Mouse driver EGA support - Define Default Reg.
                                                            Table
        0FAh    Microsoft Mouse driver EGA support - Interrogate Driver
        0FEh    Get Virtual Buffer Address         (Topview/DesQview/Taskview)
        0FFh    Update Video Buffer                (Topview/DesQview/Taskview)
```

Interrupt 10h Video I/O - services to handle video output

(0:0040h)
The ROM video routines in the original PC BIOS are designed for use with the Colour Graphics Adapter and incorporate code to test for the horizontal retrace before writing. The check is performed no matter what actual display adapter is installed. The ROM character table for the first 128 characters is located at 0FA6Eh in the PC. Int 01Fh can be used to point to a second table of 128 characters. CS, SS, DS, ES, BX, CX, DX are preserved during call. All others are destroyed.

```
Function 00h        Determine or Set Video State
entry    AH         00h     set video mode
         AL                 display mode:                   CGA|PCjr|MDA|MCGA|EGA|VGA|8514
                    00h     40x25 B/W text              8x8 CGA|PCjr|   |    |EGA|
16 Colour                   40x25, 320x400 graphics                     |MCGA|
16 Colour                   40x25, 360x400 graphics                     |    |   |VGA|
                            40x25 B/W tet              8x14 | ATI VIP
16 Colour           01h     40x25 colour text          8x8 CGA|PCjr|   |    |EGA|   |
16 Colour                   40x25                      8x14 | ATI VIP
                    02h     80x25 B/W text             8x8 CGA|PCjr|   |    |EGA|
16 Colour                   640x400 80x25              8x8              |MCGA|
16 Colour                   720x400 80x25                               |    |   |VGA|
                            80x25 B/W                  8x14 | ATI VIP
16 Colour           03h     80x25 colour text          8x8 CGA|PCjr|   |MCGA|EGA|VGA
4 Colour            04h     320x200 colour graphics        CGA|PCjr|   |    |EGA
4 tone grey         05h     320x200 B/W graphics       8x8 CGA|PCjr|   |    |EGA
2 Colour            06h     640x200 B/W graphics       8x8 CGA|PCjr|   |    |EGA
monochrome          07h     80x25 monochrome text      9x14           |MDA |EGA|VGA
16 Colour           08h     160x200 colour graphics        CGA|PCjr|
16 Colour           09h     320x200 colour graphics            |PCjr|   |    |   |VGA
4 Colour            0Ah     640x200 colour graphics            |PCjr|
N/A                 0Bh     BIOS font load                                   |EGA|VGA
N/A                 0Ch     BIOS font load                                   |EGA|VGA
16 Colour           0Dh     320x200 graphics 40x25     8x8                   |EGA|VGA
16 Colour           0Eh     640x200 graphics 80x25     8x8                   |EGA|VGA
monochrome          0Fh     640x350 graphics 80x25     8x14                  |EGA|VGA
16&64 Colour        10h     640x350 colour   80x25     8x14                  |EGA|VGA
2 Colour            11h     640x480 graphics                      |MCGA|    |   |VGA
                13h = 40x25 8x8 320x200 256/256k          A000 VGA,MCGA,ATI VIP
                14h = 80x25 8x8 640x200                   Lava Chrome II EGA
                    =       640x400   16                  Tecmar VGA/AD
16 Colour           12h     640x480 graphics           8x16  |    |   |    |   |VGA|
16&64 Colour                640x480   80x30            8x16  ATI EGA Wonder
256Colour           13h     320x200 graphics           8x8       |    |MCGA|   |VGA|8514
                    14h-20h used by EGA and VGA graphics modes
                    14h     640x200   80x25            8x8   Lava Chrome II EGA
                    15h     640x350   80x25            8x14  Lava Chrome II EGA
                    16h     640x350   80x25            8x14  Lava Chrome II EGA
```

16 Colour		800x600			Tecmar VGA/AD
	17h	640x480	80x34	8x14	Lava Chrome II EGA
		132x25			Tecmar VGA/AD
monochrome	18h	132x44		8x8	Tseng Labs EVA
		640x480	80x34	8x14	Lava Chrome II EGA
16 Colour		1024x768			Tecmar VGA/AD
monochrome	19h	132x25		8x14	Tseng Labs EVA
monochrome	1Ah	132x28		8x13	Tseng Labs EVA
256 Colour		640x350			Tecmar VGA/AD
256 Colour	1Bh	640x400			Tecmar VGA/AD
256 Colour	1Ch	640x480			Tecmar VGA/AD
256 Colour	1Dh	800x600			Tecmar VGA/AD
monochrome	21h	Hercules Graphics, Graphics Page 1			
monochrome	22h	Hercules Graphics, Graphics Page 2			
	22h	132x44		8x8	Tseng Labs EVA
		132x44		8x8	Ahead Systems EGA2001
		132x43			Allstar Peacock (VGA)
	23h	132x25		6x14	Tseng Labs EVA
		132x25		8x14	Ahead Systems EGA2001
16 Colour		132x25		8x8	ATI EGA Wonder/ ATI VIP
		132x28			Allstar Peacock (VGA)
	24h	132x28		6x13	Tseng Labs EVA
		132x25			Allstar Peacock (VGA)
	25h	640x480	80x60	8x8	Tseng Labs EVA
16 Colour		640x480	80x60		VEGA VGA
	26h		80x60	8x8	Tseng Labs EVA
		640x480	80x60	8x8	Ahead Systems EGA2001
			80x60		Allstar Peacock (VGA)
16 Colour	27h	720x512			VEGA VGA
monochrome			132x25	8x8	ATI EGA Wonder, ATI VIP
	28h	unknown			VEGA VGA
16 Colour	29h	800x600			VEGA VGA
16 Colour		800x600			Allstar Peacock (VGA)
	2Ah		100x40		Allstar Peacock (VGA)
256 Colour	2Dh	640x350			VEGA VGA
256 Colour	2Eh	640x480			VEGA VGA
256 Colour	2Fh	720x512			VEGA VGA
256 Colour	30h	800x600			VEGA VGA
		unknown			AT&T 6300
16 Colour		640x400	80x25	8x16	Logitech EGA
16 Colour	31h	1056x350	132x25	8x14	Logitech EGA
16 Colour	32h	640x400	80x25	8x16	Logitech EGA
16 Colour	33h	640x480	80x30	8x16	Logitech EGA
16 Colour			132x44	8x8	ATI EGA Wonder/ATI VIP
monochrome	34h	720x348	90x25	8x14	Logitech EGA
16 Colour	35h	720x350	90x25	8x16	Logitech EGA
16 Colour	36h	960x720			VEGA VGA
16 Colour	37h	1024x768			VEGA VGA
monochrome			132x44	8x8	ATI EGA Wonder/ATI VIP
2 Colour	40h	640x400	80x25	8x16	Compaq Portable II
2 Colour		640x400	80x25	8x16	AT&T 6300, AT&T VDC600
			80x43		VEGA VGA, Tecmar VGA/AD
			80x43		Video7 V-RAM VGA
			80x43		Tatung VGA
16 Colour	41h	640x200			AT&T 6300
			132x25		VEGA VGA
			132x25		Tatung VGA
			132x25		Video7 V-RAM VGA
16 Colour	42h	640x400	80x25	8x16	AT&T 6300, AT&T VDC600
			132x43		VEGA VGA
16 Colour		640x400	80x25	8x16	Logitech EGA
			132x43		Tatung VGA
			132x43		Video7 V-RAM VGA
	43h	unsupported 640x200 of 640x400 viewport			AT&T 6300
			80x60		VEGA VGA
16 Colour		640x400	80x25	8x16	Logitech EGA
			80x60		Tatung VGA
			80x60		Video7 V-RAM VGA
	44h	disable VDC and DEB output			AT&T 6300
		100x60			VEGA VGA
4 Colour		320x200	40x25	8x16	Logitech EGA

Video Subsystems and Programming

Colours	Mode	Resolution	Text	Font	Card
			100x60		Tatung VGA
			100x60		Video7 V-RAM VGA
4 Colour	45h	320x200	40x25	8x16	Logitech EGA
			132x28		Tatung VGA
			132x28		Video7 V-RAM VGA
2 Colour	46h	640x400	80x25	8x16	Logitech EGA
2 Colour		800x600	100x40	8x15	AT&T VDC600
16 Colour	47h	800x600	100x37	8x16	AT&T VDC600
2 Colour	48h	640x400	80x50	8x8	AT&T 6300, AT&T VDC600
	49h	640x480	80x30	8x16	Lava Chrome II EGA
	4Dh		120x25		VEGA VGA
	4Eh		120x43		VEGA VGA
	4Fh		132x25		VEGA VGA
monochrome	50h		132x25	9x14	Ahead Systems EGA2001
16 Colour		640x480		8x16	Paradise EGA-480
monochr.			80x43		VEGA VGA
monochr.?		640x480			Taxan 565 EGA
			80x34		Lava Chrome II EGA
	51h		80x30	8x16	Paradise EGA-480
monochrome			132x25		VEGA VGA
16 Colour		640x480	80x34	8x14	ATI EGA Wonder
			80x30		Lava Chrome II EGA
monochrome	52h		132x44	9x8	Ahead Systems EGA2001
monochrome			132x43		VEGA VGA
16 Colour		752x410	94x29	8x14	ATI EGA Wonder
			80x60		Lava Chrome II EGA
16 Colour	53h	800x560	100x40	8x14	ATI EGA Wonder/ATI VIP
			132x43		Lava Chrome II EGA
	54h		132x43	8x8	Paradise EGA-480
16 Colour			132x43	7x9	Paradise VGA 256k
16 Colour			132x43	8x9	Paradise VGA on multisync
			132x43		Taxan 565 EGA
16 Colour		800x600	100x42	8x14	ATI EGA Wonder
			132x25		Lava Chrome II EGA
			132x43		AST VGA Plus
			132x43		Hewlett-Packard D1180A
16 Colour			132x43	7x9	AT&T VDC600
	55h		132x25	8x14	Paradise EGA-480
16 Colour			132x25	7x16	Paradise VGA 256k
16 Colour			132x25	8x16	Paradise VGA on multisync
			132x25		Taxan 565 EGA
			132x25		AST VGA Plus
			132x25		Hewlett-Packard D1180A
16 Colour			132x25	7x16	AT&T VDC600
16 Colour			80x66	8x8	ATI VIP 256k
		752x410	94x29	8x14	Lava Chrome II EGA
2 Colour	56h		132x43	8x8	NSI Smart EGA+
4 Colour			132x43	7x9	Paradise VGA
4 Colour			132x43	8x9	Paradise VGA on multisync
monochrome			132x43		Taxan 565 EGA
2 Colour			132x43	7x9	AT&T VDC600
4 Colour	57h		132x25	8x14	NSI Smart EGA+
4 Colour			132x25	7x16	Paradise VGA
4 Colour			132x25	8x16	Paradise VGA on multisync
monochrome			132x25		Taxan 565 EGA
2 Colour			132x25	7x16	AT&T VDC600
16 Colour	58h	800x600	100x75		Paradise VGA 256k
16 Colour			80x33	8x14	ATI EGA Wonder/ATI VIP
16 Colour		800x600	100x75	8x8	AT&T VDC600
16 Colour		800x600			AST VGA Plus
16 Colour		800x600			Hewlett-Packard D1180A
	59h	800x600	100x75		Paradise VGA
2 Colour		800x600	100x75	8x8	AT&T VDC600
2 Colour		800x600		8x8	AST VGA Plus
2 Colour		800x600		8x8	Hewlett-Packard D1180A
16 Colour			80x66	8x8	ATI VIP 256k
256 Colour	5Eh	640x400			Paradise VGA, VEGA VGA
256 Colour		640x400			AST VGA Plus
256 Colour		640x400	80x25	8x16	AT&T VDC600
256 Colour	5Fh	640x480			Paradise VGA
256 Colour		640x480			AST VGA Plus

```
256 Colour            640x480                          Hewlett-Packard D1180A
256 Colour            640x480      80x30        8x16   AT&T VDC600 (512K)
              60h     ?x400        80x?                Corona/Cordata BIOS
                                                       v4.10+
                      752x410                          VEGA VGA
              60h     400 line graphics+80col text     Corona/Cordata BIOS
                                                       v4.10+
                      752x410                          VEGA VGA
 16 Colour            752x410                          Tatung VGA
 16 Colour            752x410                          Video7 V-RAM VGA
              61h     400 line graphics                Corona/Cordata BIOS
                                                       v4.10+
                      720x540                          VEGA VGA
 16 Colour            720x540                          Tatung VGA
 16 Colour            720x540                          Video7 V-RAM VGA
              62h     800x600                          VEGA VGA
 16 Colour            800x600                          Tatung VGA
 16 Colour            800x600                          Video7 V-RAM VGA
  2 Colour    63h     1024x768                         Video7 V-RAM VGA
  4 Colour    64h     1024x768                          Video7 V-RAM VGA
 16 Colour    65h     1024x768                         Video7 V-RAM VGA
256 Colour    66h     640x400                          Tatung VGA
256 Colour            640x400                          Video7 V-RAM VGA
256 Colour    67h     640x480                          Video7 V-RAM VGA
256 Colour    69h     720x540                          Video7 V-RAM VGA
              70h     extended mode set                Everex Micro Enhancer EGA
                  AX      0070h
                  BL      mode (graphics mode if graphics res. listed)
                          00h              640x480 multisync
                          01h              752x410 multisync
                          02h      reserved
                          03h      80x34         multisync
                          04h      80x60         multisync
                          05h      94x29         multisync
                          06h      94x51         multisync
                          07h      reserved
                          08h      reserved
                          09h      80x44         EGA
                          0Ah      132x25        EGA
                          0Bh      132x44        EGA
                          0Ch      132x25        CGA
                          0Dh      80x44         TTL mono
                          0Eh      132x25        TTL mono
                          0Fh      132x44        TTL mono
 16 Colour    71h     800x600      100x35       8x16   NSI Smart EGA+
  2 Colour    74h     640x400                          Toshiba 3100
              7Eh     Special Mode Set                 Paradise VGA, AT&T VDC600
                  BX      horizontal dimension of the mode desired
                  CX      vertical dimension of the mode desired
                          (both BX/CX in pixels for graphics modes, rows
                          for text modes)
                  DX      number of colours of the mode desired
                          (use 00h for monochrome modes)
                  return AL   7Eh      if successful (AT&T VDC600)
                         BH   7Eh      if successful (Paradise VGA)
              7Fh     Special Function Set       | Paradise VGA, AT&T VDC600
                  BH      00h    Set VGA Operation
                          01h    Set Non-VGA Operation
                          02h    Query Mode Status
                  return BL   00h     if operating in VGA mode
                              01h     if non-VGA mode.
                          CH     total video RAM size in 64k byte units
                          CL     video RAM used by the current mode
                          03h    Lock Current Mode
                                 Allows current mode (VGA or non-VGA) to
                                 survive reboot.
                          04h    Enter CGA Mode (AT&T VDC600 only)
                          05h    Enter MDA Mode (AT&T VDC600 only)
                  BH      0Ah,0Bh,0Ch,0Dh,0Eh,0Fh
                          write Paradise registers 0,1,2,3,4,5
                          (port 03CEh indices A,B,C,D,E,F)
```

```
                BL      value to set in the Paradise register.
                BH      1Ah,1Bh,1Ch,1Dh,1Eh,1Fh
                        read Paradise registers 0,1,2,3,4,5
                        (port 03CEh indices A,B,C,D,E,F)
                return AL      7Fh      if successful (AT&T VDC600)
                       BH      7Fh      if successful (Paradise VGA)
                       BL              value of the Paradise register
                note    colour modes (0,1,2,3,4,5,6) will set non-VGA CGA
                        operation. Monochrome mode 7 will set non-VGA
                        MDA/Hercules operation.
        82h     80x25 B&W                        AT&T VDC overlay mode *
        83h     80x25                            AT&T VDC overlay mode *
        86h     640x200 B&W                      AT&T VDC overlay mode *
        0C0h    640x400    2/prog palette        AT&T VDC overlay mode *
        0C4h    disable output                   AT&T VDC overlay mode *
        0D0h    640x400                          DEC VAXmate AT&T mode
```
note 1. If the high bit in AL is set, the display buffer is not cleared when a new mode is selected. This may be used to mix modes on the display; for example, characters of two difference sizes might be displayed
  2. Modes 8-10 are available on the PCjr, Tandy 1000, and PS/2
  3. IBM claims 100% software and hardware emulation of the CGA with the MCGA chipset. All registers may be read and written as CGA. All charactersare double-scanned to give 80x25 with 400 line resolution. The attributes for setting border colour may be set on MCGA, but the borders will remain the default colour (they cannot actually be set)
  4. The IBM Colour Graphics Adapter (CGA) is too slow for the screen to be updated before the vertical retrace of the monitor is completed. If the video RAM is addressed directly, the screen will have 'snow' or interference. IBM's default is to turn the adapter off when it is being updated, ie 'flickering' when the display is scrolled.
  5. The vertical retrace signal may be ignored when using the MCGA adapter. The MCGA will not generate snow when written to. There is no flicker with the MCGA.
  6. The PCjr Video Gate Array uses a user-defined block of main system RAM from 4 to 32k in size instead of having dedicated memory for the display. Vertical retrace may be ignored when writing to the PCjr. There is no flicker with the PCjr display.
  7. The Hercules Graphics Card has 750x348 resolution
  8. The Hercules Graphics Card takes 64k beginning at B:000 (same as MDA)
  9. The CGA, MCGA, and VGA adapters use hardware address B:800
 10. The BIOS clears the screen when the mode is set or reset.
 11. For AT&T VDC overlay modes, BL contains the DEB mode, which may be 06h, 40h, or 44h
 12. Int 10 will take the shapes of the first 128 characters (00h-7Fh) from the table located in ROM at absolute address F000:FA6E. The EGA and VGA have hardware capability to change this.
 13. The presence or absence of colour burst is only significant when a compo site monitor is being used. For RGB monitors, there is no functional difference between modes 00h and 01h or modes 02h and 03h.
 14. On the CGA, two palettes are available in mode 04h and one in mode 05h.
 15. The Corona built-in hi-res mono adapter similar to the Hercules but not identical. The Corona graphics memory address is not fixed; instead one of the control registers must be loaded with the buffer address. This makes it impossible to run most commercial graphics software, unless there is specifically a Corona option. The design was actually quite impressive - you could do hi-speed animation by switching buffers (similar to switching pages on other configurations) but you could use as many as you could fit in available memory, at 32k per page. In addition, the mono text buffer is always available, and independent of graphics, making it easy to overlay text and graphics on the same screen. Unfortunately the Corona never really took off, and no one else picked up on the design.

```
Function 01h    Set Cursor Type - set the size of the cursor or turn it off
  entry   AH      01h
          CH      bit values:
            bits 0-4        top line for cursor in character cell
                 5-6        blink attribute
                            0,0     normal
                            0,1     invisible (no cursor)
                            1,0     slow      (not used on original IBM PC)
```

```
                       1,1       fast      (may be erratic on Tandy 1000TX)
              CL      bit values:
              bits 0-4      bottom line for cursor in character cell
   return  none
   note 1. The ROM BIOS default cursors are:   start    end
                          monochrome mode 07h:    11      12
                          text modes 00h-03h:      6       7
        2. The blinking in text mode is caused by hardware and cannot be turned off,
           though some kludges can temporarily fake a nonblinking cursor.
        3. The cursor is automatically turned off in graphics mode.
        4. The cursor can be turned off in several ways. On the MDA, CGA, and VGA,
           setting register CH = 20h causes the cursor to disappear. Techniques
           that involve setting illegal starting and ending lines for the current
           display mode tend to be unreliable. Another method of turning off the
           cursor in text mode is to position it to a non-displayable address, such
           as (X,Y)=(0,25).
        5. For the EGA, MCGA, and VGA in text modes 00h-03h, the BIOS accepts cursor
           start and end values as though the character cell were 8x8, and remaps
           the values as appropriate for the true character cell dimensions. This
           mapping is called cursor emulation. One problems is that the BIOS remaps
           BIOS cursor shape in 43 line modes, but returns the unmapped cursor shape.

   Function 02h    Set Cursor Position - reposition the cursor to (X,Y)
   entry    AH     02h
            BH     video page
                   00h       graphics mode
                   03h       modes 2 and 3
                   07h       modes 0 and 1
            DH     row       (Y=0-24)
            DL     column    (X=0-79 or 0-39)
   return   none
   note 1. (0,0) is upper left corner of the screen
        2. A separate cursor is maintained for each display page, and each can be
           set independently with this function regardless of the currently active
           page.
        3. The maximum value for each text coordinate depends on the video adapter
           and current display mode, as follows:
           19,24    08h
           39,24    00h, 01h, 04h, 05h, 09h, 0Dh, 13h
           79,26    02h, 03h, 06h, 07h, 0Ah, 0Eh, 0Fh, 10h,
           79,29    11h, 12h

   Function 03h    Read Cursor Position - return the position of the cursor
   entry    AH     03h
            BH     page number
                   00h       in graphics modes
                   03h       in modes 2 & 3
                   07h       in modes 0 & 1
   return   CH     top line for cursor      (bits 4-0)
            CL     bottom line for cursor   (bits 4-0)
            DH     row number       (Y=0-24)
            DL     column number    (X=0-79 or 0-39)
   note     A separate cursor is maintained for each display page, and each can be
            checked independently with this function regardless of the currently
            active page.

   Function 04h    Read Light Pen - fetch light pen information      (CGA, Jr, EGA)
   entry    AH     04h
   return   AH     00h    light pen not triggered
            AH     01h    light pen is triggered, values in registers
            BX     pixel column                (X=0-319,639)    graphics mode
            CH     raster line                 (Y=0-199)        old graphics modes
            CX     (EGA) raster line (0-nnn)                    new graphics modes
            DH     row of current position     (Y=0-24)         text mode
            DL     column of current position  (X=0-79 or 0-39) text mode
   note 1. Not supported on PS/2.
        2. The range of coordinates returned by this function depends on the current
           display mode.
        3. On the CGA, the graphics coordinates returned by this function are not
           continuous. The y coordinate is always a multiple of two; the x
           coordinate is either a multiple of four (for 320-by-200 graphics modes)
```

Video Subsystems and Programming

or a multiple of eight (for 640-by-200 graphics modes).
4. Careful selection of background and foreground colours is necessary to obtain maximum sensitivity from the light pen across the full screen width.

```
Function 05h    Select Active Page - set page number for services 6 and 7
entry   AH      05h
        AL      number of new active page
                0-7     modes 00h and 01h (CGA)
                0-3     modes 02h and 03h (CGA)
                0-7     modes 02h and 03h (EGA)
                0-7     mode 0Dh (EGA)
                0-3     mode 0Eh (EGA)
                0-1     mode 0Fh (EGA)
                0-1     mode 10h (EGA)
                0       set address of graphics bitmap buffer (modes 60h,61h)
                        BX      segment of buffer
                0Fh     get address of graphics bitmap buffer (modes 60h,61h)
                        BX      segment of buffer
for PCjr, most Tandy 1000s only:
        AL      80h     to read CRT/CPU page registers
                81h     to set CPU page register to value in BL
                82h     to set CRT page register to value in BH
                83h     to set both CPU and page registers
                        (and Corona/Cordata BIOS v4.10+)
Corona/Cordata BIOS v4.10+
                00h     set address of graphics bitmap buffer (video modes
                        60h,61h)
                        BX      segment of buffer
                0Fh     get address of graphics bitmap buffer (video modes
                        60h,61h)
        BH      CRT page number for subfunctions 82h and 83h
        BL      CPU page register for subfunctions 81h and 83h
return  standard PC     none
        PCjr    if called with AH bit 7=1 then
                BH      CRT page register (if AL = 80h)
                BL      CPU page register (if AL = 80h)
        DX      segment of graphics bitmap buffer (video modes 60h,61h; AL=0Fh)
note 1. Mono adapter has only one display page
     2. CGA has four 80x25 text pages or eight 40x25 text pages
     3. A separate cursor is maintained for each display page
     4. Switching between pages does not affect their contents
     5. Higher page numbers indicate higher memory positions

Function 06h    Scroll Page Up - scroll up or initialize a display 'window'
entry   AH      06h
        AL      number of lines blanked at bottom of page
                00h     blank entire window
        BH      attributes to be used on blank line
        CH      row     (Y) of upper left corner or window
        CL      column  (X) of upper left corner of window
        DH      row     (Y) of lower right corner of window
        DL      column  (X) of lower right corner of window
return  none
note 1. Push BP before scrolling, pop after
     2. Affects current video page only

Function 07h    Scroll Page Down - scroll down or clear a display 'window'
entry   AH      07h
        AL      number of lines to be blanked at top of page
                00h     blank entire window
        BH      attributes to be used on blank line
        CH      row     (Y) of upper left corner or window
        CL      column  (X) of upper left corner of window
        DH      row     (Y) of lower right corner of window
        DL      column  (X) of lower right corner of window
return  none
note 1. Push BP before scrolling, pop after
     2. Affects current video page only
```

```
Function 08h Read Character Attribute-of character at current cursor pos.
entry    AH    08h
         BH    display page number - text mode
return   AH    character attribute - text mode
         AL    ASCII code of character at current cursor position
note     In video modes that support multiple pages, characters and their
         attributes can be read from any page, regardless of the page currently
         being displayed.

Function 09h    Write Character and Attribute - at current cursor position
entry    AH    09h
         AL    ASCII code of character to display
         BH    display page number - text mode
         BL    attribute (text modes) or colour (graphics modes)
         CX    number of characters to write
return   none
note 1.  CX should not exceed actual rows available, or results may be erratic.
     2.  Setting CX to zero will cause runaway.
     3.  All values of AL result in some sort of display; the various control
         characters are not recognized as special and do not change the current
         cursor position.
     4.  Does not change cursor position when called - the cursor must be advanced
         with int 10 function 0Ah.
     5.  If used to write characters in graphics mode with bit 7 of AH set to 1
         the character will by XORed with the current display contents. This
         feature can be used to write characters and then 'erase' them.
     6.  In graphics mode the bit patterns for ASCII character codes 80h-0FFh are
         obtained from a table. On the standard PC and AT, the location is at
         interrupt vector 01Fh (0000:007Ch). For ASCII characters 00h-07Fh, the
         table is at an address in ROM. On the PCjr the table is at interrupt
         vector 44h (0000:00110h) and is in addressable RAM (may be replaced by
         the user).
     7.  All characters are displayed, including CR, LF, and BS.
     8.  In graphics modes, the dup factor in CX produces a valid result only for
         the current row. If more characters are written than there are remaining
         columns in the current row, the result is unpredictable.
     9.  For the EGA, MCGA, and VGA in graphics modes, the address of the
         character definition table is stored in the vector for int 43h.

Function 0Ah Write Character-display character(s) (use current attribute)
             at current cursor position
entry    AH    0Ah
         AL    ASCII code of character to display
         BH    display page - text mode
         BL    colour of character (graphics mode, PCjr only)
         CX    number of times to write character
return   none
note 1.  CX should not exceed actual rows available, or results may be erratic.
     2.  All values of AL result in some sort of display; the various control
         characters are not recognized as special and do not change the current
         cursor position.
     3.  If used to write characters in graphics mode with bit 7 of BL set to 1
         the character will by XORed with the current display contents. This
         feature can be used to write characters and then 'erase' them.
     4.  In graphics mode the bit patterns for ASCII character codes 80h-0FFh are
         obtained from a table. On the standard PC and AT, the location is at
         interrupt vector 01Fh (0000:007C). For ASCII characters 00h-07Fh, the
         table is at an address in ROM. On the PCjr the table is at interrupt
         vector 44h (0000:00110) and is in addressable RAM (may be replaced by
         the user).
     5.  In graphics modes, replication count in CX works correctly only if all
         characters written are contained on the same row.
     6.  All characters are displayed, including CR, LF, and BS.
     7.  For EGA, MCGA, and VGA in graphics modes, the address of the character
         definition table is stored in the vector for int 43h.
     8.  After a character is written, the cursor must be moved explicitly with Fn
         02h to the next position.

Function 0Bh    Set Colour Palette - set palette for graphics or text border
                Selects a palette, background, or border colour.
entry    AH    0Bh
```

Video Subsystems and Programming 323

```
            BH        00h       select border (text mode)
                      BL        colour 0-15, 16-31 for high-intensity characters
            BH        01h       set graphics palette with value in BL
               (CGA)  BL        0         green/red/yellow
                                1         cyan/magenta/white
    (EGA) (graphics modes)
            BH        0
            BL        has border colour (0-15) & high intensity bkgr'd colour (16-31)
            BH        1
            BL        contains palette being selected (0-1)
return      none
note 1. Valid in CGA mode 04h, PCjr modes 06h, 08h-0Ah.
     2. Although the registers in the MCGA may be set as if to change the border,
        the MCGA will not display a border no matter what register settings are
        used.
     3. In text modes, this function selects only the border colour. The
        background colour of each individual character is controlled by the
        upper 4 bits of that character's attribute byte.
     4. On the CGA and EGA, this function is valid for palette selection only in
        320-by-200 4-colour graphics modes.
     5. In 320-by-200 4-colour graphics modes, if BH=01h, the following palettes
        may be selected:
           Palette   Pixel value      Colour
              0          0            same as background
                         1            green
                         2            red
                         3            brown or yellow
              1          0            same as background
                         1            cyan
                         2            magenta
                         3            white
     6. On the CGA in 640-by-200 2-colour graphics mode, the background colour
        selected with this function actually controls the display colour for non
        zero pixels; zero pixels are always displayed as black.
     7. On the PCjr in 640-by-200 2-colour graphics mode, if BH=00h and bit 0 of
        BL is cleared, pixel value 1 is displayed as white; if bit 0 is set,
        pixel value 1 is displayed as black.

Function 0Ch     Write Dot - plot one graphics pixel
entry    AH      0Ch
         AL      dot colour code    (0/1 in mode 6, 0-3 in modes 4 and 5)
                 (set bit 7 to XOR the dot with current colour)
                 0-3 mode 04h, 05h
                 0-1 mode 06h
         BH      page number (ignored if adapter supports only one page)
         CX      column (X=0000h - 027Fh)
                 (0 - 319 in modes 4,5,13,  0 - 639 in modes 6,14,15,16)
         DX      row    (Y=0000h - 00C7h) (0 - 199 CGA)
return   none
note 1. Video graphics modes 4-6 only.
     2. The range of valid pixel values and (x,y) coordinates depends on the
        current video mode.
     3. If bit 7 of AL is set, the new pixel value will be XORed with the current
        contents of the pixel.

Function 0Dh     Read Dot - determine the colour of one graphics pixel
entry    AH      0Dh
         BH      page
         CX      column (X=0000h - 027Fh)  (0-319 or 639)
         DX      row    (Y=0000h - 00C7h)  (0-199)
return   AL      colour of dot
note 1. Only valid in graphics modes.
     2. The range of valid (x,y) coordinates and possible pixel values depends on
        the current video mode.
     3. Register BH is ignored for display modes that support only one page.

Function 0Eh     Write TTY-write one character and update cursor. Also handles
                 CR (0Dh), beep (07h), backspace (10h), and scrolling
entry    AH      0Eh
         AL      ASCII code of character to be written
         BH      page number (text)
```

```
           BL         foreground colour (video modes 6 & 7 only) (graphics)
return     none
note   1.  The ASCII codes for bell, backspace, carriage return, and line-feed are
           recognized and appropriate action taken. All other characters are
           written to the screen and the cursor is advanced to the next position.
       2.  Text can be written to any page regardless of current active page.
       3.  Automatic linewrap and scrolling are provided through this function.
       4.  This is the function used by the DOS CON console driver.
       5.  This function does not explicitly allow the use of attributes to the
           characters written. Attributes may be provided by first writing an ASCII
           27h (blank) with the desired attributes using function 09h, then over
           writing with the actual character using this function. While clumsy
           this allows use of the linewrap and scrolling services provided by this
           function.
       6.  The default DOS console driver (CON) uses this function to write text to
           the screen.

Function 0Fh       Return Current Video State - mode and size of the screen
                   Obtains the current display mode of the active video controller.
entry      AH      0Fh
return     AH      number of character columns on screen
           AL      mode currently set (see AH=00h for display mode codes)
           BH      current active display page
note   1.  If mode was set with bit 7 set ("no blanking"), the returned mode will
           also have bit 7 set.
       2.  This function can be called to obtain the screen width before clearing
           the screen with Fns 06h or 07h.

Function 10h       Set Palette Registers              (PCjr, Tandy 1000, EGA, MCGA, VGA)
entry      AH      10h
           AL      00h     Set Individual Palette Register
                           BH      colour value to store
                           BL      palette register to set
                                   (on MCGA, only BX = 0712h is supported)
                           return  none
                           note    On the MCGA, this function can only be called
                                   with BX=0712h and selects a colour register set
                                   with eight consistent colours.

                   01h     Set Border Colour    (overscan)              (Jr, EGA, VGA)
                           BH      colour value to store
                           return  none

                   02h     Set All Palette Registers and Border
                           ES:DX   pointer to 17-byte colour list
                                   bytes 0-15   values for palette regs. 0-15
                                   byte 16      value for border colour
                                                register
                           return  none
                           note    In 16-colour graphics modes, the following default
                                   palette is set up:
                               Pixel value     Colour
                                   01h         blue
                                   02h         green
                                   03h         cyan
                                   04h         red
                                   05h         magenta
                                   06h         brown
                                   07h         white
                                   08h         grey
                                   09h         light blue
                                   0Ah         light green
                                   0Bh         light cyan
                                   0Ch         light red
                                   0Dh         light magenta
                                   0Eh         yellow
                                   0Fh         intense white

                   03h     Toggle Blink/Intensity Bit            (Jr & later exc Conv.)
                           BL      00h     enable intensity
                                   01h     enable blink
```

Video Subsystems and Programming

```
           return   none

    04h    unknown

    05h    unknown

    06h    unknown

    07h    Get Palette Register Value                          (VGA)
           BL       palette register number
    return BH       palette register colour value

    08h    Get Border Colour   (overscan)                      (VGA)
    return BH       colour value

    09h    Read All Palette Registers and Overscan Register    (VGA)
           ES:DX    pointer to buffer address (17 bytes)
    return ES:DX    buffer contains palette values in bytes
                    00h-0Fh and border colour in byte 10h.

    10h    Set Individual Video DAC Colour Register       (MCGA, VGA)
           BX       register number
           CH       new value for green  (0-63)
           CL       new value for blue   (0-63)
           DH       new value for red    (0-63)
    return none
           note     If greyscale summing is enabled, the weighted
                    greyscale value for each register is calculated
                    as described under Subfn 1Bh and is stored into
                    all three components of the colour register.

    11h    unknown

    12h    Set Block of Video DAC Colour Registers        (MCGA, VGA)
           BX       starting colour register
           CX       number of registers to set
           ES:DX    pointer to a table of 3*CX bytes where each
                    3-byte group represents one byte each of red,
                    green and blue (0-63) in that order.
           return   none
           note     If greyscale summing is enabled, the weighted
                    greyscale value for each register is calculated
                    as described under Subfn 1Bh and is stored into
                    all three components of the colour register.

    13h    Set Video DAC Colour Page                           (VGA)
           BL       00h      select paging mode
                    BH       00h      select 4 pages of 64 registers
                             01h      select 16 pages of 16 registers
                    01h      select register page
                    BH       page number (00h to 03h or 00h to 0Fh)
           return   none
           note     This function not valid in mode 13h (320-by-200
                    256-colour graphics).

    14h    unknown

    15h    Read Individual Video DAC Colour Register      (MCGA, VGA)
           BX       palette register number
    return CH       green value
           CL       blue value
           DH       red value

    16h    unknown

    17h    Read Block of Video DAC Colour Registers       (MCGA, VGA)
           BX       starting palette register
           CX       number of palette registers to read
           ES:DX    pointer for palette register list (3 * CX bytes
                    in size)
    return CX       number of red, green and blue triples in buffer
```

```
                    ES:DX     address of buffer with colour list
          note      The colour list returned in the caller's buffer consists
                    of a series of 3-byte entries corresponding to the
                    colour registers. Each 3-byte entry contains the
                    register's red, green, and blue components in that order.

          18h       Set Pixel Mask (undocumented)
                    BL        new pixel value

          19h       Read Pixel Mask (undocumented)
                    BL        value read

          1Ah       Read Video DAC Colour-Page State              (VGA)
          return    BH        current page
                    BL        paging mode
                              00h       four pages of 64 registers
                              01h       sixteen pages of 16 registers

          1Bh       Perform Greyscale Summing                  (MCGA, VGA)
                    BX        starting palette register
                    CX        number of registers to convert
          return    none
          note 1.   For each colour register, the weighted sum of its red,
                    green, and blue values is calculated (30 red + 59 green
                    + 11 blue) and written back into all three components of
                    the colour register.
               2.   The original red, green, and blue values are lost.

     BH             colour value
     BL             if AL=00h      palette register to set (00h-0Fh)
                    if AL=03h      00h       to enable intensity
                                   01h       to enable blinking
     ES:DX          if AL=02h      pointer to 16-byte table of register values
                                   followed by the overscan value:
                              bytes 0-15     values for palette registers 0-15
                              byte 16        value for border register
return    none
note      DAC is Digital to Analog Convertor circuit in MCGA/VGA chips.

Function 11h       Character Generator Routine (EGA and after)
entry     AH       11h
                   The following functions will cause a mode set, completely
                   resetting the video environment, but without clearing the video
                   buffer.
          AL       00h, 10h  Load User-Specified Patterns or Fonts   (EGA, MCGA, VGA)
                             BH        number of bytes per character pattern
                             BL        block to load in map 2
                             CX        count of patterns to store
                             DX        character offset into map 2 block (1st code)
                             ES:BP     pointer to user font table
                    return   none
                    note 1.  If AL=10h, page 0 must be active. The bytes per
                             character, rows, and length of the refresh buffer are
                             recalculated.
                         2.  The controller is reprogrammed with the maximum scan line
                             (points-1), cursor start (points-2), cursor end (points-
                             1), vertical display end ((rows*points)-1), and
                             underline locations (points-1, mode 7 only).
                         3.  If subfn 10h is called at any time other than immediately
                             after a mode set, the results are unpredictable.
                         4.  On the MCGA, a subfn 00h call should be followed by a
                             subfn 03h call so that the BIOS will load the font into
                             the character generator's internal font pages.
                         5.  Subfn 10h is reserved on the MCGA. If it is called, subfn
                             00h is performed.
                         6.  Text modes only.

                   01h, 11h  Load ROM 8 by 14 Character Set         (EGA, VGA)
                             BL        block to load
                    return   none
                    note 1.  Text modes only.
```

Video Subsystems and Programming

```
             2. For AL=11h, page 0 must be active. The points (bytes per
                character), rows, and length of the refresh buffer are
                recalculated.
             3. The controller is reprogrammed with the maximum scan line
                (points-1), cursor start (points-2), cursor end (points-
                1), vertical display end ((rows*points)-1), and
                underline location (points-1, mode 7 only).
             4. If subfn 11h is called at any time other than right after
                a mode set, the results are unpredictable.
             5. Subfns 01h and 11h are reserved on the MCGA. If either is
                called, subfn 04h is performed instead.

02h, 12h        Load ROM 8x8 Double-Dot Patterns         (EGA, MCGA, VGA)
                BL      block to load
     return     none
     note    1. Text modes only.
             2. If AL=12h, page 0 must be active. The points (bytes per
                character), rows, and length of the refresh buffer are
                recalculated.
             3. The controller is reprogrammed with the maximum scan line
                (points-1), cursor start (points-2), cursor end (points-
                1), vertical display end ((rows*points)-1), and underline
                location (points-1, mode 7 only).
             4. If subfn 12h is called at any time other than right after
                a mode set, the results are unpredictable.
             5. For the MCGA, a subfn 02h call should be followed by a
                subfn 03h call so the BIOS will load the font into the
                character generator's internal font pages.
             6. Subfn 12h is reserved on the MCGA. If it is called, subfn
                02h is executed.

    03h         Set Block Specifier                      (EGA, MCGA, VGA)
                BL      block specifier select mode
(EGA/MCGA) bits 0-1     char block selected by attr bytes with bit 3=0
                2-3     char block selected by attr bytes with bit 3=1
                4-7     not used (should be 0)
    (VGA) bits 0,1,4    char block selected by attr bytes with bit 3=0
                2,3,5   char block selected by attr bytes with bit 3=1
                6-7     not used (should be 0)
     return     none
     note    1. Determines the char blocks selected by bit 3 of char
                attribute bytes in text display modes.
             2. When using a 256 character set, both fields of BL should
                select the same character block. In such cases,
                character attribute bit 3 controls the foreground
                intensity. When using 512-character sets, the fields of
                BL designate the blocks holding each half of the
                character set, and bit 3 of the character attribute
                selects the upper or lower half of the character set.
             3. When using a 512-char set, a call to int 10h/fn10h/ subfn
                00h with BX=0712h is recommended to set the colour
                planes to eight consistent colours.

04h,14h         Load ROM 8x16 Text Character Set              (MCGA,VGA)
                BL      block
     return     none
     note    1. For text modes.
             2. If AL=14h, page 0 must be active. The points (bytes per
                char), rows, and refresh buffer length are recalculated
             3. The controller is reprogrammed with the maximum scan line
                (points-1), cursor start (points-2), cursor end (points-
                1), vertical display end (rows*points -1 for 350 and 400
                line modes, or rows*points*2 -1 for 200 line modes), and
                underline location (points -1, mode 7 only).
             4. If subfn 14h is called any time other than just after a
                mode set, the results are unpredictable.
             5. For MCGA, a subfn 04h call should be followed by a subfn
                03h call so that the BIOS will load the font into the
                character generator's internal font pages.
             6. Subfn 14h is reserved on the MCGA. If it is called, subfn
                04h is executed.
```

```
20h         Set User 8x8 Graphics Chars      (int 1Fh)(EGA, MCGA, VGA)
            ES:BP    pointer to user font table
return      none
note 1.     This table is used for chars 80h-0FFh in graphics modes
            04h-06h.
     2.     If this subfn is called at any time other than just after
            a mode set, the results are unpredictable.

21h         Set int 43h for User Graphics Chars     (EGA, MCGA, VGA)
            BL       character rows specifier
                     00H      if user specified (see register DL)
                     01h      14 (0Eh) rows
                     02h      25 (19h) rows
                     03h      43 (2Bh) rows
            CX       bytes per character (points)
            DL       character rows per screen if BL=00h
            ES:BP    pointer to user table
return      none
note 1.     The video controller is not reprogrammed.
     2.     This function works for graphics modes.
     3.     If this subfn is called at any time other than right
            after a mode set, the results are unpredictable.

22h         Set int 43h for ROM 8x14 Font           (EGA, MCGA, VGA)
            BL       character rows specifier
                     00h      if user specified (see register DL)
                     01h      14 (0Eh) rows
                     02h      25 (19h) rows
                     03h      43 (2Bh) rows
            DL       character rows per screen (if BL=00h)
return      none
note 1.     The video controller is not reprogrammed.
     2.     This function works for graphics modes.
     3.     If this subfn is called at any time other than right
            after a mode set, the results are unpredictable.
     4.     When this subfn is called on the MCGA, subfn 24h is
            substituted.

23h         Set int 43h for ROM 8x8 Double Dot Font (EGA, MCGA, VGA)
            BL       character row specifier
                     00h      if user specified (see register DL)
                     01h      14 (0Eh) rows
                     02h      25 (19h) rows
                     03h      43 (2Bh) rows
            DL       character rows per screen (BL=00h)
            return   none
            note 1.  Updates the video BIOS data area. The video
                     controller is not reprogrammed.
                 2.  Provides font selection in graphics modes.
                 3.  If called at any time other than immediately
                     after a mode set the results are unpredictable.

24h         Set int 43h for 8x16 Graphics Font           (MCGA, VGA)
            BL       character row specifier
                     00h      if user specified (see register DL)
                     01h      14 (0Eh) rows
                     02h      25 (19h) rows
                     03h      43 (2Bh) rows
            DL       character rows per screen (BL=00h)
            return   none
            note 1.  Updates the video BIOS data area. The video
                     controller is not reprogrammed.
                 2.  Provides font selection in graphics modes.
                 3.  If called at any time other than immediately
                     after a mode set the results are unpredictable.

30h         Get Font Information                    (EGA, MCGA, VGA)
            BH       pointer specifier
                     00h      current int 1Fh pointer
                     01h      current int 43h pointer
```

Video Subsystems and Programming

```
                          02h     ROM 8x14 char font ptr      (EGA, VGA only)
                          03h     ROM 8x8 double dot font pointer
                                  (characters 00h-7Fh)
                          04h     ROM 8x8 double dot font (top half)
                                  (characters 80h-0FFh)
                          05h     ROM text alternate (9x14) pointer
                                                              (EGA, VGA only)
                          06h     ROM 8x16 font              (MCGA, VGA only)
                          07h     ROM alternate 9x16 font        (VGA only)
              return  CX          points (bytes per character)
                      DL          rows (character rows on screen -1)
                      ES:BP       pointer to font table

Function 12h  Alternate Select (EGA and after)
entry    AH   12h
         BL   10h     Return Configuration Information          (EGA, VGA)
              return  BH    00h     if colour mode is in effect    (3Dx)
                            01h     if mono mode is in effect      (3Bx)
                      BL    00h     if 64k EGA memory installed
                            01h     if 128k EGA memory installed
                            02h     if 192k EGA memory installed
                            03h     if 256k EGA memory installed
                            10h     EGA adapter is installed (use to check)
                      CH            feature bits (see note 2)
                      CL            switch settings (see note 3)
              note 1. Obtains information for the active video subsystem.
                   2. The feature bits are set from Input Status register 0 in
                      response to an output on the specified Feature Control
                      register bits:
                            Feature    Feature Control  Input Status
                            Bit(s)     Output Bit       Bit
                            0          0                5
                            1          0                6
                            2          1                5
                            3          1                6
                            4-7        not used
                   3. The bits in the switch settings byte indicate the state
                      of the EGA's configuration DIP switch (1=off, 0=on).
                      bit 0       configuration switch 1
                          1       configuration switch 2
                          2       configuration switch 3
                          3       configuration switch 4
                          4-7     not used
              20h     Select Alternate Print Screen Routine     (EGA, VGA)
              return  none
              note    Selects PrtSc routine for screen modes using more than
                      the default BIOS 25 lines.

              30h     Select Vertical Resolution for Text Modes       (VGA)
                      AL    00h     200 scan lines
                            01h     350 scan lines
                            02h     400 scan lines
              return  AL    12h     if function supported
                            00h     VGA not active
              note    The selected value takes effect the next time int 10h/Fn
                      00h is called to select the display mode.

              31h     Enable/Disable Default Palette Loading    (MCGA, VGA)
                      AL    00h     enable default palette loading
                            01h     disable default palette loading
              return  AL    12h     if function was supported

              32h     Enable/Disable Video Addressing           (MCGA, VGA)
                      AL    00h     enable video access
                            01h     disable video access
              return  AL    12h     if function was supported
              note    Enables or disables CPU access to the video adapter's I/O
                      ports and video refresh buffer.

              33h     Enable/Disable Default Greyscale Summing  (MCGA, VGA)
                      AL    00h     enable greyscale summing
```

```
                                01h       disable greyscale summing
                    return  AL  12h       if function was supported
                    note 1. Works for the currently active display.
                         2. When enabled, greyscale summing occurs during display
                            mode selection, palette programming, and colour register
                            loading.

                    34h     Enable/Disable Text Cursor Emulation               (VGA)
                            AL   00h      enable cursor emulation
                                 01h      disable cursor emulation
                    return  AL   12h      if function was supported
                    note 1. Works for currently active display.
                         2. When cursor emulation is enabled the BIOS automatically
                            remaps int 10h/Fn 01h (Cursor Starting & Ending Lines)
                            for the current character cell dimensions.

                    35h     Switch Active Display      (PS/2)          (MCGA, VGA)
                            AL   00h      disable initial video adapter
                                 01h      enable motherboard video adapter
                                 02h      disable active video adapter
                                 03h      enable active video adapter
                                 80h      *undocumented* set system board video
                                          active flag
                            ES:DX  128 byte save area buffer if AL=00h, 02h or 03h
                    return  AL   12h      if function was supported
                    note 1. Allows selection of one of two video adapters in the
                            system when memory or port addresses conflict.
                         2. This subfn cannot be used unless both video adapters have
                            a disable capability (int 10h/Fn12h subfn 32h).
                         3. If there is no conflict between the system board video
                            and the adapter board video in memory or port usage,
                            both video controllers can be active simultaneously.

                    36h     Enable/Disable Video Refresh                       (VGA)
                            AL   00h      enable refresh
                                 01h      disable refresh
                    return  AL   12h      if function supported
                    note    Enables or disables the video refresh for the currently
                            active display.

                    55h     unknown (used by ATI and Taxan video boards) fns 00h and
                            02h

Function 13h        Enhanced String Write              (except original PC)
entry     AH        13h
          AL        00h     Write String, Don't Move Cursor
                    01h     Write String and Update Cursor
                    02h     Write String of Alternating Characters and Attributes;
                            Don't Move Cursor
                            bit 0: set in order to move cursor after write
                            bit 1: set if string contains alternating chars and
                                   attributes
                    03h     Write String of Alternating Characters and Attributes;
                            Move Cursor
                            bit 0: set in order to move cursor after write
                            bit 1: set if string contains alternating characters and
                                   attributes
          BH        display page number
          BL        attribute (if AL=00h or 01h)
          CX        length of string
          DH        row of starting cursor position (y)
          DL        column of starting cursor position (x)
          ES:BP     pointer to start of string
return    none
note 1.   Recognizes CR, LF, BS, and bell.
     2.   This function is not available on the original IBM PC or XT unless an EGA
          or later video adapter is installed.

Function 14h        Load LCD Character Font                        (Convertible)
entry     AH        14h
          AL        00h     load user-specified font
```

Video Subsystems and Programming 331

```
                BH      number of bytes per character
                BL      00h     load main font (block 0)
                        01h     load alternate font (block 1)
                CX      number of characters to store
                DX      character offset into RAM font area
                ES:DI   pointer to character font
        AL      01h     load system ROM default font
                BL      00h     load main font (block 0)
                        01h     load alternate font (block 1)
        AL      02h     set mapping of LCD high intensity attribute
                BL      00h         ignore high intensity attribute
                        01h         map high intensity to underscore
                        02h         map high intensity to reverse video
                        03h         map high intensity to selected alternate font
return  unknown

Function 15h    Return Physical Display Parameters              (Convertible)
entry   AH      15h
return  AX      Alternate display adapter type
                0000h   none
                5140h   LCD
                5151h   mono
                5153h   CGA
        ES:DI   pointer to parameter table:
                word #      Information
                01h     monitor model number
                02h     vertical pixels per meter
                03h     horizontal pixels per meter
                04h     total number of vertical pixels
                05h     total number of horizontal pixels
                06h     horizontal pixel separation in micrometers
                07h     vertical pixel separation in micrometers

Functions 15h-19h   apparently not used

Function 1Ah    Get or Set Display Combination Code     (PS/2)  (MCGA, VGA)
                Using the compatibility BIOS of the PS/2 Models 50, 60, 80
                there is a way to determine which video controller and attached
                display are on the system. The Display Combination Code (DCC) is
                a Video BIOS function that provides the capability.
entry   AH      1Ah
        AL      00h     read display combination code
                01h     write display combination code
        BH      inactive display code (if AL=01h)
        BL      active display code   (if AL=01h)
return  AL      1Ah     indicates Compatibility BIOS is supported, any other
                        value is invalid
        BH      Display Combination Code (DCC) (if AH=00h)
                00h     no display
                01h     IBM monochrome adapter and 5151 display
                02h     IBM colour/graphics adapter w/5153 or 5154 colour display
                03h     reserved
                04h     IBM EGA, 5153 or 5154 colour display
                05h     IBM EGA, 5151 monochrome display
                06h     IBM PGA, 5175 colour display
                07h     VGA, analog monochrome display
                08h     VGA, analog colour display
                09h     reserved
                0Ah     MCGA, digital colour display
                0Bh     MCGA, analog monochrome display
                0Ch     MCGA, analog colour display
                0Dh-0FEh reserved
                0FFh    unknown display type
        BL      active display device code  (if AH=00h)
note    This function may be used to test for VGA, since it is not supported in
        earlier adapters. If AL is still 1Ah when the call completes, a VGA or
        MCGA compatible adapter is present.

Function 1Bh    Functionality/State Information         (PS/2)       (MCGA, VGA)
entry   AH      1Bh
        BX      implementation type (always 0000h)
```

```
       ES:DI    pointer to 64 byte buffer
return AL       1Bh if function supported
       ES:DI    buffer filled
                00h-03h address of functionality table  (see note 1)
                04h     current video mode
                05h-06h number of columns
                07h-08h length of regen buffer in bytes
                09h-0Ah starting address in regen buffer of upper left corner of
                        display
                0Bh-0Ch cursor position for page 0  (y,x)
                0Dh-0Eh cursor position for page 1  (y,x)
                0Fh-10h cursor position for page 2  (y,x)
                11h-12h cursor position for page 3  (y,x)
                13h-14h cursor position for page 4  (y,x)
                15h-16h cursor position for page 5  (y,x)
                17h-18h cursor position for page 6  (y,x)
                19h-1Ah cursor position for page 7  (y,x)
                1Bh     cursor starting line
                1Ch     cursor ending line
                1Dh     active display page
                1Eh-1Fh adapter base CRTC port address (3BXh mono, 3DXh colour)
                20h     current setting of register 3B8h or 3D8h
                21h     current setting of register 3B9h or 3D9h
                22h     number of character rows
                23h-24h character height in scan lines
                25h     DCC of active display
                26h     DCC of alternate (inactive) display
                27h-28h number of colours supported in current mode (0 for mono)
                29h     number of pages supported in current mode
                2Ah     number of scan lines active
                        00h     200 scan lines
                        01h     350 scan lines
                        02h     400 scan lines
                        03h     480 scan lines
                        04h-0FFh reserved
                2Bh     primary character block
                2Ch     secondary character block
                2Dh     miscellaneous flags byte
                    bit 0       all modes on all displays on (always 0 on MCGA)
                        1       greyscale summing on
                        2       monochrome display attached
                        3       default palette loading disabled
                        4       cursor emulation enabled (always 0 on MCGA)
                        5       0=intensity; 1=blinking
                        6       reserved
                        7       reserved
                2Eh-30h reserved
                31h     video memory available
                        00h     64k
                        01h     128k
                        02h     192k
                        03h     256k
                32h     save pointer state flags byte
                    bit 0       512 character set active
                        1       dynamic save area active
                        2       text mode font override active
                        3       graphics font override active
                        4       palette override active
                        5       DCC override active
                        6       reserved
                        7       reserved
                33h-3Fh reserved
note   State Functionality Table format (16 bytes)
        00h     modes supported #1
            bit 0       mode 00h supported
                1       mode 01h supported
                2       mode 02h supported
                3       mode 03h supported
                4       mode 04h supported
                5       mode 05h supported
                6       mode 06h supported
```

```
           7         mode 07h supported
   01h     modes supported #2
           bit 0     mode 08h supported
               1     mode 09h supported
               2     mode 0Ah supported
               3     mode 0Bh supported
               4     mode 0Ch supported
               5     mode 0Dh supported
               6     mode 0Eh supported
               7     mode 0Fh supported
   02h     modes supported #3
           bit 0     mode 10h supported
               1     mode 11h supported
               2     mode 12h supported
               3     mode 13h supported
               4-7   reserved
   03h to 06h reserved
   07H     scan lines available in text modes
           bit 0     200 scan lines
               1     350 scan lines
               2     400 scan lines
               3-7   reserved
   08h     total number of character blocks available in text modes
   09h     maximum number of active character blocks in text modes
   0Ah     miscellaneous BIOS functions #1
           bit 0       all modes on all displays function supported (0 on MCGA)
               1       greyscale summing function supported
               2       character font loading function supported
               3       default palette loading enable/disable supported
               4       cursor emulation function supported
               5       EGA 64-colour palette present
               6       colour palette present
               7       colour paging function supported
   0Bh     miscellaneous BIOS functions #2
           bit 0       light pen supported
               1       save/restore state function 1Ch supported (0 on MCGA)
               2       intensity blinking function supported
               3       Display Combination Code supported
               4-7     reserved
   0Ch to 0Dh reserved
   0Eh     Save pointer function flags
           bit 0       512 character set supported
               1       dynamic save area supported
               2       text font override supported
               3       graphics font override supported
               4       palette override supported
               5       DCC extension supported
               6       reserved
               7       reserved
   0Fh     reserved

Function 1Ch    Save/Restore Video State                    (PS/2 50+)  (VGA)
entry   AH      1Ch
        AL      00h     return state buffer size
                01h     save video state
                        ES:BX   buffer address
                02h     restore video state
                        ES:BX   buffer address of previously saved state
        CX      requested states   (1 byte)
           bits 0       save or restore video hardware state
                1       save or restore BIOS data areas
                2       save or restore colour registers and DAC state
                3-0Fh   reserved
return  AL      1Ch if function supported
        BX      number of 64 byte blocks needed (function 00h)
note 1. VGA only.
     2. Saves or restores the digital-to-analog converter (DAC) state and colour
        registers, BIOS video driver data area, or video hardware state.
     3. Subfn 00h is used to determine the size of buffer to contain the
        specified state information. The caller must supply the buffer.
     4. The current video state is altered during a save state operation
```

(AL=01h). If the requesting program needs to continue in the same video state, it can follow the save state request with an immediate call to restore the video state.

```
Function 40h      Set Graphics Mode (Hercules Graphics Card)
entry   AH        40h
return  unknown

Function 41h      Set Text Mode (Hercules Graphics Card)
entry   AH        41h
return  unknown

Function 42h      Clear Current Page (Hercules Graphics Card)
entry   AH        42h
return  unknown

Function 43h      Select Drawing Page (Hercules Graphics Card)
entry   AH        43h
        AL        page number (0 or 1)
return  unknown

Function 44h      Select Drawing Function (Hercules Graphics Card)
entry   AH        44h
        AL        00h     clear pixels
                  01h     set pixels
                  02h     invert pixels
return  unknown

Function 45h      Select Page to Display (Hercules Graphics Card)
entry   AH        45h
        AL        page number (0 or 1)
return  unknown

Function 46h      Draw One Pixel (Hercules Graphics Card)
entry   AH        46h
        DI        x       (0-720)
        BP        y       (0-347)
return  unknown
note    Function 44h determines operation and function 43h which page to use.

Function 47h      Find Pixel Value (Hercules Graphics Card)
entry   AH        47h
        DI        x       (0-720)
        BP        y       (0-347)
return  AL        00h     pixel clear
                  01h     pixel set
note    Function 43h specifies page that is used.

Function 48h      Move to Point (Hercules Graphics Card)
entry   AH        48h
        DI        x       (0-720)
        BP        y       (0-347)
return  unknown

Function 49h      Draw to Point (Hercules Graphics Card)
entry   AH        49h
        DI        x       (0-720)
        BP        y       (0-347)
return  unknown
note    Function 48h or 49h specify first point, 44h operation and 43h page to
        use.

Function 4Ah      Block Fill (Hercules Graphics Card)
entry   AH        4Ah
return  unknown

Function 4Bh      Display Character (Hercules Graphics Card)
entry   AH        4Bh
        AL        ASCII code for character to display
        DI        x       (0-720)
        BP        y       (0-347)
```

```
return    unknown
note      Unlike the other BIOS character functions character position is specified
          in pixels rather than rows and columns.

Function 4Ch      Draw Arc (Hercules Graphics Card)
entry    AH       4Ch
return   unknown

Function 4Dh      Draw Circle (Hercules Graphics Card)
entry    AH       4Dh
return   unknown

Function 4Eh      Fill Area (Hercules Graphics Card)
entry    AH       4Eh
return   unknown

Function 6Ah      Direct Graphics Interface Standard (DGIS)
entry    AH       6Ah
         AL       00h       Inquire Available Devices
                  BX        00h
                  CX        00h
                  DX        buffer length (may be zero)
                  ES:DI     address of buffer
         return   BX        number of bytes stored in buffer
                  CX        bytes req'd for all descriptions (0 if no DGIS)
         note     Buffer contains descriptions and addresses of
                  DGIS-compatible display(s) and printer(s)
                  01h       Redirect Character Output
                  CX        00h
                  ES:DI     address of device to send INT 10 output to
         return   CX        00h       output could not be redirected
                            not 00h   int 10h output now routed to requested
                                      display
                  02h       Inquire int 10h Output Device
                  ES:DI     0:0
         return   ES:DI     0:0       if current display is non-DGIS
                                      else address of current DGIS int 10h display

Function 6Fh      Set Video Mode (VEGA Extended EGA/VGA)
entry    AH       6F
         AL       05h
         BL       mode      resoltn     colours
                  62h       800x600     16
                  65h       1024x768    16
                  66h       640x400     256
                  67h       640x480     256
                  68h       720x540     256
                  69h       800x600     256

Function 70h      Get Video RAM Address                              (Tandy 1000)
entry    AH       70h
return   AX       Segment addresses of the following
         BX       Offset address of green plane
         CX       segment address of green plane
         DX       segment address of red/blue plane
note     (red offset = 0, blue offset = 4000)

Function 71h      Get INCRAM Addresses                               (Tandy 1000)
entry    AH       71h
return   AX       segment address of the following
         BX       segment address of INCRAM
         CX       offset address of INCRAM

Function 72h      Scroll Screen Right                                (Tandy 1000)
entry    AH       72h
         AL       number of columns blanked at left of page
                  00h       blank window
         BH       attributes to be used on blank columns
         CH,CL    row, column address of upper left corner
         DH,DL    row, column address of lower right corner
```

```
Function 73h      Scroll Screen Left                                    (Tandy 1000)
entry    AH       73h
         AL       number of columns blanked at right of page
                  00h     blank window
         BH       attributes to be used on blank columns
         CH,CL    row, column address of upper left corner
         DH,DL    row, column address of lower right corner

Function 81h      DESQview video - Get Video Buffer Segment
entry    AH       81h
         DX       4456h ('DV')
return   ES       segment of DESQview data structure for video buffer
                  byte ES:[0]    current window number (DV 2.0+)
note     This function is probably meant for internal use only, due to the magic
         value required in DX.

Function 82h      DESQview - Get Current Window Info
entry    AH       82h
         DX       4456h ('DV')
return   AH       unknown
         AL       current window number
         BH       unknown
         BL       direct screen writes
                  0       program does not do direct writes
                  1       program does direct writes, so shadow buffer not usable
         CH       unknown
         CL       current video mode
         DS       segment in DESQview for data structure
                  for DV 2.00+, structure is:
                  byte   DS:[0]    window number
                  word   DS:[1]    segment of other data structure
                  word   DS:[3]    segment of window's object handle
         ES       segment of DESQview data structure for video buffer
note     This function is probably meant for internal use only, due to the magic
         value required in DX.

Function 0BFh     Compaq Portable Extensions
entry    AH       0BFh
         AL       subfunction
                  00h     Select External Monitor
                          (all registers preserved, the internal monitor is blanked
                          and the external monitor is now the active monitor)
                  01h     Select Internal Monitor
                          (all registers preserved, the external monitor is blanked
                          and internal monitor is now active monitor)
                  02h     Set Master Mode of Current Active Video Controller
                          BH      04h     CGA
                                  05h     EGA
                                  07h     MDA
                  03h     Get Environment
                          BX      0000h
                          return  BH      active monitor
                                          00h     external
                                          01h     internal
                                  BL      master mode
                                          00h     switchable VDU not present
                                          04h     CGA
                                          05h     EGA
                                          07h     MDA
                                  CH      00h     (reserved)
                                  CL      switchable VDU mode supported (1 byte) bits:
                                          0       CGA supported
                                          1,2     reserved (1)
                                          3       MDA supported
                                          4-7     reserved (1)
                                  DH      internal monitor type
                                          00h     none
                                          01h     dual-mode monitor
                                          02h     5153 RGB monitor
                                          03h     Compaq colour monitor
                                          04h     640x400 flat panel display
```

Video Subsystems and Programming

```
              DL          external monitor type
                          00h       none
                          01h       dual-mode monitor
                          02h       5153 RGB monitor
                          03h       Compaq colour monitor
                          04h       640x400 flat panel display
      04h     Set Mode Switch Delay
              BH          switch
                          00h       enable delay
                          01h       disable delay

Function  0EFh   MSHERC.COM - Installation Check?
entry     AH     0EFh
return    DX     unknown value
note             MSHERC.COM is a program included with the PC Tech Journal high-level
                 benchmark suite that adds video modes 08h and 88h for Hercules cards,
                 and supports text in the new graphics modes.

Functions 0F0h, 0F1h, 0F2h, 0F3h, 0F4h, 0F5h, 0F6h, 0F7h, 0FAh
                 Microsoft Mouse Driver EGA Support.
                 See Chapter 14 for details.

Function 0FEh   Get Virtual Buffer Address           (text mode only)
                                                     (Topview/DesQview/Taskview)
entry     AH     0FEh
          ES:DI  pointer to assumed video buffer
return    ES:DI  pointer to actual video buffer
note   1. This alternate video buffer can be written to directly, in the same
          manner as writing to B:000 or B:800. The MT program will manage the
          actual display.
       2. There is no need to synchronize vertical retrace when writing to the
          alternate buffer; this is managed by the MT program
       3. If TopView or DESQview is not running, ES:DI is returned unchanged.
       4. TopView requires that function 0FFh be called every time you write into
          the buffer to tell TopView that something changed
       5. This function returns the address of the virtual screen in the ES:DI
          registers. If TaskView returns a virtual screen address, you can use a
          combination of BIOS functions and writing directly to the virtual screen
          which will automatically update the real screen when it is visible. You
          do not have to synchronize screen writing to the virtual screen even if
          the screen is in a colour text mode. A common way of using this function
          is to place the real screen address in the ES:DI registers, put 0FEh in
          the AH register, then issue an interrupt 10h. If neither TopView nor
          TaskView are present, the values of ES and DI will remain the same.

Function 0FFh   Update Real Display (text mode only) (TopView)
                Update Video Buffer                  (Topview/DesQview/Taskview)
entry     AH     0FFh
          CX     number of sequential characters that have been modified
          DI     offset of first character that has been modified
          ES     segment of video buffer
return    unknown
note   1. DesQview supports this call, but does not require it
       2. Avoid CX=0.
       3. This function is unnecessary in TaskView, but using it will provide
          compatibility with TopView as well. After you have written information
          directly to the virtual screen, place the start address of the changed
          information in ES:DI, the number of integers (not bytes) changed in CX,
          0FFh in AH, and call int 10h. In TopView, the screen will be updated to
          reflect your changes. In TaskView, the visible screen will automatically
          reflect your changes.
```

Appendix 1

Keyboard Scan Codes

These scan codes are generated by pressing a key on the PC's keyboard. This is the 'make' code. A 'break' code is generated when the key is released. The break scancode is 128 higher than the make code, and is generated by setting bit 7 of the scan code byte to 1.

IBM PC Keyboard Extended Codes

The keyboard returns an 0 in the ASCII code byte to indicate that the code passed in the Scan Code byte is 'special'.

Codes marked with an asterisk (*) are available only on the 'enhanced' keyboard.

key	Normal	Shift	Control	Alt	
escape	1				
1	2			0;120	
2	3			0;121	
3	4			0;122	
4	5			0;123	
5	6			0;124	
6	7			0;125	
7	8			0;126	
8	9			0;127	
9	10			0;128	
0	11			0;129	
-	12			0;130	
=	13			0;131	
tab	15	0;15	0;148*	0;165*	
backtab	none			0;15	
RETURN	28			0;166*	
Home	0;71		0;119	0;151*	7
UpArrow	0;72		0;141*	0;152*	8
PgUp	0;73		0;132	0;153*	9
grey -	0;74				0;74
LArrow	0;75		0;115	0;154*	4
keypad 5	none		none	none	5
RArrow	0;77		0;116	0;155*	6
grey +	0;78				0;78
End	0;79		0;117	0;156*	1
DnArrow	0;80		0;145*	0;160*	2
PgDn	0;81		0;118	0;161*	3
Ins	0;82		0;146*	0;162*	11
Del	0;83		0;128	0;163*	52
PrtSc	55		0;114		
L shift	42				

```
R shift         54
alt key         56
capslock        58
spacebar        57
control         29
numlock         69
scrollck        70
;               39
[               26
]               27
"               40
\               43
/               53                      0;149*          0;164*
,               51
.               52
Ctrl -                                  0;142*
Ctrl 5                                  0;143*
Ctrl +                                  0;144*
Ctrl-*                                  0;150*
a               30                                      0;30
b               48                                      0;48
c               46                                      0;46
d               32                                      0;32
e               18                                      0;18
f               33                                      0;33
g               34                                      0;34
h               35                                      0;35
i               23                                      0;23
j               36                                      0;36
k               37                                      0;37
l               38                                      0;38
m               50                                      0;50
n               49                                      0;49
o               24                                      0;24
p               25                                      0;25
q               16                                      0;16
r               19                                      0;19
s               31                                      0;31
t               20                                      0;20
u               22                                      0;22
v               47                                      0;47
w               17                                      0;17
x               45                                      0;45
y               21                                      0;21
z               44                                      0;44
F1              0;59    0;84            0;94            0;104
F2              0;60    0;85            0;95            0;105
F3              0;61    0;86            0;96            0;106
F4              0;62    0;87            0;97            0;107
F5              0;63    0;88            0;98            0;108
F6              0;64    0;89            0;99            0;109
F7              0;65    0;90            0;100           0;110
F8              0;66    0;91            0;101           0;111
F9              0;67    0;92            0;102           0;112
F10             0;68    0;93            0;103           0;113
F11             0;152   0;162           0;172           0;182   Tandy
F12             0;153   0;163           0;173           0;183   Tandy
F11             0;133   0;135           0;137           0;139   IBM
F12             0;134   0;136           0;138           0;140   IBM
```

Shift Byte

```
Right Shift     01
Left Shift      02
Control         04
Alt             08
```

A shift byte can be created by adding together as many of the above as desired. That is, the shift combination Control+Alt would be represented by a hex C, which is 04 + 08.

BIOS keystroke codes in hexadecimal

key	Normal		Shift		Control	Alt
Esc	011B		011B		011B	--
1!	0231	'1'	0221	'!'	--	7800
2@	0332	'2'	0340	'@'	0300	7900
3#	0433	'3'	0423	'#'	--	7A00
4$	0534	'4'	0524	'$'	--	7B00
5%	0635	'5'	0625	'%'	--	7C00
6^	0736	'6'	075E	'^'	071E	7D00
7&	0837	'7'	0826	'&'	--	7E00
8*	0938	'8'	092A	'*'	--	7F00
9(	0A39	'9'	0A28	'('	--	8000
0)	0B30	'0'	0B29	')'	--	8100
-_	0C2D	'-'	0C5F	'_'	0C1F	8200
=+	0D3D	'='	0D2B	'+'	--	8300
BkSp	0E08		0E08		0E7F	--
Tab	0F09		0F00		--	--
q	1071	'q'	1051	'Q'	1011	1000
w	1177	'w'	1157	'W'	1117	1100
e	1265	'e'	1245	'E'	1205	1200
r	1372	'r'	1352	'R'	1312	1300
t	1474	't'	1454	'T'	1414	1400
y	1579	'y'	1559	'Y'	1519	1500
u	1675	'u'	1655	'U'	1615	1600
i	1769	'i'	1749	'I'	1709	1700
o	186F	'o'	184F	'O'	180F	1800
p	1970	'p'	1950	'P'	1910	1900
[{	1A5B	'['	1A7B	'{'	1A1B	--
]}	1B5D	']'	1B7D	'}'	1B1D	--
Enter	1C0D		1C0D		1C0A	--
Ctrl	--		--		--	--
a	1E61	'a'	1E41	'A'	1E01	1E00
s	1F73	's'	1F53	'S'	1F13	1F00
d	2064	'd'	2044	'D'	2004	2000
f	2166	'f'	2146	'F'	2106	2100
g	2267	'g'	2247	'G'	2207	2200
h	2368	'h'	2348	'H'	2308	2300
j	246A	'j'	244A	'J'	240A	2400
k	256B	'k'	254B	'K'	250B	2500
l	266C	'l'	264C	'L'	260C	2600
;:	273B	';'	273A	':'	--	--
'"	2827	'''	2822	'"'	--	--
`~	2960	'`'	297E	'~'	--	--
Lshift	--		--		--	--
\\|	2B5C	'\\'	2B7C	'|'	2B1C	--
z	2C7A	'z'	2C5A	'Z'	2C1A	2C00
x	2D78	'x'	2D58	'X'	2D18	2D00
c	2E63	'c'	2E43	'C'	2E03	2E00
v	2F76	'v'	2F56	'V'	2F16	2F00
b	3062	'b'	3042	'B'	3002	3000
n	316E	'n'	314E	'N'	310E	3100
m	326D	'm'	324D	'M'	320D	3200
,<	332C	','	333C	'<'	--	--
.>	342E	'.'	343E	'>'	--	--
/?	352F	'/'	353F	'?'	--	--
Rshift	--		--		--	--
PrtSc	372A	'*'	--		7200	--
Alt	--		--		--	--
Space	3920	' '	3920	' '	3920	' '	3920	' '
CapsL	--		--		--	--
F1	3B00		5400		5E00	6800
F2	3C00		5500		5F00	6900
F3	3D00		5600		6000	6A00
F4	3E00		5700		6100	6B00
F5	3F00		5800		6200	6C00
F6	4000		5900		6300	6D00
F7	4100		5A00		6400	6E00
F8	4200		5B00		6500	6F00
F9	4300		5C00		6600	7000
F10	4400		5D00		6700	7100

```
NumLock     --           --            --       --
Scroll      --           --            --       --
7 Home      4700         4737    '7'   7700     --
8 up        4800         4838    '8'   --       --
9 PgUp      4900         4939    '9'   8400     --
Grey -      4A2D   '-'   4A2D    '-'   --       --
4 left      4B00         4B34    '4'   7300     --
5           --           4C35    '5'   --       --
6 right     4D00         4D36    '6'   7400     --
Grey +      4E2B   '+'   4E2B    '+'   --       --
1 End       4F00         4F31    '1'   7500     --
2 down      5000         5032    '2'   --       --
3 PgDn      5100         5133    '3'   7600     --
Ins         5200         5230    '0'   --       --
Del         5300         532E    '.'   --       --
```

An entry of "--" means you can't get that combination out of the BIOS.

Appendix 2

Standard ASCII Character Codes

dec	hex	char	control	code	dec	hex	chr	dec	hex	chr	dec	hex	chr
0	0	Ctrl-@	NUL	Null	32	20	SP	64	40	@	96	60	'
1	1	Ctrl-A	SOH	Start of Heading	33	21	!	65	41	A	97	61	a
2	2	Ctrl-B	STX	Start of Text	34	22	"	66	42	B	98	62	b
3	3	Ctrl-C	ETX	End of Text	35	23	#	67	43	C	99	63	c
4	4	Ctrl-D	EOT	End of Transmit	36	24	$	68	44	D	100	64	d
5	5	Ctrl-E	ENQ	Enquiry	37	25	%	69	45	E	101	65	e
6	6	Ctrl-F	ACK	Acknowledge	38	26	&	70	46	F	102	66	f
7	7	Ctrl-G	BEL	Bell	39	27	'	71	47	G	103	67	g
8	8	Ctrl-H	BS	Back Space	40	28	(	72	48	H	104	68	h
9	9	Ctrl-I	HT	Horizontal Tab	41	29	)	73	49	I	105	69	i
10	0A	Ctrl-J	LF	Line Feed	42	2A	*	74	4A	J	106	6A	j
11	0B	Ctrl-K	VT	Vertical Tab	43	2B	+	75	4B	K	107	6B	k
12	0C	Ctrl-L	FF	Form Feed	44	2C	,	76	4C	L	108	6C	l
13	0D	Ctrl-M	CR	Carriage Return	45	2D	-	77	4D	M	109	6D	m
14	0E	Ctrl-N	SO	Shift Out	46	2E	.	78	4E	N	110	6E	n
15	0F	Ctrl-O	SI	Shift In	47	2F	/	79	4F	O	111	6F	o
16	10	Ctrl-P	DLE	Data Line Escape	48	30	0	80	50	P	112	70	p
17	11	Ctrl-Q	DC1	Device Control 1	49	31	1	81	51	Q	113	71	q
18	12	Ctrl-R	DC2	Device Control 2	50	32	2	82	52	R	114	72	r
19	13	Ctrl-S	DC3	Device Control 3	51	33	3	83	53	S	115	73	s
20	14	Ctrl-T	DC4	Device Control 4	52	34	4	84	54	T	116	74	t
21	15	Ctrl-U	NAK	Negative Acknowledge	53	35	5	85	55	U	117	75	u
22	16	Ctrl-V	SYN	Synchronous Idle	54	36	6	86	56	V	118	76	v
23	17	Ctrl-W	ETB	End of Transmit Blk	55	37	7	87	57	W	119	77	w
24	18	Ctrl-X	CAN	Cancel	56	38	8	88	58	X	120	78	x
25	19	Ctrl-Y	EM	End of Medium	57	39	9	89	59	Y	121	79	y
26	1A	Ctrl-Z	SUB	Substitute	58	3A	:	90	5A	Z	122	7A	z
27	1B	Ctrl-[	ESC	Escape	59	3B	;	91	5B	[	23	7B	{
28	1C	Ctrl-\	FS	File Separator	60	3C	<	92	5C	\	124	7C	|
29	1D	Ctrl-]	GS	Group Separator	61	3D	=	93	5D	]	125	7D	}
30	1E	Ctrl-^	RS	Record Separator	62	3E	>	94	5E	^	126	7E	~
31	1F	Ctrl-_	US	Unit Separator	63	3F	?	95	5F	_	127	7F	DEL

ASCII = The American National Standard Code for Information Interchange

The complete document describing the ASCII standard, 'X3.4-1977: American National Standard Code for Information Interchange' can be ordered for $5.00 (plus $4 postage) from

American National Standards Institute
1430 Broadway
New York, NY 10018
212/354-3300

1968 ASCII CODE

X3.64	Dec	Oct	Hex	EBCDIC			meaning
0/0	000	000	00	00	NUL	^@	Null, Ctrl-@
0/1	001	001	01	01	SOH	^A	Start of Header
0/2	002	002	02	02	STX	^B	Start of Text
0/3	003	003	03	03	ETX	^C	End of Text
0/4	004	004	04	37	EOT	^D	End of Transmission
0/5	005	005	05	2D	ENQ	^E	Enquire, WRU
0/6	006	006	06	2E	ACK	^F	HEREIS
0/7	007	007	07	2F	BEL	^G	Bell
0/8	008	010	08	16	BS	^H	Backspace, \b
0/9	009	011	09	05	HT	^I	TAB, \t
0/10	010	012	0A	25	LF	^J	Newline, NL, \n
0/11	011	013	0B	0B	VT	^K	Vertical Tab
0/12	012	014	0C	0C	FF	^L	Form Feed, \f
0/13	013	015	0D	0D	CR	^M	Return, \r,
0/14	014	016	0E	0E	SO	^N	Shift Out
0/15	015	017	0F	0F	SI	^O	Shift in
1/0	016	020	10	10	DLE	^P	
1/1	017	021	11	11	DC1	^Q	XON, Start Reader
1/2	018	022	12	12	DC2	^R	DC2, Tape Punch ON
1/3	019	023	13	13	DC3	^S	XOFF, Stop Reader
1/4	020	024	14	3C	DC4	^T	DC4, Tape Punch OFF
1/5	021	025	15	3D	NAK	^U	Nak
1/6	022	026	16	32	SYN	^V	Sync
1/7	023	027	17	26	ETB	^W	End of Tape Block
1/8	024	030	18	18	CAN	^X	Cancel
1/9	025	031	19	19	EM	^Y	End of Medium
1/10	026	032	1A	3F	SUB	^Z	CP/M End of File
1/11	027	033	1B	27	ESC	^[	Escape, \E
1/12	028	034	1C	1C	FS	^\	File Separator
1/13	029	035	1D	1D	GS	^]	Group Separator
1/14	030	036	1E	1E	RS	^^	Record Separator
1/15	031	037	1F	1F	US	^_	Unit Separator
2/0	032	040	20	40	SP	Space	
2/1	033	041	21	5A	!	Exclamation mark	
2/2	034	042	22	7F	"	Double Quote	
2/3	035	043	23	7B	#		
2/4	036	044	24	5B	$		
2/5	037	045	25	6C	%		
2/6	038	046	26	50	&		
2/7	039	047	27	7D	'	Apostrophe, Single Quote	
2/8	040	050	28	4D	(		
2/9	041	051	29	5D	)		
2/10	042	052	2A	5C	*	Splat, Star, asterisk	
2/11	043	053	2B	4E	+		
2/12	044	054	2C	6B	,	Comma	
2/13	045	055	2D	60	-		
2/14	046	056	2E	4B	.	Period	
2/15	047	057	2F	61	/	Slash, Stroke	
3/0	048	060	30	F0	0		
3/1	049	061	31	F1	1		
3/2	050	062	32	F2	2		
3/3	051	063	33	F3	3		
3/4	052	064	34	F4	4		
3/5	053	065	35	F5	5		
3/6	054	066	36	F6	6		
3/7	055	067	37	F7	7		
3/8	056	070	38	F8	8		
3/9	057	071	39	F9	9		
3/10	058	072	3A	7A	:		
3/11	059	073	3B	5E	;		
3/12	060	074	3C	4C	<		
3/13	061	075	3D	7E	=		
3/14	062	076	3E	6E	>		
3/15	063	077	3F	6F	?	Question Mark	
4/0	064	100	40	7C	@	Commercial AT	
4/1	065	101	41	C1	A		
4/2	066	102	42	C2	B		

4/3	067	103	43	C3	C	
4/4	068	104	44	C4	D	
4/5	069	105	45	C5	E	
4/6	070	106	46	C6	F	
4/7	071	107	47	C7	G	
4/8	072	110	48	C8	H	
4/9	073	111	49	C9	I	
4/10	074	112	4A	D1	J	
4/11	075	113	4B	D2	K	
4/12	076	114	4C	D3	L	
4/13	077	115	4D	D4	M	
4/14	078	116	4E	D5	N	
4/15	079	117	4F	D6	O	
5/0	080	120	50	D7	P	
5/1	081	121	51	D8	Q	
5/2	082	122	52	D9	R	
5/3	083	123	53	E2	S	
5/4	084	124	54	E3	T	
5/5	085	125	55	E4	U	
5/6	086	126	56	E5	V	
5/7	087	127	57	E6	W	
5/8	088	130	58	E7	X	
5/9	089	131	59	E8	Y	
5/10	090	132	5A	E9	Z	
5/11	091	133	5B	AD	[	Left square bracket
5/12	092	134	5C	E0	\	Backslash
5/13	093	135	5D	BD	]	Right Square Bracket
5/14	094	136	5E	5F	^	Circumflex
5/15	095	137	5F	6D	_	Underline or Back Arrow(old)
5/16						Back Arrow on older codes
6/0	096	140	60	79	'	Accent Grave
6/1	097	141	61	81	a	
6/2	098	142	62	82	b	
6/3	099	143	63	83	c	
6/4	100	144	64	84	d	
6/5	101	145	65	85	e	
6/6	102	146	66	86	f	
6/7	103	147	67	87	g	
6/8	104	150	68	88	h	
6/9	105	151	69	89	i	
6/10	106	152	6A	91	j	
6/11	107	153	6B	92	k	
6/12	108	154	6C	93	l	
6/13	109	155	6D	94	m	
6/14	110	156	6E	95	n	
6/15	111	157	6F	96	o	
7/0	112	160	70	97	p	
7/1	113	161	71	98	q	
7/2	114	162	72	99	r	
7/3	115	163	73	A2	s	
7/4	116	164	74	A3	t	
7/5	117	165	75	A4	u	
7/6	118	166	76	A5	v	
7/7	119	167	77	A6	w	
7/8	120	170	78	A7	x	
7/9	121	171	79	A8	y	
7/10	122	172	7A	A9	z	
7/11	123	173	7B	C0	{	Left Brace
7/12	124	174	7C	4F	|	Vertical Bar, Pipe, (Confirm on some older systems)
7/13	125	175	7D	D0	}	Right Brace
7/14	126	176	7E	7E	~	Tilde (ESC on some old sys)
7/15	127	177	7F	07	^?	DEL, RUBOUT

ASCII = American Standard Code for Information Exchange

EBCDIC = Extended Binary-Coded Decimal Interchange Code

Appendix 3

ASCII Control Codes

dec	hex	char	name	control code	
0	0	☺	Ctrl-@	NULL	Null
1	1	☻	Ctrl-A	SOH	Start of Heading
2	2	♥	Ctrl-B	STX	Start of Text
3	3	♦	Ctrl-C	ETX	End of Text
4	4	♣	Ctrl-D	EOT	End of Transmit
5	5	♠	Ctrl-E	ENQ	Enquiry
6	6	•	Ctrl-F	ACK	Acknowledge
7	7	◘	Ctrl-G	BEL	Bell
8	8	○	Ctrl-H	BS	Back Space
9	9	◉	Ctrl-I	HT	Horizontal Tab
10	A	♂	Ctrl-J	LF	Line Feed
11	B	♀	Ctrl-K	VT	Vertical Tab
12	C	♪	Ctrl-L	FF	Form Feed
13	D	♫	Ctrl-M	CR	Carriage Return
14	E	☼	Ctrl-N	SO	Shift Out
15	F	►	Ctrl-O	SI	Shift In
16	10	►	Ctrl-P	DLE	Data Line Escape
17	11	◄	Ctrl-Q	DC1	Device Control 1
18	12	↕	Ctrl-R	DC2	Device Control 2
19	13	‼	Ctrl-S	DC3	Device Control 3
20	14	¶	Ctrl-T	DC4	Device Control 4
21	15	§	Ctrl-U	NAK	Negative Acknowledge
22	16	▬	Ctrl-V	SYN	Synchronous Idle
23	17	↨	Ctrl-W	ETB	End of Transmit Block
24	18	↑	Ctrl-X	CAN	Cancel
25	19	↓	Ctrl-Y	EM	End of Medium
26	1A	→	Ctrl-Z	SUB	Substitute
27	1B	←	Ctrl-[	ESC	Escape
28	1C	∟	Ctrl-\	FS	File Separator
29	1D	↔	Ctrl-]	GS	Group Separator
30	1E	▲	Ctrl-^	RS	Record Separator
31	1F	▼	Ctrl-_	US	Unit Separator

Standard ASCII Codes

dec	hex	char	dec	hex	char	dec	hex	char	dec	hex	char
0	0	NUL	32	20	space	64	40	@	96	60	'
1	1	SOH	33	21	!	65	41	A	97	61	a
2	2	STX	34	22	"	66	42	B	98	62	b
3	3	ETX	35	23	#	67	43	C	99	63	c
4	4	EOT	36	24	$	68	44	D	100	64	d
5	5	ENQ	37	25	%	69	45	E	101	65	e
6	6	ACK	38	26	&	70	46	F	102	66	f
7	7	BEL	39	27	'	71	47	G	103	67	g
8	8	BS	40	28	(	72	48	H	104	68	h

ASCII Control Codes

dec	hex	char	dec	hex	char	dec	hex	char	dec	hex	char
9	9	HT	41	29	)	73	49	I	105	69	i
10	A	LF	42	2A	*	74	4A	J	106	6A	j
11	B	VT	43	2B	+	75	4B	K	107	6B	k
12	C	FF	44	2C	,	76	4C	L	108	6C	l
13	D	CR	45	2D	-	77	4D	M	109	6D	m
14	E	SO	46	2E	.	78	4E	N	110	6E	n
15	F	SI	47	2F	/	79	4F	O	111	6F	o
16	10	DLE	48	30	0	80	50	P	112	70	p
17	11	DC1	49	31	1	81	51	Q	113	71	q
18	12	DC2	50	32	2	82	52	R	114	72	r
19	13	DC3	51	33	3	83	53	S	115	73	s
20	14	DC4	52	34	4	84	54	T	116	74	t
21	15	NAK	53	35	5	85	55	U	117	75	u
22	16	SYN	54	36	6	86	56	V	118	76	v
23	17	ETB	55	37	7	87	57	W	119	77	w
24	18	CAN	56	38	8	88	58	X	120	78	x
25	19	EM	57	39	9	89	59	Y	121	79	y
26	1A	SUB	58	3A	:	90	5A	Z	122	7A	z
27	1B	ESC	59	3B	;	91	5B	[	123	7B	{
28	1C	FS	60	3C	<	92	5C	\	124	7C	|
29	1D	GS	61	3D	=	93	5D	]	125	7D	}
30	1E	RS	62	3E	>	94	5E	^	126	7E	~
31	1F	US	63	3F	?	95	5F	_	127	7F	

Extended ASCII Codes

dec	hex	char	dec	hex	char	dec	hex	char	dec	hex	char
128	80	Ç	160	A0	á	192	C0	└	224	E0	α
129	81	ü	161	A1	í	193	C1	┴	225	E1	β
130	82	é	162	A2	ó	194	C2	┬	226	E2	Γ
131	83	â	163	A3	ú	195	C3	├	227	E3	π
132	84	ä	164	A4	ñ	196	C4	─	228	E4	Σ
133	85	à	165	A5	Ñ	197	C5	┼	229	E5	σ
134	86	å	166	A6	ª	198	C6	╞	230	E6	μ
135	87	ç	167	A7	º	199	C7	╟	231	E7	τ
136	88	ê	168	A8	¿	200	C8	╚	232	E8	Φ
137	89	ë	169	A9	⌐	201	C9	╔	233	E9	Θ
138	8A	è	170	AA	¬	202	CA	╩	234	EA	Ω
139	8B	ï	171	AB	½	203	CB	╦	235	EB	δ
140	8C	î	172	AC	¼	204	CC	╠	236	EC	∞
141	8D	ì	173	AD	¡	205	CD	═	237	ED	φ
142	8E	Ä	174	AE	«	206	CE	╬	238	EE	ε
143	8F	Å	175	AF	»	207	CF	╧	239	EF	∩
144	90	É	176	B0	░	208	D0	╨	240	F0	≡
145	91	æ	177	B1	▒	209	D1	╤	241	F1	±
146	92	Æ	178	B2	▓	210	D2	╥	242	F2	≥
147	93	ô	179	B3	│	211	D3	╙	243	F3	≤
148	94	ö	180	B4	┤	212	D4	╘	244	F4	⌠
149	95	ò	181	B5	╡	213	D5	╒	245	F5	⌡
150	96	û	182	B6	╢	214	D6	╓	246	F6	÷
151	97	ù	183	B7	╖	215	D7	╫	247	F7	≈
152	98	ÿ	184	B8	╕	216	D8	╪	248	F8	°
153	99	Ö	185	B9	╣	217	D9	┘	249	F9	·
154	9A	Ü	186	BA	║	218	DA	┌	250	FA	·
155	9B	¢	187	BB	╗	219	DB	█	251	FB	√
156	9C	£	188	BC	╝	220	DC	▄	252	FC	η
157	9D	¥	189	BD	╜	221	DD	▌	253	FD	²
158	9E	₧	190	BE	╛	222	DE	▐	254	FE	■
159	9F	ƒ	191	BF	┐	223	DF	▀	255	FF	reserved

Appendix 4

IBM PC Interrupt Usage

Interrupt	Used for	Model
00h	Divide by zero	PC, AT, PS/2
01h	Single step	PC, AT, PS/2
02h	NMI	PC, AT, PS/2
03h	Breakpoint	PC, AT, PS/2
04h	Overflow	PC, AT, PS/2
05h	ROM BIOS PrintScreen	PC, AT, PS/2
06h	Reserved	PC
07h	Reserved	PC
08h	IRQ0 timer tick	PC, AT, PS/2
09h	IRQ1 keyboard	PC, AT, PS/2
0Ah	IRQ2 reserved	PC
	IRQ2 cascade from slave 8259 PIC	AT, PS/2
0Bh	IRQ3 serial communications (COM2)	PC, AT, PS/2
0Ch	IRQ4 serial communications (COM1)	PC, AT, PS/2
0Dh	IRQ5 hard disk	PC
	IRQ5 parallel printer (LPT2)	AT
	Reserved	PS/2
0Eh	IRQ6 floppy disk	PC, AT, PS/2
0Fh	IRQ7 parallel printer (LPT1)	PC, AT, PS/2
10h	ROM BIOS video driver	PC, AT, PS/2
11h	ROM BIOS equipment check	PC, AT, PS/2
12h	ROM BIOS conventional memory size	PC, AT, PS/2
13h	ROM BIOS disk drives	PC, AT, PS/2
14h	ROM BIOS communications driver	PC, AT, PS/2
15h	ROM BIOS cassette driver	PC
	ROM BIOS I/O system extensions	AT, PS/2
16h	ROM BIOS keyboard driver	PC, AT, PS/2
17h	ROM BIOS printer driver	PC, AT, PS/2
18h	ROM BASIC	PC, AT, PS/2
19h	ROM BIOS bootstrap	PC, AT, PS/2
1Ah	ROM BIOS time of day	AT, PS/2
1Bh	ROM BIOS Ctrl-break	PC, AT, PS/2
1Ch	ROM BIOS timer tick	PC, AT, PS/2
1Dh	ROM BIOS video parameter table	PC, AT, PS/2
1Eh	ROM BIOS floppy disk parameters	PC, AT, PS/2
1Fh	ROM BIOS font (characters 80h-0FFh)	PC, AT, PS/2
20h	DOS terminate process	
21h	DOS function dispatcher	
22h	DOS terminate address	
23h	DOS Ctrl-C handler address	
24h	DOS critical-error handler address	
25h	DOS absolute disk read	
26h	DOS absolute disk write	
27h	DOS terminate and stay resident	
28h	DOS idle interrupt	
29h	DOS fast screen output	

2Ah	DOS network redirector	
2Bh-2Eh	DOS reserved	
2Fh	DOS multiplex interrupt	
30h-3Fh	DOS reserved	
40h	ROM BIOS floppy disk driver (if hard disk installed)	PC, AT, PS/2
41h	ROM BIOS hard disk parameters	PC
	ROM BIOS hard disk params (drive 0)	AT, PS/2
42h	ROM BIOS default video driver (if EGA installed)	PC, AT, PS/2
43h	EGA, MCGA, VGA character table	PC, AT, PS/2
44h	ROM BIOS font (characters 00-7Fh)	PCjr
46h	ROM BIOS hard disk params (drive 1)	AT, PS/2
4Ah	ROM BIOS alarm handler	AT, PS/2
5Ah	Cluster adapter	PC, AT
5Bh	Used by cluster program	PC, AT
60h-66h	User interrupts	PC, AT, PS/2
67h	LIM EMS driver	PC, AT, PS/2
70h	IRQ8 CMOS real-time clock	AT, PS/2
71h	IRQ9 software diverted to IRQ2	AT, PS/2
72h	IRQ10 reserved	AT, PS/2
73h	IRQ11 reserved	AT, PS/2
74h	IRQ12 reserved	AT
	IRQ12 mouse	PS/2
75h	IRQ13 80x87 math coprocessor	AT, PS/2
76h	IRQ14 hard disk controller	AT, PS/2
77h	IRQ15 reserved	AT, PS/2
80h-0F0h	BASIC	PC, AT, PS/2
0F1h-0FFh	Not used	PC, AT, PS/2

Appendix 5

List of IBM PC-XT-AT-PS/2 Diagnostic Error Codes

This list has been compiled from a variety of sources, including the IBM Technical Reference manuals, IBM Hardware Maintenance and Service manuals, technical articles, and other BBS listings.

The IBM PC family of computers (PC, Portable, XT, AT, and PS/2s) comes complete with built-in diagnostic procedures to assist you in identifying many problems that may occur with the computer's components. These diagnostics are called the Power-On Self Test (POST) and are performed whenever a PC is turned on. This test process provides error or warning messages whenever a faulty component is encountered. Two types of messages are provided: audible codes and screen messages or codes.

Audio codes consist of beeps that identify the faulty component. If your computer is functioning normally, you will hear one short beep when the system is started up. If a problem is detected, a different series of beeps will be sounded. These audio codes and corresponding problem areas are:

Audio Code	Problem Area
No beep, continuous beep, or repeating short beeps	Power Supply
1 long beep and 1 short beep	System Board
1 long beep and 2 short beeps, or 1 short beep and blank or incorrect display	Monitor adapter card and/or monitor cable and/or display
1 short beep and either the red drive LED staying on or Personal Computer BASIC statement	Drive and/or drive adapter card
1 long 3 short beeps	Enhanced Graphics Adapter card
3 long beeps	Keyboard card

On the XT and AT, the POST procedures also display system memory as it is read. The last number displayed (640KB, for example) should be the total amount of memory in your system, including system board memory and any expansion memory.

During the POST procedures, error messages or numeric codes will be displayed whenever a problem is detected. In most cases, the error code will be a three or four digit number that, when checked against the list provided in Table 1, will help identify the malfunctioning component.

All personal computer error codes for the Power On Self Test, General Diagnostics, and Advanced Diagnostics consist of a device number followed by two digits other than 00. (The device number plus 00 indicates successful completion of the test.)

Note: Not all computers can generate all codes!

```
Code    Description
0xx     Miscellaneous errors
   01x  undetermined problem errors
   02x  power supply errors

1xx     System board errors
   101  system board error - interrupt controller failure
   102  system board error - system timer 2 failure
   103  system board error - system timer 0 failure
   104  system board error - protected mode failure
   105  system board error - last 8042 DMA command not accepted
   106  system board error - converting logic test
   107  system board error - hot NMI test
   108  system board error - timer bus test
   109  Direct Memory Access (DMA) test error
   111  80C88 microprocessor failed
   121  unexpected hardware interrupts occurred
   131  cassette wrap test failed
   110  system board memory
   111  adapter memory
   112  (any adapter in system unit)
   113  (any adapter in system unit)
   121  unexpected hardware interrupts occurred
   131  cassette wrap test failed
   151  system board error; defective battery
   152  system board error; real time clock failure
   161  system options error-(Run SETUP) [Battery failure]
   162  system options not set correctly-(Run SETUP)
   163  time and date not set-(Run SETUP)
   164  memory size error-(Run SETUP)
   165  system options not set - (Run SETUP)
   166  (any adapter in system unit)
   170  LCD not in use when suspended
   171  base 128K checksum failure
   172  diskette active when suspended
   173  LCD not active when suspended
   174  LCD configuration changed
   175  LCD alternate mode failed
   199  user-indicated configuration not correct

2xx     Memory (RAM) errors
   201  memory test failed. Displayed in the form XXXXX YY 201 where XXXXX
        represents the memory bank and YY represents the bit (actual chip)
   202  memory address error
   203  memory address error
   215  (system board memory failure)
   216  (system board memory failure)

3xx     Keyboard or keyboard card errors
   301  keyboard did not respond to software reset correctly, or a stuck key
        failure was detected. If a stuck key was detected, the scancode for the
        key is displayed in hexadecimal. For example, the error code 49 301
        indicates that key 73, the PgUp key, has failed (49 hex=73 dec)
   302  user-indicated error from the keyboard test, or AT keylock is locked.
   303  keyboard or system unit error
   304  keyboard or system unit error; CMOS does not match system, or keyboard
        cable not attached
   305  PS/2 models 50 and 60 fuse or keyboard cable error, or typamatic error
   341  replace keyboard
```

List of IBM PC-XT-AT-PS/2 Diagnostic Error Codes

```
     342  replace interface cable
     343  replace enhancement card or cable

4xx      Monochrome monitor errors
     401  monochrome memory test, horizontal sync frequency test, or video test
          failed
     408  user-indicated display attributes failure
     416  user-indicated character set failure
     424  user-indicated 80 X 25 mode failure
     432  parallel port test failed (monochrome adapter)

5xx      Colour monitor errors
     501  colour memory test failed, horizontal sync frequency test, or video test
          failed
     503  CRT display adapter controlled failed
     508  user-indicated display attribute failure
     516  user-indicated character set failure
     524  user-indicated 80 X 25 mode failure
     532  user-indicated 40 X 25 mode failure
     540  user-indicated 320 X 200 graphics mode failure
     548  user-indicated 640 X 200 graphics mode failure
     564  user indicated a paging test failure

6xx      Diskette drive errors
     601  diskette power-on diagnostics test failed
     602  diskette test failed; boot record is not valid
     606  diskette verify function failed
     607  write-protected diskette
     608  bad command diskette status returned
     610  diskette initialization failed
     611  timeout - diskette status returned
     612  bad NEC controller chip - diskette status returned
     613  bad DMA - diskette status returned
     614  DMA Boundary error
     621  bad seek - diskette status returned
     622  bad CRC - diskette status returned
     623  record not found - diskette status returned
     624  bad address mark - diskette status returned
     625  bad NEC (controller) seek - diskette status returned
     626  diskette data compare error
     627  diskette change line error
     628  diskette removed

7xx      NDP (math coprocessor) errors (8087, 80287, 80387)
     701  math coprocessor test failed

8xx      undefined

9xx      Parallel printer adapter errors
     901  printer adapter data register latch error
     902  printer adapter control register latch error
     903  printer adapter register address decode error
     904  printer adapter address decode error
     910  status line(s) wrap connector error  (pn 8529228 ?)
     911  status line bit 7 wrap error
     912  status line bit 7 wrap error
     913  status line bit 6 wrap error
     914  status line bit 5 wrap error
     915  status line bit 4 wrap error
     916  printer adapter interrupt wrap failed
     917  unexpected printer adapter interrupt
     92x  feature register error (special card)

10xx     Alternate Parallel Printer Adapter (LPT2)
    1001  alternate printer port (LPT2) test failed

11xx     Asynchronous communications adapter errors
    1101  asynchronous communications adapter test failed (int. modem 8250 chip)
    1102  any serial device (system board), or internal modem failed
    1103  dial tone test 1 failed (internal modem)
    1104  dial tone test 2 failed (internal modem)
```

```
1106    any serial device (system board)
1107    communications cable (system board)
1108    any serial device (system board)
1109    any serial device (system board)
1110    modem status register not clear
1111    ring indicate failure
1112    trailing edge ring indicate failure
1113    receive and delta receive line signal detect failure
1114    receive line signal detect failure
1115    delta receive line signal detect failure
1116    line control register; all bits cannot be set
1117    line control register; all bits cannot be reset
1118    xmit holding and/or shift register is stuck on
1119    data ready stuck on
1120    interrupt enable register, all bits cannot be set
1121    interrupt enable register, all bits cannot be reset
1122    interrupt pending stuck on
1123    interrupt ID register stuck on
1124    modem control register, all bits cannot be set
1125    modem control register, all bits cannot be reset
1126    modem status register, all bits cannot be set
1127    modem status register, all bits cannot be reset
1128    interrupt ID failure
1129    cannot force overrun error
1130    no modem status interrupt
1131    invalid interrupt pending
1132    no data ready
1133    no data available interrupt
1134    no transmit holding interrupt
1135    no interrupts
1136    no received line status interrupt
1137    no receive data available
1138    transmit holding register not empty
1139    no modem status interrupt
1140    transmit holding register not empty
1141    no interrupts
1142    no IRQ4 interrupt
1143    no IRQ3 interrupt
1144    no data transferred
1145    max baud rate failed
1146    min baud rate failed
1148    timeout error
1149    invalid data returned
1150    modem status register error
1151    no DSR and delta DSR
1152    no data set ready
1153    no delta
1154    modem status register not clear
1155    no CTS and delta CTS
1156    no clear to send
1157    no delta CTS

12xx    Alternate asynchronous communications adapter errors
  1201  Alternate asynchronous communications adapter test failed
        1101 if internal modem is not installed
  1202  Dual Asynch Adapter/A (any serial device)
        1102 if internal modem is not installed
  1206  Dual Asynch Adapter/A (any serial device)
  1207  Dual Asynch Adapter/A board error
  1208  Dual Asynch Adapter/A (any serial device)
  1209  Dual Asynch Adapter/A (any serial device)

13xx    Game control adapter errors
  1301  game control adapter test failed
  1302  joystick test failed

14xx    Printer errors
  1401  printer test failed
  1402  printer not ready error
  1403  printer paper error
  1404  matrix printer failed
```

List of IBM PC-XT-AT-PS/2 Diagnostic Error Codes

```
  1405   user indicated a print-pattern error

 15xx    Synchronous data link control (SDLC) communications adapter errors
  1510   8255 port B failure
  1511   8255 port A failure
  1512   8255 port C failure
  1513   8253 timer 1 did not reach terminal count
  1514   8253 timer 1 stuck on
  1515   8253 timer 0 did not reach terminal count
  1516   8253 timer 0 stuck on
  1517   8253 timer 2 did not reach terminal count
  1518   8253 timer 2 stuck on
  1519   8273 port B error
  1520   8273 port A error
  1521   8273 command/read timeout
  1522   interrupt level 4 failure
  1523   ring Indicate stuck on
  1524   receive clock stuck on
  1525   transmit clock stuck on
  1526   test indicate stuck on
  1527   ring indicate not on
  1528   receive clock not on
  1529   transmit clock not on
  1530   test indicate not on
  1531   data set ready not on
  1532   carrier detect not on
  1533   clear to send not on
  1534   data set ready stuck on
  1536   clear to send stuck on
  1537   level 3 interrupt failure
  1538   receive interrupt results error
  1539   wrap data miscompare
  1540   DMA channel 1 error
  1541   DMA channel 1 error
  1542   error in 8273 error checking or status reporting
  1547   stray interrupt level 4
  1548   stray interrupt level 3
  1549   interrupt presentation sequence timeout

 16xx    Display emulation errors (327x, 5520, 525x)

 17xx    Fixed disk errors
  1701   fixed disk POST error
  1702   fixed disk adapter error
  1703   fixed disk drive error
  1704   fixed disk adapter or drive error
  1780   fixed disk 0 failure
  1781   fixed disk 1 failure
  1782   fixed disk controller failure
  1790   fixed disk 0 error
  1791   fixed disk 1 error

 18xx    I/O expansion unit errors
  1801   I/O expansion unit POST error
  1810   enable/disable failure
  1811   extender card wrap test failed (disabled)
  1812   high order address lines failure (disabled)
  1813   wait state failure (disabled)
  1814   enable/Disable could not be set on
  1815   wait state failure (disabled)
  1816   extender card wrap test failed (enabled)
  1817   high order address lines failure (enabled)
  1818   disable not functioning
  1819   wait request switch not set correctly
  1820   receiver card wrap test failure
  1821   receiver high order address lines failure

 19xx    3270 PC attachment card errors

 20xx    Binary synchronous communications (BSC) adapter errors
  2010   8255 port A failure
```

```
2011   8255 port B failure
2012   8255 port C failure
2013   8253 timer 1 did not reach terminal count
2014   8253 timer 1 stuck on
2016   8253 timer 2 did not reach terminal count, or timer 2 stuck on
2017   8251 Data set ready failed to come on
2018   8251 Clear to send not sensed
2019   8251 Data set ready stuck on
2020   8251 Clear to send stuck on
2021   8251 hardware reset failed
2022   8251 software reset failed
2023   8251 software "error reset" failed
2024   8251 transmit ready did not come on
2025   8251 receive ready did not come on
2026   8251 could not force "overrun" error status
2027   interrupt failure - no timer interrupt
2028   interrupt failure - transmit, replace card or planar
2029   interrupt failure - transmit, replace card
2030   interrupt failure - receive, replace card or planar
2031   interrupt failure - receive, replace card
2033   ring indicate stuck on
2034   receive clock stuck on
2035   transmit clock stuck on
2036   test indicate stuck on
2037   ring indicate stuck on
2038   receive clock not on
2039   transmit clock not on
2040   test indicate not on
2041   data set ready not on
2042   carrier detect not on
2043   clear to send not on
2044   data set ready stuck on
2045   carrier detect stuck on
2046   clear to send stuck on
2047   unexpected transmit interrupt
2048   unexpected receive interrupt
2049   transmit data did not equal receive data
2050   8251 detected overrun error
2051   lost data set ready during data wrap
2052   receive timeout during data wrap

21xx   Alternate binary synchronous communications adapter errors
2110   8255 port A failure
2111   8255 port B failure
2112   8255 port C failure
2113   8253 timer 1 did not reach terminal count
2114   8253 timer 1 stuck on
2115   8253 timer 2 did not reach terminal count, or timer  2 stuck on
2116   8251 Data set ready failed to come on
2117   8251 Clear to send not sensed
2118   8251 Data set ready stuck on
2119   8251 Clear to send stuck on
2120   8251 hardware reset failed
2121   8251 software reset failed
2122   8251 software "error reset" failed
2123   8251 transmit ready did not come on
2124   8251 receive ready did not come on
2125   8251 could not force "overrun" error status
2126   interrupt failure - no timer interrupt
2128   interrupt failure - transmit, replace card or planar
2129   interrupt failure - transmit, replace card
2130   interrupt failure - receive, replace card or planar
2131   interrupt failure - receive, replace card
2133   ring indicate stuck on
2134   receive clock stuck on
2135   transmit clock stuck on
2136   test indicate stuck on
2137   ring indicate stuck on
2138   receive clock not on
2139   transmit clock not on
2140   test indicate not on
```

List of IBM PC-XT-AT-PS/2 Diagnostic Error Codes

```
2141   data set ready not on
2142   carrier detect not on
2143   clear to send not on
2144   data set ready stuck on
2145   carrier detect stuck on
2146   clear to send stuck on
2147   unexpected transmit interrupt
2148   unexpected receive interrupt
2149   transmit data did not equal receive data
2150   8251 detected overrun error
2151   lost data set ready during data wrap
2152   receive timeout during data wrap

22xx   Cluster adapter errors

23xx   undefined

24xx   Enhanced Graphics Adapter errors (and VGA)
  2401   \
  2402   / both are used, meanings unknown

25xx   undefined

26xx   XT/370 error codes
  2601-2655   XT/370-M card   (Note: P-Processor, M-Memory, EM-Emulator)
  2657-2668   XT/370-M card
  2672        XT/370-M card
  2673-2674   XT/370-P card
  2677-2680   XT/370-P card
  2681        XT/370-M card
  2682-2694   XT/370-P card
  2697        XT/370-P card
  2698        XT/370 diagnostic diskette error
  2701-2703   XT/370-EM card

27xx   XT/370 error codes, 3277 emulator card

28xx   Distributed functions card

29xx   Colour matrix printer errors
  2901   \
  2902    - unknown
  2904   /
30xx   Primary PC Network Adapter Error
  3001   CPU failure
  3002   ROM failure
  3003   ID failure
  3004   RAM failure
  3005   HIC failure
  3006   +/- 12v failed
  3007   digital loopback failure
  3008   host detected HIC failure
  3009   sync fail & no go bit
  3010   HIC test OK & no go bit
  3011   go bit & no CMD 41
  3012   card not present
  3013   digital failure (fall thru)
  3015   analog failure
  3041   hot carrier (not this card)
  3042   hot carrier (this card)

31xx   Secondary PC Network Adapter Error
  3101   CPU failure
  3102   ROM failure
  3103   ID failure
  3104   RAM failure
  3105   HIC failure
  3106   +/- 12v failed
  3107   digital loopback failure
  3108   host detected HIC failure
  3109   sync fail & no go bit
```

```
3110  HIC test OK & no go bit
3111  go bit & no CMD 41
3112  card not present
3113  digital failure (fall thru)
3115  analog failure
3141  hot carrier (not this card)
3142  hot carrier (this card)

32xx  Display/program symbols/XGA card

33xx  Compact printer errors

36xx  GPIB card

38xx  Data acquisition card

39xx  Professional graphics adapter card (PGA)

50xx  Liquid crystal display
 5001  display buffer failed
 5002  font buffer failed
 5003  controller failed
 5004  user indicated a pel/drive test failure
 5008  user indicated a display attribute test failed
 5016  user indicated a character set test failure
 5020  user indicated an alternate character set test failure
 5024  user indicated a 80 x 25 mode test failure
 5032  user indicated a 40 x 25 mode test failure
 5040  user indicated a 320 x 200 graphics test failure
 5048  user indicated a 640 x 200 graphics test failure
 5064  user indicated a paging test failure

51xx  Portable printer
 5101  printer port failure
 5102  busy error
 5103  paper or ribbon error
 5104  time out
 5105  user indicated a print-pattern error

56xx  Financial input card, connector, 4700 keyboard, pin kbd

71xx  Voice communications adapter
 7101  I/O control register
 7102  instruction or external data memory
 7103  PC to VCA interrupt
 7104  internal data memory
 7105  DMA
 7106  internal registers
 7107  interactive shared memory
 7108  VCA to PC interrupt
 7109  DC wrap
 7111  external analog wrap & tone output
 7112  mic to spkr wrap
 7114  telephone attach test

73xx  3.5" external diskette drive

74xx  Display adapter 8514/A

850x  80286 Expanded Memory Adapter/A

851x  80286 Expanded Memory Adapter/A

852x  Memory module package on the 80286 Expanded Memory Adapter/A

860x  Personal Series 2 pointing device errors
 8601  pointing device (IBM mouse)
 8602  pointing device
 8603  system board error
 8604  system board : Pointing device
```

List of IBM PC-XT-AT-PS/2 Diagnostic Error Codes

```
100xx   Multiprotocol Adapter/A
 10002   Multiprotocol Adapter/A any serial device
 10006   Multiprotocol Adapter/A any serial device
 10007   communications cable Multiprotocol Adapter/A
 10008   Multiprotocol Adapter/A any serial device
 10009   Multiprotocol Adapter/A any serial device

101xx   Modem Adapter/A
 10102   Modem Adapter/A any serial device
 10106   Modem Adapter/A any serial device
 10108   Modem Adapter/A any serial device
 10109   Modem Adapter/A any serial device

104xx   Fixed disk adapter (ESDI) drives 0 or 1 (C or D)
 10480   fixed disk C, adapter (ESDI) or system board error
 10481   fixed disk D, adapter (ESDI) or system board error
 10482   fixed disk C or system board error
 10483   fixed disk adapter (ESDI) or system board error
 10490   fixed disk C or adapter (ESDI) error
 10491   fixed disk C or adapter (ESDI) error

 16500   6157 Tape Attachment Adapter

 16520   6157 Streaming Tape Drive

 16540   6157 Streaming Tape Drive or tape attachment adapter

 C0000   Keyboard/keyboard card

 C8000   Fixed disk/fixed disk card

 CA000   Keyboard/keyboard card
```

Appendix 6

Pinouts For Various Interfaces

PC expansion card sizes:

XT 13-1/8x4.0,   1 62 pin connector
XT/286   62 and 36 pin connectors
AT 13-1/8x4.8   62 and 36 pin connectors

Original PC slot spacing was 1 inch on centre. XT, AT and most clone systems are $^{13}/_{16}$ inch on centre. Some modem and hard disk cards are advertised as 'one slot wide' but they often refer to PC slots. Make sure the card will fit if you have the narrower slot spacing.

'Half cards' vary in size from almost as long as a standard card to no longer than the expansion connector itself. If you have a space problem (like the centre drive bay or a hard disk card with a two slot wide far end) make sure the 'half card' you buy will be short enough to actually fit.

Many XT type (8 bit) expansion cards drop down at the end of the connector and hug the motherboard closely for more room on the card. These cards will not fit in an AT type 16 bit slot since the extra connector gets in the way. When ordering cards for an AT, remember you only have two or three 8 bit slots which are able to hold these drop-down type cards.

PC/XT Slot J8

The slot next to the power supply in the XT is slightly different from the slots in the PC and the other seven slots in the XT. Timing requirements are much stricter for cards in J8, and the computer expects a 'card selected' signal to be pulled high by any card in that slot. Early PC Portables with the PC Portable motherboard (these were supposed to have been recalled and replaced with XT motherboards, but you never know!) lacked some of the memory lines, and cards with memory access won't work there at all.

Due to the different timing of the slot, some cards will not work in J8. The IBM parallel card will not work there, but many were delivered with the serial card in that location.

J8 was likely developed for the synchronous mainframe communications adapter or something similar.

8-bit Expansion Card Slot
female 62 pin female card edge

PC/XT 8 bit bus slot:

```
        GND          B1    A1   I/O CH CK
        RESET              D7
        +5VDC              D6
        IRQ2               D5
        -5VDC              D4
        DRQ2               D3
        -12VDC             D2
        -HRQ I/O CHAN      D1
        +12VDC             D0
        GND          B10   A10  I/O CH RDY
        -MEMW              AEN
        -MEMR              A19
        -IOW               A18
        -IOR               A17
        -DACK3             A16
        DRQ3               A15
        -DACK1             A14
        DRQ1               A13
        -DACK0             A12
        CLK          B20   A20  A11
        IRQ7               A10
        IRQ6               A9
        IRQ5               A8
        IRQ4               A7
        IRQ3               A6
        -DACK2             A5
        TC                 A4
        ALE                A3
        +5VDC              A2
        OSC          B30   A30  A1
        GND                A0
```

XT/286, AT 16 bit bus extension slot:
36 pin edge card connector

```
        -MEM C516    D1    C1   SBHE
        -I/O CS16    D2    C2   LA23
        IRQ10        D3    C3   LA22
        IRQ11        D4    C4   LA21
        IRQ12        D5    C5   LA20
        IRQ15        D6    C6   LA19
        IRQ14        D7    C7   LA18
        -DACK0       D8    C8   LA17
        DRQ0         D9    C9   -MEMR
        -DACK5       D10   C10  -MEMW
        DRQ5         D11   C11  SD08
        -DACK6       D12   C12  SD09
        DRQ6         D13   C13  SD10
        -DACK7       D14   C14  SD11
        DRQ7         D15   C15  SD12
        -5vdc        D16   C16  SD13
        -MASTER      D17   C17  SD14
        GND          D18   C18  SD15
```

Game Port

DB15

```
1     +5 VDC
2     button 1
3     position 0  (X Coordinate)
4     ground
5     ground
6     position 1  (Y Coordinate)
7     button 2
8     +5 VDC                       JOY-STICK 'A'

9     +5 VDC                       JOY-STICK 'B'
10    button 3
11    position 2  (X Coordinate)
12    ground
13    position 3  (Y Coordinate)
14    button 4
15    +5 VDC
```

The Kraft KC-3 joy-stick is supplied with two potentiometers. They measure 880k ohms, probably 1Meg pots. It should be noted that the effective wiper travel is very limited, say around 45 degrees from stop to stop, and the internal wiring is arranged so as to leave one end of the pot unconnected. That is to say, the wiper (middle) post is connected, and one end post is connected as well (I assume the wires would be called signal and +5v, respectively).

hard disk 34-pin

34 pin card edge connector

```
pin
#'s              function
2     RWC        reduced write current
4     HS2        head select 2 (2)
6                write gate
8                seek complete
10               track 0
12               write fault
14    HS0        head select 2  (0)
16          reserved
18    HS1        head select 2  (1)
20    IDX        index
22    RDY        ready
24               step
26    DS1        drive select 1
28    DS2        drive select 2
30          reserved
32          reserved
34               direction in
```

all odd numbers are ground

hard disk 20 pin

20-pin card edge connector

```
13    + MFM write data
14    - MFM write data
17    + MFM read data
18    - MFM read data

2,4,6,11,12,15,16,19,20 ground
all other pins unused
```

Note: The IBM AT 20-pin connector and some clones have one pin clipped off to 'key' the connector. If your card has 20 pins but your cable has only 19 holes, you can usually safely clip off the offending pin.

IBM expansion chassis
Expansion connector, IBM Expansion Chassis

If you decide to make one, pins 13 and 18 are reversed in the Technical Reference Manual. Pin 13 is WRITE DATA and pin 18 is SELECT HEAD 1.

```
            DB-62 connector
         _____
   21   ( o o o o o o o o o o o o o o o o o o o o o ) 1
   42    \ o o o o o o o o o o o o o o o o o o o o o / 22
   62     \ o o o o o o o o o o o o o o o o o o o o / 43
           _____/
```

PIN	signal	pin	signal	pin	signal
1	+E IRQ6	22	+E D5	43	+E IRQ7
2	+E DRQ2	23	+E DRQ1	44	+E D6
3	+E DIR	24	+E DRQ3	45	+E I/O CH RDY
4	+E enable	25	reserved	46	+E IRQ3
5	+E clk	26	+E ALE	47	+E D7
6	-E mem in exp	27	+E T/C	48	+E D1
7	+E A17	28	+E reset	49	+E I/O CH CK
8	+E A16	29	+E AEN	50	+E IRQ2
9	+E A5	30	+E A19	51	+E D0
10	-E DACK0	31	+E A14	52	+E D2
11	+E A15	32	+E A12	53	+E D4
12	+E A11	33	+E A16	54	+E IRQ5
13	+E A10	34	-E MEMR	55	+E IRQ4
14	+E A19	35	-E MEMW	56	+E D3
15	+E A1	36	+E A0	57	GND
16	+E A3	37	-E DACK3	58	GND
17	-E DACK1	38	+E A6	59	GND
18	+E A4	39	-E IOR	60	GND
19	-E DACK2	40	+E A8	61	GND
20	-E IOW	41	+E A2	62	GND
21	+E A13	42	+E A7		

IBM PC Tech Ref says the expansion chassis has its own clock, the clock signals are not carried over the cable. There is 1 wait state inserted to allow for the asynchronopus operation of the expansion chassis. IBM uses an amplifier and reciever card to make up for signal losses, with a very short cable it may be possible ot hook the busses directly.

5.25 inch floppy connector (to drive)
34 pin card edge connector

all odd numbers are grounds

```
        2,4,6   unused
        8       index
        10      motor enable A
        12      Drive Select B
        14      Drive Select A
        16      Motor Enable B
        18      Direction (Step Motor)
        20      Step Pulse
        22      Write Data
        24      Write Enable
        26      Track 0
        28      Write Protect
        30      Read Data
        32      Select head 1
        34      Unused
```

Colour Graphics Adapter
RGB monitor (standard digital) 8 colour, intensity signal gives 16
DB9

```
          1 o o o o 5
          6  o o o  9
```

```
1    ground
2    shield ground
3    red
4    green
5    blue
6    intensity
7    reserved
8    horizontal sync
9    vertical sync
```

Colour Graphics Adapter
RCA female
(CGA, EGA, VGA composite output)

Centre - composite video signal, approximately 1.5vDC
Outside - ground

RGB monitor (some analog)
DB-15 connector
(not IBM - some Apple)

```
          1 o o o o o o o 8
          9  o o o o o o  15
```

```
1  shield ground     6  ground        11  B&W NTSC video
2  green             7  -5v           12  colour NTSC video
3  sync              8  +12v          13  ground
4  not used          9  blue          14  -12v
5  red              10  intensity     15  +5v
```

Monochrome Display Adapter, Hercules
DB9

```
          5 o o o o 1
          6  o o o  9
```

```
1    ground
2    shield ground
3    N/C
4    N/C
5    N/C
6    + intensity
7    + video
8    + horizontal
9    - vertical
```

Signal voltages are: 0 to .6 VDC at the Low Level
                     +5 VDC at the High Level

IBM VGA

```
Pin     function
1       red
2       green
3       blue
4       reserved
5       digital ground
6       red rtn     (a return signal that informs the VGA
                    that this is a colour on monochrome monitor?)
7       green rtn
8       blue rtn
9       plug        (no function?)
10      digital ground
11      reserved
12      reserved
13      horizontal sync
14      vertical sync
15      reserved
```

Keyboard Connector
XT/AT except XT/286
DIN 5 pin round

```
1       +clock    +5vDC
2       +data     +5vDC
3       -keyboard reset (not used by keyboard)
4       ground
5       +5vDC
```

Cassette Port Connector
PC-0, PC-1, PC-2
DIN-5 round

```
pin     use
1       cassette motor control, common from relay
2       ground
3       cassette motor control, 6vDC @1A
4       data in, 500nA @+/-13v, 1000-2000 baud
5       data out, 250uA @ .68 or .75vDC
```

Light Pen Connector
6 pins CGA, Hercules

```
pin     use
1       + light pen input
2       not used
3       + light pen switch
4       ground
5       + 5v
6       + 12v
```

Disk Drive Power Connectors
4 pin special (Shugart standard)

```
           1 / O  O  O  O \ 4
             ---------------
pin     use
1       +12vDC
2       ground
3       ground
4       +5vDC
```

4 trace card edge (Sony 3.5 inch)

```
pin   use
1     +5v
2     gnd (5v)
3     gnd (12v)
4     +12v
```

Power Supply
PC, XT

```
     1    power good
     2    +5v
P    3    +12v
8    4    -12v
     5    gnd
     6    gnd
     7    gnd
     8    gnd
P    9    -5
9    10   +5
     11   +5
     12   +5
```

```
            AT VOLTAGE CHECKS
Min Vdc   Max Vdc    - LEAD    + LEAD
 +2.4      +5.2       J8-5      J8-1
 +4.8      +5.2       J8-5      J9-4
 +4.5      +5.4       J9-3      J8-6
+11.5     +12.6       J9-1      J8-3
+10.8     +12.9       J8-4      J9-2

      DISKETTE/DISK DRIVE VOLTAGE CHECKS
 +4.8      +5.2         2         4
+11.5     +12.6         3         1

         ***TOP OF DISKETTE DRIVE***

              . . . .
              1 2 3 4
```

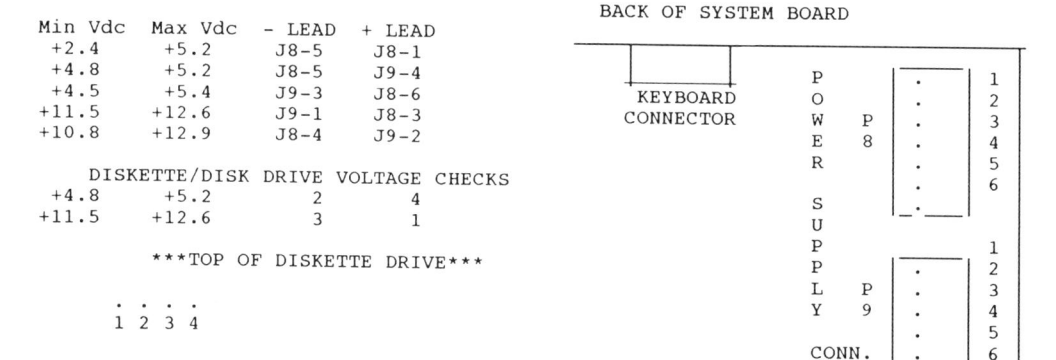

```
BACK OF SYSTEM BOARD

         KEYBOARD           P         1
         CONNECTOR          O         2
                            W  P      3
                            E  8      4
                            R         5
                                      6
                            S
                            U
                            P         1
                            P         2
                            L  P      3
                            Y  9      4
                                      5
                         CONN.        6
```

PC/AT power connectors must be terminated with the proper resistor plug if not used, XT power supplies should not be operated without a load.

Parallel Port
DB25 (Amphenol 57-30360)

```
1     STROBE (Normal=High, Data read-in when Low)
2     DATA 1
3     DATA 2
4     DATA 3
5     DATA 4
6     DATA 5
7     DATA 6
8     DATA 7
9     DATA 8
10    ACKNLG (5us pulse,low=data rcvd and printer is ready)
11    BUSY
12    PE (high=printer out of paper)
13    SLCT (printer is in the selected state)
```

Pinouts for Various Interfaces

```
14     AUTO FEED XT (low=paper auto. fed one line after printing)
15     N/C
16     0V (logic ground level)
17     chassis ground
18     N/C
19-30  ground
31     INIT (normal=high, low=printer controller reset, buffer cleared)
32     ERROR (low=paper end state, off-line state, or error state)
33     ground
34     N/C
35     +5 VDC through a 4.7K resistor
36     SLCT IN (low=data entry possible)
```

Serial Port
for PC, XT, PS/2
connector DB-25

```
              1 o o o o o o o o o o o o 13
              14 o o o o o o o o o o o o 25

1     N/C
2     transmit data
3     receive data
4     RTS (request to send)
5     CTS (clear to send)
6     DSR (data set ready)
7     signal ground
8     CD (carrier detect)
9     +transmit current loop return (20ma)
10    N/C
11    -transmit current loop data (20ma)
12    N/C
13    N/C
14    N/C
15    N/C
16    N/C
17    N/C
18    +receive current loop data (20ma)
19    N/C
20    DTR (data terminal ready)
21    N/C
22    RI (ring indicator)
23    N/C
24    N/C
25    -receive current loop return (20ma)
```

(RS232C industry standard)

Pin #	code	description	Pin #	code	description
1	AA	ground	13	SCB	sec. clear to send
2	BA	transmitted data	14	SBA	sec. transmitted data
3	BB	received data	15	DB	transmitted signal element timing (DCE)
4	CA	request to send			
5	CB	clear to send	16	SBB	sec. received data
6	CC	data set ready	17	DD	receiver signal element timing (DCE)
7	AB	signal ground			
8	CF	received line signal detector	18	-	unassigned
9	-	reserved	19	SCA	sec. request to send
10	-	reserved	20	CD	data terminal ready
11	-	unassigned	21	CG	signal quality detector
12	SCF	sec. received line signal detector	22	CE	ring indicator
			23	CH/CI	data signal rate select
			24	DA	trans. sig. timing (DTE)
			25	-	unassigned

Serial Port
DB9
AT

```
                        5 o o o o o 1
                        6 o o o o 9

Pin                              Description
1       CD      in       data carrier detect
2       RD      in       serial receive data
3       TD      out      serial transmit data
4       DTR     out      data terminal ready
5       gnd              signal ground
6       DSR     in       data set ready
7       RTS     out      request to send
8       CTS     in       clear to send
9       RI      in       ring indicator
```

RGB monitor (standard digital)
EIAJ-8 connector

```
1. intensity    5. shield ground                o   o 1
2. red          6. ground
3. green        7. horiz or composite sync      o   o
4. blue         8. vertical sync
                                                o   o

                                                o   o
```

DB9 to EIJ-8 (IBM compatible to Taxan or component TV)
adapter wiring

```
        1 == 5 gnd
        2 == 6 gnd
        3 == 2 red
        4 == 3 green
        5 == 4 blue
        6 == 1 intensity
        7 == no connection
        8 == 7 horiz sync
        9 == 8 vertical sync
```

Note: intensity signals can be either positive or negative!

Sony Multiscan monitor (analog)

```
Pin     function
1       gnd
2       gnd
3       red
4       grn
5       blu
6       gnd
7       no connection
8       horiz sync
9       vert sync
```

Various Serial Cable Pin-outs
(like symbols mean connect pins together)

```
   IBM-PC         Hayes Modem          IBM-AT         Hayes Modem
    DB-25            DB-25              DB-9             DB-25
   FGND  1 -------  1 FGND             DCD  1 <------  8 DCD
   XMT   2 ------>  2 XMT              RCV  2 <------  3 RCV
   RCV   3 <------  3 RCV              XMT  3 ------>  2 XMT
   RTS   4 ------>  4 RTS              DTR  4 ------> 20 DTR
   CTS   5 ------>  5 CTS              SGND 5 -------  7 SGND
   DSR   6 <------  6 DSR              DSR  6 <------  6 DSR
   SGND  7 -------  4 SGND             RTS  7 ------>  4 RTS
   DCD   8 <------  8 DCD              CTS  8 <------  5 CTS
   DTR  20 ------> 20 DTR              RNG  9 <------ 22 RNG
   RNG  22 <------ 22 RNG

        Null Modem Cable                     Null Modem Cable
    IBM PC          IBM PC             IBM AT           IBM AT
    DB-25            DB-25              DB-9             DB-9
   XMT   2------------  3 RCV          RCV  2------------  3 XMT
   RCV   3------------  2 XMT          XMT  3------------  2 RCV
   RTS   4-#           *- 4 RTS        RTS  7-#           *- 7 RTS
   CTS   5-#           *- 5 CTS        CTS  8-#           *- 8 CTS
   DSR   6-+           @- 6 DSR        DSR  6-+           @- 6 DSR
   DCD   8-+           @- 8 DCD        DCD  1-+           @- 1 DCD
   DTR  20-+           @-20 DTR        DTR  4-+           @- 4 DTR
   SGND  7------------  7 SGND         SGND 5------------  5 SGND

        Null Modem Cable
    IBM PC          IBM AT
    DB-25            DB-9
   XMT   2------------  2 RCV
   RCV   3------------  3 XMT
   RTS   4-#           *- 7 RTS
   CTS   5-#           *- 8 CTS
   DSR   6-+           @- 6 DSR
   DCD   8-+           @- 1 DCD
   DTR  20-+           @- 4 DTR
   SGND  7------------  5 SGND

    VT 220       Brother M 1509         P-E 6100     Brother M-1509
    DB-9            DB-25               DB-25           DB-25
   GND   1-------  1 GND                GND   1-------  1 GND
   XMT   2-------  3 RCV                XMT   2-------  2 RCV
   RCV   3-------  2 XMT                RCV   3-------  3 XMT
   DSR   6-------20 DTR                 RTS   4-------
   SGND  7-------  7 SGND               CTS   5-------
                                        DSR   6-------
                                        SGND  7-------  7 SGND
                                        DCD   8-------
                                        DTR  20-------
```

Various Serial Cable Pinouts

```
                  NEC                                 NEC
    IBM-AT     3510/3515             IBM-XT        3510/3515
     DB9          DB25                 DB25           DB25
    RCV   2-------  2 XMT             XMT   2-------  3 RCV
    XMT   3-------  3 RCV             RCV   3-------  2 XMT
    SGND  5-------  7 SGND            CTS   5-------19 2nd RTS
    CTS   8-------19 2nd RTS          SGND  7-------  7 SGND
    DCD   1 #       *  4 RTS          DSR   6 #       *  4 RTS
    DTR   4 #       *  5 CTS          DCD   8 #       *  5 CTS
    DSR   6 #       +  6 DSR          DTR  20 #       +  6 DSR
    RTS   7         +  8 DCD          RTS   7         +  8 DCD
    RNG   9         +20 DTR           RNG   9         +20 DTR
```

```
IBM-AT          NEC 7700 Series
  DB9
  DCD   1-+-----20 DTR
  DSR   6-+
  RCV   2------- 2 XMT
  XMT   3------- 3 RCV
  DTR   4-----+- 6 DSR
              +- 8 DCD
  SGND  5------- 7 SGND
  RTS   7------- 5 CTS
  CTS   8-------19 2nd RTS


IBM-AT         HP 7470A              IBM-XT          HP 7470A
  DB9           DB25                  DB25            DB25
  RCV   2------- 2 XMT                GND   1------- 1 GND
  XMT   3------- 3 RCV                XMT   2------- 3 RCV
  SGND  5------- 7 SGND               RCV   3------- 2 XMT
  DSR   6-+-----20 DTR                CTS   5-+-----20 DTR
  CTS   8-+                           DSR   6-+
                                      SGND  7------- 7 SGND


IBM-AT         HP Laserjet           IBM-XT          HP Laserjet
  RCV   2------- 2 XMT                GND   1------- 1 GND
  XMT   3------- 3 RCV                XMT   2------- 3 RCV
  SGND  5------- 7 SGND               RCV   3------- 2 XMT
  DSR   6-+-----20 DTR                CTS   5-+-----20 DTR
  CTS   8-+                           DSR   6-+
                                      SGND  7------- 7 SGND


   IBM-AT Pinout Names                 IBM-XT Pinout Names
 1 DCD   Data Carrier Detect         1 FGND  Frame Ground
 2 RCV   Receive Data                2 XMT   Transmit Data
 3 XMT   Transmit Data               3 RCV   Receive Data
 4 DTR   Data Terminal Ready         4 RTS   Request to Send
 5 SGND  Signal Ground               5 CTS   Clear to Send
 6 DSR   Data Set Ready (In)         6 DSR   Data Set Ready
 7 RTS   Request to Send             7 SGND  Signal Ground
 8 CTS   Clear to Send               8 DCD   Data Carrier Detect
 9 RNG   Ring Indicator             20 DTR   Data Terminal Ready
                                    22 RNG   Ring Indicator
```

Data Terminal to Data Communications

```
       Data Terminal     Data Comm.         Data Terminal    Data Terminal
        Equipment  <-->  Equipment           Equipment  <-->  Equipment
        Typical Configuration                Typical Configuration
       (DTE)            (DCE)               (DTE)             (DTE)
       AT  XT           Modem               AT  XT            Printer
           1 FGND----------- FGND               1 FGND--------- 1 FGND
       3   2 XMT----------->2 XMT          3   2 XMT--------->  3 RCV
       2   3 RCV<-----------3 RCV          2   3 RCV<---------  2 XMT
       7   4 RTS----------->4 RTS          7   4 RTS<---------  5 CTS
       8   5 CTS<-----------5 CTS          8   5 CTS--------->  4 RTS
       6   6 DSR<-----------6 DSR          6   6 DSR<--------- 20 DTR
       5   7 SGND-----------7 SGND         1   8 DCD<-+
       1   8 DCD<-----------8 DCD                     +-> 6 DSR
       4  20 DTR----------->20 DTR         4  20 DTR-------+-> 8 DCD
       9  22 RNG<-----------22 RNG         5   7 SGND---------7 SGND
                                           9  22 RNG          22 RNG
```

Null Modem

```
RS-232C Null Modem         RS-232C Straight         RS-232C typical
Cable Connections          through (computer        serial printer
(computer to computer)     to modem)

2  ----------- 3           2  ----------- 2         7  ----------- 7
3  ----------- 2           3  ----------- 3         2  ----------- 3
4  ----------- 5           4  ----------- 4         5  ---|
5  ----------- 4           5  ----------- 5         6  ---|------- 20
6  ----------- 20          6  ----------- 6         8  ---|
7  ----------- 7           7  ----------- 7         1  ----------- 1
20 ---------- 6            20 ---------- 20
```

Appendix 6

ANSI.SYS

ANSI.SYS is an installable console (CON) driver which understands ANSI control sequences.

ANSI.SYS replaces CON, since it is named CON and is installed as a device driver. ANSI.SYS watches all output going to the 'CON' file. When it sees its specific 'escape code' (ESC followed by a left bracket '[') it parses the following text until it sees a terminating string. If the escape code is a valid sequence, it will perform the task set by the code and then continue parsing the input stream. Invalid ANSI codes are ignored.

ANSI.SYS contains a buffer of 196 bytes under DOS 2.x or 204 bytes under DOS 3.x. You may use this buffer to store strings which you may assign to any key. The buffer is of fixed size, and so long as you do not overflow it, you may assign any length string to any key. The buffer will only contain the *ANSI.SYS significant* characters ANSI.SYS sees. The assignments to a key may be removed by assigning a NUL string to a key.

When designing ANSI.SYS, IBM selected a set of commands adopted by the American National Standards Institute, or ANSI, hence the driver's name. The driver's incorporation of ANSI standard sequences permits the use of the many programs that are designed with the standards in mind. With the new console device driver installed, the PC can use these programs. ANSI.SYS can also be used to develop programs for the PC or other systems with terminals that meet the standard. It is not necessary to include hardware-specific commands to control the display or cursor location. Program outputs can achieve the same results on any conforming hardware.

ANSI.SYS uses BIOS calls to control the screen. While putting text on the screen, ANSI.SYS watches for valid escape sequences. Such sequences follow the format:

```
            ESC [ param; param; ...; param cmd
   where:
            ESC    is the escape character chr$(27).
            [      is the left bracket character.
            param  is an ASCII decimal number, or a string in quotes.
            cmd    is a case-specific letter identifying the command.
```

Usually, zero, one, or two parameters are given. Spaces are not allowed between parameters. If parameters are omitted, they usually default to 1; however, some commands (KKR) treat the no-parameter case specially. For example, both ESC[1;1H and ESC[H send the cursor to the home position (1,1), which is the upper left.

Either single or double quotes may be used to quote a string. Each character inside a quoted string is equivalent to one numeric parameter. Quoted strings are normally used only for the Keyboard Key Reassignment command.

Control Sequences

The control sequences are valid if you issue them through standard DOS function calls that use standard input, standard output, or standard error output devices. These are the DOS function calls 01h, 02h, 06h, 07h, 09h, 0Ah, and 40h.

The following table lists the sequences understood by ANSI.SYS.

Cursor Positioning

Short	Long name	Format	Notes
CUP	cursor position	ESC[y;xH	Sets cursor position.
HVP	cursor position	ESC[y;xf	Same as CUP; not recommended.
CUU	cursor up	ESC[nA	n = # of lines to move
CUD	cursor down	ESC[nB	
CUF	cursor forward	ESC[nC	n = # of columns to move
CUB	cursor backward	ESC[nD	
DSR	Device Status, Report!	ESC[6n	Find out cursor position.
CPR	Cursor Position report	ESC[y;xR	Response to DSR, as if typed.
SCP	Save Cursor Position	ESC[s	Not nestable.
RCP	Restore Cursor Position	ESC[u	

Editing

ED	Erase in Display	ESC[2J	Clears screen.
EL	Erase in Line	ESC[K	Clears to end of line.

Mode-Setting

SGR	Set Graphics Rendition	ESC[n;n;...nm	See character attribute table.
SM	Set Mode	ESC[=nh	See screen mode table.
RM	Reset Mode	ESC[=nl	See screen mode table.
IBMKKR	Keyboard Key Reass.	ESC['string'p	

1. The first char of the string gives the key to redefine; the rest of the string is the key's new value.
2. To specify unprintable chars, give the ASCII value of the character outside of quotes, as a normal parameter.
3. IBM function keys are two byte strings; see Appendix 1. For example, ESC[0;';DIR A:';13;p redefines function key 1 to have the value 'DIR A:' followed by the ENTER key.

Character Attributes

The Set Graphics Rendition command is used to select foreground and background colours or attributes. When you use multiple parameters, they are executed in sequence, and the effects are cumulative.

Attrib code	Value
0	All attributes off (normal white on black)
1	Bold
4	Underline
5	Blink
7	Reverse Video
8	Invisible (but why?)
30-37	foregnd blk/red/grn/yel/blu/magenta/cyan/white
40-47	background

Cursor Positioning

To move the cursor to a specified position: ESC [#;#h where the first # is the desired line number and the second the desired column.

To move the cursor up without changing columns: ESC [#a where # specifies the number of lines moved.

To move the cursor to a specified horizontal and vertical position: ESC [#;#f where # means first the line number and secondly the column number.

To get a device status report: ESC [6n.

To get a cursor position report: ESC [#;#r where the first # specifies the current line and the second # specifies the current column.

To move the cursor down: ESC [#b where # specifies the number of lines moved down.

To move the cursor forward: ESC [#C where # specifies the number of columns moved.

To move the cursor backward: ESC [#d where # specifies the number of columns moved.

To save the cursor position: ESC [s and to restore it: ESC [u.

Erasing The Screen

To do a CLS (erase screen move cursor to home position): ESC [2j. To erase from cursor to end of line: ESC [k.

Set Screen/Character Colours

To set the colour/graphics attributes, enter ESC [#;#m where the first # is the desired foreground colour and the second is the desired background colour. Select colours from the list below:

```
30        black foreground
31        red foreground
32        green foreground
33        yellow foreground
34        blue foreground
35        magenta foreground
36        cyan foreground
37        white foreground

40        black background
41        red background
42        green background
43        yellow background
44        blue background
45        magenta background
46        cyan background
47        white background
```

To set additional attributes enter: ESC [#m where # is the number of the desired attribute. Select attributes from the list below:

```
0         all attributes off (white on black)
1         bold (high intensity) on
4         underscore (on monochrome or EGA display)
```

```
5        blinking
7        reverse video
8        invisible (character and box are set to the same colour)
```

Using ANSI Codes in the Prompt

PROMPT metastrings

metastring	definition special characters
$B	the '|' character
$G	the '' character
$L	the '' character
$Q	the '=' character
$$	the '$' character

System Information

$D	the date (14 characters: 3 character day-of-week, blank, 2 character month, dash, 2 character day, dash, 4 character year)
$T	the time (11 characters: 2 digit hour, colon, 2 digit minutes, colon, 2 digit seconds, point, 2 digit hundredths-of-seconds)
$N	the current default drive (1 character)
$P	the current directory path of the default drive (begins with default drive, colon, then a maximum of 63 characters of the path from the root to the current directory)
$V	the DOS version number (currently prints 39 characters)

Cursor Control

$H	backspace & erasure of the previous character
$_	a carriage return and linefeed sequence (the prompt continues on the beginning of the next screen line).

Other ASCII characters

$E	the ASCII ESCape character (alt-27)
$a	a null string (where 'a' is anything not used above)

DOS will not accept any other characters after the $ sign according to the manual, however, $aSTRING is sometimes used to display a string. The PROMPT commands are not case sensitive. ANSI.SYS escape code definitions may be mixed freely with the internal PROMPT commands. For example, PROMPT $e[s$e[1;1H$e[0m$e[K$e[7m $d / $t : $p $e[0m$e[ung.

What this does

```
$e[s         Save current cursor position
$e[1;1H      Move to upper left corner of display
$e[0m        Set normal mode display
$e[K         Erase topmost line of display
$e[7m        Set Reverse Video mode
$d           Display current date
$t           Display current time
$p           Display current drive & path
$e[0m        Set normal mode display
$e[u         Return to original cursor position
$n           Display the current drive
$g           Display the prompt character
```

Bibliography

The information presented here was gathered from megabytes of files found on BBS systems, conversations on a dozen different BBS systems, correspondence, and every reference book I could get my hands on. On occasion, a number of prestigious references didn't agree with each other. Where this has happened, I have used the latest references. There is too much information here for me to verify every fact personally. I have used my own judgement as to the reliability of the sources.

References used in preparing this book

AST EEMS Technical Reference Manual v3.2, documents 020022-001B and 000408-001B provided by AST Corporation, 1987.
Data General Programmer's Reference for MS-DOS, Rev.3, Data General Corporation (covers through DOS 3.0), p/n 069-100157 rev 00, May 1986.
IBM DOS Operations Manual Version 2.00.
IBM Technical Reference Options and Adapters - Enhanced Graphics Adapter, p/n 6280131, IBM Publications, Aug 1984.
IBM Technical Reference, *Personal Computer*, p/n 6322507 IBM Publications.
IBM Technical Reference, *Personal Computer* - PCjr, p/n 1502293 IBM Publications.
Lotus-Intel-Microsoft Expanded Memory Specification Version 3.20, part number 300275-003, provided by Intel Corp., September 1985.
Lotus-Intel-Microsoft Expanded Memory Specification 4.0, document 300275-005, provided by Intel Corp., October 1987.
Microsoft Extended Memory Specification v2.00, provided by Microsoft Corporation, 1988
MS-DOS Programmer's Reference (covers through DOS 2.00) by Microsoft, p/n 135555-001 Intel Corp. 1984
Tandy 1000 TX Technical Reference Manual, Tandy Corp., p/n 25-1514 Tandy Corp, 1987
Toshiba 1000 Technical Reference Manual, Toshiba Corp. of America, 1987
X3.4-1977: American National Standard Code for Information Interchange by American National Standards Institute (ANSI), New York, NY, 1977

FastCard IV User Manual Peripheral Marketing Inc., p/n 0527, Jan 1987.
Hercules Graphics Card User's Manual, Hercules Computer Technology, 1983.
Hercules Graphics Card Plus Owner's Manual, Hercules Computer Technology, Model GB112, 1987.
LANtastic Programmer's Information Package, 21/2/89.
LANtastic 2.46 Installation Guide.

Logitech EGA Reference Manual, EGA+Mouse Board.
MPC Operations Guide Manual #1023, Columbia Data Products, Inc., CDP, 1983
Microcomputer Products - 1987 Data Book, NEC Electronics, Inc., p/n 500105, Aug 1987
NEC uPD70108/70116 Microprocessor User's Manual, p/n 500350, October 1986, provided by NEC Electronics, Inc.
S-286 User Manual, version 2, Link Computer, 1988.
TesSeRact v1.0 documentation.
VideoTrax Installation Guide, Alpha Micro, 1987.

Advanced MSDOS, Ray Duncan, Microsoft Press, 1986.
Assembly Language Programming for the IBM Personal Computer, David J. Bradley, Prentice-Hall, 1984.
Assembly Language Subroutines for MSDOS Computers, Leo J. Scanlon, TAB Books, 1986.
Atari ST Internals, Gerits, English, & Bruckmann, Abacus Software, 1985.
Compute!'s Guide to Assembly Language Programming on the IBM PC, COMPUTE! Publications.
Compute!'s Mapping the IBM PC and PCjr, Russ Davis, COMPUTE! Publications.
DOS Power Tools, Paul Somerson, Bantam Books, 1988.
DOS: The Complete Reference, Kris Jamsa, Osborne/McGraw-Hill, 1987.
Exploring the IBM PCjr, Peter Norton, Microsoft Press, 1984.
IBM Video Subsystems, Richard Wilton, Microsoft Press, 1988.
Inside the IBM PC, Peter Norton.
Mapping the IBM PC, Russ Davies/Compute! Magazine, Compute! Books, 1986.
Microcomputer Interfacing, Bruce A. Artwick, Prentice Hall, 1980.
'Expanded Memory: Writing Programs that Break the 640k Barrier', *Microsoft Systems Journal*, Marion Hansen, Bill Krueger, Nick Stuecklen, March 1987
Operating Systems Design and Implementation, Arthur S. Tanenbaum, Prentice Hall 1987
Programmer's Guide to the IBM PC, Peter Norton, Microsoft Press, 1985.
Programmer's Problem Solver for the IBM PC, XT, & AT, Robert Jourdain, Prentice Hall, 1986.
Running MS-DOS, Van Wolverton, Microsoft Press
Supercharging MS-DOS, Van Volverton, Microsoft Press, 1986
The 8080a Bugbook, Tony-Larsen-Titus, Howard W. Sams, 1977
The 8086 Book, Russell Rector and George Alexy, Osborne/McGraw-Hill, 1980.
The IBM Personal Computer from the Inside Out, Murray Sargent III and Richard L. Shoemaker, Addison-Wesley, 1984.
The IBM ROM BIOS, Ray Duncan, Microsoft Press, 1988.
The Serious Assembler, Charles A. Crayne and Dian Gerard, Baen Books, 1985.
Tricks of the MS-DOS Masters, Waite Group, Howard W. Sams, 1987.
Turbo Pascal Express, Robert Jourdain, Brady Books, 1987.

Microsoft Macro Assembler 4.0, 5.1 documentation
Microsoft C 4.0 documentation
Borland Turbo Pascal 3.02a and 5.0 documentation, Turbo C 2.0 documentation

Magazines

A large amount of miscellaneous information came from various computer magazines. Documenting what came from where would be an experience all its own. A great deal of information came from articles by Michael Mefford, Charles Petzold, and Neil Rubenking of PC Magazine, and Ray Duncan, who gets around a lot.

Dr. Dobb's Journal (I always thought the old title, *'Doctor Dobbs' Journal of Computer Calisthe-*

nics and Orthodontia - Running Light Without Overbyte' was a killer name, but nobody asked me.)
PC Magazine
PC Resource
PC Tech Journal
Computer Language
Programmer's Journal
Byte Magazine
Computer Shopper

Computer Bulletin Board Systems

Various computer bulletin board systems, including

Byte Information Exchange (BIX)
Compuserve IBM SIG
GEnie IBM RT and Borland RT
GT Net international network
FIDO Net international network
PCanada BBS system, (Toronto, Canada)
Pecan Pi RBBS (404) 454-8756 (Atlanta, GA), Stan Young, sysop (R.I.P.)
College Corner BBS (206) 643-0804 (Seattle, WA), Jerry Houston, sysop.
Poverty Rock BBS (206) 232-1763 (Seattle WA), Rick Kunz, sysop.
Night Modulator BBS (408) 728-5598 (San Jose CA), Jim Bready, sysop.

Now that I no longer subscribe to PC-Pursuit, I'm not on any of these boards now, but they're still fine places to call.

Text Files

The text files on the following page were of use. Bear in mind that some of them may be seen under several different names. The author's name is given as it appears in the documentation (if any).

Name	Ext	Size	Date	Description	Author
10H-BUG	ASM	4680	29/01/87	bug in 2.x int 21h/fn10h	Ray Duncan
1PT4MB	INF	5120	3/10/87	1.44Mb drives	Clyde Washburn 70305,1211
2EH	ASM	2969	3/03/87	info on undoc'd int 2Eh	David Gwillim
386BUG	ARC	9216	15/10/87	bug in early 80386 chips	Compaq Corp.
8086	3	10572	5/12/88	dump of Fidonet?? 8086 conf??	[no name]
8259	ARC	2826	15/03/88	info on 8259 chip	[no name]
APICALLS	ARC	11481	8/01/88	OS/2 API function call list	Bill Earle
ASM-ADRS	ARC	6144	20/12/87	low memory vectors	Malcolm McCorquodale
ATCMDS	ARC	3072	20/03/88	Hayes 1200 baud command set	[no name]
BIOSDOC	ARC	34816	3/11/87	very good function list	David E. Powell
BIXDOS1	ARC	155648	14/12/87	BIX 'MSDOS Secrets' #1	[no name]
BUG40DOS	ARC	3200	18/08/88	bugs in DOS 4.0	'Doug'
CAS	ARC	33792	27/10/88	Communicating Applications Standard 1.0A	DCA, Intel Corp
DEBUGTUT	ARC	15655	23/04/88	DEBUG tutorial	[no name] possibly David Whitman?
DIAGNOSE	ARC	14336	1/01/86	memory error codes	Jerry Schneider, Arnold Kischi
DISK144	ARC	23086	16/10/88	info on 1.44Mb diskettes	[no name]
DISKTYPE	ARC	5073	14/04/88	IBM floppy formats	[no name]

Bibliography

Name	Type	Size	Date	Description	Author
DOOM	ARC	9216	29/09/88	hard drive information	[no name]
DOS-SIZE	ARC	787	27/03/88	size of DOS files 1.1-3.1	[no name]
DOS32	ARC	17408	31/05/88	command list for DOS 3.2	[no name]
DOS3BUGS	ARC	5639	15/10/87	acknowledged bugs in DOS 3.0 -3.2	IBM Corp.
DOS40	ARC	15625	22/07/88	IBM announcement of DOS 4.0	IBM Corp.
DOS401	ARC	18178	19/10/88	errors in DOS 4.0	IBM Corp.
DOS40B	ARC	27008	26/08/88	Compuserve thread on DOS 4.0	[no name]
DOS40FAT	ARC	1510	11/09/88	DOS 4.0 File Allocation Table	Mike Austin
DOS40FUN	ZOO	3410	31/12/99	DOS 4.0 int 24,25, etc	Pat Myrto
DOS40HLP	ARC	53376	28/08/88	DOS 4.0 command set	[no name]
DOS40TXT	ARC	46169	16/10/88	DOS 4.0 problems & info	[no name]
DOS4TIPS	ARC	1735	19/09/88	problems with DOS 4.0	IBM Corp.
DOSBUG	TXT	1024	15/10/87	info on 2.0 volume label	[no name]
DOSGUIDE	ARC	21344	21/02/88	DOS tutorial	Carrington B. Dixon
DOSINT	ARC	4201	15/03/88	list of DOS 2.0 function calls	John Chapman
DOSNOTES	ARC	5052	15/03/88	info on DOS undoc fns.	[no name]
DOSREF	ARC	9216	21/01/87	partial list of PC BIOS calls	[no name]
DOSREF	ARC	62052	23/08/86	device driver info	'Cracker'
DOSTIPS	ARC	28926	15/03/88	info on DOS	John Chapman
DOSTIPS1	ARC	159657	25/11/85	various DOS info	Dean R. Wood
DOSTIPS3	ARC	59264	25/01/88	various DOS tips (different)	Dean R. Wood
DOSUNDOC	ARC	3840	03/05/86	one of the very first interrupt lists	Spyros Sakellariadis
DRIVPARM	ARC	11264	7/01/88	info on DRIVPARM parameters	Joan Friendman
EGATEK	ARC	8704	15/03/88	IBM EGA registers	Bill Frantz
EMS40BIX	ARC	3802	21/09/87	BIX announcement of EMS 4.0	BIX
ENVIRONM	ARC	4255	18/09/88	info on DOS environment	Jan Fagerholm
ESC_CODE	ARC	3072	3/10/88	Laserjet setup codes	S. Noh
FILEIO	ARC	8192	24/07/88	TSRs and INDOS flag	[no name]
FLOPPIES	ARC	9216	2/11/87	info on floppy media	Ted Jensen
FOSSIL	ARC	9031	15/07/87	list of FOSSIL functions	Vincent Periello
FXN4BH	ASM	4503	1/01/80	odd 4Bh behaviour	Ray Duncan
HAYESET2	ARC	6479	4/09/86	modem commands	Ruth Lubow, Fowler Brown
HD-DATA	ARC	4096	19/07/87	list of hard drives & specs. I've seen many similar files. I believe the original was a file or bulletin on Sparta BBS	[no name]
HDINFO	ARC	11264	19/11/87	updated version of above, evidently by someone else	[no name]
HDNOISE	ARC	4159	11/11/87	hard disk information	Clancy Malloy
HDTIPS	ARC	9660	11/10/87	hard disk information	Barry Gordon
IBMTECH	ARC	136064	4/11/88	error codes, other info	IBM Corp.
INT-MDOS	ARC	20682	31/07/85	one of the original INT lists	Ross Greenberg
INTERRUP	ARC	157440	19/09/88	interrupt vector list	Ralf Brown
INTERRPT	ARC	42632	4/04/88	interrupt vector list. this is a very nice list and some programming information. If I'd come across it way back then it would have saved a ton of typing (sigh).	Marshall Presnell
JARGON	ARC	49274	16/07/88	dictionary of computer terms	[no name]

Name	Type	Size	Date	Description	Author
LIM-40	ARC	21504	15/10/87	info on LIM 4.0	Stephen Satchell
LISTINTS	ARC	6144	3/12/87	small interrupt list	[no name]
MCB	ARC	5120	24/07/88	info on DOS Memory Control Blocks	David Gwillim
MNP-TEXT	ARC	6144	30/09/88	MNP modem info	Mike Focke
MOUSENG	ARC	10240	13/08/88	Norton Guide file for mouse programming, with C examples	[no name]
MSLOOKUP	ARC	58368	25/12/87	interrupt and function listing	Frank Bonita
MS-OS2	ARC	25600	15/10/87	MS press release on OS/2	Microsoft Corp.
MSINT125	ARC	48128	12/01/88	interrupt vector listing	Ralf Brown
NETBIOS	ARC	17280	29/10/88	NetBIOS tutorial & summary	Tom Thompson
NOVELINT	ARC	4531	18/10/88	NetBIOS calls	Marc Guyot
OCOM_520	ARC	53632	19/08/88	FOSSIL tutorial and functions	Rick Moore
ODDITY	ARC	3072	24/07/88	int 2Eh description	Daniel Briggs
PINS	ARC	3072	18/01/88	pinouts of various connectors	[no name]
QUES40	ARC	9081	1/09/88	info on DOS 4.0	IBM Corp.
RAW_COOK	ARC	2048	15/10/87	info on DOS raw and cooked modes	[no name]
RESETSWT	TXT	3584	23/01/86	add a reset switch to a PC	Don Jenkins
RLLHINTS	ARC	12288	17/10/87	RLL controller into	Steve Sneed
RLLMISC	ARC	5120	17/10/87	info on RLL controllers	Richard Driggers
RLLSTORY	ARC	9718	31/07/88	good info on RLL coding	Pete Holzmann
SEAGATE	ARC	2048	3/03/88	specs for many Seagate drives	Jim McKown
SECRETS2	ARC	179625	17/04/88	BIX 'MS-DOS Secrets' #2	[no name]
SERCBL2	ARC	4372	16/10/88	serial cable pinouts	Lee Zeis
SM2400	ARC	2296	9/08/86	Hayes 2400 baud command set	[no name]
ST225	ARC	11264	7/10/87	optimizing ST225 and WD cont.	Neil Erbe
TANDON	ARC	3612	21/02/88	info on Tandon drives	David Welcher
TECH	ARC	27827	8/05/88	misc tech info - Fidonet?	[no name]
TOS		938	24/03/88	TOS function calls	Mike Crawford
TRYST	ARC	29312	29/10/88	DOS and hard disk info	Amy Goebel
UNDOCINT	21H	7168	14/04/87	undocumented DOS calls	Peter Holzmann
VGAPIN	ARC	1252	24/10/88	VGA pinout	'Mike'
WD-27X	ARC	6144	10/10/87	WD 27X HD controller setup	Steve Shelton
WDCONFIG	ARC	5504	11/10/87	WD-1002 WXS setup	Richard Driggers
WDCONT	ARC	11264	25/12/87	info on WD hard disk controllers	Peter Fales
XEB1210	ARC	7947	18/07/87	Xebec HD controller setup	
XEBEC	ARC	1036	30/04/88	setup for Xebec HD controller	Richard Driggers
XEBECTEC	ARC	1834	30/04/88	setup for Xebec 1210	Richard Driggers
XMS	ARC	75776	1/08/88	Microsoft Extended Memory Specification 1.0	[no name] Microsoft Corporation
XTCHARTS	ARC	12416	4/11/88	ports, charts	[no name]

NBRCV.C	Paul McGinnis	NetBIOS API calls
DESQ10.ASM	James H. LeMay	DesqView API calls
NETTUT.DOC	Charles L. Hedrick	TCP/IP network
CED10D	Chris Dunford	CED interrupt calls
INTER189.ARC	Ralf Brown	interrupt list

LANTSTIC.DOC	LANTastic adware	peer-to-peer LAN calls
GLOSSARY.ARC	no author name	computer terms

And thanks to all the people who have been good enough to furnish information and support (in alphabetical order):

Tommy Apple, Joe Felix, Ron Melson, Denis Murphy, & Ben Sansing, who all loaned me documentation and reference material for so long that some of them have forgotten to ask for their stuff back

Ben Sansing, Little Rock AR: ANSI.SYS information documentation for the NEC V20/30 chips error in register chart in Chapter 4

Pat Myrto, Seattle WA: Compaq DOS 3.31, IBM DOS 4.0 enhanced hard disk support

Mike Crawford, Little Rock AR: Atari ST TOS function calls and information

Alan R. Levinstone, Garland TX: 80286 LOADALL instruction BIOS Data Area floppy control parameters 40:8B, 40:8F, 40:90

Patrick O'Riva, San Jose CA: info on what happens to the interleave when the BIOS is finished

Klaus Overhage, Stuttgart W.Germany: FANSI-CONSOLE system calls

Special thanks to Chris Dunford, who donated his 'CED' program to the public domain. If it wasn't for CED, I would likely have abandoned MSDOS machines entirely and bought a Mac!

Dave Williams
Jacksonville, AR

Index

8255 peripheral interface chip, 310
8259 interrupt controller, 312

absolute disk read interrupt, 101
absolute disk write interrupt, 101
adapter card, 8
address space, 10
aftermarket applications, 96
alarm, 50
alternate EXEC, 104
alternate printer, AT 80287 interrupt, 24
AmigaDOS, 209
ANSI.SYS, 370
API calls, 96
append, 117
AQA EEMS, 186
arena headers, 136
ASCII (cooked)mode, 144
ASCII character codes, 342
ASCII control codes, 345
assign, 107
AT&T 80287, 24
AT&T/Olivetti, 51
Atari ST, 208
attribute field, 173
audio code, 349
AutoCAD, 4, 125
AUTOEXEC.BAT, 9

BASIC data areas, 18
binary (Raw) mode, 143
BIOS, 11
BIOS data area, 14
BIOS disk routines, 162
BIOS keystroke codes, 340
BIOS parameter block, 180
bit file allocation table, 154
block devices, 171, 176
boot, 8
boot area, 151
boot indicator, 160

boot record, 5, 159, 161
boot record, extended, 152
boot sequence, 158
bootstrap loader interrupt, 49
Borland turbo lightning API, 47
Break Handler, 7
breakpoint interrupt, 21
build BPB, 180

cassette connector, 363
cassette I/O interrupt, 34
CD-ROM extensions, 110
CGA - see colour graphics
character colours, 372
character devices, 171, 175
CHMOD, 77
CMOS RAM map, 311
colour graphics adapter, 362
colours (screen/character), 372
COM file structure, 146
COM1, 14, 23
command code field, 177
command interpreter, 6
command.com, 7, 9
command.com, resident portion, 7
command.com, transient portion, 7
communications controller (serial port), 23
Compaq DOS, 48
Compaq DOS 3.31, 102
control block, 148
control-break interrupt, 51
cooked modes, 142
cordless keyboard translation, 123
CP/M, 209
Ctrl-Break Handler, 7
Ctrl-Break exit address interrupt, 98
cursor positioning, 372

data area, 156
DEC, 4
DesQView, 44

Index

device busy loop, 41
device drivers, 171
    creating, 172
    format of, 171
    installing, 175
    structure of, 172
device header, 173
device header field, 173
device strategy, 174
disk directory entry, 155
disk functions interrupt, 25
disk transfer area (DTA), 131
diskette interrupt, 24
diskette motor statue, 15
diskette parameter table, 18
divide by zero interrupt, 20
divide overflow interrupt, 21
DOS
    3.3, 58
    4.0, 59
    address space, 130
    Arabic version, 4
    area, 151
    data areas, 18
    disk information, 151
    idle interrupt, 102
    interrupts, 54
    open handle, 190
    registers, 53
    services, 55
    services, calling, 57
    stacks, 54
doubleDOS, 97
driver.sys, 107
DUP, 80

EEMS 3.2, 186
EGS BIOS signature, 18
EMMXXXX0, 190
EMS 4.0, 197
EMS address space, 187
enhanced expanded memory, 186
environment area, 130
equipment flag, 14
equipmet check interrupt, 25
error codes (MS windows), 267
error codes, 349
error handler interrupt, 98
Error Handler, 7
error handling, critical, 107
errors, 100
event wait, 39
EXE file structure, 146
EXEC, 81
exit, 83

expanded memory, 11, 185
expansion card sizes, 358
expansion card slot , 359
expansion chassis , 361
extended boot record, 152
extended error code, 89
extended error support, 89
extended file block, 149
extended memory size, 40
extended shift status, 47

FASTOPEN, 185
FCB,57
    function calls, 140
    services, 57
    usage, 145
file allocation table, 152
file control block, see FCB
file handles, special, 142
file I/0, 143, 144
file management functions, 140
file, allocating space, 145
find first, 83
find next, 84
floppy disk formats, 157
FORCEDUP, 80
FOSSIL drivers, 29
fragmented workspace, 130
function 0, 135
function 3, 135
function call request interrupt, 55
game port , 360

GEM, 128
global descriptor table, 40
graphics adapter API, 128
graphics.com, 21

handle function calls, 140, 141
handle usage, 145
hard disk, 122
    allocation, 161
    layout, 158
hardware reset, 8
Hercules adaptor, 362
hidden file, 9

IBMBIO.COM, 6
IBMDOS.COM, 6
in-vars, 85
INIT, 178
initialization, 8
initialize and acccess serial port for Int 14, 25
input, nondestructive, 182
Intel 8255, 310

Intel communicating applications, 118
interface pinouts, 358
Interprocess Communications Area, location, 128
interrupt
    00h, 20
    01h, 20
    02h, 21
    03h, 21
    04h, 21
    05h, 21
    06h, 21
    07h, 22
    08h, 22
    09h, 22
    0Ah EGA, 23
    0Ch, 23
    0Dh, 24, 24
    0Eh, 24
    0Fh, 24
    0Hb, 23
    10h, 25, 314
    11h, 25
    12h, 25
    13h, 25
    14h, 25, 29
    15h, 34
    16h, 45
    17h, 48
    18h, 48
    19h, 49
    1Ah, 49
    1Bh, 51
    1Ch, 51
    1Dh, 51
    1Eh, 52
    1Fh, 52
    20h, 52
    21h, 55
    22h, 98
    23h, 98
    24h, 98
    25h, 101
    26h, 101
    27h, 102
    28h, 102
    29h, 103
    2Ah, 104
    2Eh, 104
    2Fh, 105
    33h, 301
    42h, 123
    43h, 123
    44h, 123
    46h, 123

interrupts:
    DOS, 54
    miscellaneous, 122
    routine, pointer to, 175
    usage, 347
    vector technique, 191
    vector, 14
    vectors, 8
invalid responses, 101
IO.SYS, 6
IOCTL, 78, 181
IRQ0, 22
IRQ0-IRQ7 relocation, 124
IRQ1, 22
IRQ3, 23
IRQ5, 24
IRQ7, 24
IRQ8 Real Time interrupt, 125
IRQ9 redirected to IRQ8, 125
IRQ10 (AT,XT/286,PS/2)reserved, 125
IRQ11 (AT,XT/286,PS/2)reserved, 125
IRQ12 Mouse Interrupt(PS/2), 125
IRQ13,Coprocessor Error(AT), 125
IRQ14, hard disk controller (AT,XT/286,PS/1), 125
IRQ15 (AT,XT/286,PS/2) reserved, 125

joystick, 39

keyboard buffer, 14
keyboard connector, 363
keyboard extended codes, 338
keyboard flag byte, 14
keyboard I/O interrupt, 45
keyboard intercept, 38
keyboard interrupt, 22
keyboard scan codes, 338
keytronic numeric keypad, 123

light pen connector, 364
LIM 3.2, 185
LIM 4.0, 185
LPT1, 14
LSEEK, 77

MacOS, 209
media check, 179
media descriptor byte, 153
media descriptor, 180
memory block move, 40
memory control block, 136
memory control blocks, 13
memory map, 10
memory size interrupt, 25
memory size, 14

Index

memory,
    enhanced expanded, 186
    expanded manager error codes, 205
    expanded service, 193
    expanded services, 192
    expanded, 185
mickeys, 300
Microsoft
    extended memory specifications, 112
    mouse driver extensions, 301
    mouse driver, 301
    networks, 117
    networks-session layer interrupt, 104
    Windows, 210
mode,
    ASCII (cooked), 144
    binary (raw), 143
    protected, 12
    raw and cooked, 142
    real, 12
Motorola 68000, 208
Motorola MC146818, 311
mouse driver, 301
mouse driver EGA support, 307
mouse programming, 300
MS-DOS, see DOS
MS-DOS.SYS, 6
multiplex - network redirection, 107
multiplex interrupt (eFh), 105, 290
multiplex, DOS 3.x internal services, 108

name/unit field, 175
netbios, 128
network interfacing, 269
network redirection, 93
next fit algorithm, 162
non-keyboard scan code translation, 123
non-destructive input, 182
non-maskable interrupt, 21
Novell Netware, 117, 125

open files, 145
OS hook, 38
    - device close, 39
    - device open, 38
    - keyboard intercept, 38
OS/2, 209
overlay manager interrupt, 122
overlay, 81
page frames, 189
parallel port, 365
partition table, 159
PC internal clock, 49
PC model identification, 18
pcAnywhere, 47

PCjr BIOS, 123
Perstor's ARLL, 161
pinouts, 358
pointer to:
    EGA graphics character table interrupt, 123
    graphics character table, 123
    screen BIOS entry interrupt, 123
    second hard disk parameter block interrupt, 123
port assignment, 12
POS, 44
POST, 41
power supply, 364
power-on Self Test, see POST
print screen interrupt, 21
print.com, 106
printer, 48
program segment prefix, 84, 130, 131, 132, 137, 148
program termination, 39
programmable option select, 44
prompt (string), 373
protected mode, switch processor, 40
protected modes, 12

quick screen output interrupt, 103

raw modes, 142
real modes, 12
real time clock, 50
real time interrupt, 125
register-level hardware access, 310
relative sector, 160
relocation table, 147
removable media, 184
request header, 176
request header length field, 177
'reserved by IBM' interrupt, 21, 22, 24
reserved memory, 14
REXX-PCAPI, 126
RGB monitor, 362
ROM, 4
ROM BASIC interrupt, 48
ROM BIOS, 18, 25
ROM tables, 19

screen colours, 372
screen, erasing, 372
screen/character colours, 372
serial port, 365
SETBLOCK, 81
SHARE, 107
single step interrupt, 20
software portability, 207

special file handles, 142
stack, 54
status field, 177
status, 183
stay resident, 70
STDAUX, 142, 171
STDERR, 142
STDIN, 142, 171
STDOUT, 142, 171
STDPN, 171
STDRN, 142
STERR, 171
storage block, 130
strategy routine, 174
system indicator, 160
system initialization, 158
system interrupts, 19, 20
system request, 39
system timer, 50

terminate address interrupt, 98
terminate and stay resident, 70, 102, 192
terminate current program interrupt, 59
Tesseract, 116
time of day interrupt, 49
timer interrupt, 22
timer tick, 51
Topview, 35, 37

unit code field, 177
UNIX, 209
user program interrupts, 125

VDISK, 49, 185
vector
    of diskette controller parameters
    interrupt, 52
    of video initialization parameters
    interrupt, 51
vertical retrace interrupt, 23
video buffer, 11
video gate array, 11
video service, 25
video subsystems, , 314

wait, 83
working tables, 8

XMA, 186
XMS, 112

Zenith 3.05, 93